HAMMOND®

UNITED STATES ATLAS

Gemini Edition

HAMMOND®
INCORPORATED
MAPLEWOOD, NEW JERSEY 07040-1396

Library of Congress Cataloging-in-Publication Data

Hammond Incorporated.
        Hammond United States atlas. – Gemini ed.
                p.   cm.
        Companion vol. to: Hammond world atlas. – Gemini ed.
        Includes index and "United States history atlas."
        ISBN 0-8437-1134-5
        1. United States – Maps. 2. United States – historical geography – Maps.
        I. Title.   II. Title: United States atlas.   III. Title: United States history atlas.
G1200. H357   1993   <G&M>
912--dc20   93-19640
                                                                    CIP
                                                                    MAP

CONTENTS

*The Hammond United States Atlas — Gemini Edition contains maps and indexes of the individual states and of the history of the United States. This volume is a companion to the Hammond World Atlas — Gemini Edition, which contains maps and indexes of the major world divisions, namely continents and countries. The pagination of this atlas continues from that of the World Atlas, although this volume has also been designed to be used on its own.

HAMMOND PUBLICATIONS ADVISORY BOARD

GAZETTEER-INDEX OF THE UNITED STATES

State	Square Miles	Square Kilometers	Population (1990)	Capital	Page Ref.
Alabama	52,423	135,775	4,040,587	Montgomery	195
Alaska	656,424	1,700,139	550,043	Juneau	196
Arizona	114,006	295,276	3,665,228	Phoenix	198
Arkansas	53,182	137,742	2,350,725	Little Rock	202
California	163,707	424,002	29,760,020	Sacramento	204
Colorado	104,100	269,620	3,294,394	Denver	208
Connecticut	5,544	14,358	3,287,116	Hartford	210
Delaware	2,489	6,447	666,168	Dover	245
District of Columbia	68	177	606,900	Washington	244
Florida	65,758	170,313	12,937,926	Tallahassee	212
Georgia	59,441	153,953	6,478,216	Atlanta	217
Hawaii	10,932	28,313	1,108,229	Honolulu	218
Idaho	83,574	216,456	1,006,749	Boise	220
Illinois	57,918	150,007	11,430,602	Springfield	222
Indiana	36,420	94,328	5,544,159	Indianapolis	227
Iowa	56,276	145,754	2,776,755	Des Moines	229
Kansas	82,282	213,110	2,477,574	Topeka	232
Kentucky	40,411	104,665	3,685,296	Frankfort	237
Louisiana	51,843	134,275	4,219,973	Baton Rouge	238
Maine	35,387	91,653	1,227,928	Augusta	243
Maryland	12,407	32,135	4,781,468	Annapolis	245
Massachusetts	10,555	27,337	6,016,425	Boston	249
Michigan	96,810	250,738	9,295,297	Lansing	250
Minnesota	86,943	225,182	4,375,099	St. Paul	255
Mississippi	48,434	125,443	2,573,216	Jackson	256
Missouri	69,709	180,546	5,117,073	Jefferson City	261
Montana	147,046	380,850	799,065	Helena	262
Nebraska	82,282	213,110	1,578,385	Lincoln	264
Nevada	110,567	286,368	1,201,833	Carson City	266
New Hampshire	9,351	24,219	1,109,252	Concord	268
New Jersey	8,722	22,590	7,730,188	Trenton	273
New Mexico	121,598	314,939	1,515,069	Santa Fe	274
New York	54,475	141,089	17,990,456	Albany	276
North Carolina	53,821	139,397	6,628,637	Raleigh	281
North Dakota	70,704	183,123	638,800	Bismarck	282
Ohio	44,828	116,103	10,847,115	Columbus	284
Oklahoma	69,903	181,049	3,145,585	Oklahoma City	288
Oregon	98,386	254,819	2,842,321	Salem	291
Pennsylvania	46,058	119,291	11,881,643	Harrisburg	294
Rhode Island	1,545	4,002	1,003,464	Providence	249
South Carolina	32,007	82,898	3,486,703	Columbia	296
South Dakota	77,358	200,358	696,004	Pierre	298
Tennessee	42,146	109,158	4,877,185	Nashville	237
Texas	268,601	695,676	16,986,510	Austin	303
Utah	84,904	219,902	1,722,850	Salt Lake City	304
Vermont	9,615	24,903	562,758	Montpelier	268
Virginia	42,769	110,771	6,187,358	Richmond	307
Washington	71,303	184,674	4,866,692	Olympia	310
West Virginia	24,231	62,759	1,793,477	Charleston	312
Wisconsin	65,503	169,653	4,891,769	Madison	317
Wyoming	97,818	253,349	453,588	Cheyenne	319
United States	3,792,575	9,822,769	254,709,873	Washington, D.C.	VI

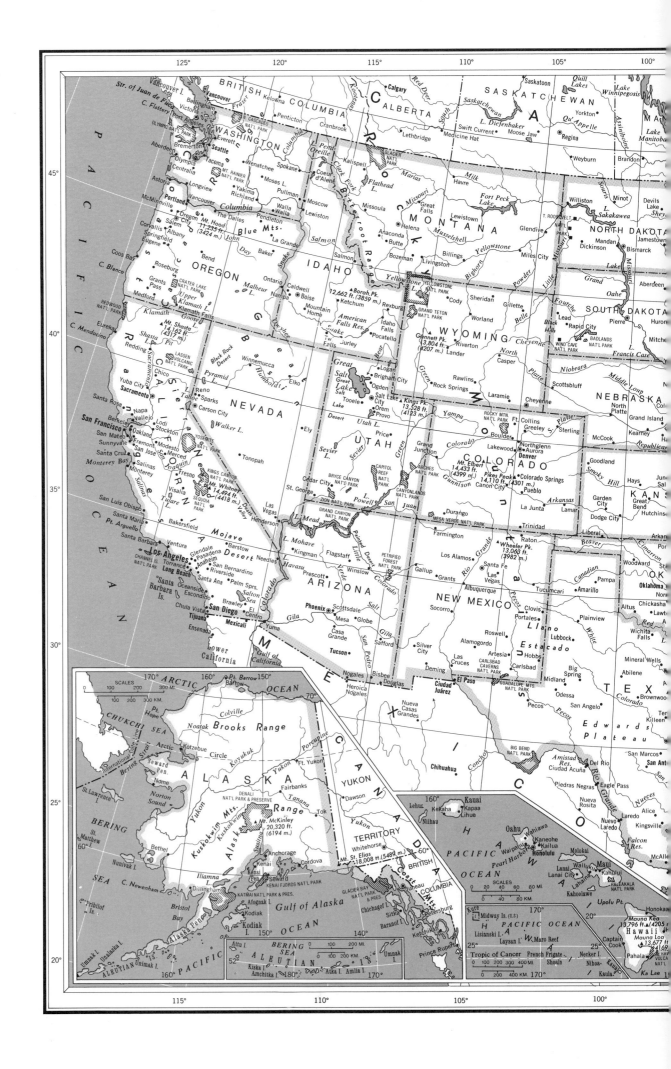

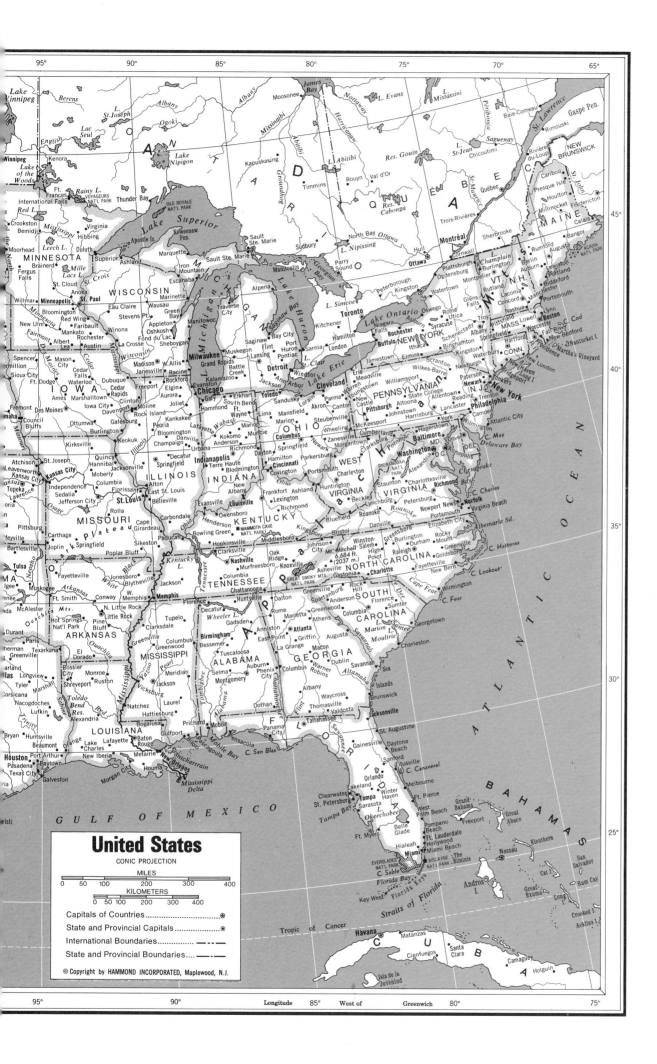

United States

CONIC PROJECTION

MILES

| 0 | 50 | 100 | 200 | 300 | 400 |

KILOMETERS

| 0 | 50 100 | 200 | 300 | 400 |

Capitals of Countries..............................⊛

State and Provincial Capitals..................◉

International Boundaries............._ _ _ _

State and Provincial Boundaries...._ _ _ _ _

© Copyright by HAMMOND INCORPORATED, Maplewood, N.J.

FACTS ABOUT THE FIFTY STATES

State Name	Admitted to Union	Settled at	Date	State Nickname	State Flower	State Bird
ALABAMA	Dec. 14, 1819	Mobile	1702	Yellowhammer State; Cotton State; Heart of Dixie	Camellia	Yellowhammer
ALASKA	Jan. 3, 1959	Sitka	1801	The Great Land; Last Frontier	Forget-me-not	Willow Ptarmigan
ARIZONA	Feb. 14, 1912	Tucson	1752	Grand Canyon State	Saguaro Cactus Blossom	Cactus Wren
ARKANSAS	June 15, 1836	Arkansas Post	1685	Land of Opportunity	Apple Blossom	Mockingbird
CALIFORNIA	Sept. 9, 1850	San Diego	1769	Golden State	Golden Poppy	California Valley Quail
COLORADO	Aug. 1, 1876	Near Denver	1858	Centennial State	Rocky Mountain Columbine	Lark Bunting
CONNECTICUT	Jan. 9, 1788	Windsor	1635	Constitution State; Nutmeg State	Mountain Laurel	Robin
DELAWARE	Dec. 7, 1787	Cape Henlopen	1627	Blue Hen State; Diamond State; First State	Peach Blossom	Blue Hen Chicken
FLORIDA	Mar. 3, 1845	St. Augustine	1565	Sunshine State; Peninsula State	Orange Blossom	Mockingbird
GEORGIA	Jan. 2, 1788	Savannah	1733	Peach State; Empire State of the South	Cherokee Rose	Brown Thrasher
HAWAII	Aug. 21, 1959	–	–	Aloha State	Hibiscus	Nene (Hawaiian Goose)
IDAHO	July 3, 1890	Coeur d'Alene	1842	Gem State	Syringa	Mountain Bluebird
ILLINOIS	Dec. 3, 1818	Kaskaskia	1720	Prairie State; Land of Lincoln	Native Violet	Cardinal
INDIANA	Dec. 11, 1816	Vincennes	1730	Hoosier State	Peony	Cardinal
IOWA	Dec. 28, 1846	Burlington	1788	Hawkeye State	Wild Rose	Eastern Goldfinch
KANSAS	Jan. 29, 1861	–	1831	Sunflower State	Sunflower	Western Meadowlark
KENTUCKY	June 1, 1792	Harrodsburg	1774	Bluegrass State	Goldenrod	Cardinal
LOUISIANA	Apr. 30, 1812	Iberville	1699	Pelican State	Magnolia	Eastern Brown Pelican
MAINE	Mar. 15, 1820	Bristol	1624	Pine Tree State	White Pine Cone and Tassel	Chickadee
MARYLAND	Apr. 28, 1788	St. Mary's	1634	Old Line State; Free State	Black-Eyed Susan	Baltimore Oriole
MASSACHUSETTS	Feb. 6, 1788	Plymouth	1620	Bay State; Old Colony	Mayflower	Chickadee
MICHIGAN	Jan. 26, 1837	Near Detroit	1650	Wolverine State	Apple Blossom	Robin
MINNESOTA	May 11, 1858	Saint Peter's River	1805	North Star State; Gopher State	Pink and White Lady's-Slipper	Common Loon
MISSISSIPPI	Dec. 10, 1817	Natchez	1716	Magnolia State	Magnolia	Mockingbird
MISSOURI	Aug. 10, 1821	St. Louis	1764	Show Me State	Hawthorn	Bluebird
MONTANA	Nov. 8, 1889	–	1809	Treasure State; Big Sky Country	Bitterroot	Western Meadowlark
NEBRASKA	Mar. 1, 1867	Bellevue	1847	Cornhusker State	Goldenrod	Western Meadowlark
NEVADA	Oct. 31, 1864	Genoa	1850	Silver State; Sagebrush State	Sagebrush	Mountain Bluebird
NEW HAMPSHIRE	June 21, 1788	Dover and Portsmouth	1623	Granite State	Purple Lilac	Purple Finch
NEW JERSEY	Dec. 18, 1787	Bergen	1617	Garden State	Purple Violet	Eastern Goldfinch
NEW MEXICO	Jan. 6, 1912	Santa Fe	1605	Land of Enchantment	Yucca	Road Runner
NEW YORK	July 26, 1788	Manhattan Island	1614	Empire State	Rose	Bluebird
NORTH CAROLINA	Nov. 21, 1789	Albemarle	1650	Tar Heel State	Dogwood	Cardinal
NORTH DAKOTA	Nov. 2, 1889	Pembina	1780	Flickertail State; Peace Garden State; Sioux State	Wild Prairie Rose	Western Meadowlark
OHIO	Mar. 1, 1803	Marietta	1788	Buckeye State	Scarlet Carnation	Cardinal
OKLAHOMA	Nov. 16, 1907	–	1889	Sooner State	Mistletoe	Scissor-Tailed Flycatcher
OREGON	Feb. 14, 1859	Astoria	1810	Beaver State	Oregon Grape	Western Meadowlark
PENNSYLVANIA	Dec. 12, 1787	Delaware River	1682	Keystone State	Mountain Laurel	Ruffed Grouse
RHODE ISLAND	May 29, 1790	Providence	1636	Little Rhody; Ocean State	Violet	Rhode Island Red
SOUTH CAROLINA	May 23, 1788	Port Royal	1670	Palmetto State	Carolina (Yellow) Jessamine	Carolina Wren
SOUTH DAKOTA	Nov. 2, 1889	Sioux Falls	1856	Coyote State; Mt. Rushmore State	Pasque	Ring-Necked Pheasant
TENNESSEE	June 1, 1796	Ft. Loudon	1757	Volunteer State	Iris	Mockingbird
TEXAS	Dec. 29, 1845	Matagorda Bay	1686	Lone Star State	Bluebonnet	Mockingbird
UTAH	Jan. 4, 1896	Salt Lake City	1847	Beehive State	Sego Lily	Sea Gull
VERMONT	Mar. 4, 1791	Ft. Dummer	1764	Green Mountain State	Red Clover	Hermit Thrush
VIRGINIA	June 26, 1788	Jamestown	1607	Old Dominion State	Dogwood	Cardinal
WASHINGTON	Nov. 11, 1889	Astoria	1811	Evergreen State	Western Rhododendron	Willow Goldfinch
WEST VIRGINIA	June 20, 1863	Wheeling	1774	Mountain State	Big Rhododendron	Cardinal
WISCONSIN	May 29, 1848	Green Bay	1670	Badger State	Wood Violet	Robin
WYOMING	July 10, 1890	Ft. Laramie	1834	Equality State	Indian Paintbrush	Meadowlark

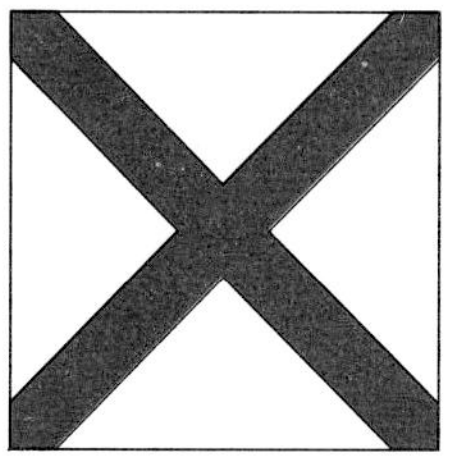

AREA 51,705 sq. mi. (133,916 sq. km.)
POPULATION 4,062,608
CAPITAL Montgomery
LARGEST CITY Birmingham
HIGHEST POINT Cheaha Mtn. 2,407 ft. (734 m.)
SETTLED IN 1702
ADMITTED TO UNION December 14, 1819
POPULAR NAME Heart of Dixie; Cotton State; Yellowhammer State
STATE FLOWER Camellia
STATE BIRD Yellowhammer

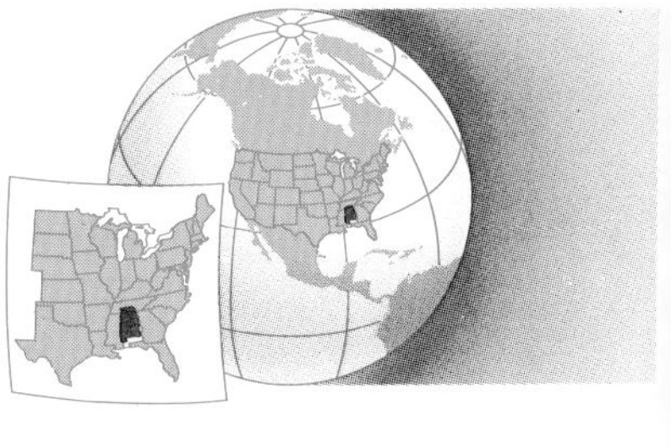

COUNTIES

Autauga 34,222 ... E5
Baldwin 98,280 ... C9
Barbour 25,417 ... H7
Bibb 16,576 ... D5
Blount 39,248 ... E2
Bullock 11,042 ... G6
Butler 21,892 ... E7
Calhoun 116,034 ... G3
Chambers 36,876 ... H5
Cherokee 19,543 ... G2
Chilton 32,458 ... E5
Choctaw 16,018 ... B6
Clarke 27,240 ... C7
Clay 13,252 ... G4
Cleburne 12,730 ... G3
Coffee 40,240 ... G8
Colbert 51,666 ... C1
Conecuh 14,054 ... E8
Coosa 11,063 ... F5
Covington 36,478 ... F8
Crenshaw 13,635 ... F7
Cullman 67,613 ... E2
Dale 49,633 ... G8
Dallas 48,130 ... D6
De Kalb 53,658 ... G2
Elmore 49,210 ... F5
Escambia 35,518 ... D8
Etowah 99,840 ... F2
Fayette 17,962 ... C3
Franklin 27,814 ... C2
Geneva 23,647 ... G8
Greene 10,153 ... C5
Hale 15,498 ... C5
Henry 15,374 ... H7
Houston 81,331 ... H8
Jackson 47,796 ... F1
Jefferson 651,525 ... E3
Lamar 15,715 ... B3
Lauderdale 79,661 ... C1
Lawrence 31,513 ... D1
Lee 87,146 ... H5
Limestone 54,135 ... E1
Lowndes 12,658 ... E6
Macon 24,928 ... G6
Madison 238,912 ... E1
Marengo 23,084 ... C6
Marion 29,830 ... C2
Marshall 70,832 ... F2
Mobile 378,643 ... B9
Monroe 23,968 ... D7
Montgomery 209,085 ... F6
Morgan 100,043 ... E2
Perry 12,759 ... D5
Pickens 20,699 ... B4
Pike 27,595 ... G7
Randolph 19,881 ... H4
Russell 46,860 ... H6
Saint Clair 41,205 ... F3
Shelby 99,358 ... E4
Sumter 16,174 ... B5
Talladega 74,107 ... F4
Tallapoosa 38,826 ... G5
Tuscaloosa 150,522 ... C4
Walker 67,670 ... D3
Washington 16,694 ... B8
Wilcox 13,568 ... D7
Winston 22,053 ... D2

CITIES and TOWNS

Abbeville▲ 3,173 ... H7
Abernant 405 ... D4
Adamsville 4,161 ... D3
Addison 626 ... D2
Adger 400 ... D4
Akron 468 ... C5
Alabaster 14,732 ... E4
Albertville 14,507 ... F2
Aldrich 500 ... E4
Alexander City 14,917 ... G5
Alexandria 600 ... G3
Aliceville 3,009 ... B4
Allgood 464 ... F3
Allsboro 300 ... B1
Alma 500 ... C8
Altoona 960 ... F2
Andalusia▲ 9,269 ... E8
Anderson 339 ... D1
Anniston▲ 26,623 ... G3
Arab 6,321 ... E2
Ardmore 1,090 ... E1
Argo 930 ... E3
Ariton 743 ... G7
Arley 338 ... D2
Ashby 500 ... E4
Ashford 1,926 ... H8
Ashland▲ 2,034 ... G4
Ashville▲ 1,494 ... F3
Athens▲ 16,901 ... E1
Atmore 8,046 ... C8
Attalla 6,859 ... F2
Auburn 33,830 ... H5
Autaugaville 681 ... E6
Avon 462 ... H8
Axis 500 ... B9
Babbie 576 ... F8
Baileyton 352 ... E2
Baker Hill 300 ... H7
Banks 195 ... G7
Barnwell 700 ... C10
Bay Minette▲ 7,168 ... C9
Bayou La Batre 2,456 ... B10
Bear Creek 913 ... C2
Beatrice 454 ... D7
Beaverton 319 ... B3
Belgreen 500 ... C2
Belk 255 ... C3
Bellamy 700 ... B6
Belle Mina 675 ... E1
Bellwood 400 ... G8
Benton 48 ... E6
Berry 1,218 ... C3
Bessemer 33,497 ... D4
Beulah 500 ... H5
Billingsley 150 ... E5
Birmingham▲ 265,968 ... D3
Black 174 ... G8
Blountsville 1,527 ... E2
Blue Mountain 221 ... G3
Blue Springs 108 ... G7
Boaz 6,928 ... F2
Boligee 268 ... C5
Bon Air 91 ... F4
Bon Secour 850 ... C10
Branchville 370 ... F3
Brantley 1,015 ... F7
Brent 2,776 ... D5
Brewton▲ 5,885 ... D8
Bridgeport 2,936 ... G1
Brighton 4,518 ... D4
Brilliant 751 ... C2
Brookside 1,365 ... E3
Brookwood 658 ... D4
Browns 375 ... D6
Brownville 2,386 ... C4
Brundidge 2,472 ... G7
Butler▲ 1,872 ... B6
Cahaba 4,778 ... D6
Calera 2,136 ... E4
Calhoun 950 ... F6
Calvert 600 ... B8
Camden▲ 2,414 ... D7
Camp Hill 1,415 ... G5
Canoe 560 ... D8
Carbon Hill 2,115 ... D3
Cardiff 72 ... E3
Carolina 201 ... E8
Carrollton▲ 1,170 ... B4
Carrville 820 ... G5
Carson 400 ... C8
Castleberry 669 ... D8
Cedar Bluff 1,174 ... G2
Centre▲ 2,893 ... G2
Centreville▲ 2,508 ... D5
Chatom▲ 1,094 ... B8
Chelsea 1,329 ... E4
Cherokee 1,479 ... C1
Chickasaw 6,649 ... B9
Childersburg 4,579 ... F4
Choccolocco 500 ... G3
Choctaw 600 ... B6
Chrysler 400 ... C8
Chunchula 700 ... B9
Citronelle 3,671 ... B8
Clanton▲ 7,669 ... E5
Clayhatchee 411 ... G8
Clayton▲ 1,564 ... G7
Cleveland 739 ... E3
Clio 1,365 ... G7
Coaling 400 ... D4
Coden 600 ... B10
Coffee Springs 294 ... G8
Coffeeville 431 ... B7
Coker 800 ... C4
Collinsville 1,429 ... G2
Columbia 922 ... H8
Columbiana▲ 2,968 ... E4
Coosada 912 ... F5
Cordova 2,623 ... D3
Cottondale 500 ... D4
Cottonton 324 ... H6
Cottonwood 1,385 ... H8
County Line 124 ... F8
County Line 199 ... E3
Courtland 803 ... D1
Cowarts 1,400 ... H8
Coy 950 ... D7
Crane Hill 355 ... D2
Creola 1,896 ... B9
Cromwell 650 ... B6
Crossville 1,350 ... G2
Cuba 390 ... B6
Cullman▲ 13,367 ... E2
Cullomburg 325 ... B7
Cusseta 650 ... H5
Dadeville▲ 3,276 ... G5
Daleville 5,117 ... G8
Daphne 11,290 ... C9
Dauphin Island 824 ... B10
Daviston 261 ... G4
Dayton 77 ... C6
De Armanville 350 ... G3
Decatur▲ 48,761 ... D1
Demopolis 7,512 ... C6
Detroit 291 ... B2
Dolomite ... D4
Dora 2,214 ... D3
Dothan▲ 53,589 ... H8
Double Springs▲ 1,138 ... D2
Douglas 474 ... F2
Dozier 483 ... F7
Dutton 243 ... G1
East Brewton 2,579 ... E8
Eclectic 1,087 ... F5
Edwardsville 118 ... H3
Elba▲ 4,011 ... F8
Elberta 458 ... C10
Eldridge 225 ... C3
Elkmont 389 ... E1
Elmore 600 ... F5
Elrod 746 ... C4
Emelle 44 ... B5
Empire 600 ... D3
Enterprise 20,123 ... G8
Epes 267 ... B5
Ethelsville 52 ... B4
Eufaula 13,220 ... H7
Eunola 199 ... G8
Eutaw▲ 2,281 ... C5
Eva 438 ... E2
Evergreen▲ 3,911 ... E8
Excel 571 ... D8
Fairfield 12,200 ... E4
Fairhope 8,485 ... C10
Fairview 383 ... E2
Falkville 1,337 ... E2
Faunsdale 96 ... C6
Fayette▲ 4,909 ... C3
Five Points 200 ... H4
Flat Rock 750 ... G1
Flint City 1,033 ... D1
Flomaton 1,811 ... D8
Florala 2,075 ... F8
Florence▲ 36,426 ... C1
Foley 4,937 ... C10
Forestdale 10,395 ... E3
Forkland 667 ... C5
Fort Davis 500 ... G6
Fort Deposit 1,240 ... E7
Fort Mitchell 900 ... H6
Fort Payne▲ 11,838 ... G2
Fosters 400 ... C4
Franklin 133 ... G6
Franklin 152 ... D7
Frisco City 1,581 ... D8
Fruitdale 500 ... B8
Fruithurst 177 ... G3
Fulton 384 ... C7
Fultondale 6,400 ... E3
Fyffe 1,094 ... G2
Gadsden▲ 42,523 ... G2
Gainesville 449 ... B5
Gallant 475 ... F2
Gantt 265 ... E8
Gantt's Quarry ... F4
Garden City 578 ... E2
Gardendale 9,251 ... E3
Gaylesville 149 ... G2
Geiger 270 ... B5
Geneva▲ 4,681 ... G8
Georgiana 1,933 ... E7
Geraldine 801 ... G2
Gilbertown 235 ... B7
Glen Allen 350 ... C3
Glencoe 4,670 ... G3
Glenwood 208 ... F7
Goldville 61 ... G4
Good Hope 1,700 ... E2
Goodsprings 360 ... D3
Goodwater 1,840 ... F4
Gordo 1,918 ... C4
Gordon 493 ... H8
Gorgas 500 ... D3
Goshen 302 ... F7
Gosport 500 ... C7
Grand Bay 3,383 ... B10
Grant 638 ... F1
Graysville 2,241 ... D3
Green Pond 750 ... D4
Greensboro▲ 3,047 ... C5
Greenville▲ 7,492 ... E7
Grimes 443 ... H8
Grove Hill▲ 1,551 ... C7
Gu-Win 243 ... C3
Guin 2,464 ... C3
Gulf Shores 3,261 ... C10
Guntersville▲ 7,038 ... F2
Gurley 1,007 ... F1
Hackleburg 1,161 ... C2
Haleburg 97 ... H8

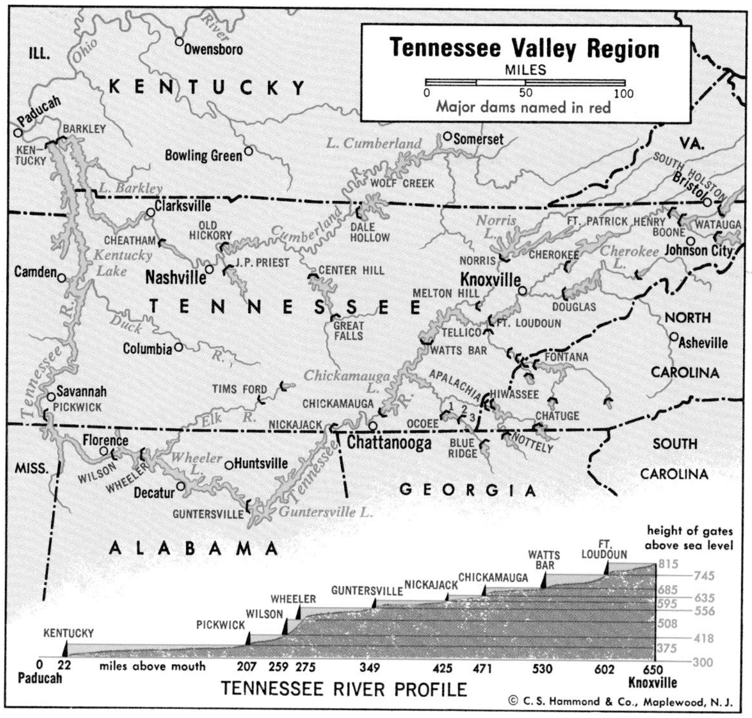
Tennessee Valley Region
MILES
0 50 100
Major dams named in red
ILL.
KENTUCKY
Owensboro
Paducah
BARKLEY
KENTUCKY
Bowling Green
L. Cumberland
Somerset
VA.
WOLF CREEK
Bristol
L. Barkley
Clarksville
OLD HICKORY
DALE HOLLOW
Norris L.
FT. PATRICK HENRY
BOONE
WATAUGA
CHEATHAM
Kentucky Lake
Nashville
J.P. PRIEST
CENTER HILL
NORRIS
CHEROKEE
Cherokee L.
Johnson City
Camden
TENNESSEE
Knoxville
MELTON HILL
DOUGLAS
Duck R.
Columbia
GREAT FALLS
TELLICO
FT. LOUDOUN
NORTH
Asheville
WATTS BAR
FONTANA
CAROLINA
Savannah
PICKWICK
TIMS FORD
Chickamauga L.
CHICKAMAUGA
APALACHIA
HIWASSEE
CHATUGE
Elk R.
NICKAJACK
OCOEE
Florence
Chattanooga
BLUE RIDGE
NOTTELY
SOUTH
MISS.
WILSON
WHEELER
Wheeler L.
Huntsville
GEORGIA
CAROLINA
Decatur
GUNTERSVILLE
Guntersville L.
ALABAMA
height of gates above sea level
KENTUCKY
PICKWICK
WILSON
WHEELER
GUNTERSVILLE
NICKAJACK
CHICKAMAUGA
WATTS BAR
FT. LOUDOUN
815
745
685
635
595
556
508
418
375
300
0 22 miles above mouth 207 259 275 349 425 471 530 602 650
Paducah
Knoxville
TENNESSEE RIVER PROFILE
© C. S. Hammond & Co., Maplewood, N. J.

Haleyville 4,452 ... C2
Hamilton▲ 5,787 ... C2
Hammondville 420 ... G1
Hanceville 2,246 ... E2
Hardaway 600 ... G6
Harpersville 772 ... F4
Hartford 2,448 ... G8
Hartselle 10,795 ... E2
Harvest 1,922 ... E1
Hatchechubbee 840 ... H6
Hatton 950 ... D1
Hayden 385 ... E3
Hayneville▲ 969 ... E6
Hazel Green 2,208 ... E1
Headland 3,266 ... H8
Heath 182 ... F8
Heflin▲ 2,906 ... G3
Heiberger 310 ... D5
Helena 3,918 ... E4
Henagar 1,934 ... G1
Higdon 925 ... G1
Highland Lake 304 ... F3
Hillsboro 587 ... D1
Hobson City 794 ... G3
Hodges 272 ... C2
Hokes Bluff 3,739 ... G3
Hollins 500 ... F4
Holly Pond 602 ... E2
Hollywood 916 ... G1
Holt 4,125 ... D4
Holy Trinity 400 ... H6
Homewood 22,922 ... E4
Hoover 39,788 ... E4
Hope Hull 975 ... F6
Horn Hill 186 ... F8
Hueytown 15,280 ... D4
Huntsville▲ 159,789 ... E1
Hurtsboro 707 ... H6
Hytop 350 ... F1
Ider 671 ... G1
Inverness 2,528 ... G6
Irondale 9,454 ... E3
Jack 5,819 ... F7
Jackson 789 ... C8
Jacksons Gap 800 ... G5
Jacksonville 10,283 ... G3
Jasper▲ 13,553 ... D3
Jemison 1,898 ... E5
Kansas 230 ... C3
Kellyton 375 ... F5
Kennedy 523 ... B3
Key 400 ... G2
Killen 1,047 ... D1
Kimberly 1,096 ... E3
Kinsey 1,679 ... H8
Kinston 595 ... F8
Laceys Spring 400 ... E1
Lafayette▲ 3,151 ... H5
Lakeview 166 ... G2
Lanett 8,985 ... H5
Langdale 2,034 ... H5
Langston 207 ... G1
Larkinsville 425 ... F1
Lavaca 500 ... B6
Leeds 9,946 ... E3
Leesburg 218 ... G2
Leighton 988 ... D1
Leroy 699 ... B8
Lester 89 ... D1
Level Plains 1,473 ... G8
Lexington 821 ... D1
Libertyville 133 ... F8
Lillian 350 ... D10
Lincoln 2,941 ... F3
Linden▲ 2,548 ... C6
Lineville 2,394 ... G4
Lipscomb 2,892 ... E4
Lisman 481 ... B6
Little River 400 ... C8
Little Shawmut 2,793 ... H5
Littleville 925 ... C1
Livingston▲ 3,530 ... B5
Loachapoka 259 ... G5
Lockhart 484 ... F8
Locust Fork 342 ... E3
Longview 475 ... E4
Louisville 728 ... G7
Lower Peach Tree 926 ... C7
Lowndesboro 139 ... E6
Loxley 1,161 ... C9
Luverne▲ 2,555 ... F7
Lynn 611 ... C2
Madison 14,904 ... E1
Madrid 211 ... H8
Magnolia Springs 800 ... C10
Malvern 570 ... G8
Manchester 400 ... D3
Maplesville 725 ... E5
Margaret 616 ... F3
Marion Junction 400 ... D6
Marion▲ 4,211 ... D5
Maylene 500 ... E4
McCalla 657 ... E4
McCullough 500 ... D8
McIntosh 250 ... B8
McKenzie 464 ... E7
McWilliams 305 ... D7
Memphis 54 ... B4
Mentone 474 ... G1
Meridianville 2,852 ... F1
Midfield 5,559 ... E4
Midland City 1,819 ... H8
Midway 455 ... H6
Mignon 1,548 ... F4
Millbrook 6,050 ... F6
Millerville 345 ... G4
Millport 1,203 ... B3
Millry 781 ... B7
Minter 450 ... D6
Mobile▲ 196,278 ... B9
Monroeville▲ 6,993 ... D7
Monrovia 500 ... E1
Montevallo 4,239 ... E4
Montgomery (cap.)▲ 187,106 ... F6
Montrose 750 ... C9
Moody 4,921 ... F3
Mooresville 54 ... E1
Morris 1,136 ... E3
Morvin 355 ... C7
Moulton▲ 3,248 ... D2
Moundville 1,348 ... C5
Mount Vernon 902 ... B8
Mountain Brook 19,810 ... E4
Mountainboro 261 ... F2
Munford 700 ... F3
Muscle Shoals 9,611 ... C1
Myrtlewood 197 ... C6
Nanafalia 500 ... B6
Napier Field 462 ... H8
Nauvoo 240 ... D3
Nectar 238 ... E3
Needham 99 ... B7
New Brockton 1,184 ... G8
New Hope 2,248 ... F1
New Market 1,094 ... F1
New Site 669 ... G4
Newbern 222 ... C5
Newton 1,580 ... G8
Newville 531 ... H8
North Johns 177 ... D4
Northport 17,366 ... C4
Notasulga 979 ... G5
Oak Grove 436 ... B9
Oak Grove 638 ... F4
Oak Hill 28 ... D7
Oakman 846 ... D3
Odenville 796 ... F3
Ohatchee 1,042 ... G3
Oneonta▲ 4,844 ... E3
Onycha 150 ... F8
Opelika▲ 22,122 ... H5
Opp 6,985 ... F8
Orange Beach 2,253 ... C10
Orrville 234 ... D6
Owens Cross Roads 695 ... E1
Oxford 9,362 ... G3
Ozark▲ 12,922 ... G8
Paint Rock 214 ... F1
Parrish 1,433 ... D3
Pelham 9,765 ... E4
Pell City▲ 8,118 ... F3
Pennington 302 ... B6
Perdido 500 ... C8
Peterman 600 ... D7
Peterson ... D4
Petrey 80 ... F7
Phenix City▲ 25,312 ... H6
Phil Campbell 1,317 ... C2
Pickensville 169 ... B4
Piedmont 5,288 ... G3
Pinckard 618 ... G8
Pine Apple 365 ... E7
Pine Hill 481 ... C7
Pinson 10,987 ... E3
Pisgah 652 ... G1
Plantersville 650 ... E5
Pleasant Grove 8,458 ... D4
Point Clear 2,125 ... C10
Pollard 100 ... D8
Powell's Crossroads 636 ... G1
Prattville▲ 19,587 ... E6
Priceville 1,323 ... E1
Prichard 34,311 ... B9
Providence 307 ... C6
Ragland 1,807 ... F3
Rainbow City 7,673 ... F3
Rainsville 3,875 ... G2
Ramer 680 ... F6
Ranburne 447 ... H3
Red Bay 3,451 ... B2
Red Level 588 ... E8
Reece City 657 ... G2
Reform 2,105 ... C4
Remlap 800 ... E3
Renfroe 400 ... F4
Repton 293 ... D8
Republic 500 ... E3
River Falls 710 ... E8

(continued on following page)

Agriculture, Industry and Resources

DOMINANT LAND USE

- Specialized Cotton
- Cotton, Livestock
- Cotton, General Farming
- Cotton, Hogs, Peanuts
- Cotton, Forest Products
- Peanuts, General Farming
- Truck and Mixed Farming
- Forests
- Swampland, Limited Agriculture

MAJOR MINERAL OCCURRENCES

Al	Bauxite	Ls	Limestone
At	Asphalt	Mi	Mica
C	Coal	Mr	Marble
Cl	Clay	Na	Salt
Fe	Iron Ore	O	Petroleum
G	Natural Gas		

⚡ Water Power
▨ Major Industrial Areas

Topography

0   30   60 MI.
0   30   60 KM.

Below Sea Level | 100 m. 328 ft. | 200 m. 656 ft. | 500 m. 1,640 ft. | 1,000 m. 3,281 ft. | 2,000 m. 6,562 ft. | 5,000 m. 16,404 ft.

River View 1,314 ....H5
Riverside 1,004 ....F3
Riverview 90 ....D8
Roanoke 6,362 ....H4
Robertsdale 2,401 ....C9
Rock Mills 600 ....H4
Rockford▲ 461 ....F5
Rogersville 1,125 ....D1
Roosevelt City 3,352 ....E4
Rosa 139 ....E3
Rural C7
Russellville▲ 7,812 ....C2
Rutledge 473 ....F7
Saginaw 475 ....E4
Saint Elmo 700 ....B10
Saint Florian 388 ....C1
Saint Stephens 700 ....B7
Salem 350 ....H5
Salitpa 550 ....C7
Samantha 400 ....C4
Samson 2,190 ....F8
Sanford 282 ....F8
Saraland 11,751 ....B9
Sardis 1,301 ....E6
Sardis 883 ....F2
Satsuma 5,194 ....B9
Sayre 700 ....E3
Scottsboro▲ 13,786 ....F1
Seale 350 ....H6
Section 777 ....G1
Selma▲ 23,755 ....E6
Selmont 3,823 ....E6
Shady Grove F7
Shawmut 2,284 ....H5
Sheffield 10,380 ....C1
Shelby 500 ....E4
Shiloh 252 ....C6
Shiloh 297 ....G2
Shorter 461 ....G6
Shorterville 400 ....H7
Silas 245 ....B7
Silverhill 556 ....C9
Sipsey 568 ....D3
Slocomb 1,906 ....G8
Smiths 3,456 ....H5
Snead 632 ....F2
Somerville 211 ....E2
South 543 ....E8
Southside 5,580 ....F3
Spanish Fort 3,732 ....C9
Spring Valley 600 ....C1
Springville 1,910 ....E3
Stapleton 975 ....C9
Steele 1,046 ....F3
Sterrett 350 ....F4
Stevenson 2,046 ....G1
Stewart 450 ....C5
Stockton 500 ....C9
Suggsville 400 ....C7
Sulligent 1,886 ....B3
Sumiton 2,604 ....D3
Summerdale 559 ....C10
Sunny South 350 ....C7
Sweet Water 243 ....C6
Sycamore 800 ....F4
Sylacauga 12,520 ....F4
Sylvania 932 ....G1
Talladega Springs 148 ....F4
Talladega▲ 18,175 ....F4
Tallassee 5,112 ....G5
Tanner 600 ....E1
Tarrant 8,046 ....E3
Taylor 1,352 ....H8
Theodore 6,509 ....B9
Thomaston 497 ....C6
Thomasville 4,301 ....C7
Thorsby 1,465 ....E5
Tibbie 675 ....B8
Town Creek 1,379 ....D1
Townley 500 ....D3
Toxey 211 ....B7
Trafford 739 ....E3
Triana 499 ....E1
Trinity 1,380 ....D1
Troy▲ 13,051 ....G7
Trussville 8,266 ....E3
Tuscaloosa▲ 77,759 ....C4
Tuscumbia▲ 8,413 ....C1
Tuskegee Institute G6
Tuskegee▲ 12,257 ....G6
Union 321 ....C5
Union Grove 119 ....E2
Union Springs▲ 3,975 ....G6
Uniontown 1,730 ....D6
Uriah 450 ....D8
Valhermoso Springs 500 ....E2
Valley 8,173 ....H5
Valley Head 577 ....G1
Vance 248 ....D4
Vandiver 700 ....F4
Verbena 500 ....E5
Vernon▲ 2,247 ....B3
Vestavia Hills 19,749 ....E4
Vina 356 ....B2
Vincent 1,767 ....F4
Vinemont E2
Vredenburgh 313 ....D7
Wadley 517 ....G4
Wadsworth 500 ....E5
Wagarville 550 ....B8
Waldo 309 ....F4
Walker Springs 500 ....C7
Walnut Grove 717 ....F2
Warrior 3,280 ....E3
Waterloo 250 ....B1
Wattsville 550 ....F3
Waverly 152 ....G5
Weaver 2,715 ....G3
Webb 1,039 ....H8
Wedowee▲ 796 ....H4
Wegra D3
Weogufka 500 ....F4
West Blocton 1,468 ....D4
West Jefferson 388 ....D3
West Point 257 ....D2
West Selmont 5,255 ....E6
Weston 384 ....B2

Westover 500 ....E4
Wetumpka▲ 4,670 ....F5
Whatley 800 ....C7
White Hall 814 ....E6
White Plains 350 ....G3
Whites Chapel 336 ....F3
Wicksburg 400 ....G8
Wilmer 494 ....B9
Wilsonville 1,185 ....E4
Wilton 602 ....E4
Winfield 3,689 ....C3
Woodland 189 ....H4
Woodstock 340 ....D4
Woodville 687 ....F1
Yantley 500 ....B6
Yellow Bluff 245 ....C7
Yellow Pine 350 ....B6
York 3,160 ....B6

OTHER FEATURES

Alabama (riv.) C8
Aliceville (dam) B4
Anniston Army Depot F3
Bankhead (lake) D4
Bartletts Ferry (dam) H5
Big Canoe (creek) F3
Big Creek (lake) B9
Black Warrior (riv.) C5
Bon Secour (bay) C10
Brookley Air Force Base B9
Buttahatchee (riv.) B3
Cahaba (riv.) D5
Cedar (pt.) B10
Chattahoochee (riv.) H8
Chattooga (riv.) H2
Cheaha (mt.) G4
Choctawhatchee (riv.) H8
Coffeeville (dam) C7
Conecuh (riv.) D8
Coosa (riv.) F4
Cowikee, North Fork (creek) H6
Cumberland (plat.) F1
Dannelly (res.) D6
Demopolis (dam) C5
Elk (riv.) D1
Escambia (creek) D8
Escambia (riv.) D9
Escatawpa (riv.) B9
Fort Gaines B10
Fort McClellan
    Military Reservation 4,128 ....G3
Fort Morgan C10
Fort Rucker 7,593 ....G8
Gainesville (dam) B5
Goat Rock (dam) H5
Goat Rock (lake) H5
Grants Pass (chan.) B10
Gunter Air Force Base F6
Guntersville (dam) F2
Guntersville (lake) F2
Harding (lake) F4
Herbes (isl.) B10
Holt (dam) D4
Horseshoe Bend
    Nat'l Mil. Park G5
Inland (lake) E3
Jordan (dam) F5
Jordan (lake) F5
Lay (dam) E5
Lewis Smith (dam) D3
Lewis Smith (lake) D2
Little (riv.) C8
Little (riv.) G2
Locust Fork (riv.) E3
Logan Martin (lake) F4
Lookout (mt.) G2
Martin (dam) G5
Martin (lake) G5
Maxwell Air Force Base F6
Mexico (gulf) E10
Mississippi (sound) B10
Mitchell (lake) F5
Mobile (bay) B10
Mobile (pt.) B10
Mobile (riv.) C9
Mulberry (creek) E5
Mulberry Fork (riv.) E3
Neely Henry (lake) F3
Oakmulgee (creek) D5
Oliver (dam) J5
Paint Rock (riv.) F1
Patsaliga (creek) F7
Pea (riv.) F8
Perdido (bay) D10
Perdido (riv.) C9
Pickwick (lake) B1
Pigeon (creek) F7
Redstone Arsenal E1
Russell Cave Nat'l Mon. G1
Sand (mt.) G1
Sandy (creek) H7
Sepulga (riv.) E7
Sipsey (riv.) B4
Sipsey Fork (riv.) D2
Tallapoosa (riv.) G5
Tennessee (riv.) C1
Tennessee-Tombigbee
    Waterway B4
Tensaw (riv.) C9
Thurlow (dam) G5
Tombigbee (riv.) B7
Town (creek) E3
Tuscaloosa (lake) D4
Tuskegee Institute
    Nat'l Hist. Site G6
Walter F. George (dam) H7
Walter F. George (res.) H7
Warrior (riv.) C5
Weiss (lake) G2
West Point (lake) H4
Wheeler (dam) D1
Wheeler (lake) D1
Wilson (dam) C1
Yates (dam) G5

▲County seat.

Alabama

SCALE
0 5 10   20   30   40 MI.

0 5 10   20   30   40 KM.

State Capitals...............⊛

County Seats.................◉

Major Limited Access Hwys.

Scale 1:1,930,000

© Copyright HAMMOND INCORPORATED, Maplewood, N.J.

Agriculture, Industry and Resources

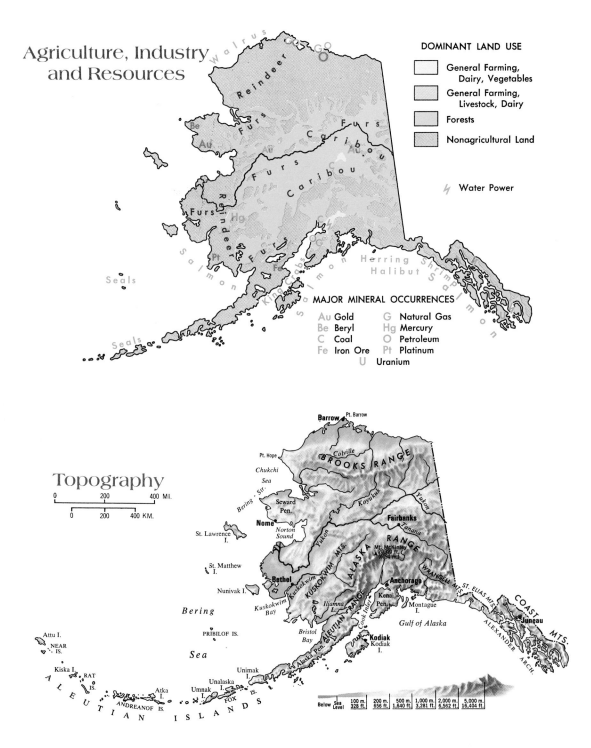

DOMINANT LAND USE

- General Farming, Dairy, Vegetables
- General Farming, Livestock, Dairy
- Forests
- Nonagricultural Land

⚡ Water Power

MAJOR MINERAL OCCURRENCES

Au	Gold	G	Natural Gas
Be	Beryl	Hg	Mercury
C	Coal	O	Petroleum
Fe	Iron Ore	Pt	Platinum
U	Uranium		

Topography

0 200 400 MI.
0 200 400 KM.

Below Sea Level | 100 m. 328 ft. | 200 m. 656 ft. | 500 m. 1,640 ft. | 1,000 m. 3,281 ft. | 2,000 m. 6,562 ft. | 5,000 m. 16,404 ft.

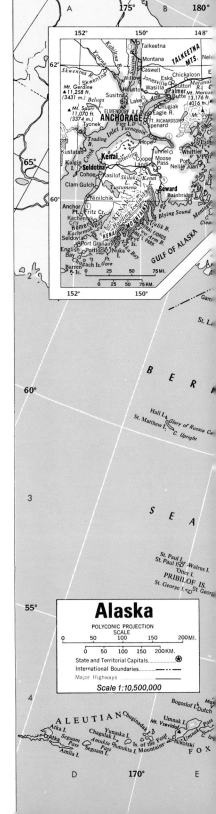

Alaska

POLYCONIC PROJECTION
SCALE
0 50 100 150 200MI.
0 50 100 150 200KM.

State and Territorial Capitals ⊛
International Boundaries
Major Highways

Scale 1:10,500,000

AREA 591,004 sq. mi. (1,530,700 sq. km.)
POPULATION 551,947
CAPITAL Juneau
LARGEST CITY Anchorage
HIGHEST POINT Mt. McKinley 20,320 ft.
(6194 m.)
SETTLED IN 1801
ADMITTED TO UNION January 3, 1959
POPULAR NAME Great Land; Last Frontier
STATE FLOWER Forget-me-not
STATE BIRD Willow Ptarmigan

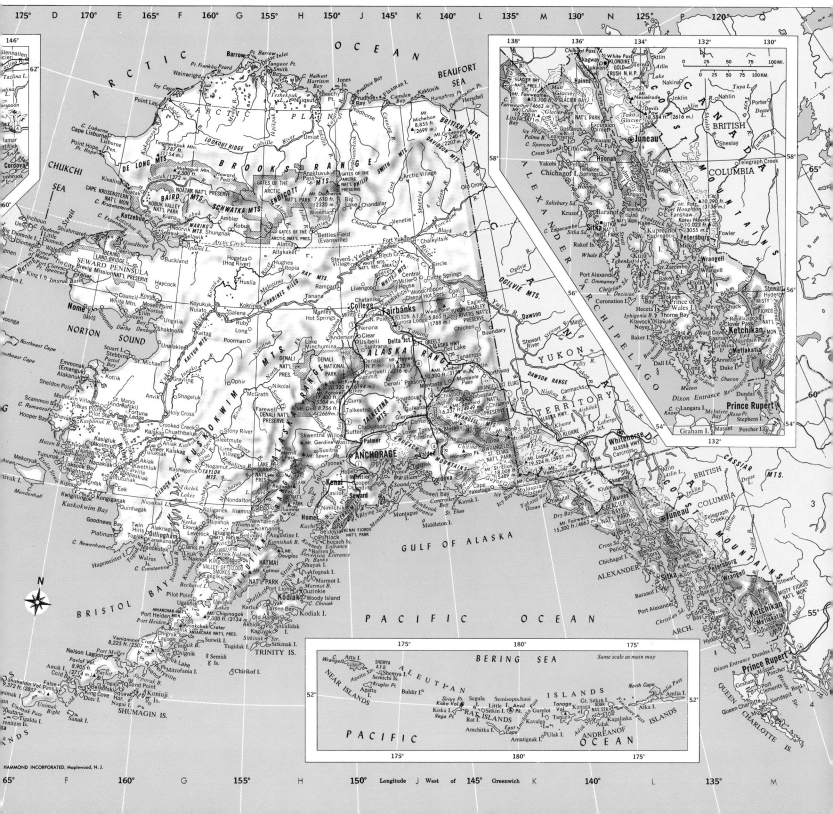

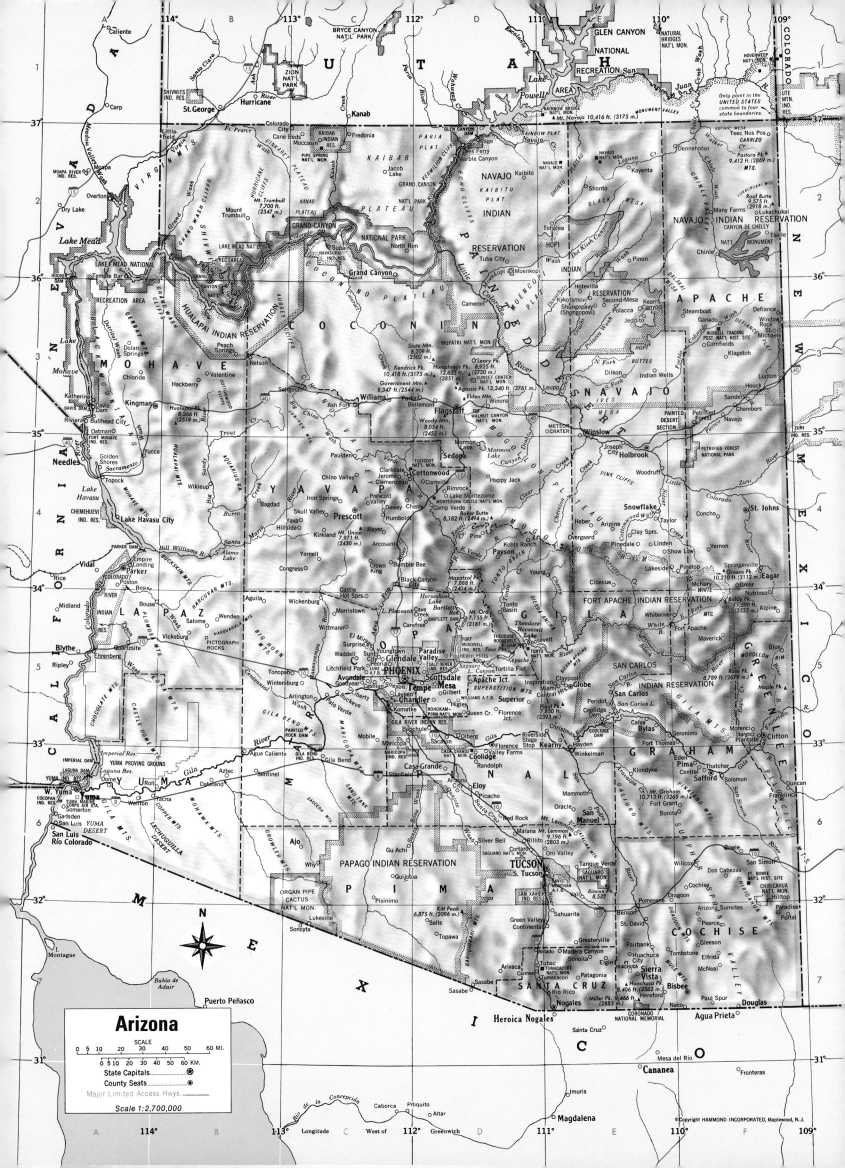

AREA 114,000 sq. mi. (295,260 sq. km.)
POPULATION 3,677,985
CAPITAL Phoenix
LARGEST CITY Phoenix
HIGHEST POINT Humphreys Pk. 12,633 ft.
(3851 m.)
SETTLED IN 1752
ADMITTED TO UNION February 14, 1912
POPULAR NAME Grand Canyon State
STATE FLOWER Saguaro Cactus Blossom
STATE BIRD Cactus Wren

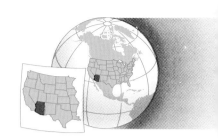

Agriculture, Industry and Resources

MAJOR MINERAL OCCURRENCES

Ab	Asbestos	Cu	Copper	Pb	Lead
Ag	Silver	Gp	Gypsum	U	Uranium
Au	Gold	Hg	Mercury	V	Vanadium
C	Coal	Mo	Molybdenum	Zn	Zinc

DOMINANT LAND USE

- Fruit, Truck and Mixed Farming
- Cotton and Alfalfa
- General Farming, Livestock, Special Crops
- Range Livestock
- Forests
- Nonagricultural Land

⚡ Water Power
▨ Major Industrial Areas

COUNTIES

Apache 61,591	F3
Cochise 97,624	F7
Coconino 96,591	C3
Gila 40,216	E5
Graham 26,554	E6
Greenlee 8,008	F5
La Paz 13,844	A5
Maricopa 2,122,101	C5
Mohave 93,497	A3
Navajo 77,658	E3
Pima 666,880	D6
Pinal 116,379	D6
Santa Cruz 29,676	E7
Yavapai 107,714	C4
Yuma 106,895	A5

CITIES and TOWNS

Agua Caliente 60	B6
Aguila 900	B5
Ajo 2,919	C6
Alpine 450	F5
Amado 75	D7
Apache Junction 18,100	D5
Arcosanti	C4
Aripine 25	E4
Arivaca 400	D7
Arizona City 1,940	D6
Arizona Sunsites 825	F7
Arlington 950	C5
Ash Fork 800	C3
Avondale 16,169	C5
Aztec 20	B6
Bagdad 1,858	B4
Bapchule 400	D5

Bellemont 210	D3
Benson 3,824	E7
Bisbee▲ 6,288	F7
Black Canyon City 1,811	C4
Blue 50	F5
Bonita 20	E6
Bouse 500	A5
Bowie 600	F6
Buckeye 5,038	C5
Bullhead City	
(Bullhead City-Riviera)	
21,951	A3
Bumble Bee 15	C4
Bylas 1,219	E5
Calva 10	E5
Cameron 493	D3
Camp Verde 6,243	D4
Cane Beds 30	B2
Carefree 1,666	C5
Carmen 200	D7
Casa Grande 19,082	D6
Cashion 3,014	C5
Castle Hot Springs 50	C5
Cave Creek 2,925	D5
Central 300	F6
Central Heights	
(Central Heights-	
Midland City) 2,791	E5
Chambers 500	F3
Chandler 90,533	D5
Cherry 20	C4
Chinle 5,059	F2
Chino Valley 4,837	C4
Chloride 225	A3
Christmas 201	E5
Cibecue 1,254	E4
Clarkdale 2,144	C4

Clay Springs 500	E4
Claypool 1,942	E5
Clemenceau 300	C4
Clifton▲ 2,840	F5
Cochise 150	F6
Colorado City 2,426	B2
Concho 100	F4
Congress 800	C4
Continental 250	D7
Coolidge 6,927	D6
Coolidge Dam 42	E5
Cornfields 200	F3
Cornville 2,089	D4
Cortaro 375	D6
Cottonwood 5,918	D4
Crown King 100	C4
Dateland 100	B6
Davis Dam 125	A3
Dennehotso 616	F2
Dewey 100	C4
Dilkon 90	E3
Dolan Springs 1,090	A3
Dome 48	A6
Dos Cabezas 30	F6
Douglas 12,822	F7
Dragoon 150	F6
Duncan 662	F6
Eagar 4,025	F4
Eden 89	F6
Ehrenberg 1,226	A5
El Mirage 5,001	C5
Elfrida 700	F7
Elgin 525	E7
Eloy 7,211	D6
Empire Landing	A4
Fairbank 100	E7
Flagstaff▲ 45,857	D3

(continued on following page)

Topography

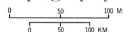

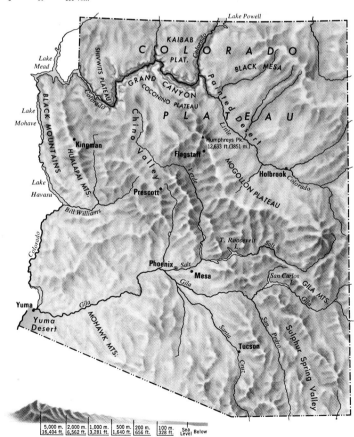

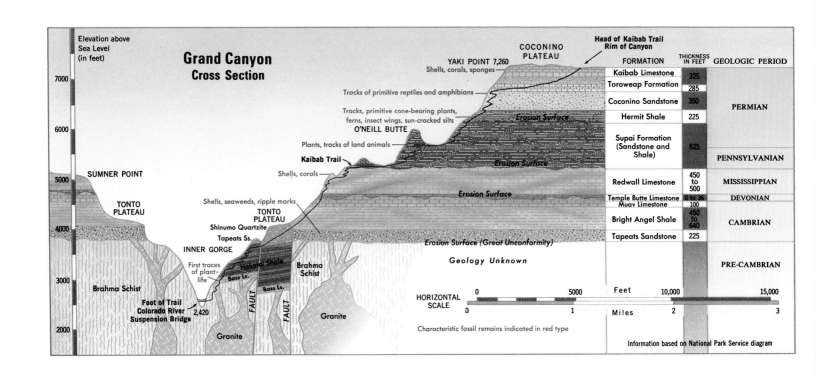

Grand Canyon Cross Section

Elevation above Sea Level (in feet)

7000, 6000, 5000, 4000, 3000, 2000

SUMNER POINT
TONTO PLATEAU
Brahma Schist
Foot of Trail
Colorado River Suspension Bridge 2,420
INNER GORGE
First traces of plant-life
Bass Ls.
Hakatai Shale
Bass Ls.
FAULT
FAULT
Shinumo Quartzite
Tapeats Ss.
Granite
Brahma Schist
Granite
Shells, seaweeds, ripple marks
TONTO PLATEAU
Shells, corals
Kaibab Trail
Plants, tracks of land animals
O'NEILL BUTTE
Tracks, primitive cone-bearing plants, ferns, insect wings, sun-cracked silts
Tracks of primitive reptiles and amphibians
Shells, corals, sponges
YAKI POINT 7,260
COCONINO PLATEAU
Head of Kaibab Trail Rim of Canyon
Erosion Surface
Erosion Surface
Erosion Surface
Erosion Surface (Great Unconformity)
Geology Unknown

FORMATION	THICKNESS IN FEET	GEOLOGIC PERIOD
Kaibab Limestone	325	PERMIAN
Toroweap Formation	285	PERMIAN
Coconino Sandstone	350	PERMIAN
Hermit Shale	225	PERMIAN
Supai Formation (Sandstone and Shale)	825	PENNSYLVANIAN
Redwall Limestone	450 to 500	MISSISSIPPIAN
Temple Butte Limestone	0 to 36	DEVONIAN
Muav Limestone	100	CAMBRIAN
Bright Angel Shale	450 to 640	CAMBRIAN
Tapeats Sandstone	225	CAMBRIAN
		PRE-CAMBRIAN

HORIZONTAL SCALE

0   5000   Feet   10,000   15,000
0   1   Miles   2   3

Characteristic fossil remains indicated in red type

Information based on National Park Service diagram

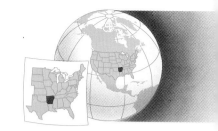

AREA 53,187 sq. mi. (137,754 sq. km.)
POPULATION 2,362,239
CAPITAL Little Rock
LARGEST CITY Little Rock
HIGHEST POINT Magazine Mtn. 2,753 ft. (839 m.)
SETTLED IN 1685
ADMITTED TO UNION June 15, 1836
POPULAR NAME Land of Opportunity
STATE FLOWER Apple Blossom
STATE BIRD Mockingbird

Agriculture, Industry and Resources

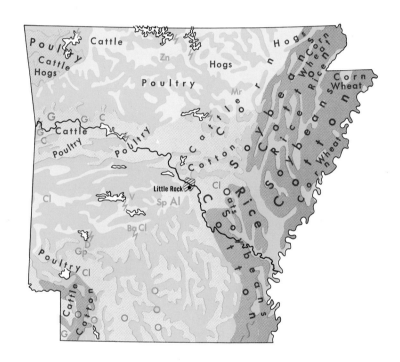

DOMINANT LAND USE

- Fruit and Mixed Farming
- Specialized Cotton
- Cotton, General Farming
- Rice, General Farming
- General Farming, Livestock, Truck Farming, Cotton
- Forests
- Swampland, Limited Agriculture

MAJOR MINERAL OCCURRENCES

Al	Bauxite	Gp	Gypsum
Ba	Barite	Mr	Marble
C	Coal	O	Petroleum
Cl	Clay	Sp	Soapstone
D	Diamonds	V	Vanadium
G	Natural Gas	Zn	Zinc
	Water Power		Major Industrial Areas

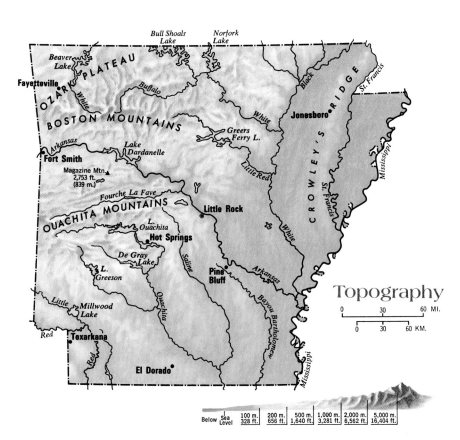

Topography

0   30   60 MI.
0   30   60 KM.

Below Sea Level | 100 m. 328 ft. | 200 m. 656 ft. | 500 m. 1,640 ft. | 1,000 m. 3,281 ft. | 2,000 m. 6,562 ft. | 5,000 m. 16,404 ft.

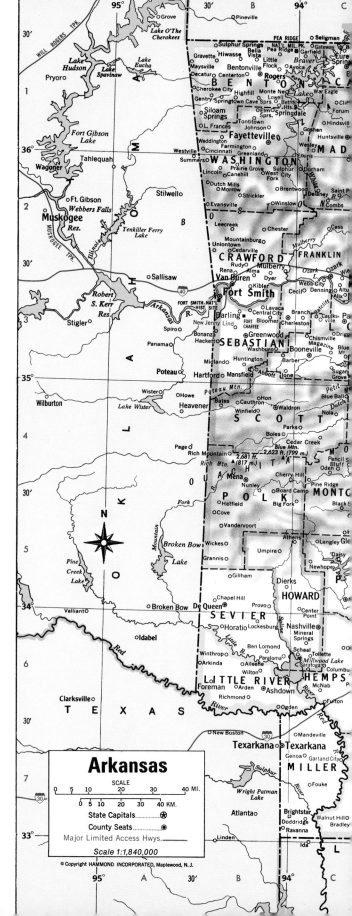

Arkansas

SCALE
0   5   10   20   30   40 MI.
0 5 10   20   30   40 KM.

State Capitals ....⊛
County Seats ....◉
Major Limited Access Hwys. _____

Scale 1:1,840,000

© Copyright HAMMOND INCORPORATED, Maplewood, N.J.

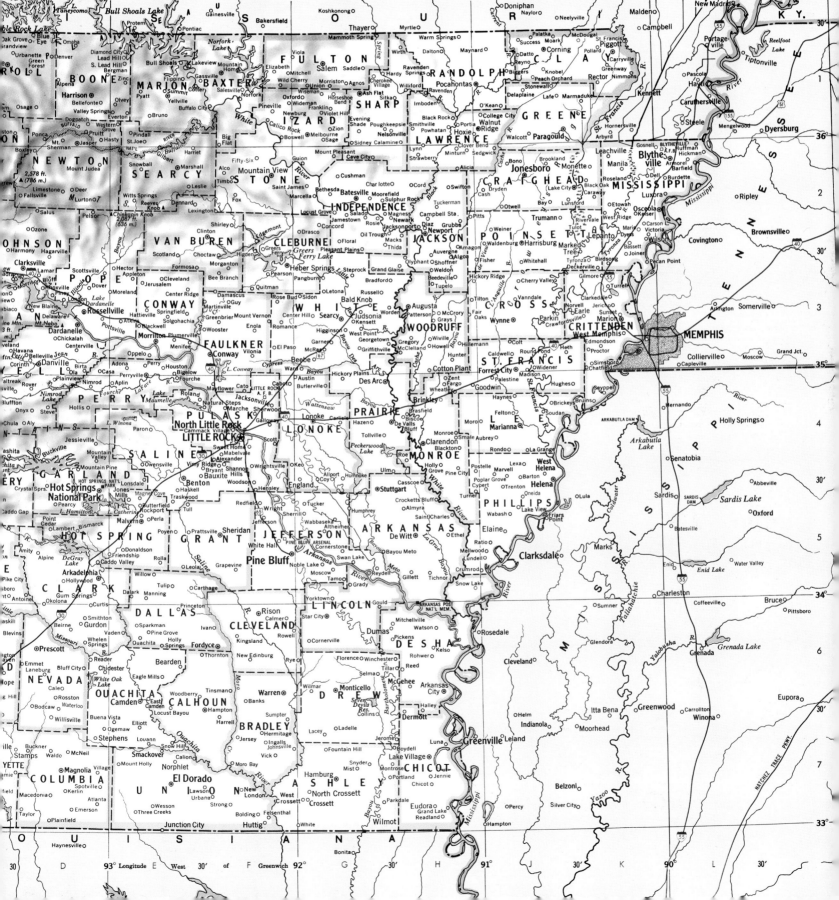

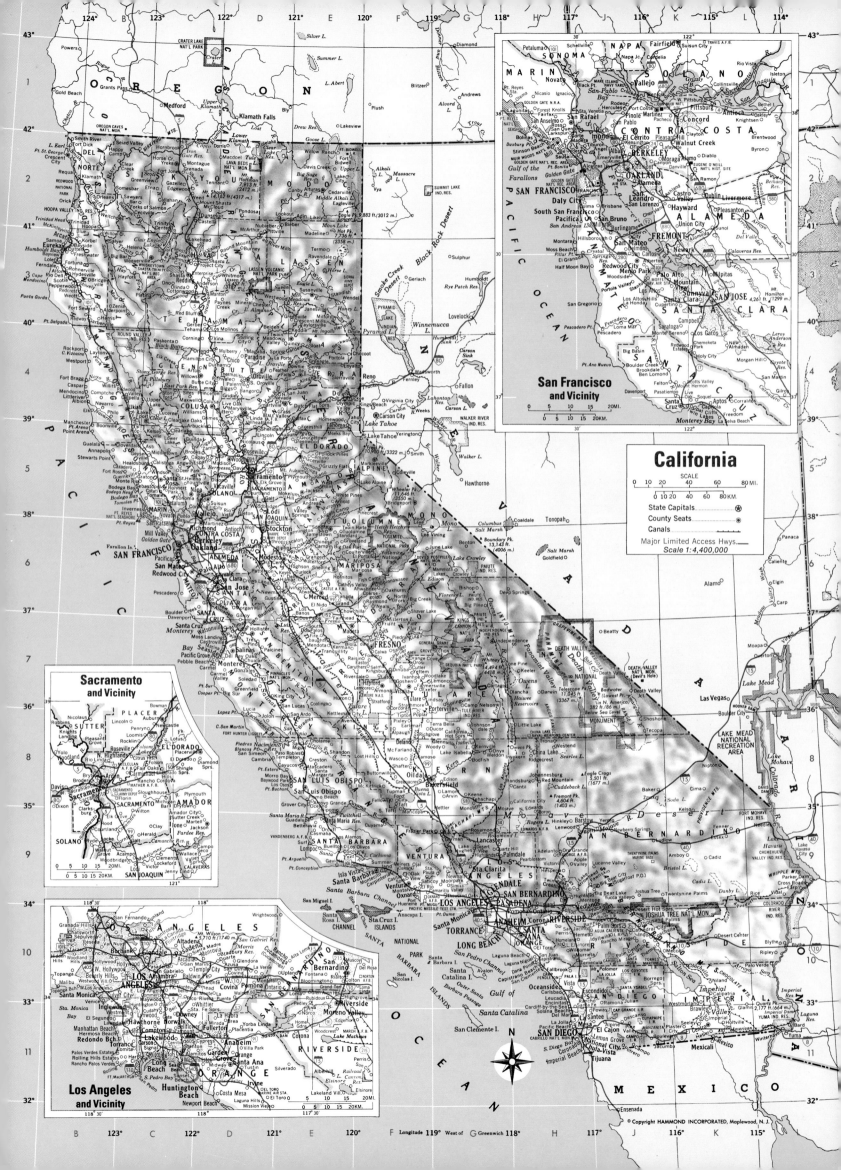

California

SCALE
0 10 20   40   60   80 MI.

0 10 20 40   60   80 KM.

State Capitals	⊛
County Seats	⊙
Canals	

Major Limited Access Hwys.

Scale 1:4,400,000

San Francisco and Vicinity

0   5   10   15   20MI.

0   5   10   15   20KM.

Sacramento and Vicinity

0   5   10   15   20MI.

0 5 10 15 20KM.

Los Angeles and Vicinity

0   5   10   15   20MI.

0   5   10   15 20KM.

© Copyright HAMMOND INCORPORATED, Maplewood, N.J.

CALIFORNIA REPUBLIC

AREA 158,706 sq. mi. (411,049 sq. km.)
POPULATION 29,839,250
CAPITAL Sacramento
LARGEST CITY Los Angeles
HIGHEST POINT Mt. Whitney 14,494 ft. (4418 m.)
SETTLED IN 1769
ADMITTED TO UNION September 9, 1850
POPULAR NAME Golden State
STATE FLOWER Golden Poppy
STATE BIRD California Valley Quail

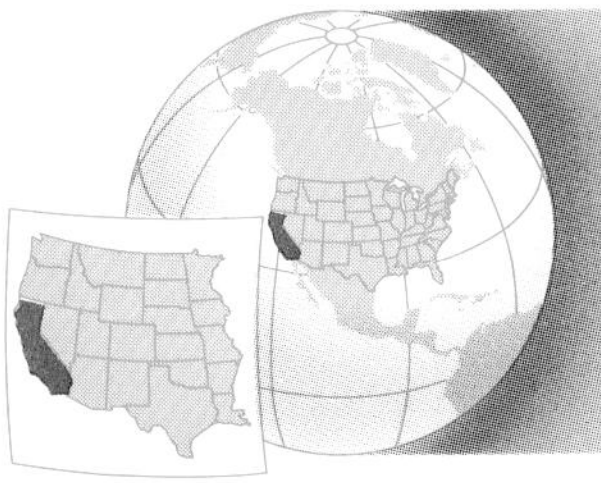

COUNTIES

Alameda 1,279,182 ....D6
Alpine 1,113 ....F5
Amador 30,039 ....E5
Butte 182,120 ....D4
Calaveras 31,998 ....E5
Colusa 16,275 ....C4
Contra Costa 803,732 ....D6
Del Norte 23,460 ....B2
El Dorado 125,995 ....E5
Fresno 667,490 ....E7
Glenn 24,798 ....C4
Humboldt 119,118 ....B3
Imperial 109,303 ....K1
Inyo 18,281 ....H7
Kern 543,477 ....G8
Kings 101,469 ....E8
Lake 50,631 ....C4
Lassen 27,598 ....E3
Los Angeles 8,863,164 ....G9
Madera 88,090 ....F6
Marin 230,096 ....C5
Mariposa 14,302 ....E6
Mendocino 80,345 ....B4
Merced 178,403 ....E6
Modoc 9,678 ....E2
Mono 9,956 ....F5
Monterey 355,660 ....D7
Napa 110,765 ....C5
Nevada 78,510 ....E4
Orange 2,410,556 ....H1
Placer 172,796 ....E4
Plumas 19,739 ....E4
Riverside 1,170,413 ....J1
Sacramento 1,041,219 ....D5
San Benito 36,697 ....D7
San Bernardino 1,418,380 ....J9
San Diego 2,498,016 ....J1
San Francisco 723,959 ....J2
San Joaquin 480,628 ....D5
San Luis Obispo 217,162 ....E8
San Mateo 649,623 ....J3
Santa Barbara 369,608 ....E9
Santa Clara 1,497,577 ....D6
Santa Cruz 229,734 ....C6
Shasta 147,036 ....C3
Sierra 3,318 ....E4
Siskiyou 43,531 ....C2
Solano 340,421 ....D5
Sonoma 388,222 ....C5
Stanislaus 370,522 ....D6
Sutter 64,415 ....D4
Tehama 49,625 ....C3
Trinity 13,063 ....B3
Tulare 311,921 ....G7
Tuolumne 48,456 ....F5
Ventura 669,016 ....F9
Yolo 141,092 ....D5
Yuba 58,228 ....D4

CITIES and TOWNS

Adelanto 8,517 ....H9
Alameda 76,459 ....J2
Alamo 12,277 ....K2
Albany 16,327 ....J2
Alhambra 82,106 ....C10
Alpine 9,695 ....J11
Alta Loma E10
Altadena 42,658 ....C10
Alturas▲ 3,231 ....E2
Amador City 196 ....C9
Anaheim 266,406 ....D11
Anderson 8,299 ....C3
Angels Camp 2,302 ....E5
Angwin 3,503 ....C5
Antioch 62,195 ....L1
Apple Valley 46,079 ....H9
Aptos 9,061 ....K4
Arbuckle 1,912 ....C4
Arcadia 48,290 ....C10
Arcata 15,197 ....A3
Arden-Arcade 92,040 ....B8
Armona 3,122 ....F7
Arnold 3,788 ....E5
Aromas 2,275 ....D7
Arroyo Grande 14,378 ....E8
Artesia 15,464 ....C11
Arvin 9,286 ....G8
Ashland 16,590 ....K2
Asti 75 ....C5
Atascadero 23,138 ....E8
Atherton 7,163 ....K3
Atwater 22,282 ....E6
Auberry 1,866 ....F6
Auburn▲ 10,592 ....C8
Avalon 2,918 ....G10
Avenal 9,770 ....E8
Azusa 41,333 ....D10
Baker 174,820 ....J8
Bakersfield▲ 105,611 ....G8
Baldwin Park 69,330 ....D10
Banning 20,570 ....J10
Barstow 21,472 ....H9
Bayview 1,318 ....A3
Baywood Park (Baywood Park–Los Osos) 10,933 ....E8
Beaumont 9,685 ....J10
Bell 34,365 ....C11
Bell Gardens 42,355 ....C11
Bellflower 61,815 ....C11
Belmont 24,127 ....J3
Belvedere 2,147 ....H2
Ben Lomond 7,884 ....K4
Benicia 24,437 ....K1
Berkeley 102,724 ....J2
Bethel Island 2,115 ....L1
Beverly Hills 31,971 ....B10
Big Bear City (Sugarloaf Post Office) 4,920 ....J9
Big Bear Lake 5,351 ....J9
Big Pine 1,158 ....G6
Biggs 1,581 ....D4
Bishop 3,475 ....G6
Bloomington 15,116 ....E10
Blue Lake 1,235 ....B3
Blythe 8,428 ....L10
Bodfish 1,283 ....G8
Bolinas 1,098 ....H1
Boron 2,101 ....H8
Borrego Springs 2,244 ....J10
Boulder Creek 6,725 ....J4
Bowman C7
Brawley 18,923 ....K11
Brea 32,873 ....D11
Brentwood 7,563 ....L2
Bridgeport▲ 525 ....F5
Brisbane 2,952 ....J2
Broderick (Broderick-Bryte) 10,194 ....B8
Bryte (Bryte-Broderick) 10,194 ....B8
Buellton 3,506 ....E9
Buena Park 68,784 ....D11
Burbank 93,643 ....C10
Burlingame 26,801 ....J2
Burney 3,423 ....D3
Buttonwillow 1,301 ....F8
Cabazon 1,588 ....J10
Calexico 18,633 ....K11
California City 5,955 ....H8
Calipatria 2,690 ....K10
Calistoga 4,468 ....C5
Calwa 6,640 ....F7
Camarillo 52,303 ....G9
Cambria 5,382 ....D8
Campbell 36,048 ....K3
Canoga Park B10
Canyon 7,938 ....K2
Capistrano Beach 6,168 ....H10
Capitola 10,171 ....K4
Cardiff-by-the-Sea 10,054 ....H10
Carlsbad 63,126 ....H10
Carmel 4,407 ....D7
Carmel Valley 4,013 ....D7
Carmichael 48,702 ....C8
Carpinteria 13,747 ....F9
Carson 83,995 ....C11
Caruthers 1,603 ....E7
Casitas Springs 1,038 ....F9
Castro Valley 48,619 ....K2
Castroville 5,272 ....D7
Cathedral City 30,085 ....J10
Cayucos 2,960 ....E8
Central Valley 4,340 ....C3
Ceres 26,314 ....D6
Cerritos 53,240 ....C11
Chatsworth B10
Chemeketa Park (Chemeketa Park-Redwood Estates) 1,847 ....K4
Cherryland 11,088 ....K2
Chester 2,082 ....D3
Chico 40,079 ....D4
China Lake 4,275 ....H8
Chinese Camp 150 ....E6
Chino 59,682 ....D10
Chowchilla 5,930 ....E6
Chula Vista 135,163 ....J11
Citrus Heights 107,439 ....C8
Claremont 32,503 ....D10
Clay 7,317 ....C9
Clayton 4,325 ....K2
Clearlake 11,804 ....C5
Clearlake Oaks 2,419 ....C4
Cloverdale 4,924 ....B5
Clovis 50,323 ....F7
Coachella 16,896 ....J10
Coalinga 8,212 ....E7
Colfax 1,306 ....E4
Colton 40,213 ....E10
Columbia 1,799 ....E5
Colusa▲ 4,934 ....C4
Commerce 12,135 ....C10
Compton 90,454 ....C11
Concord 111,348 ....K1
Corcoran 13,364 ....F7
Corning 5,870 ....C4
Corona 76,095 ....E11
Coronado 26,540 ....H11
Corralitos 2,513 ....L4
Corte Madera 8,272 ....J2
Costa Mesa 96,357 ....D11
Cotati 5,714 ....C5
Cottonwood 1,747 ....C3
Covina 43,207 ....D10
Crescent City▲ 4,380 ....A2
Crestline 8,594 ....H9
Crockett 3,228 ....J1
Crowley Lake G6
Cudahy 22,817 ....C11
Culver City 38,793 ....B10
Cupertino 40,263 ....K3
Cutler 4,450 ....F7
Cutten 1,516 ....A3
Cypress 42,655 ....D11
Daly City 92,311 ....H2
Dana Point 31,896 ....H10
Danville 31,306 ....K2
Davis 46,209 ....B8
Death Valley Junction J7
Deer Park 1,825 ....C5
Del Mar 4,860 ....H11
Del Rey Oaks 1,661 ....D7
Del Rosa F10
Delano 22,762 ....F8
Delhi 3,280 ....E6
Desert Hot Springs 11,668 ....J9
Desert View Highlands 2,154 ....G9
Diamond Springs 2,872 ....D8
Dinuba 12,743 ....F7
Dixon 10,401 ....B9
Dorris 892 ....D2
Dos Palos 4,196 ....E6
Downey 91,444 ....C11
Downieville▲ 500 ....E4
Duarte 20,688 ....D10
Dublin 23,229 ....K2
Dunsmuir 2,129 ....C2
Durham 4,784 ....D4
Earlimart 5,881 ....F8
East Blythe 1,511 ....L10
East Los Angeles 126,379 ....C10
Easton 1,877 ....F7
Edgemont E11
Edison G8
El Cajon 88,693 ....J11
El Centro▲ 31,384 ....K11
El Cerrito 4,490 ....J2
El Dorado 6,395 ....C8
El Dorado Hills 3,453 ....C8
El Granada 4,426 ....H3
El Monte 106,209 ....D10
El Rio 6,419 ....F9
El Segundo 15,223 ....B11
El Toro 62,685 ....E11
Elk 17,483 ....B4
Elk Grove 10,959 ....B9
Emeryville 5,740 ....J2
Empire D6
Encinitas 55,386 ....H10
Encino B10
Enterprise C3
Escalon 4,437 ....E6
Escondido 108,635 ....J10
Esparto 1,487 ....C5
Eureka▲ 27,025 ....A3
Exeter 7,276 ....F7
Fair Oaks 26,867 ....C8
Fairfax 6,931 ....H1
Fairfield▲ 77,211 ....K1
Fallbrook 22,095 ....H10
Farmersville 6,235 ....F7
Felton 5,350 ....K4
Ferndale 1,331 ....A3
Fillmore 11,992 ....G9
Firebaugh 4,429 ....E7
Florin 24,330 ....B8
Folsom 29,802 ....C8
Fontana 87,535 ....E10
Ford City 3,781 ....F8
Forest Knolls (Forest Knolls-Lagunitas) H1
Foresthill 1,409 ....E4
Fort Bragg 6,078 ....B4
Fortuna 8,788 ....A3
Foster City 28,176 ....J2
Fountain Valley 53,691 ....D11
Fowler 3,208 ....F7
Frazier Park 2,201 ....F9
Freedom 8,361 ....L4
Fremont 173,339 ....K3
Fresno▲ 354,202 ....F7
Fullerton 114,144 ....D11
Galt 8,889 ....C9
Garden Grove 143,050 ....D11
Gardena 49,847 ....C11
Gilroy 31,487 ....D6
Glen Avon Heights 8,444 ....E10
Glendale 180,038 ....C10
Glendora 47,828 ....D10
Goleta F9
Gonzales 4,660 ....D7
Goshen 1,809 ....F7
Granada Hills B10
Grand Terrace 10,946 ....E10
Grass Valley 9,048 ....D4
Graton 1,409 ....C5
Greenacres 7,379 ....F8
Greenfield 7,464 ....D7
Greenville 1,396 ....E3
Gridley 4,631 ....D4
Groveland 2,753 ....E6
Grover City 11,656 ....E8
Guadalupe 5,479 ....E9
Guerneville 1,966 ....B5
Gustine 3,931 ....D6
Half Moon Bay 8,886 ....H3
Hamilton City 1,811 ....C4
Hanford▲ 30,897 ....F7
Harbor City C11
Hawthorne 71,349 ....C11
Hayfork 2,605 ....B3
Hayward 111,498 ....K2
Healdsburg 9,469 ....B5
Heber 2,566 ....K11
Hemet 36,094 ....H10
Hercules 16,829 ....J1
Herlong 1,188 ....E3
Hermosa Beach 18,219 ....B11
Hesperia 50,418 ....H9
Hidden Hills 1,729 ....B10
Highgrove 3,175 ....E10
Highland 34,439 ....H9
Hillsborough 10,667 ....J2
Hilmar (Hilmar-Irwin) 3,392 ....E6
Hollister▲ 19,212 ....D7
Hollywood C10
Holt 4,820 ....D6
Holtville 4,399 ....K11
Home Gardens 7,780 ....E11
Homeland 3,312 ....H10
Hughson 3,259 ....E6
Huntington Beach 181,519 ....C11
Huntington Park 56,065 ....C11
Huron 4,766 ....E7
Idyllwild (Idyllwild-Pine Cove) 2,853 ....J10
Imperial 4,113 ....K11
Imperial Beach 26,512 ....H11
Independence▲ 748 ....H7
Indian Wells 2,647 ....J10
Indio 36,793 ....J10
Inglewood 109,602 ....B11
Inverness 1,422 ....B5
Ione 6,516 ....C9
Irvine 110,330 ....D11
Isla Vista 20,395 ....E9
Ivanhoe 3,293 ....F7
Jackson▲ 3,545 ....C9
Jamestown 2,178 ....E6
Joshua Tree 3,898 ....J9
Julian 1,284 ....J10
Kelseyville 2,861 ....C5
Kensington 4,974 ....J2
Kerman 5,448 ....E7
Kernville 1,656 ....G8
Kettleman City 1,411 ....E7
Keyes 2,878 ....E6
King City 7,634 ....D7
Kings Beach 2,796 ....F4
Kingsburg 7,205 ....F7
La Canada Flintridge 19,378 ....C10
La Crescenta (La Crescenta-Montrose) 16,968 ....C10
La Habra 51,266 ....D11
La Mesa 52,931 ....H11
La Mirada 40,452 ....D11
La Puente 36,955 ....D10
La Selva Beach 1,603 ....K4
La Verne 30,897 ....D10
Lafayette 23,501 ....K2
Laguna Beach 23,170 ....G10
Laguna Hills 46,731 ....D11
Laguna Niguel 44,400 ....H10
Lagunitas (Lagunitas-Forest Knolls) 1,821 ....H1
Lake Arrowhead 6,539 ....H9
Lake Elsinore 18,285 ....F11
Lake Isabella 3,323 ....G8
Lakeland Village 5,159 ....E11
Lakeport▲ 4,390 ....C4
Lakewood 73,557 ....C11
Lamont 11,517 ....G8
Lancaster 97,291 ....G9
Larkspur 11,070 ....H1
Lathrop 6,841 ....D6
Laton 1,415 ....F7
Lawndale 27,331 ....B11
Le Grand 1,205 ....E6
Lemon Grove 23,984 ....J11
Lemoore 13,622 ....F7
Lenwood 3,190 ....H9
Leucadia 9,478 ....H10
Lewiston 1,187 ....C3
Lincoln 7,248 ....B8
Linda 13,033 ....D4
Linden 1,339 ....D5
Lindsay 8,338 ....F7
Live Oak 11,482 ....K4
Live Oak 3,103 ....D4
Live Oak 4,320 ....K4
Livermore 56,741 ....L2
Livingston 7,317 ....E6
Locke 2,722 ....B9
Lockeford 1,852 ....C9
Lodi 51,874 ....C9
Loma Linda 17,400 ....F10
Lomita 19,382 ....C11
Lompoc 37,649 ....E9
Lone Pine 1,818 ....H7
Long Beach 429,433 ....C11
Loomis 5,705 ....C8
Los Alamitos 11,676 ....D11
Los Altos 26,303 ....K3
Los Altos Hills 7,514 ....J3
Los Angeles▲ 3,485,398 ....C10
Los Banos 14,519 ....E6
Los Gatos 27,357 ....K4
Los Molinos 1,709 ....D3
Los Osos (Los Osos-Baywood Park) 10,933 ....E8
Lost Hills 1,212 ....F8
Lower Lake 1,217 ....C5
Lucerne 2,011 ....C4
Lynwood 61,945 ....C11
Madera▲ 29,281 ....E7
Magalia 8,987 ....D4
Mammoth Lakes 4,785 ....G6
Manhattan Beach 32,063 ....B11
Manteca 40,773 ....D6
Maricopa 1,193 ....F8
Marina 26,436 ....D7
Mariposa▲ 1,152 ....F6
Markleeville▲ 500 ....F5
Martinez▲ 31,808 ....K1
Marysville▲ 12,324 ....D4
Maywood 27,850 ....C10
McCloud 1,555 ....C2
McFarland 7,005 ....F8
McKinleyville 10,749 ....A3
Mecca 1,966 ....K10
Meiners Oaks (Meiners Oaks-Mira Monte) 3,329 ....F9
Mendota 6,821 ....E7
Menlo Park 28,040 ....J3
Mentone 5,675 ....H9
Merced▲ 56,216 ....E6
Mill Valley 13,038 ....H2
Millbrae 20,412 ....J2
Milpitas 50,686 ....L3
Mira Loma 15,786 ....E10
Mission Viejo 72,820 ....D11
Modesto▲ 164,730 ....D6
Mojave 3,763 ....G8
Monrovia 35,761 ....D10
Montague 1,415 ....C2
Montara 2,552 ....H3
Montclair 28,434 ....D10
Monte Sereno 3,287 ....K4
Montebello 59,564 ....C10
Monterey 31,954 ....D7
Monterey Park 60,738 ....C10
Montrose (Montrose-La Crescenta) C10
Moorpark 25,494 ....G9
Moraga 15,852 ....K2
Moreno Valley 118,779 ....H10
Morgan Hill 23,928 ....L4
Morro Bay 9,664 ....D8
Moss Beach 3,002 ....H3
Mount Shasta 3,460 ....C2
Mountain View 67,460 ....K3
Mulberry 1,946 ....D4
Murphys 1,517 ....E5
Murrieta 1,628 ....H10
Muscoy 7,541 ....E10
Napa▲ 61,842 ....C5
National City 54,249 ....J11
Needles 5,191 ....L9
Nevada City▲ 2,855 ....D4
Newark 37,861 ....K3
Newhall 12,029 ....G9
Newman 4,151 ....D6
Newport Beach 66,643 ....D11
Nipomo 7,109 ....E8
Norco 23,302 ....E11
North Edwards 1,259 ....H8
North Highlands 42,105 ....B8
Norwalk 94,279 ....C11
Novato 47,585 ....H1
Oak View 3,606 ....F9
Oakdale 11,961 ....E6
Oakhurst 2,602 ....F6
Oakland▲ 372,242 ....J2
Oakley 18,374 ....L1
Oceano 6,169 ....E8
Oceanside 128,398 ....H10
Oildale 26,553 ....F8
Ojai 7,613 ....F9
Ontario 133,179 ....D10
Opal Cliffs 5,940 ....K4
Orange 110,658 ....D11
Orange Cove 5,604 ....F7
Orinda 16,642 ....J2
Orland 5,052 ....C4
Orosi 5,486 ....F7
Oroville▲ 11,960 ....D4
Oxnard 142,216 ....F9
Pacheco (Pacheco-Vine Hill) 3,325 ....K1
Pacific Grove 16,117 ....C7
Pacifica 37,670 ....H2
Pajaro 3,332 ....D7
Palermo 5,260 ....D4
Palm Desert 23,252 ....J10
Palm Springs 40,181 ....J10
Palmdale 68,842 ....G9
Palo Alto 55,900 ....K3
Palos Verdes Estates 13,512 ....B11
Paradise 25,408 ....D4
Paramount 47,669 ....C11
Parlier 7,938 ....F7
Pasadena 131,591 ....C10
Paso Robles 18,583 ....E8
Patterson 8,626 ....D6
Pebble Beach C7
Pedley 8,869 ....E10
Perris 21,460 ....F11
Petaluma 43,184 ....H1
Pico Rivera 59,177 ....C10
Piedmont 10,602 ....J2
Pine Valley 1,297 ....J11
Pinole 17,460 ....J1
Piru 1,157 ....G9
Pismo Beach 7,669 ....E8
Pittsburg 47,564 ....L1
Pixley 2,457 ....F8
Placentia 41,259 ....D11
Placerville▲ 8,355 ....C8
Planada 3,531 ....E6
Pleasant Hill 31,585 ....K2
Pleasanton 50,553 ....L2
Pollock Pines 4,291 ....E5
Pomona 131,723 ....D10
Poplar (Poplar-Cotton Center) 1,901 ....F7

(continued on following page)

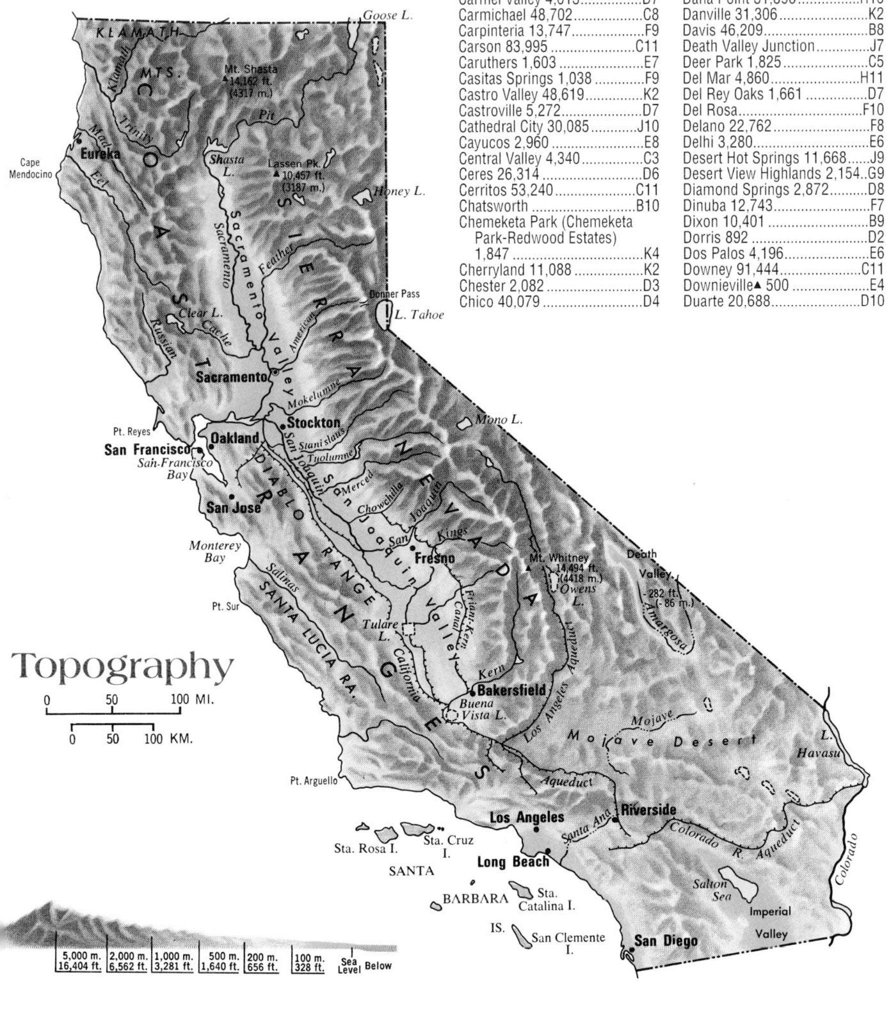
Goose L.
KLAMATH
MTS.
Mt. Shasta 14,162 ft. (4317 m.)
Pit
Trinity
Eureka
Cape Mendocino
Eel
Shasta L.
Lassen Pk. 10,457 ft. (3187 m.)
Honey L.
Sacramento
Feather
SIERRA
COAST
Clear L.
Cache
Russian
American
Donner Pass
L. Tahoe
Sacramento
Mokelumne
Stockton
Pt. Reyes
San Francisco
San Francisco Bay
Oakland
Stanislaus
Tuolumne
Merced
Mono L.
San Joaquin
DIABLO
Chowchilla
NEVADA
San Jose
Kings
Fresno
RANGE
Mt. Whitney 14,494 ft. (4418 m.)
Owens L.
Death Valley
282 ft. (86 m.)
Monterey Bay
Salinas
SANTA LUCIA RA.
Pt. Sur
Tulare L.
Amargosa
Topography
0 50 100 MI.
0 50 100 KM.
Kern
Bakersfield
Buena Vista L.
Mojave
Mojave Desert
Havasu L.
Pt. Arguello
Aqueduct
Los Angeles
Riverside
Santa Ana
Sta. Rosa I.
Sta. Cruz I.
SANTA BARBARA IS.
Long Beach
Sta. Catalina I.
San Clemente I.
Salton Sea
Imperial Valley
San Diego
Colorado
5,000 m. 16,404 ft.
2,000 m. 6,562 ft.
1,000 m. 3,281 ft.
500 m. 1,640 ft.
200 m. 656 ft.
100 m. 328 ft.
Sea Level
Below

Agriculture, Industry and Resources

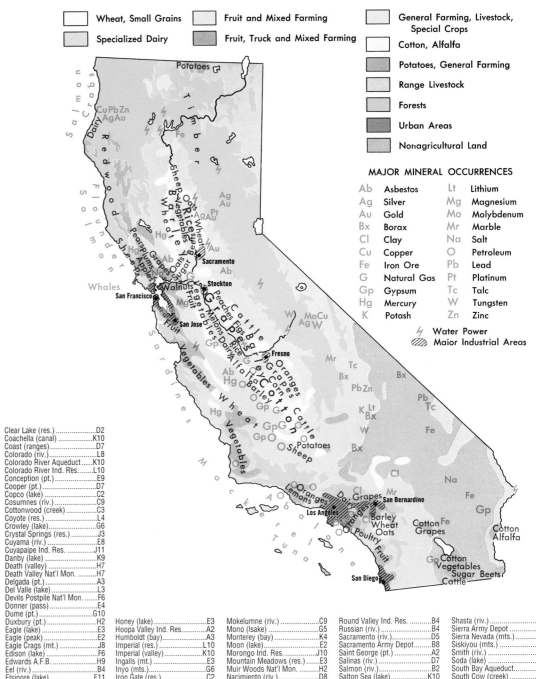

DOMINANT LAND USE

Wheat, Small Grains	Fruit and Mixed Farming
Specialized Dairy	Fruit, Truck and Mixed Farming

General Farming, Livestock, Special Crops
Cotton, Alfalfa
Potatoes, General Farming
Range Livestock
Forests
Urban Areas
Nonagricultural Land

MAJOR MINERAL OCCURRENCES

Ab	Asbestos	Lt	Lithium
Ag	Silver	Mg	Magnesium
Au	Gold	Mo	Molybdenum
Bx	Borax	Mr	Marble
Cl	Clay	Na	Salt
Cu	Copper	O	Petroleum
Fe	Iron Ore	Pb	Lead
G	Natural Gas	Pt	Platinum
Gp	Gypsum	Tc	Talc
Hg	Mercury	W	Tungsten
K	Potash	Zn	Zinc

Water Power
Major Industrial Areas

▲County seat

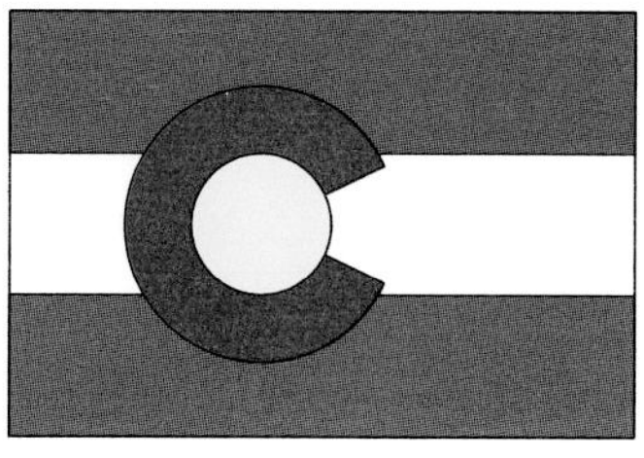

AREA 104.091 sq. mi. (269,596 sq. km.)
POPULATION 3,307,912
CAPITAL Denver
LARGEST CITY Denver
HIGHEST POINT Mt. Elbert 14,433 ft. (4399 m.)
SETTLED IN 1858
ADMITTED TO UNION August 1, 1876
POPULAR NAME Centennial State
STATE FLOWER Rocky Mountain Columbine
STATE BIRD Lark Bunting

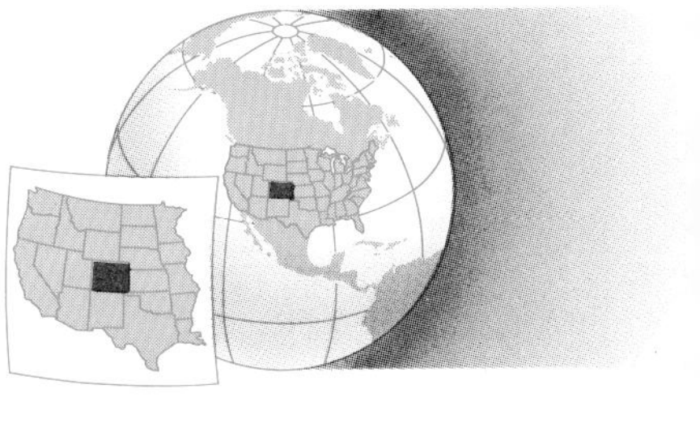

COUNTIES

Adams 265,038 ... L3
Alamosa 13,617 ... H7
Arapahoe 391,511 ... L3
Archuleta 5,345 ... E8
Baca 4,556 ... O8
Bent 5,048 ... N7
Boulder 225,339 ... J2
Chaffee 12,684 ... G5
Cheyenne 2,397 ... O5
Clear Creek 7,619 ... H3
Conejos 7,453 ... G8
Costilla 3,190 ... J8
Crowley 3,946 ... M6
Custer 1,926 ... J6
Delta 20,980 ... D5
Denver 467,610 ... K3
Dolores 1,504 ... C7
Douglas 60,391 ... K4
Eagle 21,928 ... F3
El Paso 397,014 ... K5
Elbert 9,646 ... L4
Fremont 32,273 ... J5
Garfield 29,974 ... C3
Gilpin 3,070 ... H3
Grand 7,966 ... G2
Gunnison 10,273 ... E5
Hinsdale 467 ... E7
Huerfano 6,009 ... K7
Jackson 1,605 ... G1
Jefferson 438,430 ... J3
Kiowa 1,688 ... O6
Kit Carson 7,140 ... O4
La Plata 32,284 ... D8
Lake 6,007 ... G4
Larimer 186,136 ... H1
Las Animas 13,765 ... L8
Lincoln 4,529 ... M5
Logan 17,567 ... N1
Mesa 93,145 ... B5
Mineral 558 ... F7
Moffat 11,357 ... C1
Montezuma 18,672 ... B8
Montrose 24,423 ... C6
Morgan 21,939 ... M2
Otero 20,185 ... M7
Ouray 2,295 ... D6
Park 7,174 ... H4
Phillips 4,189 ... P1
Pitkin 12,661 ... F4
Prowers 13,347 ... P7
Pueblo 123,051 ... K6
Rio Blanco 5,972 ... C3
Rio Grande 10,770 ... G7
Routt 14,088 ... E1
Saguache 4,619 ... G6
San Juan 745 ... D7
San Miguel 3,653 ... C6
Sedgwick 2,690 ... P1
Summit 12,881 ... G3
Teller 12,468 ... J5
Washington 4,812 ... N3
Weld 131,821 ... L1
Yuma 8,954 ... P2

CITIES and TOWNS

Agate 90 ... M4
Aguilar 520 ... K8
Akron▲ 1,599 ... N2
Alamosa▲ 7,579 ... H8
Allenspark 200 ... J2
Alma 148 ... G4
Almont 135 ... F5
Amherst 85 ... P1
Anton 875 ... N3
Antonito 1,103 ... H8
Arapahoe 300 ... P5
Arlington 37 ... N6
Arriba 220 ... N4
Arriola 5,672 ... B8
Arvada 89,235 ... J3
Aspen▲ 5,049 ... F4
Atwood 100 ... N1
Ault 1,107 ... K1
Aurora 222,103 ... K3
Austin ... D5
Avon 1,798 ... F3
Avondale 750 ... L6
Bailey 150 ... H4
Barnesville 20 ... L2
Basalt 1,128 ... E4
Bayfield 1,090 ... D8
Bedrock 45 ... B6
Beecher Island 5 ... P3
Bellvue 250 ... J1
Bennett 1,757 ... L3
Berthoud 2,990 ... J2
Berthoud Pass 40 ... H3
Bethune 173 ... P4
Beulah 650 ... K6
Black Forest 8,143 ... K4
Black Hawk 227 ... J3
Blanca 272 ... H8
Blue River 440 ... G4
Bonanza 16 ... G6
Boncarbo 200 ... K8
Bond 65 ... F3
Boone 341 ... L6
Boulder▲ 83,312 ... J2
Bowie 18 ... D5
Boyero 12 ... N5
Brandon 30 ... P6
Branson 58 ... M8
Breckenridge▲ 1,285 ... G4
Briggsdale 85 ... L1
Brighton▲ 14,203 ... K3
Bristol 200 ... P6
Brookside 183 ... J6
Broomfield 24,638 ... J3
Brush 4,165 ... M2
Buckingham 5 ... L1
Buena Vista 1,752 ... G5
Buffalo Creek 150 ... J4
Burlington▲ 2,941 ... P4
Burns 100 ... F3
Byers 1,065 ... L3
Cahone 200 ... B7
Calhan 562 ... L4
Campo 121 ... O8
Canon City▲ 12,687 ... J6
Capulin 600 ... G8
Carbondale 3,004 ... E4
Carr 49 ... K1
Cascade 1,479 ... K5
Castle Rock▲ 8,708 ... K4
Cedaredge 1,380 ... D5
Center 1,963 ... G7
Central City▲ 335 ... J3
Chama 239 ... J8
Cheraw 265 ... N6
Cheyenne Wells▲ 1,128 ... P5
Chimney Rock 76 ... E8
Chivington 20 ... O6
Chromo 115 ... F8
Cimarron 50 ... D6
Clark 20 ... F1
Clifton 12,671 ... C4
Climax 975 ... G4
Coal Creek 157 ... J6
Coaldale 153 ... H6
Coalmont 50 ... F1
Cokedale 116 ... K8
Collbran 228 ... C4
Colona 54 ... D6
Colorado City 1,149 ... K6
Colorado Springs▲ 281,140 ... K5
Columbine 23,969 ... E1
Commerce City 16,466 ... K3
Como 30 ... H4
Conejos▲ 200 ... G8
Cope 110 ... O3
Cornish 15 ... L2
Cortez▲ 7,284 ... B8
Cotopaxi 250 ... H6
Cowdrey 80 ... G1
Craig▲ 8,091 ... D2
Crawford 221 ... D5
Creede▲ 362 ... E7
Crested Butte 878 ... E5
Crestone 39 ... H7
Cripple Creek▲ 584 ... J5
Crook 148 ... O1
Crowley 225 ... M6
Cuchara 43 ... J8
Dacono 2,228 ... K2
Dailey 20 ... O1
De Beque 257 ... C4
Deckers 4 ... J4
Deer Trail 476 ... M3
Del Norte▲ 1,674 ... G7
Delhi 10 ... M7
Delta▲ 3,789 ... D5
Denver (cap.)▲ 467,610 ... K3
Deora 2 ... O7
Dillon 553 ... H3
Dinosaur 324 ... B2
Divide 700 ... J5
Dolores 866 ... C8
Dove Creek▲ 643 ... A7
Doyleville 75 ... F6
Drake 300 ... J2
Durango▲ 12,430 ... D8
Eads▲ 780 ... O6
Eagle▲ 1,580 ... F3
Eaton 1,959 ... K1
Eckley 211 ... P2
Edgewater 4,613 ... J3
Edwards 250 ... F3
Egnar 50 ... B7
Elbert 200 ... L4
Eldora 100 ... H3
Elizabeth 818 ... K4
Elk Springs 18 ... C2
Empire 401 ... H3
Englewood 29,387 ... K3
Erie 1,258 ... K2
Estes Park 3,184 ... J2
Eureka 25 ... D7
Evans 5,877 ... K2
Evergreen 7,582 ... J3
Fairplay▲ 387 ... H4
Farisita 116 ... J7
Federal Heights 9,342 ... J3
Firestone 1,358 ... K2
Firstview 6 ... O5
Flagler 564 ... N4
Fleming 344 ... O1
Florence 2,987 ... J6
Florissant 130 ... J5
Fort Collins▲ 87,758 ... J1
Fort Garland 700 ... J8
Fort Lupton 5,159 ... K2
Fort Lyon 500 ... N6
Fort Morgan▲ 9,068 ... M2
Fountain 9,984 ... K5
Fowler 1,154 ... L6
Foxton 12 ... J4
Franktown 200 ... K4
Fraser 575 ... H3
Frederick 988 ... K2
Freshwater (Guffey) 24 ... H5
Frisco 1,601 ... G3
Fruita 4,045 ... B4
Galeton 200 ... K1
Garcia 75 ... J8
Gardner 100 ... J7
Garfield 30 ... G5
Gateway 7,510 ... B5
Genoa 167 ... N4
Georgetown▲ 891 ... H3
Gilcrest 1,084 ... K2
Gill 250 ... L2
Gilman 160 ... G3
Glade Park 100 ... B5
Glen Haven 110 ... H2
Glendevey 50 ... H1
Glenwood Springs▲ 6,561 ... E4
Golden▲ 13,116 ... J3
Goodrich 85 ... M2
Gould 12 ... G2
Granada 513 ... P6
Granby 966 ... H2
Grand Junction▲ 29,034 ... B4
Grand Lake 259 ... H2
Granite 47 ... G4
Grant 50 ... H4
Greeley▲ 60,536 ... K2
Green Mountain Falls 663 ... K5
Greenland 21 ... K4
Greystone 2 ... B1
Grover 135 ... L1
Guffey 24 ... H5
Gulnare 6 ... K8
Gunnison▲ 4,636 ... E5
Gypsum 1,750 ... F3
Hale 4 ... P3
Hamilton 100 ... D2
Hartman 108 ... P6
Hartsel 69 ... H4
Hasty 150 ... O6
Haswell 62 ... N6
Haxtun 952 ... O1
Hayden 1,444 ... E2
Hereford 50 ... L1
Hesperus 250 ... C8
Hillrose 169 ... N2
Hillside 79 ... H6
Hoehne 400 ... L8
Holly 877 ... P6
Holyoke▲ 1,931 ... P1
Hooper 112 ... H7
Hot Sulphur Springs▲ 347 ... H2
Hotchkiss 744 ... D5
Howard 200 ... H6
Hoyt 60 ... L2
Hudson 918 ... K2
Hugo▲ 660 ... N4
Hygiene 450 ... J2
Idaho Springs 1,834 ... H3
Idalia 125 ... P3
Ignacio 720 ... D8
Iliff 174 ... N1
Jamestown 251 ... J2
Jansen 267 ... K8
Jaroso 50 ... H8
Jefferson 50 ... H4
Joes 100 ... O3
Johnstown 1,579 ... K2
Julesburg▲ 1,295 ... P1
Karval 51 ... N5
Keenesburg 570 ... L2
Keota 5 ... L1
Kersey 980 ... L2
Kim 76 ... N8
Kiowa▲ 275 ... L4
Kirk 30 ... P3
Kit Carson 305 ... O5
Kremmling 1,166 ... G2
Kutch 2 ... M5
La Garita 10 ... G7
La Jara 725 ... H8
La Junta▲ 7,637 ... M7
La Salle 1,783 ... K2
La Veta 726 ... J8
Lafayette 14,548 ... K3
Laird 105 ... P2
Lake City▲ 223 ... E6
Lake George 500 ... J5
Lakewood 126,481 ... J3
Lamar▲ 8,343 ... O6
Laporte 950 ... J1
Larkspur 232 ... K4
Las Animas▲ 2,481 ... N6
Lasauces 150 ... H8
Lavalley 237 ... J8
Lawson 108 ... H3
Lay 40 ... D2
Lazear 60 ... D5
Leadville▲ 2,629 ... G4
Lebanon 50 ... B8
Lewis 150 ... B8
Limon 1,831 ... M4
Lincoln Park 3,728 ... J6
Lindon 60 ... N3
Littleton▲ 33,685 ... K3
Livermore 150 ... J1
Lochbuie 1,168 ... K2
Log Lane Village 667 ... M2
Loma 265 ... B4
Longmont 42,942 ... J2
Longview 10 ... J4
Louisville 12,361 ... J3
Louviers 300 ... K4
Loveland 37,352 ... J2
Lucerne 135 ... K2
Lycan 4 ... P7
Lyons 1,227 ... J2
Mack 380 ... B4
Maher 75 ... D5
Malta 200 ... G4
Manassa 988 ... H8
Mancos 842 ... C8
Manitou Springs 4,535 ... J5
Manzanola 437 ... M6
Marble 64 ... E4
Marvel 176 ... C8
Masonville 200 ... J2
Masters 50 ... L2

(continued on following page)

Agriculture, Industry and Resources

DOMINANT LAND USE

- Specialized Wheat
- Wheat, Range Livestock
- Wheat, Grain Sorghums, Range Livestock
- Dry Beans, General Farming
- Sugar Beets, Dry Beans, Livestock, General Farming
- Fruit, Mixed Farming
- General Farming, Livestock, Special Crops
- Range Livestock
- Forests
- Urban Areas
- Nonagricultural Land

MAJOR MINERAL OCCURRENCES

Ag	Silver	Mi	Mica
Au	Gold	Mo	Molybdenum
Be	Beryl	Mr	Marble
C	Coal	O	Petroleum
Cl	Clay	Pb	Lead
Cu	Copper	U	Uranium
F	Fluorspar	V	Vanadium
Fe	Iron Ore	W	Tungsten
G	Natural Gas	Zn	Zinc

Water Power
Major Industrial Areas

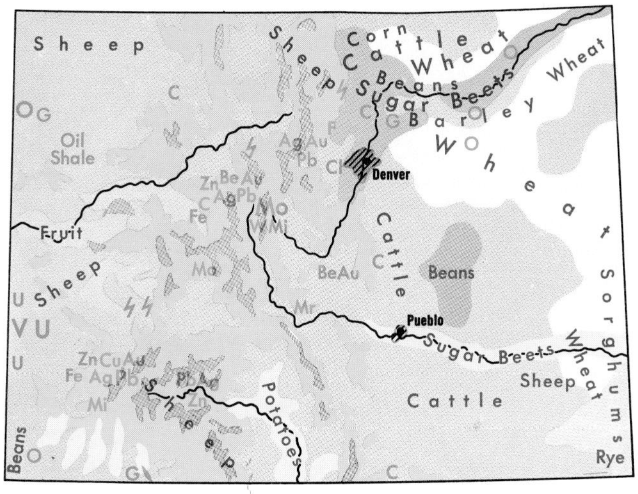

Topography

0   50   100 MI.

0   50   100 KM.

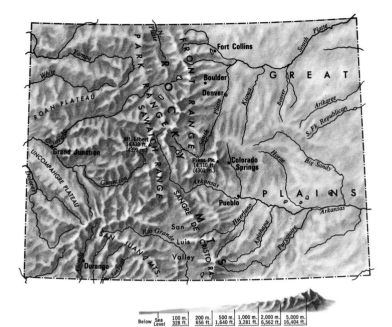

Below Sea Level	100 m. 328 ft.	200 m. 656 ft.	500 m. 1,640 ft.	1,000 m. 3,281 ft.	2,000 m. 6,562 ft.	5,000 m. 16,404 ft.

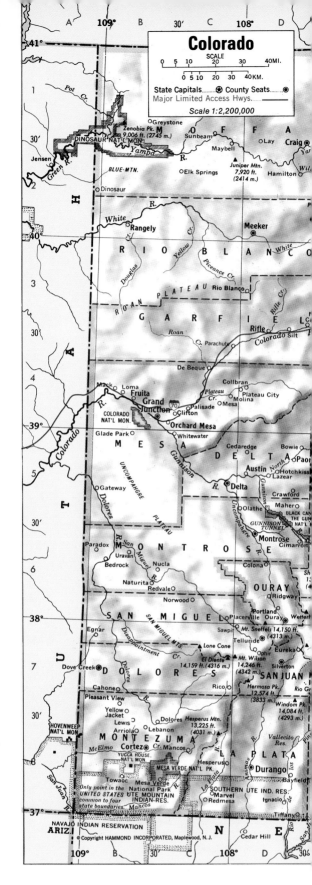

Colorado
SCALE
0 5 10   20   30   40MI.
0 5 10 20   30   40KM.
State Capitals ⊛ County Seats ⊛
Major Limited Access Hwys.
Scale 1:2,200,000

© Copyright HAMMOND INCORPORATED, Maplewood, N.J.

Matheson 120 ....M4
Maybell 130 ....C2
McClave 125 ....O6
McCoy 62 ....F3
Mead 456 ....K2
Meeker▲ 2,098 ....D2
Meredith 47 ....F4
Merino 238 ....N2
Mesa 120 ....C4
Mesa Verde National Park 45..C8
Mesita 70 ....H8
Milliken 1,605 ....K2
Milner 196 ....F2
Minturn 1,066 ....G3
Model 200 ....L8
Moffat 99 ....H6
Molina 200 ....D4
Monte Vista 4,324 ....G7
Montezuma 6 ....H3
Montrose▲ 8,854 ....D6
Monument 1,020 ....K4
Morrison 465 ....J3
Mosca 100 ....H7
Nathrop 150 ....H5
Naturita 434 ....B6
Nederland 1,099 ....H3
New Castle 679 ....E3
New Raymer 80 ....M1
Ninaview 2 ....N7
Niwot 2,666 ....J2
North Avondale 110 ....L6
North La Junta 1,076 .....N7
Northglenn 27,195 ....K3
Norwood 429 ....C6
Nucla 656 ....B6
Nunn 324 ....K1
Oak Creek 673 ....F2
Ohio 100 ....F5
Olathe 1,263 ....D5
Olney Springs 340 ....M6
Ophir 69 ....D7
Orchard 2,218 ....L2
Orchard Mesa 5,977 ......C4
Ordway▲ 1,025 ....M6
Ortiz 163 ....H8
Otis 451 ....O2
Ouray▲ 644 ....D6
Ovid 349 ....P1
Padroni 100 ....N1
Pagosa Junction 15 ......E8
Pagosa Springs▲ 1,207 ..E8
Palisade 1,871 ....C4
Palmer Lake 1,480 ....J4
Paoli 29 ....P1
Paonia 1,403 ....D5
Parachute 658 ....C4
Paradox 250 ....B6
Parkdale 21 ....H6
Parker 5,450 ....K4
Parlin 100 ....F6
Parshall 80 ....G2
Peetz 179 ....N1
Penrose 2,235 ....K6
Peyton 250 ....K4
Phippsburg 300 ....F2
Pierce 823 ....K1

Pine 100 ....J4
Pinecliffe 375 ....J3
Pinon 50 ....K6
Pitkin 53 ....F5
Placerville 50 ....D6
Plateau City 35 ....D4
Platner 30 ....N2
Platteville 1,515 ....K2
Pleasant View 300 ....B7
Poncha Springs 244 .....G6
Portland D6
Portland 17 ....K6
Powderhorn 100 ....E6
Pritchett 153 ....O8
Proctor 25 ....N1
Pryor 50 ....K8
Pueblo▲ 98,640 ....K6
Radium 22 ....G3
Ramah 94 ....L4
Rand 50 ....G2
Rangely 2,278 ....B2
Raymer (New Raymer) ...M1
Red Cliff 297 ....G4
Red Feather Lakes 150 ..H1
Red Mesa 100 ....C8
Red Wing 200 ....J7
Redstone 115 ....E4
Redvale 300 ....B6
Rico 92 ....C7
Ridgway 423 ....D6
Rifle 4,636 ....D3
Rio Blanco 4 ....C3
Rockvale 321 ....H6
Rocky Ford 4,162 ....M6
Roggen 100 ....L2
Romeo 341 ....G8
Rush 40 ....L5
Rye 168 ....K7
Saguache▲ 584 ....G6
Saint Elmo 75 ....G5
Salida▲ 4,737 ....H6
San Acacio 50 ....J8
San Isabel 8 ....K7
San Luis▲ 800 ....J8
San Pablo 150 ....J8
Sanford 750 ....H8
Sargents 31 ....F6
Sawpit 36 ....D7
Sedalia 200 ....K4
Sedgwick 183 ....O1
Segundo 200 ....K8
Seibert 181 ....O4
Severance 106 ....K1
Shawnee 100 ....H4
Sheridan 4,976 ....J3
Sheridan Lake 95 ....P6
Silt 1,095 ....D4
Silver Cliff 322 ....J6
Silver Plume 134 ....H3
Silverthorne 1,768 ....G3
Silverton▲ 716 ....D7
Simla 481 ....M4
Slater 10 ....E1
Snowmass 1,449 ....E4

Snyder 200 ....M2
Somerset 200 ....E5
South Fork 500 ....F7
Springfield▲ 1,475 ....O8
Starkville 104 ....L8
Steamboat Springs▲ 6,695 ..F2
Sterling▲ 10,362 ....N1
Stoneham 35 ....M1
Stonington 27 ....P8
Strasburg 1,005 ....L3
Stratton 649 ....O4
Sugar City 252 ....M6
Sunbeam 19 ....C1
Superior 255 ....J3
Swink 584 ....M7
Tabernash 250 ....H3
Telluride▲ 1,309 ....D7
Tennessee Pass 5 ....G4
Texas Creek 80 ....H6
Thatcher 50 ....L7
Thornton 55,031 ....K3
Tiffany 24 ....D8
Timnath 190 ....J2
Timpas 25 ....M7
Tincup 8 ....F5
Toponas 55 ....F2
Towaoc 700 ....B8
Towner 61 ....P6
Trinchera 30 ....L8
Trinidad▲ 8,580 ....L8
Truckton 10 ....L5
Twin Lakes 40 ....G4
Two Buttes 63 ....P7
Tyrone 9 ....L8
Uravan 500 ....B6
Utleyville 2 ....O8
Vail 3,659 ....G3
Valdez 12 ....K8
Vernon 50 ....P3
Victor 258 ....J5
Vilas 105 ....P8
Villa Grove 37 ....G6
Villegreen 6 ....M8
Vineland 100 ....K6
Virginia Dale 2 ....J1
Vona 100 ....P3
Wagon Wheel Gap 20 ...F7
Walden▲ 890 ....G1
Walsenburg▲ 3,300 ......K7
Walsh 692 ....P8
Ward 159 ....H2
Weldona 200 ....M2
Wellington 1,340 ....K1
Westcliffe▲ 312 ....J6
Westcreek 2 ....J4
Westminster 74,625 ......J3
Weston 150 ....K8
Wetmore 150 ....J6
Wheat Ridge 29,419 ......J3
Whitewater 300 ....C5
Wiggins 499 ....L2
Wild Horse 13 ....N5
Wiley 406 ....O6
Williamsburg 253 ....J6
Windsor 5,062 ....J2
Winter Park 528 ....H3

Wolcott 30 ....F3
Woodland Park 4,610 ....J4
Woodrow 24 ....M3
Woody Creek 400 ....F4
Wray▲ 1,998 ....P2
Yampa 317 ....F2
Yellow Jacket 115 ....B7
Yoder 25 ....L5
Yuma 2,719 ....O2

OTHER FEATURES

Adams (mt.) H6
Adobe Creek (res.) N6
Air Force Academy 9,062 ..K5
Alamosa (creek) G8
Alva B. Adams (tunnel) ..H2
Animas (riv.) D8
Antero (mt.) G5
Antero (res.) H5
Antora (peak) G6
Apishapa (riv.) L8
Arapaho Nat'l Rec. Area..G2
Arapahoe (peak) H2
Arikaree (riv.) O3
Arkansas (riv.) P6
Arkansas Divide (mts.) ..L4
Baker (mt.) B8
Bald (mt.) H4
Bear (creek) H7
Beaver (creek) M3
Bennett (peak) G7
Bent's Old Fort
  Nat'l Hist. Site M6
Big Grizzly (creek) G1
Big Sandy (creek) N4
Big Thompson (riv.) H2
Bijou (creek) L3
Black Canyon of the Gunnison
  Nat'l Mon. D5
Black Squirrel (creek) L5
Blanca (peak) H7
Blue (mt.) B2
Blue (riv.) G3
Blue Mesa (res.) E5
Bonny (res.) P3
Box Elder (creek) K4
Cache la Poudre (riv.) ...H1
Cameron (peak) H1
Carbon (peak) E5
Castle (peak) F5
Cebolla (creek) E6
Cedar (creek) M1
Chacuaco (creek) M8
Cheesman (lake) J4
Clay (creek) O7
Cochetopa (creek) F6
Colorado (riv.) A5
Colorado Nat'l Mon. B4
Conejos (peak) G8
Conejos (riv.) G8
Crestone (peak) H7
Crow (creek) L1
Culebra (peak) J8
Curecanti Nat'l Rec. Area..F6

Del Norte (peak) F7
De Weese (plat.) J6
Dinosaur Nat'l Mon. B2
Disappointment (creek) ..B7
Dolores (riv.) B5
Douglas (creek) B3
Eagle (riv.) E3
Elbert (mt.) G4
El Diente (peak) C7
Eleven Mile Canyon (res.) ..H5
Elk (riv.) F1
Empire (res.) L2
Ent A.F.B. K5
Ethel (mt.) F1
Evans (mt.) H3
Florissant Fossil Beds
  Nat'l Mon. J5
Fort Carson 11,309 ....K5
Fountain (creek) K5
Frenchman (creek) P1

Frenchman, North Fork
  (creek) O1
Frenchman, South Fork
  (creek) O1
Front (range) H1
Gore (range) G3
Graham (peak) E8
Granby (lake) G2
Great Sand Dunes Nat'l Mon...H7
Green (riv.) A2
Green Mountain (res.) ...G3
Gunnison (riv.) C5
Gunnison (tunnel) D6
Gunnison, North Fork (riv.)...D5
Handies (peak) E7
Harvard (mt.) G5
Hermosa (peak) D7
Hesperus (mt.) C8
Holy Cross (mt.) F4
Horse (creek) M5

Horse Creek (res.) N6
Horsetooth (res.) J1
Hovenweep Nat'l Mon. ...A8
Huerfano (riv.) J8
Illinois (riv.) G1
Jackson Lake (res.) L2
James (mt.) H3
John Martin (res.) N6
Juniper (mt.) C1
Kiowa (creek) L2
Kit Carson (mt.) H7
La Garita (mts.) F7
Lake Fork, Gunnison (riv.)...E6
Landsman (creek) P4
La Plata (peak) G5
La Plata (mts.) C8
Laramie (mts.) H1
Laramie (riv.) H1
Lincoln (mt.) H3
Lone Cone (mt.) C7

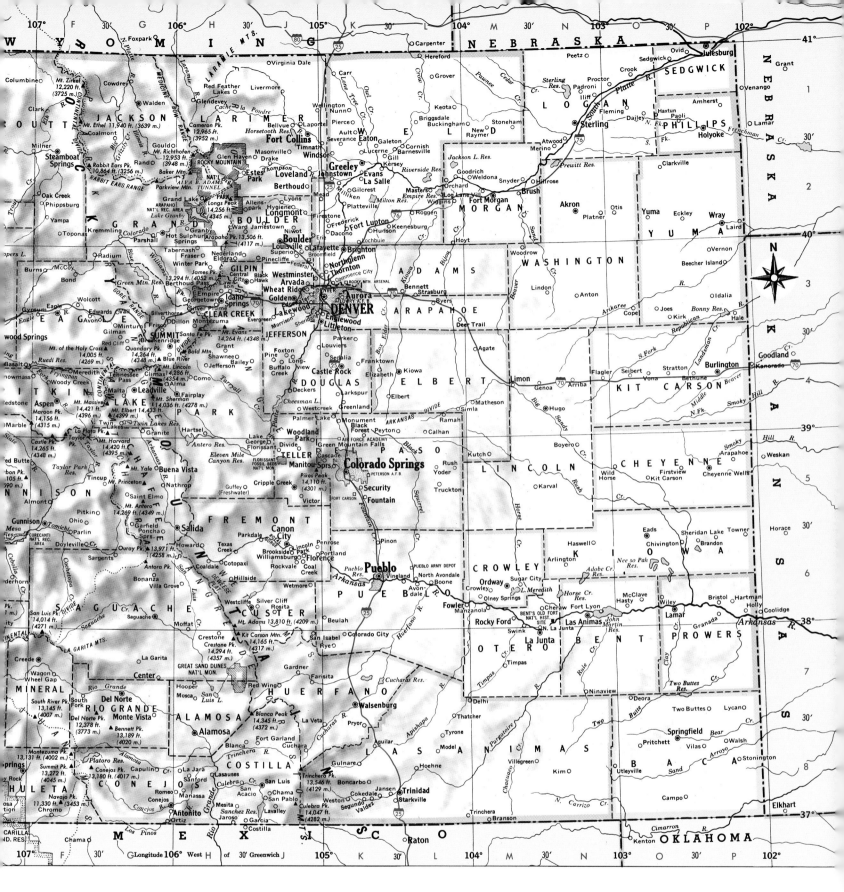

Connecticut

SCALE

0 — 5 — 10 — 15 MI.

0 — 5 — 10 — 15 KM.

State Capitals ⊛

Major Limited Access Hwys. ⎯⎯⎯

Scale 1:610,000

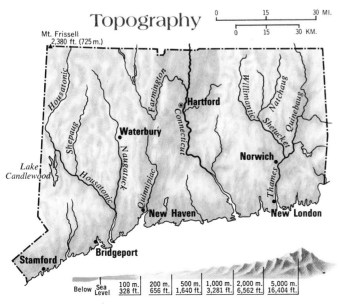

Topography

0 — 15 — 30 MI.

0 — 15 — 30 KM.

Mt. Frissell
2,380 ft. (725 m.)

Below	Sea Level	100 m. 328 ft.	200 m. 656 ft.	500 m. 1,640 ft.	1,000 m. 3,281 ft.	2,000 m. 6,562 ft.	5,000 m. 16,404 ft.

AREA 5,018 sq. mi. (12,997 sq. km.)
POPULATION 3,295,669
CAPITAL Hartford
LARGEST CITY Bridgeport
HIGHEST POINT Mt. Frissell (S. Slope) 2,380 ft.
(725 m.)
SETTLED IN 1635
ADMITTED TO UNION January 9, 1788
POPULAR NAME Constitution State; Nutmeg State
STATE FLOWER Mountain Laurel
STATE BIRD Robin

© Copyright HAMMOND INCORPORATED, Maplewood, N.J.

Milldale 975	D2	Poquonock Bridge 2,770	G3
Milton 600	C1	Portland 5,645	E2
Mohegan 700	G3	Portland ● 8,418	E2
Monroe ● 16,896	C3	Preston 5,006	H2
Monroe P.O. (Stepney)	B3	Prospect ● 7,775	D2
Montowese	D3	Putnam 6,835	H1
Montville 1,711	G3	Putnam ● 9,031	H1
Montville ● 16,673	G3	Putnam Heights 500	H1
Moodus 1,170	F2	Quaker Hill 2,052	G3
Moosup 3,289	H2	Quinebaug 1,031	H1
Morningside Park	G3	Quinnipiac	D3
Morris ● 2,039	C2	Redding ● 7,927	B3
Mystic 2,618	H3	Redding Ridge 550	B3
Naugatuck 30,625	C3	Ridgefield 6,363	B3
New Britain 75,491	E2	Ridgefield ● 20,919	B3
New Canaan ● 17,864	B4	Riverside	A4
New Fairfield ● 12,911	B3	Rockfall 900	E2
New Hartford 1,269	C1	Rockville	F1
New Hartford ● 5,769	C1	Rocky Hill ● 16,554	E2
New Haven 130,474	D3	Rogers 650	H1
New London 28,540	G3	Round Hill 900	A4
New Milford 5,775	B2	Rowayton	B4
New Milford ● 23,629	B2	Roxbury ● 1,825	B2
New Preston 1,217	B2	Salem ● 3,310	F3
Newington ● 29,208	E2	Salisbury ● 4,090	B1
Newtown 1,800	B3	Sandy Hook	B3
Newtown ● 20,779	B3	Saugatuck	B4
Niantic 3,048	G3	Saybrook Point 700	F3
Nichols	C4	Scantic 500	E1
Noank 1,406	G3	Scotland ● 1,215	G2
Norfolk ● 2,060	C1	Seymour ● 14,288	C3
Noroton	B4	Sharon ● 2,928	B1
Noroton Heights	B4	Shelton 35,418	C3
North Bloomfield 500	E1	Sherman ● 2,809	B2
North Branford ● 12,996	E3	Short Beach	D3
North Franklin 500	G2	Simsbury 5,577	D1
North Granby 1,455	D1	Simsbury ● 22,023	D1
North Grosvenor Dale 1,705	H1	Somers 1,643	F1
North Guilford	E3	Somers ● 9,108	F1
North Haven ● 22,249	D3	Somersville 750	F1
North Lyme	F3	South Coventry (Coventry)	
North Stonington ● 4,884	H3	1,257	F1
North Wilton 900	B4	South Glastonbury	E2
North Woodbury 900	C2	South Killingly 500	H1
Northfield 600	C2	South Norwalk	B4
Northford	D3	South Wilton	B4
Northville 700	B2	South Windham 1,644	G2
Norwalk 78,331	B4	South Windsor ● 22,090	E1
Norwich ● 37,391	G2	South Woodstock 1,112	G1
Norwichtown	G2	Southbury ● 15,818	C3
Oakdale 608	G3	Southington ● 38,518	D2
Oakville 8,741	C2	Southport	B4
Occum	G2	Stafford ● 11,091	F1
Old Greenwich	A4	Stafford Springs 4,100	F1
Old Lyme ● 6,535	F3	Staffordville 500	G1
Old Mystic 600	H3	Stamford 108,056	A4
Old Saybrook 1,820	F3	Stepney	B3
Old Saybrook ● 9,552	F3	Sterling ● 2,357	H2
Oneco 550	H2	Stonington 1,100	H3
Orange ● 12,830	C3	Stonington ● 16,919	H3
Oxford ● 8,685	C3	Stony Creek	E3
Pawcatuck 5,289	H3	Storrs 12,198	F1
Pequabuck 642	C2	Stratford ● 49,389	C4
Plainfield 2,856	H2	Suffield 1,353	E1
Plainfield ● 14,363	H2	Suffield ● 11,427	E1
Plainville ● 17,392	D2	Taftville	G2
Plantsville	D2	Talcottville 875	F1
Pleasure Beach 1,356	G3	Tariffville 1,477	D1
Plymouth ● 11,822	C2	Terryville 5,426	C2
Pomfret ● 3,102	H1	Thamesville	G2
Poquonock	E1	Thomaston ● 6,947	C2

Thompson ● 8,668	H1	Colebrook River (lake)	C1
Thompsonville 8,458	E1	Congamond (lakes)	E1
Tolland 11,001	F1	Connecticut (riv.)	E2
Torringford	C1	Dennis (hill)	C1
Torrington 33,687	C1	Easton (res.)	B3
Totoket 950	D3	Eight Mile (riv.)	F3
Trumbull ● 32,016	C4	Farmington (riv.)	D1
Uncasville 1,597	G3	French (riv.)	H1
Union ● 612	F1	Frissell (mt.)	B1
Union City	C2	Gaillard (lake)	D3
Unionville	D2	Gardner (lake)	G2
Vernon Center	F1	Hammonasset (pt.)	E3
Vernon ● 29,841	F1	Hammonasset (res.)	E3
Versailles 540	G2	Haystack (mt.)	C1
Voluntown ● 2,113	H2	Highland (lake)	C1
Wallingford 17,827	D3	Hockanum (riv.)	E1
Wallingford ● 40,822	D3	Hop (riv.)	F1
Warehouse Point	D1	Housatonic (riv.)	C3
Warren ● 1,226	B2	Lillinonah (lake)	B3
Washington ● 3,905	D1	Little (riv.)	G2
Washington Depot 900	B2	Long Island (sound)	C4
Waterbury 108,961	C2	Mad (riv.)	C1
Waterford 2,736	G3	Mashapaug (lake)	G1
Waterford ● 17,930	G3	Mason (isl.)	H3
Watertown ● 20,456	C2	Mattabesset (riv.)	E2
Watertown 1,079	H2	Mianus (riv.)	A4
Weatogue 2,521	D1	Mohawk (mt.)	B1
West Avon	D1	Moosup (riv.)	H2
West Granby 567	D1	Mount Hope (riv.)	G1
West Hartford ● 60,110	D1	Mudge (pond)	B1
West Haven 54,021	D3	Mystic (riv.)	H3
West Mystic 3,595	H3	Natchaug (riv.)	G1
West Norwalk 950	B4	Naugatuck (riv.)	C3
West Simsbury 2,149	D1	Nepaug (res.)	D1
West Suffield	E1	Niantic (riv.)	G3
Westbrook 2,060	E3	Norwalk (riv.)	B4
Westbrook ● 5,414	F3	Pachaug (pond)	H2
Westfield	E2	Pawcatuck (riv.)	H3
Weston ● 8,648	B4	Pequabuck (riv.)	D2
Westport ● 24,410	B4	Pequonnock (riv.)	C3
Wethersfield ● 25,651	E2	Pocotopaug (lake)	E2
Whitneyville	D3	Quaddick (res.)	H1
Willimantic 14,746	G2	Quinebaug (riv.)	H2
Willington ● 5,979	F1	Quinnipiac (riv.)	D3
Wilton 15,989	B4	Rippowam (riv.)	A4
Winchester ● 11,524	C1	Sachem (head)	E4
Windham ● 22,039	G2	Salmon (brook)	D1
Windsor 17,531	E1	Salmon (riv.)	F2
Windsor ● 27,817	E1	Saugatuck (res.)	B3
Windsor Locks ● 12,358	E1	Scantic (riv.)	E1
Winnipauk 650	B4	Shenipsit (lake)	F1
Winsted 8,254	C1	Shepaug (riv.)	B2
Winthrop 750	E3	Shetucket (riv.)	G2
Wolcott ● 13,700	D2	Silvermine (riv.)	B4
Woodbridge ● 7,924	D3	Spectacle (lakes)	B2
Woodbury 1,212	C2	Still (riv.)	B3
Woodbury ● 8,131	C2	Still (riv.)	C1
Woodmont 1,770	D4	Talcott (range)	D1
Woodstock ● 6,008	H1	Thames (riv.)	G3
Yalesville	C2	Thomaston (res.)	C2
Yantic	G2	Titicus (riv.)	A3
		Trap Falls (riv.)	C3
OTHER FEATURES		Twin (lakes)	B1
		Wamgumbaug (lake)	F1
Aspetuck (res.)	B4	Waramaug (lake)	B2
Bantam (lake)	C2	West Rock Ridge (hills)	D3
Barkhamsted (res.)	D1	Willimantic (riv.)	F1
Bear (mt.)	B1	Wononskopomuc (lake)	B1
Byram (riv.)	A4	Yantic (riv.)	G2
Candlewood (lake)	A2	
Coast Guard Academy	G3	● Population of town or township

Agriculture, Industry and Resources

DOMINANT LAND USE

- Specialized Dairy
- Dairy, Poultry, Mixed Farming
- Forests
- Urban Areas

MAJOR MINERAL OCCURRENCES

Cl Clay   Mi Mica

Major Industrial Areas

Gales Ferry 1,191	G3	Ivoryton	F3
Gaylordsville 960	A2	Jewett City 3,349	H2
Georgetown 1,694	B4	Kensington 8,306	D2
Glastonbury 7,082	E2	Kent ● 2,918	B2
Glastonbury ● 27,901	E2	Killingly ● 15,889	H1
Glenville	A4	Killingworth ● 4,814	E3
Goshen ● 2,329	C1	Lake Pocotopaug 3,029	F2
Granby 1,912	D1	Lakeville	B1
Granby ● 9,369	D1	Lebanon ● 6,041	G2
Greenfield Hill	B4	Ledyard 14,913	G3
Greenwich ● 58,441	A4	Leetes Island 500	E3
Grosvenor Dale 700	H1	Lisbon ● 3,790	G2
Groton 9,837	G3	Litchfield 1,378	C2
Groton ● 45,144	G3	Litchfield ● 8,365	C2
Guilford 2,588	E3	Long Hill	C3
Guilford ● 19,848	E3	Lords Point 500	H3
Haddam ● 6,769	E3	Lyons Plain 700	B4
Hamden ● 52,434	D3	Madison 2,139	E3
Hampton ● 1,578	G1	Madison ● 15,485	E3
Hanover 500	G2	Manchester 31,058	E1
Hartford (cap.) 139,739	E1	Manchester ● 51,618	E1
Hartland ● 1,866	D1	Mansfield ● 21,103	F1
Harwinton 3,293	C1	Mansfield Center 1,043	G1
Harwinton ● 5,228	C1	Marion 900	D2
Hawleyville 600	B3	Marlborough 1,039	F2
Hazardville 5,179	E1	Marlborough ● 5,535	F2
Hebron ● 7,079	F2	Meriden 59,479	D2
Higganum 1,692	E2	Middlebury ● 6,145	C2
Highland Park 500	F1	Middlefield ● 3,925	E2
Hockanum	E2	Middletown 42,762	E2
Huntington	C3	Milford 48,168	C4
Indian Neck	D3	Mill Plain 750	A3

Florida

SCALE

0 5 10 20 30 40 50MI.

0 5 10 20' 30 40 50KM.

State Capitals...........⊛

County Seats...........◉

Canals...........

Major Limited Access Hwys.———

Scale 1:2,550,000

Western Part of Florida

Same scale as main map

ⓒ Copyright HAMMOND INCORPORATED, Maplewood, N.J.

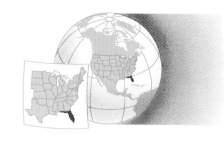

AREA 58,664 sq. mi. (151,940 sq. km.)
POPULATION 13,003,362
CAPITAL Tallahassee
LARGEST CITY Jacksonville
HIGHEST POINT (Walton County) 345 ft. (105 m.)
SETTLED IN 1565
ADMITTED TO UNION March 3, 1845
POPULAR NAME Sunshine State; Peninsula State
STATE FLOWER Orange Blossom
STATE BIRD Mockingbird

Topography

(continued on following page)

Agriculture, Industry and Resources

DOMINANT LAND USE

- Fruit, Truck & Mixed Farming
- Truck & Mixed Farming
- Truck Farming
- Cotton, Tobacco, Hogs, Peanuts
- Peanuts, General Farming
- General Farming, Forest Products, Truck Farming, Cotton
- Livestock Grazing
- Forests
- Swampland, Limited Agriculture
- Urban Areas
- Nonagricultural Land

MAJOR MINERAL OCCURRENCES

Cl Clay
Ls Limestone
O Petroleum
P Phosphates
Pe Peat
Ti Titanium
Zr Zirconium

⚡ Water Power   ▨ Major Industrial Areas

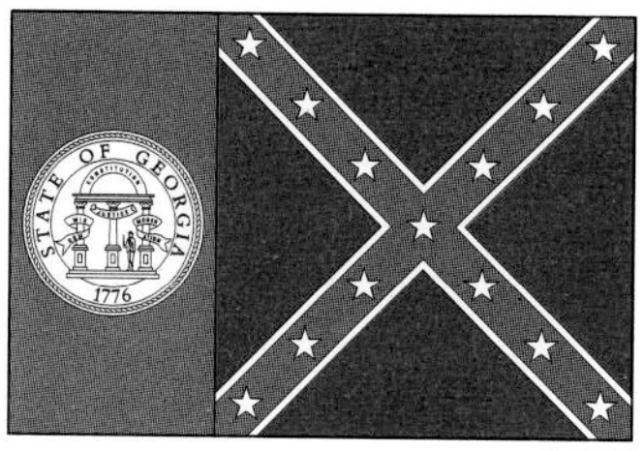

AREA 58,910 sq. mi. (152,577 sq. km.)
POPULATION 6,508,419
CAPITAL Atlanta
LARGEST CITY Atlanta
HIGHEST POINT Brasstown Bald 4,784 ft. (1458 m.)
SETTLED IN 1733
ADMITTED TO UNION January 2, 1788
POPULAR NAME Empire State of the South; Peach State
STATE FLOWER Cherokee Rose
STATE BIRD Brown Thrasher

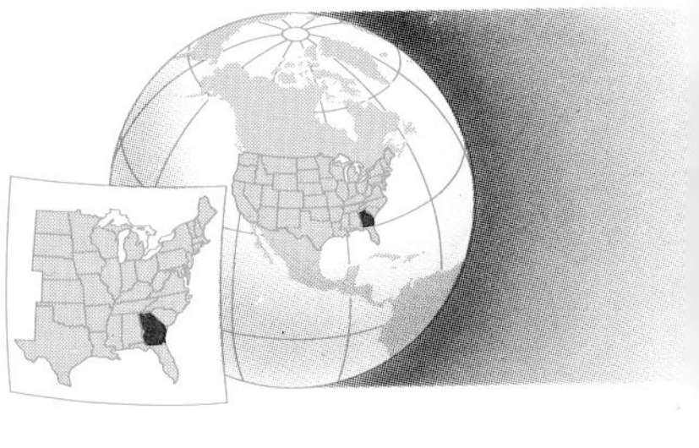

COUNTIES

Appling 15,744 H7
Atkinson 6,213 G8
Bacon 9,566 G7
Baker 3,615 D8
Baldwin 39,530 F4
Banks 10,308 E2
Barrow 29,721 E2
Bartow 55,911 C2
Ben Hill 16,245 F7
Berrien 14,153 F8
Bibb 149,967 E5
Bleckley 10,430 F6
Brantley 11,077 J8
Brooks 15,398 E9
Bryan 15,438 K6
Bulloch 43,125 J6
Burke 20,579 J4
Butts 15,326 E4
Calhoun 5,013 C7
Camden 30,167 J9
Candler 7,744 H6
Carroll 71,422 B3
Catoosa 42,464 B1
Charlton 8,496 H9
Chatham 216,935 K6
Chattahoochee 16,934 C6
Chattooga 22,242 B1
Cherokee 90,204 D2
Clarke 87,594 F3
Clay 3,364 B7
Clayton 182,052 D3
Clinch 6,160 G9
Cobb 447,745 C3
Coffee 29,592 G8
Colquitt 36,645 E8
Columbia 66,031 H3
Cook 13,456 F8
Coweta 53,853 C4
Crawford 8,991 E5
Crisp 20,011 E7
Dade 13,147 A1
Dawson 9,429 D2
De Kalb 483,024 D3
Decatur 25,511 C9
Dodge 17,607 F6
Dooly 9,901 E6
Dougherty 96,311 D7
Douglas 71,120 C3
Early 11,854 C8
Echols 2,334 G9
Effingham 25,687 K6
Elbert 18,949 G2
Emanuel 20,546 H5
Evans 8,724 J6
Fannin 15,992 D1
Fayette 62,415 C4
Floyd 81,251 B2
Forsyth 44,083 D2
Franklin 16,650 F2
Fulton 648,951 D3
Gilmer 13,368 D1
Glascock 2,357 G4
Glynn 62,496 J8
Gordon 35,072 C2
Grady 20,279 D9
Greene 11,793 F3
Gwinnett 352,910 D2
Habersham 27,621 E1
Hall 95,428 E2
Hancock 8,908 G4
Haralson 21,966 B3
Harris 17,788 C5
Hart 19,712 G2
Heard 8,628 B4
Henry 58,741 D4
Houston 89,208 E6
Irwin 8,649 F7
Jackson 30,005 E2
Jasper 8,453 E4
Jeff Davis 12,032 G7
Jefferson 17,408 H4
Jenkins 8,247 J5
Johnson 8,329 G5
Jones 20,739 E5
Lamar 13,038 D4
Lanier 5,531 F8
Laurens 39,988 G6
Lee 16,250 D7
Liberty 52,745 J7
Lincoln 7,442 H3
Long 6,202 J7
Lowndes 75,981 F9
Lumpkin 14,573 D1
Macon 13,114 D6
Madison 21,050 F2
Marion 5,590 C6
McDuffie 20,119 H4
McIntosh 8,634 K7
Meriwether 22,411 C4
Miller 6,280 C8
Mitchell 20,275 D8
Monroe 17,113 E4
Montgomery 7,163 G6
Morgan 12,883 F3
Murray 26,147 C1
Muscogee 179,278 C6
Newton 41,808 E3
Oconee 17,618 F3
Oglethorpe 8,929 F3
Paulding 41,611 C3
Peach 21,189 E5
Pickens 14,432 D2
Pierce 13,328 H8
Pike 10,224 D4
Polk 33,815 B3
Pulaski 8,108 E6
Putnam 14,137 F4
Quitman 2,209 B7
Rabun 11,648 F1
Randolph 8,023 C7
Richmond 189,719 H4
Rockdale 54,091 D3
Schley 3,588 D6
Screven 13,842 J5
Seminole 9,010 C9
Spalding 54,457 D4
Stephens 23,257 F1
Stewart 5,654 C6
Sumter 30,228 D6
Talbot 6,524 C5
Taliaferro 1,915 G3
Tattnall 17,722 H6
Taylor 7,642 D5
Telfair 11,000 G7
Terrell 10,653 D7
Thomas 38,986 E9
Tift 34,998 E7
Toombs 24,072 H6
Towns 6,754 E1
Treutlen 5,994 G6
Troup 55,536 B4
Turner 8,703 E7
Twiggs 9,806 F5
Union 11,993 E1
Upson 26,300 D5
Walker 58,340 B1
Walton 38,586 E3
Ware 35,471 H8
Warren 6,078 G4
Washington 19,112 G4
Wayne 22,356 J7
Webster 2,263 C6
Wheeler 4,903 G6
White 13,006 E1
Whitfield 72,462 B1
Wilcox 7,008 F7
Wilkes 10,597 G3
Wilkinson 10,228 F5
Worth 19,745 E8

CITIES and TOWNS

Abbeville▲ 907 F7
Acworth 4,519 C2
Adairsville 2,131 C2
Adel▲ 5,093 F8
Adrian 615 G5
Ailey 579 G6
Alamo▲ 855 G6
Alapaha 812 F8
Albany▲ 78,122 D7
Aldora 127 D4
Allenhurst 594 J7
Allentown 273 F5
Alma▲ 3,663 G7
Alpharetta 13,002 D2
Alston 160 H6
Alto 651 E2
Alvaton 91 C4
Ambrose 288 G7
Americus▲ 16,512 D6
Andersonville 277 D6
Appling▲ 150 H3
Arabi 433 E7
Aragon 902 B2
Arcade 697 E2
Arco 6,189 J8
Argyle 206 G8
Arlington 1,513 C8
Armuchee 600 B2
Arnoldsville 275 F3
Ashburn▲ 4,827 E7
Athens▲ 45,734 F3
Atlanta (cap.)▲ 394,017 K1
Attapulgus 380 D9
Auburn 3,139 E2
Augusta▲ 44,639 J4
Austell 4,173 J1
Avalon 159 F1
Avera 215 G4
Avondale Estates 2,209 L1
Baconton 623 D8
Bainbridge▲ 10,712 C9
Baldwin 1,439 E2
Ball Ground 905 D2
Barnesville▲ 4,747 D4
Barney 146 E8
Bartow 292 G5
Barwick 385 E9
Baxley▲ 3,841 H7
Bellville 192 H6
Belvedere 18,089 L1
Benevolence 138 C7
Berkeley Lake 791 D3
Berlin 480 E8
Bethlehem 348 E3
Between 82 E3
Bibb City 597 B5
Bishop 158 F3
Blackshear▲ 3,263 H8
Blairsville▲ 564 E1
Blakely▲ 5,595 C8
Bloomingdale 2,271 K6
Blue Ridge▲ 1,336 D1
Bluffton 138 C7
Blythe 300 H4
Bogart 1,018 E3
Boston 1,395 E9
Bostwick 307 E3
Bowdon 1,981 B3
Bowersville 311 F2
Bowman 791 G2
Box Springs 518 C5
Braselton 418 E2
Braswell 247 C3
Bremen 4,356 B3
Brinson 238 C9
Bronwood 513 D7
Brookfield 600 F8
Brookhaven K1
Brooklet 1,013 J6
Brooks 328 D4
Broxton 1,211 G7
Brunswick▲ 16,433 K8
Buchanan▲ 1,009 B3
Buckhead 176 F3
Buena Vista▲ 1,472 D6
Buford 8,771 D2
Butler▲ 1,673 D5
Byromville 452 E6
Byron 2,276 E5
Cadwell 458 G6
Cairo▲ 9,035 D9
Calhoun▲ 7,135 C1
Calvary 500 D9
Camak 220 G4
Camilla▲ 5,008 D8
Campton E3
Canon 737 F2
Canton▲ 4,817 C2
Carl 263 E3
Carlton 282 F2
Carnesville▲ 514 F2
Carrollton▲ 16,029 C3
Carters 12,035 C1
Cartersville▲ 9,247 C2
Cataula 500 C5
Cave Spring 950 B2
Cecil 376 F8
Cedar Grove A1
Cedartown▲ 7,978 B2
Center 3,251 F2
Centerville 2,622 E5
Centralhatchee 301 B4
Chalybeate Springs 265 C5
Chamblee 7,668 K1
Charles H6
Chatsworth▲ 2,865 C1
Chauncey 312 F6
Chester 1,072 F6
Chickamauga 2,149 B1
Chula 500 E7
Clarkesville▲ 1,151 F1
Clarkston 5,385 L1
Claxton▲ 2,464 J6
Clayton▲ 1,613 F1
Clermont 402 E2
Cleveland▲ 1,653 E1
Climax 226 D9
Clyattville 500 F9
Cobb 338 E7
Cobbtown 494 H6
Cochran▲ 4,390 F6
Cohutta 529 C1
Colbert 443 F2
Coleman 137 C7
Colemans Lake H5
College Park 20,457 K2
Collins 528 H6
Colquitt▲ 1,991 C8
Columbus▲ 179,278 C6
Comer 939 F2
Commerce 4,108 E2
Concord 211 D4
Conley 5,528 K2
Constitution K2
Conyers▲ 7,380 D3
Coolidge 610 E8
Coosa 600 B2
Cordele▲ 10,321 E7
Corinth 136 B4
Cornelia 3,219 E1
Cotton 122 D8
Covington▲ 10,026 E3
Crandall C1
Crawford 694 F3
Crawfordville▲ 577 G3
Crosland E8
Crystal Springs 500 B2
Culloden 242 D5
Cumming▲ 2,828 D2
Cusseta▲ 1,107 C6
Cuthbert▲ 3,730 C7
Dacula 2,217 E3
Dahlonega▲ 3,086 D1
Daisy 138 J6
Dallas▲ 2,810 C3
Dalton▲ 21,761 C1
Damascus 290 C8
Danielsville▲ 318 F2
Danville 480 F5
Darien▲ 1,783 K8
Dasher 659 F9
Davisboro 407 G5
Dawson▲ 5,295 D7
Dawsonville▲ 467 D2
De Soto 258 D7
Dearing 547 H4
Decatur▲ 17,336 K1
Deenwood 2,055 H8
Deepstep 111 G4
Demorest 1,088 F1
Denton 335 G7
Dexter 475 G6
Dickey C7
Dillard 199 F1
Dixie 259 E9
Dock Junction (Arco) J8
Doerun 899 E8
Donalsonville▲ 2,761 C8
Dooling 28 E6
Doraville 7,626 K1
Douglas▲ 10,464 G7
Douglasville▲ 11,635 C3
Dry Branch 700 F5
Du Pont 177 G9
Dublin▲ 16,312 G5
Ducktown D2
Dudley 430 F5
Duluth 9,029 D2
Dunwoody 26,302 K1
Durand 206 C5
East Dublin 2,524 G5
East Ellijay 303 C1
East Juliette E4
East Newnan 1,173 C4
East Point 34,402 K2
Eastman▲ 5,153 F6
Eastville E3
Eatonton▲ 4,737 F4
Eden 990 K6
Edge Hill 22 G4
Edison 1,182 C7
Elberta 1,559 E5
Elberton▲ 5,682 G2
Elizabeth 950 J1
Ellabell 500 K6
Ellaville▲ 1,724 D6
Ellenton 227 E8
Ellenwood L2
Ellerslie 700 C5
Ellijay▲ 1,178 C1
Emerson 1,201 C2
Enigma 611 F8
Ephesus 324 B4

(continued on following page)

Agriculture, Industry and Resources

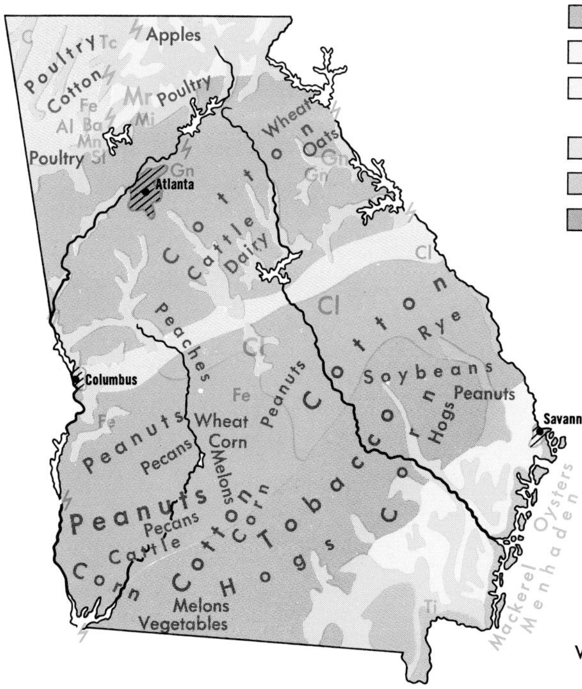

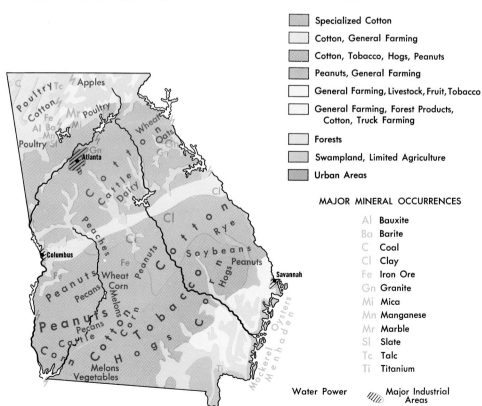

DOMINANT LAND USE

- Specialized Cotton
- Cotton, General Farming
- Cotton, Tobacco, Hogs, Peanuts
- Peanuts, General Farming
- General Farming, Livestock, Fruit, Tobacco
- General Farming, Forest Products, Cotton, Truck Farming
- Forests
- Swampland, Limited Agriculture
- Urban Areas

MAJOR MINERAL OCCURRENCES

- Al Bauxite
- Ba Barite
- C Coal
- Cl Clay
- Fe Iron Ore
- Gn Granite
- Mi Mica
- Mn Manganese
- Mr Marble
- Sl Slate
- Tc Talc
- Ti Titanium

Water Power

Major Industrial Areas

Eton 315 C1
Euharlee 850 C2
Evans 13,713 H3
Experiment 3,762 D4
Fair Oaks 6,996 J1
Fairburn 4,013 J2
Fairmount 657 C2
Fargo 800 G9
Farmington F3
Farrar E4
Fayetteville▲ 5,827 C4
Felton 500 B3
Finleyson 101 F6
Fitzgerald▲ 8,612 F7
Fleming 279 K7
Flemington 440 K7
Flippen 600 D3
Flovilla 602 E4
Flowery Branch 1,251 E2
Floyd J1
Folkston▲ 2,285 H9
Forest Park 16,925 K2
Forsyth▲ 4,268 E4
Fort Gaines▲ 1,248 C7
Fort Oglethorpe 5,880 B1
Fort Valley▲ 8,198 E5
Franklin Springs 475 F2
Franklin▲ 876 B4
Funston 248 E8
Gainesville▲ 17,885 E2
Garden City 7,410 K6
Garfield 255 H5
Gay 133 C4
Geneva 182 C5
Georgetown▲ 913 B7
Gibson▲ 679 G4
Gillsville 113 E2
Gilmore J1
Girard 195 J4
Glenn 3,676 B4
Glennville 4,144 J7
Glenwood 824 G6
Glenwood 881 L1
Glynco J8
Good Hope 181 E3
Gordon 2,468 F5
Grantville 1,180 C4
Gray▲ 2,189 F4
Grayson 529 E3
Graysville 193 B1
Greensboro▲ 2,860 F3
Greenville▲ 1,167 C4
Griffin▲ 21,347 D4
Grovetown 3,596 H4
Gumbranch 291 J7
Guyton 740 K6
Haddock 800 F4
Hagan 787 J6
Hahira 1,353 F9
Hamilton▲ 454 C5
Hampton 2,694 D4
Hapeville 5,483 K2
Haralson 139 C4
Hardwick (Midway-
Hardwick) 8,977 F4
Harlem 2,199 H4
Harrison 414 G5
Hartwell▲ 4,555 G2
Hawkinsville▲ 3,527 E6
Hazlehurst▲ 4,202 G7
Helen 300 E1
Helena 1,256 G6
Hephzibah 2,466 H4
Hiawassee▲ 547 E1
Higgston 274 G6
Hilltonia 402 J5
Hinesville▲ 21,603 J7
Hiram 1,389 C3
Hoboken 440 H8
Hogansville 2,976 C4
Holly Springs 2,406 D2
Homeland 981 H9
Homer▲ 742 F2
Homerville▲ 2,560 G8
Hoschton 642 E2
Howell F9
Hull 156 F2
Ideal 554 D6
Ila 297 F2
Indian Springs 1,273 E4
Industrial City 1,054 C1
Inman 500 D4
Iron City 503 C8
Irwinton▲ 641 F5
Isle of Hope 975 K7
Ivey 1,053 F5
Jackson▲ 4,076 E4
Jacksonville 128 G7
Jakin 137 C8
Jasper▲ 1,772 D2
Jefferson▲ 2,763 F2
Jeffersonville▲ 1,545 F5
Jenkinsburg 213 E4
Jersey 149 E3
Jesup▲ 8,958 J7
Jonesboro▲ 3,635 D4
Juliette 600 E4
Junction City 182 C5
Juno 522 D2
Kennesaw 8,936 C2
Keysville 284 H4
Kingsland 4,699 J9
Kingston 616 C2
Kite 297 G5
Knoxville▲ 75 E5
La Fayette▲ 6,313 B1
La Grange▲ 25,597 B4
Lake City 2,733 K2
Lake Park 500 F9
Lakeland▲ 2,467 F8
Lavonia 1,840 F2
Lawrenceville▲ 16,848 D3
Leary 701 C8
Lebanon 800 D2
Leesburg▲ 1,452 D7
Leland J1
Lenox 783 F8
Leslie 445 D7
Lexington▲ 230 F3
Lilburn 9,301 D3
Lilly 138 E6
Lincoln Park 1,755 D5
Lincolnton▲ 1,476 G3
Lindale 4,187 B2
Linwood 342 B1
Lithia Springs 11,403 C3
Lithonia 2,448 D3
Lizella 975 E5
Locust Grove 1,681 D4
Loganville 3,180 E3
Lollie G6
Lone Oak 161 C4
Lookout Mountain 1,636 B1
Louisville▲ 2,429 H4
Lovejoy 754 D4
Lovett G5
Ludowici▲ 1,291 J7
Lula 1,018 E2
Lumber City 1,429 G7
Lumpkin▲ 1,250 C6
Luthersville 741 C4
Lyerly 493 B2
Lyons▲ 4,502 H6
Mableton 25,725 J1
Macon▲ 106,612 E5
Madison▲ 3,483 F3
Manassas 123 H6
Manchester 4,104 C5
Mansfield 341 E4
Marietta▲ 44,129 J1
Marlow 500 K6
Marshallville 1,457 D6
Martin 243 F2
Martinez 33,731 H3
Matthews H4
Maxeys 180 F3
Maysville 728 E2
McCaysville 1,065 D1
McDonough▲ 2,929 D4
McIntosh 500 K7
McIntyre 552 F5
McRae▲ 3,007 G6
Meansville 250 D4
Mechanicsville L1
Meigs 1,120 D8
Meldrim 510 K6
Menlo 538 B2
Merrillville E9
Metcalf E9
Metter▲ 3,707 H6
Middleton G2
Midville 620 H5
Midway 863 K7
Milan 1,056 G6
Milledgeville▲ 17,727 F4
Millen▲ 3,808 J5
Milner 321 D4
Milstead D3
Mineral Bluff 153 D1
Mitchell 181 G4
Modoc H5
Molena 439 D4
Monroe▲ 9,759 E3
Montezuma 4,506 E6
Monticello▲ 2,289 E4
Montrose 117 F5
Moreland 366 C4
Morgan▲ 252 C7
Morganton 295 D1
Morrow 5,168 K2
Morven 536 E9
Moultrie▲ 14,865 E8
Mount Airy 543 F1
Mount Berry B2
Mount Bethel K1
Mount Vernon▲ 1,914 G6
Mount Zion 511 B3
Mountain City 784 F1
Mountain Park 554 D2
Mountain View K2
Muntville 168 C4
Murrayville 550 E2
Nahunta▲ 1,049 H8
Nashville▲ 4,782 F8
Naylor 111 F9
Nelson 486 D2
New Holland 950 E2
Newborn 404 E3
Newington 319 J5
Newnan▲ 12,497 C4
Newton▲ 703 D8
Nicholls 1,003 G7
Nicholson 535 F2
Norcross 5,947 D3
Norman Park 711 E8
Normantown H6
North Canton 950 C2
North High Shoals 268 F3
Norwood 238 G4
Nunez 135 H5
Oak Park 269 J6
Oakfield 113 E7
Oakman 150 C1
Oakwood 1,464 E2
Ochlocknee 588 E9
Ocilla▲ 3,182 F7
Oconee 234 G5
Odessadale 142 C5
Odum 388 H7
Oglethorpe▲ 1,302 D6
Ohoopee H6
Oliver 242 J5
Omaha 116 C6
Omega 912 E8
Orchard Hill 239 D4
Oxford 1,945 E3
Palmetto 2,612 C3
Panthersville 9,874 L1
Parrott 140 D7
Patterson 626 H8
Pavo 774 E9
Payne 192 E5
Peachtree City 19,027 C4
Pearson▲ 1,714 G8
Pelham 3,869 D8
Pembroke▲ 1,503 J6
Pendergrass 298 E2
Penfield F3
Perry▲ 9,452 E6
Phillipsburg 1,044 E8
Piedmont D4
Pine Lake 810 D3
Pine Mountain 875 C5
Pine Park D9
Pinehurst 388 E6
Pineora 387 K6
Pineview 594 F6
Pitts 214 E7
Pittsburg L1
Plainfield 128 F6
Plains 716 D6
Plainville 231 C2
Pocotalago F2
Pooler 4,453 K6
Port Wentworth 4,012 K6
Portal 522 J5
Porterdale 1,278 E3
Poulan 962 E8
Powder Springs 6,893 C3
Preston▲ 388 C6
Primrose 30 C4
Pulaski 264 J6
Putney 3,108 D8
Quitman▲ 5,292 E9
Raleigh C5
Ranger 153 C2
Ray City 603 F8
Rayle 107 G3
Rebecca 148 E7
Red Oak 950 J2
Register 195 J6
Reidsville▲ 2,469 H6
Remerton 463 F9
Reno D9
Rentz 364 G6
Resaca 410 C1
Rest Haven 176 E2
Reynolds 1,166 D5
Rhine 466 F7
Riceboro 745 K7
Richland 1,668 C6
Richmond Hill 2,934 K7
Riddleville 79 G5
Rincon 2,697 K6
Ringgold▲ 1,675 B1
Riverdale 9,359 K2
Riverside 74 B2
Riverside 99 E8
Roberta 939 D5
Rochelle 1,510 F7
Rockmart 3,356 B2
Rocky Face 500 C1
Rocky Ford 197 J5
Rocky Mount 56 C4
Rome▲ 30,326 B2
Roopville 248 B4
Rossville 3,601 B1
Roswell 47,923 D2
Royston 2,758 F2
Ruckersville G2
Russell 871 E3
Rutledge 659 E3
Saint George 600 H9
Saint Marks 36 C4
Saint Marys 8,187 J9
Saint Simons Island 12,026 K8
Sale City 324 D8
Sandersville▲ 6,290 G5
Sandy Springs 67,842 K1
Santa Claus 154 H6
Sardis 1,116 J5
Sargent 800 C4
Sasser 335 D7
Savannah▲ 137,560 L6
Scotland 244 G6
Scott 8,636 G5
Scottdale 8,770 L1
Screven 819 H7
Sea Island 600 K8
Senoia 956 C4
Seville 209 E7
Shady Dale 180 E4
Shannon 1,703 B2
Sharon 94 G3
Sharpsburg 224 C4
Shellman 1,162 C7
Shiloh 329 C5
Siloam 329 F3
Silver Creek 500 B2
Six Flags Over Georgia J1
Sky Valley 187 F1
Smithonia F2
Smithville 804 D7
Smyrna 30,981 K1
Snellville 12,084 D3
Social Circle 2,755 E3
Soperton▲ 2,797 G6
Sparks 1,205 F8
Sparta▲ 1,710 F4
Spring Place 246 C1
Springfield▲ 1,415 K6
Stapleton 330 H4
Statenville▲ 700 G9
Statesboro▲ 15,854 J6
Statham 1,360 E3
Stillmore 615 H6
Stockbridge 3,359 D3
Stockton 532 G9
Stone Mountain 6,494 D3
Stonewall 950 J2
Sugar Hill 4,557 E2
Sugar Valley C1
Summertown 153 H5
Summerville▲ 5,025 B2
Sumner 209 E7
Sunny Side 215 D4
Surrency 253 H7
Suwanee 2,412 D2
Swainsboro▲ 7,361 H5
Sycamore 417 E7
Sylvania▲ 2,871 J5
Sylvester▲ 5,702 E7
Talbotton▲ 1,046 C5
Talking Rock 62 D1
Tallapoosa 2,805 B3
Tallulah Falls 147 F1
Talmo 189 E2
Tarrytown 130 H6
Tate 950 D2
Taylorsville 269 C2
Tazewell D6
Tell J2
Temple 1,870 B3
Tennille 1,552 G5
The Rock 88 D5
Thomaston▲ 9,127 D5
Thomasville▲ 17,457 E9
Thomson▲ 6,862 H4
Thunderbolt 2,786 K6
Tifton▲ 14,215 F8
Tiger 301 F1
Tignall 711 G3
Toccoa▲ 8,266 F1
Toco Hills K1
Toomsboro 617 F5
Towns G7
Trenton▲ 1,994 A1
Trion 1,661 B1
Tunnel Hill 970 C1
Turin 189 C4
Twin City 1,466 H5
Ty Ty 579 E8
Tybee Island 2,842 L6
Tyrone 2,724 C4
Unadilla 1,620 E6
Union City 8,375 J2
Union Point 1,753 F3
Unionville 2,710 F8
Uvalda 561 H6
Valdosta▲ 39,806 F9
Van Wert 303 B3
Vanna F2
Varnell 358 C1
Vernonburg 74 K7
Vidalia 11,078 H6
Vidette H4
Vienna▲ 2,708 E
Villa Rica 6,542 C
Vinings 7,417 K
Waco 461 B
Wadley 2,473 H
Waleska 700 D
Walnut Grove 458 E
Walthourville 2,024 J
Waresboro 582 H
Warm Springs 407 C
Warner Robins 43,726 E
Warrenton▲ 2,056 G
Warwick 501 E
Watkinsville▲ 1,600 E
Waverly 769 J
Waverly Hall 913 C
Waycross▲ 16,410 H
Waynesboro▲ 5,701 J
Welcome All J
Wesley H
West Point 3,571 B
Weston 42 C
Whigham 605 D
White 542 C
White Plains 286 F
White Sulphur Springs 118 C
Whitesburg 643 B
Willacoochee 1,205 G
Williamson 295 D
Wilmington Island 11,230 L
Winder▲ 7,373 E
Winterville 876 F
Woodbine▲ 1,212 J
Woodbury 1,429 C
Woodland 552 D
Woodstock 4,361 D
Woodville 415 F
Woolsey 120 D
Wrens 2,414 H
Wrightsville▲ 2,331 G
Yatesville 409 D
Young Harris 604 E
Zebulon▲ 1,035 D

OTHER FEATURES

Alapaha (riv.) F
Allatoona (lake) C
Altamaha (riv.) H
Andersonville Nat'l Hist. Site D
Atlanta Naval Air Sta.
Banks (lake) F
Bartletts Ferry (dam) E
Blackshear (lake) E
Blue Ridge (mts.) D
Brasstown Bald (mt.) E
Burton (lake) E
Carters (lake) C
Chattahoochee (riv.) E
Chattahoochee River
Nat'l Rec. Area K
Chattooga (riv.) A
Chattooga (riv.)
Chatuge (lake) E
Chickamauga and Chattanooga
Nat'l Mil. Park E
Coosa (riv.) A
Coosawattee (riv.) C
Cumberland (isl.) K
Cumberland Island
Nat'l Seashore K
Dobbins A.F.B.
Doboy (sound) K
Etowah (riv.) C
Flint (riv.) D
Fort Benning E
Fort Frederica Nat'l Mon. K
Fort Gordon 9,140 H
Fort McPherson K
Fort Pulaski Nat'l Mon. L
Fort Stewart 13,774
Goat Rock (lake) E
Harding (lake) E
Hartwell (lake) C
Jekyll (isl.) K
Jimmy Carter Nat'l Hist. Site D
Kennesaw Mtn. Nat'l
Battlefield Park
Martin Luther King, Jr.,
Nat'l Hist. Site K
Moody A.F.B. 1,288
Morgan Falls (dam) K
Nottely (lake) D
Ochlockonee (riv.)
Ocmulgee (riv.)
Ocmulgee Nat'l Mon.
Oconee (riv.)
Ogeechee (riv.)
Okefenokee (swamp) K
Oliver (lake)
Oostanaula (riv.)
Ossabaw (sound)
Rabun (lake)
Robins A.F.B. 3,092
Saint Andrew (sound)
Saint Catherines (isl.)
Saint Mary's (riv.)
Saint Simons (isl.)
Sapelo (isl.)
Satilla (riv.) C
Savannah (riv.)
Sea (isls.)
Seminole (lake)
Sidney Lanier (lake)
Sinclair (lake)
Skidaway (isl.)
Springer (mt.)
Strom Thurmond (lakes)
Suwannee (riv.) G
Walter F. George (res.)
Wassaw (sound)
Weiss (lake)
West Point (lake)

▲County seat

Topography

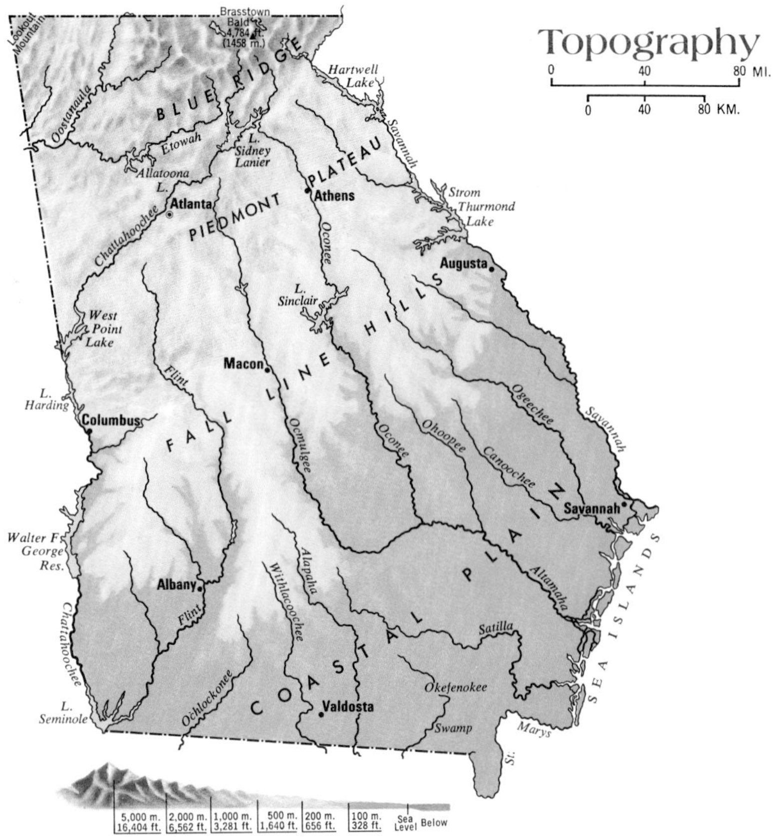

0 40 80 MI.
0 40 80 KM.
Brasstown Bald 4,784 ft. (1458 m.)
Lookout Mountain
BLUE RIDGE
Hartwell Lake
Oostanaula
Etowah
Allatoona L.
L. Sidney Lanier
Savannah
PLATEAU
Athens
Atlanta
Chattahoochee
PIEDMONT
Strom Thurmond Lake
Oconee
Augusta
L. Sinclair
HILLS
West Point Lake
Flint
Macon
LINE
L. Harding
Columbus
FALL
Ocmulgee
Ogeechee
Ohoopee
Canoochee
Savannah
Savannah
Walter F. George Res.
Albany
Flint
Withlacoochee
Alapaha
Altamaha
SEA ISLANDS
Chattahoochee
Satilla
COASTAL PLAIN
Okefenokee
Swamp
L. Seminole
Ochlockonee
Valdosta
St. Marys
5,000 m. 16,404 ft.
2,000 m. 6,562 ft.
1,000 m. 3,281 ft.
500 m. 1,640 ft.
200 m. 656 ft.
100 m. 328 ft.
Sea Level
Below

Georgia

SCALE

0 5 10   20   30   40 MI.

0 5 10   20   30   40 KM.

State Capitals .... ⊛

County Seats .... ⊙

Major Limited Access Hwys. ———

Scale 1:2,210,000

© Copyright Hammond Incorporated, Maplewood, N.J.

COUNTIES

Hawaii 120,317................K7
Honolulu 836,231..........D3
Kalawao 130.................G1
Kauai 51,177................A1
Maui 100,374...............J1

CITIES and TOWNS

Aiea 8,906....................B3
Aina Haina...................F2
Ala Moana...................C4
Anahola 1,181..............C1
Barbers Point 2,218.......E2
Captain Cook 2,595.......G5
Eleele 1,489.................C2
Ewa 14,315..................A4
Ewa Beach 14,369.........A4
Haena 200....................C1
Haiku 4,509..................J2
Haina 333....................H3
Hakalau......................J4
Halawa Heights............B3
Halawa, Hawaii 50........G3
Haleiwa 2,442..............E1
Halfway House 150........H6
Haliimaile 841..............J2
Hana 683.....................K2
Hanalei 461.................C1

Hanamaulu 3,611..........C1
Hanapepe 1,395............C2
Hauula 3,479................E1
Hawaii Kai..................F2
Hawaii National Park 250..J6
Hawi 924.....................G3
Hickam Housing 6,553....B4
Hilo▲ 37,808................J5
Holualoa 3,834.............G5
Honaunau 2,373............G6
Honohina 125...............J4
Honokaa 2,186.............H4
Honokahua 309............H1
Honokohau 200.............G5
Honokohau 309.............J1
Honolulu (cap.)▲ 365,272..C4
Honomu 532.................J4
Hoolehua....................G1
Huehue 100.................G5
Hulopoe Bay................H2
Huumula 50.................H5
Iroquois Point 4,188.......A4
Iwilei.........................C4
Kaaawa 1,138..............F1
Kaanapali 579..............H2
Kahakuloa 75...............J1
Kahala........................D5
Kahaluu 3,068..............E2
Kahuku 2,063..............E1

Kahului 16,889.............J2
Kailua (Kailua Kona),
 Hawaii 9,126.............F5
Kailua Kona.................F5
Kailua, Oahu 36,818.......F2
Kaimuki.....................D4
Kainaliu 512................G5
Kalae 150....................G1
Kalaheo 3,592..............C2
Kalaoa 4,490................G5
Kalapana 75.................J6
Kalaupapa▲ 170...........G1
Kalihi 435...................C4
Kamalo 60...................H1
Kamuela 1,179..............G4
Kapaa 8,149................D1
Kapaahu 850................J6
Kapaau 1,083...............G3
Kapalama...................C4
Kapoho 300.................K5
Kapulena 125...............H4
Kaumakani 803.............C2
Kaunakakai 2,658..........G1
Kaupakulua 600............K2
Kaupo 65.....................K2
Kawaihae 56................G4
Kawailoa 200...............E1
Keaau 1,584.................J5

Kealakekua 1,453..........G5
Kealia 550...................G6
Kealia, Kauai 300..........D1
Keanae 280..................K2
Keauhou.....................F5
Kekaha 3,506...............C2
Keokea 500..................G6
Keokea 750..................J2
Kihei 11,107................J2
Kilauea 1,685...............C1
Kipahulu 75.................K2
Koali 60......................K2
Kohala (Kapaau)...........G3
Kokomo 500................K2
Koloa 1,791.................C2
Koloa Landing..............C2
Kualapuu 1,661.............G1
Kukaiau 75..................H4
Kukuihaele 316.............H3
Kula 800.....................J2
Kunia 550....................D2
Kurtistown 910.............J5
Lahaina 9,073..............H2
Laie 5,577...................E1
Lanai City 2,400............H2
Laupahoehoe 508..........J4
Lawai 1,787.................C2
Lihue▲ 5,536...............C2
Lower Paia 1,500...........J1
Maalaea 443.................J2

Maili 6,059...................D2
Makaha 7,990..............D2
Makaiwa.....................H2
Makakilo 9,828.............E2
Makapala....................G3
Makawao 5,405............K2
Makaweli 500...............B2
Makena 100.................J2
Makiki........................C4
Mana.........................B2
Manele Bay.................H2
Maunaloa 405..............G1
Maunawili 4,847...........F2
Mililani Town 29,359......E2
Milolii 120...................G6
Moiliili.......................C4
Mokapu 11,615............F2
Mokuleia 1,776............D1
Mountain View 3,075.....J5
Naalehu 1,027..............H7
Nanakuli 9,575............D2
Napili-Honokowai 4,332..H1
Ninole 75....................J4
Olowalu 750................H2
Ookala 401..................J4
Opihikao 125...............K6
Paauhau 350................H4
Paauilo 620.................H4
Pacific Heights 5,305.....C4
Pacific Palisades...........E2

Pahala 1,520................H6
Pahoa 1,027.................J5
Paia 2,091...................J2
Papa 1,634..................G6
Papaaloa....................J4
Papaikou 1,567.............J5
Paukaa 495..................J5
Pauwela 468................K2
Peahi 308....................K2
Pearl City 30,993...........B3
Pepeekeo 1,813............J4
Poipu 975....................C2
Princeville 1,244...........C1
Puako 397...................G4
Puhi 1,210...................C2
Pukalani 5,879.............C2
Punaluu 672................H7
Puuanahulu 56.............G4
Puuiki 75....................K2
Puunene 572................J2
Puunui.......................C4
Puuwai 200.................A2
Schofield Barracks 19,597..E2
Spreckelsville 350.........J1
Sunset Beach...............E1
Ulumalu 201................K2
Ulupalakua 75..............J2
Volcano 1,516..............J6
Wahiawa 17,386...........E2
Waiakoa......................J2

Waialae.......................D4
Waialua, Oahu 3,943......E1
Waianae 8,758.............D2
Waihee 4,004...............J2
Waikane 717................E2
Waikapu 729................J2
Waikiki 50....................H4
Waikiki.......................C4
Wailea, Hawaii 150.......J4
Wailea-Makena, Maui 3,799..J2
Wailua 2,018................D2
Wailuku▲ 10,688.........J2
Waimalu 29,967...........B3
Waimanalo 3,508..........F2
Waimanalo Beach 4,185..F2
Waimea (Kamuela), Hawaii
 1,840.......................G4
Waimea 200.................C1
Waimea, Kauai 5,972.....B2
Wainaku 1,243.............J5
Wainiha 715.................C1
Waiohinu 200...............G7
Waipio 11,812..............H3
Waipio Acres 5,304........E2
Whitmore Village 3,373...E1

OTHER FEATURES

Alalakeiki (chan.)..........J3

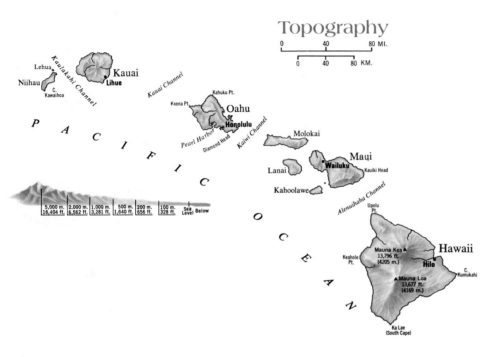

Topography

Agriculture, Industry and Resources

DOMINANT LAND USE

Diversified Tropical Cash Crops

Livestock Grazing

Forests

Urban Areas

Nonagricultural Land

///// Major Industrial Areas

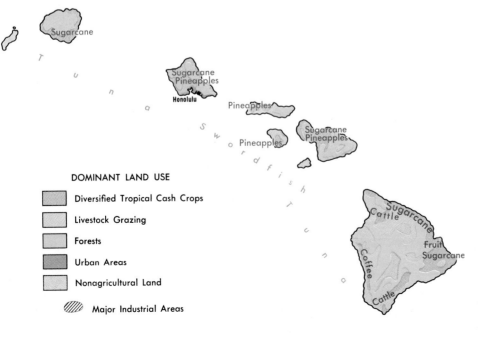

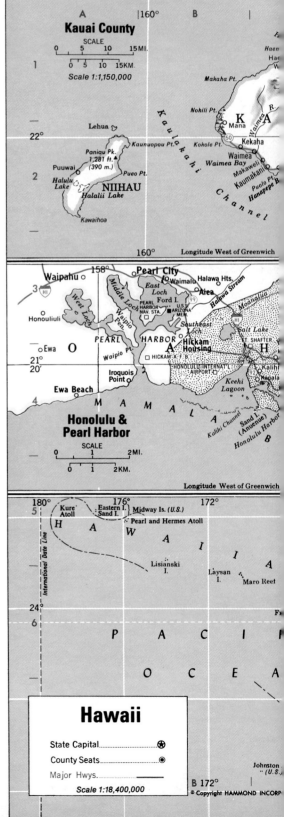

Kauai County

SCALE
0 5 10 15 MI.
0 5 10 15KM.
Scale 1:1,150,000

NIIHAU

Longitude West of Greenwich

Honolulu & Pearl Harbor

SCALE
0 1 2 MI.
0 1 2 KM.

Longitude West of Greenwich

Hawaii

State Capital..................⊛

County Seats..................◉

Major Hwys.

Scale 1:18,400,000

© Copyright HAMMOND INCORP.

Alenuihaha (chan.) E7
Anuenue (Sand) (isl.) C4
Auau (chan.) H2
Barbers Point Naval Air Sta. E2
Diamond (head) C5
East Loch (inlet) B3
Ford (isl.) B3
Fort Shafter 2,952 ....C3
French Frigate (shoals) C6
Gardner Pinnacles (isls.) C6
Halalii (lake) A2
Halawa (bay) H1
Haleakala (crater) K2
Haleakala Nat'l Park K2
Hawaii (isl.) H5
Hawaii Volcanoes Nat'l Park H6
Hickam A.F.B. B4
Hilo (bay) J5
Honolulu (harb.) C4
Honolulu Int'l Airport B4
Ilio (pt.) G1
Kaala (mt.) D1
Kahala (pt.) D1
Kahana (bay) F1
Kaiwi (chan.) E6
Ka Lae (cape) G7
Kalaupapa Nat'l Hist. Park H1
Kalohi (chan.) G1
Kaloko-Honokohau Nat'l Hist. Park F5

Kamakou (peak) H1
Kanapou (bay) J3
Kaneohe Bay U.S.M.C. Air Station F2
Kau (des.) J6
Kauai (chan.) E6
Kauai (isl.) C1
Kauiki (head) K2
Kaula (isl.) D6
Kaulakahi (chan.) B2
Kawaihae (bay) G4
Kawaihoa (cape) A2
Kawaikini (peak) C1
Keahi (pt.) A4
Kealaikahiki (chan.) H3
Kealakekua (bay) F6
Keanapapa (pt.) G2
Keehi (lag.) B4
Kiholo (bay) F4
Kilauea (crater) H6
Kohala (mts.) G4
Koko (head) F2
Konahuanui (peak) D3
Koolau (range) E2
Kumukahi (cape) K5
Kure (atoll) A5
Laau (pt.) G1
Lanai (isl.) H2
Lanaihale (mt.) H2
Laysan (isl.) B6

Lisianski (isl.) B5
Lua Makika (mt.) J3
Maalaea (bay) J2
Makaha (pt.) B1
Makahuena (pt.) C2
Makapuu (pt.) F2
Mamala (bay) B4
Manana (isl.) F2
Maro (reef) C6
Maui (isl.) J2
Mauna Kea (mt.) H4
Mauna Loa (mt.) G6
Middle Loch (inlet) A3
Moanalua (stream) B3
Mokapu (pen.) F2
Mokuaweoweo (crater) H6
Molokai (isl.) G1
Molokini (isl.) J2
Necker (isl.) D6
Nihoa (isl.) D6
Niihau (isl.) A2
Oahu (isl.) E1
Pailolo (chan.) H1
Palolo (stream) D4
Paniau (peak) A2
Pearl (harb.) A3
Pearl and Hermes (atoll) B5
Pearl Harbor Naval Sta. B3
Wheeler A.F.B. 2,600 ....E1

Puolo (pt.) C2
Puuhonua O Honaunau Nat'l Hist. Park F6
Puu Keahiakahoe (mt.) D3
Puukohola Heiau Nat'l Hist. Park G4
Puu Kukui (mt.) J2
Red Hill (mt.) K2
Roundtop (mt.) C4
Salt (lake) B3
Sand (isl.) B4
South (Ka Lae) (cape) G7
Southeast Loch (inlet) A3
Sugarloaf (hill) C4
Tantalus (mt.) D4
Upolu (pt.) G3
U.S.S. Arizona Memorial B3
Waialeale (mt.) C1
Waikiki (beach) C4
Waimanu (bay) B2
Waimea (bay) C2
Wainiha (riv.) C1
Waipio (bay) H3
Waipio (pen.) A3
Waipio (pt.) A4
West Loch (inlet) A3

▲County seat

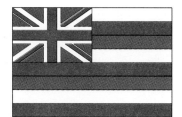

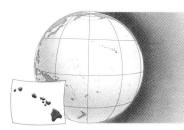

AREA 6,471 sq. mi. (16,760 sq. km.)
POPULATION 1,115,274
CAPITAL Honolulu
LARGEST CITY Honolulu
HIGHEST POINT Mauna Kea 13,796 ft. (4205 m.)
SETTLED IN —
ADMITTED TO UNION August 21, 1959
POPULAR NAME Aloha State
STATE FLOWER Hibiscus
STATE BIRD Nene (Hawaiian Goose)

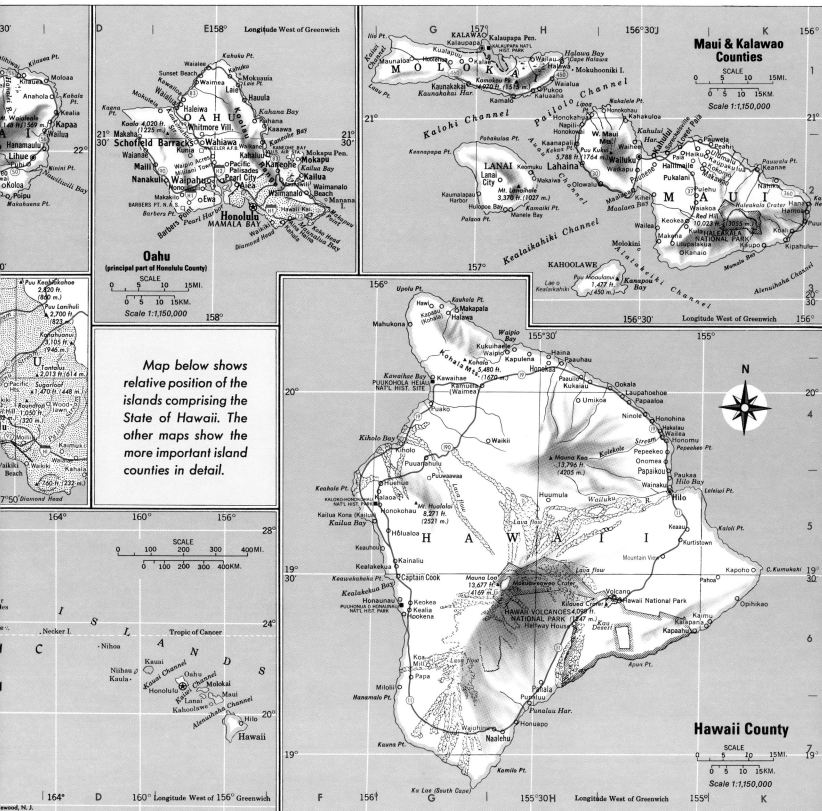

Map below shows relative position of the islands comprising the State of Hawaii. The other maps show the more important island counties in detail.

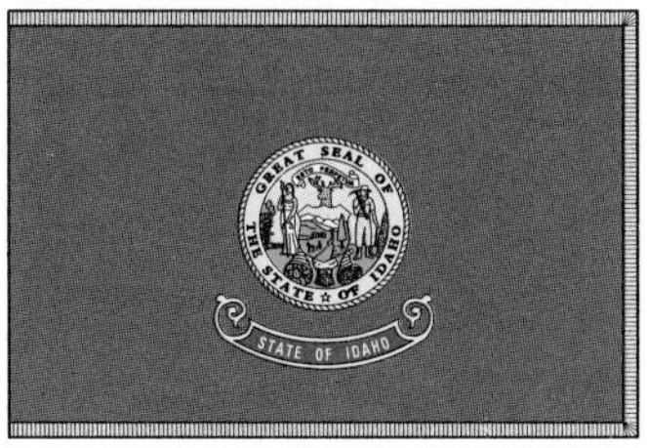

AREA 83,564 sq. mi. (216,431 sq. km.)
POPULATION 1,011,986
CAPITAL Boise
LARGEST CITY Boise
HIGHEST POINT Borah Pk. 12,662 ft. (3859 m.)
SETTLED IN 1842
ADMITTED TO UNION July 3, 1890
POPULAR NAME Gem State
STATE FLOWER Syringa
STATE BIRD Mountain Bluebird

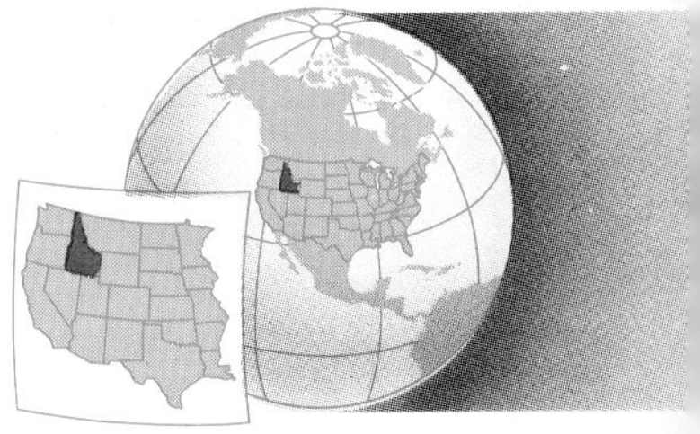

COUNTIES

Ada 205,775 B6
Adams 3,254 B5
Bannock 66,026 F7
Bear Lake 6,084 G7
Benewah 7,937 B2
Bingham 37,583 F6
Blaine 13,552 D6
Boise 3,509 C6
Bonner 26,622 B1
Bonneville 72,207 G6
Boundary 8,332 B1
Butte 2,918 E6
Camas 727 D6
Canyon 90,076 B6
Caribou 6,963 G7
Cassia 19,532 E7
Clark 762 F5
Clearwater 8,505 C3
Custer 4,133 D5
Elmore 21,205 C6
Franklin 9,232 G7
Fremont 10,937 G5
Gem 11,844 B6
Gooding 11,633 D6
Idaho 13,783 C4
Jefferson 16,543 F6
Jerome 15,138 D7
Kootenai 69,795 B2
Latah 30,617 B3
Lemhi 6,899 D4
Lewis 3,516 B3
Lincoln 3,308 D6
Madison 23,674 G6
Minidoka 19,361 E7
Nez Perce 33,754 B3
Oneida 3,492 F7
Owyhee 8,392 B7
Payette 16,434 B5
Power 7,086 F7
Shoshone 13,931 B2
Teton 3,439 G6
Twin Falls 53,580 D7
Valley 6,109 C5
Washington 8,550 B5

CITIES and TOWNS

Aberdeen 1,406 F7
Acequia 106 E7
Ahsahka 160 B3
Albion 305 E7
American Falls▲ 3,757 E7
Ammon 5,002 G6
Arco▲ 1,016 E6
Arimo 311 F7
Ashton 1,114 G5
Athol 346 B2
Atomic City 25 F6
Bancroft 393 G7
Basalt 407 F6
Bayview 350 B2
Bellevue 1,275 D6
Bern 154 G7
Blackfoot▲ 9,646 F6
Bliss 185 D7
Bloomington 197 G7
Boise (cap.)▲ 102,160 B6
Bonners Ferry▲ 2,193 B1
Bovill 256 B3
Bruneau 160 C7
Buhl 3,516 D7
Burgdorf B4
Burke 150 C2
Burley▲ 8,702 E7
Butte City 59 E6
Calder 200 B2
Caldwell▲ 18,400 B6
Cambridge 374 B5
Carey 800 E6
Cascade▲ 877 C5
Castleford 179 C7
Cataldo 150 B2
Challis▲ 1,073 D5
Chatcolet 72 B2
Chester 300 G5
Chilly E5
Chubbuck 7,791 F7
Clark Fork 448 B1
Clarkia 175 B2
Clayton 26 D5
Clifton 228 F7
Coeur d'Alene▲ 24,563 B2
Colburn 250 B1
Conda 200 G7
Coolin 150 B1
Cottonwood 822 B3
Council▲ 831 B5
Craigmont 542 B3
Crouch 75 B5
Culdesac 280 B3
Dalton Gardens 1,951 B2
Dayton 357 F7
Deary 529 B3
Declo 279 E7
Dietrich 127 D7
Dingle 300 G7
Donnelly 135 B5
Dover 294 B1
Downey 626 F7
Driggs▲ 846 G6
Drummond 37 G5
Dubois▲ 420 F5
Eagle 3,327 B6
East Hope 215 B1
Eden 314 D7
Elk City 500 C4
Elk River 149 B3
Emida 175 B2
Emmett▲ 4,601 B6
Fairfield▲ 371 D6
Ferdinand 135 B3
Fernan Lake 178 B2
Fernwood 608 B2
Filer 1,511 D7
Firth 429 F6
Fort Hall 2,681 F6
Franklin 478 G7
Fruitland 2,400 B6
Fruitvale 200 B5
Garden City 6,369 B6
Garden Valley 250 C5
Genesee 725 B3
Geneva 220 G7
Georgetown 558 G7
Gilmore E5
Glenns Ferry 1,304 C7
Gooding▲ 2,820 D7
Grace 973 G7
Grand View 330 B7
Grangeville▲ 3,226 B4
Greenleaf 648 B6
Grimes Pass C5
Hagerman 600 D7
Hailey▲ 3,687 D6
Hamer 79 F6
Hammett 180 C7
Hansen 848 D7
Harrison 226 B2
Hauser 380 A2
Hayden 3,744 B2
Hayden Lake 338 B2
Hazelton 394 E7
Headquarters 165 C3
Heise 84 G6
Heyburn 2,714 E7
Hollister 144 D7
Homedale 1,963 A6
Hope 99 B1
Horseshoe Bend 643 B6
Huetter 82 B2
Idaho City▲ 322 C6
Idaho Falls▲ 43,929 F6
Inkom 769 F7
Iona 1,049 G6
Irwin 108 G6
Island Park 159 G5
Jerome▲ 6,529 D7
Juliaetta 488 B3
Kamiah 1,157 B3
Kellogg 2,591 B2
Kendrick 325 B3
Ketchum 2,523 D6
Kimberly 2,367 D7
Kooskia 692 C3
Kootenai 327 B1
Kuna 1,955 B6
Laclede 400 B1
Lake Fork 250 B5
Lapwai 932 B3
Lava Hot Springs 420 F7
Leadore 74 E5
Lewiston▲ 28,082 A3
Lewisville 471 F6
Lost River (Grouse) 29 E6
Lowman 180 C5
Mackay 574 E6
Macks Inn 200 G5
Malad City▲ 1,946 F7
Malta 171 E7
Marsing 798 B6
McCall 2,005 C5
McCammon 722 F7
Meadows 250 B5
Melba 252 B6
Menan 601 F6
Meridian 9,596 B6
Middleton 1,851 B6
Midvale 110 B5
Minidoka 67 E7
Monteview 200 F6
Montpelier 2,656 G7
Moore 190 E6
Moreland 600 F6
Moscow▲ 18,519 B3
Mountain Home▲ 7,913 C6
Moyie Springs 415 B1
Mud Lake 179 F6
Mullan 821 C2
Murphy▲ 200 B6
Murtaugh 114 D7
Nampa 28,365 B6
Naples 250 B1
New Meadows 534 B4
New Plymouth 1,313 B6
Newdale 377 G6
Nezperce▲ 453 B3
Nordman 300 B1
North Fork 250 D4
Notus 380 B6
Oakley 635 D7
Ola 175 B5
Oldtown 151 A1
Onaway 203 B3
Orofino▲ 2,868 B3
Osburn 1,579 B2
Oxford 44 F7
Paris▲ 581 G7
Parker 288 G6
Parma 1,597 B6
Patterson 4 E5
Paul 901 E7
Payette▲ 5,592 B5
Pearl 8 B6
Peck 160 B3
Pierce 746 C3
Pinehurst 1,722 B2
Placerville 14 C6
Plummer 804 B2
Pocatello▲ 46,080 F7
Ponderay 449 B1
Post Falls 7,349 A2
Potlatch 790 A3
Preston▲ 3,710 G7
Priest River 1,560 A1
Rathdrum 2,000 A2
Reubens 46 B3
Rexburg▲ 14,302 G6
Richfield 383 D6
Rigby▲ 2,681 F6
Riggins 443 B4
Ririe 596 G6
Roberts 557 F6
Rockland 264 F7
Rupert▲ 5,455 E7
Sagle 600 B1
Saint Anthony▲ 3,010 G6
Saint Charles 211 G7
Saint Maries▲ 2,442 B2
Salmon▲ 2,941 D4
Samuels 467 B1
Sandpoint▲ 5,203 B1
Shelley 3,536 F6
Shoshone▲ 1,249 D7
Silver City 1 B6
Smelterville 464 B2
Soda Springs▲ 3,111 G7
Spencer 11 F5
Spirit Lake 790 A2
Stanley 71 D5
Star 500 B6
State Line 26 A2
Stites 204 C3
Sugar City 1,275 G6
Sun Valley 938 D6
Swan Valley 141 G6
Sweet 290 B6
Tendoy 155 E5
Tensed 90 B2
Terreton 400 F6
Teton 570 G6
Tetonia 132 G6
Thatcher 300 G7
Thornton 177 G6
Troy 699 B3
Twin Falls▲ 27,591 D7
Ucon 895 F6
Victor 292 G6
Wallace▲ 1,010 C2
Wardner 246 B2
Warm Lake 200 C5
Warm River 9 G5
Wayan 175 G7
Weippe 532 C3
Weiser▲ 4,571 B5
Wendell 1,963 D7
Weston 390 F7
White Bird 108 B4
Wilder 1,232 A6
Winchester 262 B3
Worley 182 B2

OTHER FEATURES

Albeni Falls (dam) B1
Albion (mts.) E7
Allan (mt.) D4
American Falls (res.) F6
Anderson Ranch (res.) C6
Antelope (creek) E6
Arrowrock (res.) C6
Auger (falls) D7
Badger (peak) E7
Bald (mt.) D5
Bannock (creek) F7
Bannock (peak) F7
Bannock (range) F7
Bargamin (creek) C4
Battle (creek) B7
Bear (lake) G7
Bear (riv.) G7
Bear River (range) G7
Beaver (creek) F5
Beaverhead (mts.) E4
Big (creek) C4
Big Boulder (creek) B7
Big Elk (peak) G6
Big Hole (mts.) G6
Big Lost (riv.) E6
Big Southern (butte) E6
Big Wood (riv.) D6
Birch (creek) F5
Birch Creek (valley) E5
Bitterroot (range) D3
Blackfoot (res.) G7
Black Pine (mts.) E7
Blue Nose (mt.) D4
Boise (mts.) B6
Boise (riv.) B6
Borah (peak) E5
Boulder (mts.) D6
Brownlee (dam) B5
Bruneau (riv.) C7
Camas (creek) D5
Camas (creek) D6
Camas (creek) F5
Canyon (creek) C6
Cape Horn (mt.) C5
Caribou (mt.) G6
Caribou (range) G6
Cascade (res.) C5
Castle (creek) B7
Castle (peak) D5
Cedar Creek (peak) E7
Cedar Creek (res.) D7
Centennial (mts.) F5
Chesterfield (res) F7
Clearwater (mts.) C3
Clearwater (riv.) B3
Coeur d'Alene (lake) B2
Coeur d'Alene (mts.) C2
Coeur d'Alene (riv.) B2
Cottonwood (butte) C4
Craig (mts.) B4
Crane Creek (res.) B5
Craters of the Moon Nat'l Mon. E6
Deadwood (res.) C5
Deep (creek) B7
Deep (creek) F7
Deep Creek (mts.) F7
Diamond (peak) E5
Duck Valley Ind. Res. B7
Dworshak (res.) C3
East Sister (peak) C2
Eighteen Mile (peak) E5
Fish Creek (res.) E6
Fort Hall Ind. Res. F6
Goldstone (mt.) E4
Goose (creek) E7
Goose Creek (mts.) E7
Grand Canyon of the Snake River (canyon) B4
Grays (lake) G6
Grays Lake Outlet (creek) G6
Greylock (mt.) C6
Hayden (lake) B2
Hells (canyon) B4
Hells Canyon Nat'l Rec. Area B4
Henrys (lake) G5
Henrys Fork, Snake (riv.) G5
Hunter (peak) D3
Hyndman (peak) D6
Indian (creek) C5
Island Park (res.) G5
Jarbidge (riv.) C7
Johnson (creek) C5
Jordan (creek) A7
Kootenai (riv.) C1
Lemhi (pass) E5
Lemhi (range) E5
Lemhi (riv.) E5
Little Lost (riv.) E5
Little Owyhee (riv.) B7
Little Salmon (riv.) B4
Little Weiser (riv.) B5
Little Wood (riv.) D6
Lochsa (riv.) C3
Lolo (creek) C3
Lolo (pass) D3
Lone Pine (peak) D5
Lookout (mt.) D5
Lookout (mt.) F5
Lost River (range) E5
Lost Trail (pass) D4
Lowell (lake) B6
Lower Goose Creek (res.) D7
Lower Granite (lake) A3
Lucky Peak (lake) B6
Mackay (res.) E6
Magic (res.) D6
Malad (riv.) F7
Marsh (creek) F7
McGuire (mt.) D4
Meade (peak) G7
Meadow (creek) C4
Medicine Lodge (creek) F5
Middle Fork (peak) D5
Monument (peak) B4
Moose (creek) D3
Mores (creek) C6
Mormon (mt.) C4
Mountain Home (res.) C6
Mountain Home A.F.B. 5,936 C6
Moyie (riv.) B1
Mud (lake) F6
National Reactor Testing Sta. F6
Nez Perce Nat'l Hist. Park C3
Norton (peak) D6
Orofino (creek) C3
Owyhee (mts.) B6
Owyhee, East Fork (riv.) B7
Oxbow (dam) B5
Pack (riv.) B1
Pahsimeroi (riv.) E5
Palisades (res.) G6
Palouse (riv.) B3
Panther (creek) D4
Payette (lake) C4
Payette (mts.) B5
Payette (riv.) B6
Peale (mts.) G7
Pend Oreille (lake) B1
Pend Oreille (mt.) B1
Pend Oreille (riv.) A1
Pilot (peak) C4
Pilot (peak) C6
Pilot Knob (mt.) C4
Pinyon (peak) C5
Pioneer (mts.) D6
Pot (mt.) C3
Potlatch (riv.) B3
Priest (lake) B1
Priest (riv.) B1
Purcell (mts.) B1
Pyramid (peak) E4
Raft (riv.) E7
Rainbow (mt.) C5
Ranger (peak) D3
Rays (lake) F6
Red (riv.) C4
Redfish (lake) D5
Reynolds (creek) B6
Rhodes (peak) D3
Rock (creek) F7
Rocky (mts.) D1
Rocky Ridge (mt.) C3
Ryan (peak) D6
Saddle (mt.) D3
Saddle (mt.) F6
Sailor (creek) C7
Saint Joe (riv.) B2
Saint Maries (riv.) B2
Salmon (falls) C7
Salmon (riv.) B4
Salmon Falls (creek) D7
Salmon Falls Creek (res.) D7
Salmon River (mts.) C5
Sawtooth (range) C6
Sawtooth Nat'l Rec. Area D5
Secesh (riv.) C4
Selkirk (mts.) B1
Selway (riv.) C3
Seven Devils (mts.) B4
Shoshone (falls) D7
Sleeping Deer (mt.) D5
Smith (creek) B1
Smoky (mts.) D6
Snake (riv.) A3
Snake River (plain) D7
Snake River (range) G6
Spirit (lake) B2
Squaw (creek) B5
Squaw (peak) D4
Steamboat (mt.) C4
Steel (mt.) C6
Strike, C.J. (res.) C7
Sublett (mts.) E7
Sunset (peak) E6
Taylor (mt.) D5
Teton (riv.) G6
Thompson (peak) C5
Trinity (mt.) C6
Trout (creek) B1
Twin (falls) D7
Twin Peaks (mt.) D5
Walcott (lake) E7
Waugh (mt.) D4
Weiser (riv.) B5
White Knob (mts.) E6
Wickahoney (creek) C7
Willow (creek) G6
Wilson Lake (res.) D7
Yankee Fork, Salmon (riv.) D5
Yellowstone Nat'l Park H5

▲County seat

Agriculture, Industry and Resources

MAJOR MINERAL OCCURRENCES

Ag Silver
Au Gold
Co Cobalt
Cu Copper
Fe Iron Ore
Hg Mercury
Mo Molybdenum
P Phosphates
Pb Lead
Sb Antimony
Th Thorium
Ti Titanium
V Vanadium
W Tungsten
Zn Zinc

Water Power

DOMINANT LAND USE

Wheat, General Farming
Wheat, Peas
Specialized Dairy
Potatoes, Beans, Sugar Beets, Livestock, General Farming
General Farming, Dairy, Hay, Sugar Beets
General Farming, Livestock, Special Crops
General Farming, Dairy, Range Livestock
Range Livestock
Forests

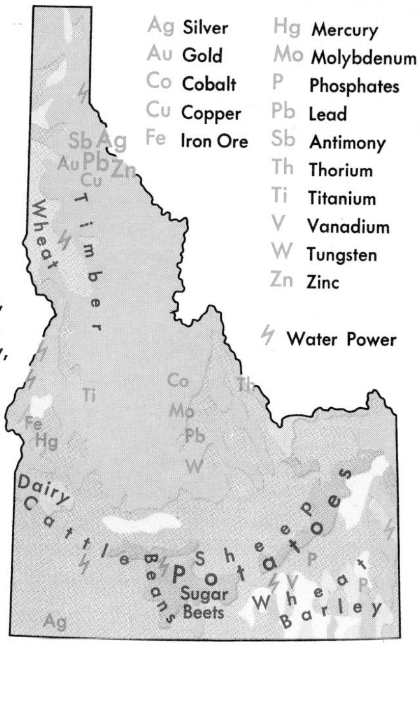

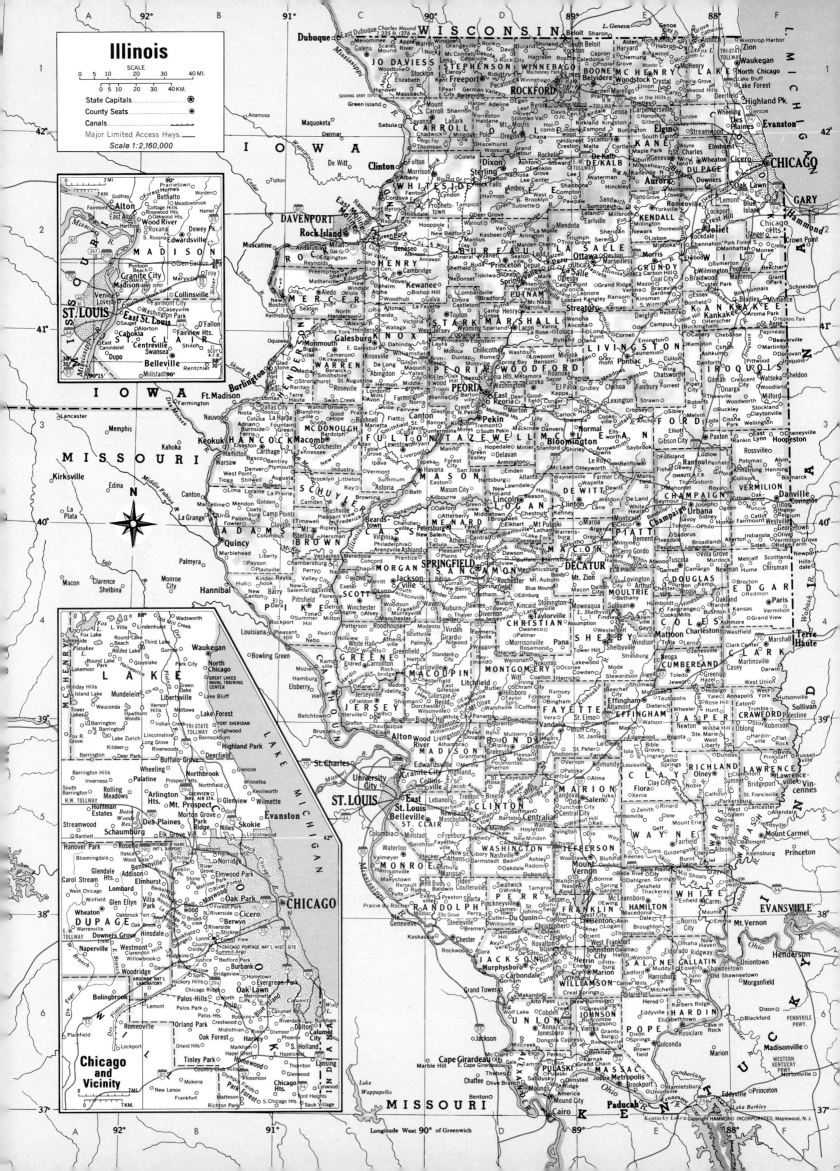

ILLINOIS

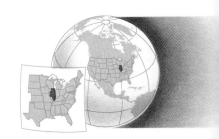

AREA 56,345 sq. mi. (145,934 sq. km.)
POPULATION 11,466,682
CAPITAL Springfield
LARGEST CITY Chicago
HIGHEST POINT Charles Mound 1,235 ft. (376 m.)
SETTLED IN 1720
ADMITTED TO UNION December 3, 1818
POPULAR NAME Prairie State; Land of Lincoln
STATE FLOWER Native Violet
STATE BIRD Cardinal

COUNTIES

Adams 66,090 ....B4
Alexander 10,626 ....D6
Bond 14,991 ....D5
Boone 30,806 ....E1
Brown 5,836 ....C4
Bureau 35,688 ....D2
Calhoun 5,322 ....C4
Carroll 16,805 ....D1
Cass 13,437 ....C3
Champaign 173,025 ....E3
Christian 34,418 ....D4
Clark 15,921 ....F4
Clay 14,460 ....E5
Clinton 33,944 ....D5
Coles 51,644 ....E4
Cook 5,105,067 ....F2
Crawford 19,464 ....F4
Cumberland 10,670 ....E4
De Kalb 74,624 ....E1
De Witt 16,516 ....E3
Douglas 19,464 ....E4
Du Page 658,858 ....E2
Edgar 19,595 ....F4
Edwards 7,440 ....E5
Effingham 31,704 ....E4
Fayette 20,893 ....D4
Ford 14,275 ....E3
Franklin 40,319 ....E5
Fulton 38,080 ....C3
Gallatin 6,909 ....E6
Greene 15,317 ....C4
Grundy 32,337 ....E2
Hamilton 8,499 ....E5
Hancock 21,373 ....B3
Hardin 5,189 ....E6
Henderson 8,096 ....C3
Henry 51,159 ....C2
Iroquois 30,787 ....F3

Jackson 61,067 ....D6
Jasper 10,609 ....E4
Jefferson 37,020 ....E5
Jersey 20,539 ....C4
Jo Daviess 21,821 ....C1
Johnson 11,347 ....E6
Kane 317,471 ....E2
Kankakee 96,255 ....F2
Kendall 39,413 ....E2
Knox 56,393 ....C3
La Salle 106,913 ....E2
Lake 516,418 ....E1
Lawrence 15,972 ....F5
Lee 34,392 ....D2
Livingston 39,301 ....E3
Logan 30,798 ....D3
Macon 117,206 ....E4
Macoupin 47,679 ....D4
Madison 249,238 ....D5
Marion 41,561 ....E5
Marshall 12,846 ....D2
Mason 16,269 ....D3
Massac 14,752 ....E6
McDonough 35,244 ....C3
McHenry 183,241 ....E1
McLean 129,180 ....E3
Menard 11,164 ....D3
Mercer 17,290 ....C2
Monroe 22,422 ....C5
Montgomery 30,728 ....D4
Morgan 36,397 ....C4
Moultrie 13,930 ....E4
Ogle 45,957 ....D1
Peoria 182,827 ....D3
Perry 21,412 ....D5
Piatt 15,548 ....E4
Pike 17,577 ....C4
Pope 4,373 ....E6
Pulaski 7,523 ....D6
Putnam 5,730 ....D2

Randolph 34,583 ....D5
Richland 16,545 ....E5
Rock Island 148,723 .....C2
Saint Clair 267,531 .....D5
Saline 26,551 ....E6
Sangamon 178,386 ....D4
Schuyler 7,498 ....C3
Scott 5,644 ....C4
Shelby 22,261 ....E4
Stark 6,534 ....D2
Stephenson 48,052 ....D1
Tazewell 123,692 ....D3
Union 17,619 ....D6
Vermilion 88,257 ....F3
Wabash 13,111 ....F5
Warren 19,181 ....C3
Washington 14,965 ....D5
Wayne 17,241 ....E5
White 16,522 ....E5
Whiteside 60,186 ....D2
Will 357,313 ....F2
Williamson 57,733 ....E6
Winnebago 252,913 ....D1
Woodford 32,653 ....D3

CITIES and TOWNS

Abingdon 3,597 ....C3
Addison 32,058 ....B5
Albany 835 ....C2
Albers 700 ....D5
Albion▲ 2,116 ....E5
Aledo▲ 3,681 ....C2
Alexis 908 ....C2
Algonquin 11,663 ....E1
Alhambra 709 ....D5
Allendale 476 ....F5
Alorton 2,960 ....B2
Alpha 753 ....C2
Alsip 18,227 ....B6
Altamont 2,296 ....E4
Alton 32,905 ....A2
Altona 559 ....C2
Amboy 2,377 ....D2
Andalusia 1,052 ....C2
Andover 579 ....C2
Anna 4,805 ....D6
Annawan 802 ....C2
Antioch 6,105 ....E1
Arcola 2,678 ....E4
Arenzville 432 ....C4
Argenta 940 ....E4
Arlington Heights 75,460 ...B5
Aroma Park 690 ....F2
Arthur 2,112 ....E4
Ashkum 650 ....E3
Ashland 1,257 ....C4
Ashley 583 ....D5
Ashmore 800 ....F4
Ashton 1,042 ....D2
Assumption 1,244 ....E4
Astoria 1,205 ....C3
Athens 1,404 ....D4
Atkinson 950 ....C2
Atlanta 1,616 ....D3
Atwood 1,253 ....E4
Auburn 3,724 ....D4
Augusta 614 ....C3
Aurora 99,581 ....E2
Ava 674 ....D6
Aviston 924 ....D5
Avon 957 ....C3
Baldwin 426 ....D5
Bannockburn 1,388 ......B5
Barrington 9,504 ....A5
Barrington Hills 4,202 ...A5
Barry 1,391 ....B4
Bartlett 19,373 ....A5
Bartonville 5,643 ......D3
Batavia 17,076 ....E2
Beardstown 5,270 ....C3
Beckemeyer 1,070 ....D5
Bedford Park 566 ....B6
Beecher 2,032 ....F2
Beecher City 437 ....E4
Belgium 511 ....F3
Belleville▲ 42,785 .....B3
Bellwood 20,241 ....B5
Belvidere▲ 15,958 ......E1
Bement 1,668 ....E4
Benld 1,604 ....D4
Bensenville 17,767 .....B5
Benton▲ 7,216 ....E6
Berkeley 5,137 ....B5
Berwyn 45,426 ....B6
Bethalto 9,507 ....D5
Bethany 1,369 ....E4
Blandinsville 762 ......C3
Bloomingdale 16,614 ....A5
Bloomington▲ 51,972 ....D3
Blue Island 21,203 .....B6
Blue Mound 1,161 ....D4
Bluffs 774 ....C4
Bluford 747 ....E5
Bolingbrook 40,843 .....A6
Bourbon 13,934 ....E4
Bourbonnais 13,280 .....F2
Bowen 462 ....B3
Braceville 587 ....E2
Bradford 678 ....D2
Bradley 10,792 ....F2
Braidwood 3,584 ....E2
Breese 3,567 ....D5
Bridgeport 2,118 ....F5
Bridgeview 14,402 ......B6
Brighton 2,270 ....C4
Brimfield 797 ....D3
Broadview 8,713 ....B6
Brookfield 18,876 ......B6
Brooklyn (Lovejoy) 1,144 ...A2
Brookport 1,070 ....E6
Brownstown 668 ....E5
Buckley 557 ....F3
Buckner 478 ....E6
Buda 563 ....D2
Buffalo 503 ....D4
Buffalo Grove 36,427 ...B5
Bunker Hill 1,722 ......D4
Burbank 27,600 ....B6
Burnham 3,916 ....C6

Burr Ridge 7,669 ....B6
Bushnell 3,288 ....C3
Byron 2,284 ....D1
Cahokia 17,550 ....A3
Cairo▲ 4,846 ....D6
Calumet City 37,840 ....C6
Calumet Park 8,418 .....C6
Cambria 1,230 ....D6
Cambridge▲ 2,124 ....C2
Camp Point 1,230 ....B3
Canton 13,922 ....C3
Capron 682 ....E1
Carbon Cliff 1,492 .....C2
Carbondale 27,033 ......D6
Carlinville▲ 5,416 .....D4
Carlyle▲ 3,474 ....D5
Carmi▲ 5,564 ....E5
Carol Stream 31,716 ....A5
Carpentersville 23,049 ...E1
Carrier Mills 2,268 ....E6
Carrollton▲ 2,507 ......C4
Carterville 3,630 ......D6
Carthage▲ 2,657 ....B3
Cary 10,043 ....E1
Casey 2,914 ....F4
Caseyville 4,419 ....B2
Catlin 2,173 ....F3
Cave in Rock 381 ....E6
Cedarville 751 ....D1
Central City 1,390 .....D5
Centralia 14,274 ......D5
Centreville 7,489 ......B3
Cerro Gordo 1,436 ......E4
Chadwick 557 ....D1
Champaign 63,502 ....E3
Chandlerville 689 ......C3
Channahon 4,266 ....E2
Chapin 632 ....C4
Charleston▲ 20,398 .....E4
Chatham 6,074 ....D4
Chatsworth 1,186 ....E3
Chebanse 1,082 ....F3
Chenoa 1,732 ....E3
Cherry 487 ....D2
Cherry Valley 1,615 ....D1
Chester▲ 8,194 ....D6
Chicago Heights 33,072 ...C6
Chicago Ridge 13,643 ...B6
Chicago▲ 2,783,726 ....C5
Chillicothe 5,959 ......D3
Chrisman 1,136 ....F4
Christopher 2,774 ......D6
Cicero 67,436 ....B5
Cisne 645 ....E5
Cissna Park 805 ....F3
Clarendon Hills 6,994 ...B6
Clay City 929 ....E5
Clayton 726 ....B3
Clifton 1,347 ....F3
Clinton▲ 7,437 ....E3
Coal City 3,907 ....E2
Coal Valley 2,683 ......C2
Cobden 1,090 ....D6
Coffeen 736 ....D4
Colchester 1,645 ....C3
Colfax 854 ....E3
Collinsville 22,446 ....B2
Colona 2,237 ....C2
Columbia 5,524 ....C5
Cordova 638 ....C2
Cornell 556 ....E3
Cortland 963 ....E2
Coulterville 984 ....D5
Country Club Hills 15,431 ...B6
Countryside 5,716 ......B6
Cowden 599 ....E4
Creal Springs 791 ......E6
Crescent City 541 ......F3
Crest Hill 10,643 ......E2
Creston 535 ....D2
Crestwood 10,823 ....B6
Crete 6,773 ....F2
Creve Coeur 5,938 ......D3
Crossville 805 ....F5
Crystal Lake 24,512 ....E1
Cuba 1,440 ....C3
Cullom 568 ....E3
Cutler 523 ....D5
Dahlgren 512 ....E5
Dakota 549 ....D1
Dallas City 1,037 ......B3
Dalton City 573 ....E4
Dalzell 587 ....D2
Danforth 457 ....E3
Danvers 981 ....D3
Danville▲ 33,828 ......F3
Darien 18,341 ....B6
Davis 541 ....D1
Dawson 536 ....D4
De Kalb 34,925 ....E2
De Land 458 ....E3
De Soto 1,500 ....D6
Decatur▲ 83,885 ....E4
Deer Creek 630 ....D3
Deer Park 2,887 ....A5
Deerfield 17,327 ......B5
Delavan 1,642 ....D3
Depue 1,729 ....D2

Des Plaines 53,223 .....B5
Dieterich 568 ....E4
Divernon 1,178 ....D4
Dix 456 ....E5
Dixmoor 3,647 ....C6
Dixon▲ 15,144 ....D2
Dolton 23,930 ....C6
Dongola 728 ....D6
Dow 465 ....C4
Dowell 480 ....D6
Downers Grove 46,858 ...A6
Downs 620 ....E3
Du Quoin 6,697 ....D5
Dundee (East and West
  Dundee) 6,169 ....E1
Dunlap 851 ....D3
Dupo 3,164 ....A3
Durand 1,100 ....D1
Dwight 4,230 ....E2
Earlville 1,435 ....E2
East Alton 7,063 ......D5
East Cape Girardeau 451 ...D6
East Carondelet 630 ....A3
East Dubuque 1,914 .....C1
East Dundee (Dundee) 2,721 ..E1
East Galesburg 813 .....C3
East Hazelcrest 1,570 ...C6
East Moline 20,147 .....C2
East Peoria 21,378 .....D3
East Saint Louis 40,944 ...A2
Edgewood 502 ....E5
Edinburg 982 ....D4
Edwards 14,579 ....D3
Edwardsville▲ 12,480 ...B2
Effingham▲ 11,851 .....E4
El Paso 2,499 ....D3
Elburn 1,275 ....E2
Eldorado 4,536 ....E6
Elgin 77,010 ....E1
Elizabeth 641 ....C1
Elizabethtown▲ 427 ....E6
Elk Grove Village 33,429 ...B5
Elkhart 475 ....D3
Elkville 958 ....D6
Elmhurst 42,029 ....B5
Elmwood 1,841 ....D3
Elmwood Park 23,206 ....B5
Elsah 851 ....A2
Elwood 951 ....E2
Emden 459 ....D3
Energy 1,106 ....E6
Enfield 683 ....E5
Equality 748 ....E6
Erie 1,572 ....C2
Essex 482 ....E2
Eureka▲ 4,435 ....D3
Evanston 73,233 ....C5
Evansville 844 ....D5
Evergreen Park 20,874 ...B6
Fairbury 3,643 ....E3
Fairfield▲ 5,439 ......E5
Fairmont 2,894 ....A2
Fairmont City 2,140 ....B2
Fairmount 678 ....F3
Fairview 510 ....C3
Fairview Heights 14,351 ...B3
Farina 575 ....E5
Farmer City 2,114 ......E3
Farmersville 698 ......D4
Farmington 2,535 ......C3
Findlay 787 ....E4
Fisher 1,526 ....E3
Fithian 512 ....F3
Flanagan 987 ....E3
Flat Rock 421 ....F5
Flora 5,054 ....E5
Flossmoor 8,651 ....B6
Ford Heights 4,259 ....C6
Forest Homes 1,701 ....B2
Forest Park 14,918 ....B5
Forest View 743 ....B6
Forrest 1,124 ....E3
Forreston 1,361 ....D1
Forsyth 1,275 ....D4
Fox Lake 7,478 ....A4
Fox River Grove 3,551 ...A5
Frankfort 7,180 ....B6
Franklin 634 ....C4
Franklin Grove 968 ....D2
Franklin Park 18,485 ...B5
Freeburg 3,115 ....D5
Freeport▲ 25,840 .....D1
Fulton 3,698 ....C2
Galatia 983 ....E6
Gale 3,647 ....D6
Galena▲ 3,876 ....C1
Galesburg▲ 33,530 .....C3
Galva 2,742 ....D2
Gardner 1,237 ....E2
Geneseo 5,990 ....C2
Geneva▲ 12,617 ....E2
Genoa 3,083 ....E1
Georgetown 3,678 ......F4
German Valley 480 .....D1
Germantown 1,167 ......D5
Gibson City 3,498 .....E3
Gifford 845 ....E3
Gilberts 987 ....E1

Gillespie 3,645 ....D4
Gilman 1,816 ....E3
Glasford 1,115 ....D3
Glen Carbon 7,731 .....B2
Glen Ellyn 24,944 .....A5
Glencoe 8,499 ....B5
Glendale Heights 27,973 ...A5
Glenview 37,093 ....B5
Glenwood 9,289 ....C6
Godfrey 5,436 ....A2
Golconda▲ 823 ....E6
Golden 565 ....B3
Golf 454 ....B5
Goodfield 454 ....D3
Goreville 872 ....E6
Grafton 918 ....C5
Grand Ridge 560 ....E2
Grand Tower 775 ....D6
Grandview 1,647 ....D4
Granite City 32,862 ....A2
Grant Park 1,024 ......F2
Granville 1,407 ....D2
Grayslake 7,388 ....B4
Grayville 2,043 ....E5
Green Oaks 2,101 ......B4
Green Rock 2,615 ......C2
Green Valley 745 ......D3
Greenfield 1,162 ......C4
Greenup 1,616 ....E4
Greenview 848 ....D3
Greenville▲ 4,806 .....D5
Gridley 1,304 ....E3
Griggsville 1,218 .....C4
Gurnee 13,701 ....B4
Hamel 530 ....B2
Hamilton 3,281 ....B3
Hammond 527 ....E4
Hampshire 1,843 ....E1
Hampton 1,601 ....C2
Hanna City 1,205 ......D3
Hanover 908 ....C1
Hanover Park 32,895 ....A5
Hardin▲ 1,071 ....C4
Harrisburg▲ 9,289 ....E6
Harristown 1,319 ......D4
Hartford 1,676 ....A2
Harvard 5,975 ....E1
Harvey 29,771 ....B6
Harwood Heights 7,680 ...B5
Havana▲ 3,610 ....D3
Hawthorn Woods 4,423 ...B5
Hazel Crest 13,334 .....B6
Hebron 809 ....E1
Hecker 534 ....D5
Hegeler 1,853 ....F3
Hennepin▲ 669 ....D2
Henry 2,591 ....D2
Herrick 466 ....E4
Herrin 10,857 ....E6
Herscher 1,278 ....E2
Heyworth 1,627 ....E3
Hickory Hills 13,021 ...B6
Highland 7,525 ....D5
Highland Park 30,575 ...B5
Highwood 5,331 ....B5
Hillcrest 828 ....D2
Hillsboro▲ 4,400 .....D4
Hillsdale 489 ....C2
Hillside 7,672 ....B5
Hinckley 1,682 ....E2
Hinsdale 16,029 ....B6
Hodgkins 1,963 ....B6
Hoffman 492 ....D5
Hoffman Estates 46,561 ...A5
Holiday Hills 807 .....A4
Homer 1,264 ....F3
Hometown 4,769 ....B6
Homewood 19,278 ....B6
Hoopeston 5,871 ....F3
Hopedale 805 ....D3
Hopkins Park 601 ......F2
Hoyleton 508 ....D5
Hudson 1,006 ....E3
Hull 514 ....B4
Humboldt 470 ....E4
Hunt 2,453 ....E4
Huntley 1,646 ....E1
Hurst 842 ....D6
Hutsonville 622 ....F4
Illiopolis 934 ....D4
Ina 489 ....E5
Industry 571 ....C3
Inverness 6,503 ....A5
Ipava 483 ....C3
Irving 516 ....D4
Irvington 827 ....D5
Island Lake 4,449 .....A4
Itasca 6,947 ....B5
Jacksonville▲ 19,324 ..C4
Jerome 1,206 ....D4
Jerseyville▲ 7,382 ....C4
Johnston City 3,706 ....E6
Joliet▲ 76,836 ....F2
Jonesboro▲ 1,728 .....D6
Joppa 492 ....E6
Joy 452 ....C2
Junction City 539 .....D5
Justice 11,137 ....B6

(continued on following page)

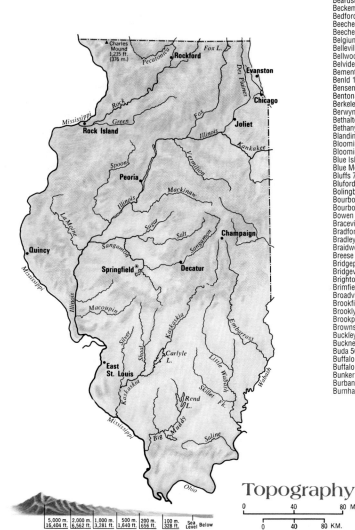

▲ Charles Mound 1,235 ft. (376 m.)

Rockford
Evanston
Chicago
Joliet
Rock Island
Peoria
Champaign
Quincy
Springfield
Decatur
East St. Louis

Rivers/features: Pecatonica, Fox L., Des Plaines, Rock, Green, Mississippi, Fox, Illinois, Kankakee, Spoon, Mackinaw, Vermilion, La Moine, Sangamon, Sugar, Salt, Sangamon, Illinois, Macoupin, Silver, Shoal, Kaskaskia, Carlyle L., Little Wabash, Embarrass, Skillet Fk., Wabash, Rend L., Big Muddy, Saline, Mississippi, Ohio

Topography

0   40   80 MI.
0   40   80 KM.

| 5,000 m. 16,404 ft. | 2,000 m. 6,562 ft. | 1,000 m. 3,281 ft. | 500 m. 1,640 ft. | 200 m. 656 ft. | 100 m. 328 ft. | Sea Level | Below |

Agriculture, Industry and Resources

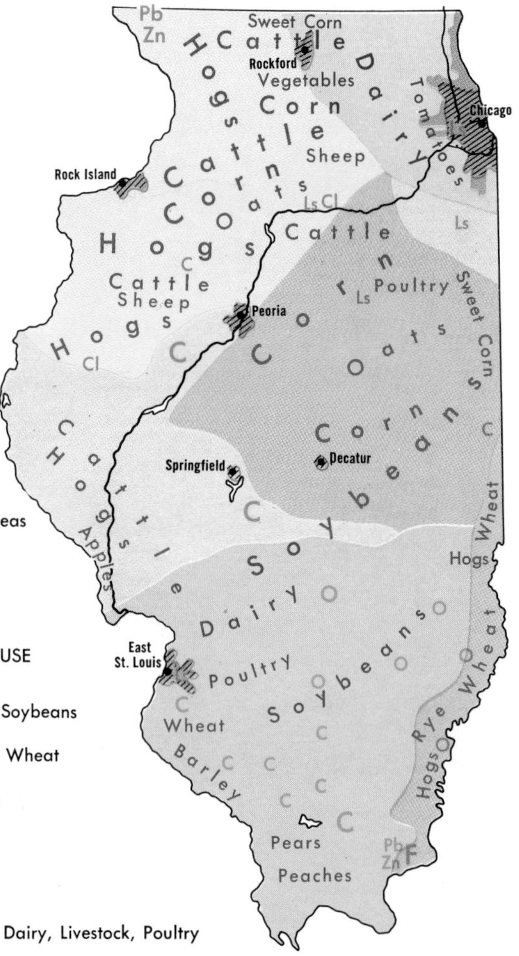

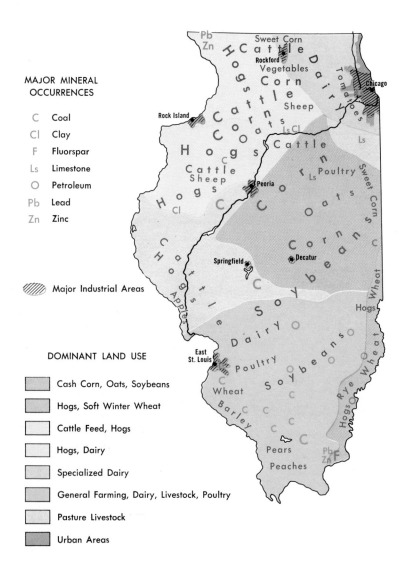

MAJOR MINERAL OCCURRENCES

C Coal
Cl Clay
F Fluorspar
Ls Limestone
O Petroleum
Pb Lead
Zn Zinc

Major Industrial Areas

DOMINANT LAND USE

Cash Corn, Oats, Soybeans
Hogs, Soft Winter Wheat
Cattle Feed, Hogs
Hogs, Dairy
Specialized Dairy
General Farming, Dairy, Livestock, Poultry
Pasture Livestock
Urban Areas

Kane 456 ..... C4
Kankakee▲ 27,575 ..... F2
Kansas 887 ..... F4
Karnak 581 ..... E6
Kaskaskia 32 ..... C6
Keithsburg 747 ..... B2
Kenilworth 2,402 ..... B5
Kewanee 12,969 ..... C2
Keyesport 440 ..... D5
Kildeer 2,257 ..... A5
Kincaid 1,353 ..... D4
Kingston 562 ..... E1
Kinmundy 879 ..... E5
Kirkland 1,011 ..... E1
Kirkwood 884 ..... C3
Knoxville 3,243 ..... C3
La Grange 15,362 ..... B6
La Grange Park 12,861 ..... B5
La Harpe 1,407 ..... C3
La Moille 654 ..... D2
La Salle 9,717 ..... E2
Lacon▲ 1,986 ..... D2
Ladd 1,283 ..... D2
Lake Barrington 3,855 ..... A5
Lake Bluff 5,513 ..... B4
Lake Catherine 1,515 ..... E1
Lake Forest 17,836 ..... B4
Lake Villa 2,857 ..... A4
Lake Zurich 14,947 ..... A5
Lake in the Hills 5,866 ..... E1
Lakemoor 1,322 ..... A4
Lakewood 1,609 ..... E4
Lanark 1,382 ..... D1
Lansing 28,086 ..... C6
Latham 482 ..... D4
Lawrenceville▲ 4,897 ..... F5
Le Roy 2,777 ..... E3
Leaf River 546 ..... D1
Lebanon 3,688 ..... D5
Leland 862 ..... E2
Lemont 7,348 ..... B6
Lena 2,605 ..... D1
Lenzburg 510 ..... D5
Lewistown▲ 2,572 ..... C3
Lexington 1,809 ..... E3
Liberty 541 ..... B4
Libertyville 19,174 ..... B4
Lincoln▲ 15,418 ..... D3
Lincolnshire 4,931 ..... B5
Lincolnwood 11,365 ..... B5
Lindenhurst 8,038 ..... B4
Lisle 19,512 ..... A6
Litchfield 6,883 ..... D4
Livingston 928 ..... D5
Loami 802 ..... D4
Lockport 9,401 ..... B6
Lomax 473 ..... B3
Lombard 39,408 ..... B5
London Mills 485 ..... C3
Long Grove 4,740 ..... B5
Lostant 510 ..... D2
Louisville▲ 1,098 ..... E5
Lovejoy 1,233 ..... A2
Loves Park 15,462 ..... E1
Lovington 1,143 ..... E4
Lyndon 615 ..... D2
Lynwood 6,535 ..... C6
Lyons 9,828 ..... B6
Machesney Park 19,033 ..... D1
Mackinaw 1,331 ..... D3
Macomb▲ 19,952 ..... C3
Macon 1,282 ..... E4
Madison 4,629 ..... A2
Mahomet 3,103 ..... E3
Malta 865 ..... E2
Manhattan 2,059 ..... F2
Manito 1,711 ..... D3
Mansfield 929 ..... E3
Manteno 3,488 ..... F2
Maple Park 641 ..... E2
Marengo 4,768 ..... E1
Marine 972 ..... D5
Marion▲ 14,545 ..... E6
Marissa 2,375 ..... D5
Markham 13,136 ..... B6
Maroa 1,602 ..... E3
Marquette Heights 3,077 ..... D3
Marseilles 4,811 ..... E2
Marshall▲ 3,555 ..... F4
Martinsville 1,161 ..... F4
Maryville 2,576 ..... B2
Mascoutah 5,511 ..... D5
Mason City 2,323 ..... D3
Matherville 708 ..... C2
Matteson 11,378 ..... B6
Mattoon 18,441 ..... E4
Maywood 27,139 ..... B5
Mazon 764 ..... E2
McCullom Lake 1,033 ..... E1
McHenry 16,177 ..... E1
McLean 797 ..... D3
McLeansboro▲ 2,677 ..... E5
Meadowbrook 1,082 ..... B2
Mechanicsburg 538 ..... D4
Medora 420 ..... C4
Melrose Park 20,859 ..... B5
Melvin 466 ..... E3
Mendon 854 ..... B3
Mendota 7,018 ..... D2
Meredosia 1,134 ..... C4
Merrionette Park 2,065 ..... B6
Metamora 2,520 ..... D3
Metropolis▲ 6,734 ..... E6
Middletown 436 ..... D3
Midlothian 14,372 ..... B6
Milan 5,831 ..... C2
Milford 1,512 ..... F3
Milledgeville 1,076 ..... D1
Millington 470 ..... E2
Millstadt 2,566 ..... B3
Minier 1,155 ..... D3
Minonk 1,982 ..... D3
Minooka 2,561 ..... E2
Mokena 6,128 ..... B6
Moline 43,202 ..... C2
Momence 2,968 ..... F2
Monee 1,044 ..... F2
Monmouth▲ 9,489 ..... C3
Montgomery 4,267 ..... E2
Monticello▲ 4,549 ..... E3
Morris▲ 10,270 ..... E2
Morrison▲ 4,363 ..... C2
Morrisonville 1,113 ..... D4
Morton 13,799 ..... D3
Morton Grove 22,408 ..... B5
Mound City▲ 765 ..... D6
Mounds 1,407 ..... D6
Mount Auburn 544 ..... D4
Mount Carmel▲ 8,287 ..... F5
Mount Carroll▲ 1,726 ..... D1
Mount Morris 2,919 ..... D1
Mount Olive 2,126 ..... D4
Mount Prospect 53,170 ..... B5
Mount Pulaski 1,610 ..... D3
Mount Sterling▲ 1,922 ..... C4
Mount Vernon▲ 16,988 ..... E5
Mount Zion 4,522 ..... E4
Moweaqua 1,785 ..... E4
Mulberry Grove 660 ..... D5
Mundelein 21,215 ..... A4
Murphysboro▲ 9,176 ..... D6
Murrayville 673 ..... C4
Naperville 85,351 ..... A6
Naplate 609 ..... E2
Nashville▲ 3,202 ..... D5
Nauvoo 1,108 ..... B3
Neoga 1,678 ..... E4
Neponset 529 ..... D2
New Athens 2,010 ..... D5
New Baden 2,602 ..... D5
New Berlin 797 ..... D4
New Boston 620 ..... B2
New Haven 459 ..... E6
New Lenox 9,627 ..... B6
New Millford 463 ..... D1
New Windsor C2
Newark 840 ..... E2
Newman 960 ..... F4
Newton▲ 3,154 ..... E5
Niantic 647 ..... D4
Niles 28,284 ..... B5
Noble 756 ..... E5
Nokomis 2,534 ..... D4
Normal 40,023 ..... E3
Norridge 14,459 ..... B5
Norris City 1,341 ..... E6
North Aurora 5,940 ..... E2
North Barrington 1,787 ..... A5
North Chicago 34,978 ..... B4
North Pekin 1,556 ..... D3
North Riverside 6,005 ..... B5
North Utica (Utica) 848 ..... E2
Northbrook 32,308 ..... B5
Northfield 4,635 ..... B5
Northlake 12,505 ..... B5
O'Fallon 16,073 ..... B2
Oak Brook 9,178 ..... B6
Oak Forest 26,203 ..... B6
Oak Grove 626 ..... C2
Oak Lawn 56,182 ..... B6
Oak Park 53,648 ..... B5
Oakbrook Terrace 1,907 ..... B5
Oakland 996 ..... F4
Oakwood 1,533 ..... F3
Oakwood Hills 1,498 ..... E1
Oblong 1,616 ..... F5
Odell 1,030 ..... E2
Odin 1,150 ..... D5
Ogden 671 ..... F3
Oglesby 3,619 ..... D2
Ohio 426 ..... D2
Okawville 1,274 ..... D5
Olney▲ 8,664 ..... E5
Olympia Fields 4,248 ..... B6
Onarga 1,281 ..... F3
Oneida 723 ..... C2
Oquawka▲ 1,442 ..... B3
Orangeville 451 ..... D1
Oreana 847 ..... E4
Oregon▲ 3,891 ..... D1
Orient 428 ..... E6
Orion 1,821 ..... C2
Orland Hills 5,510 ..... B6
Orland Park 35,720 ..... B6
Oswego 3,876 ..... E2
Ottawa▲ 17,451 ..... E2
Palatine 39,253 ..... B5
Palestine 1,619 ..... F4
Palmyra 722 ..... C4
Palos Heights 11,478 ..... B6
Palos Hills 17,803 ..... B6
Palos Park 4,199 ..... B6
Pana 5,796 ..... D4
Paris▲ 8,987 ..... F4
Park City 4,677 ..... B4
Park Forest 24,656 ..... B6
Park Forest South 6,245 ..... F2
Park Ridge 36,175 ..... B5
Patoka 656 ..... D5
Pawnee 2,384 ..... D4
Pawpaw 791 ..... E2
Paxton▲ 4,289 ..... E3
Payson 1,114 ..... B4
Pearl City 670 ..... D1
Pecatonica 1,760 ..... D1
Pekin▲ 32,254 ..... D3
Peoria Heights 6,930 ..... D3
Peoria▲ 113,504 ..... D3
Peotone 2,947 ..... F2
Percy 925 ..... D5
Perry 491 ..... C4
Peru 9,302 ..... D2
Pesotum 558 ..... E4
Petersburg▲ 2,261 ..... D4
Philo 1,028 ..... E3
Phoenix 2,217 ..... C6
Pierron 554 ..... D5
Pinckneyville▲ 3,372 ..... D5
Piper City 760 ..... E3
Pittsburg 602 ..... E6
Pittsfield▲ 4,231 ..... C4
Plainfield 4,557 ..... A6
Plano 5,104 ..... E2
Pleasant Hill 1,030 ..... C4
Pleasant Plains 701 ..... D4
Plymouth 521 ..... C3
Pocahontas 837 ..... D5
Polo 2,514 ..... D1
Pontiac▲ 11,428 ..... E3
Pontoon Beach 4,013 ..... A2
Poplar Grove 743 ..... E1
Port Byron 1,002 ..... C2
Posen 4,226 ..... B6
Potomac 753 ..... F3
Prairie City 497 ..... C3
Prairie Grove 654 ..... E1
Prairie du Rocher 540 ..... C5
Preston 2,750 ..... D5
Princeton▲ 7,197 ..... D2
Princeville 1,421 ..... D3
Prophetstown 1,749 ..... D2
Prospect Heights 15,239 ..... B5
Quincy▲ 39,681 ..... B4
Ramsey 963 ..... D4
Rankin 619 ..... F3
Ransom 438 ..... E2
Rantoul 17,212 ..... E3
Rapids City 932 ..... C2
Ray 820 ..... C3
Raymond 957 ..... D4
Red Bud 2,918 ..... D5
Reynolds 583 ..... C2
Richmond 1,016 ..... E1
Richton Park 10,523 ..... B6
Ridge Farm 939 ..... F4
Ridgway 1,103 ..... E6
River Forest 11,669 ..... B5
River Grove 9,961 ..... B5
Riverdale 13,671 ..... C6
Riverside 8,774 ..... B6
Riverton 2,638 ..... D4
Riverwoods 2,868 ..... B5
Roanoke 1,910 ..... D3
Robbins 7,498 ..... B6
Robinson▲ 6,740 ..... F5
Rochelle 8,769 ..... D2
Rochester 2,676 ..... D4
Rock Falls 9,654 ..... D2
Rock Island▲ 40,552 ..... C2
Rockdale 1,709 ..... E2
Rockford▲ 139,426 ..... D1
Rockton 2,928 ..... E1
Rolling Meadows 22,591 ..... A5
Rome 1,902 ..... D3
Romeoville 14,074 ..... B6
Roodhouse 2,139 ..... C4
Roscoe 2,079 ..... D1
Roselle 20,819 ..... A5
Rosemont 3,995 ..... B5
Roseville 1,151 ..... C3
Rosewood Heights 4,821 ..... B2
Rosiclare 1,378 ..... E6
Rossville 1,334 ..... F3
Round Lake 3,550 ..... A4
Round Lake Beach 16,434 ..... A4
Round Lake Park 4,045 ..... A4
Roxana 1,562 ..... B2
Royalton 1,191 ..... D6
Rushville▲ 3,229 ..... C3
Sadorus 469 ..... E4
Saint Anne 1,153 ..... F2
Saint Charles 22,501 ..... E2
Saint David 603 ..... C3
Saint Elmo 1,473 ..... E4
Saint Francisville 851 ..... F5
Saint Jacob 752 ..... D5
Saint Joseph 2,052 ..... E3
Saint Libory 525 ..... D5
Salem▲ 7,470 ..... E5
San Jose 519 ..... D3
Sandoval 1,535 ..... D5
Sandwich 5,567 ..... E2
Sauk Village 9,926 ..... C6
Savanna 3,819 ..... C1
Savoy 2,674 ..... E3
Saybrook 767 ..... E3
Schaumburg 68,586 ..... A5
Schiller Park 11,189 ..... B5
Schram City 692 ..... D4
Seneca 1,878 ..... E2
Sesser 2,087 ..... D5
Shabbona 897 ..... E2
Shannon 887 ..... D1
Shawneetown▲ 1,575 ..... E6
Sheffield 951 ..... D2
Shelbyville▲ 4,943 ..... E4
Sheldon 1,109 ..... F3
Sheridan 1,288 ..... E2
Sherman 2,080 ..... D4
Sherrard 697 ..... C2
Shiloh 2,655 ..... B3
Shipman 624 ..... C4
Shorewood 6,264 ..... E2
Sidell 584 ..... F4
Sidney 1,027 ..... E3
Silvis 6,926 ..... C2
Skokie 59,432 ..... B5
Sleepy Hollow 3,241 ..... E1
Smithton 1,587 ..... C5
Somonauk 1,263 ..... E2
Sorento 596 ..... D5
South Barrington 2,937 ..... A5
South Beloit 4,072 ..... E1
South Chicago Heights 3,597 ..... C6
South Elgin 7,474 ..... E2
South Holland 22,105 ..... C6
South Jacksonville 3,187 ..... C4
South Pekin 1,184 ..... D3
South Roxana 1,961 ..... B2
South Wilmington 698 ..... E2
Sparta 4,853 ..... D5
Spaulding 440 ..... D4
Spring Bay 439 ..... D3
Spring Grove 1,066 ..... E1
Spring Valley 5,246 ..... D2
Springfield (cap.)▲ 105,227 ..... D4
Stanford 620 ..... D3
Staunton 4,806 ..... D5
Steeleville 2,059 ..... D6
Steger 8,584 ..... F2
Sterling 15,132 ..... D2
Stewardson 660 ..... E4
Stickney 5,678 ..... B6
Stillman Valley 848 ..... D1
Stockton 1,871 ..... C1
Stone Park 4,383 ..... B5
Stonington 1,006 ..... D4
Strasburg 473 ..... E4
Streamwood 30,987 ..... A5
Streator 14,121 ..... E2
Stronghurst 799 ..... C3
Sugar Grove 2,005 ..... E2
Sullivan▲ 4,354 ..... E4
Summerfield 509 ..... D5
Summit-Argo 10,110 ..... B6
Sumner 1,083 ..... F5
Sunnyside 1,529 ..... A4
Swansea 8,201 ..... B3
Sycamore▲ 9,708 ..... E2
Tallula 598 ..... D4
Tamaroa 780 ..... D5
Tamms 748 ..... D6
Tampico 833 ..... D2
Taylor Springs 670 ..... D4
Taylorville 11,133 ..... D4
Teutopolis 1,417 ..... E4
Thayer 730 ..... D4
Thebes 461 ..... D6
Third Lake 1,248 ..... B4
Thomasboro 1,250 ..... E3
Thompsonville 602 ..... E6
Thomson 538 ..... C2
Thornton 2,778 ..... C6
Tilden 919 ..... D5
Tilton 2,729 ..... F3
Tinley Park 37,121 ..... B6
Tiskilwa 830 ..... D2
Toledo▲ 1,199 ..... E4
Tolono 2,605 ..... E3
Toluca 1,315 ..... D2
Tonica 715 ..... E2
Toulon▲ 1,328 ..... D2
Tovey 533 ..... D4
Towanda 856 ..... E3
Tower Hill 601 ..... E4
Tower Lakes 1,333 ..... A4
Tremont 2,088 ..... D3
Trenton 2,481 ..... D5
Troy 6,046 ..... B2
Tuscola▲ 4,155 ..... E4
Union 542 ..... E1
Urbana▲ 36,344 ..... E3
Ursa 506 ..... B3
Utica E2
Valier 708 ..... D5
Valmeyer 897 ..... C5
Vandalia▲ 6,114 ..... D5
Venice 3,571 ..... A2
Vermont 806 ..... C3
Vernon Hills 15,319 ..... B4
Versailles 480 ..... C4
Vienna▲ 1,446 ..... E6
Villa Grove 2,734 ..... E4
Villa Park 22,253 ..... B5
Viola 964 ..... C2
Virden 3,635 ..... D4
Virginia▲ 1,767 ..... C4
Wadsworth 1,826 ..... B4
Walnut 1,463 ..... D2
Wamac 1,501 ..... D5
Wapella 608 ..... E3
Warren 1,550 ..... C1
Warrensburg 1,274 ..... D4
Warrenville 11,333 ..... A6
Warsaw 1,882 ..... B3
Washburn 1,075 ..... D3
Washington 10,099 ..... D3
Washington Park 7,431 ..... B2
Wataga 879 ..... C2
Waterloo▲ 5,072 ..... C5
Waterman 1,074 ..... E2
Watseka▲ 5,424 ..... F3
Watson 646 ..... E4
Wauconda 6,294 ..... A4
Waukegan▲ 69,392 ..... B4
Waverly 1,402 ..... D4
Wayne 1,541 ..... E2
Wayne City 1,099 ..... E5
Waynesville 440 ..... D3
Wenona 950 ..... E2
West Chicago 14,796 ..... A5
West City 747 ..... E5
West Dundee (Dundee) 3,728 ..... E1
West Frankfort 8,526 ..... E6
West Salem 1,042 ..... F5
Westchester 17,301 ..... B5
Western Springs 11,984 ..... B6
Westfield 676 ..... F4
Westmont 21,228 ..... B6
Westville 3,387 ..... F3
Wheaton▲ 51,464 ..... A5
Wheeling 29,911 ..... B5
White Hall 2,814 ..... C4
Williamsfield 571 ..... C3
Williamsville 1,140 ..... D4
Willisville 577 ..... D6
Willow Springs 4,509 ..... B6
Willowbrook 1,808 ..... B6
Wilmette 26,690 ..... B5
Wilsonville 609 ..... D4
Winchester▲ 1,769 ..... C4
Windsor (New Windsor) 774 ..... C2
Windsor 1,228 ..... E4
Winfield 7,096 ..... A5
Winnebago 1,840 ..... D1
Winnetka 12,174 ..... B5
Winthrop Harbor 6,240 ..... F1
Witt 866 ..... D4
Wonder Lake 1,024 ..... E1
Wood Dale 12,425 ..... B5
Wood River 11,490 ..... B2
Woodhull 808 ..... C2
Woodlawn 582 ..... D5
Woodridge 26,256 ..... B6
Woodson 472 ..... C4
Woodstock▲ 14,353 ..... E1
Worden 896 ..... B2
Worth 11,208 ..... B6
Wyanet 1,017 ..... D2
Wyoming 1,462 ..... D2
Yates City 760 ..... C3
Yorkville▲ 3,925 ..... E2
Zeigler 1,746 ..... D6
Zion 19,775 ..... F1

OTHER FEATURES

Apple (creek) C4
Apple (riv.) C1
Argonne Nat'l Laboratory B6
Big Bureau (riv.) D2
Big Muddy (riv.) D6
Bonpas (creek) F5
Cache (riv.) D6
Calumet (lake) C6
Carlyle (lake) D5
Chanute A.F.B. E3
Charles Mound (hill) C1
Chicago Portage Nat'l Hist. Site B6
Crab Orchard (lake) E6
Des Plaines (riv.) A6
Du Page (riv.) E2
Edwards (riv.) C2
Embarras (riv.) E4
Fort Sheridan B5
Fox (lake) A4
Fox (riv.) E2
Fox (riv.) E5
Glenview Naval Air Sta. B5
Granite City Army Depot A2
Great Lakes Naval Trng. Ctr. B4
Green (riv.) D2
Henderson (riv.) C2
Illinois (riv.) C4
Illinois-Mississippi (canal) C2
Iroquois (riv.) F3
Kankakee (riv.) F2
Kaskaskia (riv.) E4
La Moine (riv.) C3
Little Wabash (riv.) E5
Mackinaw (riv.) E3
Macoupin (riv.) C4
Michigan (lake) F1
Mississippi (riv.) C5
O'Hare International Airport B5
Ohio (riv.) E6
Plum (riv.) C1
Pope (creek) C2
Rend (lake) D5
Rock (creek) D2
Rock (riv.) C2
Saline (riv.) E6
Salt (creek) D3
Sangamon (riv.) C3
Savanna Army Depot C1
Scott A.F.B. 7,245 ..... B3
Shelbyville (lake) E4
Shoal (creek) D5
Spoon (riv.) C3
Wabash (riv.) F5

▲County seat

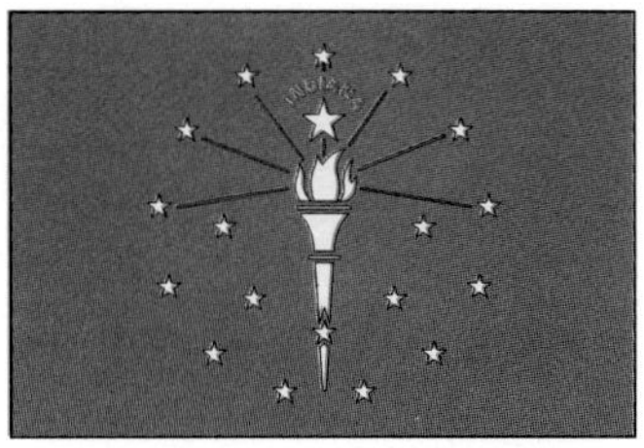

AREA 36,185 sq. mi. (93,719 sq. km.)
POPULATION 5,564,228
CAPITAL Indianapolis
LARGEST CITY Indianapolis
HIGHEST POINT 1,257 ft. (383 m.) (Wayne County)
SETTLED IN 1730
ADMITTED TO UNION December 11, 1816
POPULAR NAME Hoosier State
STATE FLOWER Peony
STATE BIRD Cardinal

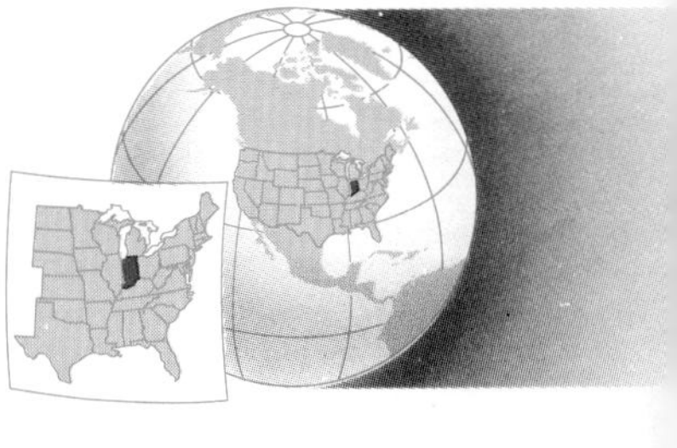

COUNTIES

Adams 31,095 H3
Allen 300,836 G2
Bartholomew 63,657 F6
Benton 9,441 C3
Blackford 14,067 G4
Boone 38,147 E4
Brown 14,080 E6
Carroll 18,809 D3
Cass 38,413 E3
Clark 87,777 F8
Clay 24,705 C6
Clinton 30,974 E4
Crawford 9,914 E8
Daviess 27,533 C7
De Kalb 35,324 H2
Dearborn 38,835 H6
Decatur 23,645 G6
Delaware 119,659 G4
Dubois 36,616 D8
Elkhart 156,198 F1
Fayette 26,015 G5
Floyd 64,404 F8
Fountain 17,808 C4
Franklin 19,580 G6
Fulton 18,840 E2
Gibson 31,913 B8
Grant 74,169 F3
Greene 30,410 D6
Hamilton 108,936 E4
Hancock 45,527 F5
Harrison 29,890 E8
Hendricks 75,717 D5
Henry 48,139 G5
Howard 80,827 E4
Huntington 35,427 G3
Jackson 37,730 E7
Jasper 24,960 C2
Jay 21,512 G4
Jefferson 29,797 G7
Jennings 23,661 F7
Johnson 88,109 E6
Knox 39,884 C7
Kosciusko 65,294 F2
LaPorte 108,632 D1
Lagrange 29,477 G1
Lake 475,594 C2
Lawrence 42,836 E7
Madison 130,669 F4
Marion 797,159 E5
Marshall 42,182 E2
Martin 10,369 D7
Miami 36,897 E3
Monroe 108,978 D6
Montgomery 34,436 D4
Morgan 55,920 E6
Newton 13,551 C3
Noble 37,877 G2
Ohio 5,315 H7
Orange 18,409 E7
Owen 17,281 D6
Parke 15,410 C5
Perry 19,107 D8
Pike 12,509 C8
Porter 128,932 C2
Posey 25,968 B8
Pulaski 12,643 D2
Putnam 30,315 D5
Randolph 27,148 G4
Ripley 24,616 G6
Rush 18,129 G5
Saint Joseph 241,617 E1
Scott 20,991 F7
Shelby 40,307 F5
Spencer 19,490 C9
Starke 22,747 D2
Steuben 27,446 G1
Sullivan 18,993 C6
Switzerland 7,738 G7
Tippecanoe 130,598 D4
Tipton 16,119 E4
Union 6,976 H5
Vanderburgh 165,058 B8
Vermillion 16,773 C5
Vigo 106,107 C6
Wabash 35,069 F3
Warren 8,176 C4
Warrick 44,920 C8
Washington 23,717 E7
Wayne 71,951 G5
Wells 25,948 G3
White 23,265 D3
Whitley 27,651 F2

CITIES and TOWNS

Abington 200 H5
Adams 250 F6
Adamsboro 325 E3
Advance 520 D5
Akron 1,001 E2
Alamo 112 C5
Albany 2,357 G4
Albion▲ 1,823 G2
Alexandria 5,709 F4
Altona 156 G2
Ambia 249 C4
Amboy 370 F3
Americus 150 D3
Amity 200 E6
Amo 380 D5
Anderson▲ 59,459 F4
Andersonville 225 G5
Andrews 1,118 F3
Angola▲ 5,824 G1
Anthony 130 G4
Arcadia 1,468 E4
Arcola 300 G2
Ardmore 800 E1
Argos 1,642 E2
Arlington 500 F5
Ashley 767 G1
Athens 145 E2
Atlanta 703 E4
Attica 3,457 C4
Atwood 300 F2
Auburn▲ 9,379 G2
Aurora 3,825 H6
Austin 4,310 F7
Avilla 1,366 G2
Avoca 400 D7
Azalia 194 F6
Bainbridge 682 D5
Bargersville 1,681 E5
Batesville 4,720 G6
Battle Ground 806 D3
Bear Branch 150 G7
Bedford▲ 13,817 E7
Beech Grove 13,383 E5
Bellmore 160 C5
Bennetts Switch 138 E3
Benton 220 F2
Berne 3,559 H3
Bethany 90 E5
Beverly Shores 622 D1
Bicknell 3,357 C7
Bippus 300 F3
Birdseye 472 D8
Black Oak C1
Blanford 500 B5
Blocher 400 F7
Bloomfield▲ 2,592 D6
Blooming Grove 300 G5
Bloomingdale 341 C5
Bloomington▲ 60,633 D6
Blountsville 155 G4
Blue Ridge 219 F5
Bluffton▲ 9,020 G3
Boggstown 200 F5
Boone Grove 220 C2
Boonville▲ 6,724 C8
Borden F8
Boston 159 H5
Boswell 767 C3
Bourbon 1,672 E2
Bowling Green 200 D6
Bradford 350 E8
Brazil▲ 7,640 C5
Bremen 4,725 E2
Bridgeton 250 C5
Bright 3,945 H6
Brimfield 292 G2
Bringhurst 275 E3
Bristol 1,133 F1
Brook 899 C3
Brooklyn 1,162 E5
Brooksburg 79 G7
Brookston 1,804 D3
Brookville▲ 2,529 G6
Brownsburg 7,628 E5
Brownstown▲ 2,872 F7
Brownsville 250 H5
Bruceville 471 C7
Bryant 273 G3
Buck Creek 225 D4
Buckskin 200 C8
Buffalo 500 D3
Bunker Hill 1,010 E3
Burket 200 F2
Burlington 568 E4
Burnettsville 401 D3
Burney 300 F6
Burns City 140 D7
Burns Harbor 788 C1
Burrows 250 E3
Butler 2,601 H2
Butlerville 300 F6
Byron 200 C5
Cadiz 202 G5
Cambridge City 2,091 G5
Camden 607 D3
Cammack 250 G4
Campbellsburg 606 E7
Cannelburg 97 C7
Cannelton▲ 1,786 D9
Carbon 350 C5
Carefree 26 E8
Carlisle 613 C7
Carmel 25,380 E5
Cartersburg 300 E5
Carthage 887 F5
Cassville 159 E3
Cates 125 C4
Cayuga 1,083 C5
Cedar Grove 246 H6
Cedar Lake 8,885 C2
Celestine 150 D8
Centenary 150 B5
Center 278 E4
Centerpoint 242 C6
Centerton 250 E5
Centerville 2,398 H5
Chalmers 525 D3
Chandler 3,099 C8
Chapel Hill 175 E6
Charlestown 5,889 F8
Charlottesville 300 F5
Chelsea 200 F7
Chester 2,730 H5
Chesterfield 2,701 F4
Chesterton 9,124 D1
Chili 280 F3
Chrisney 511 C8
Churubusco 1,781 G2
Cicero 3,268 E4
Clarks Hill 716 D4
Clarksburg 300 G6
Clarksville 19,833 F8
Clay City 929 C6
Claypool 411 F2
Clayton 610 D5
Clear Creek 200 E6
Clear Lake 272 H1
Clifford 308 F6
Clinton 5,040 C5
Cloverdale 1,681 D5
Cloverland 175 C5
Clymers 150 E3
Coal City 225 D6
Coalmont 450 C6
Coatesville 469 D5
Coesse 150 G2
Colburn 300 D3
Colfax 727 D4
Collegeville 993 C3
Columbia City▲ 5,706 G2
Columbus▲ 31,802 E6
Commiskey 150 F7
Connersville▲ 15,550 G5
Converse 1,144 F3
Correct 131 G7
Cortland 175 F7
Corunna 241 G2
Cory 2,661 C6
Corydon▲ 2,724 E8
Covington▲ 2,747 C4
Cowan 428 G4
Craigville 130 G3
Crandall 147 E8
Crane 216 D7
Crawfordsville▲ 13,584 D4
Cromwell 520 F2
Cross Plains 254 G7
Crothersville 1,687 F7
Crown Point▲ 17,728 C2
Crumstown 175 E1
Culver 1,404 E2
Cumberland 1,624 F5
Cutler 140 D4
Cynthiana 669 B8
Dale 1,553 D8
Daleville 1,681 F4
Dana 612 C5
Danville▲ 4,345 D5
Darlington 740 D4
Darmstadt 1,346 B8
Dayton 996 D4
Decatur▲ 8,644 H3
Decker 281 B7
Deer Creek 250 E3
Deerfield 300 H4
Delaware 135 G6
Delong 156 E2
Delphi▲ 2,531 D3
Demotte 2,482 C2
Denham 140 D2
Denver 504 E3
Depauw 150 E8
Deputy 200 F7
Desoto 385 G4
Dillsboro 1,200 G6
Donaldson 320 E2
Doolittle Mills 200 D8
Dublin 805 G5
Dubois 550 D8
Dugger 936 C6
Dundee 160 F4
Dune Acres 263 C1
Dunkirk 2,739 G4
Dunlap 5,705 F1
Dunreith 205 F5
Dupont 391 G7
Dyer 10,923 C1
Eagletown 306 E4
Earl Park 443 C3
East Chicago 33,892 C1
East Enterprise 250 H7
East Germantown (Pershing) 372 G5
Eaton 1,614 G4
Economy 151 G5
Edgewood 2,057 F4
Edinburgh 4,536 E6
Edwardsport 380 C7
Edwardsville 700 F8
Elberfeld 635 C8
Elizabeth 153 F8
Elizabethtown 495 F6
Elkhart 43,627 F1
Ellettsville 3,275 D6
Elnora 679 C7
Elrod 200 G6
Elston 500 D4
Elwood 9,494 F4
Eminence 200 D5
English▲ 614 E8
Etna 578 F2
Etna Green 522 E2
Eugene 400 B5
Evansville▲ 126,272 C9
Everton 500 G5
Fair Oaks 175 C2
Fairbanks 165 B6
Fairland 1,348 F5
Fairmount 3,130 F4
Fairview 1,446 G7
Fairview Park 1,545 C5
Farmersburg 1,159 C6
Farmland 1,412 G4
Fayetteville 180 D7
Ferdinand 2,318 D8
Fillmore 497 D5
Finly 400 F5
Fishers 7,508 E5
Flat Rock 323 F6
Flora 2,179 E3
Florence 155 H7
Floyds Knobs 500 F8
Fontanet 325 C5
Forest 400 E4
Fort Branch 2,447 B8
Fort Wayne▲ 173,072 G2
Fortville 2,690 F5
Fountain 766 C4
Fountain City 839 H5
Fountaintown 225 F5
Fowler▲ 2,333 C3
Fowlerton 306 F4
Francesville 969 D3
Francisco 560 B8
Frankfort▲ 14,754 E4
Franklin▲ 12,907 E6
Frankton 1,736 F4
Fredericksburg 155 E8
Freelandville 600 C7
Freetown 600 E7
Fremont 1,407 H1
French Lick 2,087 D7
Fulton 371 E3
Galena 1,231 F8
Galveston 1,609 E3
Garrett 5,349 G2
Gary 116,646 C1
Gas City 6,296 F4
Gaston 979 G4
Geneva 1,280 H3
Gentryville 277 C8
Georgetown 2,092 F8
Gessie 144 C4
Glenwood 285 G5
Glezen 300 C8
Goldsmith 235 E4
Goodland 1,033 C3
Goshen▲ 23,797 F1
Gosport 764 D6
Grabill 751 H2
Grandview 761 C9
Granger 20,241 E1
Grantsburg 189 E8
Gravelton 150 F2
Greencastle▲ 8,984 D5
Greendale 3,881 H6
Greenfield▲ 11,657 F5

(continued on following page)

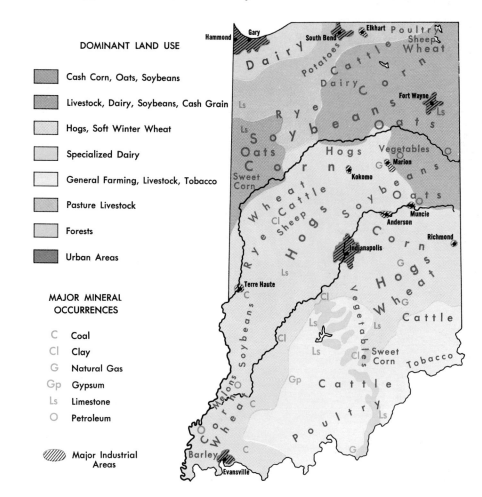

Agriculture, Industry and Resources

DOMINANT LAND USE

- Cash Corn, Oats, Soybeans
- Livestock, Dairy, Soybeans, Cash Grain
- Hogs, Soft Winter Wheat
- Specialized Dairy
- General Farming, Livestock, Tobacco
- Pasture Livestock
- Forests
- Urban Areas

MAJOR MINERAL OCCURRENCES

- C Coal
- Cl Clay
- G Natural Gas
- Gp Gypsum
- Ls Limestone
- O Petroleum

Major Industrial Areas

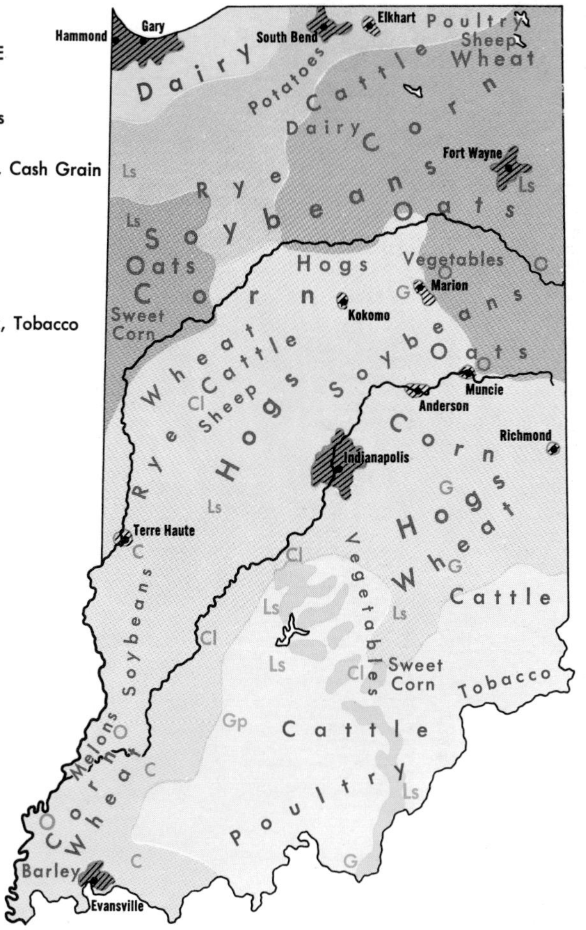

Greens Fork 416 ..... H5
Greensboro 204 ..... G5
Greensburg▲ 9,286 ..... G6
Greentown 2,172 ..... E4
Greenville 508 ..... F8
Greenwood 26,265 ..... E5
Griffin 171 ..... B8
Griffith 17,916 ..... C1
Grovertown 150 ..... D2
Gwynneville 250 ..... F5
Hagerstown 1,835 ..... G5
Hamilton 684 ..... H1
Hamlet 789 ..... D2
Hammond 84,236 ..... B1
Hanna 550 ..... D2
Hanover 3,610 ..... F7
Hardinsburg 322 ..... E8
Harlan 840 ..... H2
Harmony 645 ..... C5
Harrodsburg 400 ..... D6
Hartford City▲ 6,960 ..... G4
Hartsville 391 ..... F6
Hatfield 800 ..... C9
Haubstadt 1,455 ..... B8
Hayden 300 ..... F7
Haysville 600 ..... D8
Hazelwood 650 ..... D5
Hazleton 357 ..... B8
Hebron 3,183 ..... C2
Helmsburg 150 ..... E6
Heltonville 400 ..... E7
Hemlock 300 ..... F4
Henryville 1,132 ..... F7
Hibbard 150 ..... E2
Highland 23,696 ..... B1
Hillisburg 180 ..... E4
Hillsboro 499 ..... C4
Hillsdale 500 ..... C5
Hoagland 600 ..... H3
Hobart 21,822 ..... C1
Hobbs 200 ..... F4
Holland 675 ..... C8
Hollandsburg 150 ..... C5
Holton 451 ..... G6
Homer 235 ..... F5
Hope 2,171 ..... F6
Hortonville 240 ..... E4
Houston 200 ..... E6
Howe 800 ..... G1
Hudson 438 ..... G1
Hudson Lake 1,347 ..... C1
Huntertown 1,330 ..... G2
Huntingburg 5,242 ..... D8
Huntington▲ 16,389 ..... G3
Huntsville 1,200 ..... G4
Huron 250 ..... D7
Hymera 771 ..... C6
Idaville 655 ..... D3
Independence 150 ..... C4
Indian Village 142 ..... E1
Indianapolis (cap.)▲ 741,952 .. E5
Ingalls 889 ..... F5
Inglefield 378 ..... B8
Inwood 150 ..... E2
Ireland 600 ..... C8
Jamestown 764 ..... D5
Jasonville 2,200 ..... C6
Jasper▲ 10,030 ..... D8
Jefferson 21,841 ..... D8
Jeffersonville▲ 21,220 ..... F8
Jolietville 300 ..... E4
Jonesboro 2,073 ..... F4
Jonesville 221 ..... F6
Kempton 362 ..... E4
Kendallville 7,773 ..... G2
Kennard 382 ..... G5
Kent 1,798 ..... F7
Kentland▲ 1,936 ..... C3
Kewanna 542 ..... E2
Keystone 204 ..... G3
Kimmell 250 ..... F2
Kingman 561 ..... C5
Kingsbury 258 ..... D1
Kingsford Heights 1,486 ..... D2
Kirklin 707 ..... E4
Knightstown 2,048 ..... F5
Knightsville 740 ..... C5
Knox▲ 3,705 ..... D2
Kokomo▲ 44,962 ..... E4
Koontz Lake 1,615 ..... D2
Kouts 1,603 ..... C2
La Crosse 677 ..... D2
La Fontaine 909 ..... F3
Ladoga 1,124 ..... D5
Lafayette▲ 43,764 ..... D4
Lagrange▲ 2,382 ..... F1
Lagro 496 ..... F3
Lake Bruce 160 ..... E2
Lake James 400 ..... H1
Lake Station 13,899 ..... C1
Lake Village 900 ..... C2
Laketon 500 ..... F3
Lakeville 655 ..... E1
Lancaster 275 ..... F7
Landess 150 ..... F3
Lanesville 512 ..... E8
Laotto 361 ..... G2
Lapaz 562 ..... E2
Lapel 1,742 ..... F4
LaPorte▲ 21,507 ..... D1
Laconia 75 ..... E8
Larwill 219 ..... F2
Laurel 544 ..... G6
Lawrence 26,763 ..... E5
Lawrenceburg▲ 4,375 ..... H6
Leavenworth 320 ..... E8
Lebanon▲ 12,059 ..... D4
Lee 584 ..... D3
Leesburg 629 ..... F2
Leesville 164 ..... E7
Leiters Ford 280 ..... E2
Leo 500 ..... G2
Leopold 175 ..... D8
Leroy 400 ..... C2
Letts 247 ..... F6
Lewis 437 ..... C6
Lewisville 577 ..... G5
Lexington F7
Liberty Center 275 ..... G3
Liberty Mills 200 ..... F2
Liberty▲ 2,051 ..... H5
Ligonier 3,443 ..... F2
Lincoln City 160 ..... C8
Lincolnville 150 ..... F3
Linden 718 ..... D4
Linn Grove 175 ..... H3
Linton 5,814 ..... C6
Linwood 157 ..... F4
Lisbon 200 ..... G2
Little York 155 ..... F7
Livonia 136 ..... E7
Lizton 410 ..... D5
Logan 16,812 ..... H6
Logansport▲ 17,731 ..... E3
Long Beach 2,044 ..... D1
Loogootee 2,884 ..... D7
Losantville 253 ..... G4
Lowell 6,430 ..... C2
Lucerne 135 ..... E3
Lydick E1
Lyford 400 ..... C5
Lynn 1,183 ..... H4
Lynnville 640 ..... C8
Lyons 753 ..... C7
Mackey 89 ..... C8
Macy 218 ..... E3
Madison▲ 12,006 ..... G7
Majenica 150 ..... G3
Manchester 250 ..... H6
Manilla 350 ..... F5
Mansfield 200 ..... C5
Marco 150 ..... C7
Marengo 856 ..... E8
Mariah Hill 300 ..... D8
Marietta 234 ..... F6
Marion▲ 32,618 ..... F3
Markle 1,208 ..... G3
Markleville 412 ..... F5
Marshall 379 ..... C5
Martinsburg 200 ..... E8
Martinsville▲ 11,677 ..... D6
Matthews 571 ..... F4
Mauckport 95 ..... E8
Maxinkuckee 150 ..... E2
Maxwell 300 ..... F5
Mays 156 ..... G5
McCordsville 684 ..... F5
Mecca 331 ..... C5
Mechanicsburg 150 ..... G5
Medaryville 689 ..... D2
Medora 805 ..... E7
Mellott 222 ..... C4
Memphis 300 ..... F8
Mentone 912 ..... E2
Merom 257 ..... B6
Merrillville 27,257 ..... C2
Metamora 350 ..... G6
Metz 200 ..... H1
Mexico 1,003 ..... E3
Miami 350 ..... E3
Michiana Shores 378 ..... D1
Michigan City 33,822 ..... C1
Michigantown 472 ..... E4
Middlebury 2,004 ..... F1
Middletown 2,333 ..... F4
Midland 250 ..... C6
Milan 1,529 ..... G6
Milford 126 ..... F2
Milford 177 ..... F6
Mill Creek 208 ..... D1
Millersburg 854 ..... F1
Millhousen 151 ..... G6
Milltown 917 ..... E8
Millville 275 ..... G5
Milroy 750 ..... G6
Milton 634 ..... G5
Mishawaka 42,608 ..... E1
Mitchell 4,669 ..... E7
Modoc 218 ..... G4
Mongo 225 ..... G1
Monon 1,585 ..... D3
Monroe 788 ..... H3
Monroe City 538 ..... C7
Monroeville 1,232 ..... H3
Monrovia 800 ..... E5
Monterey 230 ..... D2
Montezuma 1,134 ..... C5
Montgomery 351 ..... C7
Monticello▲ 5,237 ..... D3
Montmorenci 300 ..... D4
Montpelier 1,880 ..... G3
Mooreland 465 ..... G5
Moores Hill 649 ..... G6
Mooresville 5,541 ..... E5
Morgantown 978 ..... E6
Morocco 1,044 ..... C3
Morris 980 ..... G6
Morristown 989 ..... F5
Mount Auburn 138 ..... G5
Mount Ayr 151 ..... C3
Mount Carmel 108 ..... H6
Mount Etna 111 ..... F3
Mount Summit 238 ..... G4
Mount Vernon▲ 7,217 ..... B9
Mulberry 1,262 ..... D4
Muncie▲ 71,035 ..... G4
Munster 19,949 ..... B1
Murray 136 ..... G3
Nabb 150 ..... F7
Napoleon 238 ..... G6
Nappanee 5,510 ..... E2
Nashville▲ 873 ..... E6
Needmore 200 ..... E7
New Albany▲ 36,322 ..... F8
New Amsterdam 30 ..... E8
New Carlisle 1,446 ..... E1
New Castle▲ 17,753 ..... G5
New Chicago 2,066 ..... C1
New Goshen 500 ..... B5
New Harmony 846 ..... B8
New Haven 9,320 ..... H2
New Lebanon 150 ..... C6
New Lisbon 300 ..... G5
New London 200 ..... E4
New Marion 200 ..... G6
New Market 614 ..... D5
New Middletown 82 ..... E8
New Palestine 671 ..... F5
New Paris 1,007 ..... F2
New Pekin 1,095 ..... F7
New Point 296 ..... G6
New Providence (Borden) 270 ..... F8
New Richmond 312 ..... D4
New Ross 331 ..... D5
New Salem 200 ..... G5
New Salisbury 350 ..... E8
New Trenton 200 ..... H6
New Washington 800 ..... F7
New Waverly 162 ..... E3
New Whiteland 4,097 ..... E5
New Winchester 180 ..... D5
Newbern 150 ..... F6
Newberry 207 ..... C7
Newburgh 2,880 ..... C9
Newport▲ 627 ..... C5
Newtonville 136 ..... D8
Newtown 243 ..... C4
Newville 150 ..... H2
Noblesville▲ 17,655 ..... F4
North Grove 91 ..... F3
North Judson 1,582 ..... D2
North Liberty 1,366 ..... E1
North Manchester 6,383 ..... F3
North Salem 499 ..... D5
North Terre Haute 4,331 ..... C5
North Vernon 5,311 ..... F6
North Webster 881 ..... F2
Norway 300 ..... D3
Notre Dame E1
Nulltown 235 ..... G5
Oakford 325 ..... E4
Oakland City 2,810 ..... C8
Oaktown 655 ..... C7
Oakville 220 ..... G4
Odon 1,475 ..... C7
Ogden Dunes 1,499 ..... C1
Oldenburg 715 ..... G6
Onward 63 ..... E3
Oolitic 1,424 ..... E7
Ora 200 ..... D2
Orange 200 ..... G5
Orestes 458 ..... F4
Orland 361 ..... G1
Orleans 2,083 ..... D7
Osceola 1,999 ..... E1
Osgood 1,688 ..... G6
Ossian 2,428 ..... G3
Oswego 150 ..... F2
Otis 250 ..... D1
Otisco 425 ..... F7
Otterbein 1,291 ..... C4
Otwell 600 ..... C8
Owensburg 785 ..... D7
Owensville 1,053 ..... B8
Oxford 1,273 ..... C3
Packertown 150 ..... F2
Palestine 800 ..... F2
Palmyra 621 ..... E8
Paoli▲ 3,542 ..... E7
Paragon 515 ..... D6
Parker City 1,323 ..... G4
Patoka 704 ..... B8
Patricksburg 250 ..... D6
Patriot 190 ..... H7
Paxton 200 ..... C6
Pekin 950 ..... E7
Pendleton 2,309 ..... F5
Pennville 637 ..... G4
Perkinsville 175 ..... F4
Perrysville 443 ..... C4
Pershing 425 ..... E2
Pershing G5
Peru▲ 12,843 ..... E3
Petersburg▲ 2,449 ..... C7
Petroleum 212 ..... G3
Pierceton 1,030 ..... F2
Pilot Knob 150 ..... E8
Pimento 150 ..... C6
Pine Lake 1,676 ..... D1
Pine Village 134 ..... C4
Pittsboro 815 ..... D5
Pittsburg 175 ..... D3
Plainfield 10,433 ..... E5
Plainville 444 ..... C7
Pleasant Lake 800 ..... H1
Pleasant Mills 175 ..... H3
Plymouth▲ 8,303 ..... E2
Poe 162 ..... G3
Poland 230 ..... C6
Poneto 236 ..... G3
Portage 29,060 ..... C1
Porter 3,118 ..... C1
Portland▲ 6,483 ..... H4
Poseyville 1,089 ..... B8
Pottawattomie Park 281 ..... C1
Prairie Creek 275 ..... C6
Prairieton 200 ..... B6
Preble 150 ..... H3
Princes Lakes 1,055 ..... E6
Princeton▲ 8,127 ..... B8
Providence 250 ..... E6
Putnamville 250 ..... D5
Quincy 250 ..... D6
Ragsdale 135 ..... C7
Ramsey 550 ..... E8
Ray 200 ..... H1
Rays Crossing 157 ..... F5
Reddington 400 ..... F6
Redkey 1,383 ..... G4
Reelsville 210 ..... D5
Remington 1,247 ..... C3
Rensselaer▲ 5,045 ..... C3
Reynolds 528 ..... D3
Richland 500 ..... C9
Richmond▲ 38,705 ..... H5
Ridgeville 808 ..... G4
Rigdon 150 ..... F4
Riley 232 ..... C6
Rising Sun▲ 2,311 ..... H7
Roachdale 902 ..... D5
Roann 447 ..... F3
Roanoke 1,018 ..... G3
Rochester▲ 5,969 ..... E2
Rockfield 300 ..... D3
Rockport▲ 2,315 ..... C9
Rockville▲ 2,706 ..... C5
Rolling Prairie 550 ..... D1
Rome 1,138 ..... D9
Rome City 1,319 ..... G1
Romney 250 ..... D4
Rosedale 783 ..... C5
Roseland 706 ..... E1
Roselawn 200 ..... C2
Rossville 1,175 ..... D4
Royal Center 859 ..... E3
Royerton 300 ..... G4
Rushville▲ 5,533 ..... G5
Russellville 336 ..... D5
Russiaville 988 ..... E4
Saint Anthony 470 ..... D8
Saint Bernice 500 ..... C5
Saint Henry 560 ..... D8
Saint Joe 452 ..... H2
Saint John 4,921 ..... C2
Saint Leon 493 ..... H6
Saint Louis Crossing 150 ..... F6
Saint Mary-of-the-Woods 920 ..... B6
Saint Marys E1
Saint Meinrad 910 ..... D8
Saint Paul 1,032 ..... F6
Saint Peter 175 ..... H6
Saint Philip 400 ..... B9
Saint Wendel 250 ..... B8
Salamonia 138 ..... H4
Salem 5,619 ..... H3
Salem▲ 5,290 ..... E7
Saltillo 117 ..... E7
San Pierre 325 ..... D2
Sandborn 455 ..... C7
Santa Claus 927 ..... D8
Saratoga 266 ..... H4
Sardinia 133 ..... F6
Schererville 19,926 ..... C2
Schneider 310 ..... C2
Schnellville 250 ..... D8
Scipio 200 ..... F6
Scott 5,334 ..... F1
Scottsburg▲ 5,068 ..... F7
Sedalia 160 ..... E4
Seelyville 1,090 ..... C6
Sellersburg 5,745 ..... F8
Selma 800 ..... G4
Servia 212 ..... F3
Seymour 15,576 ..... F7
Shadeland 1,674 ..... C4
Shamrock Lakes 207 ..... G4
Sharpsville 769 ..... E4
Shelburn 1,147 ..... C6
Shelby 15,336 ..... C2
Shelbyville▲ 14,989 ..... F6
Shepardsville 325 ..... B5
Sheridan 2,046 ..... E4
Shideler 275 ..... G4
Shipshewana 524 ..... F1
Shirley 817 ..... F5
Shirley City (Woodburn) H2
Shoals▲ 853 ..... D7
Sidney 167 ..... F2
Silver Lake 528 ..... F2
Sims 250 ..... F4
Smith Valley E5
Smithville 500 ..... D6
Solsberry 200 ..... D6
Somerset 350 ..... F3
Somerville 223 ..... C8
South Bend▲ 105,511 ..... E1
South Milford 270 ..... G1
South Whitley 1,482 ..... F2
Southport 1,969 ..... E5
Spartanburg 201 ..... H4
Speed 13,092 ..... F8
Speedway 12,641 ..... E5
Spelterville 200 ..... C5
Spencer▲ 2,609 ..... D6
Spencerville 400 ..... G2
Spiceland 757 ..... F5
Spring Grove 420 ..... H5
Spring Lake 216 ..... F5
Springport 194 ..... G4
Springville 279 ..... D7
Spurgeon 149 ..... C8
Stanford 200 ..... D6
Star City 351 ..... D3
State Line 182 ..... C4
Staunton 592 ..... C6
Stendal 175 ..... C8
Stewartsville 225 ..... B8
Stilesville 298 ..... D5
Stillwell 225 ..... D1
Stinesville 204 ..... D6
Stockwell 310 ..... D4
Straughn 318 ..... G5
Stroh 350 ..... G1
Sullivan▲ 4,663 ..... C6
Sulphur 257 ..... E8
Sulphur Springs 345 ..... G4
Sumava Resorts 300 ..... C2
Summitville 1,010 ..... F4
Sunman 623 ..... G6
Swayzee 1,059 ..... F4
Sweetser 924 ..... F3
Switz City 257 ..... C6
Syracuse 2,729 ..... F2
Talma 170 ..... E2
Taylorsville 1,044 ..... F6
Tell City 8,088 ..... D9
Tennyson 267 ..... C8
Terhune 150 ..... E4
Terre Haute▲ 57,483 ..... C6
Thayer 350 ..... C2
Thorntown 1,506 ..... D4
Tippecanoe 320 ..... E2
Tipton▲ 4,751 ..... E4
Tocsin 160 ..... G3
Topeka 912 ..... F1

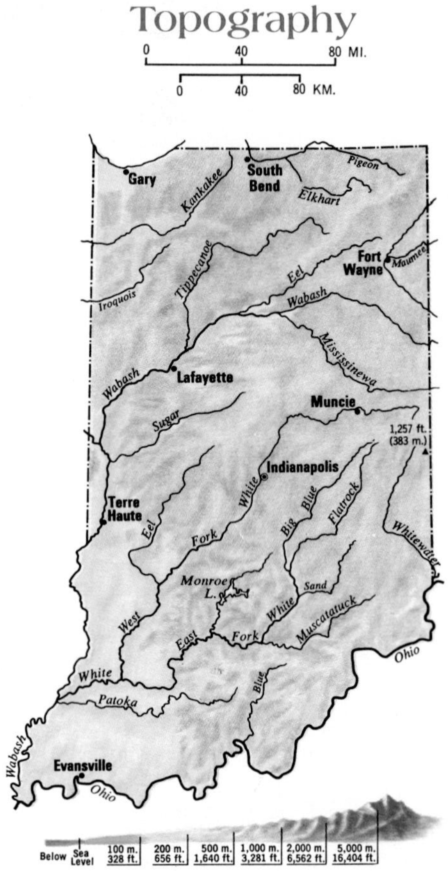

Town of Pines 789 ..... D1
Trafalgar 531 ..... E6
Trail Creek 2,463 ..... D1
Tri Lakes 3,299 ..... G2
Troy 465 ..... D9
Tunnelton 150 ..... E7
Twelve Mile 240 ..... E3
Tyner 245 ..... E2
Underwood 550 ..... F7
Union 3,612 ..... C8
Union City 3,908 ..... H4
Union Mills 650 ..... D2
Uniondale 289 ..... G3
Unionville 225 ..... E6
Universal 392 ..... C5
Upland 3,295 ..... F4
Urbana 400 ..... F3
Utica 411 ..... F8
Valeene 150 ..... E8
Vallonia 550 ..... E7
Valparaiso▲ 24,414 ..... C2
Van Buren 934 ..... F3
Veedersburg 2,192 ..... C4
Velpen 375 ..... C8
Vera Cruz 83 ..... G3
Vernon▲ 370 ..... F7
Versailles▲ 1,791 ..... G6
Vevay▲ 1,393 ..... G7
Vicksburg 175 ..... C6
Vienna 175 ..... F7
Vincennes▲ 19,859 ..... C7
Wabash▲ 12,127 ..... F3
Wadesville 450 ..... B8
Wakarusa 1,667 ..... F1
Waldron 850 ..... F6
Walesboro 214 ..... F6
Walkerton 2,061 ..... E2
Wallace 89 ..... C5
Wallen 945 ..... G2
Walton 1,053 ..... E3
Wanatah 852 ..... D2
Warren 1,185 ..... G3
Warrington 200 ..... F5
Warsaw▲ 10,968 ..... F2
Washington▲ 10,838 ..... C7
Waterloo 2,040 ..... G2
Watson 200 ..... F8
Waveland 474 ..... D5
Wawaka 320 ..... F2
Wawasee 600 ..... F2
Wawpecong 175 ..... F4
Waynetown 911 ..... C4
Webster 350 ..... H5
West Baden Springs 675 ..... D7
West College Corner 686 ..... H5
West Harrison 318 ..... H6
West Lafayette 25,907 ..... D4
West Lebanon 760 ..... C4
West Middleton 327 ..... E4
West Terre Haute 2,495 ..... B6
Westfield 3,304 ..... E4
Westphalia 300 ..... C7
Westpoint 375 ..... C4
Westport 1,478 ..... F6
Westville 5,255 ..... D1
Wheatfield 621 ..... C2
Wheatland 439 ..... C7
Wheeler 540 ..... C1
Wheeling 180 ..... G4
Wheeling 500 ..... C8
Whiteland 2,446 ..... E5
Whitestown 476 ..... E5
Whitewater 111 ..... H5
Whiting 5,155 ..... C1
Wilkinson 446 ..... F5
Williams 425 ..... D7
Williamsport▲ 1,798 ..... C4
Willow Branch 145 ..... F5
Wilmington 600 ..... H6
Winamac▲ 2,262 ..... D2
Winchester▲ 5,095 ..... G4
Windfall 779 ..... F4
Windsor 150 ..... G4
Wingate 275 ..... C4
Winona Lake 4,053 ..... F2
Winslow 875 ..... C8
Wirt 150 ..... G7
Wolcott 886 ..... C3
Wolcottville 879 ..... G1
Wolflake 230 ..... F2
Woodburn 1,321 ..... H2
Woodland 400 ..... E1
Woodlawn Heights 109 ..... F4
Worthington 1,473 ..... C6
Wyandotte 26 ..... E8
Wyatt 250 ..... E1
Yankeetown 250 ..... C9
Yeoman 131 ..... D3
Yoder 250 ..... G3
Yorktown 4,106 ..... G4
Young America 259 ..... E3
Youngstown 350 ..... C6
Zanesville 575 ..... G3
Zenas 225 ..... G6
Zionsville 5,281 ..... E5

OTHER FEATURES

Anderson (riv.) D8
Bass (lake) D2
Beanblossom (creek) D6
Big (creek) B8
Big Blue (riv.) F5
Big Pine (creek) C3
Big Raccoon (creek) C5
Big Walnut (creek) D5
Blue (riv.) E8
Brookville (lake) G6
Buck (creek) E8
Busseron (creek) C7
Camp (creek) E6
Cedar (creek) G2
Clifty (creek) F6
Coal (coal) C4
Crooked (creek) D2
Cypress (pond) B8
Deer (creek) E3
Deer (creek) D5
Eagle (creek) E4
Eel (riv.) C6
Eel (riv.) F3
Elkhart (riv.) F1
Fawn (riv.) G1
Flatrock (creek) F5
Fort Benjamin Harrison E5
Freeman (lake) D3
Geist (res.) F5
George Rogers Clark Nat'l Hist. Park B7
Graham (creek) F7
Grissom A.F.B. 4,271 ..... E3
Huntington (lake) F3
Indian (creek) D6
Indian (creek) E8
Indiana Dunes Nat'l Lakeshore C1
Iroquois (riv.) B3
Jefferson Proving Ground G7
Kankakee (riv.) C2
Lemon (lake) E6
Lincoln Boyhood Nat'l Mem. C8
Little (riv.) G3
Little Elkhart (riv.) F1
Little Pigeon (creek) C9
Little Vermilion (riv.) B5
Lost (riv.) D7
Maria (creek) C7
Maumee (riv.) H2
Maxinkuckee (lake) E2
Michigan (lake) C1
Mill (creek) D5
Mississinewa (lake) F3
Mississinewa (riv.) F3
Monroe (lake) E6
Morse (res.) E4
Muscatatuck (riv.) E7
Ohio (riv.) B9
Patoka (riv.) C8
Pigeon (creek) C8
Pigeon (riv.) F1
Pipe (creek) F4
Prairie (creek) C7
Richland (creek) D6
Saint Joseph (riv.) E1
Saint Joseph (riv.) H2
Saint Marys (lake) H3
Saint Marys (riv.) H3
Salamonie (lake) F3
Salamonie (riv.) G4
Salt (creek) E6
Sand (creek) F6
Shafer (lake) D3
Silver (creek) F8
Sugar (creek) B3
Sugar (creek) C5
Sugar (creek) F5
Tippecanoe (riv.) E2
Vermilion (riv.) B4
Vernon Fork (creek) F7
Wabash (riv.) B7
Wawasee (lake) F2
White (riv.) B8
White, East Fork (riv.) C7
White, West Fork (riv.) C7
Whitewater (riv.) H6
Wildcat (creek) E4

▲County seat

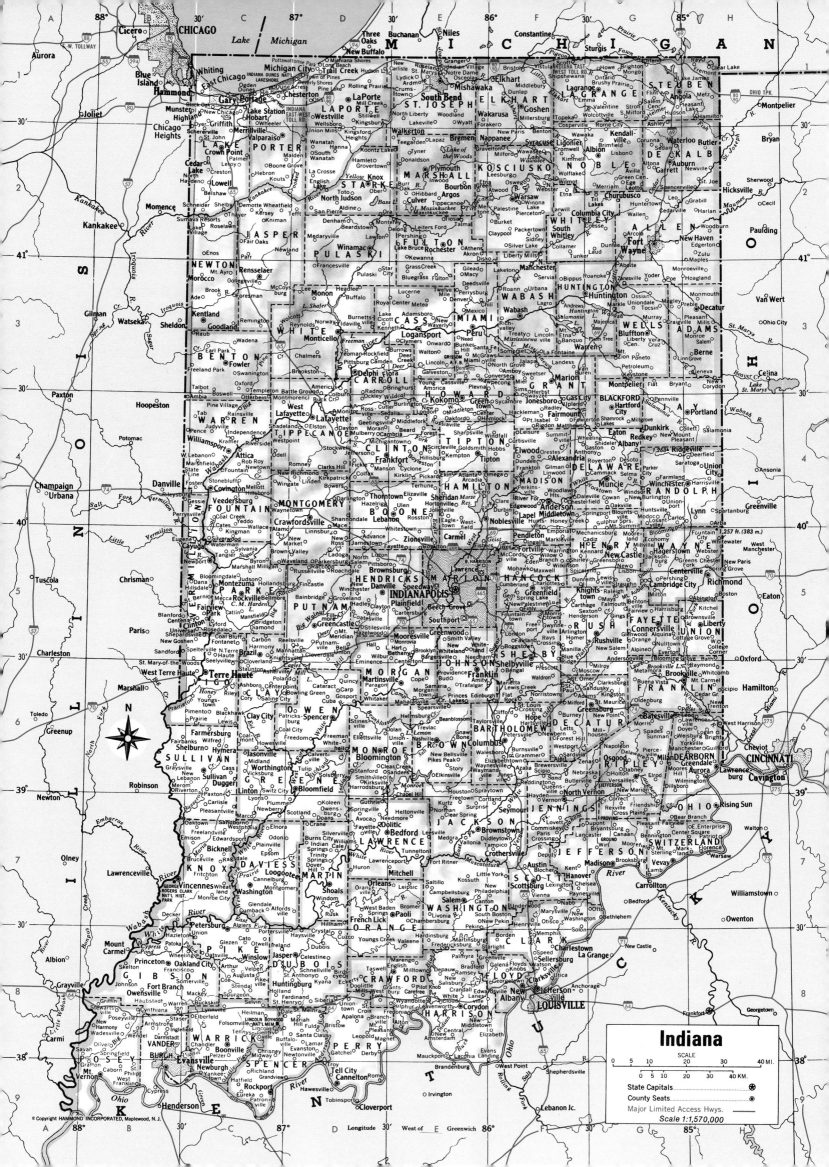

Indiana

SCALE

0 5 10   20   30   40 MI.

0 5 10   20   30   40 KM.

State Capitals .... ⊛

County Seats .... ◉

Major Limited Access Hwys. ———

Scale 1:1,570,000

© Copyright HAMMOND INCORPORATED, Maplewood, N.J.

IOWA

AREA 56,275 sq. mi. (145,752 sq. km.)
POPULATION 2,787,424
CAPITAL Des Moines
LARGEST CITY Des Moines
HIGHEST POINT (Osceola Co.) 1670 ft. (509 m.)
SETTLED IN 1788
ADMITTED TO UNION December 28, 1846
POPULAR NAME Hawkeye State
STATE FLOWER Wild Rose
STATE BIRD Eastern Goldfinch

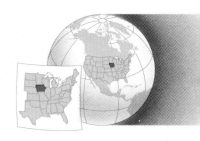

Iowa

SCALE
0 5 10 20 30 40 MI.
0 5 10 20 30 40 KM.

State Capitals .... ⊛
County Seats .... ◉
Major Limited Access Hwys. ____
Scale 1:1,700,000

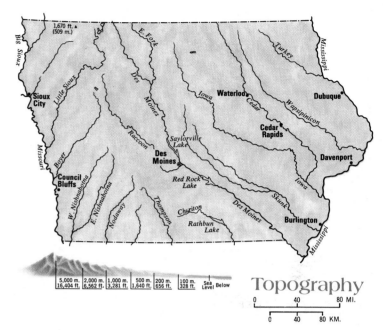

5,000 m. 2,000 m. 1,000 m. 500 m. 200 m. 100 m. Sea Below
16,404 ft. 6,562 ft. 3,281 ft. 1,640 ft. 656 ft. 328 ft. Level

Topography

0 40 80 MI.
0 40 80 KM.

(continued on following page)

© Copyright HAMMOND INCORPORATED, Maplewood, N.J.

Agriculture, Industry and Resources

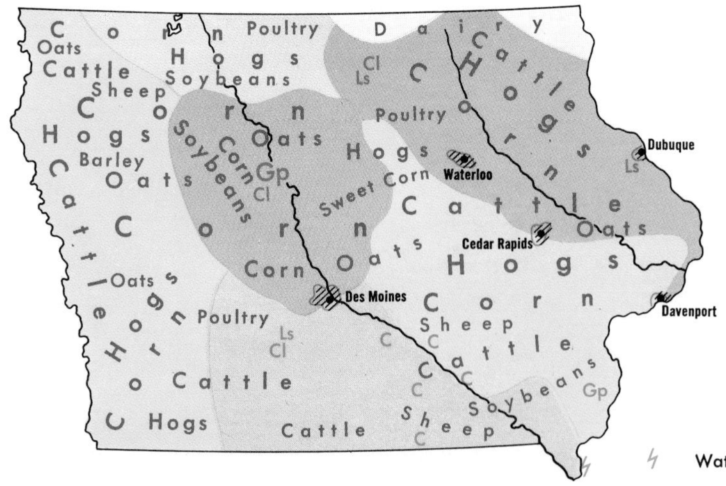

DOMINANT LAND USE

- Cattle Feed, Hogs
- Cash Corn, Oats, Soybeans
- Hogs, Dairy
- Livestock, Cash Grain
- Dairy, Livestock
- Pasture Livestock

MAJOR MINERAL OCCURRENCES

- C Coal
- Cl Clay
- Gp Gypsum
- Ls Limestone

Water Power

Major Industrial Areas

Guthrie Center▲ 1,614 ....D5
Guttenberg 2,257 ....L3
Halbur 215..............................D4
Hamburg 1,248........................B7
Hampton▲ 4,133 ....G3
Hancock 201...........................C6
Hanlontown 193 ....G2
Harcourt 306...........................E4
Harlan▲ 5,148.........................C5
Harper 147 ....J6
Harpers Ferry 284 ....L2
Harris 170...............................C2
Hartford 768...........................G6
Hartley 1,632 ....C2
Harvey 235 ....H6
Hastings 187...........................C6
Havelock 217 ....D3
Haverhill 144 ....H5
Hawarden 2,439......................A2
Hawkeye 460...........................J3
Hazleton 733...........................K3
Hedrick 810.............................J6
Henderson 206 ....B6
Hiawatha 4,986.......................K4
Hills 662 ....K5
Hillsboro 151 ....K7
Hinton 697..............................A3
Holland 215 ....H4
Holstein 1,449 ....B4
Holy Cross 304 ....L3
Hopkinton 695 ....L4
Hornick 222 ....A4
Hospers 643 ....B2
Hubbard 814...........................G4
Hudson 2,037 ....H4
Hull 1,724 ....A2
Humboldt 4,438 ....E3
Humeston 553.........................G7
Huxley 2,047 ....F5
Ida Grove▲ 2,357 ....B4
Independence▲ 5,972 ....K4
Indianola▲ 11,340 ....F6
Inwood 824 ....A2
Ionia 304 ....J2
Iowa City▲ 59,738...................L5
Iowa Falls 5,424 ....G3
Ireton 597 ....A3
Irwin 394 ....C5
Jamaica 232............................E5
Janesville 822 ....J3
Jefferson▲ 4,292.....................E4
Jesup 2,121 ....J4
Jewell 1,106............................F4
Johnston 4,702 ....F5
Joice 245.................................G2
Kalo 1,942...............................E4
Kalona 1,862...........................K6
Kamrar 203 ....F4
Kanawha 763...........................F3
Kellerton 314...........................E7
Kelley 246 ....F5
Kellogg 626 ....H5
Kensett 298 ....G2
Keokuk▲ 12,451......................L8
Keosauqua▲ 1,020 ....J7
Keota 1,000 ....K6
Keswick 284............................J6
Keystone 568 ....J5
Kimballton 289 ....D5
Kingsley 1,129.........................A3
Kirkville 177............................H6
Kiron 301 ....C4
Klemme 587 ....F3
Knoxville▲ 8,232.....................G6
La Motte 219...........................M4
La Porte City 2,128..................J4
Lacona 357..............................G6
Ladora 308..............................J5
Lake City 1,841 ....D4
Lake Mills 2,143......................F2

Lake Park 996.........................C2
Lake View 1,303 ....C4
Lakeside 522...........................C3
Lakota 281 ....E2
Lambs Grove 212 ....G5
Lamoni 2,319..........................E7
Lamont 471 ....K3
Lanesboro 182 ....D4
Lansing 1,007 ....L2
Larchwood 739.......................A2
Larrabee 175...........................B3
Latimer 430 ....G3
Laurel 271 ....H5
Laurens 1,550 ....D3
Lawler 517 ....J2
Lawton 482.............................A4
Le Claire 2,734 ....N5
Le Grand 854..........................H5
Le Mars▲ 8,454 ....A3
Ledyard 164............................E2
Lehigh 536 ....E4
Leighton 142 ....H6
Leland 311 ....F2
Lenox 1,303............................D7
Leon▲ 2,047............................F7
Lester 257...............................A2
Letts 390.................................L6
Lewis 433 ....C6
Libertyville 264 ....K7
Lidderdale 202........................D4
Lime Springs 438....................J2
Lincoln 173.............................H4
Linden 201 ....E5
Lineville 289 ....G7
Linn Grove 194 ....C3
Lisbon 1,452...........................L5
Liscomb 258...........................H4
Little Rock 493........................B2
Little Sioux 205.......................B5
Livermore 436.........................E3
Lockridge 270.........................K7
Logan▲ 1,401 ....B5
Lohrville 453...........................D4
Lone Rock 185.........................E2
Lone Tree 979.........................L6
Long Grove 605 ....M5
Lorimor 377............................E6
Lost Nation 467 ....M5
Lovilia 551 ....H6
Low Moor 280.........................N5
Lowden 726 ....L5
Lu Verne 328 ....E3
Luana 190...............................K2
Lucas 224...............................G6
Luther 154...............................F5
Luxemburg 257.......................L3
Lynnville 393 ....H5
Lytton 320 ....D4
Macedonia 262 ....C6
Madrid 2,395...........................F5
Magnolia 204..........................B5
Malcom 447 ....H5
Mallard 360 ....D3
Malvern 1,210.........................B7
Manchester▲ 5,137..................L3
Manilla 898.............................C5
Manly 1,349............................G2
Manning 1,484........................C5
Manson 1,844 ....D3
Mapleton 1,294........................B4
Maquoketa▲ 6,111..................M4
Marathon 320 ....C3
Marble Rock 361 ....H3
Marcus 1,171...........................B3
Marengo▲ 2,270 ....J5
Marion 20,403 ....K4
Marne 149 ....C6
Marquette 479..........................L2
Marshalltown▲ 25,178 ....G4
Martelle 290 ....L4

Martensdale 491 ....F6
Martinsburg 157 ....J6
Mason City▲ 29,040 ....G2
Masonville 129 ....K4
Massena 372 ....D6
Maurice 243............................A3
Maxwell 788 ....G5
Maynard 513...........................K3
Maysville 170..........................M5
McCallsburg 292 ....G4
McCausland 308 ....M5
McClelland 139.......................B6
McGregor 797.........................L2
McIntire 147............................H2
Mechanicsville 1,012 ....L5
Mediapolis 1,637 ....L6
Melbourne 669 ....G5
Melcher 1,302 ....G6
Melrose 150 ....G7
Melvin 250..............................B2
Menlo 356...............................E5
Meriden 193 ....B3
Merrill 729..............................A3
Meservey 292 ....G3
Middle 386..............................K5
Middletown 487 ....L7
Miles 409................................N4
Milford 2,170 ....C2
Miller 188 ....F2
Millersburg 184.......................J5
Milo 864 ....G6
Milton 506...............................J7
Minburn 346 ....E5
Minden 498.............................C6
Mingo 252 ....G5
Missouri Valley 2,888 ....B5
Mitchell 170............................H2
Mitchellville 1,670 ....G5
Modale 289.............................B5
Mondamin 403 ....B5
Monmouth 169 ....M4
Monona 1,520..........................L2
Monroe 1,739..........................G5
Montezuma▲ 1,651 ....H5
Monticello 3,522 ....L4
Montour 312............................H5
Montrose 957 ....L7
Moorhead 259 ....B5
Moorland 209 ....E4
Moravia 679 ....H7
Morning Sun 841 ....L6
Moulton 613............................H7
Mount Auburn 134...................J4
Mount Ayr▲ 1,796...................E7
Mount Pleasant▲ 8,027...........L7
Mount Union 140.....................L6
Mount Vernon 3,657................K5
Moville 1,306..........................A4
Murray 731 ....F6
Muscatine▲ 22,881 ....L6
Mystic 545..............................H7
Nashua 1,476...........................J3
Neola 894 ....B6
Nevada▲ 6,009 ....G5
New Albin 534.........................L2
New Hampton▲ 3,660 ....J2
New Hartford 683 ....H3
New Liberty 139......................M5
New London 1,922...................L7
New Market 454 ....D7
New Providence 240...............G4
New Sharon 1,136 ....H6
New Vienna 376 ....L3
New Virginia 433 ....F6
Newell 1,089...........................D3
Newhall 854............................K5
Newton▲ 14,789......................H5
Nichols 366.............................L6
Nodaway 153...........................D7
Nora Springs 1,505 ....H2

North Buena Vista 145 ....L3
North English 944 ....J5
North Liberty 2,926.................K5
Northwood▲ 1,940 ....G2
Norwalk 5,726.........................F6
Norway 583 ....K5
Numa 151 ....G7
Oakland 1,496.........................C6
Oakland Acres 152..................H5
Oakville 442 ....L6
Ocheyedan 539 ....B2
Odebolt 1,158 ....C4
Oelwein 6,493.........................K3
Ogden 1,909 ....E4
Okoboji 775 ....C2
Olds 205 ....K6
Olin 663 ....L5
Ollie 207..................................J6
Onawa▲ 2,936 ....A4
Onslow 216.............................M4
Oran 4,940 ....J3
Orange City▲ 4,588................A2
Orient 376 ....E6
Orleans 560 ....C2
Osage▲ 3,439 ....H2
Osceola▲ 4,164 ....F6
Oskaloosa▲ 10,632.................H6
Ossian 810..............................K2
Otho 529.................................E4
Ottumwa▲ 24,488 ....J6
Oxford 663..............................K5
Oxford Junction 581 ....M4
Pacific Junction 548 ....B6
Packwood 208.........................J6
Palmer 230.............................D3
Palo 514 ....K4
Panama 201............................B5
Panora 1,100 ....E5
Parkersburg 1,804..................H3
Parnell 209..............................J5
Paton 255 ....E4
Patterson 128..........................F6
Paullina 1,134.........................B3
Pella 9,270..............................H6
Peosta 128..............................M4
Perry 6,652 ....E5
Persia 312...............................B5
Peterson 390 ....C3
Pierson 341 ....B3
Pilot Mound 199......................F4
Pisgah 268..............................B5
Plainfield 455 ....J3
Pleasant Hill 3,671..................G5
Pleasant Plain 128 ....K6
Pleasantville 1,536..................G6
Plymouth 453 ....G2
Pocahontas▲ 2,085 ....D3
Polk City 1,908........................F5
Pomeroy 762...........................D3
Portsmouth 209.......................C5
Postville 1,472 ....K2
Prairie City 1,360....................G5
Prairieburg 213 ....L4
Prescott 287 ....D6
Preston 1,025..........................N4
Primghar▲ 950 ....B2
Princeton 806 ....N5
Protivin 305.............................J2
Pulaski 221 ....J7
Quasqueton 579 ....K4
Quimby 334 ....B3
Radcliffe 574 ....G4
Rake 238 ....F2
Randall 161 ....F4
Randolph 243 ....B7
Raymond 619...........................J4
Readlyn 773 ....J3
Reasnor 191 ....G5
Red Oak▲ 6,264......................C6
Redfield 883............................E5

Reinbeck 1,605.......................H4
Rembrandt 229........................C3
Remsen 1,513 ....B3
Renwick 287 ....E3
Rhodes 272.............................G5
Riceville 827 ....H2
Richland 522...........................K6
Rickardsville 171 ....M3
Ridgeway 295 ....K2
Ringsted 481 ....D2
Rippey 275...............................E5
Riverdale 433 ....N5
Riverside 824..........................K6
Riverton 333 ....B7
Robins 875 ....K4
Rock Falls 130 ....G2
Rock Rapids▲ 2,601 ....A2
Rock Valley 2,540...................A2
Rockford 863...........................H2
Rockwell 1,008........................G3
Rockwell City▲ 1,981..............D4
Roland 1,035............................F4
Rolfe 721 ....D3
Rose Hill 171...........................J6
Rowan 189..............................F3
Rowley 272.............................K4
Royal 466 ....C2
Rudd 429................................H2
Runnells 306 ....G5
Russell 531.............................G7
Ruthven 707 ....D2
Rutland 149 ....E3
Ryan 382 ....K4
Sabula 710 ....N4
Sac City▲ 2,492 ....C4
Sageville 288 ....M3
Saint Ansgar 1,063..................H2
Saint Anthony 112..................G4
Saint Charles 537 ....F6
Saint Donatus 145 ....M4
Saint Lucas 174 ....K2
Saint Olaf 111 ....L3
Saint Paul 120..........................L7
Salem 453...............................K7
Salix 367................................A4
Sanborn 1,345 ....B2
Schaller 768...........................C4
Schleswig 851 ....B4
Scranton 583 ....D4
Searsboro 164.........................H5
Sergeant Bluff 2,772...............A4
Seymour 869 ....G7
Shambaugh 190 ....D7
Sheffield 1,174 ....G3
Shelby 637..............................C5
Sheldahl 315 ....F5
Sheldon 4,937 ....B2
Shell Rock 1,385 ....H3
Shellsburg 765 ....K4
Shenandoah 5,572..................C7
Sherrill 148.............................M3
Shueyville 223 ....K5
Sibley▲ 2,815 ....B2
Sidney▲ 1,253 ....B7
Sigourney▲ 2,111 ....J6
Silver City 252 ....B6
Sioux Center 5,074 ....A2
Sioux City▲ 80,505 ....A3
Sioux Rapids 761....................C3
Slater 1,268.............................F5
Sloan 938 ....A4
Smithland 235 ....B4
Soldier 205 ....B5
Solon 1,050 ....L5
Somers 161 ....E4
South English 224....................J6
Spencer▲ 11,066 ....C2
Spillville 387...........................J2
Spirit Lake▲ 3,871 ....C2
Springville 1,068.....................L4

Stacyville 481 ....H2
Stanhope 447 ....F4
Stanton 692 ....C7
Stanwood 646.........................L5
State Center 1,248...................G5
Steamboat Rock 335 ....G4
Stockport 260 ....K7
Stockton 187 ....M5
Storm Lake▲ 8,769 ....C3
Story City 2,959 ....F4
Stout 192................................H3
Stratford 715............................F4
Strawberry Point 1,357...........K3
Stuart 1,522 ....E6
Sully 841 ....H5
Sumner 2,078 ....J3
Superior 128...........................D2
Sutherland 714 ....B3
Swaledale 190 ....G3
Swea City 634 ....E2
Swisher 645............................K5
Tabor 957 ....B7
Tama 2,697 ....H5
Templeton 321 ....D5
Terril 383 ....C2
Thompson 498.........................F2
Thor 205 ....E3
Thornton 431...........................G3
Thurman 239 ....B7
Tiffin 460 ....K5
Tingley 179 ....E7
Tipton▲ 2,998 ....L5
Titonka 612.............................E2
Toledo▲ 2,380 ....H4
Traer 1,552...............................J4
Treynor 897 ....B6
Tripoli 1,188.............................J3
Truesdale 132 ....C3
Truro 391 ....F6
Underwood 515 ....B6
Union 448...............................G4
Unionville 133.........................H7
University Heights 1,042.........K5
University Park 604 ....H6
Urbana 595 ....K4
Urbandale 23,500.....................F5
Ute 395 ....B4
Vail 388...................................C4
Van Horne 695 ....J4
Van Meter 751 ....E5
Van Wert 249 ....F7
Ventura 590..............................F2
Victor 966 ....J5
Villisca 1,332 ....C7
Vincent 185.............................E3
Vinton▲ 5,103 ....J4
Volga 306.................................L3
Wadena 236.............................K3
Wahpeton 484 ....C2
Walcott 1,356 ....M5
Walford 303............................K5
Walker 673 ....K4
Wall Lake 875 ....C4
Wallingford 196 ....D2
Walnut 857 ....C6
Wapello▲ 2,013.........................L6
Washington▲ 7,074 ....K6
Washta 284.............................B3
Waterloo▲ 66,467 ....J4
Waterville 140..........................L2
Waucoma 277 ....J2
Waukee 2,512 ....F5
Waukon▲ 4,019 ....L2
Waverly▲ 8,539.........................J3
Wayland 838............................K6
Webb 167 ....D3
Webster City▲ 7,894 ....F4
Weldon 151..............................F7
Wellman 1,085........................K6
Wellsburg 682 ....H4

Welton 177 ....M5
Wesley 444 ....E2
West 862.................................J5
West Bend 941 ....D3
West Branch 1,908 ....L5
West Burlington 3,083 ....L7
West Chester 178 ....K6
West Des Moines 31,702 ....F5
West Liberty 2,935..................L5
West Okoboji 263 ....C2
West Point 1,079 ....K7
West Union▲ 2,490.................K3
Westfield 160..........................A3
Westgate 207..........................K3
Westphalia 144 ....C5
Westside 348...........................C4
What Cheer 762 ....J6
Wheatland 723.........................M5
Whiting 683 ....A4
Whittemore 535 ....E2
Whitten 137 ....H4
Williams 368 ....F3
Williamsburg 2,174..................J5
Williamson 166........................G6
Wilton 2,577 ....M5
Windsor Heights 5,190 ....F5
Winfield 1,051.........................L6
Winterset▲ 4,196 ....E6
Winthrop 742...........................K4
Wiota 160 ....D6
Woden 259..............................F2
Woodbine 1,500 ....B5
Woodburn 240 ....F7
Woodward 1,197 ....E5
Woolstock 212 ....F3
Worthington 439......................L4
Wyoming 659 ....L4
Yale 220..................................E5
Zearing 614 ....G4

OTHER FEATURES

Big Sioux (riv.)........................A3
Boyer (riv.)..............................B5
Cedar (riv.).............................K4
Chariton (riv.) G7
Clear (lake) G2
Des Moines (riv.)......................J7
Eagle (lake) F2
East Nishnabotna (riv.) C6
Effigy Mounds Nat'l Mon.........L2
Five Island (lake) D2
Floyd (riv.) A3
Herbert Hoover Nat'l
Hist. Site L5
Iowa (riv.)...............................H4
Little Sioux (riv.).....................B3
Lost Island (lake)....................D2
Mississippi (riv.) L7
Missouri (riv.) A5
Nodaway (riv.) D7
Palo Alto (lake) D2
Platte (riv.)..............................D8
Raccoon (riv.)..........................D4
Rathbun (lake).........................G7
Red Rock (lake).......................G6
Rock (riv.)...............................A2
Sac and Fox Ind. Res. H5
Skunk (riv.).............................K6
Spirit (lake).............................C2
Storm (lake)............................C3
Summit (lake) E6
Thompson (riv.) E7
Trumbull (lake) C2
Turkey (riv.)............................K2
Upper Iowa (riv.).....................K2
Wapsipinicon (riv.)..................J3
West Nishnabotna (riv.)..........C6

▲County seat

KANSAS

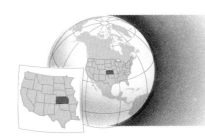

AREA 82,277 sq. mi. (213,097 sq. km.)
POPULATION 2,485,600
CAPITAL Topeka
LARGEST CITY Wichita
HIGHEST POINT Mt. Sunflower 4,039 ft. (1231 m.)
SETTLED IN 1831
ADMITTED TO UNION January 29, 1861
POPULAR NAME Sunflower State
STATE FLOWER Sunflower
STATE BIRD Western Meadowlark

Agriculture, Industry and Resources

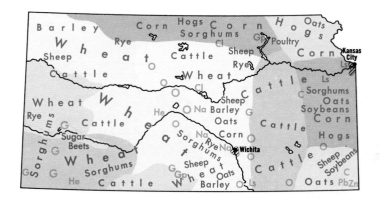

DOMINANT LAND USE

- Specialized Wheat
- Wheat, General Farming
- Wheat, Range Livestock
- Wheat, Grain Sorghums, Range Livestock
- Cattle Feed, Hogs
- Livestock, Cash Grain
- Livestock, Cash Grain, Dairy
- General Farming, Livestock, Cash Grain
- General Farming, Livestock, Special Crops
- Range Livestock

MAJOR MINERAL OCCURRENCES

C	Coal	Ls	Limestone
Cl	Clay	Na	Salt
G	Natural Gas	O	Petroleum
Gp	Gypsum	Pb	Lead
He	Helium	Zn	Zinc

////// Major Industrial Areas

COUNTIES

...llen 15,654	G4	Altoona 456	G4
...nderson 7,803	G3	Americus 891	F3
...tchison 16,932	G2	Ames 65	E2
...arber 5,874	D4	Andale 566	E4
...arton 29,382	D3	Andover 4,047	E4
...ourbon 14,966	H4	Angola 55	G4
...rown 11,128	G2	Anthony▲ 2,516	D4
...utler 50,580	F4	Arcadia 338	H4
...hase 3,021	F3	Argonia 529	E4
...hautauqua 4,407	F4	Arkansas City 12,762	E4
...herokee 21,374	H4	Arlington 457	D4
...heyenne 3,243	A2	Arma 1,542	H4
...lark 2,418	C4	Ash Valley 50	C3
...lay 9,158	E2	Ashland▲ 1,032	C4
...loud 11,023	E2	Assaria 387	E3
...offey 8,404	G3	Atchison▲ 10,656	G2
...omanche 2,313	C4	Athol 86	D2
...owley 36,915	F4	Atlanta 232	F4
...rawford 35,568	H4	Attica 716	D4
...ecatur 4,021	B2	Atwood▲ 1,388	B2
...ickinson 18,958	E3	Auburn 908	G3
...oniphan 8,134	G2	Augusta 7,876	F4
...ouglas 81,798	G3	Aurora 101	E2
...dwards 3,787	C4	Axtell 432	F2
...k 3,327	F4	Baileyville 130	F2
...lis 26,004	C3	Baldwin City 2,961	G3
...lsworth 6,586	D3	Barnard 129	D2
...nney 33,070	B3	Barnes 167	F2
...ord 27,463	C4	Bartlett 107	G4
...ranklin 21,994	G3	Basehor 1,591	G2
...eary 30,453	F3	Bassett 20	G4
...ove 3,231	B3	Bavaria 100	E3
...raham 3,543	C2	Baxter Springs 4,351	H4
...rant 7,159	A4	Bazine 373	C3
...ray 5,396	B4	Beagle 88	G3
...reeley 1,774	A3	Beattie 221	F2
...reenwood 7,847	F4	Beaumont 112	F4
...amilton 2,388	A3	Beaver 57	D3
...arper 7,124	D4	Beeler 80	B3
...arvey 31,028	E3	Belle Plaine 1,649	E4
...askell 3,886	B4	Belleville▲ 2,517	E2
...odgeman 2,177	C3	Beloit▲ 4,066	D2
...ackson 11,525	G2	Belpre 116	C4
...efferson 15,905	G2	Belvue 207	F2
...ewell 4,251	D2	Bendena 125	G2
...ohnson 355,054	H3	Benedict 16	G4
...earny 4,027	A3	Bennington 568	E2
...ngman 8,292	D4	Bentley 360	E4
...owa 3,660	C4	Benton 669	E4
...abette 23,693	G4	Bern 190	F2
...ne 2,375	B3	Berryton 150	G3
...eavenworth 64,371	G2	Beverly 131	E2
...ncoln 3,653	D2	Big Bow 55	A4
...nn 8,254	H3	Bird City 467	A2
...ogan 3,081	A3	Bison 252	C3
...von 34,732	F3	Blaine 50	F2
...arion 12,888	E3	Bloom 65	C4
...arshall 11,705	F2	Blue Mound 251	H3
...cPherson 27,268	E3	Blue Rapids 1,131	F2
...eade 4,247	B4	Bluff City 69	E4
...iami 23,466	H3	Bogue 150	C2
...itchell 7,203	D2	Bonner Springs 6,413	H2
...ontgomery 38,816	G4	Brazilton 91	H4
...orris 6,198	F3	Bremen 60	F2
...orton 3,480	A4	Brewster 296	A2
...emaha 10,446	F2	Bridgeport 95	E3
...eosho 17,035	G4	Bronson 343	H4
...ess 4,033	C3	Brookville 226	E3
...orton 5,947	C2	Brownell 44	C3
...sage 15,248	G3	Bucklin 710	C4
...sborne 4,867	D2	Bucyrus 135	H3
...tawa 5,634	E2	Buffalo 293	G4
...awnee 7,555	C3	Buhler 1,277	E3
...illips 6,590	C2	Bunker Hill 111	D3
...ottawatomie 16,128	F2	Burden 518	F4
...ratt 9,702	D4	Burdett 248	C3
...awlins 3,404	A2	Burdick 100	F3
...eno 62,389	D4	Burlingame 1,074	G3
...epublic 6,482	E2	Burlington▲ 2,735	G3
...ce 10,610	D3	Burns 226	F3
...ley 67,139	F2	Burr Oak 278	D2
...ooks 6,039	C2	Burrton 866	E3
...ush 3,842	C3	Bushong 57	F3
...ussell 7,835	D3	Bushton 341	D3
...aline 49,301	E3	Byers 46	D4
...cott 5,289	B3	Caldwell 1,351	E4
...edgwick 403,662	E4	Cambridge 74	F4
...eward 18,743	B4	Caney 2,062	G4
...awnee 160,976	G2	Canton 794	E3
...heridan 3,043	B2	Carbondale 1,526	G3
...herman 6,926	A2	Carlton 39	E3
...mith 5,078	D2	Carlyle 75	G4
...afford 5,365	D3	Cassoday 95	F3
...anton 2,333	A4	Catharine 121	C3
...evens 5,048	A4	Cedar 25	D2
...umner 25,841	E4	Cedar Point 39	F3
...homas 8,258	A2	Cedar Vale 760	F4
...rego 3,694	C3	Centerville 104	H3
...abaunsee 6,603	F3	Centralia 452	F2
...allace 1,821	A3	Chanute 9,488	G4
...ashington 7,073	E2	Chapman 1,264	E3
...ichita 2,758	A3	Chase 577	D3
...ilson 10,289	G4	Chautauqua 132	F4
...oodson 4,116	G4	Cheney 1,560	E4
...yandotte 161,993	H2	Cherokee 651	H4
		Cherryvale 2,464	G4
		Chetopa 1,357	G4

CITIES and TOWNS

		Chicopee 300	H4
...bbyville 123	D4	Cimarron▲ 1,626	B4
...bilene▲ 6,242	E3	Circleville 153	G2
...da 120	E2	Claflin 678	D3
...dmire 147	F3	Clay Center▲ 4,613	E2
...genda 81	E2	Clayton 91	B2
...gra 322	C2	Clearview City	G3
...amota 50	B3	Clearwater 1,875	E4
...bert 229	C3	Clifton 561	E2
...den 182	D3	Climax 57	F4
...exander 85	C3	Clyde 793	E2
...iceville 60	G3	Coats 127	D4
...len 191	F3	Codell 90	C2
...ma▲ 871	F2	Coffeyville 12,917	G4
...mena 423	C2	Colby▲ 5,396	A2
...amota 50	B3	Coldwater▲ 939	C4
...ta Vista 477	F3	Collyer 144	B2
...tamont 1,048	G4	Colony 447	G3
...ton 115	D2	Columbus▲ 3,268	H4

Colwich 1,091	E4	Denton 166	G2	Elgin 118	F4	Falun 89	E3
Concordia▲ 6,167	E2	Derby 14,699	E4	Elk City 334	G4	Farlington 80	H4
Conway 1,384	E3	Detroit 90	E3	Elk Falls 122	G4	Florence 636	E3
Conway Springs 1,313	E4	Devon 108	H4	Elkhart▲ 2,318	A4	Fontana 131	H3
Coolidge 90	A3	Dexter 320	F4	Ellinwood 2,329	D3	Ford 247	C4
Copeland 290	B4	Dighton▲ 1,361	B3	Ellis 1,814	C3	Formoso 128	D2
Corning 142	F2	Dodge City▲ 21,129	B4	Ellsworth▲ 2,294	D3	Fort Dodge 400	C4
Cottonwood Falls▲ 889	F3	Dorrance 195	D3	Elmdale 83	F3	Fort Leavenworth	H2
Council Grove▲ 2,228	F3	Douglass 1,722	F4	Elmont 112	G2	Fort Scott▲ 8,362	H4
Courtland 343	E2	Dover 192	G3	Elsmore 91	G4	Fowler 571	B4
Coyville 78	G4	Downs 1,119	D2	Elwood 1,079	H2	Frankfort 927	F2
Crestline 85	H4	Dresden 73	B2	Elyria 100	E3	Franklin 400	H4
Cuba 242	E2	Dunlap 65	F3	Emmett 165	F2	Frederick 18	D3
Cullison 120	D4	Durham 119	E3	Emporia▲ 25,512	F3	Fredonia▲ 2,599	G4
Culver 162	E2	Dwight 365	F3	Englewood 96	C4	Freeport 8	E4
Cummings 150	G2	Earlton 69	G4	Ensign 192	B4	Frontenac 2,588	H4
Cunningham 535	D4	Easton 405	G2	Enterprise 865	E3	Fulton 191	H4
Damar 112	C2	Eastborough 896	E4	Erie▲ 1,276	G4	Galatia 47	D3
Danville 56	E4	Easton 405	G2	Esbon 167	D2	Galena 3,308	H4
De Soto 2,291	H3	Edgerton 1,244	H3	Eskridge 518	F3	Galesburg 160	G4
Dearing 428	G4	Edmond 37	C2	Eudora 3,006	G3	Galva 651	E3
Deerfield 677	A4	Edna 438	G4	Eureka▲ 2,974	F4	Garden City▲ 24,097	B4
Delia 172	G2	Edson 55	A2	Everest 310	G2	Garden Plain 731	E4
Delphos 494	E2	Edwardsville 3,979	H2	Fairview 306	F2	Gardner 3,191	H3
Denison 225	G2	Effingham 540	G2	Fairway 4,173	H2	Garfield 236	C3
Dennis 96	G4	El Dorado▲ 11,504	F4	Fall River 113	G4	Garland 112	H4
		Elbing 184	E3				

Garnett▲ 3,210	G3
Gas 505	G4
Gaylord 173	D2
Gem 104	B2
Geneseo 382	D3
Geuda Springs 219	E4
Girard▲ 2,794	H4
Glade 101	C2
Glasco 556	E2
Glen Elder 448	D2
Goddard 1,804	E4
Goessel 506	E3
Goff 156	G2
Goodland▲ 4,983	A2
Gorham 284	D3
Gove▲ 103	B3
Grainfield 357	B2
Grandview Plaza 1,233	F2
Grantville 220	G2
Great Bend▲ 15,427	D3
Greeley 339	G3
Green 150	E2
Greenleaf 353	E2
Greensburg▲ 1,792	C4
Grenola 256	F4
Gridley 356	G3

(continued on following page)

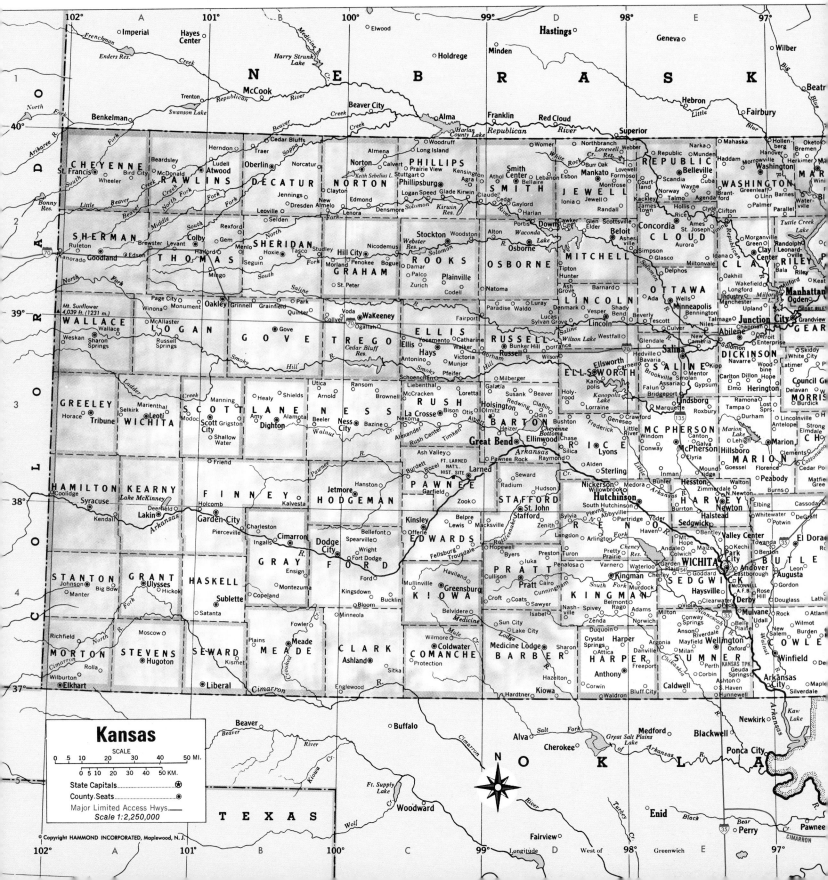

Kansas

SCALE

0 5 10   20   30   40   50 MI.

0 5 10 20   30   40 50 KM.

State Capitals .... ⊛

County Seats .... ◉

Major Limited Access Hwys. _____

Scale 1:2,250,000

© Copyright HAMMOND INCORPORATED, Maplewood, N.J.

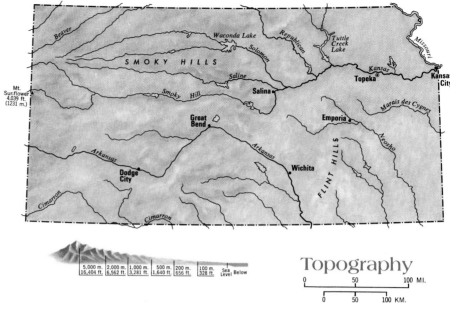

Topography

KENTUCKY

COUNTIES

Adair 15,360 L6
Allen 14,628 J7
Anderson 14,571 M5
Ballard 7,902 C6
Barren 34,001 K7
Bath 9,692 O4
Bell 31,506 O7
Boone 57,589 M3
Bourbon 19,236 N4
Boyd 51,150 R4
Boyle 25,641 M5
Bracken 7,766 N3
Breathitt 15,703 P5
Breckinridge 16,312 J5
Bullitt 47,567 K5
Butler 11,245 H6
Caldwell 13,232 F6
Calloway 30,735 E7
Campbell 83,866 N3
Carlisle 5,238 C7
Carroll 9,292 L3
Carter 24,340 P4
Casey 14,211 M6
Christian 68,941 F7
Clark 29,496 N4
Clay 21,746 O6
Clinton 9,135 L7
Crittenden 9,196 E6
Cumberland 6,784 L7
Daviess 87,189 G5
Edmonson 10,357 J6
Elliott 6,455 P4
Estill 14,614 O5
Fayette 225,366 M5
Fleming 12,292 O4
Floyd 43,586 R5
Franklin 43,781 M4
Fulton 8,271 C7
Gallatin 5,393 M3
Garrard 11,579 M5
Grant 15,737 M3
Graves 33,550 D7
Grayson 21,050 J5
Green 10,371 K6
Greenup 36,742 R3
Hancock 7,864 H5
Hardin 89,240 K5
Harlan 36,574 P7
Harrison 16,248 N4
Hart 14,890 K6
Henderson 43,044 F5
Henry 12,823 L4
Hickman 5,566 C7
Jackson 11,955 N6
Jefferson 664,937 K4
Jessamine 30,508 M5
Johnson 23,248 R5
Kenton 142,031 M3
Knott 17,906 R6
Knox 29,676 O7
Larue 11,679 K6
Laurel 43,438 N6
Lawrence 13,998 R4
Lee 7,422 O5
Leslie 13,642 P6
Letcher 27,000 R6
Lewis 13,029 P3
Lincoln 20,045 M6
Livingston 9,062 E6
Logan 24,416 H7
Lyon 6,624 E7
Madison 57,508 N5
Magoffin 13,077 P5
Marion 16,499 L5
Marshall 27,205 E7
Martin 12,526 R5
Mason 16,666 O3
McCracken 62,879 D6
McCreary 15,603 N7
McLean 9,628 G5
Meade 24,170 J5
Menifee 5,092 O5
Mercer 19,148 M5
Metcalfe 8,963 K7
Monroe 11,401 K7
Montgomery 19,561 O4
Morgan 11,648 P5
Muhlenberg 31,318 G6
Nelson 29,710 K5
Nicholas 6,725 N4
Ohio 21,105 H6
Oldham 33,263 L4
Owen 9,035 M3
Owsley 5,036 O6
Pendleton 12,036 N3
Perry 30,283 P6
Pike 72,583 S6
Powell 11,686 O5
Pulaski 49,489 M6
Robertson 2,124 N3
Rockcastle 14,803 N6
Rowan 20,353 P4
Russell 14,716 L6
Scott 23,867 M4
Shelby 24,824 L4
Simpson 15,145 H7
Spencer 6,801 L4
Taylor 21,146 L6
Todd 10,940 G7
Trigg 10,361 F7
Trimble 6,090 L3
Union 16,557 F5
Warren 76,673 H6
Washington 10,441 L5
Wayne 17,468 M7
Webster 13,955 F5
Whitley 33,326 N7
Wolfe 6,503 O5
Woodford 19,955 M4

CITIES and TOWNS

Adairville 906 H7
Ages 500 P7
Albany▲ 2,062 L7
Alexandria▲ 5,592 N3
Allen 229 R5
Allensville 218 G7
Amburgey 500 R6
Anchorage 2,082 L2
Annville 470 O6
Arjay 975 O7
Arlington 449 D7
Ashland 23,622 R4
Auburn 1,273 H7
Audubon Park 1,520 J2
Augusta 1,336 N3
Austin 500 K7
Auxier 900 R5
Bancroft 582 K1
Banner 950 R5
Barbourmeade 1,402 K1
Barbourville▲ 3,658 O7
Bardstown▲ 6,801 L5
Bardwell▲ 819 D7
Barlow 706 D6
Baskett 550 F5
Beattyville▲ 1,131 O5
Beauty 800 S5
Beaver Dam 2,904 H6
Bedford▲ 761 L3
Bee Spring 500 J6
Beechwood Village 1,263 K2
Belcher 500 S6
Belfry 800 S5
Bellemeade 927 L2
Bellevue 6,997 S1
Benham 717 R7
Benton▲ 3,899 E7
Berea 9,126 N5
Berry 240 N3
Betsy Layne 975 R5
Big Creek 700 O6
Blaine 271 R4
Blandville 95 D7
Bloomfield 845 L5
Blue Ridge Manor 565 L2
Boldman 510 R5
Bonnieville 300 K6
Bonnyman 800 P6
Boone 232 N5
Booneville▲ 191 O6
Bowling Green▲ 40,641 H7
Bradford 199 N3
Bradfordsville 331 L6
Brandenburg▲ 1,857 J4
Bremen 267 G6
Briensburg E7
Broadfields 273 K2
Brodhead 1,140 N6
Bromley 1,137 S2
Brooks 2,464 K4
Brooksville▲ 670 N3
Brownsboro Farm 670 L1
Brownsville 897 J6
Buechel 7,081 K2
Buffalo K6
Bulan 800 P6
Burgin 1,009 M5
Burkesville▲ 1,815 L7
Burlington▲ 6,070 R2
Burnside 695 M6
Butler 625 N3
Cadiz▲ 2,148 F7
Calhoun▲ 854 G5
California 130 N3
Calvert City 2,531 E6
Camargo 1,022 O4
Campbellsburg 604 L3
Campbellsville▲ 9,577 L6
Campton▲ 484 O5
Caney 549 P5
Caneyville 642 J6
Cannel City 600 P5
Carlisle▲ 1,639 N4
Carrollton▲ 3,715 L3
Carter P4
Catlettsburg▲ 2,231 R4
Cave City 1,953 K6
Cawood 800 P7
Center 383 K6
Centertown 462 G6
Centerville S6
Central City 4,979 G6
Cerulean F7
Clarkson 611 J6
Clay 1,173 F6
Clay City 1,258 O5
Clearfield 1,250 P4
Clinton▲ 1,547 D7
Clover Bottom 600 N5
Cloverport 1,207 H5
Coal Run 262 R5
Cold Spring 2,880 T2
Columbia▲ 3,845 L6
Columbus 252 C7
Combs 900 P6
Corbin 7,419 N7
Corinth 137 M3
Corydon 790 F5
Covington 43,264 S2
Crab Orchard 825 M6
Crescent Springs 2,179 R2
Crestview 356 S2
Crestview Hills 2,546 R2
Crestwood 1,435 L4
Crittenden 731 M3
Crofton 699 G6
Cumberland 3,112 R6
Cynthiana▲ 6,497 N4
Danville▲ 12,420 M5
Dawson Springs 3,129 F6
Dayton 6,576 T1
Devondale 1,164 K2
Dexter E7
Dixon▲ 552 F5
Dorton 750 R6
Douglass Hills 5,549 L2
Dover 297 O3
Drakesboro 565 H6
Dry Ridge 1,601 M3
Earlington 1,833 F6
East Bernstadt 550 N6
Echols 576 H6
Eddyville▲ 1,889 E6
Edgewood 8,143 S2
Edmonton▲ 1,477 K7
Elizabethtown▲ 18,167 K5
Elkhorn City 813 S6
Elkton▲ 1,789 G7
Elsmere 6,847 R2
Eminence 2,055 L4
Eolia 875 R6
Erlanger 15,979 R2
Essie 650 P6
Eubank 354 M6
Evarts 1,063 P7
Ewing 268 O4
Fairdale 6,563 K4
Fairfield 142 L5
Fairview 119 G7
Fairview 198 S2
Fallsburg R4
Falmouth▲ 2,378 N3
Fancy Farm 800 D7
Farmington 600 D7
Fedscreek 950 S6
Ferguson 934 M6
Fincastle 838 L1
Flat 7,799 O5
Flat Lick 600 O7
Flatwoods 8,354 R4
Fleming (Fleming-Neon) 759 R6
Flemingsburg▲ 3,071 O4
Florence 18,624 R2
Ford 522 N5
Fordsville 561 H5
Forest Hills 454 L2
Fort Knox 21,495 K5
Fort Mitchell 7,438 S2
Fort Thomas 16,032 S2
Fort Wright 6,570 S2
Fountain Run 259 K7
Frankfort (cap.)▲ 25,968 M4
Franklin▲ 7,607 J7
Fredonia 490 E6
Frenchburg▲ 625 O5
Fullerton 950 P3
Fulton 3,078 D7
Gamaliel 462 K7
Garrison 700 P3
Georgetown▲ 11,414 M4
Germantown 213 O3
Ghent 365 L3
Gilbertsville E7
Glasgow▲ 12,351 J7
Glencoe 257 M3
Glenview 653 K1
Goose Creek 321 L1
Goshen 2,447 K4
Gramoor 1,167 K1
Grand Rivers 351 E7
Gray 2,911 O7
Grayson▲ 3,510 R4
Greensburg▲ 1,990 K6
Greenup▲ 1,158 R3
Greenville▲ 4,689 G6
Guthrie 1,504 G7
Hammond 510 O7
Hanson 450 G6
Hardin 595 E7
Hardinsburg▲ 1,906 H5
Hardy 900 S5
Harlan▲ 2,686 P7
Harold 520 R5
Harrodsburg▲ 7,335 M5
Hartford▲ 2,532 H6
Hatfield 700 S5
Hawesville▲ 998 H5
Hazard▲ 5,416 P6
Hazel 460 E7
Hebron 930 R2
Helton 600 P7
Henderson▲ 25,945 F5
Hickman▲ 2,689 C7
Hickory 152 D7
Highland Heights 4,223 T2
Hima 600 O6
Himyar 545 O7
Hindman▲ 798 R6
Hiseville 220 K6
Hitchins 750 R4
Hodgenville▲ 2,721 K5
Hollow Creek 991 K4
Hopkinsville▲ 29,809 F7
Horse Cave 2,284 K6
Houston Acres 496 K2
Hustonville 313 M6
Hyden▲ 375 P6
Independence▲ 10,444 M3
Indian Hills 1,074 K1
Inez▲ 511 S5
Irvine▲ 2,836 O5
Irvington 1,180 J5
Island 446 G6
Ivel 850 R5
Jackson▲ 2,466 P5
Jamestown▲ 1,641 L7
Jeff 23,221 P6
Jeffersontown 15,795 L2
Jeffersonville 1,854 O5
Jenkins 2,751 R6
Junction City 1,983 M5
Keavy 900 N6
Keene 393 M5
Kenton 358 N3
Kenton Vale 145 S2
Kenvir 800 P7
Kevil 337 D6
King 399 O7
Kingsley 464 K2
Kitts 800 P7
Kuttawa 535 E6
La Center 1,040 C6
La Fayette 106 F7
La Grange▲ 3,853 L4
Lackey R6
Lake 3,131 O6
Lakeside Park 3,062 R2
Lancaster▲ 3,421 M5
Lawrenceburg▲ 5,911 M4
Leatherwood 800 P6
Lebanon Junction 1,741 K5
Lebanon▲ 5,695 L5
Leitchfield▲ 4,965 J6
Lejunior 597 P7
Lewisburg 772 G6
Lewisport 1,778 H5
Lexington▲ 204,165 N4
Liberty▲ 1,937 M6
Littcarr 645 R6
Livermore 1,534 G5
Livingston 241 N6
Lockport 84 M4
London▲ 5,757 N6
Lone Oak 465 D6
Lookout 600 S6
Lookout Heights S2
Loretto 820 L5
Lothair 600 P6
Louisa▲ 1,990 R4
Louisville▲ 269,063 J2
Loyall 1,100 P7
Ludlow 4,736 S2
Lynch 1,166 R7
Mackville 200 L5
Madisonville▲ 16,200 F6
Majestic 600 S5
Manchester▲ 1,634 O6
Marion▲ 3,320 E6
Marshes Siding 800 M7
Martha 650 R4
Martin 694 R5
Mary 177 O5
Mason 1,119 M3
Mayfield▲ 9,935 D7
Maysville▲ 7,169 O3
McAndrews 975 S5
McCarr 592 S5
McHenry 414 H6
McKee▲ 870 O6
McRoberts 1,101 R6
McVeigh 650 S5
Meadow Vale 798 L1
Meally 550 R5
Melbourne 660 T2
Mentor 169 N3
Meta 600 S5
Middlesboro 11,328 O7
Middletown 5,016 L2
Midway 1,290 M4
Millersburg 937 N4
Millstone 550 R6
Milton 563 L3
Minor Lane Heights 1,675 K4
Monterey 164 M4
Monticello▲ 5,357 M7
Moorland 467 L2
Morehead▲ 8,357 P4
Morgan 3,776 N3
Morganfield▲ 3,781 E5
Morgantown▲ 2,284 H6
Mortons Gap 987 F6
Mount Olivet▲ 384 N3
Mount Sterling▲ 5,362 N4
Mount Vernon▲ 2,654 N6
Mount Washington 5,226 K
Mouthcard 900 S
Muldraugh 1,376 J
Munfordville▲ 1,556 J
Murray▲ 14,439 E
Nebo 227 F
Neon (Neon-Fleming) R
New Castle▲ 893 L
New Concord 800 E
New Haven 796 K
New Hope L
Newport 18,871 S
Nicholasville▲ 13,603 N
North Middletown 602 N
Northfield 898 K
Nortonville 1,209 G
Oak Grove 2,863 G
Oakland 202 J
Oil Springs 900 P
Okolona 18,902 K
Oldtown 570 R
Olive Hill 1,809 P
Owensboro▲ 53,549 G
Owenton▲ 1,306 M
Owingsville▲ 1,491 O
Paducah▲ 27,256 D
Paintsville▲ 4,354 R
Paris▲ 8,730 N
Park City 549 J
Park Hills 3,321 S
Parksville 560 M
Parkway Village 707 J
Pembroke 640 G
Perryville 815 M
Petersburg M
Pewee Valley 1,283 L
Phelps 1,298 S
Philpot 700 H
Pikeville▲ 6,324 S
Pine Knot 1,549 M
Pineville▲ 2,198 O
Pittsburg N
Plantation 830 K
Pleasure Ridge Park 25,131 J
Pleasureville 761 L
Plum Springs 361 J
Powderly 748 G
Premium 729 R
Preston 3,558 O
Prestonsburg▲ 4,011 R
Prestonville 205 L
Princeton▲ 6,940 F
Prospect 2,788 K
Providence 4,123 F
Raceland 2,256 R
Radcliff 19,772 K
Ravenna 804 O
Raywick 157 L
Richmond▲ 21,155 N
Riverwood 506 K
Robards 701 F
Rochester 191 H
Rockholds 775 N
Rockport 385 H
Rolling Fields 593 K
Rolling Hills 1,135 L
Russell 4,014 R
Russell Springs 2,363 L
Russellville▲ 7,454 H
Ryland Heights 279 M
Sacramento 563 G
Sadieville 255 M
Saint Charles 316 F
Saint Matthews 15,800 K

Agriculture, Industry and Resources

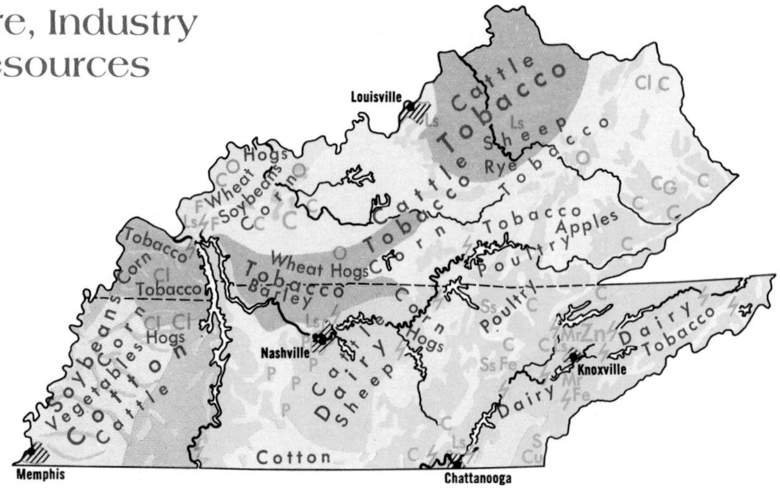

DOMINANT LAND USE

- Hogs, Soft Winter Wheat
- Tobacco, General Farming
- General Farming, Livestock, Tobacco
- General Farming, Livestock, Dairy
- General Farming, Livestock, Fruit, Tobacco
- Specialized Cotton
- Cotton, General Farming
- Cotton, Livestock
- Forests
- Swampland, Limited Agriculture

MAJOR MINERAL OCCURRENCES

C	Coal	G	Natural Gas	P	Phosphates
Cl	Clay	Ls	Limestone	S	Pyrites
Cu	Copper	Mr	Marble	Ss	Sandstone
F	Fluorspar	O	Petroleum	Zn	Zinc
Fe	Iron Ore				

Water Power

Major Industrial Areas

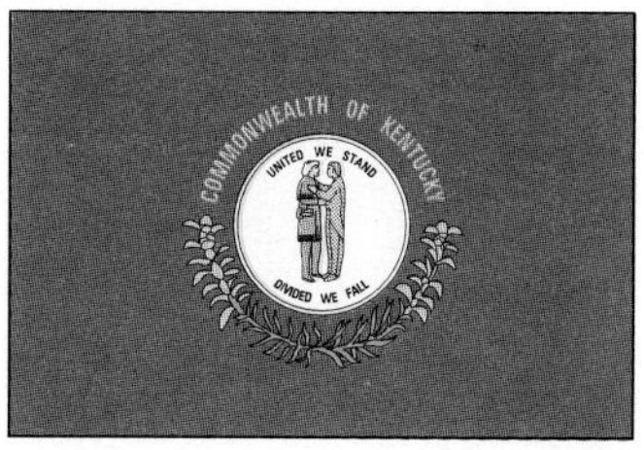

KENTUCKY

AREA 40,409 sq. mi. (104,659 sq. km.)
POPULATION 3,698,969
CAPITAL Frankfort
LARGEST CITY Louisville
HIGHEST POINT Black Mtn. 4,145 ft. (1263 m.)
SETTLED IN 1774
ADMITTED TO UNION June 1, 1792
POPULAR NAME Bluegrass State
STATE FLOWER Goldenrod
STATE BIRD Cardinal

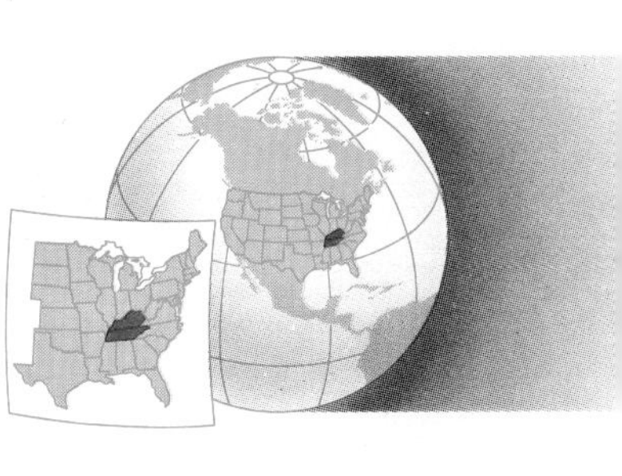

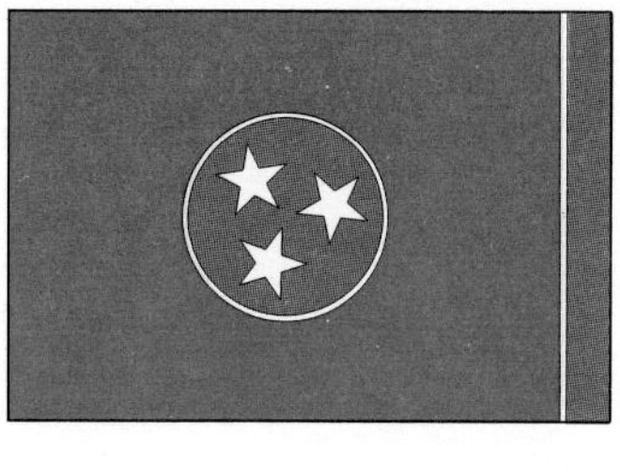

TENNESSEE

AREA 42,144 sq. mi. (109,153 sq. km.)
POPULATION 4,896,641
CAPITAL Nashville
LARGEST CITY Memphis
HIGHEST POINT Clingmans Dome 6,643 ft. (2025 m.)
SETTLED IN 1757
ADMITTED TO UNION June 1, 1796
POPULAR NAME Volunteer State
STATE FLOWER Iris
STATE BIRD Mockingbird

Saint Regis Park 1,756 .... K2
Salem 770 .... E6
Salt Lick 342 .... O4
Salyersville▲ 1,917 .... P5
Sanders 231 .... M3
Sandy Hook▲ 548 .... P4
Sardis 171 .... O3
Science Hill 628 .... M6
Scottsville▲ 4,278 .... J7
Sebree 1,510 .... F5
Seco R6
Sedalia D7
Seneca Gardens 684 .... K2
Sextons Creek 975 .... O6
Sharpsburg 315 .... O4
Shelbyville▲ 6,238 .... L4
Shepherdsville▲ 4,805 .... K4
Shively 15,535 .... K4
Silver Grove 1,102 .... T2
Simpson 907 .... P5
Simpsonville 642 .... L4
Slaughters 235 .... F6
Smilax 987 .... P6
Smithfield 115 .... L4
Smithland▲ 384 .... E6
Smiths Grove 703 .... J6
Somerset▲ 10,733 .... M6
Sonora 295 .... K5
South 202 .... J6
South Carrollton 262 .... G6
South Portsmouth 900 .... P3
South Shore 1,318 .... R3
South Williamson 1,016 .... S5
Southgate 3,266 .... T2
Sparta 133 .... M3
Spottsville 914 .... G5
Springfield▲ 2,875 .... L5
Springlee 451 .... K2
Staffordsville 700 .... R5
Stamping Ground 698 .... M4
Stanford▲ 2,686 .... M5
Stanton▲ 2,795 .... O5
Stearns 1,550 .... N7
Stone 900 .... S5
Strathmoor Village 361 .... K2
Sturgis 2,184 .... F5
Tateville 680 .... M7
Taylor Mill 5,530 .... S2
Taylorsville▲ 774 .... L4
Thealka 600 .... R5
Thornhill 146 .... K1
Tollesboro 808 .... O3
Tompkinsville▲ 2,861 .... K7
Trenton 378 .... G7
Tyner 590 .... O6
Union 1,001 .... M3
Uniontown 1,008 .... F5
Upton 719 .... K6
Valley Station 22,840 .... K4
Van 1,050 .... R6
Van Lear 2,035 .... R5
Vanceburg▲ 1,713 .... P3
Verda 1,133 .... P7
Versailles▲ 7,269 .... M4
Vicco 244 .... P6
Villa Hills 7,739 .... R2
Vine Grove 3,586 .... K5
Virgie 600 .... R6
Visalia 190 .... N3
Wallins Creek 261 .... O7
Walton 2,034 .... M3
Warfield 364 .... S5
Warsaw▲ 1,202 .... M3
Washington 795 .... O3
Water Valley 321 .... D7
Waverly 345 .... F5
Wayland 359 .... R6
Weeksbury 850 .... R6
Wellington 593 .... O5
Wellington 653 .... K2
West Buechel 1,587 .... K2
West Liberty▲ 1,887 .... P5
West Point 1,216 .... J4
West Somerset 850 .... M6
Westwood 734 .... R4
Westwood 826 .... L1
Wheatcroft 206 .... F5
Wheelwright 721 .... R6
White Plains 598 .... G6
Whitesburg▲ 1,636 .... R6
Whitesville 682 .... H5
Whitley City▲ 1,133 .... N7
Wickliffe▲ 851 .... C7
Wilders 633 .... S2
Willard R4
Williamsburg▲ 5,493 .... N7
Williamstown▲ 3,023 .... M3
Willisburg 223 .... L5
Wilmore 4,215 .... M5
Winchester▲ 15,799 .... N5
Windy Hills 2,452 .... K1
Wingo 568 .... D7
Winston Park S2
Wolf Creek 600 .... J4
Woodbine 900 .... N7
Woodburn 343 .... J7
Woodbury 117 .... H6
Woodland Hills 714 .... L2
Woodlawn (Oakdale) 308 .... D6
Woodlawn 331 .... T2
Woodlawn Park 1,099 .... K2
Wooton 750 .... P6
Worthington 1,751 .... R3
Worthville 191 .... L3
Wurtland 1,221 .... R3
Zebulon 750 .... S5

OTHER FEATURES

Abraham Lincoln Birthplace Nat'l Hist. Site K5
Barkley (dam) E6
Barkley (lake) F7
Barren (riv.) H6
Barren River (lake) J7
Beech Fork (riv.) L5
Big Sandy (riv.) R4
Black (mt.) R7
Buckhorn (lake) O6
Chaplin (riv.) L5
Clarks, East Fork (riv.) E7
Cove Run (lake) P4
Cumberland (lake) M7
Cumberland (mt.) P7
Cumberland (riv.) K8
Cumberland Gap Nat'l Hist. P7
Dale Hollow (lake) L7
Dewey (lake) R5
Dix (riv.) M5
Drakes (creek) J7
Dry (creek) R2
Eagle (creek) M3
Fishtrap (lake) S6
Fort Campbell G7
Grayson (lake) P4
Green (riv.) G6
Green River (lake) L6
Herrington (lake) M5
Hinkston (creek) N4
Kentucky (dam) E7
Kentucky (lake) E8
Kentucky (riv.) M3
Land Between The Lakes Rec. Area E7
Laurel River (lake) N6
Lexington Blue Grass Army Depot N4
Licking (riv.) N3
Mammoth Cave Nat'l Park J6
Mayfield (creek) C7
Mississippi (riv.) 10
Mud (riv.) H7
Nolin (lake) K6
Nolin (riv.) J6
Obion (creek) C7
Ohio (riv.) F5
Paint Lick (riv.) M5
Panther (creek) G5
Pine (mt.) O7
Pond (riv.) G6
Red (riv.) G7
Red (riv.) O5
Rockcastle (riv.) N6
Rolling Fork (riv.) K5
Rough (riv.) H5
Rough River (lake) J5
Salt (riv.) K5
Tennessee (riv.) D6
Tradewater (riv.) F6
Tug Fork (riv.) S5

TENNESSEE

COUNTIES

Anderson 68,250 .... N8
Bedford 30,411 .... J9
Benton 14,524 .... E8
Bledsoe 9,669 .... L9
Blount 85,969 .... O9
Bradley 73,712 .... M1
Campbell 35,079 .... N8
Cannon 10,467 .... J9
Carroll 27,514 .... E9
Carter 51,505 .... S8
Cheatham 27,140 .... G8
Chester 12,819 .... D1
Claiborne 26,137 .... O8
Clay 7,238 .... K7
Cocke 29,141 .... P9
Coffee 40,339 .... J9
Crockett 13,378 .... C9
Cumberland 34,736 .... L9
Davidson 510,784 .... H8
De Kalb 13,589 .... K9
Decatur 10,472 .... E9
Dickson 35,061 .... G8
Dyer 34,854 .... C8
Fayette 25,559 .... C1
Fentress 14,669 .... M8
Franklin 34,725 .... J1
Gibson 46,315 .... D9
Giles 25,741 .... G1
Grainger 17,095 .... O8
Greene 55,853 .... R8
Grundy 13,362 .... K1
Hamblen 50,480 .... P8
Hamilton 285,536 .... L1
Hancock 6,739 .... P7
Hardeman 23,377 .... C1
Hardin 22,633 .... E1
Hawkins 44,565 .... P8
Haywood 19,437 .... C9
Henderson 21,844 .... E9
Henry 27,888 .... E8
Hickman 16,754 .... G9
Houston 7,018 .... F8
Humphreys 15,795 .... F8
Jackson 9,297 .... K8
Jefferson 33,016 .... P8
Johnson 13,766 .... T7
Knox 335,749 .... O9
Lake 7,129 .... B8
Lauderdale 23,491 .... B9
Lawrence 35,303 .... G1
Lewis 9,247 .... F9
Lincoln 28,157 .... H1
Loudon 31,255 .... N9
Macon 15,906 .... J7
Madison 77,982 .... D9
Marion 24,860 .... K1
Marshall 21,539 .... H1
Maury 54,812 .... G9
McMinn 42,383 .... M1
McNairy 22,422 .... D1
Meigs 8,033 .... M9
Monroe 30,541 .... N1
Montgomery 100,498 .... G8
Moore 4,721 .... J1
Morgan 17,300 .... M8
Obion 31,717 .... C8
Overton 17,636 .... L8
Perry 6,612 .... F9
Pickett 4,548 .... M7
Polk 13,643 .... N1
Putnam 51,373 .... K8
Rhea 24,344 .... M9
Roane 47,227 .... M9
Robertson 41,494 .... H7
Rutherford 118,570 .... J9
Scott 18,358 .... M8
Sequatchie 8,863 .... L1
Sevier 51,043 .... O9
Shelby 826,330 .... B1
Smith 14,143 .... J8
Stewart 9,479 .... F7
Sullivan 143,596 .... S7
Sumner 103,281 .... J8
Tipton 37,568 .... B9
Trousdale 5,920 .... J8
Unicoi 16,549 .... S8
Union 13,694 .... O8
Van Buren 4,846 .... L9
Warren 32,992 .... K9
Washington 92,315 .... R8
Wayne 13,935 .... F1
Weakley 31,972 .... D8
White 20,090 .... L9
Williamson 81,021 .... H9
Wilson 67,675 .... J8

CITIES and TOWNS

Adams 587 .... G7
Adamsville 1,745 .... E10
Afton 800 .... R8
Alamo▲ 2,426 .... C9
Alcoa 6,400 .... N9
Alexandria 730 .... J8
Algood 2,399 .... K8
Allardt 609 .... M8
Allons 600 .... L8
Altamont▲ 679 .... K10
Apison 750 .... L10
Ardmore 866 .... H10
Arlington 1,541 .... B10
Armathwaite 700 .... M8
Arthur 500 .... O7
Ashland City▲ 2,552 .... G8
Athens▲ 12,054 .... M10
Atoka 659 .... B10
Atwood 1,066 .... D9
Auburntown 240 .... J9
Baileyton 309 .... R8
Banner Hill 1,717 .... R8
Bartlett 26,989 .... B10
Bath Springs 800 .... E10
Baxter 1,289 .... K8
Bean Station 500 .... P8
Beechgrove 550 .... J9
Beersheba Springs 596 .... K10
Bell Buckle 326 .... J9
Belle Meade 2,839 .... H8
Bells 1,643 .... C9
Benton▲ 992 .... M10
Berry Hill 802 .... H8
Berry's Chapel 2,703 .... H9
Bethel Springs 755 .... D10
Big Sandy 505 .... E8
Birchwood 550 .... M10
Blaine 1,326 .... O8
Bloomingdale 10,953 .... R7
Bloomington Springs 800 .... K8
Blountville▲ 2,605 .... S7
Bluff City 1,390 .... S8
Bolivar▲ 5,969 .... C10
Braden 354 .... B10
Bradford 1,154 .... D8
Braemar S8
Brentwood 16,392 .... H8
Briceville 850 .... N8
Brighton 717 .... B10
Bristol 23,421 .... S7
Brownsville▲ 10,019 .... C9
Bruceton 1,586 .... E8
Buena Vista 500 .... E9
Bulls Gap 659 .... P8
Burlison 394 .... B9
Burns 1,127 .... G8
Butler 500 .... T8
Byrdstown▲ 998 .... L7
Calhoun 552 .... M10
Camden▲ 3,643 .... E8
Carthage▲ 2,386 .... K8
Caryville 1,751 .... N8
Castalian Springs 650 .... J8
Cedar Hill 347 .... H7
Celina▲ 1,493 .... K7
Centertown 332 .... K9
Centerville▲ 3,616 .... G9
Chapel Hill 833 .... H9
Charleston 653 .... M10
Charlotte▲ 854 .... G8
Chattanooga▲ 152,466 .... K10
Chuckey 500 .... R8
Church Hill 4,834 .... R7
Clairfield 650 .... O7
Clarksburg 321 .... E9
Clarksville▲ 75,494 .... G7
Cleveland▲ 30,354 .... M10
Clifton 620 .... F10
Clinton▲ 8,972 .... N8
Coalfield 712 .... N8
Coalmont 813 .... K10
Cokercreek 500 .... N10
College Grove 580 .... H9
Collegedale 5,048 .... M10
Collierville 14,427 .... B10
Collinwood 1,014 .... F10
Colonial Heights 6,716 .... R8
Columbia▲ 28,583 .... G9
Concord 8,569 .... N9
Cookeville▲ 21,744 .... L8
Copperhill 362 .... N10
Cordova 600 .... B10
Cornersville 683 .... H10
Corryton 500 .... O8
Counce 975 .... E10
Covington▲ 7,487 .... B9
Cowan 1,738 .... K10
Crab Orchard 876 .... M9
Crockett Mills 500 .... C9
Cross Plains 1,025 .... H7
Crossville▲ 6,930 .... L9
Crump 2,028 .... E10
Cumberland City 319 .... F8
Cumberland Gap 210 .... O8
Cypress Inn 500 .... F10
Dandridge▲ 1,540 .... O8
Dayton▲ 5,671 .... L9
Decatur▲ 1,361 .... M9
Decaturville▲ 879 .... E9
Decherd 2,196 .... J10
Dickson 8,791 .... G8
Dover▲ 1,341 .... F8
Dowelltown 308 .... K8
Doyle 345 .... K9
Dresden▲ 2,488 .... D8
Drummonds 800 .... A10
Duck River 750 .... G9
Ducktown 421 .... N10
Dunlap▲ 3,731 .... L10
Dyer 2,204 .... D8
Dyersburg▲ 16,317 .... C8
Eads 550 .... B10
Eagleton Village 5,169 .... O9
Eagleville 462 .... H9
East Ridge 21,101 .... L11
Eastview 563 .... D10
Elgin 700 .... M8
Elizabethton▲ 11,931 .... S8
Elk Valley 750 .... N7
Elkton 448 .... H10
Ellendale 850 .... B10
Embreeville Junction R8
Emory Gap 500 .... M9
Englewood 1,611 .... M10
Enville 211 .... E10
Erin▲ 1,586 .... F8
Erwin▲ 5,015 .... S8
Estill Springs 1,408 .... J10
Ethridge 565 .... G10
Etowah 3,815 .... M10
Eva 500 .... E8
Fairfield 2,209 .... J9
Fairview 4,210 .... G9
Fall Branch 1,203 .... R8
Farner 750 .... N10
Fayetteville▲ 6,921 .... H10
Finger 279 .... D10
Finley 1,014 .... B8
Flintville 500 .... H10
Forest Hills 4,231 .... H8
Fort Pillow 700 .... B9
Fowlkes 700 .... C9
Franklin▲ 20,098 .... H9
Friendship 467 .... C9
Friendsville 792 .... N9
Gadsden 561 .... D9
Gainesboro▲ 1,002 .... K8
Gallatin▲ 18,794 .... H8
Gallaway 762 .... B10
Garland 194 .... B9
Gates 608 .... C9
Gatlinburg 3,417 .... O9
Germantown 32,893 .... B10
Gibson 281 .... D9
Gilt Edge 447 .... B9
Gleason 1,402 .... D8
Goodlettsville 8,177 .... H8
Gordonsville 891 .... K8
Grand Junction 365 .... C10
Grandview M9
Graysville 1,301 .... L10
Greenback 611 .... N9
Greenbrier 2,873 .... H8
Greeneville▲ 13,532 .... R8
Greenfield 2,105 .... D8
Grimsley 650 .... L8
Gruetli 1,810 .... K10
Guys 497 .... D10
Habersham 750 .... N8
Halls 2,431 .... C9
Halls Crossroads O8
Hampshire 788 .... G9
Hampton 2,236 .... S8
Harriman 7,119 .... M9
Harris 7,191 .... C8
Harrison 6,206 .... L10
Harrogate (Shawanee) 2,657 .. O8
Hartsville▲ 2,188 .... J8
Helenwood 675 .... M8
Henderson▲ 4,760 .... D10
Hendersonville 32,188 .... H8
Henning 802 .... B9
Henry 317 .... E8
Hickory Valley 159 .... C10
Hixson L10
Hohenwald▲ 3,760 .... F9
Hollow Rock 902 .... E8
Hornbeak 445 .... C8
Hornsby 313 .... D10
Humboldt 9,651 .... D9
Huntingdon▲ 4,180 .... E8
Huntland 885 .... J10
Huntsville▲ 660 .... N8
Hurricane Mills 850 .... F9
Iron City 402 .... F10
Jacksboro▲ 1,568 .... N8
Jackson▲ 48,949 .... D9
Jamestown▲ 1,862 .... M8
Jasper▲ 2,780 .... K10
Jefferson City 5,494 .... P8
Jellico 2,447 .... N7
Johnson City 49,381 .... S8
Jones 3,091 .... C9
Jonesborough▲ 2,829 .... R8
Karns 1,458 .... N9
Kenton 1,366 .... C8
Kimball 1,243 .... K10
Kimberlin Heights 500 .... O9
Kingsport 36,365 .... R7
Kingston Springs 1,529 .... G8
Kingston▲ 4,552 .... N9
Knoxville▲ 165,121 .... O9
Kodak 700 .... O9
La Follette 7,192 .... N8
La Grange 167 .... C10
La Vergne 7,499 .... H9
Laager 675 .... K10
Lafayette▲ 3,641 .... J7
Lake City 2,166 .... N8
Lakeland 1,204 .... B10
Lakesite 732 .... L10
Lakewood 2,009 .... H8
Lawrenceburg▲ 10,412 .... G10
Lebanon▲ 15,208 .... J8
Lenoir City 6,147 .... N9
Leoma 600 .... G10
Lewisburg▲ 9,879 .... H10
Lexington▲ 5,810 .... E9
Liberty 391 .... K8
Linden▲ 1,099 .... F9
Livingston▲ 3,809 .... L8
Lobelville 830 .... F9
Long Island S7
Lookout Mountain 1,901 .... L11
Loretto 1,515 .... G10
Loudon▲ 4,026 .... N9
Louisville 500 .... N9
Luttrell 812 .... O8
Lutts 740 .... F10
Lyles 500 .... G9
Lynchburg▲ 668 .... J10
Lynnville 344 .... G10
Madisonville▲ 3,033 .... N9
Malesus 600 .... D9
Manchester▲ 7,709 .... J10
Martel 500 .... N9
Martin 8,600 .... D8
Maryville▲ 19,208 .... O9
Mascot 2,138 .... O8
Mason 337 .... B10
Maury City 782 .... C9
Maynardville▲ 1,298 .... O8
McDonald 500 .... M10
McEwen 1,442 .... F8
McKenzie 5,168 .... E8
McLemoresville 280 .... D9
McMinnville▲ 11,194 .... K9
Medina 658 .... D9
Medon 137 .... D10
Memphis▲ 610,337 .... B10
Michie 677 .... E10
Middleton 536 .... D10
Midway 2,953 .... P8
Milan 7,512 .... D9
Milledgeville 279 .... E10
Milligan College 600 .... S8
Millington 17,866 .... B10
Minor Hill 372 .... G10
Mitchellville 193 .... J7
Monteagle 1,138 .... K10
Monterey 2,559 .... L8
Morley 600 .... N7
Morrison 570 .... K9
Morrison City 2,032 .... R7
Morristown▲ 21,385 .... P8
Moscow 384 .... C10
Mosheim 1,451 .... R8
Mount Carmel 4,082 .... R8
Mount Juliet 5,389 .... H8
Mount Pleasant 4,278 .... G9
Mountain City▲ 2,169 .... T8
Munford 2,326 .... B10
Murfreesboro▲ 44,922 .... J9
Murray Lake Hills L10
Nashville (cap.)▲ 488,374 .... H8
Neubert 800 .... O9
New Hope 854 .... K11
New Johnsonville 1,643 .... E8
New Market 1,086 .... O8
New Tazewell 1,864 .... O8
Newbern 2,515 .... C8
Newport▲ 7,123 .... P9
Niota 745 .... M9
Norma 118 .... N8
Normandy 118 .... J10
Norris 1,303 .... N8
Oak Hill 4,301 .... H8
Oak Ridge 27,310 .... N8
Oakdale 268 .... M9
Oakland 392 .... B10
Obion 1,241 .... C8
Oliver Springs 3,433 .... N8
Oneida 3,502 .... N7
Ooltewah 4,903 .... M10
Orebank 1,284 .... R7
Orlinda 469 .... H7
Orme 150 .... K10
Pall Mall 750 .... M7
Palmer 769 .... K10
Paris▲ 9,332 .... E8
Parrotsville 121 .... P8
Parsons 2,033 .... E9
Pegram 1,371 .... H8
Petersburg 514 .... H10
Petros 1,286 .... M8
Philadelphia 463 .... M9
Pickwick Dam 650 .... E10
Pigeon Forge 3,027 .... O9
Pikeville▲ 1,771 .... L9
Piperton 612 .... B10
Pittman Center 478 .... P9
Pleasant Hill 494 .... L9
Pleasant View 625 .... G8
Portland 5,165 .... H7
Powder Springs 600 .... O8
Powell 7,534 .... N8
Powells Crossroads 1,098 .... L10
Primm Springs 750 .... G9
Pulaski▲ 7,895 .... G10
Puryear 592 .... E8
Ramer 337 .... D10
Red Bank 12,322 .... L10
Red Boiling Springs 905 .... K7
Rheatown R8
Ridgely 1,775 .... B8
Ridgeside 400 .... L10
Ripley▲ 6,188 .... B9
Rives 344 .... C8
Roan Mountain 1,220 .... S8
Rockford 646 .... O9
Rockwood 5,348 .... M9
Rogersville▲ 4,149 .... P8
Rosemark 950 .... B10
Rossville 291 .... B10
Russellville 1,069 .... P8
Rutherford 1,303 .... C8
Rutledge▲ 903 .... P8
Saint Joseph 789 .... G10
Sale Creek 900 .... L10
Saltillo 383 .... E10
Samburg 374 .... C8
Sardis 305 .... E10
Saulsbury 106 .... C10
Saundersville H8
Savannah▲ 6,547 .... E10
Scotts Hill 594 .... E10
Selmer▲ 3,838 .... D10
Sequatchie 800 .... K10
Sevierville▲ 7,178 .... P9
Sewanee 2,128 .... K10
Seymour 7,026 .... O9
Sharon 1,047 .... D8
Shelbyville▲ 14,049 .... H10
Sherwood 900 .... K10
Signal Mountain 7,034 .... L10
Smithville▲ 3,791 .... K9
Smyrna 13,647 .... H9
Sneedville▲ 1,446 .... P7
Soddy-Daisy (Daisy-Soddy) 8,240 .... L10
Somerville▲ 2,047 .... C10
South Carthage 851 .... K8
South Cleveland 5,372 .... M10
South Clinton 1,671 .... N8
South Fulton 2,688 .... D8
South Pittsburg 3,295 .... K10
Southside 800 .... G8
Sparta▲ 4,681 .... K9
Spencer▲ 1,125 .... L9
Spring City 2,199 .... M9
Spring Hill 1,464 .... H9
Springfield▲ 11,227 .... H8
Stanton 487 .... C10
Stantonville 264 .... E10
Strawberry Plains 680 .... O8
Sullivan Gardens 2,513 .... R8
Summertown 850 .... G10
Surgoinsville 1,499 .... R8
Sweetwater 5,066 .... N9
Talbott 975 .... P8
Tazewell▲ 2,150 .... O8
Tellico Plains 657 .... N10
Ten Mile 700 .... M9
Tennessee Ridge 1,271 .... F8
Tiftona L11
Tipton 2,149 .... B10
Tiptonville▲ 2,438 .... B8
Toone 279 .... D10
Townsend 329 .... O9
Tracy City 1,556 .... K10
Treadway 712 .... P8
Trenton▲ 4,836 .... D9
Trezevant 874 .... D8
Trimble 694 .... C8
Troy 1,047 .... C8
Tullahoma 16,761 .... J10
Tusculum 1,918 .... R8
Union City▲ 10,513 .... C8
Vanleer 369 .... G8
Victoria 800 .... K10
Viola 123 .... K9
Vonore 605 .... N9
Walden 1,523 .... L10
Walterhill 1,043 .... J9
Wartburg▲ 932 .... M8
Wartrace 494 .... J9

(continued on following page)

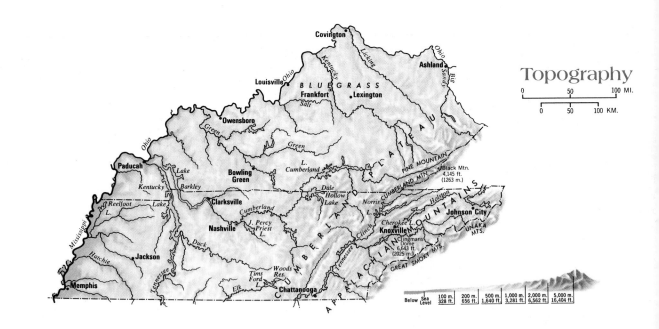

Topography

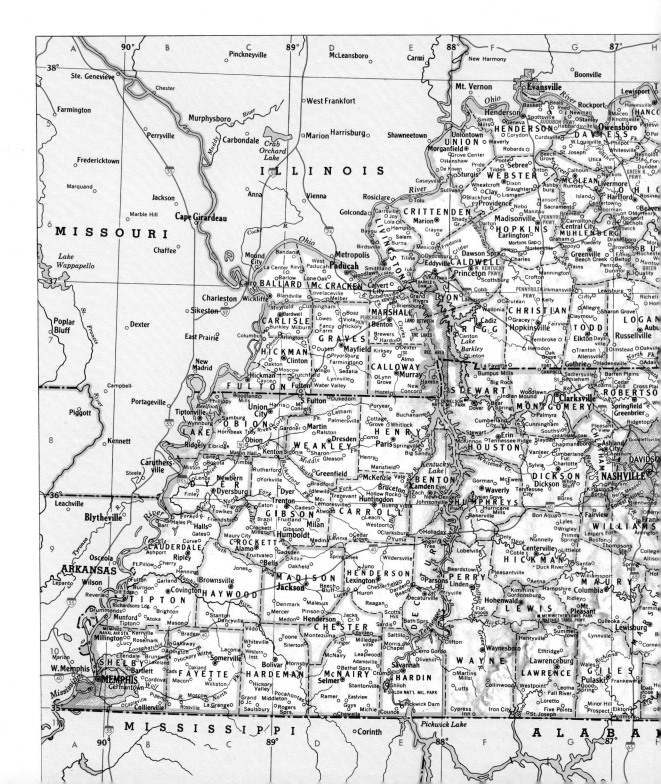

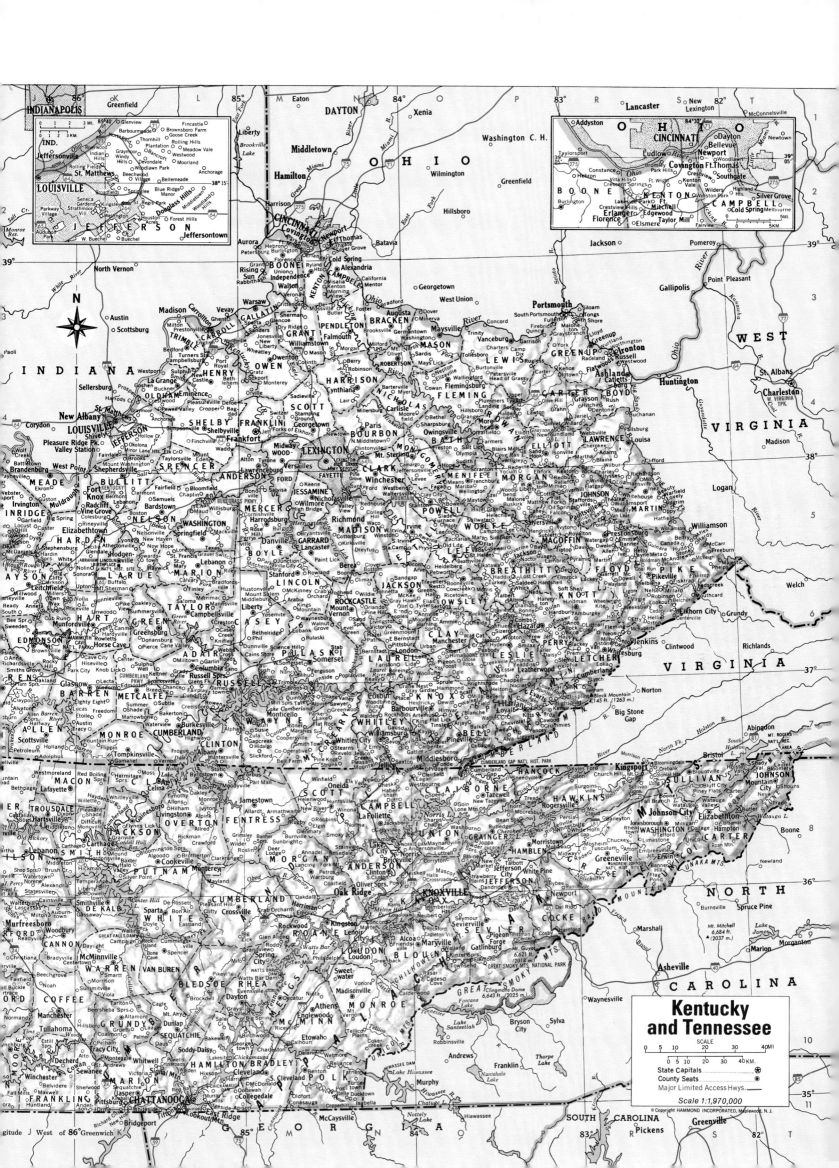

Kentucky and Tennessee

SCALE
0 5 10 20 30 40MI
0 5 10 20 30 40 KM.
State Capitals ⊛
County Seats ◉
Major Limited Access Hwys.

Scale 1:1,970,000

© Copyright HAMMOND INCORPORATED, Maplewood, N.J.

Topography

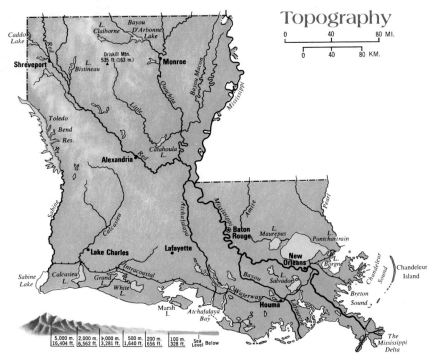

Shreveport • Monroe •

Driskill Mtn. 535 ft. (163 m.)

Alexandria •

Baton Rouge •

Lake Charles • Lafayette •

New Orleans

Houma •

Chandeleur Island

Chandeleur Sound

Breton Sound

The Mississippi Delta

Toledo Bend Res.

Sabine Lake

| 5,000 m. 16,404 ft. | 2,000 m. 6,562 ft. | 1,000 m. 3,281 ft. | 500 m. 1,640 ft. | 200 m. 656 ft. | 100 m. 328 ft. | Sea Level | Below |

Louisiana

SCALE

0 5 10 20 30 40 MI.

0 5 10 20 30 40 KM.

State Capitals .... ⊛
Parish Seats .... ◉
Canals .... ▬▬▬
Major Limited Access Hwys. ▬▬▬

Scale 1:2,000,000

PARISHES

Acadia 56,427	F6
Allen 21,390	E5
Ascension 50,068	L3
Assumption 22,084	H7
Avoyelles 41,393	G4
Beauregard 29,692	D5
Bienville 16,387	D2
Bossier 80,721	C1
Caddo 252,437	C1
Calcasieu 167,223	D6
Caldwell 10,761	F2
Cameron 9,336	D7
Catahoula 12,287	G3
Claiborne 17,095	D1
Concordia 22,981	G4
De Soto 25,727	C2
East Baton Rouge 366,191	K1
East Carroll 11,772	H1
East Feliciana 19,015	H5
Evangeline 33,343	F5
Franklin 24,141	G2
Grant 16,703	E3
Iberia 63,752	G7
Iberville 32,159	H6
Jackson 17,321	E2
Jefferson 454,592	K7
Jefferson Davis 32,168	E6
La Salle 17,004	F3
Lafayette 150,017	F6
Lafourche 82,483	K7
Lincoln 39,763	E1
Livingston 58,806	L2
Madison 15,682	H2
Morehouse 34,803	G1
Natchitoches 39,863	D3
Orleans 557,927	L6
Ouachita 139,241	F2
Plaquemines 26,049	L8
Pointe Coupee 24,045	G5
Rapides 135,282	E4
Red River 10,433	D2
Richland 22,187	G2
Sabine 25,280	C3
Saint Bernard 64,097	L7
Saint Charles 37,259	K7
Saint Helena 9,827	J5
Saint James 21,495	L3
Saint John the Baptist 31,924	M3
Saint Landry 84,128	F5
Saint Martin 40,214	G6
Saint Mary 64,253	H7
Saint Tammany 110,869	L6
Tangipahoa 80,698	K5
Tensas 8,525	H2
Terrebonne 94,393	J8
Union 21,167	F1
Vermilion 48,458	F7
Vernon 53,475	D4
Washington 44,207	L5
Webster 43,631	D1
West Baton Rouge 19,086	H6
West Carroll 12,922	G1
West Feliciana 12,186	H5
Winn 17,253	E3

CITIES and TOWNS

Abbeville▲ 11,187	F7
Abita Springs 1,296	L6
Acme 235	G4
Acy 570	L3
Addis 1,222	J2
Adeline 200	G7

Akers 150	N2
Albany 645	M1
Alberta 150	D2
Alexandria▲ 49,188	E4
Allen 175	D3
Alto 132	G2
Alton 500	L6
Amelia 2,447	H7
Amite▲ 4,301	K5
Anacoco 823	D4
Anandale 100	F4
Andrew 100	F6
Angie 235	L5
Angola 600	G5
Ansley 100	E2
Arabi 8,787	P4
Arbroth 250	H5
Arcadia▲ 3,079	E1
Archibald 425	G2
Archie 280	G3
Arcola 200	K5
Arnaudville 1,444	G6
Ashland 289	D2
Athens 278	E1
Atlanta 118	E3
Avery Island 500	G7
Bains 400	H5
Baker 13,233	K1
Baldwin 2,379	G7
Ball 3,305	F4
Bancroft 114	C5
Baptist 150	M1
Baratoria 1,160	K7
Basile 1,808	E5
Baskin 243	G2
Bastrop▲ 13,916	G1
Batchelor 500	G5
Baton Rouge (cap.)▲ 219,531	K2
Bayou Barbary 200	M2
Bayou Cane 15,876	J7
Bayou Goula 850	J3
Bayou Vista 4,733	H7
Baywood 100	K1
Beaver 350	J1
Beekman 150	G1
Bel 150	D6
Belcher 249	C1
Bell City 400	D6
Belle Alliance	H6
Belle Chasse 8,512	O4
Belle D'Eau 120	F4
Belle Rose 900	K3
Bellwood 150	D2
Belmont 350	C3
Benson 200	C3
Bentley 120	E3
Benton▲ 2,047	C1
Bernice 1,543	E1
Bertrandville 175	L7
Berwick 4,375	H7
Bethany 300	B2
Bienville 316	D2
Blanchard 1,175	C1
Bogalusa 14,280	L5
Bolinger 200	C1
Bonita 265	G1
Boothville 300	M8
Bordelonville 350	G4
Bosco 480	F2
Bossier City 52,721	C1
Boudreaux 275	J8
Bourg 2,073	J7
Boutte 2,702	N4
Boyce 1,361	E4
Braithwaite 350	P4
Branch 200	F6

Breaux Bridge 6,515	G6
Brittany 475	L3
Broussard 3,213	G6
Brusly 1,824	J2
Bryceland 103	E1
Buckeye 280	F4
Bunkie 5,044	F5
Buras (Buras-Triumph) 4,137	L8
Burnside 500	L3
Bush 275	L5
Cade 175	G6
Calcasieu 400	D6
Calhoun 350	F2
Calumet 100	H7
Calvin 207	E3
Cameron▲ 2,041	D7
Campti 929	D3
Cankton 323	F6
Carencro 5,429	G6
Carlisle 975	L7
Carville 1,108	K3
Castor 196	D2
Cecelia 550	G6
Center Point 850	F4
Centerville 600	H7
Central 546	L3
Chacahoula 150	J7
Chalmette▲ 31,860	P4
Charenton 1,584	H7
Chase 200	G2
Chataignier 281	F5
Chatham 617	F2
Chauvin 3,375	J8
Cheneyville 1,005	F4
Chopin 175	E4
Choudrant 557	F1
Church Point 4,677	F6
Clarence 577	E3
Clarks 650	F2
Clay 400	E2
Clayton 917	G3
Clear Lake 100	D3
Clinton▲ 1,904	H5
Clio 125	M2
Cloutierville 100	E3
Colfax▲ 1,696	E3
Collinston 375	G1
Columbia▲ 386	F2
Convent▲ 400	L3
Converse 436	C2
Corey 110	F2
Cotton Valley 1,130	D1
Cottonport 2,600	F5
Couchwood 150	D1
Coushatta▲ 1,845	D2
Covington▲ 7,691	K5
Cow Island 200	F7
Cravens 200	E5
Creole 175	D7
Crescent 300	G3
Creston 135	E3
Crowley▲ 13,983	F6
Crowville 400	G2
Cullen 1,642	D1
Curtis 110	C2
Cut Off 5,325	K7
Dalcour 275	P4
Danville 100	H5
Darrow 500	K3
Davant 600	L7
De Quincy 3,474	D6
De Ridder▲ 9,868	D5
Deerford 100	K1
Delcambre 1,978	G7
Delhi 3,169	H2
Delta 234	J2

Denham Springs 8,381	L2
Des Allemands 2,504	N4
Destrehan 8,031	N4
Deville 1,113	F4
Diamond 370	L7
Dixie 330	C1
Dixie Inn 347	D1
Dodson 350	E2
Donaldsonville▲ 7,949	K3
Donner 500	J7
Downsville 101	F1
Doyline 884	D1
Dry Creek 300	D5
Dry Prong 380	E3
Dubach 843	E1
Dubberly 253	D1
Dulac 3,273	J8
Dunn 225	G2
Duplessis 500	K2
Duson 1,465	F6
East Hodge 421	E2
East Point 100	D2
Easton 365	F5
Echo 525	F4
Edgard▲ 2,753	M3
Edgefield 207	D2
Edgerly 250	C6
Effie 300	F4
Elizabeth 414	E5
Elm Grove 100	C2
Elm Park 200	H5
Elmer 200	E4
Elton 1,277	E6
Empire 2,654	L8
Enterprise 375	G3
Epps 541	G1
Erath 2,428	F7
Eros 177	F2
Erwinville 790	H5
Esther 745	F7
Estherwood 745	F6
Ethel 250	H5
Eunice 11,162	F6
Eva 100	G4
Evangeline 400	F6
Evans 500	D5
Evergreen 283	F5
Extension 950	G3
Fairbanks 300	F1
Farmerville▲ 3,334	F1
Fenton 265	E6
Ferriday 4,111	G3
Fields 125	C5
Fisher 277	D3
Flatwoods 360	E4
Flora 300	D3
Fluker 400	K5
Folsom 469	K5
Forbing 100	C2
Fordoche 869	G5
Forest 263	H1
Forest Hill 408	E4
Fort Jesup 100	C3
Fort Necessity 150	G2
Franklin▲ 9,004	G7
Franklinton▲ 4,007	K5
French Settlement 829	L2
Frierson 700	C2
Frost 500	L2
Fryeburg 150	L2
Fullerton 120	D4
Galliano 4,294	K8
Galvez 200	L2
Garden City 225	H7
Garyville 3,181	M3

(continued)

AREA 47,752 sq. mi. (123,678 sq. km.)
POPULATION 4,238,216
CAPITAL Baton Rouge
LARGEST CITY New Orleans
HIGHEST POINT Driskill Mtn. 535 ft. (163 m.)
SETTLED IN 1699
ADMITTED TO UNION April 30, 1812
POPULAR NAME Pelican State
STATE FLOWER Magnolia
STATE BIRD Eastern Brown Pelican

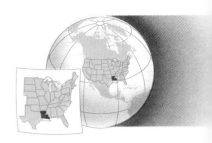

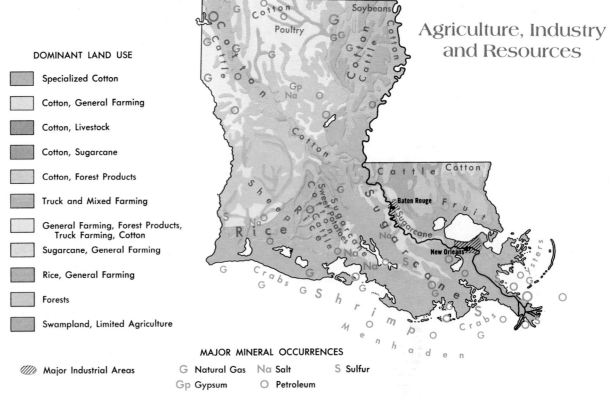

Agriculture, Industry and Resources

DOMINANT LAND USE

- Specialized Cotton
- Cotton, General Farming
- Cotton, Livestock
- Cotton, Sugarcane
- Cotton, Forest Products
- Truck and Mixed Farming
- General Farming, Forest Products, Truck Farming, Cotton
- Sugarcane, General Farming
- Rice, General Farming
- Forests
- Swampland, Limited Agriculture

Major Industrial Areas

MAJOR MINERAL OCCURRENCES

- G   Natural Gas
- Na Salt
- S   Sulfur
- Gp Gypsum
- O   Petroleum

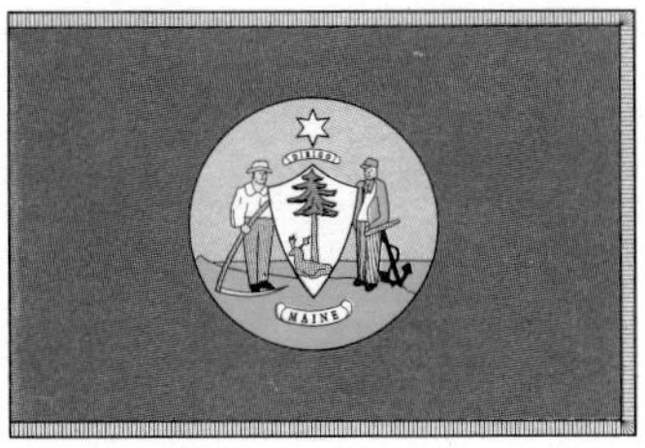

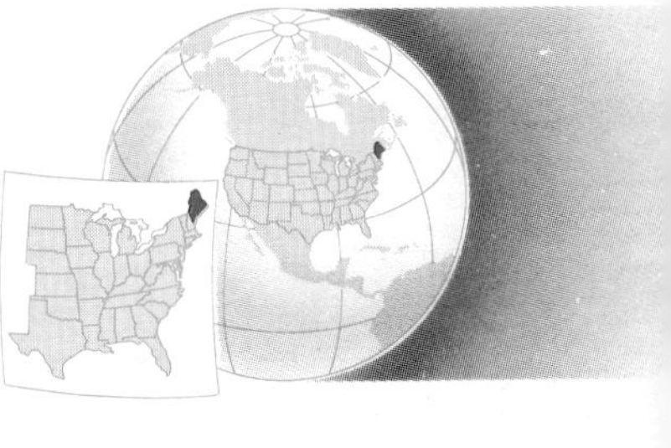

AREA 33,265 sq. mi. (86,156 sq. km.)
POPULATION 1,233,223
CAPITAL Augusta
LARGEST CITY Portland
HIGHEST POINT Katahdin 5,268 ft. (1606 m.)
SETTLED IN 1624
ADMITTED TO UNION March 15, 1820
POPULAR NAME Pine Tree State
STATE FLOWER White Pine Cone & Tassel
STATE BIRD Chickadee

COUNTIES

Androscoggin 105,259 C7
Aroostook 86,936 F2
Cumberland 243,135 C8
Franklin 29,008 B5
Hancock 46,948 G6
Kennebec 115,904 D7
Knox 36,310 E7
Lincoln 30,357 D7
Oxford 52,602 B7
Penobscot 146,601 F5
Piscataquis 18,653 E4
Sagadahoc 33,535 D7
Somerset 49,767 C4
Waldo 33,018 E6
Washington 35,308 H6
York 164,587 B9

CITIES and TOWNS

Abbot Village• 576 D5
Acton 850 B8
Acton• 1,727 B8
Addison 350 H6
Addison• 1,114 H6
Albion• 1,736 E6
Alexander• 478 H5
Alfred 1,890 B9
Alfred• 2,238 B9
Allagash• 359 F1
Alna• 571 D7
Alton• 771 F5
Amherst• 226 G6
Andover 350 B6
Andover• 953 B6
Anson 950 D6
Anson• 2,382 D6
Appleton• 1,069 E7
Argyle 202 F5
Ashland 750 G2
Ashland• 1,542 G2
Athens 300 D6
Athens• 897 D6
Atkinson• 332 E5
Auburn▲ 24,309 C7
Augusta (cap.)▲ 21,325 D7
Aurora• 82 G6
Bailey Island 500 D8
Bancroft H4
Bancroft• 66 H4
Bangor▲ 33,181 F6
Bar Harbor 2,685 G7
Bar Harbor• 2,768 G7
Bar Mills 800 C8
Baring 235 J5
Baring• 275 J5
Bass Harbor 450 G7
Bath▲ 9,799 D8
Bayside F7
Beals• 667 H7
Beddington• 43 H6
Belfast▲ 6,355 F7
Belgrade 950 D7
Belgrade• 2,375 D7
Belgrade Lakes 700 D6
Belmont• 652 E7
Benedicta• 225 G4
Benton• 2,312 D6
Berwick 2,378 B9
Berwick• 5,995 B9
Bethel 750 B7
Bethel• 2,329 B7
Biddeford 20,710 B9
Biddeford Pool 500 C9
Bingham 1,074 D5
Bingham• 1,071 D5
Birch Harbor 300 H7
Blaine-Mars Hill 1,921 H2
Blaine• 784 H2
Blanchard 78 D5
Blue Hill 850 F7
Blue Hill• 1,941 F7
Bolsters Mills 150 B7
Boothbay 200 D8
Boothbay• 2,648 D8
Boothbay Harbor 1,267 D8
Bowdoinham• 2,192 D7
Bowerbank• 72 E5
Bradford 150 F5
Bradford• 1,103 F5
Bradley• 1,136 F6
Brewer 9,021 F6
Bridgewater• 647 H3
Bridgton 1,639 B7
Bridgton• 2,195 B7
Brighton• 94 D5
Bristol 450 D8
Bristol• 2,326 D8
Brooklin• 785 F7
Brooks 900 E6
Brooksville• 760 F7
Brookton 175 H4
Brownfield 300 B8
Brownfield• 1,034 B8
Brownville 600 E5
Brownville• 1,506 E5
Brownville Junction 950 E5
Brunswick 10,990 C8
Brunswick• 14,683 C8
Bryant Pond 600 B7
Buckfield• 1,566 C7
Bucks Harbor 300 J6
Bucksport 2,853 F6
Bucksport• 2,989 F6
Burlington• 360 G5
Burnham• 961 E6
Buxton• 6,494 C8
Byron• 111 B6
Calais 3,963 J5
Cambridge• 490 E5
Camden 3,743 F7
Camden• 4,022 F7
Canaan• 1,636 D6
Canton• 951 C7
Cape Neddick 2,193 B9
Cape Porpoise 500 C9
Caratunk 98 C5
Cardville 223 F5
Caribou 9,415 G2
Carmel• 1,906 E6
Carrabassett Valley• 325 C5
Carroll• 185 G5
Carthage• 458 C6
Cary• 235 H4
Casco 400 B7
Casco• 3,018 B7
Castine• 1,161 F7
Centerville• 30 H6
Chapman• 422 G2
Charleston• 1,187 F5
Charlotte• 271 J5
Chebeague Island 900 C8
Chelsea• 2,497 D7
Cherryfield• 1,183 H6
Chester• 442 F5
Chesterville• 1,012 C6
China 2,918 E7
China• 3,713 E7
Chisholm 1,653 C7
Clifton• 607 G6
Clinton 1,305 D6
Clinton• 1,485 D6
Columbia• 437 H6
Columbia Falls• 552 H6
Cooper• 124 H6
Coopers Mills 200 E7
Corea 375 H7
Corinna• 2,196 E6
Cornish• 1,178 B8
Cornville• 1,008 D6
Costigan 200 F5
Cranberry Isles• 189 G7
Crawford• 89 H5
Crescent Lake 325 C7
Criehaven F8
Crouseville 450 G2
Crystal• 303 G4
Cumberland Center 2,015 C8
Cumberland Center• 1,890 C8
Cundys Harbor 150 D8
Cushing• 988 E7
Cutler 400 J6
Cutler• 779 J6
Damariscotta• 1,811 E7
Damariscotta-Newcastle 1,567 E7
Danforth 650 H4
Danforth• 710 H4
Deblois• 73 H6
Dedham• 1,229 F6
Deer Isle 600 F7
Deer Isle• 1,829 F7
Denmark• 855 B8
Dennysville• 355 J6
Derby 300 E5
Detroit• 751 E6
Dexter 3,118 E5
Dexter• 2,650 E5
Dixfield 1,725 C6
Dixfield• 1,300 C6
Dixmont• 1,007 E6
Dover-Foxcroft▲ 2,974 E5
Dover-Foxcroft• 3,077 E5
Dresden• 1,332 D7
Dry Mills 700 C8
Dryden 675 C6
Dyer Brook• 243 G3
Eagle Lake 675 F1
Eagle Lake• 942 F1
East Andover 250 B6
East Baldwin 175 B8
East Blue Hill 150 G7
East Boothbay 800 D8
East Corinth 525 F5
East Dixfield 250 C6
East Eddington 200 F6
East Hiram 198 B8
East Holden 600 F6
East Lebanon 950 B9
East Limington 200 B8
East Livermore 500 C7
East Machias 850 J6
East Machias• 1,218 J6
East Madison 400 D6
East Millinocket 2,361 F4
East Millinocket• 2,075 F4
East Parsonfield 400 B8
East Peru 200 C7
East Poland 200 C7
East Stoneham 300 B7
East Sullivan 496 G6
East Vassalboro 300 D7
East Waterboro 365 B8
East Wilton 650 C6
Easton• 1,291 H2
Eastport 1,965 K6
Eddington 250 F6
Eddington• 1,947 F6
Edgecomb• 993 D8
Edmunds 430 J6
Eliot• 5,329 B9
Ellsworth▲ 5,975 F6
Enfield 150 F5
Enfield• 1,476 F5
Etna• 977 E6
Eustis• 616 B5
Exeter• 937 E6
Fairbanks 400 C6
Fairfield 3,169 D6
Fairfield Center 975 D6
Fairfield• 2,794 D6
Falmouth 1,655 C8
Falmouth• 7,610 C8
Farmingdale 2,014 D7
Farmingdale• 2,070 D7
Farmington▲ 3,583 C6
Farmington• 4,197 C6
Farmington Falls 500 C6
Fayette• 855 C7
Five Islands 225 D8
Fort Fairfield 2,282 H2
Fort Fairfield• 1,729 H2
Fort Kent 2,375 F1
Fort Kent• 2,123 F1
Fort Kent Mills 200 F1
Foxcroft 2,974 E5
Frankfort• 1,020 F6
Franklin 350 G6
Franklin• 1,141 G6
Freedom• 593 E7
Freeport 1,906 C8
Freeport• 1,829 C8
Frenchboro• 44 G7
Frenchville 980 G1
Frenchville• 1,338 G1
Friendship 700 E7
Friendship• 1,099 E7
Fryeburg 1,644 A7
Fryeburg• 1,580 A7
Gardiner• 6,746 D7
Garland 300 E5
Garland• 1,064 E5
Georgetown 190 D8
Georgetown• 914 D8
Gilead• 204 B7
Glen Cove 250 E7
Glenburn• 3,198 F6
Goodwins Mills 340 B8
Goose Rocks Beach 200 C9
Gorham 4,052 C8
Gorham• 3,618 C8
Gouldsboro 498 H7
Gouldsboro• 1,986 H7
Grand Isle 600 G1
Grand Isle• 558 G1
Grand Lake Stream• 174 H5
Gray 525 C8
Gray• 5,904 C8
Great Pond• 59 G6
Greene• 3,661 C7
Greenville• 1,839 D5
Greenville 1,601 D5
Greenville Junction 650 D5
Guilford 1,235 E5
Guilford• 1,082 E5
Hallowell 2,534 D7
Hamlin• 204 H1
Hampden 3,538 F6
Hampden• 3,895 F6
Hampden Highlands 950 F6
Hancock• 1,757 G6
Hanover• 272 B7
Harmony 450 D6
Harmony• 838 D6
Harpswell• 5,012 D8
Harrington• 893 H6
Harrison• 1,951 B7
Hartford• 722 C7
Hartland 1,041 D6
Hartland• 1,038 D6
Haynesville• 243 G4
Hebron• 878 C7
Hermon• 3,755 F6
Highland Lake 600 C8
Hiram 175 B8
Hiram• 1,260 B8
Hodgdon• 1,257 H3
Hollis Center• 2,892 B8
Hope 175 E7
Hope• 1,017 E7
Houlton▲ 5,730 H3
Houlton• 5,627 H3
Howland 1,502 F5
Howland• 1,304 F5
Hudson• 1,048 F5
Hulls Cove 200 G7
Island Falls• 897 G3
Isle Au Haut• 57 F7
Islesboro 200 F7
Islesboro• 579 F7
Jackman 700 C4
Jackman• 920 C4
Jacksonville 200 J6
Jay 850 C7
Jay• 5,080 C7
Jefferson• 2,111 D7
Jonesboro• 585 J6
Jonesport 1,050 H6
Jonesport• 1,525 H6
Keegan 450 G1
Kenduskeag• 1,234 E6
Kennebunk 3,294 B9
Kennebunk• 4,206 B9
Kennebunk Beach 200 C9
Kennebunkport 1,685 C9
Kennebunkport• 1,100 C9
Kents Hill 300 D7
Kezar Falls 680 B8
Kingfield• 1,114 C6
Kingman 246 G4
Kingsbury• 13 D5
Kittery 5,465 B9
Kittery• 5,151 B9
Kittery Point 1,093 B9
Knox• 681 E6
Lagrange 250 F5
Lagrange• 509 F5
Lake View• 23 F5
Lamoine• 1,311 G7
Lee• 832 G5
Leeds• 1,669 C7
Levant• 1,627 F6
Lewiston 39,757 C7
Liberty 200 E7
Liberty• 790 E7
Lille 300 G1
Limerick• 1,688 B8
Limestone 1,334 H2
Limestone• 1,245 H2
Limington• 2,796 B8
Lincoln 3,524 G5
Lincoln• 3,399 G5
Lincoln Center 325 G5
Lincolnville 800 E7
Lincolnville• 1,809 E7
Lincolnville Center 200 E7
Linneus• 810 H3
Lisbon• 9,457 C7
Lisbon Falls 4,674 D7
Lisbon-Lisbon Center 1,865 C7
Litchfield• 2,650 D7
Little Deer Isle 475 F7
Little Falls-South Windham 1,715 C8
Littleton• 956 H3
Livermore 280 C7
Livermore• 1,950 C7
Livermore Falls 2,441 C7
Livermore Falls• 1,935 C7
Locke Mills 600 B7
Lovell 180 B7
Lovell• 888 B7
Lowell• 267 F5
Lubec 900 K6
Lubec• 1,853 K6
Ludlow• 430 G3
Machias▲ 1,277 J6
Machias• 1,773 J6
Machiasport 374 H6
Machiasport• 1,166 H6
Macwahoc• 114 G4
Madawaska 4,165 G1
Madawaska• 3,653 G1
Madison 2,788 D6
Madison• 2,956 D6
Madrid• 178 B6
Manchester• 2,099 D7
Mapleton• 1,853 G2
Mars Hill• 1,760 H2
Mars Hill-Blaine 1,717 H2
Masardis• 305 G3

(continued on following page)

Agriculture, Industry and Resources

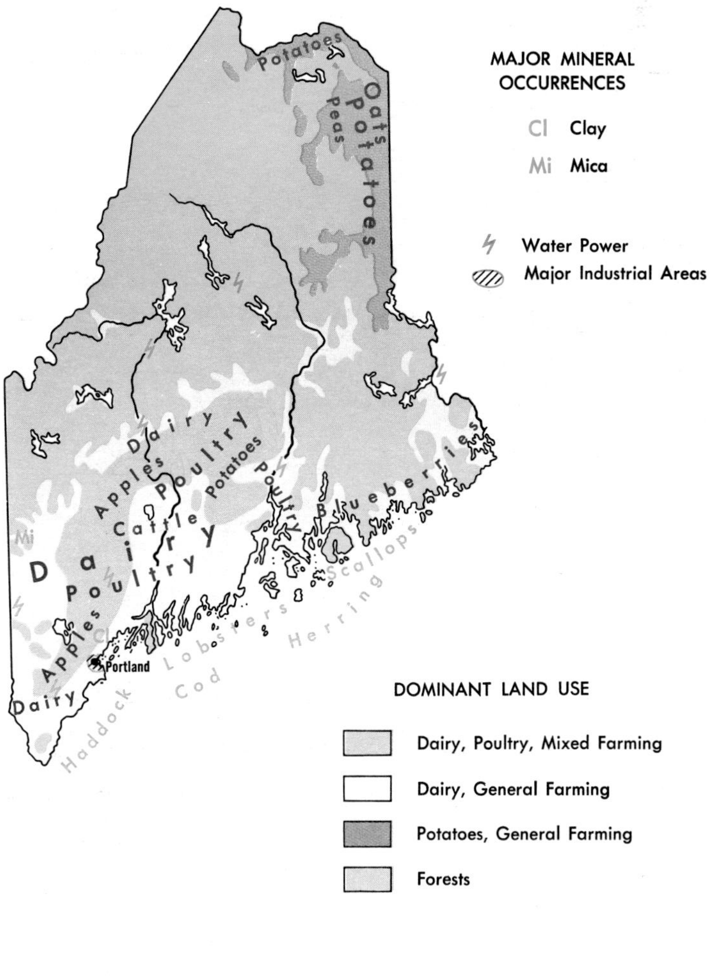
Potatoes
Peas
Oats
Potatoes
Dairy
Poultry
Apples
Cattle
Potatoes
Poultry
Blueberries
Scallops
Lobsters
Herring
Cod
Haddock
Apples
Poultry
Dairy
Apples
Dairy
Portland
Mi
Cl
MAJOR MINERAL OCCURRENCES
Cl Clay
Mi Mica
Water Power
Major Industrial Areas
DOMINANT LAND USE
Dairy, Poultry, Mixed Farming
Dairy, General Farming
Potatoes, General Farming
Forests

Matinicus 66 F8
Mattawamkeag• 830 G5
Mechanic Falls 2,198 C7
Mechanic Falls• 2,388 C7
Meddybemps• 133 J5
Medford 194 F5
Medway• 1,922 G4
Mercer• 593 D6
Mexico 3,207 B6
Mexico• 2,302 B6
Milbridge• 1,305 H6
Milford 1,688 F6
Milford• 2,228 F6
Millinocket• 6,922 F4
Milo 2,255 F5
Milo• 2,129 F5
Minot 250 C7
Minot• 1,664 C7
Minturn 150 G7
Monhegan• 88 E8
Monmouth 500 D7
Monmouth• 3,353 C7
Monroe• 802 E6
Monson• 744 E5
Monticello• 872 H3
Montville• 877 E7
Moody 500 B9
Moose River• 233 C4
Morrill• 644 E7
Mount Desert 150 G7
Mount Desert• 1,899 G7
Mount Vernon• 1,362 D7
Naples• 2,860 B8
New Gloucester 400 C8
New Gloucester• 3,916 C8
New Harbor 850 E8
New Limerick• 524 G3
New Portland 300 C6
New Portland• 789 C6
New Sharon• 1,175 C6
New Sweden 175 G2
New Sweden• 715 G2
New Vineyard• 661 C6
Newburgh• 1,317 F6
Newcastle• 1,538 E7
Newcastle-Damariscotta
1,411 E7
Newfield 200 B8
Newfield• 1,042 B8
Newport 1,748 E6
Newport• 1,843 E6
Newry• 316 B6
Nobleboro• 1,455 D7
Norridgewock 1,318 D6
Norridgewock• 1,496 D6
North Anson 950 D6
North Belgrade 300 D7
North Berwick 1,436 B9
North Berwick• 1,568 B9
North Bridgton 300 B7
North Cutler 153 J6
North Fryeburg 250 B7
North Haven 400 F7
North Haven• 332 F7
North Jay 800 C6
North Limington 400 B8
North Livermore 250 C7
North Lubec 250 J6
North New Portland 500 C6
North Penobscot 403 F7
North Raymond 225 C8
North Turner 350 C7
North Vassalboro 950 D7
North Waldoboro 250 E7
North Waterboro 200 B8
North Waterford 390 B7
North Wayne 175 C7
North Whitefield 300 D7
North Windham 4,077 C8
North Yarmouth 500 C8
North Yarmouth• 2,429 C8
Northeast Harbor 800 G7
Northfield• 99 H6
Northport• 1,201 E7
Norway 2,653 B7
Norway• 3,023 B7
Oakfield• 846 G3
Oakland 3,387 D6
Oakland• 3,510 D6
Ocean Park 200 C9
Ogunquit 974 B9
Olamon 150 F5
Old Orchard Beach 6,023 C9
Old Orchard Beach• 7,789 C9
Old Town 8,317 F6
Oquossoc 150 B6
Orient• 157 H4
Orland 200 F6
Orland• 1,805 F6
Orono 9,891 F6
Orono• 9,789 F6
Orrington 250 F6
Orrington• 3,309 F6
Orrs Island 600 D8
Otisfield• 1,136 B7
Otter Creek 260 G7
Owls Head• 1,574 F7
Oxbow• 69 G3
Oxford 550 B7
Oxford• 1,284 B7
Palermo• 1,021 E7
Palmyra• 1,867 E6
Paris• 4,492 B7
Parkman• 790 D5
Passadumkeag• 428 F5
Patten 1,057 F4
Patten• 1,256 F4
Pejepscot 200 D8
Pemaquid 200 E8
Pembroke 300 J6
Pembroke• 852 J6
Penobscot 150 F7
Penobscot• 1,131 F7
Perham• 395 G2
Perry• 758 J6
Peru• 1,541 C6
Phillips• 1,148 C6
Phippsburg 1,527 D8
Phippsburg• 1,815 D8
Pine Point 650 C8
Pittsfield 3,117 E6
Pittsfield• 3,222 E6
Pittston• 2,444 D7
Plymouth• 1,152 E6
Poland 500 C7
Poland• 4,342 C7
Port Clyde 400 E8
Portage• 562 G2
Porter 225 B8
Porter• 1,301 B8
Portland▲ 64,358 C8
Pownal• 1,262 C8
Prentiss• 245 G5
Presque Isle 10,550 H2
Princeton• 973 H5
Prospect• 542 F6
Prospect Harbor 445 H7
Randolph• 1,949 D7
Rangeley 900 B6
Rangeley• 103 B6
Raymond 550 B8
Raymond• 3,311 B8
Readfield 300 D7
Readfield• 2,033 D7
Red Beach 210 J5
Richmond 1,578 D7
Richmond• 1,775 D7
Richmond Corner 200 D7
Ripley• 445 E5
Robbinston 200 J5
Robbinston• 495 J5
Robinsons 160 H3
Rockland▲ 7,972 E7
Rockport 875 E7
Rockport• 2,854 E7
Rockville 250 E7
Rockwood 265 D4
Rome• 758 D6
Roque Bluffs• 234 H6
Round Pond 400 E8
Roxbury• 437 B6
Rumford 6,256 B6
Rumford• 5,419 B6
Rumford Center 325 B7
Rumford Point 320 B6
Sabattus 1,234 C7
Sabattus• 3,696 C7
Saco 15,181 C8
Saint Agatha• 1,035 G1
Saint Albans• 1,400 E6
Saint David 915 G1
Saint Francis• 839 E1
Saint George 700 E7
Saint George• 1,948 E7
Saint John• 322 F1
Sandy Point 350 F7
Sanford 10,268 B9
Sanford• 10,296 B9
Sangerville• 1,398 E5
Scarborough 2,280 C8
Scarborough• 2,586 C8
Seal Cove 215 G7
Seal Harbor 500 G7
Searsmont 400 E7
Searsmont• 938 E7
Searsport 1,348 F7
Searsport• 1,151 F7
Sebago Lake 800 B8
Sebec• 554 E5
Seboeis• 40 F5
Sedgwick• 905 F7
Shapleigh• 1,911 B8
Shawmut 500 D6
Sheepscott 150 D7
Sheridan 300 F2
Sherman 1,021 G4
Sherman• 1,027 G4
Sherman Mills 600 G4
Sherman Station 650 F4
Shirley Mills 242 D5
Shirley Mills• 208 D5
Sidney• 2,593 D7
Sinclair• 264 G1
Skowhegan▲ 6,517 D6
Skowhegan• 6,990 D6
Smithfield• 865 D6
Smyrna Mills• 354 G3
Soldier Pond 500 F1
Solon• 916 D6
Somerville• 458 D7
Somesville (Mount Desert)
150 D7
Sorrento• 295 G7
South Berwick 2,120 B9
South Berwick• 5,877 B9
South Bridgton 373 B8
South Bristol• 825 D8
South Casco 750 B8
South China 225 D7
South Eliot 3,112 B9
South Harpswell 650 C8
South Hiram 350 B8
South Hope 200 E7
South La Grange 150 F5
South Lebanon 200 A9
South Lincoln 150 F5
South Monmouth 400 D7
South Orrington 400 F6
South Paris▲ 2,320 C7
South Penobscot 150 F7
South Portland 23,163 C8
South Sanford 3,929 B9
South Thomaston• 1,227 E7
South Waldoboro 300 E7
South Waterford 300 B7
South Windham (Little Falls-
South Windham) C8
Southport 400 D8
Southport• 645 D8
Southwest Harbor 1,052 G7
Southwest Harbor• 1,952 G7
Springfield• 406 G5
Springvale 3,542 B9
Stacyville 155 F4
Stacyville• 480 F4
Standish 700 B8
Standish• 7,678 B8
Starks• 508 D6
Steep Falls 500 B8
Stetson• 847 E6
Steuben 190 H6
Steuben• 1,084 H6
Stillwater 700 F6
Stockholm• 286 G1
Stockton Springs 500 F7
Stockton Springs• 1,383 F7
Stonington• 1,252 F7
Stow• 283 A7
Stratton 600 B5
Strong• 1,217 C6
Sullivan• 1,118 G6
Sumner• 761 C7
Sunset 165 F7
Surry• 1,004 F7
Swans Island• 348 G7
Swanville• 1,130 E6
Sweden• 222 B7
Temple• 560 C6
Tenants Harbor 900 E8
Thomaston 2,348 E7
Thomaston• 2,445 E7
Thorndike• 702 E6
Topsfield• 235 H5
Topsham 4,657 D8
Topsham• 6,147 D8
Tremont 175 G7
Tremont• 1,324 G7
Trenton• 1,060 G7
Trevett 400 D8
Troy• 802 E6
Turner 400 C7
Turner• 4,315 C7
Union 300 E7
Union• 1,989 E7
Unity• 36 E6
Upper Frenchville 405 G1
Upton• 70 B6
Van Buren 3,282 G1
Van Buren• 2,759 G1
Vanceboro• 201 J4
Vassalboro• 3,679 D7
Veazie• 1,633 F6
Vienna• 417 D6
Vinalhaven• 1,072 F7
Waite• 119 H5
Waldo• 626 E7
Waldoboro 1,195 E7
Waldoboro• 1,420 E7
Walnut Hill 400 C8
Waltham• 276 G6
Warren 770 E7
Warren• 3,192 E7
Washburn 1,221 G2
Washburn• 1,880 G2
Washington• 1,185 E7
Waterboro 700 B8
Waterboro• 4,510 B8
Waterford• 1,299 B7
Waterville 17,173 D6
Wayne 175 D7
Wayne• 1,029 D7
Weeks Mills 235 E7
Weld• 430 C6
Wellington• 270 D5
Wells 950 B9
Wells• 7,778 B9
Wells Beach 600 B9
Wesley• 146 H6
West Baldwin 198 B8
West Bath• 1,716 D8
West Bethel 160 B7
West Brooksville 156 F7
West Buxton 185 B8
West Enfield 609 F5
West Farmington 700 C6
West Forks• 63 D5
West Franklin 350 G6
West Gouldsboro 225 G7
West Jonesport 400 H6
West Kennebunk 750 B9
West Lubec 275 J6
West Minot 400 C7
West Newfield 300 B8
West Paris• 1,514 B7
West Peru 700 C7
West Poland 250 C7
West Rockport 350 E7
West Scarborough 500 C8
West Tremont 250 G7
Westbrook 16,121 C8
Westfield• 589 G2
Weston• 207 H4
Whitefield 550 D7
Whitefield• 1,931 D7
Whiting• 407 J6
Whitneyville• 241 H6
Willimantic• 170 E5
Wilton 4,382 C6
Wilton• 2,453 C6
Windsor• 1,895 D7
Winn 250 G5
Winn• 479 G5
Winslow 5,903 D6
Winslow• 5,436 D6
Winter Harbor• 1,157 G7
Winterport 1,126 F6
Winterport• 1,274 F6
Winterville• 217 F2
Winthrop 3,264 C7
Winthrop• 2,819 C7
Wiscasset 975 D7
Wiscasset• 1,233 D7
Woodland• 1,287 H5
Woolwich• 2,570 D8
Wyman Dam 300 D5
Yarmouth 2,981 C8
Yarmouth• 3,338 C8
York 4,530 B9
York Beach 900 B9
York Harbor 2,555 B9
York• 9,818 B9

OTHER FEATURES

Abraham (mt.) C5
Acadia Nat'l Park G7
Allagash (lake) D3
Allagash (riv.) E2
Androscoggin (riv.) C7
Aroostook (riv.) G2
Attean (pond) C4
Baker (lake) D3
Baskahegan (lake) H5
Bear (riv.) B6
Big (brook) E2
Big (lake) H5
Big Black (riv.) D2
Bigelow (bight) C9
Big Spencer (mt.) E4
Black (pond) D3
Blue (mt.) C6
Blue Hill (bay) G7
Bog (lake) H6
Brassua (lake) D4
Casco (bay) C8
Cathance (lake) J6
Caucomgomoc (lake) D3
Center (pond) E5
Chamberlain (lake) E3
Chemquasabamticook (lake) D3
Chesuncook (lake) E3
Chiputneticook (lakes) H4
Clayton (lake) D2
Clifford (lake) H5
Cold Stream (pond) G5
Crawford (lake) H5
Cross (isl.) J6
Cross (lake) G1
Cupsuptic (riv.) B5
Dead (riv.) C5
Deer (isl.) F7
Duck (isls.) G7
Eagle (lake) E3
Eagle (lake) F1
East Machias (riv.) H6
East Musquash (lake) H5
Elizabeth (cape) C8
Ellis (pond) B6
Ellis (riv.) B6
Embden (pond) D6
Endless (lake) F5
Englishman (bay) J6
Eskutassis (pond) G5
Fifth (lake) H5
Fish (riv.) F2
Fish River (lake) F2
Flagstaff (lake) C5
Fourth (lake) H5
Frenchman (bay) G7
Gardner (lake) J6
Georges (isls.) E8
Graham (lake) G6
Grand (lake) H4
Grand Falls (lake) H5
Grand Lake Seboeis (lake) F3
Grand Manan (chan.) K6
Great Moose (lake) D6
Great Wass (isl.) J7
Green (isl.) F8
Harrington (lake) E4
Haut (isl.) G7
Indian (pond) D4
Islesboro (isl.) F7
Jo-Mary (lakes) E4
Katahdin (mt.) F4
Kennebec (riv.) D7
Kezar (lake) B7
Kezar (pond) B7
Kingsbury (pond) D5
Little Black (riv.) E1
Little Madawaska (riv.) G2
Lobster (lake) E4
Long (lake) B7
Long (lake) E2
Long (lake) G1
Long (pond) C4
Long (pond) D6
Long (pond) E5
Long Falls (dam) C5
Longfellow (mts.) B6
Loon (lake) D3
Loring A.F.B. 7,829 H2
Lower Roach (pond) E4
Lower Sysladobsis (lake) G5
Machias (bay) J6
Machias (riv.) F2
Machias (riv.) H6
Machias Seal (isl.) J7
Madagascal (pond) G5
Marshall (isl.) G7
Matinicus Rock (isl.) F8
Mattamiscontis (lake) F4
Mattawamkeag (lake) G4
Mattawamkeag (riv.) G4
Meddybemps (lake) J5
Metinic (isl.) E8
Millinocket (lake) F3
Millinocket (lake) F4
Molunkus (lake) G4
Monhegan (isl.) E8
Moose (pond) B7
Moose (riv.) D4
Moosehead (lake) D4
Mooseleuk (stream) F2
Mooselookmeguntic (lake) B6
Mopang (lake) H6
Mount Desert (isl.) G7
Mount Desert Rock (isl.) G8
Moxie (lake) D5
Munsungan (lake) E3
Muscongus (bay) E8
Musquacook (lakes) E2
Nahmakanta (lake) E4
Nicatous (lake) G5
Nollesemic (lake) F4
Old (stream) H6
Onawa (lake) E5
Parlin (pond) C5
Parmachenee (lake) B5
Passamaquoddy (bay) J5
Passamaquoddy Ind. Res. J6
Pemadumcook (lake) E4
Penobscot (bay) F7
Penobscot (lake) C4
Penobscot (riv.) F5
Penobscot Ind. Res. F6
Pierce (pond) C5
Piscataqua (riv.) B9
Piscataquis (riv.) E5
Pleasant (lake) E3
Pleasant (lake) G3
Pleasant (lake) H5
Pleasant (riv.) H6
Pocomoonshine (lake) H5
Portage (lake) F2
Presque Isle A.F.B. G2
Priestly (lake) E2
Pushaw (lake) F6
Ragged (isl.) F8
Ragged (lake) E4
Rainbow (lake) E4
Rangeley (lake) B6
Richardson (lakes) B6
Rocky (lake) J6
Round (pond) E2
Rowe (lake) F2
Saco (riv.) B8
Saint Croix (riv.) J5
Saint Croix Island Nat'l Mon. J5
Saint Francis (riv.) E1
Saint Froid (lake) F2
Saint John (pond) D3
Saint John (riv.) G1
Salmon Falls (riv.) B9
Sandy (riv.) C6
Schoodic (lake) F5
Scraggly (lake) F3
Scraggly (lake) H5
Seal (isl.) F8
Sebago (lake) B8
Sebasticook (lake) E6
Seboeis (lake) F5
Seboeis (riv.) F3
Seboomook (lake) D4
Shallow (lake) E3
Small (cape) D8
Sourdnahunk (lake) F3
Spencer (pond) D4
Spencer (stream) C5
Spider (lake) E3
Squa Pan (lake) G2
Square (lake) G1
Sunday (riv.) B6
Swift (riv.) B6
Sysladobsis, Lower (lake) G5
Third (lake) H5
Twin (lakes) F4
Umbagog (lake) A6
Umcalcus (lake) G3
Umsaskis (lake) E2
Union, West Branch (riv.) G6
Vinalhaven (isl.) F7
Wassataquoik (stream) F4
Webb (lake) C6
Webster (brook) E3
West Grand (lake) H5
West Musquash (lake) H5
West Quoddy (head) K6
Wilson (ponds) E5
Winnecook (lake) E6
Wooden Ball (isl.) F8
Wyman (lake) C5
Wytopitlock (lake) G4

▲County seat.
•Population of town or township.

Topography

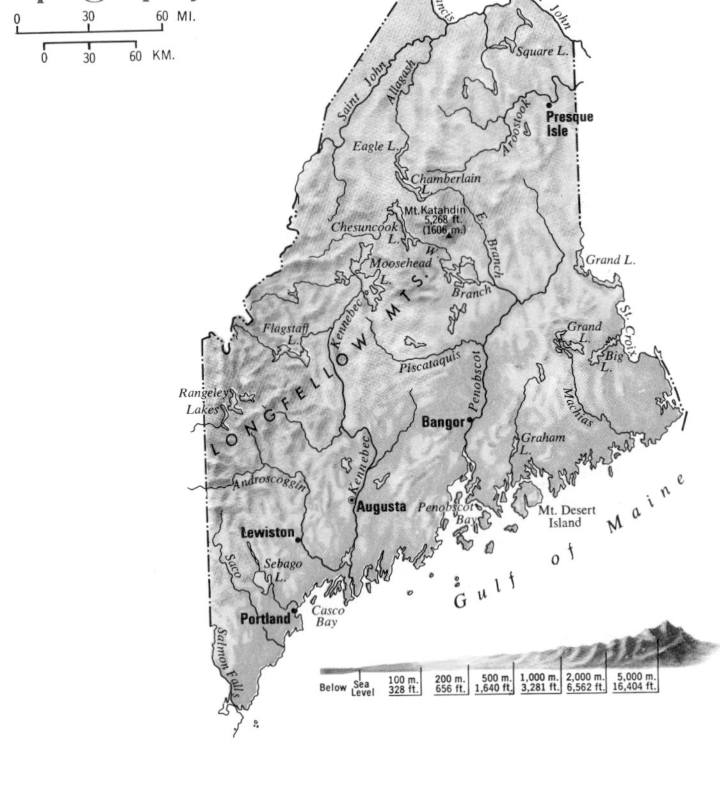

0 30 60 MI.
0 30 60 KM.
St. Francis
Saint John
Square L.
Allagash
Saint John
Aroostook
Presque Isle
Eagle L.
Chamberlain
Mt. Katahdin 5,268 ft. (1606 m.)
Chesuncook L.
Moosehead L.
E. Branch
W. Branch
Grand L.
Flagstaff L.
Kennebec
LONGFELLOW MTS.
Piscataquis
Penobscot
Grand L.
Big L.
St. Croix
Rangeley Lakes
Machias
Bangor
Graham L.
Androscoggin
Kennebec
Augusta
Penobscot Bay
Mt. Desert Island
Gulf of Maine
Lewiston
Saco
Sebago L.
Portland
Casco Bay
Salmon Falls
Below Sea Level
100 m. 328 ft.
200 m. 656 ft.
500 m. 1,640 ft.
1,000 m. 3,281 ft.
2,000 m. 6,562 ft.
5,000 m. 16,404 ft.

Maine

SCALE

0 5 10 20 30 40 MI.

0 5 10 20 30 40 KM.

State Capitals .... ⊛

County Seats .... ⊙

Major Limited Access Hwys. ....

Scale 1:1,680,000

® Copyright HAMMOND INCORPORATED, Maplewood, N.J.

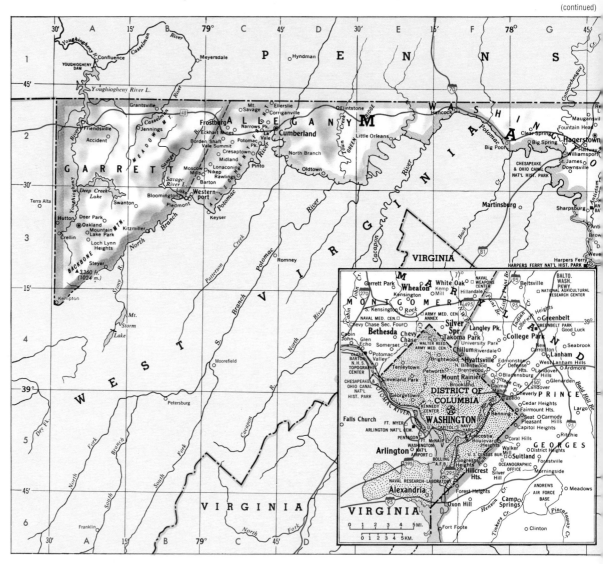

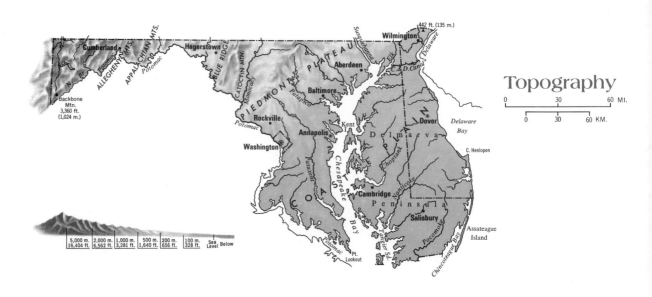

Topography

0   30   60 MI.

0   30   60 KM.

MARYLAND

AREA 10,460 sq. mi. (27,091 sq. km.)
POPULATION 4,798,622
CAPITAL Annapolis
LARGEST CITY Baltimore
HIGHEST POINT Backbone Mtn. 3,360 ft. (1024 m.)
SETTLED IN 1634
ADMITTED TO UNION April 28, 1788
POPULAR NAME Old Line State; Free State
STATE FLOWER Black-eyed Susan
STATE BIRD Baltimore Oriole

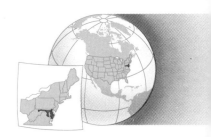

DELAWARE

AREA 2,044 sq. mi. (5,294 sq. km.)
POPULATION 668,696
CAPITAL Dover
LARGEST CITY Wilmington
HIGHEST POINT Ebright Road 442 ft. (135 m.)

SETTLED IN 1627
ADMITTED TO UNION December 7, 1787
POPULAR NAME First State; Diamond State
STATE FLOWER Peach Blossom
STATE BIRD Blue Hen Chicken

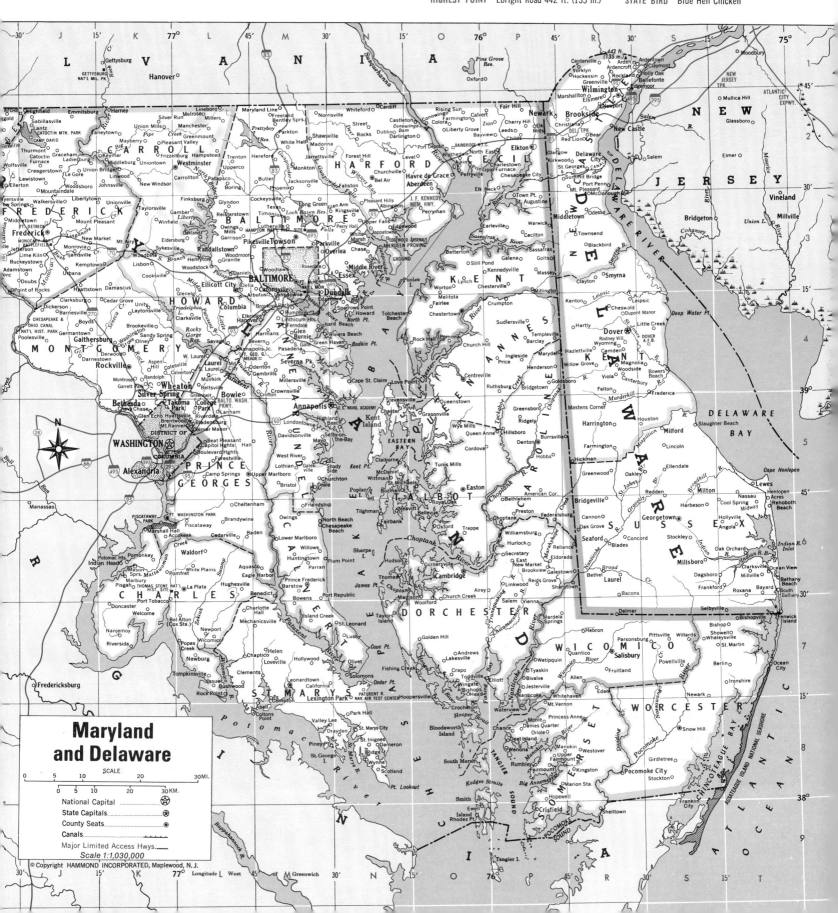

Maryland and Delaware

SCALE

0   5   10   20   30MI.

0   5   10   20   30 KM.

National Capital .... ⊛
State Capitals .... ⊛
County Seats .... ◉
Canals ....
Major Limited Access Hwys. ___
Scale 1:1,030,000

© Copyright HAMMOND INCORPORATED, Maplewood, N.J.

Joppatowne 11,084 ....N3
Keedysville 464 ....H3
Kemp Mill F3
Kemptown 250 ....J3
Kennedyville 225 ....P3
Kensington 1,713 ....E4
Keymar 200 ....K2
Kingsville 3,550 ....N3
Kitzmiller 275 ....B3
Knoxville 500 ....H3
La Plata▲ 5,841 ....L6
La Vale (La Vale-Narrows Park) 4,694 ....C2
Landover 5,052 ....G4
Landover Hills 2,074 ....G4
Langley Park 17,474 ....F4
Lanham (Lanham-Seabrook) 16,792 ....G4
Lansdowne (Lansdowne-Baltimore Highlands) 15,509 ....M3
Largo 9,475 ....G5
Laurel 19,438 ....L4
Laytonsville 248 ....K4
Le Gore 500 ....J2
Leeds 177 ....P2
Leitersburg 350 ....H2
Leonardtown▲ 1,475 ....M7
Level 250 ....O2
Lewistown 600 ....J2
Lexington Park 9,943 ....M7
Libertytown 400 ....J3
Lime Kiln 230 ....J3
Lineboro 300 ....L2
Linkwood 250 ....P6
Linthicum Heights 7,547 ....M4
Little Orleans 600 ....E2
Loch Lynn Heights 461 ....A3
Lonaconing 1,122 ....C2
Londontowne 6,992 ....M5
Long Green 1,626 ....M3
Loveville 600 ....M7
Luke 184 ....B3
Lutherville (Lutherville-Timonium) 16,442 ....M3
Madison 350 ....O6
Manchester 2,810 ....L2
Manokin 270 ....P8
Mapleville 200 ....H2
Marbury 1,244 ....K6
Mardela Springs 360 ....P7
Marion Station 400 ....R8
Marshall Hall 325 ....K6
Marydel 143 ....P4
Maryland City 6,813 ....L4
Maryland Line 281 ....M2
Massey 280 ....P3
Maugansville 1,707 ....H2
Mayo 2,537 ....M5
McDaniel 275 ....N5
Meadows 200 ....G5
Mechanicsville 784 ....M7
Middle River 24,616 ....N3
Middleburg 200 ....K2
Middletown 1,834 ....J3
Midland 574 ....C2
Millersville 380 ....M4
Millington 409 ....P3
Monkton 307 ....M2
Montrose K4
Morningside 930 ....G5
Moscow Mills 260 ....B2
Mount Airy 3,730 ....K3
Mount Pleasant 400 ....J3
Mount Rainier 7,954 ....F4
Mount Savage 1,640 ....C2
Mount Vernon 900 ....P8
Mountain Lake Park 1,938 ....A3
Mountaindale 400 ....J2
Muirkirk 950 ....L4
Myersville 464 ....H3
Nanjemoy 238 ....K7
Nanticoke 450 ....P7
Narrows Park (Narrows Park-La Vale) C2
Neavitt 300 ....N6
New Carrollton 12,002 ....G4
New Market 328 ....J3
New Windsor 757 ....K2
Newark 900 ....S7
Newburg 550 ....L7
Nikep 200 ....C2
North Beach 1,173 ....N6
North Brentwood 512 ....F4
North East 1,913 ....P2
North Potomac 18,456 ....K4
Oakland 2,242 ....L3
Oakland▲ 1,741 ....A3
Ocean City 5,146 ....T7
Odenton 12,833 ....M4
Oella 600 ....L3
Oldtown 200 ....D2
Olivet 200 ....N7
Olney 23,019 ....K4
Orchard Beach 200 ....M4
Overlea 12,137 ....N3
Owings 9,474 ....M6
Owings Mills 9,526 ....L3
Oxford 699 ....O6
Oxon Hill 35,794 ....F6
Park Hall 775 ....N8
Parkton 290 ....M2
Parkville 31,617 ....M3
Parran 200 ....M6
Parsonsburg 200 ....R7
Pasadena 10,012 ....M4
Perry Hall 22,723 ....N3
Perryman 2,160 ....O3
Perryville 2,456 ....O2
Petersville 320 ....H3
Phoenix 165 ....M2
Pikesville 24,815 ....M3
Piney Point 950 ....M8
Pinto 175 ....C2
Piscataway 500 ....L6
Pisgah 650 ....K6
Pittsville 602 ....S7
Pleasant Hills 2,591 ....N3
Pleasant Valley 200 ....L2
Plum Point 200 ....N6
Pocomoke City 3,922 ....R8
Point of Rocks 210 ....J3
Pomfret 600 ....L6
Pomonkey 410 ....K6
Poolesville 3,796 ....J4
Port Deposit 685 ....O2
Potomac Heights 1,524 ....K6
Potomac Park (Potomac Park-Bowling Green) 2,275 ....C2
Potomac Valley E4
Powellville 400 ....S7
Preston 437 ....P6
Prince Frederick▲ 1,885 ....M6
Princess Anne▲ 1,666 ....P8
Pumphrey 5,483 ....M4
Quantico 200 ....R7
Queen Anne 250 ....O5
Queenstown 453 ....O5
Randallstown 26,277 ....L3
Randolph K4
Rawlings 500 ....C2
Reid 320 ....H2
Reisterstown 19,314 ....L3
Ridge 1,034 ....N8
Ridgely 933 ....P5
Ringgold 200 ....H2
Rising Sun 1,263 ....O2
Ritchie 950 ....G5
Riverdale 5,185 ....F4
Riviera Beach 11,376 ....N4
Rock Hall 1,584 ....O4
Rocks 450 ....N2
Rockville▲ 44,835 ....K4
Rohrersville 525 ....H3
Rosedale 18,703 ....M3
Rosemont 256 ....H3
Royal Oak 600 ....O6
Rumbley 200 ....P8
Sabillasville 450 ....J2
Saint Inigoes 750 ....N8
Saint Leonard 244 ....N7
Saint Marys City N8
Saint Michaels 1,301 ....N5
Salisbury▲ 20,592 ....R7
Sandy Spring (Sandy Spring-Ashton) 2,659 ....K4
Savage (Savage-Guilford) 9,669 ....L4
Scotland 475 ....N8
Seabrook (Seabrook-Lanham) G4
Seat Pleasant 5,359 ....G5
Secretary 528 ....P6
Selby-on-the-Bay 3,101 ....N5
Severn 24,499 ....M4
Severna Park 25,879 ....M4
Shady Side 4,107 ....M5
Sharpsburg 659 ....G3
Sharptown 609 ....R6
Silver Run 350 ....K2
Silver Spring 76,046 ....F4
Smithsburg 1,221 ....H2
Snow Hill▲ 2,217 ....S8
Solomons 250 ....N7
Somerset 993 ....E4
South Gate 27,564 ....M4
South Kensington 8,777 ....E4
South Laurel 18,591 ....L4
Sparrows Point N4
Stevensville 1,862 ....N5
Still Pond 350 ....O3
Stockton 400 ....S8
Street 200 ....N2
Sudlersville 428 ....P4
Suitland (Suitland-Silver Hill) 35,111 ....F5
Swanton 223 ....A3
Sykesville 2,303 ....K3
Takoma Park 16,700 ....F4
Taneytown 3,695 ....K2
Taylors Island 400 ....N7
Texas 300 ....M3
Thurmont 3,398 ....J2
Tilghman 979 ....N6
Timonium (Timonium-Lutherville) M3
Toddville 500 ....O7
Tompkinsville 200 ....L7
Towson▲ 49,445 ....M3
Trappe 974 ....O6
Tuxedo 500 ....G5
Union Bridge 910 ....K2
Union Mills 225 ....K2
Uniontown 250 ....K2
Unionville 200 ....K3
University Park 2,243 ....F4
Upper Fairmount 500 ....P8
Upper Falls 550 ....N3
Upper Marlboro▲ 745 ....M5
Upperco 500 ....L2
Vale Summit 175 ....C2
Valley Lee 600 ....M8
Vienna 264 ....P7
Waldorf 15,058 ....L6
Walker Mill 10,920 ....F5
Walkersville 4,145 ....J3
Warwick 550 ....P3
Washington Grove 434 ....K4
Welcome 438 ....K7
Wenona 270 ....P8
West Lanham Hills 350 ....G4
West Laurel 4,151 ....L4
West River 300 ....M5
Westernport 2,454 ....B3
Westminster▲ 13,068 ....L2
Westover 450 ....R8
Wheaton (Wheaton-Glenmont) 53,720 ....E3
White Hall 360 ....M2
White Marsh 8,183 ....N3
White Oak 18,671 ....F3
White Plains 3,560 ....L6
Whiteford 500 ....N2
Wicomico 210 ....L7
Willards 708 ....S7
Williamsport 2,103 ....G2
Willows 250 ....M6
Winfield 200 ....K3
Wingate 225 ....O7
Wittman 544 ....N5
Woodbine 872 ....K3
Woodlawn 5,329 ....M3
Woodmoor L3
Woodsboro 513 ....J2
Woolford 330 ....O7
Worton 200 ....O3
Wye Mills 315 ....O5
Wynne 450 ....N8
Yellow Springs 940 ....H3
Zion 225 ....P2

OTHER FEATURES

Aberdeen Proving Ground 5,267 ....N3
Allegheny Front (mts.) C2
Andrews A.F.B. 10,228 ....G5
Antietam (creek) H2
Antietam Nat'l Battlefield H3
Back (riv.) N4
Backbone (mt.) A3
Bainbridge N.T.C O2
Bald Hill Branch (riv.) G4
Big Annemessex (riv.) P8
Big Pipe (creek) K2
Bloodsworth (isl.) O8
Blue Ridge (mts.) H3
Bodkin (pt.) N4
Bush (creek) J3
Cabin John (creek) D4
Camp David J2
Casselman (riv.) B2
Catoctin (creek) H3
Catoctin Mt. Park J2
Cedar (pt.) N7
Census Bureau F5
Chesapeake (bay) N7
Chesapeake and Delaware (canal) R2
Chesapeake and Ohio Canal Nat'l Hist. Park J4
Chester (riv.) O4
Chicamacomico (riv.) P7
Chincoteague (bay) S8
Choptank (riv.) O6
Clara Barton Nat'l Hist. Site E4
Conococheague (bay) G1
Conowingo (dam) O2
Cove (pt.) N7
Deep Creek (lake) A3
Deer (creek) N2
Dividing (creek) R8
Eastern (bay) N5
Elk (riv.) P3
Fishing (bay) O7
Fort Detrick J3
Fort George G. Meade 12,509 ....L4
Fort McHenry Nat'l Mon. M3
Fort Ritchie 1,249 ....H2
Fort Washington Park L6
Great Seneca (creek) J4
Greenbelt Park G4
Green Ridge (mts.) E2
Gunpowder (riv.) N3
Gunpowder Falls (creek) M2
Hampton Nat'l Hist. Site M3
Harpers Ferry Nat'l Hist. Park G3
Henson (creek) F6
Honga (riv.) O7
Hooper (str.) O8
Indian (creek) G4
James (pt.) N6
Kedges (strs) O8
Kent (isl.) N5
Kent (pt.) N5
Liberty (lake) L3
Linganore (creek) J3
Little Choptank (riv.) N6
Little Gunpowder Falls (creek) M2
Little Paint Branch (riv.) F4
Little Patuxent (riv.) L4
Loch Raven (res.) M3
Lookout (pt.) N8
Manokin (riv.) P8
Marshyhope (creek) P6
Mattawoman (creek) K6
Meadow (mt.) B2
Middle Patuxent (riv.) L3
Monocacy (riv.) J3
Monocacy Nat'l Battlefield J3
Nanticoke (riv.) P7
Nassawango (creek) S8
National Agricultural Research Center G3
Naval Academy, U.S. 5,420 ....N5
Naval Medical Center E4
Naval Weapons Center F3
North (pt.) N4
Oceanographic Office F5
Oxon Run (riv.) F5
Paint Branch (riv.) F4
Patapsco (riv.) M4
Patuxent (riv.) M7
Patuxent River Nav. Air Test Ctr. N7
Piscataway (creek) G6
Piscataway Park K6
Pocomoke (riv.) S8
Pocomoke (sound) P9
Pooles (isl.) O3
Poplar (isl.) N5
Potomac (riv.) M8
Prettyboy (res.) M2
Rock (creek) K4
Rocky Gorge (res.) L4
Saint George (isl.) M8
Saint Marys (riv.) N8
Sassafras (riv.) P3
Savage (riv.) B2
Savage River (lake) B2
Severn (riv.) N4
Sharps (isl.) N6
Smith (isl.) O8
South Marsh (isl.) O8
Susquehanna (riv.) N1
Tangier (sound) P8
Thomas Stone Nat'l Hist. Site K6
Tinkers (creek) F6
Topographic Center E4
Town (creek) D2
Transquaking (riv.) P7
Triadelphia (lake) L4
Tuckahoe (creek) P5
Walter Reed Army Medical Center Annex E4
Wicomico (riv.) L7
Wicomico (riv.) R7
Winters Run (creek) N2
Youghiogheny (riv.) A3
Youghiogheny River (lake) A2
Zekiah Swamp (riv.) L7

DELAWARE

COUNTIES

Kent 110,993 ....R
New Castle 441,946 ....R
Sussex 113,229 ....S

CITIES and TOWNS

Arden 477 ....R
Ardencroft 282 ....R
Ardentown 325 ....S
Bear 200 ....R
Bellefonte 1,243 ....S
Bethany Beach 326 ....T
Bethel 178 ....R
Blades 834 ....R
Bowers Beach 198 ....S
Bridgeville 1,210 ....R
Brookside 15,307 ....R
Camden 1,899 ....R
Centerville 800 ....R
Cheswold 321 ....R
Christiana 500 ....R
Clarksville 350 ....T
Claymont 9,800 ....S
Clayton 1,163 ....R
Concord 200 ....R
Cool Spring 200 ....T
Dagsboro 398 ....S
Delaware City 1,682 ....R
Delmar 962 ....R
Dover (cap.)▲ 27,630 ....R
Dupont Manor 1,059 ....R
Edgemoor 5,853 ....S
Ellendale 313 ....S
Elsmere 5,935 ....R
Farmington 122 ....R
Felton 683 ....R
Fenwick Island 186 ....T
Frankford 591 ....S
Frederica 761 ....S
Georgetown▲ 3,732 ....S
Glasgow 350 ....R
Greenville 230 ....R
Greenwood 578 ....R
Harbeson 300 ....S
Harrington 2,311 ....R
Hockessin 950 ....R
Houston 487 ....S
Kenton 232 ....R
Kirkwood 350 ....R
Laurel 3,226 ....R
Leipsic 236 ....S
Lewes 2,295 ....T
Lincoln 757 ....S
Little Creek 167 ....S
Magnolia 211 ....R
Middletown 3,834 ....R
Midway 250 ....T
Milford 6,040 ....S
Millsboro 1,643 ....S
Millville 206 ....T
Milton 1,417 ....S
New Castle 4,837 ....R
Newark 25,098 ....P
Newport 1,240 ....R
Oak Orchard 350 ....T
Ocean View 606 ....T
Odessa 303 ....R
Port Penn 300 ....R
Rehoboth Beach 1,234 ....T
Rodney Village 1,745 ....R
Roxana 250 ....T
Saint Georges 450 ....R
Seaford 5,689 ....R
Selbyville 1,335 ....S
Smyrna 5,231 ....R
South Bethany 148 ....T
Townsend 322 ....R
Viola 153 ....R4
Wilmington▲ 71,529 ....R2
Woodside 140 ....R4
Wyoming 977 ....R4

OTHER FEATURES

Broad (creek) R6
Broadkill (riv.) S5
Chesapeake and Delaware (canal) R2
Choptank (riv.) P5
Deep Water (pt.) S4
Delaware (bay) T5
Delaware (riv.) R3
Dover A.F.B. S4
Henlopen (cape) T5
Indian (riv.) S6
Indian River (bay) T6
Indian River (inlet) T6
Leipsic (riv.) R4
Mispillion (riv.) S5
Murderkill (riv.) R5
Nanticoke (riv.) R6
Saint Jones (riv.) R4
Smyrna (res.) R3

DISTRICT OF COLOMBIA

CITIES and TOWNS

Georgetown E5
Washington D.C. (cap), U.S. 609,909 ....F5

OTHER FEATURES

Anacostia (riv.) F5
Bolling A.F.B. F5
Fort Lesley J. McNair E5
Kennedy Center A5
Naval Yard F5
U.S. Capitol F5
Walter Reed Army Med. Ctr. E4

▲County seat.

Agriculture, Industry and Resources

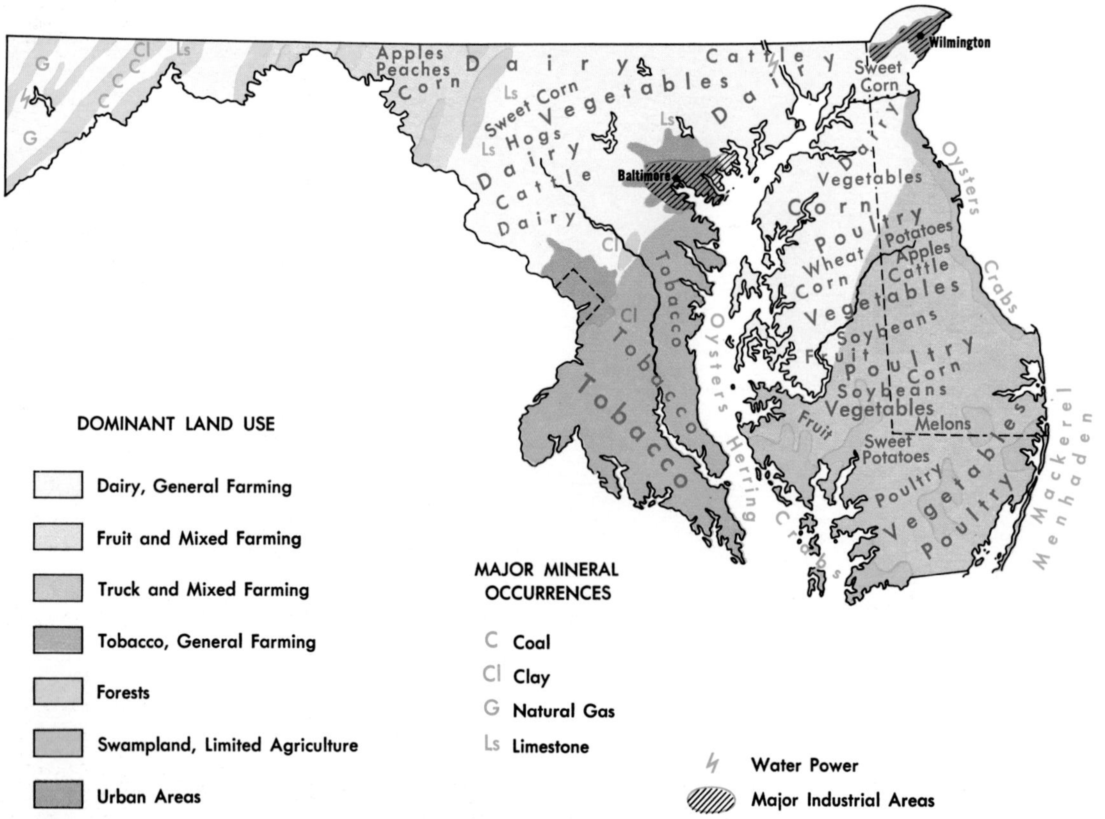

Wilmington
Baltimore
Apples
Peaches
Corn
Dairy
Cattle
Vegetables
Sweet Corn
Hogs
Sweet Corn
Poultry
Potatoes
Wheat
Soybeans
Fruit
Melons
Sweet Potatoes
Tobacco
Oysters
Crabs
Herring
Mackerel
Menhaden
DOMINANT LAND USE
Dairy, General Farming
Fruit and Mixed Farming
Truck and Mixed Farming
Tobacco, General Farming
Forests
Swampland, Limited Agriculture
Urban Areas
MAJOR MINERAL OCCURRENCES
C Coal
Cl Clay
G Natural Gas
Ls Limestone
Water Power
Major Industrial Areas

MASSACHUSETTS

AREA 8,284 sq. mi. (21,456 sq. km.)
POPULATION 6,029,051
CAPITAL Boston
LARGEST CITY Boston
HIGHEST POINT Mt. Greylock 3,491 ft.
(1064 m.)
SETTLED IN 1620
ADMITTED TO UNION February 6, 1788
POPULAR NAME Bay State; Old Colony
STATE FLOWER Mayflower
STATE BIRD Chickadee

RHODE ISLAND

AREA 1,212 sq. mi. (3,139 sq. km.)
POPULATION 1,005,984
CAPITAL Providence
LARGEST CITY Providence
HIGHEST POINT Jerimoth Hill 812 ft.
(247 m.)
SETTLED IN 1636
ADMITTED TO UNION May 29, 1790
POPULAR NAME Little Rhody; Ocean State
STATE FLOWER Violet
STATE BIRD Rhode Island Red

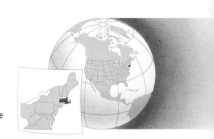

Agriculture, Industry and Resources

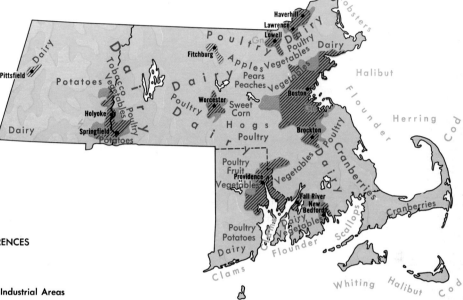

DOMINANT LAND USE

- Specialized Dairy
- Dairy, Poultry, Mixed Farming
- Forests
- Urban Areas

MAJOR MINERAL OCCURRENCES

Gn Granite

⚡ Water Power   ⬛ Major Industrial Areas

(continued on following page)

Vineyard Haven 1,762	M7
Waban •	B7
Wakefield • 24,825	C5
Wales • 1,566	F4
Walpole 5,495	B8
Walpole • 20,212	B8
Waltham 57,878	B6
Ware 6,533	E3
Ware • 9,808	E3
Wareham 19,232	L5
Wareham • 18,457	L5
Wareham Center 2,607	L5
Warren 1,516	F4
Warren • 4,437	F4
Warwick • 740	E2
Washington • 615	B3
Watertown • 33,284	C6
Waverley	B6
Wayland • 11,874	A7
Webster 11,849	G4
Webster • 16,196	G4
Wellesley • 26,615	B7
Wellesley Hills	B7
Wellfleet • 2,493	O5
Wendell • 899	E2
Wenham • 4,212	L2
West Acton 975	H3
West Barnstable 1,508	N6
West Boxford 950	K2
West Boylston • 6,611	G3
West Bridgewater • 6,389	K4
West Brookfield 1,419	F4
West Brookfield • 3,532	F4
West Chatham 1,504	O6
West Chelmsford	J2
West Concord 5,761	A6
West Dennis 2,307	O6
West Falmouth 1,752	M6
West Groton 950	H2
West Hanover	L4
West Harwich 883	O6
West Mansfield 950	K5
West Medway	J4
West Newbury • 3,421	L1
West Newton	B7
West Springfield 27,537	D4
West Stockbridge • 1,483	A3
West Tisbury • 1,704	M7
West Townsend 950	H2
West Upton-Upton	H4
West Wareham 2,059	L5
West Warren	F4
West Yarmouth 5,409	N6
Westborough 3,917	H3
Westborough • 14,133	H3
Westfield • 38,372	D4
Westford • 16,392	J2
Westhampton • 1,327	C3
Westminster • 6,191	G2
Weston • 10,200	B6
Westport 13,852	K6
Westport • 13,763	K6
Westwood 12,557	B8
Weymouth 54,063	D8
Whately • 1,375	D3
Whitinsville 5,639	H4
Whitman • 13,240	L4
Wilbraham 3,352	E4
Wilbraham • 12,635	E4
Williamsburg • 2,515	C3
Williamstown 4,791	B2
Williamstown • 8,220	B2
Wilmington • 17,654	C5
Winchendon 4,316	F2
Winchendon • 8,805	F2
Winchester • 20,267	C6
Windsor • 770	B2
Winthrop • 18,127	D6
Woburn 35,943	C6
Woods Hole 1,080	M6
Worcester▲ 169,759	H3
Worthington • 1,156	C3
Wrentham • 9,006	J4
Yarmouth Port 4,271	N6
Yarmouth • 21,174	O6

OTHER FEATURES

Adams Nat'l Hist. Site	D7
Agawam (riv.)	M5
Allerton (pt.)	E7
Ann (cape)	M2
Ashmere (lake)	B3
Assabet (riv.)	H3
Assawompset (pond)	L5
Batchelor (brook)	D3
Berkshire (hills)	B4
Big (pond)	B4
Bigelow (bight)	M1
Blackstone (riv.)	G3
Blue (hills)	C8
Boston (bay)	E6
Boston (harb.)	D7
Boston Nat'l Hist. Park	D6
Brewster (isls.)	E7
Buel (lake)	A4
Buzzards (bay)	L7
Cambridge (res.)	B6
Cape Cod (bay)	N5
Cape Cod (canal)	N5
Cape Cod Nat'l Seashore	P5
Chappaquiddick (isl.)	N7
Charles (riv.)	C7
Chicopee (riv.)	D4
Cobble Mountain (res.)	C4
Cochituate (lake)	A7
Cod (cape)	O4
Concord (riv.)	J2
Congamond (lakes)	D4
Connecticut (riv.)	D2
Cuttyhunk (isl.)	L7
Deer (isl.)	E7
Deerfield (riv.)	C2
East (pt.)	E6
East Chop (pt.)	M7
Eastern (pt.)	M2
Elizabeth (isls.)	L7
Everett (mt.)	A4
Falls (riv.)	D2
Fort Devens 8,973	H2
Fresh (pond)	C6
Gammon (pt.)	N6
Gay Head (prom.)	L7
Grace (mt.)	E2
Great (pt.)	O7
Green (pt.)	B2
Greylock (mt.)	B2
Gurnet (pt.)	M4
Hingham (bay)	E7
Holyoke (range)	D3
Hoosac (mts.)	B2
Hoosic (riv.)	A1
Housatonic (riv.)	A4
Ipswich (riv.)	L2
John F. Kennedy Nat'l Hist. Site	C7
Knightville (res.)	C3
Laurence G. Hanscom Field	B6
Little (riv.)	C4
Logan Int'l Airport	D7
Long (isl.)	E7
Long (pt.)	O4
Long (pond)	L5
Longfellow Nat'l Hist. Site	C6
Lowell Nat'l Hist. Park	J2
Maine (gulf)	M2
Manhan (riv.)	D4
Manomet (pt.)	N5
Marblehead (neck)	F6
Martha's Vineyard (isl.)	M7
Massachusetts (bay)	M4
Merrimack (riv.)	K1
Mill (riv.)	C3
Mill (riv.)	D3
Millers (riv.)	E2
Minute Man Nat'l Hist. Park	B6
Mishaum (pt.)	L6
Monomonac (lake)	G2
Monomoy (isl.)	O6
Monomoy (pt.)	O6
Mount Hope (bay)	K6
Muskeget (chan.)	N7
Muskeget (isl.)	N7
Mystic (lake)	C6
Mystic (riv.)	C6
Nahant (bay)	E6
Nantucket (isl.)	O8
Nantucket (sound)	N6
Nashawena (isl.)	L7
Nashua (riv.)	H3
Naushon (isl.)	L7
Neponset (riv.)	C8
Nomans Land (isl.)	L7
Nonamesset (isl.)	M6
North (riv.)	D2
North (riv.)	L4
Onota (lake)	A3
Otis (res.)	B4
Otis A.F.B.	M6
Pasque (isl.)	L7
Plum (isl.)	L2
Plymouth (bay)	M5
Poge (cape)	N7
Pontoosuc (lake)	A3
Quabbin (res.)	E3
Quaboag (riv.)	F4
Quincy (bay)	D7
Quinebaug (riv.)	F4
Race (riv.)	N4
Salem Maritime Nat'l Hist. Site	E5
Saugus Iron Works Nat'l Hist. Site	D6
Shawshine (riv.)	K2
Silver (lake)	L4
South (riv.)	D2
South Weymouth Nav. Air Sta.	E8
Springfield Armory Nat'l Hist. Site	D4
Squibnocket (pt.)	M7
Stillwater (riv.)	G3
Sudbury (res.)	H3
Sudbury (riv.)	A6
Swift (riv.)	E4
Taconic (mts.)	A2
Taunton (riv.)	K5
Thompson (isl.)	D7
Toby (isl.)	E3
Tom (mt.)	D4
Tuckernuck (isl.)	N7
Vineyard (sound)	L7
Wachusett (mt.)	G3
Wachusett (res.)	G3
Walden (pond)	A6
Ware (riv.)	F3
Watuppa (pond)	K6
Webster (lake)	G4
Wellfleet (harb.)	O5
West (riv.)	H4
West Chop (pt.)	M7
Westfield (riv.)	C3
Westover A.F.B.	D4
Weweantic (riv.)	L5
Whitman (riv.)	F2
Winter I. Coast Guard Air Sta.	E5

RHODE ISLAND

COUNTIES

Bristol 48,859	J6
Kent 161,135	H6
Newport 87,194	K6
Providence 596,270	H5
Washington 110,006	H7

CITIES and TOWNS

Anthony	H6
Apponaug	J6
Arctic	J6
Arnold Mills	J5
Ashaway 1,584	G7
Ashton	J5
Barrington • 15,849	J6
Block Island •	H8
Bradford 1,604	H7
Bristol▲ 21,625	J6
Centerdale	H5
Central Falls 17,637	J5
Charlestown 6,478	H7
Conimicut	J6
Coventry (Washington) 31,083	H6
Coventry Center	H6
Cranston 76,060	J5
East Greenwich▲ • 11,865	J6
East Providence 50,380	J5
Esmond	J5
Exeter • 5,461	H6
Georgiaville	H5
Greenville 8,303	H5
Harrisville 1,654	H5
Hillsgrove	J6
Hope Valley 1,446	H6
Hopkinton • 6,873	H7
Island Park	J6
Jamestown 4,999	J6
Jamestown • 4,040	J6
Kingston 6,504	J7
La Fayette	H6
Little Compton • 3,339	K6
Lonsdale	J5
Manville	H5
Middletown • 19,460	J6
Narragansett 14,985	J7
Narragansett • 12,088	J7
Natick	H6
New Shoreham (Block Island) • 836	H8
Newport 28,227	J6
North Kingstown • 23,786	J6
North Providence • 32,090	H5
North Tiverton	K6
Norwood	J6
Oakland Beach	J6
Pascoag 5,011	H5
Pawtucket 72,644	J5
Peace Dale-Wakefield 7,134	J7
Pontiac	J6
Portsmouth • 16,857	J6
Providence (cap.)▲ 160,728	H5
Riverside	J6
Rumford	J5
Tiverton 7,259	K6
Tiverton • 14,312	K6
Valley Falls 11,175	J5
Wakefield-Peace Dale 7,134	J7
Warren • 11,385	J6
Warwick 85,427	J6
Watch Hill 300	G7
West Kingston 950	H7
West Warwick 29,268	H6
Westerly▲ 16,477	G7
Westerly • 21,605	G7
Woonsocket▲ 43,877	J4

OTHER FEATURES

Black Rock (pt.)	H8
Block (isl.)	H8
Block Island (sound)	H8
Brenton (pt.)	J7
Conanicut (isl.)	J6
Dickens (pt.)	H8
Durfee (hill)	G5
Grace (pt.)	J6
Jerimoth (hill)	G5
Judith (pt.)	J7
Mount Hope (bay)	K6
Narragansett (bay)	J6
Noyes (pt.)	H7
Pawcatuck (riv.)	G7
Prudence (isl.)	J6
Rhode Island (isl.)	J6
Rhode (sound)	J6
Roger Williams Nat'l Mem.	J5
Sakonnet (pt.)	K7
Sakonnet (riv.)	K7
Sandy (pt.)	H8
Scituate (res.)	H5
Touro Synagogue Nat'l Hist. Site	J7
Watch Hill (pt.)	G7

▲County seat or Shire town
• Population of town or township

© Copyright HAMMOND INCORPORATED, Maplewood, N.J.

Topography

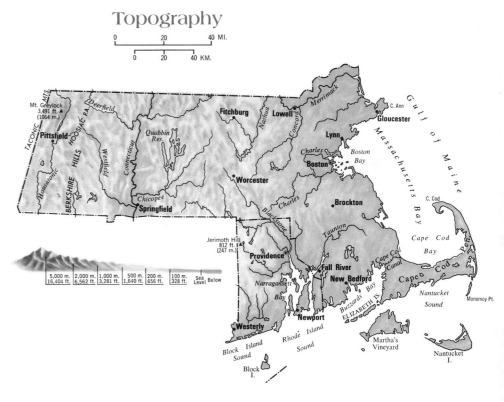

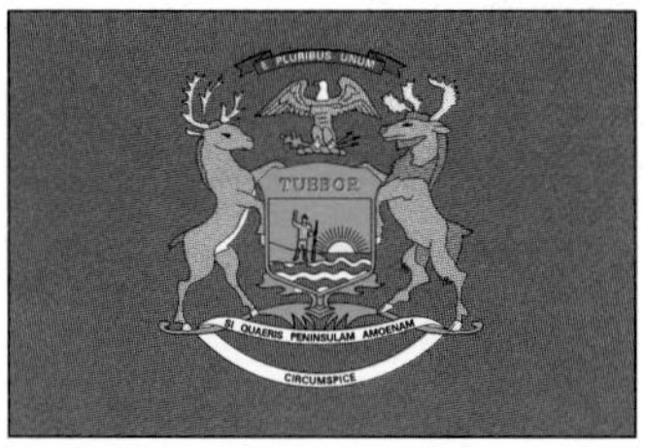
E PLURIBUS UNUM
TUEBOR
SI QUAERIS PENINSULAM AMOENAM
CIRCUMSPICE

AREA 58,527 sq. mi. (151,585 sq. km.)
POPULATION 9,328,784
CAPITAL Lansing
LARGEST CITY Detroit
HIGHEST POINT Mt. Curwood 1,980 ft. (604 m.)
SETTLED IN 1650
ADMITTED TO UNION January 26, 1837
POPULAR NAME Wolverine State
STATE FLOWER Apple Blossom
STATE BIRD Robin

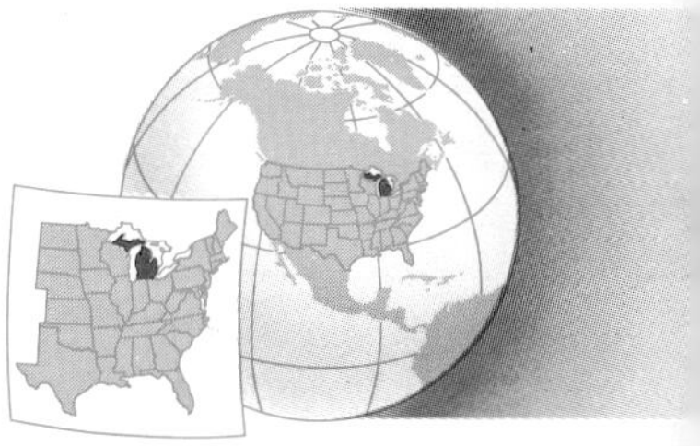

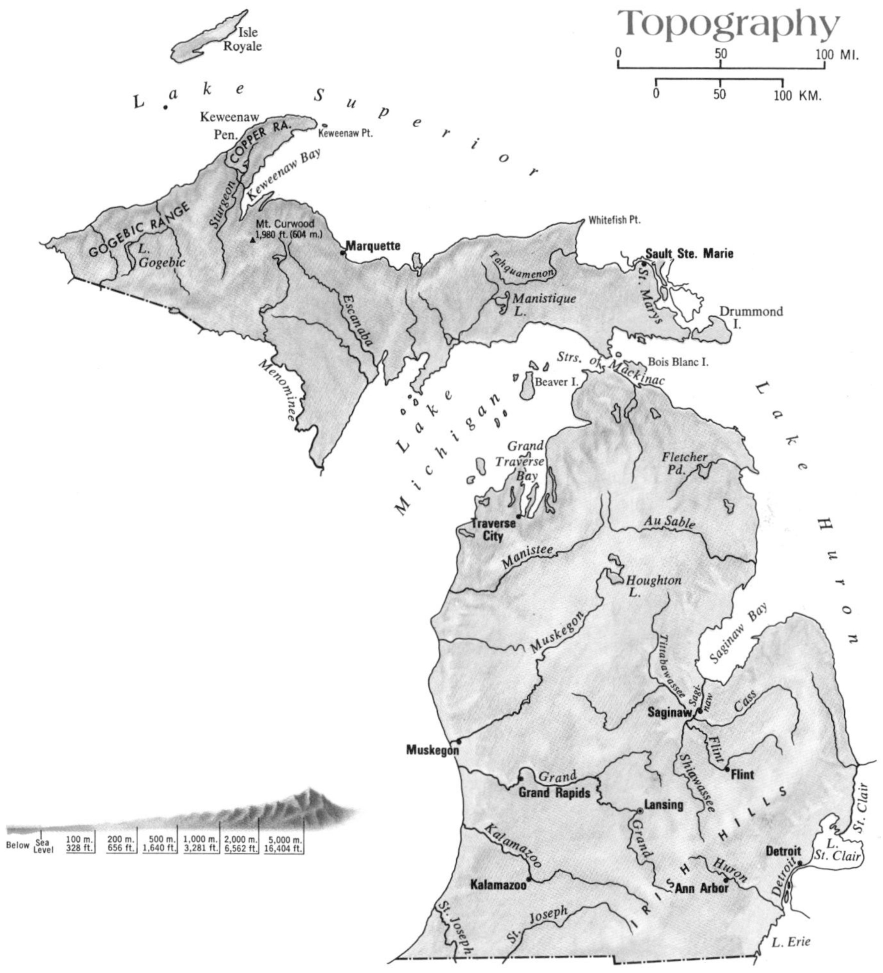
Topography
0 50 100 MI.
0 50 100 KM.
Isle Royale
Lake Superior
Keweenaw Pen.
Keweenaw Pt.
COPPER RA.
Keweenaw Bay
GOGEBIC RANGE
L. Gogebic
Sturgeon
Mt. Curwood 1,980 ft. (604 m.)
Marquette
Whitefish Pt.
Tahquamenon
Sault Ste. Marie
St. Marys
Drummond I.
Manistique L.
Escanaba
Menominee
Strs. of Mackinac
Bois Blanc I.
Beaver I.
Lake Michigan
Lake Huron
Grand Traverse Bay
Fletcher Pd.
Traverse City
Au Sable
Manistee
Houghton L.
Muskegon
Tittabawassee
Saginaw Bay
Saginaw
Cass
Flint
Shiawassee
Muskegon
Grand
Grand Rapids
Lansing
HILLS
IRISH
St. Clair
L. St. Clair
Detroit
Huron
Ann Arbor
Kalamazoo
St. Joseph
L. Erie
Below Sea Level
100 m. 328 ft.
200 m. 656 ft.
500 m. 1,640 ft.
1,000 m. 3,281 ft.
2,000 m. 6,562 ft.
5,000 m. 16,404 ft.

COUNTIES

Alcona 10,145 ..... F4
Alger 8,972 ..... C2
Allegan 90,509 ..... D6
Alpena 30,605 ..... F4
Antrim 18,185 ..... D3
Arenac 14,931 ..... F4
Baraga 7,954 ..... A2
Barry 50,057 ..... D6
Bay 111,723 ..... E5
Benzie 12,200 ..... C4
Berrien 161,378 ..... C7
Branch 41,502 ..... D7
Calhoun 135,982 ..... D6
Cass 49,477 ..... C7
Charlevoix 21,468 ..... D3
Cheboygan 21,398 ..... E3
Chippewa 34,604 ..... E2
Clare 24,952 ..... E5
Clinton 57,883 ..... E6
Crawford 12,260 ..... E4
Delta 37,780 ..... C2
Dickinson 26,831 ..... B2
Eaton 92,879 ..... E6
Emmet 25,040 ..... E3
Genesee 430,459 ..... F5
Gladwin 21,896 ..... E4
Gogebic 18,052 ..... F2
Grand Traverse 64,273 ..... D4
Gratiot 38,982 ..... E5
Hillsdale 43,431 ..... E7
Houghton 35,446 ..... G1
Huron 34,951 ..... F5
Ingham 281,912 ..... E6
Ionia 57,024 ..... D6
Iosco 30,209 ..... F4
Iron 13,175 ..... G2
Isabella 54,624 ..... E5
Jackson 149,756 ..... E6
Kalamazoo 223,411 ..... D6
Kalkaska 13,497 ..... D4
Kent 500,631 ..... D5
Keweenaw 1,701 ..... A1
Lake 8,583 ..... D5
Lapeer 74,768 ..... F5
Leelanau 16,527 ..... D4
Lenawee 91,476 ..... E7
Livingston 115,645 ..... F6
Luce 5,763 ..... D2
Mackinac 10,674 ..... D2
Macomb 717,400 ..... G6
Manistee 21,265 ..... C4
Marquette 70,887 ..... B2
Mason 25,537 ..... C4
Mecosta 37,308 ..... D5
Menominee 24,920 ..... B3
Midland 75,651 ..... E5
Missaukee 12,147 ..... D4
Monroe 133,600 ..... F7
Montcalm 53,059 ..... D5
Montmorency 8,936 ..... E3
Muskegon 158,983 ..... C5
Newaygo 38,202 ..... D5
Oakland 1,083,592 ..... F6
Oceana 22,454 ..... C5
Ogemaw 18,681 ..... E4
Ontonagon 8,854 ..... F1
Osceola 20,146 ..... D5
Oscoda 7,842 ..... E4
Otsego 17,957 ..... E3
Ottawa 187,768 ..... C6
Presque Isle 13,743 ..... F3
Roscommon 19,776 ..... E4
Saginaw 211,946 ..... E5
Saint Clair 138,802 ..... G6
Saint Joseph 56,083 ..... D7
Sanilac 39,928 ..... G5
Schoolcraft 8,302 ..... C2
Shiawassee 69,770 ..... E6
Tuscola 55,498 ..... F5
Van Buren 66,814 ..... C6
Washtenaw 282,937 ..... F6
Wayne 2,111,687 ..... F6
Wexford 26,360 ..... D4

CITIES and TOWNS

Addison 632 ..... E7
Adrian▲ 22,097 ..... F7
Akron 421 ..... F5
Alabaster 46 ..... F4
Alanson 677 ..... E3
Albion 10,066 ..... E6
Algonac 4,551 ..... G6
Allegan▲ 4,547 ..... D6
Allen 201 ..... E7
Allen Park 31,092 ..... B7
Alma 9,034 ..... E5
Almont 2,354 ..... F6
Alpena▲ 11,354 ..... F3
Alpha 219 ..... A2
Anchorville 3,202 ..... G6
Ann Arbor▲ 109,592 ..... F6
Applegate 297 ..... G5
Arcadia 780 ..... C4
Armada 1,548 ..... G6
Ashley 518 ..... E5
Athens 990 ..... D6
Atlanta▲ 475 ..... E3
Atlantic Mine 809 ..... G1
Au Gres 838 ..... F4
Au Sable 1,542 ..... F4
Auburn 1,855 ..... F5
Auburn Heights 7,500 ..... F6
Augusta 927 ..... D6
Averill 800 ..... E5
Bad Axe▲ 3,484 ..... G5
Baldwin▲ 821 ..... D5
Bancroft 599 ..... E6
Bangor 1,922 ..... C6
Baraga 1,231 ..... G1
Bark River 800 ..... B3
Baroda 657 ..... C7
Barryton 393 ..... D5
Barton Hills 320 ..... F6
Battle Creek 53,540 ..... D6
Bay City▲ 38,936 ..... F5
Bay Port 750 ..... F5
Beal City 345 ..... D5
Bear Lake 339 ..... C4
Beaverton 1,150 ..... E5
Beechwood 2,676 ..... C6
Belding 5,969 ..... D5
Bellaire▲ 1,104 ..... D4
Belleville 3,270 ..... F6
Bellevue 1,401 ..... E6
Benton Harbor 12,818 ..... C6
Benton Heights 5,465 ..... C6
Benzonia 449 ..... D4
Berkley 16,960 ..... B6
Berrien Springs 1,927 ..... C7
Bessemer▲ 2,272 ..... F2
Beulah▲ 421 ..... C4
Beverly Hills 10,610 ..... B6
Big Rapids▲ 12,603 ..... D5
Birch Run 992 ..... F5
Birmingham 19,997 ..... B6
Bitely 750 ..... D5
Blissfield 3,172 ..... F7
Bloomfield Hills 4,288 ..... B6
Bloomingdale 503 ..... C6
Boyne City 3,478 ..... E3
Boyne Falls 369 ..... E3
Breckenridge 1,301 ..... E5
Breedsville 213 ..... C6
Bridgeport 8,569 ..... F5
Bridgman 2,140 ..... C7
Brighton 5,686 ..... F6
Britton 694 ..... F6
Bronson 2,342 ..... D7
Brooklyn 1,027 ..... E6
Brown City 1,244 ..... G5
Buchanan 4,992 ..... C7
Buckley 402 ..... D4
Burlington 294 ..... D6
Burr Oak 882 ..... D7
Burt 1,169 ..... F5
Burton 27,617 ..... F6
Byron 573 ..... E6
Byron Center 900 ..... D6
Cadillac▲ 10,104 ..... D4
Caledonia 885 ..... D6
Calumet 818 ..... A1
Camden 482 ..... E7
Capac 1,583 ..... G5
Carleton 2,770 ..... F6
Carney 197 ..... B3
Caro▲ 4,054 ..... F5
Carrollton 6,521 ..... E5
Carson City 1,158 ..... E5
Carsonville 583 ..... G5
Caseville 857 ..... F5
Casnovia 376 ..... D5
Caspian 1,031 ..... G2
Cass City 2,276 ..... F5
Cassopolis▲ 1,822 ..... C7
Cedar Springs 2,600 ..... D5
Cement City 493 ..... E6
Center Line 9,026 ..... B6
Central Lake 954 ..... D3
Centreville▲ 1,516 ..... D7
Charlevoix▲ 3,116 ..... D3
Charlotte▲ 8,083 ..... E6
Chatham 268 ..... B2
Cheboygan▲ 4,999 ..... E3
Chelsea 3,772 ..... E6
Chesaning 2,567 ..... E5
Clare 3,021 ..... E5
Clarkston 1,005 ..... F6
Clarksville 360 ..... D6
Clawson 13,874 ..... B6
Clayton 384 ..... E7
Clifford 354 ..... F5
Climax 677 ..... D6
Clinton 2,475 ..... F6
Clio 2,629 ..... F5
Coldwater▲ 9,607 ..... D7
Coleman 1,237 ..... E5
Coloma 1,679 ..... C6
Colon 1,224 ..... D7
Columbiaville 934 ..... F5
Comstock• 11,162 ..... D6
Concord 944 ..... E6
Constantine 2,032 ..... D7
Coopersville 3,421 ..... C5
Copemish 222 ..... D4
Copper City 198 ..... A1
Corunna▲ 3,091 ..... E6
Croswell 2,174 ..... G5
Crystal 800 ..... E5
Crystal Falls▲ 1,922 ..... A2
Curtis 800 ..... D2
Custer 312 ..... C5
Cutlerville 11,228 ..... D6
Daggett 260 ..... B3
Dansville 437 ..... E6
Davison 5,693 ..... F5
De Tour Village 407 ..... E3
De Witt 3,964 ..... E6
Dearborn 89,286 ..... B7
Dearborn Heights 60,838 ..... B7
Decatur 1,760 ..... C6
Deckerville 1,015 ..... G5
Deerfield 922 ..... F7
Detroit Beach 2,113 ..... F7
Detroit▲ 1,027,974 ..... B7
Dexter 1,497 ..... F6
Dimondale 1,247 ..... E6
Dollar Bay 950 ..... G1
Douglas 1,040 ..... C6
Dowagiac 6,409 ..... D6
Drayton Plains F6
Drummond Island• 746 ..... F3
Dryden 628 ..... F6
Dundee 2,664 ..... F7
Durand 4,283 ..... E6
Eagle River▲ 20 ..... A1
East Detroit 35,283 ..... B6
East Grand Rapids 10,807 ..... D6
East Jordan 2,240 ..... D3
East Kingsford A3
East Lansing 50,677 ..... E6
East Tawas 2,887 ..... F4
Eastlake 473 ..... C4
Eastwood 6,340 ..... D6
Eaton Rapids 4,695 ..... E6
Eau Claire 494 ..... C6
Ecorse 12,180 ..... B7
Edmore 1,126 ..... E5
Edwardsburg 1,142 ..... C7
Elberta 478 ..... C4
Elk Rapids 1,626 ..... D4
Elkton 958 ..... F5
Ellsworth 418 ..... D3
Elsie 957 ..... E5
Emmett 297 ..... G6
Empire 355 ..... C4
Erie 750 ..... F7
Escanaba▲ 13,659 ..... C3
Essexville 4,088 ..... F5
Estral Beach 430 ..... F7
Evart 1,744 ..... D5
Ewen 821 ..... F2
Fair Haven 1,505 ..... G6
Fair Plain 8,051 ..... C6
Fairgrove 592 ..... F5
Farmington 10,132 ..... F6
Farmington Hills 74,652 ..... F6
Farwell 851 ..... E5
Fennville 1,023 ..... C6
Fenton 8,444 ..... F6
Ferndale 25,084 ..... B6
Ferrysburg 2,919 ..... C5
Fife Lake 394 ..... D4
Flat Rock 7,290 ..... F6
Flint▲ 140,761 ..... F5
Flushing 8,542 ..... F5
Fountain 165 ..... C4
Fowler 912 ..... E5
Fowlerville 2,648 ..... F6
Frankenmuth 4,408 ..... F5
Frankfort 1,546 ..... C4
Franklin 2,626 ..... B6
Fraser 13,899 ..... B6
Freeland 1,421 ..... E5
Freeport 458 ..... D6
Fremont 3,875 ..... D5
Fruitport 1,090 ..... C5
Gaastra 376 ..... G2
Gagetown 337 ..... F5
Gaines 427 ..... F6
Galesburg 1,863 ..... D6
Galien 596 ..... C7
Garden 268 ..... C3
Garden City 31,846 ..... F6
Gaylord▲ 3,256 ..... E3
Gibraltar 4,297 ..... F6
Gladstone 4,565 ..... C3
Gladwin▲ 2,682 ..... E5
Gobles 769 ..... D6
Goodrich 916 ..... F6
Grand Blanc 7,760 ..... F6
Grand Haven▲ 11,951 ..... C5
Grand Ledge 7,579 ..... E6
Grand Rapids▲ 189,126 ..... D5
Grandville 15,624 ..... D6
Grant 764 ..... D5
Grass Lake 903 ..... E6
Grayling▲ 1,944 ..... E4
Greenville 8,101 ..... D5
Grosse Ile 9,781 ..... B7
Grosse Pointe 5,681 ..... B7
Grosse Pointe Farms 10,092 ..... B6
Grosse Pointe Park 12,857 ..... B7
Grosse Pointe Shores 2,955 ..... B6
Grosse Pointe Woods 17,715 ..... B6
Gulliver 962 ..... D2
Gwinn 2,370 ..... B2
Hamilton 950 ..... C6
Hamtramck 18,372 ..... B6
Hancock 4,547 ..... G1
Hanover 481 ..... E6
Harbor Beach 2,089 ..... G5
Harbor Springs 1,540 ..... D3
Harper Woods 14,903 ..... B6
Harrison▲ 1,835 ..... E4
Harrisville▲ 470 ..... F4
Hart▲ 1,942 ..... C5
Hartford 2,341 ..... C6
Haslett 10,230 ..... E6
Hastings▲ 6,549 ..... D6
Hazel Park 20,051 ..... B6
Hemlock 1,601 ..... E5
Hermansville 950 ..... B3
Hersey 354 ..... D5
Hesperia 846 ..... D5
Highland Park 20,121 ..... B6
Hillman 643 ..... F3
Hillsdale▲ 8,170 ..... E7
Holland 30,745 ..... C6
Holly 5,595 ..... F6
Holt 11,744 ..... E6
Homer 1,758 ..... E6
Honor 292 ..... D4
Hopkins 546 ..... D6
Houghton Lake 3,353 ..... E4
Houghton Lake Heights E4
Houghton▲ 7,498 ..... G1
Howard City 1,351 ..... D5
Howell▲ 8,184 ..... E6
Hubbardston 404 ..... E5
Hubbell 1,174 ..... A1
Hudson 2,580 ..... E7
Hudsonville 6,170 ..... D6
Huntington Woods 6,419 ..... B6
Ida 970 ..... F7
Imlay City 2,921 ..... F5
Indian River 950 ..... E3
Inkster 30,772 ..... B7
Interlochen 600 ..... D4
Ionia▲ 5,935 ..... D6
Iron Mountain▲ 8,525 ..... B3
Iron River 2,095 ..... G2
Ironwood 6,849 ..... F2
Ishpeming 7,200 ..... B2
Isle Royale National Park E1
Ithaca▲ 3,009 ..... E5
Jackson▲ 37,446 ..... E6
Jenison 17,882 ..... D6
Jonesville 2,283 ..... E6
Kalamazoo▲ 80,277 ..... D6
Kaleva 484 ..... C4
Kalkaska▲ 1,952 ..... D4
Keego Harbor 2,932 ..... F6
Kent City 899 ..... D5
Kentwood 37,826 ..... D6
Kinde 473 ..... G5
Kingsford 5,480 ..... A3
Kingsley 738 ..... D4
Kingston 439 ..... F5
L'Anse▲ 2,151 ..... G1
Laingsburg 1,148 ..... E6
Lake Ann 217 ..... D4
Lake City▲ 858 ..... D4
Lake George 950 ..... E5
Lake Linden 1,203 ..... A1
Lake Michigan Beach 1,694 ..... C6
Lake Odessa 2,256 ..... D6
Lake Orion 3,057 ..... F6
Lakeview 1,108 ..... D5
Lakewood Club 659 ..... C5

(continued on following page)

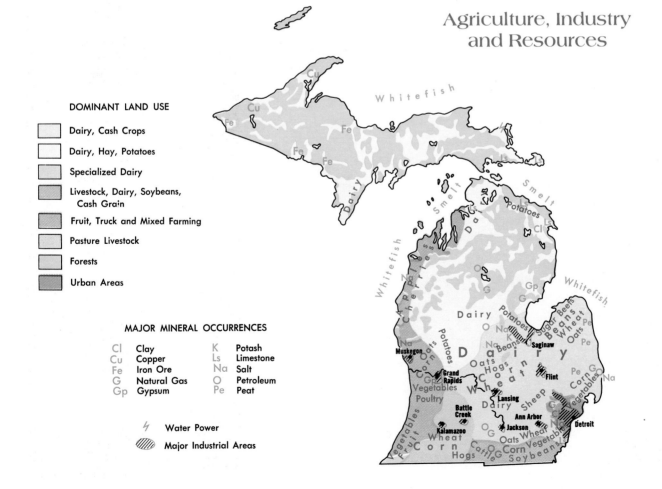

DOMINANT LAND USE

Dairy, Cash Crops
Dairy, Hay, Potatoes
Specialized Dairy
Livestock, Dairy, Soybeans, Cash Grain
Fruit, Truck and Mixed Farming
Pasture Livestock
Forests
Urban Areas

MAJOR MINERAL OCCURRENCES

Cl Clay
Cu Copper
Fe Iron Ore
G   Natural Gas
Gp Gypsum
K   Potash
Ls Limestone
Na Salt
O   Petroleum
Pe Peat

⚡ Water Power
▨ Major Industrial Areas

Agriculture, Industry and Resources

AREA 84,402 sq. mi. (218,601 sq. km.)
POPULATION 4,387,029
CAPITAL St. Paul
LARGEST CITY Minneapolis
HIGHEST POINT Eagle Mtn. 2,301 ft. (701 m.)
SETTLED IN 1805
ADMITTED TO UNION May 11, 1858
POPULAR NAME North Star State; Gopher State
STATE FLOWER Pink & White Lady's-Slipper
STATE BIRD Common Loon

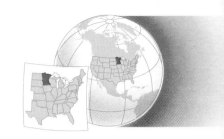

COUNTIES

Aitkin 12,425 .... E4
Anoka 243,641 .... E5
Becker 27,881 .... C4
Beltrami 34,384 .... C2
Benton 30,185 .... D5
Big Stone 6,285 .... B5
Blue Earth 54,044 .... D6
Brown 26,984 .... D6
Carlton 29,259 .... F4
Carver 47,915 .... E6
Cass 21,791 .... D4
Chippewa 13,228 .... C5
Chisago 30,521 .... F5
Clay 50,422 .... B4
Clearwater 8,309 .... C3
Cook 3,868 .... H3
Cottonwood 12,694 .... C6
Crow Wing 44,249 .... D4
Dakota 275,227 .... E6
Dodge 15,731 .... F7
Douglas 28,674 .... C5
Faribault 16,937 .... D7
Fillmore 20,777 .... F7
Freeborn 33,060 .... E7
Goodhue 40,690 .... F6
Grant 6,246 .... B5
Hennepin 1,032,431 ...... E5
Houston 18,497 .... G7
Hubbard 14,939 .... D3
Isanti 25,921 .... E5
Itasca 40,863 .... E3
Jackson 11,677 .... C7
Kanabec 12,802 .... E5
Kandiyohi 38,761 .... C5
Kittson 5,767 .... B2
Koochiching 16,299 ...... E2
Lac qui Parle 8,924 ...... B6
Lake 10,415 .... G3
Lake of the Woods 4,076 ... D2
Le Sueur 23,239 .... E6
Lincoln 6,890 .... B6
Lyon 24,789 .... C6
Mahnomen 5,044 .... C3
Marshall 10,993 .... B2
Martin 22,914 .... D7
McLeod 32,030 .... D6
Meeker 20,846 .... D5
Mille Lacs 18,670 .... E5
Morrison 29,604 .... D4
Mower 37,385 .... F7
Murray 9,660 .... C6
Nicollet 28,076 .... D6
Nobles 20,098 .... C7
Norman 7,975 .... B3
Olmsted 106,470 ..... F7
Otter Tail 50,714 ..... C4
Pennington 13,306 ... B2
Pine 21,264 .... E4
Pipestone 10,491 .... B6
Polk 32,498 .... B3
Pope 10,745 .... C5
Ramsey 485,765 .... E5
Red Lake 4,525 ..... B3
Redwood 17,254 ... C6
Renville 17,673 ..... C6
Rice 49,183 .... E6
Rock 9,806 .... B7
Roseau 15,026 ..... C2
Saint Louis 222,229 . F3
Scott 57,846 .... E6
Sherburne 41,945 .. E5
Sibley 14,366 ...... D6
Stearns 118,791 ... D5
Steele 30,729 ..... E7
Stevens 10,634 ... B5
Swift 10,724 ...... C5
Todd 23,363 ...... D4
Traverse 4,463 ... B5
Wabasha 19,744 .. F6
Wadena 13,154 .. D4
Waseca 18,079 .. E6
Washington 145,896 . F5
Watonwan 11,682 .... D7
Wilkin 7,516 .... B4
Winona 47,828 .... G6
Wright 68,710 .... D5
Yellow Medicine 11,684 .... B6

CITIES and TOWNS

Ada▲ 1,708 .... B3
Adams 756 .... F7
Adrian 1,141 .... C7
Afton 2,645 .... F6
Aitkin▲ 1,698 .... E4
Akeley 393 .... D3
Albany 1,548 .... D5
Albert Lea▲ 18,310 .. E7
Alberta 136 .... B5
Albertville 1,251 .... E5
Alborn 500 .... F4
Alden 623 .... E7
Aldrich 70 .... D4
Alexandria▲ 7,838 . C5
Alpha 105 .... D7
Altura 349 .... G6
Alvarado 356 ..... B2
Amboy 517 .... D7
Andover 15,216 .. E5
Annandale 2,054 . D5
Anoka▲ 17,192 ... E5
Apple Valley 34,598 . G6
Appleton 1,552 ... C5
Arco 104 .... B6
Argyle 636 .... B2
Arlington 1,886 .. D6
Arnold 2,891 .... F4
Ashby 469 ...... C4
Askov 343 ...... F4
Atwater 1,053 .. D5
Audubon 411 ... C4
Aurora 1,965 ... F3
Austin▲ 21,907 . E7
Avoca 150 ...... C7
Avon 970 .... D5
Babbitt 1,562 .... G3
Backus 240 .... D4
Badger 381 .... B2
Bagley▲ 1,388 .... C3
Balaton 737 .... C6
Barnesville 2,066 ... B4
Barnum 482 .... F4
Barrett 350 .... B5
Barry 40 .... B5
Battle Lake 698 ... C4
Baudette▲ 1,146 .. D2
Baxter 3,695 ...... D4
Bayport 3,200 .... F5
Beardsley 297 ... B5
Beaver Bay 147 .. G3
Beaver Creek 249 . B7
Becker 902 .... E5
Bejou 110 .... B3
Belgrade 700 .... C5
Belle Plaine 3,149 . E6
Bellechester 110 . F6
Bellingham 247 . B5
Beltrami 137 ... B3
Belview 383 .... C6
Bemidji▲ 11,245 . D3
Bena 147 ...... D3
Benson▲ 3,235 . C5
Bertha 507 .... C4
Bethel 394 ... E5
Big Falls 341 .. E2
Big Lake 3,113 . E5
Bigelow 232 .. C7
Bigfork 384 .. E3
Bingham Lake 155 . C7
Bird Island 1,326 . D6
Biscay 113 .... D6
Biwabik 1,097 . F3
Blackduck 718 . D3
Blaine 38,975 . G5
Blomkest 183 . D6
Blooming Prairie 2,043 . E7
Bloomington 86,335 .... G6
Blue Earth▲ 3,745 .... D7
Bluffton 187 .... C4
Bock 115 .... E5
Borup 119 .... B3
Bovey 662 .... E3
Bowlus 360 .... D5
Boy River 43 .... D3
Boyd 251 .... C6
Braham 1,139 .... E5
Brainerd▲ 12,353 ...... D4
Branch 2,400 .... F5
Brandon 441 .... C5
Breckenridge▲ 3,708 . B4
Breezy Point 432 .... D4
Brewster 532 .... C7
Bricelyn 426 .... D7
Brook Park 125 .... F5
Brooklyn Center 28,887 . G5
Brooklyn Park 56,381 .. G5
Brooks 158 .... B3
Brookston 107 ..... F4
Brooten 589 .... C5
Browerville 782 ... D4
Browns Valley 804 . B5
Brownsdale 695 .. E7
Brownsville 415 .. G7
Brownton 781 .... D6
Bruno 89 .... F4
Buckman 201 .... D5
Buffalo Lake 734 . D6
Buffalo▲ 6,856 .. E5
Buhl 915 .... F3
Burnsville 51,288 . E6
Burtrum 172 .... D5
Butterfield 509 . D7
Byron 2,441 ... F6
Caledonia▲ 2,846 . G7
Callaway 212 .. C3
Calumet 382 .. E3
Cambridge▲ 5,094 . E5
Campbell 233 .. B4
Canby 1,826 ... B6
Cannon Falls 3,232 . F6
Canton 362 ... F7
Carlos 361 ... C5
Carlton▲ 923 . F4
Carver 744 .. E6
Cass Lake 923 . D3
Cedar Mills 80 . D6
Center City▲ 451 . F5
Centerville 1,633 . E5
Ceylon 461 ... D7
Champlin 16,849 . G5
Chandler 316 .. C7
Chanhassen 11,732 . F6
Chaska▲ 11,339 . F6
Chatfield 2,226 . F7
Chickamaw Beach 132 . D4
Chisago City 2,009 . E5
Chisholm 5,290 . E3
Chokio 521 ... B5
Circle Pines 4,704 . G5
Clara City 1,307 . C6
Claremont 530 . E6
Clarissa 637 ... C4
Clarkfield 924 . C6
Clarks Grove 675 . E7
Clear Lake 315 . E5
Clearbrook 560 . C3
Clearwater 597 . D5
Clements 191 . D6
Cleveland 699 . E6
Climax 264 ... B3
Clinton 574 .. B5
Clitherall 109 .... C4
Clontarf 172 .... C5
Cloquet 10,885 .... F4
Coates 186 .... E6
Cobden 62 .... D6
Cohasset E3
Cokato 2,180 .... D5
Cold Spring 2,459 ..... D5
Coleraine 1,041 .... E3
Cologne 563 .... E6
Columbia Heights 18,910 . G5
Comfrey 433 .... D6
Comstock 123 ...... B4
Conger 143 .... E7
Cook 680 .... F3
Coon Rapids 52,978 . G5
Corcoran 5,199 .... F5
Correll 60 .... B5
Cosmos 610 ...... D6
Cottage Grove 22,935 . F6
Cotton 982 ...... F3
Cottonwood 924 . C6
Courtland 412 .. D6
Cromwell 221 .. F4
Crookston▲ 8,119 . B3
Crosby 2,073 .. D4
Crosslake 1,132 . E4
Crystal 23,788 . G5
Currie 303 .... C6
Cuyuna 172 .. E4
Cyrus 328 ... C5
Dakota 360 .. G7
Dalton 234 .. C4
Danube 562 . C6
Danvers 98 . C5
Darfur 128 .. D6
Darwin 252 . D5
Dassel 1,082 . D5
Dawson 1,626 . B6
Day 4,443 .... E5
Dayton 4,070 . G5
De Graff 149 .. C5
Deephaven 3,653 . G5
Deer Creek 303 . C4
Deer River 838 . E3
Deerwood 524 . E4
Delano 2,709 . E5
Delavan 245 . D7
Delhi 69 ..... C6
Dellwood 887 . F5
Denham 36 .. F4
Dennison 152 . E6
Dent 177 ... C4
Detroit Lakes▲ 6,635 . C4
Dexter 303 .. F7
Dilworth 2,562 . B4
Dodge Center 1,954 . F6
Donaldson 57 . B2
Donnelly 221 . B5
Doran 78 ... B4
Dover 416 .. F7
Dovray 60 .. C6
Duluth▲ 85,493 . F4
Dumont 126 . B5
Dundas 473 . E6
Dundee 107 . C7
Dunnell 187 . D7
Eagan 47,409 . G6
Eagle Bend 524 . D4
Eagle Lake 1,703 . E6
East Bethel 8,050 . E5
East Grand Forks 8,658 . B3
East Gull Lake 687 . D4
Easton 229 . E7
Echo 304 .. C6
Eden Prairie 39,311 . G6
Eden Valley 732 . D5
Edgerton 1,106 . B7
Edina 46,070 . G5
Effie 130 .. E3
Eitzen 221 . G7
Elba 220 .. F6
Elbow Lake▲ 1,186 . B5
Elgin 733 . F6
Elizabeth 152 . B4
Elk River▲ 11,143 . E5
Elko 223 .. E6
Elkton 142 . F7
Ellendale 549 . E7
Ellsworth 580 . C7
Elmdale 130 . D5
Elmore 709 . D7
Elrosa 205 . C5
Ely 3,968 . G3
Elysian 445 . E6
Emily 613 . E4
Emmons 439 . E7
Erhard 191 . B4
Erskine 422 . B3
Esko 500 .. F4
Evan 83 ... D6
Evansville 566 . C4
Eveleth 4,064 . F3
Excelsior 2,367 . E6
Eyota 1,448 . F7
Fairfax 1,276 . D6
Fairmont▲ 11,265 .... D7
Falcon Heights 5,380 ...... G5
Faribault▲ 17,085 .... E6
Farmington 5,940 .... E6
Farwell 74 .... C5
Federal Dam 118 .... D3
Felton 211 .... B4
Fergus Falls▲ 12,362 ..... B4
Fertile 853 .... B3
Fifty Lakes 299 .... D4
Finlayson 242 .... F4
Fisher 413 .... B3
Flensburg 213 .... D5
Floodwood 574 ...... F4
Florence 53 .... B6
Florenton 635 ...... F5
Foley▲ 1,854 .... D5
Forada 171 .... C6
Forest Lake 5,833 . F5
Foreston 354 ..... E5
Fort Ripley 92 ... D4
Fosston 1,529 ... C3
Fountain 327 ... F7
Foxhome 160 .. B4
Franklin 512 .. C6
Frazee 1,176 .. C4
Freeborn 321 . E7
Freeport 556 . D5
Fridley 28,335 . G5
Frost 236 .. D7
Fulda 1,212 . C7
Garfield 203 . C5
Garrison 138 . E4
Garvin 149 . C6
Gary 200 .. B3
Gaylord▲ 1,935 . D6
Geneva 444 . E7
Genola 85 . D5
Georgetown 107 . B3
Ghent 316 . C6
Gibbon 712 . D6
Gilbert 1,934 . F3
Gilman 192 . E5
Glen 4,648 . E4
Glencoe▲ 4,396 . D6
Glenville 778 . E7
Glenwood▲ 2,573 . C5
Glyndon 862 . B4
Golden Valley 20,971 . G5
Gonvick 302 . C3
Good Thunder 561 . D6
Goodhue 533 . F6
Goodridge 115 . C2
Goodview 2,878 . G6
Graceville 671 . B5
Granada 374 . D7
Grand Marais▲ 1,171 . G2
Grand Meadow 967 . F7
Grand Rapids▲ 7,976 . E3
Granite Falls▲ 3,083 . C6
Grasston 119 . E5
Green Isle 239 . E6
Greenbush 800 . B2
Greenfield 1,450 . F5
Greenwald 209 . D5
Grey Eagle 353 . D5
Grove City 547 . D5
Grygla 220 . C2
Gully 128 . C3
Hackensack 245 . D4
Hadley 94 . C7
Hallock▲ 1,304 . A2
Halma 73 . B2
Halstad 611 . B3
Ham Lake 8,924 . E5
Hamburg 492 . D6
Hamel F5
Hammond 205 . F6
Hampton 363 . E6
Hancock 723 . C5
Hanley Falls 246 . C6
Hanover 787 . E5
Hanska 443 . D6
Harding 76 . E4
Hardwick 234 . B7
Harmony 1,081 . F7
Harris 843 . F5
Hartland 270 . E7
Hastings▲ 15,445 . F6
Hatfield 66 . B7
Hawley 1,655 . B4
Hayfield 1,283 . F7
Hayward 246 . E7
Hazel Run 81 . C6
Hector 1,145 . D6
Heidelberg 73 . E6
Henderson 746 . E6
Hendricks 684 . B6
Hendrum 309 . B3
Henning 738 . C4
Henriette 78 . E5
Herman 485 . B5
Hermantown 6,761 . F4
Heron Lake 730 . C7
Hewitt 269 . C4
Hibbing 18,046 . F3

(continued on following page)

Agriculture, Industry and Resources

DOMINANT LAND USE

- Wheat, General Farming
- Dairy, Livestock
- Dairy, Hay, Potatoes
- Cattle Feed, Hogs
- Livestock, Cash Grain
- Forests
- Swampland, Limited Agriculture
- Urban Areas

MAJOR MINERAL OCCURRENCES

Cl Clay
Fe Iron Ore
Gn Granite
Ls Limestone
Mn Manganese

⚡ Water Power
▨ Major Industrial Areas

Hill City 469 ....E4
Hillman 45....E4
Hills 607 ....B7
Hinckley 946 ....E4
Hitterdal 242....B4
Hoffman 576....C5
Hokah 687 ....G7
Holdingford 561 ....D5
Holland 216 ....B6
Hollandale 289....E7
Holloway 123....C5
Holt 88....B2
Hopkins 16,534 ....G5
Houston 1,013....G7
Howard Lake 1,343....D5
Hoyt Lakes 2,348 ....F3
Hugo 4,417 ....E5
Humboldt 74....A2
Hutchinson 11,523 ....D6
Ihlen 101....B7
Independence 2,822....F5
Indus....E2
International Falls▲ 8,325 ....E2
Inver Grove Heights 22,477 ....E6
Iona 158 ....C7
Iron 133 ....F3
Ironton 553....D4
Isanti 1,228....E5
Island View 150 ....E2
Isle 566....E4
Ivanhoe▲ 751....B6
Jackson▲ 3,559 ....C7
Janesville 1,969 ....E6
Jasper 599....B7
Jeffers 443....C6
Jenkins 262 ....D4
Johnson 46....B5
Jordan 2,909....E6
Kandiyohi 506....D5
Karlstad 881 ....B2
Kasota 655 ....D6
Kasson 3,514 ....F6
Keewatin 1,118 ....E3
Kelliher 348 ....D3
Kellogg 423 ....G6
Kelly Lake 900....F3
Kennedy 337....B2
Kenneth 81 ....B7
Kensington 295....C5
Kent 131 ....B4
Kenyon 1,552....E6
Kerkhoven 732....C5
Kerrick 56....F4
Kettle River 190 ....E4
Kiester 606....E7
Kilkenny 167 ....E6
Kimball 690 ....D5
Kingston 131 ....D5
Kinney 257 ....F3
La Crescent 4,311....G7
La Prairie 438....E3
La Salle 98....D6
Lafayette 462....D6
Lake Benton 693....B6
Lake Bronson 272....B2
Lake City 4,391 ....F6
Lake Crystal 2,084....D6
Lake Elmo 5,903 ....F6
Lake Henry 90 ....D5
Lake Lillian 229....C6
Lake Park 638....B4
Lake Saint Croix Beach 1,078..F6
Lake Shore 693 ....D4
Lake Wilson 319 ....B7
Lakefield 1,679 ....C7
Lakeland 2,000....F6
Lakeville 24,854 ....E6
Lamberton 972 ....C6
Lancaster 342 ....B2
Lanesboro 858 ....G7
Laporte 101 ....D3
Lastrup 112 ....D4
Lauderdale 2,700....G5
Le Center▲ 2,006 ....E6
Le Roy 904....F7
Le Sueur 3,714 ....E6
Lengby 112....C3
Leonard 26 ....C3
Leonidas 70....F3
Lester Prairie 1,180 ....D6
Lewiston 1,298....G7
Lewisville 255....D7
Lexington 2,279....G5
Lilydale 506 ....G5
Lindstrom 2,461....F5
Lino Lakes 8,807 ....G5
Lismore 248 ....B7
Litchfield▲ 6,041 ....D5
Little Falls▲ 7,232....D5
Little Rock 714 ....D5
Littlefork 838....E2
Long Beach 204....C5
Long Lake 1,984 ....F5
Long Prairie▲ 2,786....D5
Longville 224....D4
Lonsdale 1,252 ....E6
Loretto 404 ....F5
Louisburg 42 ....B5
Lowry 233....C5
Lucan 235....C6
Luverne▲ 4,382 ....B7
Lyle 504 ....F7
Lynd 287....C6
Mabel 745....G7
Madelia 2,237 ....D6
Madison Lake 643....E6
Madison▲ 1,951 ....B5
Magnolia 155....B7
Mahnomen▲ 1,154 ....C3
Mahtomedi 5,569....F5
Manchester 69 ....E7
Manhattan Beach 61 ....E4
Mankato▲ 31,477....E6
Mantorville▲ 874....F6
Maple Grove 38,736 ....G5
Maple Lake 1,394 ....D5
Maple Plain 2,005 ....F5
Mapleton 1,526....E7
Mapleview 206....E7
Maplewood 30,954....G5
Marble 618....E3
Marietta 211 ....B5
Marine on Saint Croix 602....F5
Marshall▲ 12,023 ....C6
Mayer 471....E6
Maynard 419....C6
Mazeppa 722....F6
McGrath 62....E4
McGregor 376....E4
McIntosh 665 ....C3
McKinley 116 ....F3
Meadowlands 92 ....F3
Medford 733 ....E6
Medicine Lake 385....G5
Medina (Hamel) 3,096....F5
Meire Grove 124 ....C5
Melrose 2,561 ....D5
Menahga 1,076....C4
Mendota 164 ....G5
Mendota Heights 9,431 ....G6
Mentor 94....B3
Middle River 285 ....B2
Miesville 135....F6
Milaca▲ 2,182....E5
Milan 353....C5
Millerville 104 ....C4
Millville 163....F6
Milroy 297 ....C6
Miltona 181....C4
Minneapolis▲ 368,383....G5
Minneiska 127 ....G6
Minneota 1,417....C6
Minnesota City 258....G6
Minnesota Lake 681 ....E7
Minnetonka 48,370....G5
Minnetrista 3,439....F5
Mizpah 100....D3
Montevideo▲ 5,499....C6
Montgomery 2,399 ....E6
Monticello 4,941 ....E5
Montrose 1,008 ....E5
Moorhead▲ 32,295....B4
Moose Lake 1,206....F4
Mora▲ 2,905 ....E5
Morgan 965....D6
Morris▲ 5,613....C5
Morristown 784 ....E6
Morton 448....C6
Motley 441 ....D4
Mound 9,634 ....E6
Mounds View 12,541....G5
Mountain Iron 3,362 ....F3
Mountain Lake 1,906....D7
Murdock 282 ....C5
Myrtle 72....E7
Nashua 63....B4
Nashwauk 1,026 ....E3
Nassau 83....B5
Naytahwaush 378 ....C3
Nelson 177 ....C5
Nerstrand 210....E6
Nevis 375 ....D4
New Auburn 363....D6
New Brighton 22,207....G5
New Germany 353 ....E6
New Hope 21,853....G5
New London 971 ....C5
New Market 227....E6
New Munich 314 ....D5
New Prague 3,569....E6
New Richland 1,237....E7
New Trier 96....F6
New Ulm▲ 13,132 ....D6
New York Mills 940....C4
Newfolden 345....B2
Newport 3,720 ....F6
Nicollet 795 ....D6
Nielsville 100 ....B3
Nimrod 65 ....D4
Nisswa 1,391....D4
Norcross 86....B5
North Branch 1,867....F5
North Mankato 10,164....D6
North Oaks 3,386 ....G5
North Redwood 203 ....D6
North Saint Paul 12,376 ....G5
Northfield 14,684....E6
Northome 283 ....D3
Northrop 276....D7
Norwood 1,351 ....E6
Oak Park 3,486 ....E5
Oakdale 18,374 ....E5
Odessa 155....B5
Odin 102....D7
Ogema 164 ....C3
Ogilvie 510....E5
Okabena 223....C7
Oklee 441....C3
Olivia▲ 2,623 ....C6
Onamia 676....E4
Ormsby 159....D7
Oronoco 727 ....F6
Orr 265....F2
Ortonville▲ 2,205....B5
Osakis 1,256....C5
Oslo 362 ....A2
Osseo 2,704 ....G5
Ostrander 276 ....F7
Ottertail 313....C4
Owatonna▲ 19,386 ....E6
Palisade 144 ....E4
Park Rapids▲ 2,863....D4
Parkers Prairie 956....C4
Payne 2,275 ....F3
Paynesville 2,140....D5
Pease 178 ....E5
Pelican Lakes (Breezy Point) D4
Pelican Rapids 1,886....B4
Pemberton 228 ....E7
Pengilly 625....E3
Pennock 476....C5
Pequot Lakes 843....D4
Perham 2,075 ....C4
Perley 132....B3
Peterson 259 ....G7
Pierz 1,014 ....D5
Pillager 306 ....D4
Pine City▲ 2,613....F5
Pine Island 2,125 ....F6
Pine River 871 ....D4
Pipestone▲ 4,554 ....B7
Plainview 2,768....F6
Plato 355 ....D6
Pleasant Lake 79 ....D5
Plummer 277....B3
Plymouth 50,889....G5
Ponemah 704 ....D2
Porter 210....B6
Preston▲ 1,530 ....F7
Princeton 3,719 ....E5
Prinsburg 502....C6
Prior Lake 11,482 ....E6
Proctor 2,974....F4
Quamba 124 ....E5
Racine 288 ....F7
Ramsey 12,408....E5
Randall 571 ....D4
Randolph 331 ....E6
Ranier 199 ....E2
Ray 668....E2
Raymond 723 ....C5
Red Lake Falls▲ 1,481 ....B3
Red Wing▲ 15,134....F6
Redby 787 ....D3
Redwood Falls▲ 4,859....C6
Regal 51 ....D5
Remer 342....E3
Renville 1,315....C6
Revere 117 ....C6
Rice 610 ....D5
Richfield 35,710 ....G6
Richmond 965....D5
Richville 121 ....C4
Riverton 122....D4
Robbinsdale 14,396....G5
Rochester▲ 70,745 ....F6
Rock Creek 1,040....F5
Rockford 2,665 ....F5
Rockville 579....D5
Rogers 698 ....E5
Rollingstone 697 ....G6
Ronneby 58....E5
Roosevelt 180....C2
Roscoe 141 ....D5
Rose Creek 363....F7
Roseau▲ 2,396 ....C2
Rosemount 8,622 ....E6
Roseville 33,485....G5
Rothsay 443 ....B4
Round Lake 463....C7
Royalton 802....D5
Rush City 1,497....F5
Rushford 1,485 ....G7
Rushmore 381 ....C7
Russell 394....C6
Ruthton 328....B6
Rutledge 152....F4
Sabin 495 ....B4
Sacred Heart 603....C6
Saint Anthony 7,727 ....G5
Saint Anthony 81....D5
Saint Bonifacius 1,180 ....F5
Saint Charles 2,642....F7
Saint Clair 633 ....E6
Saint Cloud▲ 48,812....D5
Saint Francis 2,538 ....E5
Saint Hilaire 298 ....B2
Saint James▲ 4,364....D7
Saint Joseph 3,294....D5
Saint Leo 111....C6
Saint Louis Park 43,787 ....G5
Saint Martin 274....D5
Saint Michael 2,506 ....E5
Saint Paul (cap.)▲ 272,235....G6
Saint Paul Park 4,965 ....G6
Saint Peter▲ 9,421 ....E6
Saint Rosa 75 ....D5
Saint Stephen 607 ....D5
Saint Vincent 116....A2
Sanborn 459....C6
Sandstone 2,057 ....F4
Sargeant 78....F7
Sartell 5,393 ....D5
Sauk Centre 3,581 ....C5
Sauk Rapids 7,825 ....D5
Savage 9,906....G6
Scanlon 878....F4
Seaforth 87 ....C6
Sebeka 662....C4
Sedan 63....C5
Shafer 368....F5
Shakopee▲ 11,739 ....F6
Shelly 225....B3
Sherburn 1,105 ....D7
Shevlin 157....C3
Shoreview 24,587....G5
Shorewood 5,917....F5
Silver Bay 1,894 ....G3
Silver Lake 764....D6
Skyline 272....D6
Slayton▲ 2,147 ....C7
Sleepy Eye 3,694 ....D6
Sobieski 199....D5
Solway 74 ....C3
Soudan 900....F3
South Haven 193....D5
South International Falls 2,806....E2
South Saint Paul 20,197....G6
Spicer 1,020 ....C5
Spring Grove 1,153 ....G7
Spring Hill 77....D5
Spring Lake 6,532....E5
Spring Lake Park 6,477....E5
Spring Park 1,571 ....F5
Spring Valley 2,461 ....F7
Springfield 2,173 ....C6
Squaw Lake 139....D3
Stacy 1,081....E5
Staples 2,754....D4
Starbuck 1,143 ....C5
Steen 176 ....B7
Stephen 707 ....A2
Stewart 566 ....D6
Stewartville 4,520....F7
Stillwater▲ 13,882....F5
Stockton 529 ....G6
Storden 283....C6
Strandquist 98 ....B2
Strathcona 40 ....B2
Sturgeon Lake 230....F4
Sunburg 117....C5
Sunfish Lake 413 ....E6
Swanville 324 ....D5
Taconite 310 ....E3
Tamarack 53 ....E4
Taopi 83 ....F7
Taunton 175 ....B6
Taylors Falls 694 ....F5
Tenstrike 184....D3
Thief River Falls▲ 8,010....B2
Thomson 132....F4
Tintah 74....B5
Tonka Bay 1,472 ....F5
Tower 502....F3
Tracy 2,059....C6
Trail 67 ....C3
Trimont 745....D7
Trommald 80....D4
Trosky 120....B7
Truman 1,292....D7
Turtle River 62....D3
Twin Lakes 154....E7
Twin Valley 821 ....B3
Two Harbors▲ 3,651 ....G3
Tyler 1,257....B6
Ulen 547 ....B3
Underwood 284....C4
Upsala 371 ....D5
Urbank 73....C4
Utica 220....G7
Vadnais Heights 11,041....G5
Vergas 287 ....C4
Vermillion 510....F6
Verndale 560....C4
Vernon Center 339....D7
Vesta 302....C6
Victoria 2,354....F6
Viking 103....B2
Villard 247 ....C5
Vining 84 ....C4
Virginia 9,410....F3
Wabasha▲ 2,384 ....G6
Wabasso 684....C6
Waconia 3,498....E6
Wadena▲ 4,131 ....C4
Wahkon 197....E4
Waite Park 5,020....D5
Waldorf 243....E7
Walker▲ 950....D3
Walnut Grove 625....C6
Walters 86....E7
Waltham 170....F7
Wanamingo 847....F6
Wanda 103 ....C6
Warba 137 ....E3
Warren▲ 1,813 ....B2
Warroad 1,679....C2
Waseca▲ 8,385....E6
Watertown 2,408 ....E6
Waterville 1,771 ....E6
Watkins 849 ....D5
Watson 211 ....C5
Waubun 330 ....C3
Waverly 600....E5
Wayzata 3,806....G5
Welcome 790 ....D7
Wells 2,465....E7
Wendell 159....B4
West Concord 871 ....F6
West Saint Paul 19,248 ....G5
West Union 54....C5
Westbrook 853 ....C6
Westport 47....C5
Whalan 94 ....G7
Wheaton▲ 1,615....B5
White Bear Lake 24,704....G5
White Earth 319....C3
Wilder 83....C7
Willernie 584 ....G5
Williams 212....D2
Willmar▲ 17,531....C5
Willow River 284....F4
Wilmont 351 ....C7
Wilton 171 ....C3
Windom▲ 4,283....C7
Winger 167....B3
Winnebago 1,565 ....D7
Winona▲ 25,399....G6
Winsted 1,581 ....D6
Winthrop 1,279 ....D6
Winton 169....G3
Wolf Lake 35....C4
Wolverton 158....B4
Wood Lake 406....C6
Woodbury 20,075 ....F6
Woodstock 159....B7
Worthington▲ 9,977 ....C7
Wrenshall 296....F4
Wright 144....E4
Wykoff 493....F7
Wyoming 2,142....F5
Young America 1,354 ....E6
Zemple 63....E3
Zim 1,350....F3
Zumbro Falls 237 ....F6
Zumbrota 2,312 ....F6

OTHER FEATURES

Ash (riv.) F2
Bald Eagle (lake)....G3
Basswood (lake)....G2
Battle (riv.)....D3
Baudette (riv.)....D2
Bear (riv.)....E3
Bemidji (lake) D3
Benton (lake) B6
Big Fork (riv.)....E2
Big Sandy (lake)....E4
Big Stone (lake) B5
Birch (lake)....G3
Black (riv.)....D2
Blue Earth (riv.) D7
Bois de Sioux (riv.) B4
Bowstring (lake)....E3
Buffalo (riv.)....B4
Burntside (lake)....F3
Cass (lake)....D3
Cedar (riv.)....F7
Chippewa (riv.) C5
Christina (lake) C4
Clearwater (riv.)....C3
Cloquet (riv.)....F4
Cobb (riv.)....E7
Cottonwood (riv.)....C6
Crooked (creek)....F4
Crooked (lake) G2
Crow (riv.)....F5
Crow Wing (riv.)....D4
Cuyuna (range)....D4
Dead (lake) C4
Deer (lake) E3
Des Moines (riv.) C7
Eagle (mt.)....G2
East Swan (riv.)....F3
Elbow (lake)....C3
Emily (lake)....C5
Fond du Lac Ind. Res. F4
Grand Portage Ind. Res. G2
Grand Portage Nat'l Mon. G2
Green (lake)....D
Greenwood (lake) ....G
Gull (lake)....D
Heron (lake)....C
Hill (riv.)....C
Independence (lake)....F
Isabella (lake) ....G
Itasca (lake) C
Kabetogama (lake) ....E
Kanaranzi (creek)....C
Kettle (riv.) ....F
Knife (lake) ....G
La Croix (lake)....F
Lac qui Parle (lake) C
Lac qui Parle (riv.) ....B
Lake of the Woods (lake)....D
Leaf (riv.)....C
Leech (lake)....D
Leech Lake Ind. Res. ....D
Lida (lake)....C
Little Fork (riv.) ....E
Little Rock (creek) C
Long (lake) ....D
Long (lake)....F
Long Prairie (riv.) ....D
Lost (riv.)....C
Lower Red (lake) C
Maple (lake)....B
Maple (riv.) ....E
Marsh (lake) ....B
Mary (lake) C
Mesabi (range)....E
Middle (riv.)....B
Mille Lacs Ind. Res....E
Mille Lacs (lake)....E
Miltona (lake)....C
Minneapolis-Saint Paul Airport ....G
Minnesota (riv.) ....E
Minnetonka (lake) F5
Minnewaska (lake)....C5
Misquah (hills) ....F
Mississippi (riv.)....D
Moose (riv.)....C
Mud (lake) C
Mud (riv.)....C
Muskeg (bay)....C
Mustinka (riv.) B5
Nemadji (riv.) ....F
Nett (lake) ....E
Nett Lake Ind. Res....E
North (lake)....F
Otter Tail (lake) C4
Otter Tail (riv.) B4
Partridge (riv.)....G
Pelican (lake) C4
Pelican (lake)....D4
Pelican (riv.)....F
Pelican (riv.) B4
Pelican (riv.)....F
Pepin (lake)....F
Pigeon (riv.)....G
Pike (riv.) ....F
Pipestone Nat'l Mon....B
Pokegama (lake) ....E
Pomme de Terre (riv.) C5
Poplar (riv.) C
Prairie (riv.)....E
Rainy (lake)....E
Rainy (riv.)....D
Rapid (riv.) ....D
Redeye (riv.)....D4
Red Lake (riv.) B2
Red Lake Ind. Res....C2
Red River of the North (riv.) ...A2
Redeye (riv.)....D4
Redwood (riv.)....C6
Reno (lake) C5
Rice (lake)....E4
Rock (riv.)....B7
Root (riv.)....G7
Roseau (riv.)....B2
Rum (riv.) E5
Saganaga (lake)....H2
Saint Croix (riv.)....F5
Saint Louis (riv.) F4
Sand (creek)....F5
Sand Hill (riv.)....B3
Sarah (lake)....F5
Schoolcraft C3
Shakopee (creek)....C5
Shell (riv.)....C4
Shetek (lake)....C6
Sleepy Eye (creek) C6
Snake (riv.) A2
Snake (riv.) E4
South Fowl (lake)....G1
Star (lake) C4
Sturgeon (riv.)....F3
Superior (lake)....G3
Swan (lake)....D6
Tamarac (riv.) A2
Tamarack (riv.) D2
Thief (lake)....C2
Thief (riv.)....B2
Traverse (lake)....B5
Trout (lake) F2
Two Rivers (riv.)....A1
Upper Red (lake) D2
Vermilion (lake)....F3
Vermilion (range) F3
Vermilion (riv.)....F2
Voyageurs Nat'l Park....F2
Wabatawangang (lake) D3
West Swan (riv.) F3
White Earth Ind. Res....C3
Whiteface (riv.)....F3
Whitefish (lake) D4
White Iron (lake)....G3
Wild Rice (lake)....F4
Wild Rice (riv.)....B3
Willow (riv.) E4
Winnibigoshish (lake)....D3
Woods (lake) D1
Zumbro (riv.)....F6

▲County seat

Topography

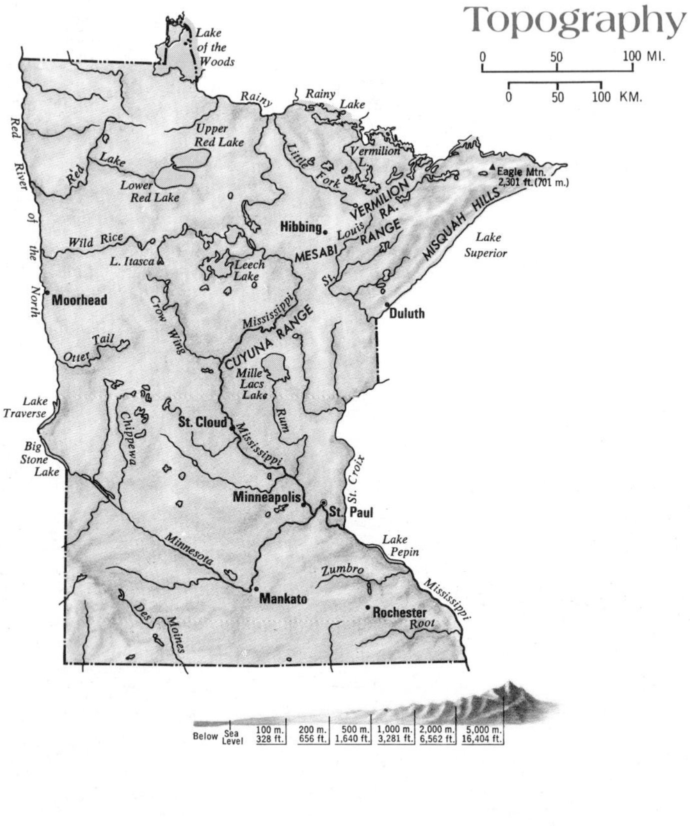

0 50 100 MI.
0 50 100 KM.
Lake of the Woods
Rainy
Rainy Lake
Upper Red Lake
Red Lake
Lower Red Lake
Red River of the North
Little Fork
Vermilion
VERMILION RA.
Eagle Mtn. 2,301 ft. (701 m.)
Hibbing
Louis
MESABI RANGE
MISQUAH HILLS
Lake Superior
Wild Rice
L. Itasca
Leech Lake
Moorhead
Crow Wing
Mississippi
St.
Duluth
Otter Tail
CUYUNA RANGE
Mille Lacs Lake
Lake Traverse
Chippewa
St. Cloud
Rum
Big Stone Lake
Minneapolis
St. Paul
St. Croix
Lake Pepin
Minnesota
Zumbro
Mankato
Rochester
Root
Des Moines
Below Sea Level
100 m. 328 ft.
200 m. 656 ft.
500 m. 1,640 ft.
1,000 m. 3,281 ft.
2,000 m. 6,562 ft.
5,000 m. 16,404 ft.

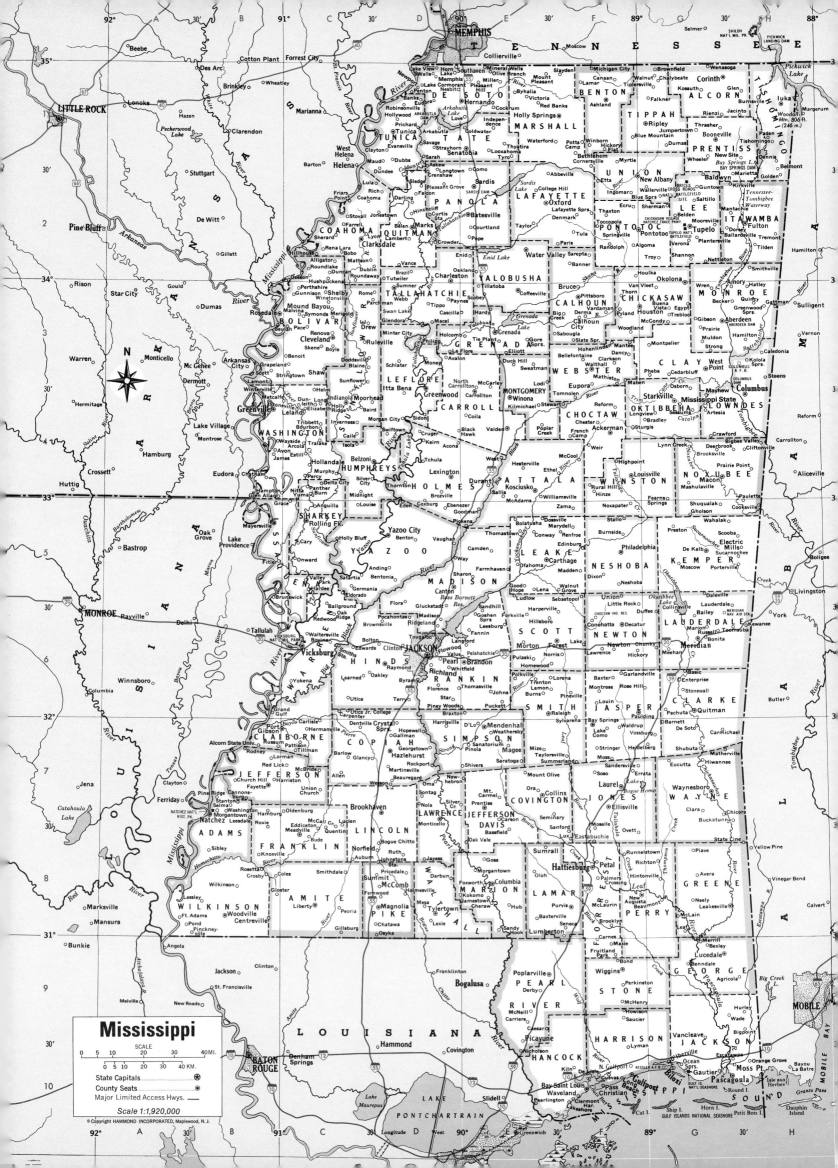

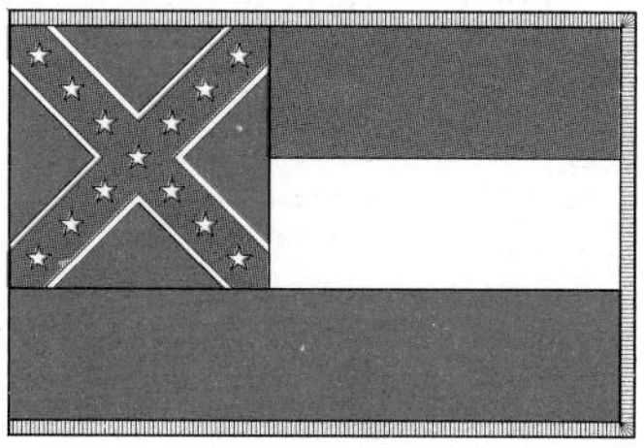

AREA 47,689 sq. mi. (123,515 sq. km.)
POPULATION 2,586,443
CAPITAL Jackson
LARGEST CITY Jackson
HIGHEST POINT Woodall Mtn. 806 ft. (246 m.)
SETTLED IN 1716
ADMITTED TO UNION December 10, 1817
POPULAR NAME Magnolia State
STATE FLOWER Magnolia
STATE BIRD Mockingbird

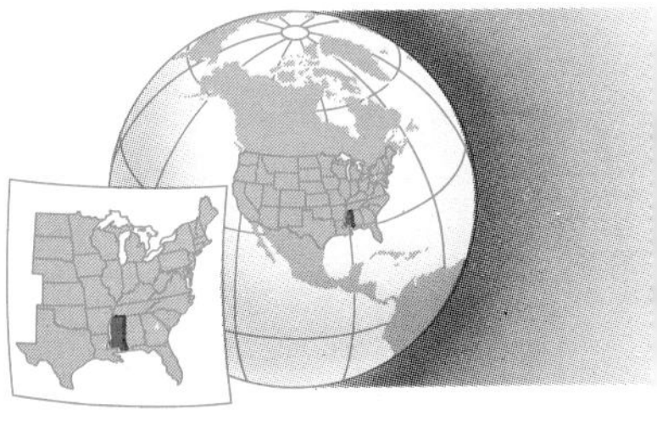

Topography

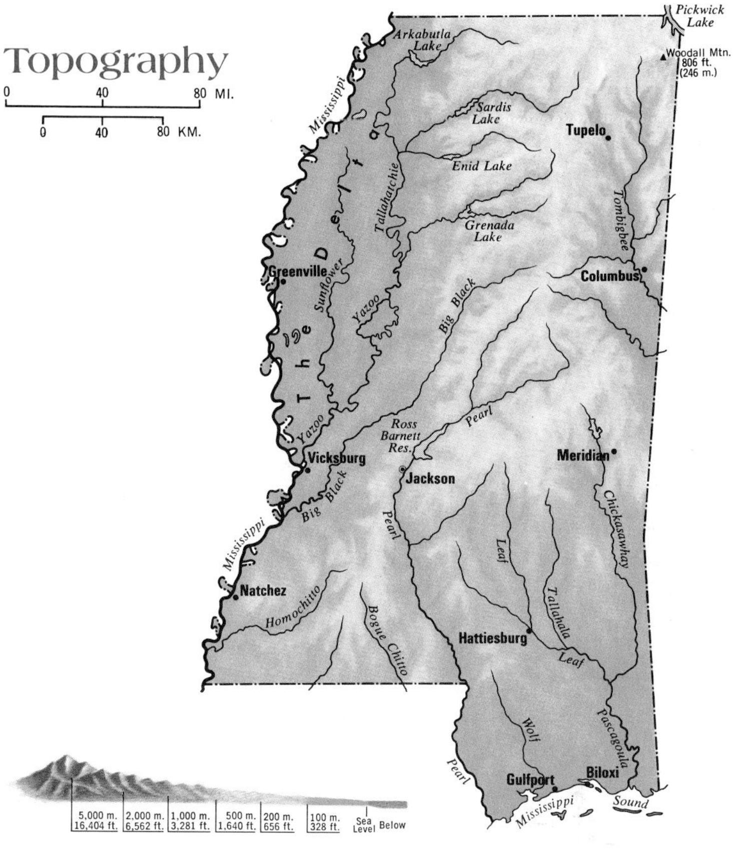

COUNTIES

Adams 35,356 B8
Alcorn 31,722 G1
Amite 13,328 C8
Attala 18,481 E4
Benton 8,046 F1
Bolivar 41,875 C3
Calhoun 14,908 F3
Carroll 9,237 E4
Chickasaw 18,085 G3
Choctaw 9,071 F4
Claiborne 11,370 C7
Clarke 17,313 G6
Clay 21,120 G3
Coahoma 31,665 C2
Copiah 27,592 D7
Covington 16,527 E7
De Soto 53,930 E1
Forrest 68,314 F8
Franklin 8,377 C8
George 16,673 G9
Greene 10,220 G8
Grenada 21,555 E3
Hancock 31,760 E10
Harrison 165,365 F10
Hinds 254,441 D6
Holmes 21,604 D4
Humphreys 12,134 C4
Issaquena 1,909 B5
Itawamba 20,017 H2
Jackson 115,243 G9
Jasper 17,114 F6
Jefferson 8,653 B7
Jefferson Davis 14,051 E7
Jones 62,031 F7
Kemper 10,356 G5
Lafayette 31,826 E2
Lamar 30,424 E8
Lauderdale 75,555 G6
Lawrence 12,458 D7
Leake 18,436 E5
Lee 65,581 G2
Leflore 37,341 D3
Lincoln 30,278 D8
Lowndes 59,308 H4
Madison 53,794 D5
Marion 25,544 E8
Marshall 30,361 E1
Monroe 36,582 H3
Montgomery 12,388 E4
Neshoba 24,800 F5
Newton 20,291 F6
Noxubee 12,604 G4
Oktibbeha 38,375 G4
Panola 29,996 E2
Pearl River 38,714 E9
Perry 10,865 G8
Pike 36,882 D8
Pontotoc 22,237 F2
Prentiss 23,278 G1
Quitman 10,490 D2
Rankin 87,161 E6
Scott 24,137 E6
Sharkey 7,066 C5
Simpson 23,953 E7
Smith 14,798 E6
Stone 10,750 F9
Sunflower 32,867 C3
Tallahatchie 15,210 D3
Tate 21,432 E1
Tippah 19,523 G1
Tishomingo 17,683 H1
Tunica 8,164 D1
Union 22,085 F2
Walthall 14,352 D8
Warren 47,880 C6
Washington 67,935 C4
Wayne 19,517 G7
Webster 10,222 F3
Wilkinson 9,678 B8
Winston 19,433 F4
Yalobusha 12,033 E2
Yazoo 25,506 D5

CITIES and TOWNS

Abbeville 399 F2
Aberdeen▲ 6,837 H3
Ackerman▲ 1,573 F4
Acona 200 D4
Agricola 200 G9
Alcorn State University B7
Algoma 420 G2
Alligator 187 C2
Amory 7,093 H3
Anguilla 883 C5
Arcola 564 C4
Arkabutla 400 D1
Artesia 484 G4
Ashland▲ 490 F1
Askew 300 D1
Auburn 500 C8
Avalon 100 D3
Avera 150 G8
Avon 400 B4
Bailey 320 G6
Baird 150 C4
Baldwyn 3,204 G2
Ballardsville 105 H2
Banks 100 D1
Banner 120 F2
Bassfield 249 E8
Batesville▲ 6,403 E2
Baxterville 100 E8
Bay Saint Louis▲ 8,063 F10
Bay Springs▲ 1,729 F7
Beaumont 1,054 G8
Beauregard 206 D7
Becker 350 G3
Belden 241 G2
Belen 400 D2
Bellefontaine 400 F3
Belmont 1,554 H1
Belzoni▲ 2,536 C4
Benndale 500 G9
Benoit 641 C3
Benton 390 D5
Bentonia 518 D5
Beulah 460 B3
Bexley 130 G9
Big Creek 123 F3
Bigbee Valley 370 H4
Bigpoint 350 H9
Biloxi 46,319 G10
Blue Mountain 667 G1
Blue Springs 140 G2
Bobo 200 C2
Bogue Chitto 689 D8
Bolatusha 87 E5
Bolton 637 D6
Bond 350 F9
Bonita 300 G6
Booneville▲ 7,955 G1
Bourbon 200 C4
Boyle 651 C3
Brandon▲ 11,077 E6
Braxton 141 D6
Brazil 229 D2
Brookhaven▲ 10,243 C7
Brooklyn 450 F8
Brooksville 1,098 G4
Brownfield 125 G1
Brownsville 200 D6
Brozville 150 D4
Bruce 2,127 F3
Brunswick 90 C5
Buckatunna 500 G7
Bude 969 C8
Burns 949 E6
Burnsville 889 H1
Byhalia 955 E1
Byram 250 D6
Caesar 80 E9
Caledonia 821 H3
Calhoun City 1,838 F3
Camden 150 E5
Canaan 200 F1
Cannonsburg 240 B7
Canton▲ 10,062 D5
Carlisle 425 C7
Carpenter 200 C6
Carriere 900 E9
Carrollton▲ 221 E4
Carson 400 E7
Carthage▲ 3,819 E5
Cary 392 C5
Cascilla 230 D3
Cedarbluff 175 G3
Centreville 1,771 B8
Chalybeate 350 G1
Charleston▲ 2,328 D2
Chatawa 300 D8
Chatham 150 B4
Cheraw 100 E8
Chunky 292 G6
Church Hill 350 B7
Clara 275 G7
Clarksdale▲ 19,717 D2
Clarkson 100 F3
Clermont Harbor 550 F10
Cleveland▲ 15,384 C3
Cliftonville 280 H4
Clinton 21,847 D6
Coahoma 254 C2
Cockrum 150 E1
Coffeeville▲ 825 E3
Coldwater 1,502 E1
Coles 150 C8
College Hill 150 E2
Collins▲ 2,541 E7
Collinsville 1,364 G6
Columbia▲ 6,815 E8
Columbus▲ 23,799 H3
Como 1,387 E1
Conehatta 925 F6
Corinth▲ 11,820 G1
Courtland 329 E2
Coxburg 300 D5
Crawford 668 G4
Crenshaw 978 D2
Crosby 465 B8
Crowder 758 D2
Cruger 548 D4
Crystal Springs 5,643 D7
Cuevas 200 F10
Curtis Station 350 D2
D'Iberville 6,566 G10
D'Lo 421 E7
Daleville 210 G5
Dancy 116 F3
Darbun 100 D8
Darling 275 D2
De Kalb▲ 1,073 G5
De Lisle 450 F10
De Soto 150 G7
Decatur▲ 1,248 F6
Delta City 310 C4
Dennis 150 H1
Dentville 175 C7
Derby 298 E9
Derma 959 F3
Dixon 125 F5
Doddsville 149 C3
Dorsey 100 H2
Drew 2,349 C3
Dublin 100 C2
Duck Hill 586 E3
Duffee 175 G6
Dumas 407 G1
Duncan 416 C2
Dundee 600 D1
Dunleith 140 C4
Durant 2,838 E4
Eastabuchie 200 F8
Ebenezer 200 D5
Ecru 696 F2
Eden 88 D5
Edinburg 200 F5
Edwards 1,279 C6
Egypt 100 G3
Electric Mills 100 G5
Elizabeth 500 C4
Elliott 200 E3
Ellisville▲ 3,634 F7
Enid E2
Enterprise 477 G6
Errata 85 F7
Escatawpa 3,902 G10
Estill 100 C4
Ethel 454 F4
Eudora 200 D1
Eupora 2,145 F3
Falcon 167 D2
Falkner 232 G1
Fannin 250 E6
Farrell 300 C2
Fayette▲ 1,853 B7
Fernwood 500 D8
Fitler 175 B5
Flora 1,482 D5
Florence 1,831 D6
Flowood 2,860 D6
Forest▲ 5,060 F6
Forkville 185 E6
Foxworth 800 E8
French Camp 320 F4
Friars Point 1,334 C2
Fulton▲ 3,387 H2
Gallman D7
Garlandville 150 F6
Gattman 120 H3
Gautier 10,088 G10
Georgetown 332 D7
Glen 165 H1
Glen Allan 650 B4
Glendora 220 D3
Gloster 1,323 B8
Gluckstadt 150 D5
Golden 202 H2
Good Hope 125 E5
Goodman 1,256 E5
Gore Springs 125 E3
Goshen Springs 100 E6
Goss 100 E8
Grace 325 C5
Grapeland 200 B3
Greenville▲ 45,226 B4
Greenwood Springs 170 H3
Greenwood▲ 18,906 D4
Grenada▲ 10,864 E3
Gulfport▲ 40,775 F10
Gunnison 611 C3
Guntown 692 G2
Hamburg 150 B7
Hamilton 500 H3
Hampton 200 B4
Hardee 100 C5
Harperville 200 E6
Harriston 500 C7
Harrisville 500 D7
Hatley 529 H3
Hattiesburg▲ 41,882 F8
Hazlehurst▲ 4,221 D7
Heidelberg 981 F7
Helm 80 C4
Hermanville 750 C7
Hernando▲ 3,125 E1
Hickory 493 F6
Hickory Flat 535 F1
Hillsboro 800 E6
Hintonville 300 F8
Hiwannee 250 G7
Hohenlinden 96 F3
Hollandale 3,576 C4
Holly Bluff 700 C5
Holly Ridge 350 C4
Holly Springs▲ 7,261 E1
Hollywood 80 D1
Hopewell 250 D7
Horn Lake 9,069 D1
Houlka G2
Houston▲ 3,903 G3
Howison 300 F9
Hub 80 E8
Hurley 500 H9
Independence 150 E1
Indianola▲ 11,809 C4
Ingomar 150 F2
Inverness 1,174 C4
Isola 732 C4
Itta Bena 2,377 D4
Iuka▲ 3,122 H1
Jackson (cap.)▲ 196,637 D6
James 100 B4
Jayess 200 D8
Johns 90 E6
Jonestown 1,467 D2
Jumpertown 438 G1
Kewanee 250 H6
Kilmichael 826 E4
Kiln 1,262 F10
Kirkville 200 H2
Kokomo 250 E8
Kolola Springs 100 H3
Kosciusko▲ 6,986 E4
Kossuth 245 G1
Lafayette Springs 80 F2
Lake 369 F6
Lake Como 150 F7
Lake Cormorant 300 D1
Lake View 125 D1
Lakeshore 550 F10
Lamar 200 F1
Lambert 1,131 D2
Lamont 400 B3
Langford 100 E6
Lauderdale 600 G5
Laurel▲ 18,827 F7
Lawrence 250 F6
Le Flore 99 D3
Leaf 250 G8
Leakesville▲ 1,129 G8
Learned 111 C6
Leland 6,366 C4
Lemon 90 E6
Lena 175 E5
Lessley 100 B8
Lexington▲ 2,227 D4
Liberty▲ 624 C8
Long 15,804 C4
Long Beach 7,967 F10
Longtown 150 D1
Longview 800 G4
Looxahoma 200 E1
Lorena 90 F6
Lorman 350 B7
Louin 289 F6
Louise 343 C5
Louisville▲ 7,169 G4
Lucedale▲ 2,592 G9
Ludlow 350 E5
Lula 224 C2
Lumberton 2,121 E8
Lyman 1,117 F10
Lyon 446 D2
Maben 752 F3
Macon▲ 2,256 G4
Madden 450 F5
Madison 7,471 D6
Magee 3,607 E7
Magnolia▲ 2,245 D8
Malvina 100 C3
Mantachie 651 H2
Mantee 134 F3
Marietta 287 H2
Marion 1,359 G6
Marks▲ 1,758 D2
Marydell 99 F5
Mashulaville 227 G4
Matherville 150 G7
Mathiston 818 F3
Mattson 200 C2
Maxie 233 F9
Mayersville▲ 329 B5
Mayhew 150 G4
McAdams 350 E4
McCall Creek 250 C7
McCarley 250 E3
McComb 11,591 D8
McCondy 150 G3
McCool 169 F4
McHenry 660 F9
McLain 536 G8
McLaurin 100 F8
McNeill 800 E9
Meadville▲ 453 C8
Meehan 100 G6
Mendenhall▲ 2,463 E7
Meridian▲ 41,036 G6
Merigold 572 C3
Merrill 100 G9
Metcalfe 1,092 B4
Michigan City 350 F1
Midnight 500 C4
Mineral Wells 250 E1
Minter City 150 D3
Mississippi State G4
Mize 312 E7
Money 350 D3
Monticello▲ 1,755 D7
Montpelier 175 G3
Montrose 106 F6
Mooreville 200 G2
Moorhead 2,417 C4
Morgan City 139 D4
Morgantown 32,880 B7
Morgantown 325 E8
Morton 3,212 E6
Moselle 525 F8
Moss 17,837 F7
Moss Point 18,998 G10
Mound Bayou 2,222 C3
Mount Olive 914 E7
Mount Pleasant 250 E1
Murphy 100 C4
Myrtle 358 F1
Natchez▲ 19,460 B7
Neely 270 G8
Nesbit 366 D1
Neshoba 250 F5
Nettleton 2,462 G2
New Albany▲ 6,775 G2
New Augusta▲ 668 F8
New Houlka (Houlka) 558 G2
New Site 100 H1
Newhebron 470 D7
Newton 3,701 F6
Nicholson 400 E10
Nitta Yuma 150 C4
Nola 120 D7
North Carrollton 578 E3
North Gulfport 4,966 F10
Noxapater 441 F5
Oak Ridge 350 C6
Oak Vale E8
Oakland 553 E2
Oakley 133 D6
Ocean Springs 14,658 G10
Ofahoma 350 E5
Okolona▲ 3,267 G2
Olive Branch 3,567 E1
Oloh 93 E8
Oma 200 D7
Ora 15,676 E7
Osyka 483 D8
Ovett 600 F8
Oxford▲ 9,984 F2
Pace 354 C3
Pachuta 268 G6
Paden 123 H1
Palmers Crossing 2,765 F8
Panther Burn 300 C4
Parchman 200 D3
Paris 253 F2
Pascagoula▲ 25,899 G10
Pass Christian 5,557 F10
Pattison 540 C7
Paulding▲ 630 F6
Paulette 230 H4
Paynes 100 D3
Pearl 19,588 D6
Pearlington 1,603 E10
Pelahatchie 1,553 E6
Penton 175 D1
Peoria 100 C8
Perkinston 950 F9
Petal 7,883 F8
Pheba 280 G3
Philadelphia▲ 6,758 F5
Philipp 975 D3
Piave 150 G8
Picayune 10,633 E9
Pickens 1,285 E5
Pine Ridge 175 B7
Pineville 80 F6
Piney Woods 450 D6
Pinola E7
Pittsboro▲ 277 F3
Plantersville 1,046 G2
Pleasant Grove 100 D2
Pleasant Hill 400 E1
Polkville 129 E6

(continued on following page)

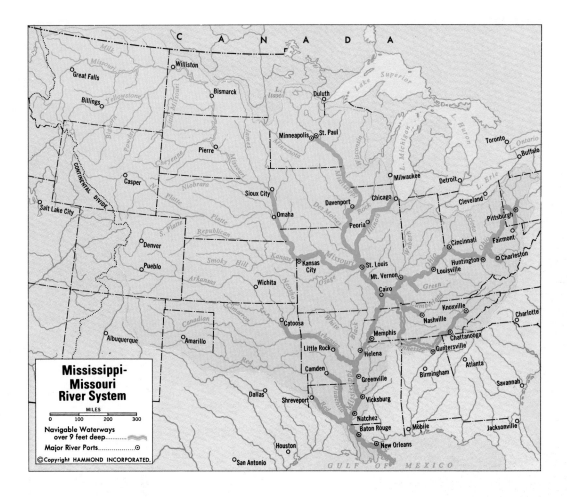

Mississippi-Missouri River System

MILES
0   100   200   300

Navigable Waterways over 9 feet deep
Major River Ports
© Copyright HAMMOND INCORPORATED.

Agriculture, Industry and Resources

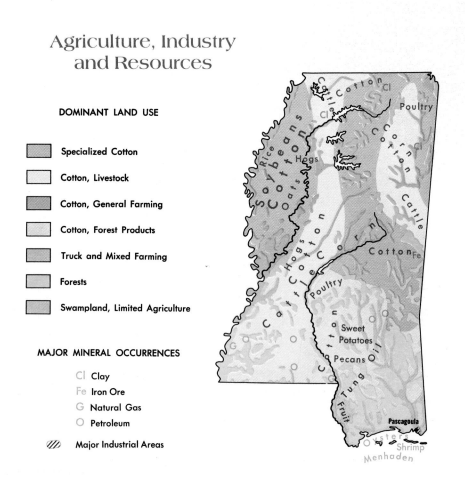

DOMINANT LAND USE

- Specialized Cotton
- Cotton, Livestock
- Cotton, General Farming
- Cotton, Forest Products
- Truck and Mixed Farming
- Forests
- Swampland, Limited Agriculture

MAJOR MINERAL OCCURRENCES

- Cl Clay
- Fe Iron Ore
- G Natural Gas
- O Petroleum
- /// Major Industrial Areas

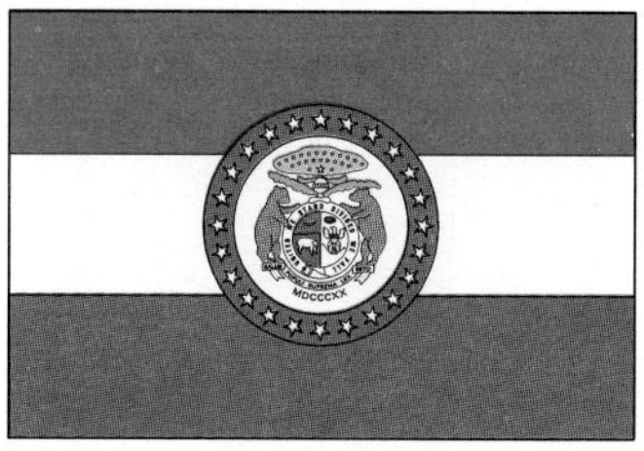

AREA 69,697 sq. mi. (180,515 sq. km.)
POPULATION 5,137,804
CAPITAL Jefferson City
LARGEST CITY St. Louis
HIGHEST POINT Taum Sauk Mtn. 1,772 ft. (540 m.)
SETTLED IN 1764
ADMITTED TO UNION August 10, 1821
POPULAR NAME Show Me State
STATE FLOWER Hawthorn
STATE BIRD Bluebird

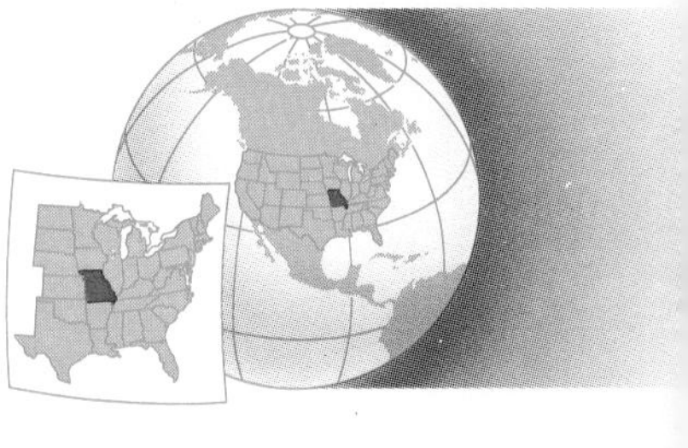

COUNTIES

Adair 24,577 G2
Andrew 14,632 C3
Atchison 7,457 B2
Audrain 23,599 J4
Barry 27,547 E9
Barton 11,312 D7
Bates 15,025 D6
Benton 13,859 F6
Bollinger 10,619 M8
Boone 112,379 H4
Buchanan 83,083 C3
Butler 38,765 M9
Caldwell 8,380 E3
Callaway 32,809 J5
Camden 27,495 G6
Cape Girardeau 61,633 N8
Carroll 10,748 F4
Carter 5,515 L9
Cass 63,808 D5
Cedar 12,093 E7
Chariton 9,202 F3
Christian 32,644 F9
Clark 7,547 J2
Clay 153,411 D4
Clinton 16,595 D3
Cole 63,579 H6
Cooper 14,835 G5
Crawford 19,173 K7
Dade 7,449 E8
Dallas 12,646 F7
Daviess 7,865 E3
De Kalb 8,222 D3
Dent 13,702 J7
Douglas 11,876 G9
Dunklin 33,112 M1
Franklin 80,603 K6
Gasconade 14,006 J6
Gentry 6,848 D2
Greene 207,949 F8
Grundy 10,536 E2
Harrison 8,469 E2
Henry 20,044 E6
Hickory 7,335 F7
Holt 6,034 B2
Howard 9,631 G4
Howell 31,447 J9
Iron 10,726 L7
Jackson 633,232 R5
Jasper 90,465 D8
Jefferson 171,380 L6
Johnson 42,514 E5
Knox 4,482 H2
Laclede 27,158 G7
Lafayette 31,107 E4
Lawrence 30,236 E8
Lewis 10,233 J2
Lincoln 28,892 L4
Linn 13,885 F3
Livingston 14,592 E3
Macon 15,345 G3
Madison 11,127 M8
Maries 7,976 J6
Marion 27,682 J3
McDonald 16,938 D9
Mercer 3,723 E2
Miller 20,700 H6
Mississippi 14,442 O9
Moniteau 12,298 G5
Monroe 9,104 H3
Montgomery 11,355 K5
Morgan 15,574 G6
New Madrid 20,928 N9
Newton 44,445 D9
Nodaway 21,709 C2
Oregon 9,470 K9
Osage 12,018 J6
Ozark 8,598 H9
Pemiscot 21,921 N1
Perry 16,648 N7
Pettis 35,437 F5
Phelps 35,248 J7
Pike 15,969 K4
Platte 57,867 C4
Polk 21,826 F7
Pulaski 41,307 H7
Putnam 5,079 F2
Ralls 8,476 J3
Randolph 24,370 G3
Ray 21,971 E4
Reynolds 6,661 L8
Ripley 12,303 L9
Saint Charles 144,107 M2
Saint Clair 8,622 E6
Saint Francois 42,600 M7
Saint Louis 974,180 O3
Saint Louis (city county) 452,801 P3
Sainte Genevieve 15,180 M7
Saline 23,523 F4
Schuyler 4,236 G2
Scotland 4,822 H2
Scott 39,376 N8
Shannon 7,613 K8
Shelby 6,942 H3
Stoddard 28,895 N9
Stone 19,078 F9
Sullivan 6,326 F2
Taney 25,561 F9
Texas 21,476 J8
Vernon 19,041 D7
Warren 19,534 K5
Washington 20,380 L7
Wayne 11,543 L8
Webster 23,753 G8
Worth 2,440 D2
Wright 16,758 H8

CITIES and TOWNS

Adrian 1,582 D6
Advance 1,139 N8
Affton 21,106 P4
Agency 642 C3
Alba 465 D8
Albany▲ 1,958 D2
Alexandria 341 K2
Alma 446 E4
Altamont 188 D3
Altenburg 307 O7
Alton▲ 692 K9
Amazonia 257 C3
Amoret 212 C6
Amsterdam 237 D6
Anderson 1,432 D9
Annapolis 363 L8
Anniston 288 O9
Appleton City 1,280 D6
Arbyrd 597 M10
Arcadia 609 L7
Archie 799 D5
Argyle 178 J6
Armstrong 310 G4
Arnold 18,828 M6
Asbury 220 C8
Ash Grove 1,128 E8
Ashland 1,252 H5
Atlanta 411 H3
Augusta 263 L5
Aurora 6,459 E9
Auxvasse 821 J4
Ava▲ 2,938 G9
Avondale 550 P5
Bakersfield 292 H9
Ballwin 21,816 N3
Baring 182 H2
Barnard 234 C2
Barnett 215 G6
Bates City 197 E5
Battlefield 1,526 F8
Bel-Nor 2,935 P2
Bel-Ridge 3,199 P2
Bell City 469 N8
Bella Villa 708 R4
Belle 1,218 J6
Bellefontaine 10,922 N2
Bellefontaine Neighbors 12,082 R2
Bellflower 413 K4
Belton 18,150 C5
Benton City 139 J4
Benton▲ 575 O8
Berger 247 K5
Berkeley 12,450 P2
Bernie 1,847 M9
Bertrand 692 O9
Bethany▲ 3,005 E2
Beverly 660 O4
Bevier 643 G3
Billings 989 F8
Birch Tree 599 K9
Birmingham 222 R5
Bismarck 1,579 L7
Black 6,128 L7
Black Jack 5,293 R1
Blackburn 308 F4
Blackwater 221 G5
Blairstown 185 E5
Bland 651 J6
Blodgett 202 O8
Bloomfield▲ 1,800 M9
Bloomsdale 353 M6
Blue Springs 40,153 R6
Bogard 228 E4
Bolckow 253 C2
Bolivar▲ 6,845 F7
Bonne Terre 3,871 L7
Boonville▲ 7,095 G5
Bosworth 334 F4
Bourbon 1,188 K6
Bowling Green▲ 2,976 K4
Brandsville 167 J9
Branson 3,706 F9
Brashear 318 H2
Braymer 886 E3
Breckenridge 418 E3
Breckenridge Hills 5,404 O2
Brentwood 8,150 P3
Bridgeton 17,779 O2
Bridgeton Terrace 334 O2
Bronaugh 211 C7
Brookfield 4,888 F3
Browning 331 F2
Brunswick 1,074 F4
Bucklin 616 G3
Buckner 2,873 R5
Buffalo▲ 2,414 F7
Bunceton 341 G5
Bunker 390 K8
Burlington Junction 634 B2
Butler▲ 4,099 D6
Butterfield 248 E9
Cabool 2,006 H8
Cainsville 387 E2
Cairo 282 H4
Caledonia 142 L7
Calhoun 450 E6
California▲ 3,465 H5
Callao 332 G3
Calverton Park 1,404 P2
Camden 238 D4
Camden Point 373 C4
Camdenton▲ 2,561 G6
Cameron 4,831 D3
Campbell 2,165 M9
Canalou 319 N9
Canton 2,623 J2
Cape Girardeau 34,438 O8
Cardwell 792 M10
Carl Junction 4,123 C8
Carrollton▲ 4,406 E4
Carterville 2,013 D8
Carthage▲ 10,747 D8
Caruth 7,389 N10
Caruthersville▲ 7,958 N10
Carytown 149 D8
Cassville▲ 2,371 E9
Cedar City 427 H5
Cedar Hill Lakes 227 L6
Center 552 J3
Centertown 356 H5
Centerview 214 E5
Centerville▲ 89 L8
Centralia 3,414 H4
Chaffee 3,059 N8
Chamois 449 J5
Charlack 1,388 P2
Charleston▲ 5,085 O9
Chesterfield 37,991 N2
Chilhowee 335 E5
Chillicothe▲ 8,804 E3
Chula 183 F3
Circle City 154 N9
Clarence 1,026 H3
Clark 257 H4
Clarksburg 358 G5
Clarksdale 287 D3
Clarkson Valley 2,508 N3
Clarksville 480 K4
Clarkton 1,113 M10
Claycomo 1,668 P5
Clayton▲ 13,874 P3
Clearmont 175 C1
Cleveland 506 C5
Clever 580 F8
Clinton▲ 8,703 E6
Cobalt City 254 M7
Cole Camp 1,054 F6
Collins 144 E7
Columbia▲ 69,101 H5
Commerce 173 O8
Conception Junction 236 C2
Concord 19,859 P4
Concordia 2,160 E5
Conway 629 G7
Cool Valley 1,407 P2
Cooter 451 N10
Corder 485 E4
Cottleville 2,936 M2
Country Club Village 1,234 C3
Cowgill 257 E3
Craig 346 B2
Crane 1,218 E9
Creighton 289 D6
Crestwood 11,234 O3
Creve Coeur 12,304 O2
Crocker 1,077 H7
Cross Timbers 168 F6
Crystal City 4,088 M6
Crystal Lake Park 506 O3
Cuba 2,537 K6
Curryville 261 K4
Dadeville 220 E8
De Kalb 222 C3
De Soto 5,993 L6
Dearborn 480 C3
Deepwater 441 E6
Dellwood 5,245 R2
Delta 450 N8
Des Arc 173 L8
Des Peres 8,395 O3
Desloge 4,150 M7
Dexter 7,559 N9
Diamond 775 D9
Diehlstadt 145 N9
Diggins 258 G8
Dixon 1,585 H6
Doniphan▲ 1,713 L9
Doolittle 599 J7
Downing 359 H2
Drexel 936 C6
Dudley 271 M9
Duenweg 940 D8
Duquesne 1,229 D8
Eagleville 275 D2
East Lynne 289 D5
East Prairie 3,416 O9
Easton 232 C3
Edgar Springs 215 J7
Edgerton 565 C3
Edina▲ 1,283 H2
Edmundson 1,111 O2
El Dorado Springs 3,830 E7
Eldon 4,419 G6
Ellington 994 L8
Ellisville 7,545 M3
Ellsinore 405 L9
Elmo 179 B1
Elsberry 1,898 L4
Elvins 1,391 L7
Eminence▲ 582 K8
Emma 194 F5
Eolia 389 L4
Essex 531 N9
Esther 1,071 M7
Eugene 141 H6
Eureka 4,683 M4
Everton 325 E8
Ewing 463 J2
Excelsior Springs 10,354 R4
Exeter 597 D9
Fair Grove 919 F8
Fair Play 442 E7
Fairfax 699 B2
Fairview 298 D9
Farber 418 J4
Farley 217 O4
Farmington▲ 11,598 M7
Fayette▲ 2,888 G4
Fenton 3,346 O4
Ferguson 22,286 P2
Ferrelview 338 O4
Festus 8,105 M6
Fillmore 256 C2
Fisk 422 M9
Flat 4,823 J7
Flat River 4,443 M7
Fleming 130 D4
Flemington 141 F7
Flinthill 219 L5
Florissant 51,206 P1
Foley 209 L4
Fordland 523 G8
Forest City 380 B3
Foristell 144 L5
Forsyth▲ 1,175 F9
Foster 161 D6
Frankford 396 K4
Franklin 181 G4
Fredericktown▲ 3,950 M7
Freeburg 446 J6
Freeman 480 C5
Freistatt 166 E8
Fremont 201 K9
Frohna 162 N7
Frontenac 3,374 O3
Fulton▲ 10,033 J5
Gainesville▲ 659 G9
Galena▲ 401 F9
Gallatin▲ 1,864 E3
Galt 296 F2
Garden City 1,225 D5
Gasconade 253 J5
Gerald 888 K6
Gideon 1,104 N10
Gilliam 212 F4
Gilman City 393 D2
Gladstone 26,243 P5
Glasgow 1,295 G4
Glenaire 597 R5
Glendale 5,945 P3
Glenwood 195 G1
Golden 794 E9
Golden City 900 D8
Goodman 1,094 C9
Gordonville 345 N8
Gower 1,249 C3
Graham 204 C2
Grain Valley 1,898 S6
Granby 1,945 D9
Grandin 233 L9
Grandview 24,967 P6
Grant City▲ 998 D2
Grantwood 904 O4
Gray Summit 2,505 L6
Green Castle 285 G2
Green City 671 F2
Green Ridge 452 F5
Greenfield▲ 1,416 E8
Greentop 425 H2
Greenville▲ 437 M8
Greenwood 1,505 R6
Hale 480 F3
Half Way 157 F7
Hallsville 917 H4
Halltown 161 E8
Hamilton 1,737 E3
Hanley Hills 2,325 P2
Hannibal 18,004 K3
Hardin 598 E4
Harrisburg 169 H4
Harrisonville▲ 7,683 D5
Hartville▲ 495 G8
Hawk Point 472 K5
Hayti 3,280 N10
Hayti Heights 893 N10
Haywood City 263 N9
Hazelwood 15,324 P2
Henrietta 412 E4
Herculaneum 2,263 M6
Hermann▲ 2,754 K5
Hermitage▲ 512 F7
Higbee 639 H4
Higginsville 4,693 E4
High Hill 204 K5

(continued on following page)

Agriculture, Industry and Resources

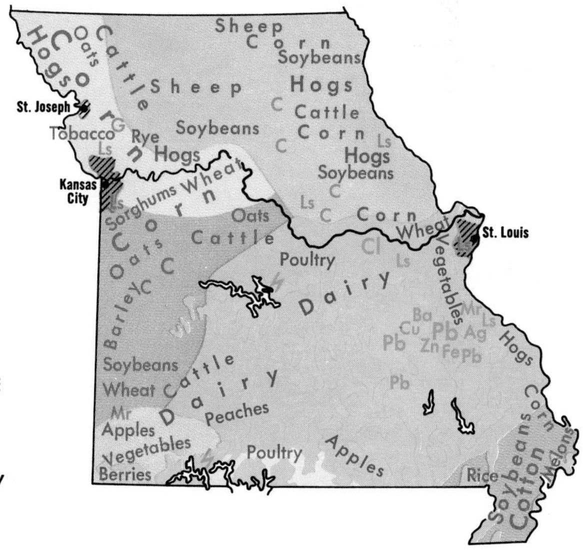

DOMINANT LAND USE

- Cattle Feed, Hogs
- Livestock, Cash Grain, Dairy
- Pasture Livestock
- Specialized Cotton
- General Farming, Dairy, Livestock, Poultry
- General Farming, Livestock, Truck Farming, Cotton
- Fruit and Mixed Farming
- Forests
- Urban Areas

MAJOR MINERAL OCCURRENCES

Ag	Silver	G	Natural Gas
Ba	Barite	Ls	Limestone
C	Coal	Mr	Marble
Cl	Clay	Pb	Lead
Cu	Copper	Zn	Zinc
Fe	Iron Ore		

Water Power — Major Industrial Areas

High Ridge 4,423 ....M6
Hillsboro▲ 1,625 ....L6
Hillsdale 1,948 ....R2
Holcomb 531 ....N10
Holden 2,389 ....E5
Holland 237 ....N10
Holliday 139 ....H3
Hollister 2,628 ....F9
Holt 311 ....D4
Holts Summit 2,292 ....H5
Homestown 230 ....N10
Hopkins 575 ....C1
Horine 1,043 ....M6
Hornersville 629 ....M10
Houston Lake 303 ....O5
Houston▲ 2,118 ....J8
Houstonia 283 ....F5
Howardville 440 ....N9
Hughesville 174 ....F5
Humansville 1,084 ....E7
Hume 287 ....C6
Hunnewell 219 ....J3
Huntleigh 392 ....O3
Huntsville▲ 1,567 ....H4
Hurdland 212 ....H2
Hurricane Deck 210 ....G6
Iberia 650 ....H7
Illmo 1,368 ....O8
Imperial 4,156 ....M6
Independence▲ 112,301 ....R5
Iron Gates 309 ....L7
Irondale 474 ....L7
Ironton▲ 1,539 ....L7
Jackson▲ 9,256 ....N8
Jameson 149 ....E2
Jamesport 570 ....E2
Jamestown 298 ....G4
Jasper 994 ....D8
Jefferson City (cap.)▲ 35,481 ....H5
Jennings 15,905 ....R2
Jerico Springs 247 ....E7
Jonesburg 630 ....K5
Joplin 40,961 ....C8
Junction City 326 ....M7
Kahoka▲ 2,195 ....J2
Kansas City 435,146 ....P5
Kearney 1,790 ....D4
Kelso 526 ....O8
Kennett▲ 10,941 ....M10
Keytesville▲ 564 ....G4
Kidder 241 ....E3
Kimberling City 1,590 ....F9
Kimmswick 135 ....M6
King City 986 ....D2
Kingston▲ 279 ....E3
Kingsville 279 ....D5
Kinloch 2,702 ....P2
Kirksville▲ 17,152 ....H2
Kirkwood 27,291 ....O3
Knob Noster 2,261 ....E5
Knox City 262 ....H2
Koshkonong 198 ....J9
La Belle 655 ....J2
La Grange 1,102 ....K2
La Monte 995 ....F5
La Plata 1,401 ....H2
Laclede 410 ....F3
Laddonia 581 ....J4
Ladue 8,847 ....P3
Lake Lotawana 2,141 ....R6
Lake Ozark 681 ....G6
Lake Saint Louis 7,400 ....L5
Lake Tapawingo 761 ....R6
Lake Waukomis 1,027 ....P5

Lake Winnebago 748 ....R6
Lakeshire 1,467 ....P4
Lamar Heights 176 ....D8
Lamar▲ 4,168 ....D8
Lanagan 501 ....C9
Lancaster▲ 785 ....H1
Laredo 205 ....E2
Lathrop 1,794 ....D3
Laurie 507 ....G6
Lawson 1,876 ....D4
Leadington 201 ....M7
Leadwood 1,247 ....L7
Leasburg 289 ....K6
Lebanon▲ 9,983 ....G7
Lee's Summit 46,418 ....R6
Leeton 632 ....E5
Lemay 18,005 ....R4
Levasy 279 ....S5
Lewistown 453 ....J2
Lewis and Clark Village 131 ....C3
Lexington▲ 4,860 ....E4
Liberal 684 ....D7
Liberty▲ 20,459 ....R5
Licking 1,328 ....J8
Lilbourn 1,378 ....N9
Lincoln 874 ....F6
Linn Creek 232 ....G6
Linn▲ 1,148 ....J5
Linneus▲ 364 ....F3
Lockwood 1,041 ....E8
Lohman 154 ....H5
Lone Jack 392 ....S6
Louisiana 3,967 ....K4
Lowry City 723 ....E6
Ludlow 147 ....E3
Lutesville 865 ....M8
Mackenzie 148 ....P3
Macks Creek 272 ....G7
Macon▲ 5,571 ....H3
Madison 518 ....H4
Maitland 338 ....B2
Malta Bend 289 ....F4
Malden 5,123 ....M9
Manchester 6,542 ....O3
Mansfield 1,429 ....G8
Maplewood 9,962 ....P3
Marble Hill▲ 1,447 ....N8
Marceline 2,645 ....F3
Marionville 1,920 ....E8
Marlborough 1,949 ....P3
Marquand 278 ....M8
Marshall▲ 12,711 ....F4
Marshfield▲ 4,374 ....G8
Marston 691 ....N9
Marthasville 674 ....L5
Martinsburg 337 ....J4
Maryland Heights 25,407 ....O3
Maryville▲ 10,663 ....C2
Matthews 614 ....N9
Maysville▲ 1,176 ....D3
Mayview 279 ....E4
McFall 142 ....D2
Meadville 360 ....F3
Mehlville 27,557 ....P4
Memphis▲ 2,094 ....H2
Mendon 207 ....F3
Mercer 297 ....E2
Meta 249 ....H6
Mexico▲ 11,290 ....J4
Miami 142 ....F4
Middletown 217 ....J4
Milan▲ 1,767 ....F2
Mill Spring 252 ....L8

Miller 753 ....E8
Mindenmines 346 ....C8
Mine La Motte 125 ....M7
Miner 1,218 ....N9
Mineral Point 384 ....L7
Missouri City 348 ....R5
Moberly 12,839 ....G4
Mokane 186 ....J5
Moline Acres 2,710 ....R2
Monett 6,529 ....E9
Monroe City 2,701 ....J3
Montgomery City▲ 2,281 ....K5
Monticello▲ 106 ....J2
Montrose 440 ....E6
Morehouse 1,068 ....N9
Morley 683 ....N8
Morrison 160 ....J5
Morrisville 293 ....F8
Mosby 194 ....R4
Moscow Mills 924 ....K5
Mound City 1,273 ....B2
Moundville 140 ....C7
Mount Vernon▲ 4,682 ....E8
Mountain Grove 4,182 ....H8
Mountain View 2,036 ....J8
Murphy 9,342 ....O4
Napoleon 233 ....E4
Naylor 842 ....L9
Neelyville 381 ....M9
Nelson 181 ....F4
Neosho▲ 9,254 ....D9
Nevada▲ 8,597 ....D7
New Bloomfield 480 ....J5
New Cambria 223 ....G3
New Florence 801 ....K5
New Franklin 1,107 ....G4
New Hampton 320 ....D2
New Haven 1,757 ....K5
New London▲ 988 ....K3
New Madrid▲ 3,350 ....O9
New Melle 486 ....L5
Newburg 589 ....J7
Newtonia 204 ....D9
Niangua 459 ....G8
Nixa 4,707 ....F8
Noel 1,169 ....D9
Norborne 856 ....E4
Normandy 4,480 ....R2
North Kansas City 4,130 ....P5
Northmoor 441 ....O5
Northwoods 5,106 ....R2
Norwood 449 ....H8
Novelty 143 ....H2
Novinger 542 ....G2
O'Fallon 18,698 ....L5
Oak Grove 4,067 ....S6
Oak Grove 402 ....K6
Oak Ridge 202 ....N7
Oakland 1,593 ....P3
Oaks 130 ....P5
Oakview 351 ....P5
Oakwood 212 ....P5
Oakwood Manor 137 ....P5
Oakwood Park 213 ....P5
Odessa 3,695 ....E5
Old Monroe 242 ....L5
Olivette 7,573 ....O2
Olympian Village 752 ....M6
Oran 1,164 ....N8
Oregon▲ 935 ....B2
Oronogo 595 ....D8
Orrick 935 ....D4
Osage Beach 2,599 ....G6
Osborn 400 ....D3

Osceola▲ 755 ....E6
Otterville 507 ....G5
Overland 17,987 ....O2
Owensville 2,325 ....K6
Ozark▲ 4,243 ....F8
Pacific 4,350 ....L5
Pagedale 3,771 ....P2
Palmyra▲ 3,371 ....J3
Paris▲ 1,486 ....J4
Parkdale 270 ....F6
Parkville 2,402 ....O5
Parkway 277 ....L6
Parma 995 ....N9
Parnell 157 ....C2
Patton 414 ....M8
Pattonsburg 502 ....D2
Peculiar 1,777 ....D5
Perry 711 ....J4
Perryville▲ 6,933 ....N7
Pevely 2,831 ....M6
Phillipsburg 170 ....G7
Pickering 171 ....C2
Piedmont 2,166 ....L8
Pierce City 1,382 ....E8
Pilot Grove 714 ....G5
Pilot Knob 783 ....L7
Pine 5,092 ....K9
Pine Lawn 6,600 ....R2
Pineville▲ 580 ....D9
Platte City▲ 2,947 ....C4
Platte Woods 427 ....O5
Plattsburg▲ 2,248 ....D3
Pleasant Hill 3,827 ....D5
Pleasant Hope 360 ....F8
Pleasant Valley 2,731 ....R5
Polo 539 ....D3
Poplar Bluff▲ 16,996 ....L9
Portage Des Sioux 503 ....M5
Portageville 3,401 ....N10
Potosi▲ 2,683 ....L7
Prairie Home 215 ....G5
Princeton▲ 1,021 ....E2
Purcell 359 ....D8
Purdin 217 ....F3
Purdy 977 ....E9
Puxico 819 ....M9
Queen City 704 ....H2
Qulin 384 ....M9
Ravenwood 409 ....C2
Raymondville 425 ....J8
Raymore 5,592 ....D5
Raytown 30,601 ....P6
Rayville 170 ....E4
Reeds Spring 411 ....F9
Renick 195 ....H4
Republic 6,292 ....E8
Rhineland 157 ....J5
Rich Hill 1,317 ....D6
Richland 2,029 ....H7
Richmond Heights 10,448 ....P3
Richmond▲ 5,738 ....D4
Ridgeway 379 ....D2
Risco 434 ....N9
Rivermines 459 ....L7
Riverside 3,010 ....O5
Riverview 3,242 ....R2
Rocheport 255 ....H5
Rock Hill 5,217 ....P3
Rock Port▲ 1,438 ....B2
Rockaway Beach 275 ....F9
Rockville 193 ....D6
Rogersville 995 ....G8
Rolla▲ 14,090 ....J7
Rosebud 380 ....K6

Rosendale 186 ....C2
Rushville 306 ....B3
Russellville 869 ....H6
Saginaw 384 ....C8
Saint Ann 14,489 ....O2
Saint Charles▲ 54,555 ....N1
Saint Clair 3,917 ....K6
Saint Elizabeth 257 ....H6
Saint George 1,270 ....P4
Saint James 3,256 ....J6
Saint John 7,466 ....P2
Saint Joseph▲ 71,852 ....C3
Saint Louis▲ 396,685 ....R3
Saint Martins 717 ....H5
Saint Marys 461 ....M7
Saint Paul 1,192 ....L5
Saint Peters 45,779 ....M1
Saint Robert 1,730 ....H7
Saint Thomas 263 ....H6
Sainte Genevieve▲ 4,411 ....M6

Salem▲ 4,486 ....J7
Salisbury 1,881 ....G4
Sappington 10,917 ....O4
Sarcoxie 1,330 ....D8
Savannah▲ 4,352 ....C3
Schell City 292 ....D6
Scott City 4,292 ....O8
Sedalia▲ 19,800 ....F5
Sedgewickville 138 ....N7
Seligman 593 ....D9
Senath 1,622 ....M10
Seneca 1,885 ....C9
Seymour 1,636 ....G8
Shelbina 2,172 ....H3
Shelbyville▲ 582 ....H3
Sheldon 464 ....D7
Sheridan 174 ....C1
Shrewsbury 6,416 ....P3
Sibley 367 ....S5
Sikeston 17,641 ....N9

Silex 197 ....K4
Skidmore 404 ....B2
Slater 2,186 ....G4
Smithton 532 ....F5
Smithville 2,525 ....D4
South West City 600 ....D9
Spanish Lake 20,322 ....R1
Sparta 751 ....F9
Spickard 326 ....F2
Springfield▲ 140,494 ....F8
Stanberry 1,310 ....C2
Steele 2,395 ....N10
Steelville▲ 1,465 ....K7
Stewartsville 732 ....C3
Stockton▲ 1,579 ....E7
Stotts City 235 ....D8
Stoutland 207 ....G7
Stover 964 ....G6
Strafford 1,166 ....F8
Sturgeon 838 ....H4

Topography

0   40   80 MI.

0   40   80 KM.

5,000 m. 2,000 m. 1,000 m. 500 m. 200 m. 100 m. Sea Below
16,404 ft. 6,562 ft. 3,281 ft. 1,640 ft. 656 ft. 328 ft. Level

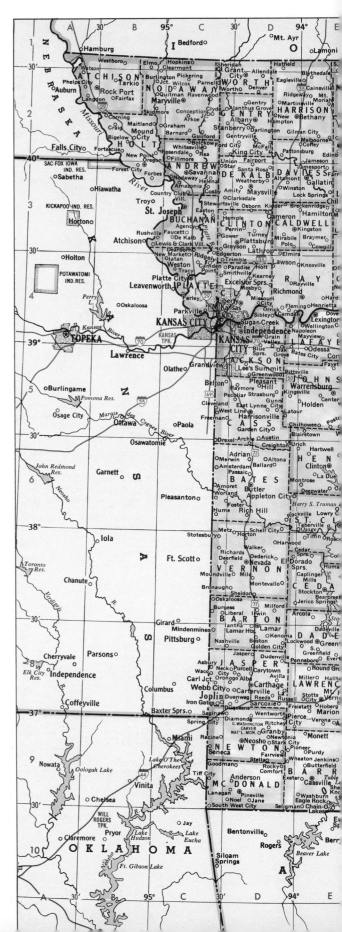

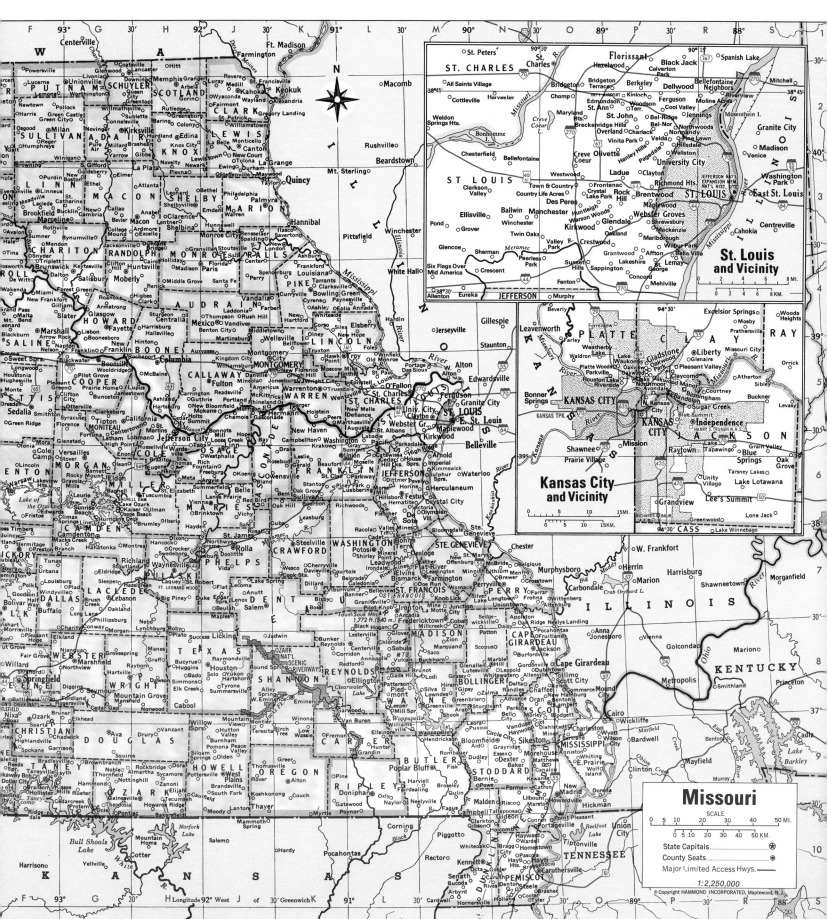

Agriculture, Industry and Resources

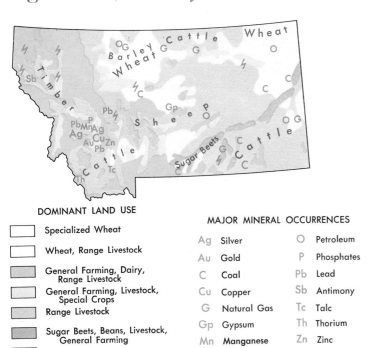

DOMINANT LAND USE

- Specialized Wheat
- Wheat, Range Livestock
- General Farming, Dairy, Range Livestock
- General Farming, Livestock, Special Crops
- Range Livestock
- Sugar Beets, Beans, Livestock, General Farming
- Forests

MAJOR MINERAL OCCURRENCES

Ag	Silver	O	Petroleum
Au	Gold	P	Phosphates
C	Coal	Pb	Lead
Cu	Copper	Sb	Antimony
G	Natural Gas	Tc	Talc
Gp	Gypsum	Th	Thorium
Mn	Manganese	Zn	Zinc

⚡ Water Power

COUNTIES

Beaverhead 8,424 ....C5
Big Horn 11,337 ....J5
Blaine 6,728 ....G2
Broadwater 3,318 ....E4
Carbon 8,080 ....G5
Carter 1,503 ....M5
Cascade 77,691 ....E3
Chouteau 5,452 ....F3
Custer 11,697 ....L4
Daniels 2,266 ....L2
Dawson 9,505 ....M3
Deer Lodge 10,278 ....C5
Fallon 3,103 ....M4
Fergus 12,083 ....G3
Flathead 59,218 ....B2
Gallatin 50,463 ....E5
Garfield 1,589 ....J3
Glacier 12,121 ....C2
Golden Valley 912 ....G4
Granite 2,548 ....C4
Hill 17,654 ....F2
Jefferson 7,939 ....D4
Judith Basin 2,282 ....F4
Lake 21,041 ....B3
Lewis and Clark 47,495 ......D3
Liberty 2,295 ....E2
Lincoln 17,481 ....A2
Madison 5,989 ....D5
McCone 2,276 ....L3
Meagher 1,819 ....F4
Mineral 3,315 ....B4
Missoula 78,981 ....C4
Musselshell 4,106 ....H4
Park 14,562 ....F5
Petroleum 519 ....H3
Phillips 5,163 ....J2
Pondera 6,433 ....D2
Powder River 2,090 ....L5
Powell 6,620 ....D4
Prairie 1,383 ....L4
Ravalli 25,010 ....B4
Richland 10,716 ....M3
Roosevelt 10,999 ....L2
Rosebud 10,505 ....K4
Sanders 8,669 ....A3
Sheridan 4,732 ....M2
Silver Bow 33,941 ....D5
Stillwater 6,536 ....G5
Sweet Grass 3,154 ....G5
Teton 6,271 ....D3
Toole 5,046 ....E2
Treasure 874 ....J4
Valley 8,239 ....K2
Wheatland 2,246 ....G4
Wibaux 1,191 ....M4
Yellowstone 113,419 ....H4

CITIES and TOWNS

Absarokee 1,067 ....G5
Acton 50 ....H5
Alberton 354 ....B3
Alder 120 ....D5
Alzada 52 ....M5
Amsterdam 130 ....E5
Anaconda-Deer Lodge County▲ ...C4
Angela 50 ....K4
Antelope 83 ....M2
Apgar 25 ....B2
Arlee 489 ....B3
Armington 75 ....F3
Ashland 484 ....K5
Augusta 497 ....D3
Avon 125 ....D4
Babb 150 ....C2
Bainville 165 ....M2
Baker▲ 1,818 ....M4
Ballantine 380 ....J5
Bannack 2 ....C5
Basin 350 ....D4
Bearcreek 37 ....G5
Becket 35 ....G4
Belfry 300 ....H5
Belgrade 3,411 ....E5
Belt 571 ....E3
Biddle 28 ....L5
Big Arm 250 ....B3
Big Sandy 740 ....G2
Big Sky 50 ....E5
Big Timber▲ 1,557 ....G5
Bigfork 1,080 ....C2
Billings▲ 81,151 ....H5
Birney 100 ....K5
Black Eagle 1,500 ....E3
Blackfoot 100 ....D2
Bloomfield 28 ....M3
Bonner-West Riverside 1,669 .C4

Boulder▲ 1,316 ....E4
Box Elder 300 ....F2
Boyd 32 ....G5
Bozeman▲ 22,660 ....E5
Brady 450 ....E2
Bridger 692 ....H5
Broadus▲ 572 ....L5
Broadview 133 ....H4
Brockton 365 ....M2
Brockway 55 ....L3
Browning 1,170 ....C2
Busby 409 ....J5
Butte-Silver Bow County▲ 33,336 ...D5
Bynum 49 ....D3
Camas Prairie 160 ....B3
Cameron 150 ....D4
Canyon Creek 100 ....D4
Canyon Ferry 100 ....E4
Cardwell 34 ....E5
Carter 70 ....E3
Cartersville 115 ....K4
Cascade 729 ....E3
Charlo 358 ....B3
Chester▲ 942 ....E2
Chinook▲ 1,512 ....G2
Choteau▲ 1,741 ....D3
Christina 60 ....F3
Circle▲ 805 ....L3
Clancy 550 ....E4
Clinton 250 ....C4
Clyde Park 282 ....F5
Coffee Creek 62 ....F3
Colstrip 3,035 ....K5
Columbia Falls 2,942 ....B2
Columbus▲ 1,573 ....G5
Condon 300 ....C3
Conner 420 ....B5
Conrad▲ 2,891 ....D2
Cooke City 120 ....G5
Coram 450 ....C2
Corvallis 500 ....C4
Craig 100 ....D3
Crane 163 ....M3
Creston 60 ....C2
Crow Agency 1,446 ....J5
Culbertson 796 ....M2
Custer 300 ....J4
Cut Bank▲ 3,329 ....D2
Dagmar 35 ....M2

Topography

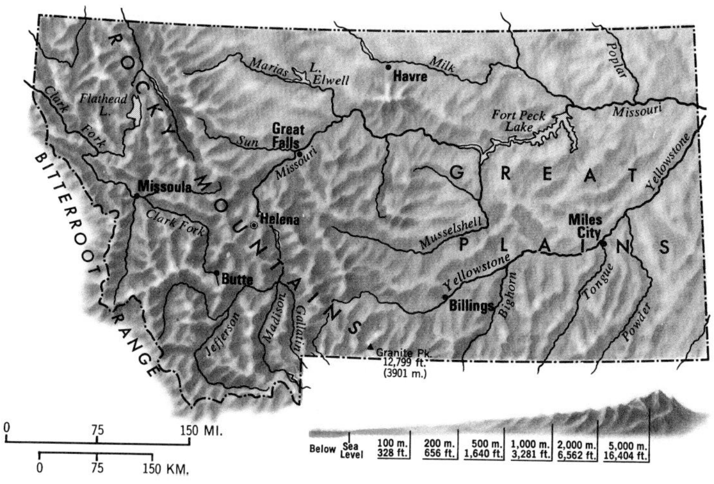

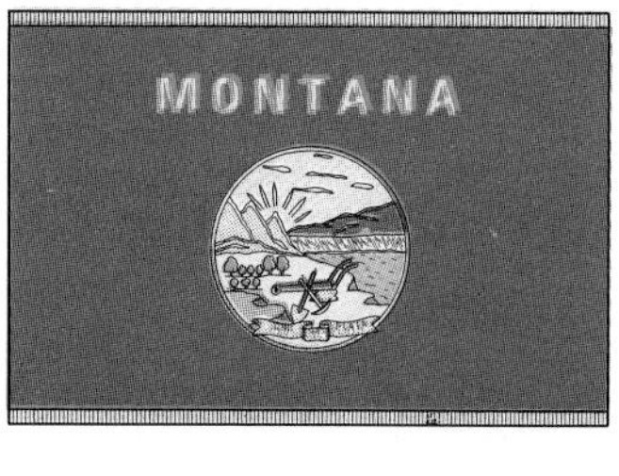

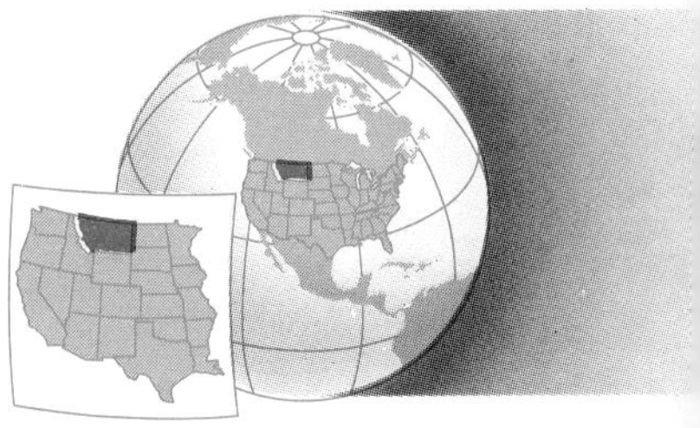

AREA 147,046 sq. mi. (380,849 sq. km.)
POPULATION 803,655
CAPITAL Helena
LARGEST CITY Billings
HIGHEST POINT Granite Pk. 12,799 ft. (3901 m.)
SETTLED IN 1809
ADMITTED TO UNION November 8, 1889
POPULAR NAME Treasure State; Big Sky Country
STATE FLOWER Bitterroot
STATE BIRD Western Meadowlark

Darby 625 ..... B4
Dayton 140 ..... B3
De Borgia 300 ..... A3
Decker 150 ..... K5
Deer Lodge▲ 3,378 ..... D4
Dell 29 ..... D6
Delpine 33 ..... F4
Denton 350 ..... G3
Dillon▲ 3,991 ..... D5
Divide 275 ..... D5
Dixon 550 ..... B3
Dodson 137 ..... H2
Drummond 264 ..... D4
Dupuyer 105 ..... D2
Dutton 392 ..... E3
East Glacier Park 326 ..... C2
East Helena 1,538 ..... E4
Edgar 220 ..... H5
Ekalaka▲ 439 ..... M5
Elliston 250 ..... D4
Elmo 250 ..... B3
Emigrant 80 ..... F5
Ennis 773 ..... E5
Epsie 60 ..... L5
Essex 48 ..... C2
Eureka 1,043 ..... B2
Fairfield 660 ..... D3
Fairview 869 ..... M3
Fallon 225 ..... L4
Fishtail 46 ..... G5
Flaxville 88 ..... L2
Florence 700 ..... B4
Floweree 48 ..... E3
Forestgrove 100 ..... H3
Forsyth▲ 2,178 ..... K4
Fort Belknap 422 ..... H2
Fort Benton▲ 1,660 ..... F3
Fort Peck 325 ..... K2
Fort Shaw 200 ..... E3
Fort Smith 300 ..... J5
Fortine 250 ..... A2
Four Buttes 50 ..... L2
Frazer 403 ..... K2
Frenchtown 300 ..... B3
Froid 195 ..... M2
Fromberg 370 ..... H5
Galata 100 ..... E2
Galen 210 ..... D4
Gallatin Gateway 600 ..... E5
Gardiner 600 ..... F5
Garneill 61 ..... G4
Garrison 300 ..... D4
Garryowen 200 ..... J5
Geraldine 299 ..... F3
Geyser 125 ..... F3
Gildford 250 ..... F2
Glasgow▲ 3,572 ..... K2
Glen 4,802 ..... D5
Glendive▲ 5,978 ..... M3
Goldcreek 100 ..... D4
Grant 25 ..... C5
Grantsdale 500 ..... B4
Grass Range 159 ..... H3
Great Falls▲ 55,097 ..... E3
Greenough 120 ..... C4
Greycliff 37 ..... G5
Hall 130 ..... C4
Hamilton▲ 2,737 ..... B4
Hardin▲ 2,940 ..... J5
Harlem 882 ..... H2
Harlowton▲ 1,049 ..... F4
Harrison 94 ..... E5
Hathaway 55 ..... K4
Haugan 90 ..... A3
Havre▲ 10,201 ..... G2
Hays 333 ..... H2
Heart Butte 499 ..... C2
Helena (cap.)▲ 24,569 ..... E4
Helmville 250 ..... C4
Heron 79 ..... A2
Highwood 150 ..... F3
Hilger 38 ..... G3
Hingham 181 ..... F2
Hinsdale 260 ..... K2
Hobson 226 ..... G4
Hodges 50 ..... M4
Hogeland 35 ..... H2
Homestead 50 ..... M2
Hot Springs 411 ..... B3
Hungry Horse 700 ..... C2
Huntley 250 ..... H5
Huson 97 ..... B3
Hysham▲ 361 ..... J4
Ingomar 48 ..... J4
Intake 60 ..... M3
Inverness 150 ..... F2
Jackson 210 ..... C5
Jardine 30 ..... F5
Jeffers 70 ..... E5
Jefferson City 162 ..... E4
Jefferson Island 25 ..... E5
Joliet 522 ..... G5
Joplin 300 ..... F2
Jordan▲ 494 ..... J3
Judith Gap 133 ..... G4
Kalispell▲ 11,917 ..... B2
Kevin 185 ..... D2
Kila 350 ..... B2
Kinsey 100 ..... L4
Kirby 30 ..... J5
Klein 250 ..... H4
Kremlin 304 ..... F2
Lakeside 663 ..... B2
Lakeview 28 ..... E6
Lambert 203 ..... M3
Lame Deer 1,918 ..... K5
Landusky 40 ..... H3
Laurel 5,686 ..... H5
Laurin 60 ..... D5
Lavina 151 ..... H4
Lewistown▲ 6,051 ..... G3
Libby▲ 2,532 ..... A2
Lima 265 ..... D6
Lincoln 473 ..... D4
Lindsay 50 ..... L3
Livingston▲ 6,701 ..... F5
Locate 55 ..... L4
Lodge Grass 517 ..... J5
Lodge Pole 292 ..... H2
Logan 53 ..... E5
Lohman 25 ..... G2
Lolo 2,746 ..... B4
Lolo Hot Springs 25 ..... B4
Loma 200 ..... F3
Lonepine 50 ..... B3
Lothair 29 ..... E2
Malta▲ 2,340 ..... J2
Manhattan 1,034 ..... E5
Marion 450 ..... B2
Martinsdale 75 ..... F4
Marysville 76 ..... D4
Maxville 44 ..... C4
McAllister 55 ..... E5
McLeod 150 ..... G5
Medicine Lake 357 ..... M2
Melrose 350 ..... D5
Melstone 166 ..... H4
Melville 100 ..... F4
Miles City▲ 8,461 ..... L4
Mill Iron 66 ..... M5
Milltown 300 ..... C4
Missoula▲ 42,918 ..... C4
Moccasin 57 ..... F3
Molt 31 ..... H5
Monarch 120 ..... F3
Moore 211 ..... G4
Musselshell 117 ..... H4
Myers 120 ..... J4
Nashua 375 ..... K2
Neihart 53 ..... F4
Nibbe 30 ..... H4
Norris 55 ..... E5
North Havre 1,230 ..... G2
Noxon 800 ..... A3
Nye 50 ..... G5
Oilmont 50 ..... E2
Olney 200 ..... B2
Opheim 145 ..... K2
Oswego 75 ..... L2
Outlook 109 ..... M2
Ovando 300 ..... C3
Pablo 1,298 ..... B3
Paradise 400 ..... B3
Park City 800 ..... H5
Peerless 110 ..... L2
Pendroy 100 ..... D2
Perma 50 ..... B3
Philipsburg▲ 925 ..... C4
Plains 992 ..... B3
Plentywood▲ 2,136 ..... M2
Plevna 140 ..... M4
Polaris 53 ..... C5
Polson▲ 3,283 ..... B3
Pompeys Pillar 300 ..... J5
Pony 130 ..... E5
Poplar 881 ..... L2
Potomac 80 ..... C4
Power 159 ..... E3
Pray 40 ..... F5
Proctor 150 ..... B3
Pryor 654 ..... H5
Radersburg 104 ..... E4
Ramsay 95 ..... D4
Rapelje 50 ..... G5
Ravalli 150 ..... B3
Raymond 26 ..... M2
Raynesford 35 ..... F3
Red Lodge▲ 1,958 ..... G5
Redstone 40 ..... M2
Reedpoint 160 ..... G5
Regina 83 ..... J3
Reserve 80 ..... M2
Rexford 132 ..... A2
Richey 259 ..... L3
Richland 48 ..... K2
Ringling 102 ..... F4
Roberts 312 ..... G5
Rocky Boy 150 ..... G2
Rollins 200 ..... B3
Ronan 1,547 ..... C3
Roscoe 40 ..... G5
Rosebud 259 ..... K4
Roundup▲ 1,808 ..... H4
Roy 200 ..... H3
Rudyard 450 ..... F2
Ryegate▲ 260 ..... G4
Saco 261 ..... J2
Saint Ignatius 778 ..... C3
Saint Regis 500 ..... A3
Saint Xavier 200 ..... J5
Saltese 90 ..... A3
Sand Coulee 600 ..... E3
Sanders 50 ..... J4
Santa Rita 120 ..... D2
Savage 300 ..... M3
Scobey▲ 1,154 ..... L2
Seeley Lake 900 ..... C3
Shawmut 66 ..... G4
Sheffield 49 ..... K4
Shelby▲ 2,763 ..... E2
Shepherd 200 ..... H5
Sheridan 652 ..... D5
Sidney▲ 5,217 ..... M3
Silesia 90 ..... H5
Silver Star 125 ..... D5
Simms 200 ..... E3
Simpson 70 ..... F2
Somers 700 ..... B2
Sonnette 42 ..... L5
Springdale 45 ..... F5
Square Butte 48 ..... F3
Stanford▲ 529 ..... F3
Stark 51 ..... B3
Stevensville 1,221 ..... C4
Stockett 500 ..... E3
Stryker 96 ..... B2
Suffolk 45 ..... G3
Sula 200 ..... B5
Sun River 300 ..... E3
Sunburst 437 ..... E2
Superior▲ 881 ..... B3
Swan Lake 100 ..... C3
Sweetgrass 250 ..... E2
Terry▲ 659 ..... L4
Thompson Falls▲ 1,319 ..... A3
Three Forks 1,203 ..... E5
Thurlow 84 ..... K4
Toston 70 ..... E4
Townsend▲ 1,635 ..... E4
Trego 50 ..... B2
Trident 50 ..... E5
Trout Creek 300 ..... A3
Troy 953 ..... A2
Turner 150 ..... H2
Twin Bridges 374 ..... D5
Twodot 285 ..... F4
Ulm 450 ..... E3
Utica 30 ..... F4
Valier 519 ..... D2
Vananda 50 ..... K4
Vandalia 35 ..... J2
Vaughn 2,270 ..... E3
Victor 700 ..... B4
Vida 50 ..... L3
Virgelle 28 ..... F2
Virginia City▲ 142 ..... E5
Volborg 125 ..... L5
Wagner 32 ..... H2
Walkerville 605 ..... D4
Warmsprings 500 ..... D4
Waterloo 102 ..... D5
West Glacier 150 ..... C2
West Yellowstone 913 ..... E6
Westby 253 ..... M2
White Sulphur Springs▲ 963 ..... E4
Whitefish 4,368 ..... B2
Whitehall 1,067 ..... D5
Whitetail 150 ..... L2
Whitewater 100 ..... J2
Whitlash 50 ..... E2
Wibaux▲ 628 ..... M3
Wickes 60 ..... D4
Willow Creek 150 ..... E5
Wilsall 250 ..... F5
Windham 63 ..... F3
Winifred 150 ..... G3
Winnett▲ 188 ..... H4
Winston 120 ..... E4
Wisdom 140 ..... C5
Wise River 150 ..... C5
Wolf Creek 500 ..... D3
Wolf Point▲ 2,880 ..... L2
Woodside 75 ..... B4
Worden 600 ..... H5
Wyola 350 ..... J5
Zurich 60 ..... G2

OTHER FEATURES

Absaroka (range) F5
Allen (mt.) C2
Arrow (creek) F3
Ashley (lake) B2
Battle (creek) G1
Bearhat (mt.) C2
Bears Paw (mts.) G2
Beartooth (mts.) G5
Beaver (creek) J2
Beaverhead (riv.) D5
Benton (lake) E3
Big (lake) G5
Big Belt (mts.) E4
Big Dry (creek) K3
Big Hole (riv.) C5
Big Hole Nat'l Battlefield C5
Bighorn (lake) H5
Bighorn (riv.) J5
Bighorn Canyon Nat'l Rec. Area H5
Big Muddy (riv.) M2
Big Porcupine (creek) J4
Birch (creek) D2
Birch Creek (res.) D2
Bitterroot (range) B4
Bitterroot (riv.) B4
Blackfeet Ind. Res. D2
Blackfoot (riv.) C4
Blackmore (mt.) F5
Bowdoin (lake) J2
Boxelder (creek) H3
Boxelder (creek) M5
Bynum (res.) D2
Cabinet (mts.) A2
Canyon Ferry (lake) E4
Clark Canyon (res.) D6
Clark Fork (riv.) A3
Clarks Fork, Yellowstone (riv.) G6
Cottonwood (creek) E2
Cow (creek) G2
Crazy peak) F4
Crow Ind. Res. H5
Cut Bank (creek) D2
Douglas (mt.) F5
Earthquake (lake) E6
Electric (peak) F6
Elwell (lake) E2
Emigrant (peak) F5
Ennis (lake) E5
Flathead (lake) C3
Flathead (riv.) B2
Flathead, North Fork (riv.) B2
Flathead, South Fork (riv.) C3
Flathead Ind. Res. B3
Flatwillow (creek) H4
Fort Belknap Ind. Res. H2
Fort Peck (lake) K3
Fort Union Trading Post Nat'l Hist. Site N2
Frances (lake) D2
Freezeout (lake) D3
Frenchman (riv.) J1
Fresno (res.) F2
Gallatin (peak) E5
Gallatin (riv.) E5
Georgetown (lake) C4
Gibson (res.) D3
Glacier Nat'l Park C2
Granite (peak) F5
Grant-Kohrs Ranch Nat'l Hist. Site D4
Hauser (lake) E4
Haystack (peak) A3
Hebgen (lake) E6
Helena (lake) E4
Holter (lake) D4
Hungry Horse (res.) C2
Hurricane (mt.) D2
Hyalite (peak) E5
Jackson (mt.) C2
Jefferson (riv.) D5
Judith (riv.) G3
Koocanusa (lake) A2
Kootenai (riv.) A2
Lemhi (pass) C6
Lewis and Clark (range) C3
Lima (res.) D6
Little Bighorn (riv.) J5
Little Bitterroot (lake) B2
Little Dry (creek) K3
Little Missouri (riv.) M5
Lockhart (mt.) D3
Lodge (creek) G1
Lolo (pass) B4
Lone (mt.) E5
Lost Trail (pass) B5
Lower Red Rock (lake) E6
Lower Saint Mary (lake) C2
Madison (riv.) E5
Malmstrom A.F.B. 5,938 ..... E3
Marias (riv.) D2
Martinsdale (res.) F4
Mary Ronan (lake) B3
McDonald (lake) B2
McGloughlin (peak) C4
McGregor (lake) B3
Medicine (lake) M2
Milk (riv.) J2
Mission (range) C3
Missouri (riv.) L3
Musselshell (riv.) J3
Nelson (res.) J2
Ninepipe (res.) C3
Northern Cheyenne Indian Reservation K5
O'Fallon (creek) L4
Pishkun (res.) D3
Poplar (riv.) L2
Porcupine (creek) K2
Powder (riv.) L4
Purcell (mts.) A2
Railley (mt.) C3
Red Rock (lakes) E6
Red Rock (riv.) D6
Redwater (riv.) L3
Rock (creek) C4
Rocky (mts.) D4
Rocky Boy's Ind. Res G2
Rosebud (creek) K4
Ruby (riv.) D5
Ruby River (res.) D5
Sage (creek) F2
Saint Mary (lake) C2
Saint Mary (riv.) C1
Sandy (creek) F2
Sheep (mt.) C2
Shields (riv.) F4
Siyeh (mt.) C2
Smith (riv.) E3
Sphinx (mt.) E5
Stillwater (riv.) G5
Stimson (mt.) C2
Sun (riv.) D3
Swan (lake) C3
Teton (riv.) E3
Tongue (riv.) K5
Upper Red Rock (lake) E6
Ward (peak) A3
Waterton-Glacier Int'l Peace Park C2
Whitefish (lake) B2
Willow (creek) E2
Willow Creek (res.) D3
Yellowstone (riv.) M3
Yellowstone National Park F6

▲County seat

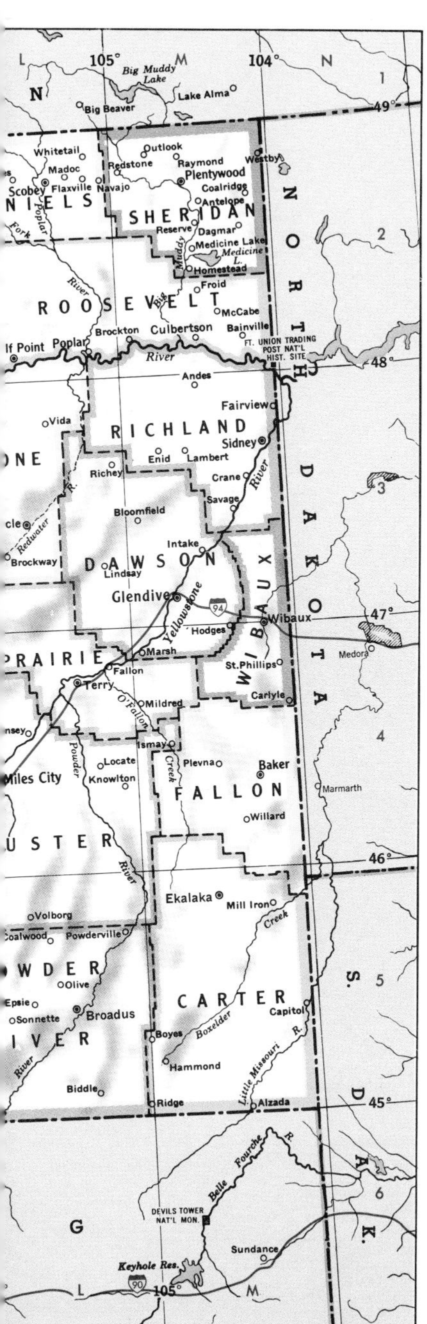

COUNTIES

Adams 29,625 F4
Antelope 7,965 F2
Arthur 462 C3
Banner 852 A3
Blaine 675 E3
Boone 6,667 F3
Box Butte 13,130 A2
Boyd 2,835 F2
Brown 3,657 E2
Buffalo 37,447 E4
Burt 7,868 H3
Butler 8,601 G3
Cass 21,318 H4
Cedar 10,131 G2
Chase 4,381 C4
Cherry 6,307 C2
Cheyenne 9,494 A3
Clay 7,123 F4
Colfax 9,139 G3
Cuming 10,117 H3
Custer 12,270 E3
Dakota 16,742 H2
Dawes 9,021 A2
Dawson 19,940 E4
Deuel 2,237 B3
Dixon 6,143 H2
Dodge 34,500 H3
Douglas 416,444 H3
Dundy 2,582 C4
Fillmore 7,103 G4
Franklin 3,938 F4
Frontier 3,101 D4
Furnas 5,553 E4
Gage 22,794 H4
Garden 2,460 B3
Garfield 2,141 F3
Gosper 1,928 E4
Grant 769 C3
Greeley 3,006 F3
Hall 48,925 F4
Hamilton 8,862 F4
Harlan 3,810 E4
Hayes 1,222 C4
Hitchcock 3,750 C4
Holt 12,599 F2
Hooker 793 C3
Howard 6,055 F3
Jefferson 8,759 G4
Johnson 4,673 H4
Kearney 6,629 F4
Keith 8,584 C3
Keya Paha 1,029 E2
Kimball 4,108 A3
Knox 9,534 G2
Lancaster 213,641 H4
Lincoln 32,508 D4
Logan 878 D3
Loup 683 E3
Madison 32,655 G3
McPherson 546 C3
Merrick 8,042 F3
Morrill 5,423 A3
Nance 4,275 F3
Nemaha 7,980 J4
Nuckolls 5,786 F4
Otoe 14,252 H4
Pawnee 3,317 H4
Perkins 3,367 C4
Phelps 9,715 E4
Pierce 7,827 G2
Platte 29,820 G3
Polk 5,675 G3
Red Willow 11,705 D4
Richardson 9,937 J4
Rock 2,019 E2
Saline 12,715 G4
Sarpy 102,583 H3
Saunders 18,285 H3
Scotts Bluff 36,025 A3
Seward 15,450 G4
Sheridan 6,750 B2
Sherman 3,718 F3
Sioux 1,549 A2
Stanton 6,244 G3
Thayer 6,635 G4
Thomas 851 D3
Thurston 6,936 H2
Valley 5,169 E3
Washington 16,607 H3
Wayne 9,364 G2
Webster 4,279 F4
Wheeler 948 F3
York 14,428 G4

CITIES and TOWNS

Adams 472 H4
Ainsworth▲ 1,870 D2
Albion▲ 1,916 F3
Alda 540 F4
Alexandria 224 G4
Allen 331 H2
Alliance▲ 9,765 A2
Alma▲ 1,226 E4
Alvo 164 H4
Amherst 231 E4
Anselmo 189 E3
Ansley 555 E3
Arapahoe 1,001 E4
Arcadia 385 F3
Arlington 1,178 H3
Arnold 679 D3
Arthur▲ 128 C3
Ashland 2,136 H3
Ashton 251 F3
Atkinson 1,380 E2
Auburn▲ 3,443 J4
Aurora▲ 3,810 F4
Avoca 254 H4
Axtell 707 E4
Bancroft 494 H2
Bartlett▲ 131 F3
Bartley 339 D4
Bassett▲ 739 E2
Battle Creek 997 G3
Bayard 1,196 A3
Beatrice▲ 12,354 H4
Beaver City▲ 707 E4
Beaver Crossing 448 G4
Bee 209 G4
Beemer 672 H3
Belden 149 G2
Belgrade 157 G3
Bellevue 30,982 J3
Bellwood 395 G3
Benedict 230 G3
Benkelman▲ 1,193 C4
Bennet 544 H4
Bennington 866 H3
Bertrand 708 E4
Big Springs 495 B3
Bladen 280 F4
Blair▲ 6,860 H3
Bloomfield 1,181 G2
Blue Hill 810 F4
Blue Springs 431 H4
Boys Town 794 H3
Bradshaw 330 G4
Brady 331 D3
Brainard 326 G3
Brewster▲ 22 D3
Bridgeport▲ 1,581 A3
Broadwater 160 B3
Brock 143 H4
Broken Bow▲ 3,778 E3
Brownville 148 J4
Brule 411 C3
Bruning 332 G4
Bruno 141 G3
Brunswick 182 G2
Burwell▲ 1,278 E3
Butte▲ 452 F2
Cairo 733 F3
Callaway 539 D3
Cambridge 1,107 D4
Campbell 432 F4
Carleton 144 G4
Carroll 237 G2
Cedar Bluffs 591 H3
Cedar Creek 334 H3
Cedar Rapids 396 F3
Center▲ 112 G2
Central City▲ 2,868 F3
Ceresco 825 H3
Chadron▲ 5,588 B2
Chambers 341 F2
Chapman 292 F3
Chappell▲ 979 B3
Chester 351 G4
Clarks 379 G3
Clarkson 699 G3
Clatonia 296 H4
Clay Center▲ 825 F4
Clearwater 401 F2
Cody 177 C2
Coleridge 596 G2
Columbus▲ 19,480 G3
Concord 156 H2
Cook 333 H4
Cordova 147 G4
Cortland 393 H4
Cozad 3,823 E4
Craig 228 H3
Crawford 1,115 A2
Creighton 1,223 G2
Creston 220 G3
Crete 4,841 G4
Crofton 820 G2
Culbertson 795 C4
Curtis 791 D4
Dakota City▲ 1,470 H2
Dalton 282 B3
Dannebrog 324 F3
Davenport 383 G4
Davey 160 H4
David City▲ 2,522 G3
Dawson 157 J4
Daykin 188 G4
De Witt 598 G4
Decatur 641 H3
Denton 161 H4
Deshler 892 G4
Diller 298 H4
Dix 229 A3
Dodge 693 H3
Doniphan 736 F4
Dorchester 614 G4
Douglas 199 H4
Dunbar 171 J4
Duncan 387 G3
Dwight 227 G3
Eagle 1,047 H4
Edgar 600 F4
Edison 148 E4
Elba 196 F3
Elgin 731 F3
Elkhorn 1,398 H3
Elm Creek 852 E4
Elmwood 584 H4
Elsie 153 C4
Elwood▲ 679 E4
Emerson 791 H2
Endicott 163 G4
Eustis 452 D4
Ewing 449 F2
Exeter 661 G4
Fairbury▲ 4,335 G4
Fairfield 458 G4
Fairmont 708 G4
Falls City▲ 4,769 J4
Farnam 188 D4
Farwell 152 F3
Filley 157 H4
Firth 471 H4
Fordyce 190 G2
Fort Calhoun 648 J3
Franklin▲ 1,112 E4
Fremont▲ 23,680 H3
Friend 1,111 G4
Fullerton▲ 1,452 F3
Funk 198 E4
Garland 247 G4
Geneva▲ 2,310 G4
Genoa 1,082 G3
Gering▲ 7,946 A3
Gibbon 1,525 F4
Giltner 367 F4
Glenvil 304 F4
Goehner 192 G4
Gordon 1,803 B2
Gothenburg 3,232 D4
Grafton 167 G4
Grand Island▲ 39,386 F4
Grant▲ 1,239 C4
Greeley▲ 562 F3
Greenwood 531 H3
Gresham 253 G3
Gretna 2,249 H3
Guide Rock 290 F4
Gurley 198 B3
Hadar 291 G2
Haigler 225 C4
Hallam 309 H4
Hampton 432 G4
Hardy 206 G4
Harrisburg▲ 75 A3
Harrison▲ 291 A2
Hartington▲ 1,583 G2
Harvard 976 F4
Hastings 22,837 F4
Hay Springs 693 B2
Hayes Center▲ 259 C4
Hebron▲ 1,765 G4
Hemingford 953 A2
Henderson 999 G4
Henry 145 A2
Herman 186 H3
Hershey 579 D3
Hickman 1,081 H4
Hildreth 364 E4
Holbrook 233 D4
Holdrege▲ 5,671 E4
Holstein 207 F4
Homer 553 H2
Hooper 850 H3
Hordville 164 G3
Hoskins 307 G2
Howells 615 H3
Hubbard 199 H2
Humboldt 1,003 J4
Humphrey 741 G3
Hyannis▲ 210 C3
Imperial▲ 2,007 C4
Indianola 672 D4
Inglewood 286 H3
Inman 159 F2
Jackson 230 H2
Johnson 323 J4
Juniata 811 F4
Kearney▲ 24,396 E4
Kenesaw 818 F4
Kennard 371 H3
Kimball▲ 2,574 A3
La Vista 9,840 J3
Laurel 981 G2
Lawrence 323 F4
Leigh 447 G3
Lewellen 307 B3
Lexington▲ 6,601 E4
Lincoln (cap.)▲ 191,972 H4
Lindsay 321 G3
Litchfield 314 E3
Lodgepole 368 B3
Long Pine 396 E2
Loomis 376 E4
Louisville 998 H3
Loup City▲ 1,104 E3
Lyman 452 A3
Lynch 296 F2
Lyons 1,144 H3
Macy 836 H2
Madison▲ 2,135 G3
Madrid 288 C4
Malcolm 181 H4
Manley 170 H4
Marquette 211 G4
Mason City 160 E3
Max 285 C4
Maxwell 410 D3
Maywood 313 D4
McCook▲ 8,112 D4
McCool Junction 372 G4
Mead 513 H3
Meadow Grove 332 G2
Merna 377 E3
Merriman 151 C2
Milford 1,886 H4
Milligan 328 G4
Minatare 807 A3
Minden▲ 2,749 F4
Mitchell 1,743 A3
Monroe 309 G3
Morrill 974 A3
Mullen▲ 554 C2
Murdock 267 H4
Murray 418 J4
Nebraska City▲ 6,547 J4
Nehawka 260 H4
Neligh▲ 1,742 G2
Nelson▲ 627 F4
Nemaha 188 J4
Newcastle 271 H2
Newman Grove 787 G3
Newport 136 E2
Nickerson 291 H3
Niobrara 376 G2
Norfolk 21,476 G2
North Bend 1,249 H3
North Loup 361 F3
North Platte▲ 22,605 D3
O'Neill▲ 4,049 F2
Oakdale 362 F2
Oakland 1,279 H3
Oconto 147 E3
Odell 291 H4
Ogallala▲ 5,095 C3
Ohiowa 146 G4
Omaha▲ 335,795 J3
Orchard 439 F2
Ord▲ 2,481 F3
Orleans 490 E4
Osceola▲ 879 G3
Oshkosh▲ 986 B3
Osmond 774 G2
Otoe 196 H4
Overton 547 E4
Oxford 949 E4
Page 191 F2
Palisade 381 C4
Palmer 753 F3
Palmyra 545 H4
Panama 207 H4
Papillion▲ 10,372 J3
Pawnee City▲ 1,008 H4
Paxton 536 C3
Pender▲ 1,208 H2
Peru 1,110 J4
Petersburg 388 G3
Phillips 316 F4
Pickrell 201 H4
Pierce▲ 1,615 G2
Pilger 361 G2
Plainview 1,333 G2
Platte Center 387 G3
Plattsmouth▲ 6,412 J3
Pleasant Dale 253 G4
Pleasanton 372 E4
Plymouth 455 G4
Polk 345 G3
Ponca▲ 877 H2
Potter 388 A3
Prague 282 H3
Ralston 6,236 J3
Randolph 983 G2
Ravenna 1,317 F4
Raymond 167 H4
Red Cloud▲ 1,204 F4
Republican City 199 E4
Rising City 341 G3
Riverdale 208 E4
Riverton 162 F4
Rosalie 178 H2
Rose 247 E2
Roseland 254 F4
Rulo 191 J4
Rushville▲ 1,127 B2
Ruskin 187 G4
Saint Edward 822 G3
Saint Paul▲ 2,009 F3
Salem 160 J4
Santee 365 G2
Sargent 710 E3
Schuyler▲ 4,052 G3
Scotia 318 F3
Scottsbluff 13,711 A3
Scribner 950 H3
Seward▲ 5,634 H4
Shelby 690 G3
Shelton 954 F4
Shickley 360 G4
Shubert 237 J4
Sidney▲ 5,959 B3
Silver Creek 625 G3
Snyder 280 H3
South Sioux City 9,677 H2
Spalding 592 F3
Spencer 536 F2
Sprague 157 H4
Springfield 1,426 H3
Springview▲ 304 E2
Stamford 188 E4
Stanton▲ 1,549 G3
Staplehurst 281 G4
Stapleton▲ 299 D3
Stella 248 J4
Sterling 451 H4
Stockville▲ 32 D4
Stratton 427 C4
Stromsburg 1,241 G3
Stuart 650 E2
Sumner 210 E4
Superior 2,397 F4
Sutherland 1,032 C3
Sutton 1,353 G4
Swanton 145 H4
Syracuse 1,646 H4
Table Rock 308 H4
Talmage 246 H4
Taylor▲ 186 E3
Tecumseh▲ 1,702 H4
Tekamah▲ 1,852 H3
Terrytown 656 A3
Thedford▲ 243 D3
Tilden 895 G2

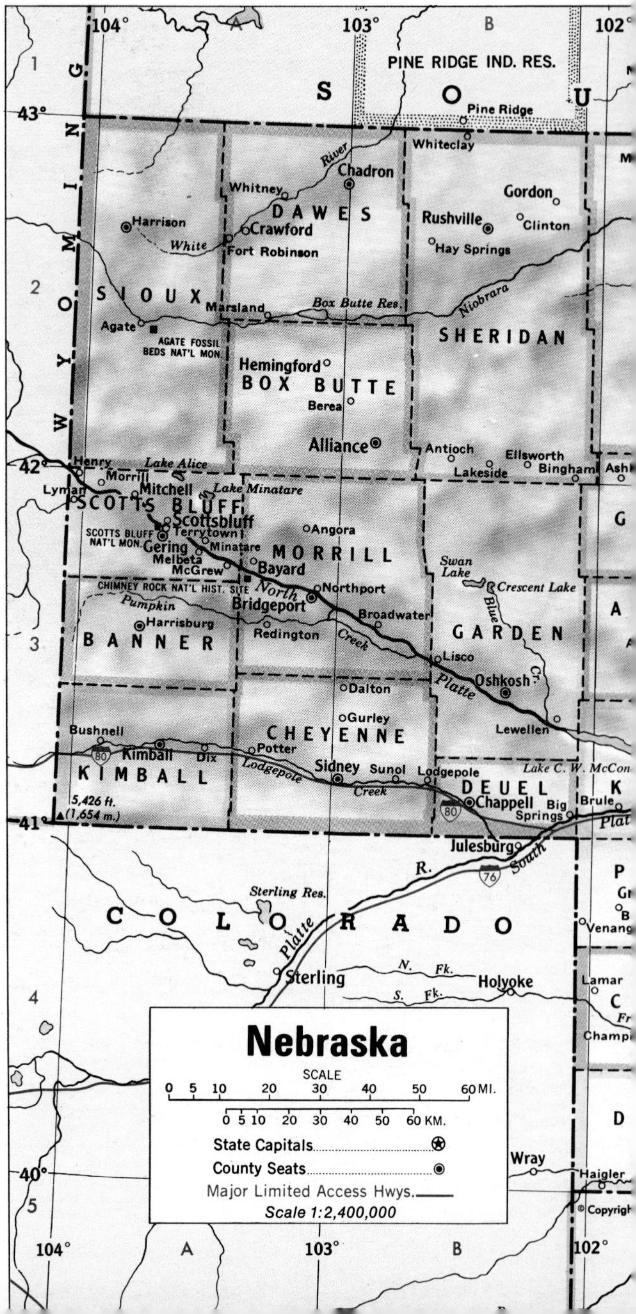

Agriculture, Industry and Resources

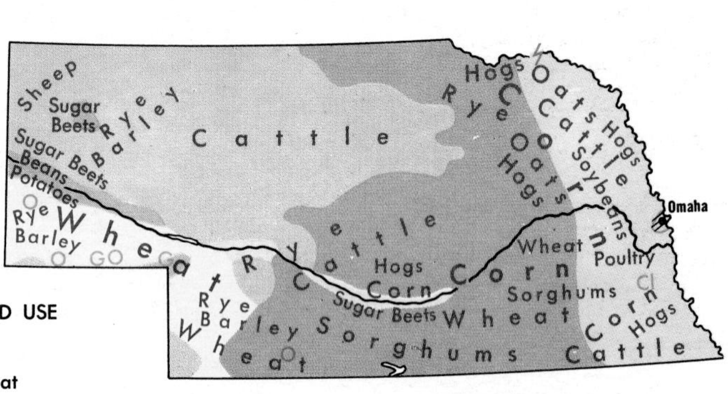

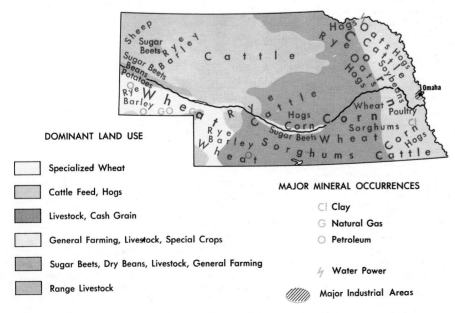

DOMINANT LAND USE

- Specialized Wheat
- Cattle Feed, Hogs
- Livestock, Cash Grain
- General Farming, Livestock, Special Crops
- Sugar Beets, Dry Beans, Livestock, General Farming
- Range Livestock

MAJOR MINERAL OCCURRENCES

- Cl Clay
- G Natural Gas
- O Petroleum
- Water Power
- Major Industrial Areas

AREA 77,355 sq. mi. (200,349 sq. km.)
POPULATION 1,584,617
CAPITAL Lincoln
LARGEST CITY Omaha
HIGHEST POINT (Kimball Co.) 5,246 ft. (1654 m.)
SETTLED IN 1847
ADMITTED TO UNION March 1, 1867
POPULAR NAME Cornhusker State
STATE FLOWER Goldenrod
STATE BIRD Western Meadowlark

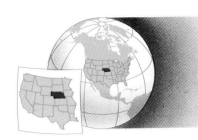

Topography

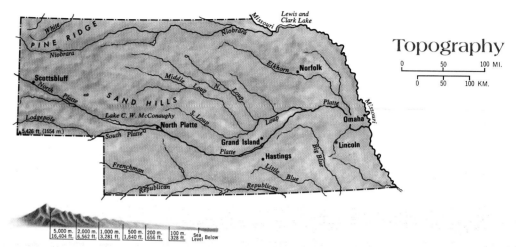

5,000 m.	2,000 m.	1,000 m.	500 m.	200 m.	100 m.	Sea Level	Below
16,404 ft.	6,562 ft.	3,281 ft.	1,640 ft.	656 ft.	328 ft.		

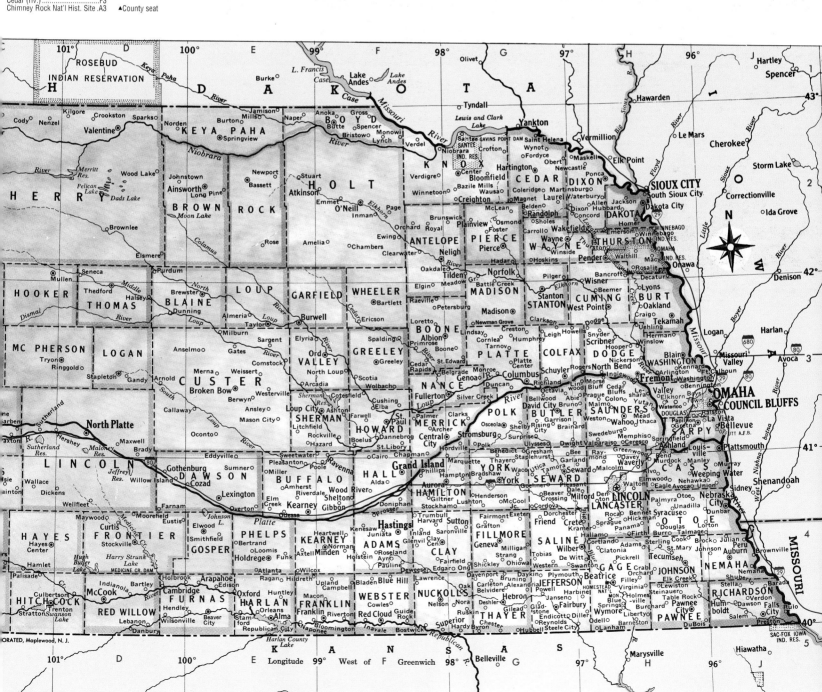

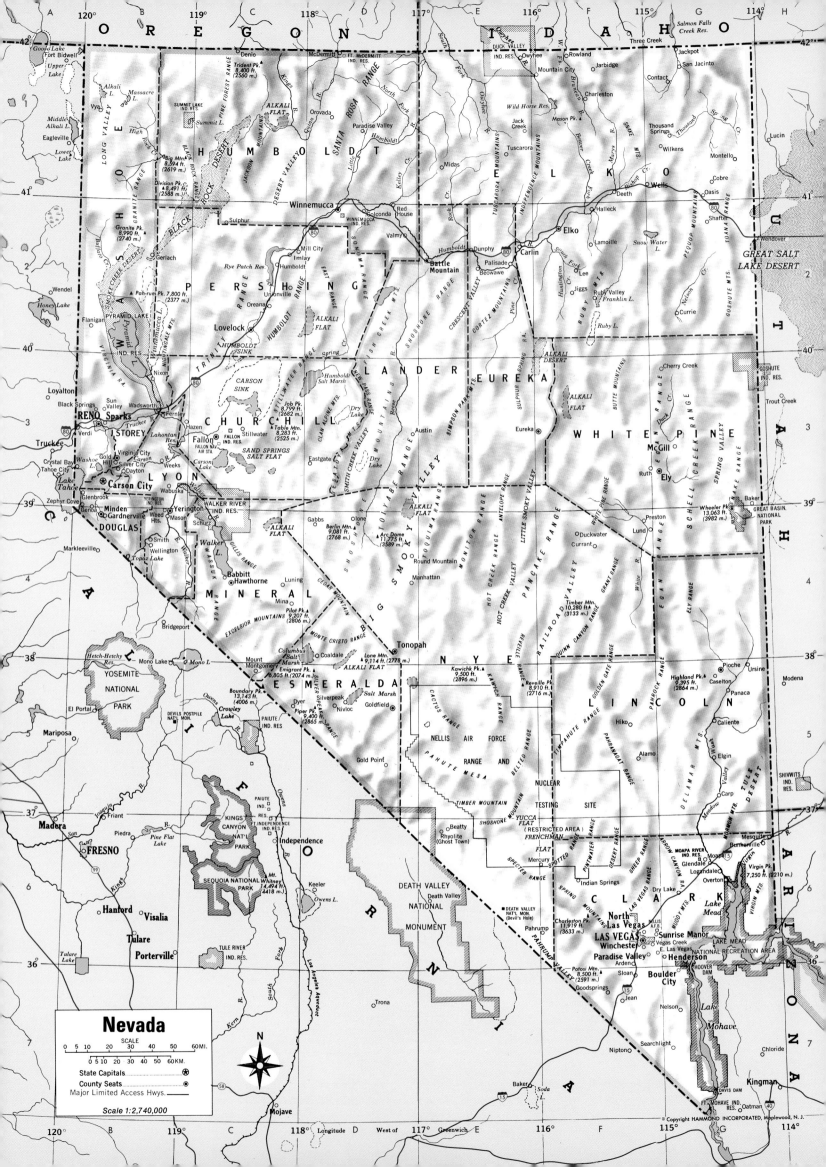

Nevada

SCALE

0 5 10   20   30   40   50   60 MI.

0 5 10 20   30   40   50   60 KM.

State Capitals ....⊛

County Seats ....◉

Major Limited Access Hwys. ─────

Scale 1:2,740,000

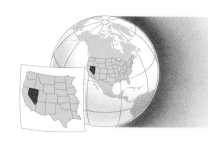

AREA 110,561 sq. mi. (286,353 sq. km.)
POPULATION 1,206,152
CAPITAL Carson City
LARGEST CITY Las Vegas
HIGHEST POINT Boundary Pk. 13,143 ft.
(4006 m.)
SETTLED IN 1850
ADMITTED TO UNION October 31, 1864
POPULAR NAME Silver State; Sagebrush
State
STATE FLOWER Sagebrush
STATE BIRD Mountain Bluebird

MAJOR MINERAL OCCURRENCES

Ag Silver
Au Gold
Ba Barite
Cu Copper
Gp Gypsum
Hg Mercury
Lt Lithium
Mg Magnesium
Mo Molybdenum
Na Salt
O Petroleum
Pb Lead
S Sulfur
W Tungsten   ⚡ Water Power
Zn Zinc

DOMINANT LAND USE

General Farming, Dairy, Livestock
General Farming, Livestock, Special Crops
Range Livestock
Forests
Nonagricultural Land

Agriculture, Industry and Resources

Topography

0   60   120 MI.
0   60   120 KM.

5,000 m. | 2,000 m. | 1,000 m. | 500 m. | 200 m. | 100 m. | Sea | Below
16,404 ft. | 6,562 ft. | 3,281 ft. | 1,640 ft. | 656 ft. | 328 ft. | Level

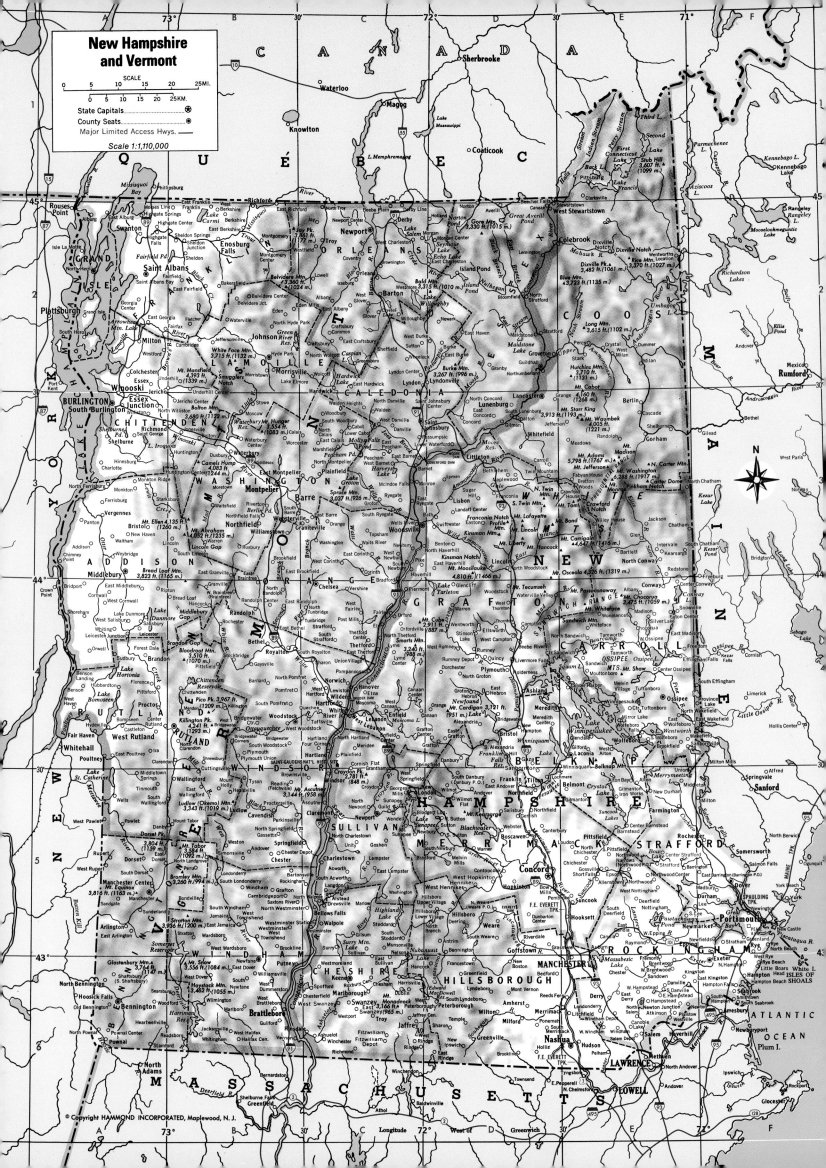

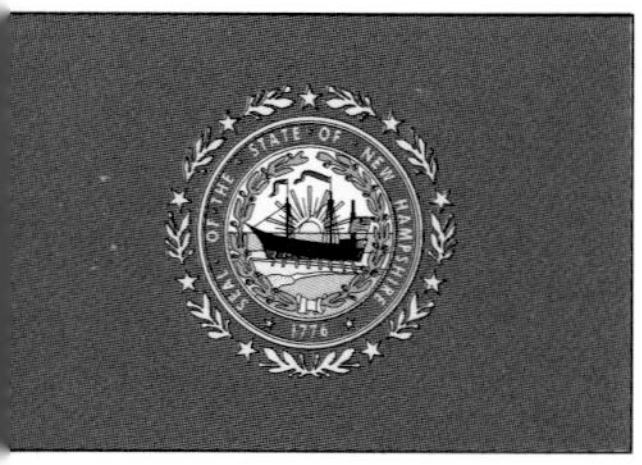

NEW HAMPSHIRE

AREA 9,279 sq. mi. (24,033 sq. km.)
POPULATION 1,113,915
CAPITAL Concord
LARGEST CITY Manchester
HIGHEST POINT Mt. Washington 6,288 ft. (1917 m.)
SETTLED IN 1623
ADMITTED TO UNION June 21, 1788
POPULAR NAME Granite State
STATE FLOWER Purple Lilac
STATE BIRD Purple Finch

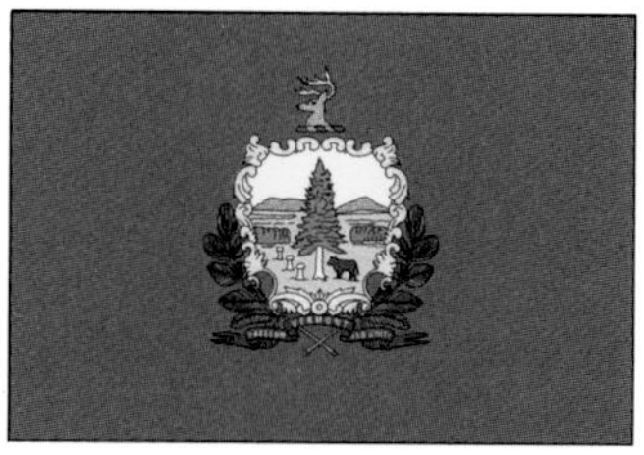

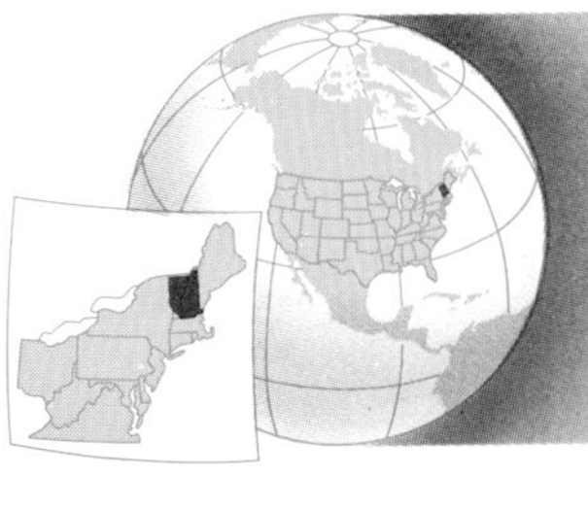

VERMONT

AREA 9,614 sq. mi. (24,900 sq. km.)
POPULATION 564,964
CAPITAL Montpelier
LARGEST CITY Burlington
HIGHEST POINT Mt. Mansfield 4,393 ft. (1339 m.)
SETTLED IN 1764
ADMITTED TO UNION March 4, 1791
POPULAR NAME Green Mountain State
STATE FLOWER Red Clover
STATE BIRD Hermit Thrush

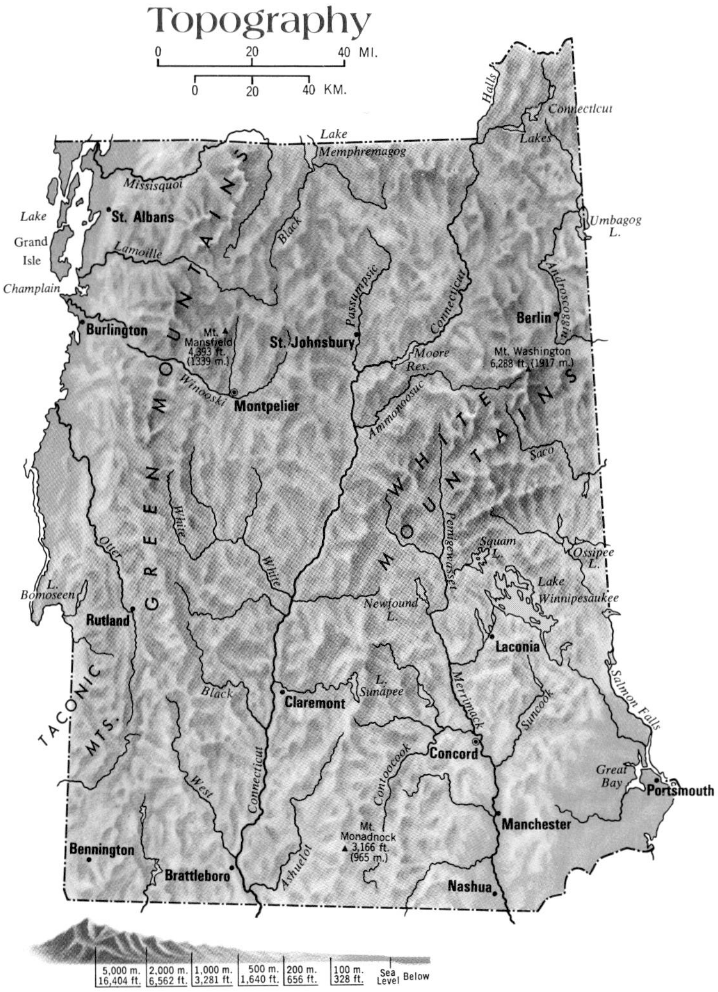

NEW HAMPSHIRE

COUNTIES

Belknap 49,216 .... D4
Carroll 35,410 .... E4
Cheshire 70,121 .... C6
Coos 34,828 .... E2
Grafton 74,929 .... D4
Hillsborough 336,073 .... D6
Merrimack 120,005 .... D5
Rockingham 245,845 .... E5
Strafford 104,233 .... E5
Sullivan 38,592 .... C5

CITIES and TOWNS

Acworth• 776 .... C5
Albany• 536 .... E4
Alexandria• 1,190 .... D4
Allenstown• 4,649 .... E5
Alstead• 1,721 .... C5
Alton Bay 500 .... E5
Alton• 3,286 .... E5
Amherst• 9,068 .... D6
Andover• 1,883 .... D5
Antrim 1,325 .... D5
Antrim• 2,360 .... D5
Ashland 1,915 .... D4
Ashland• 1,807 .... D4
Ashuelot 810 .... C6
Atkinson• 5,188 .... E6
Auburn• 4,085 .... E5
Barnstead• 3,100 .... E5
Barrington• 6,164 .... F5
Bartlett• 2,290 .... E3
Bath• 784 .... D3
Bedford• 12,563 .... D6
Beebe River 355 .... D4
Belmont• 5,796 .... E5
Bennington• 1,236 .... D5
Benton• 330 .... D3
Berlin 11,824 .... E3
Bethlehem• 2,033 .... D3
Boscawen• 3,586 .... D5
Bow Mills 802 .... D5
Bradford• 1,405 .... D5
Brentwood• 2,590 .... E6
Bretton Woods E3
Bridgewater• 796 .... D4
Bristol 1,483 .... D4
Bristol• 2,537 .... D4
Brookfield• 518 .... E4
Brookline• 2,410 .... D6
Campton• 2,377 .... D4
Canaan• 3,045 .... C4
Candia• 3,557 .... E5
Canobie Lake 500 .... E6
Canterbury• 1,687 .... D5
Carroll• 528 .... D3
Cascade 350 .... E3
Center Barnstead 400 .... E5
Center Conway 558 .... E4
Center Harbor• 996 .... E4
Center Ossipee• 800 .... E4
Center Tuftonboro 300 .... E4
Charlestown 1,173 .... C5
Charlestown• 4,630 .... C5
Chatham• 268 .... E3
Chester• 2,691 .... E6
Chesterfield• 3,112 .... C6
Chichester• 1,942 .... E5
Chocorua 575 .... E4
Claremont 13,902 .... C5
Clarksville• 232 .... E1
Colebrook 2,444 .... E2
Colebrook• 2,459 .... E2
Concord• (cap.) 36,006 .... D5
Contoocook 1,334 .... D5
Conway 1,604 .... E4
Conway• 7,940 .... E4
Cornish Flat 450 .... C4
Croydon• 627 .... C5
Dalton• 827 .... D3
Danbury• 881 .... D4
Danville• 2,534 .... E6
Deerfield• 3,124 .... E5
Deering• 1,707 .... D5
Derry 20,446 .... E6
Derry• 29,603 .... E6
Dorchester• 392 .... D4
Dover▲ 25,042 .... F5
Dublin• 1,474 .... C6
Dummer• 327 .... E2
Durham 9,236 .... F5
Durham• 11,818 .... F5
East Andover 500 .... D5
East Hampstead 900 .... E6
East Kingston• 1,352 .... F6
East Lempster 300 .... C5
East Sullivan 300 .... C6
East Swanzey 500 .... C6
East Wolfeboro 400 .... E4
Easton• 223 .... D3
Eaton (Eaton Center) 362 .... E4
Ellsworth• 74 .... D4
Enfield 1,560 .... C4
Enfield• 3,979 .... C4
Epping 1,384 .... E5
Epping• 5,162 .... E5
Epsom• 3,591 .... E5
Errol• 292 .... E2
Etna 550 .... C4
Exeter▲ 9,556 .... F6
Exeter• 12,481 .... F6
Farmington 3,567 .... E5
Farmington• 5,739 .... E5
Fitzwilliam• 2,011 .... C6
Fitzwilliam Depot 350 .... C6
Francestown• 1,217 .... D6
Franconia• 811 .... D3
Franklin 8,304 .... D5
Freedom• 935 .... E4
Fremont• 2,576 .... E6
Georges Mills 375 .... C5
Gerrish 500 .... D5
Gilford• 5,867 .... E4
Gilmanton• 2,609 .... E5
Gilmanton Iron Works 300 .... E5
Gilsum• 745 .... C5
Glen 600 .... E3
Goffstown• 14,621 .... D5
Gorham 1,910 .... E3
Gorham• 3,173 .... E3
Goshen• 742 .... C5
Grafton• 923 .... D4
Grantham• 1,247 .... C5
Grasmere 400 .... D5
Greenfield• 1,519 .... D6
Greenland• 2,768 .... F5
Greenville 1,135 .... D6
Greenville• 2,231 .... D6
Groton• 318 .... D4
Groveton 1,255 .... D2
Guild 500 .... C5
Hampstead• 6,732 .... E6
Hampton 7,989 .... F6
Hampton• 12,278 .... F6
Hampton Beach 975 .... F6
Hampton Falls• 1,503 .... F6
Hancock• 1,604 .... C6
Hanover 6,538 .... C4
Hanover• 9,212 .... C4
Harrisville• 981 .... C6
Haverhill• 4,164 .... C3
Hebron• 386 .... D4
Henniker 1,693 .... D5
Henniker• 4,151 .... D5
Hill• 814 .... D4
Hillsboro 1,826 .... D5
Hillsboro• 4,498 .... D5
Hinsdale 1,718 .... C6
Hinsdale• 3,936 .... C6
Holderness• 1,694 .... D4
Hollis• 5,705 .... D6
Hooksett 2,573 .... E5
Hooksett• 8,767 .... E5
Hopkinton• 4,806 .... D5
Hudson 7,626 .... E6
Hudson• 19,530 .... E6
Intervale 725 .... E3
Jackson• 678 .... E3
Jaffrey 2,558 .... C6
Jaffrey• 5,361 .... C6
Jaffrey Center 340 .... C6
Jefferson• 965 .... D3
Kearsarge 350 .... E3
Keene▲ 22,430 .... C6
Kingston• 5,591 .... E6
Laconia▲ 15,743 .... E4
Lancaster▲ 1,859 .... D3
Lancaster• 3,522 .... D3
Landaff• 350 .... D3
Langdon• 580 .... C5
Lebanon 12,183 .... C4
Lee• 3,729 .... F5
Lempster• 947 .... C5
Lincoln• 1,229 .... D3
Lisbon 1,246 .... D3
Lisbon• 1,664 .... D3
Litchfield• 5,516 .... E6
Littleton 4,633 .... D3
Littleton• 5,827 .... D3
Lochmere 300 .... D5
Londonderry• 19,781 .... E6
Loudon• 4,114 .... E5
Lyman• 388 .... D3
Lyme• 1,496 .... C4
Lyndeborough• 1,294 .... D6
Madbury• 1,404 .... F5
Madison• 1,704 .... E4
Manchester 99,567 .... E6
Marlborough 1,211 .... C6
Marlborough• 1,927 .... C6
Marlow• 650 .... C5
Melvin Village 450 .... E4
Meredith 1,654 .... D4
Meredith• 4,837 .... D4
Meriden 800 .... C4
Merrimack• 22,156 .... D6
Middleton• 1,183 .... E5
Milan• 1,295 .... E2
Milford 8,015 .... D6
Milford• 11,795 .... D6
Milton• 3,691 .... F5
Milton Mills 450 .... F4
Mirror Lake 350 .... E4
Monroe• 746 .... C3
Mont Vernon• 1,812 .... D6
Moultonboro• 2,956 .... E4
Nashua▲ 79,662 .... D6
Nelson• 535 .... C5
New Boston• 3,214 .... D6
New Castle• 840 .... F5
New Durham• 1,974 .... E5
New Hampton• 1,606 .... D4
New Ipswich• 4,014 .... D6
New London 3,180 .... D5
New London• 2,935 .... D5
Newbury• 1,347 .... C5
Newfields• 888 .... F5
Newington• 990 .... F5
Newmarket 4,917 .... F5
Newmarket• 7,157 .... F5
Newport▲ 3,772 .... C5
Newport• 6,110 .... C5
Newton Junction 450 .... E6
Newton• 3,473 .... E6
North Chichester 450 .... E5
North Conway 2,032 .... E3
North Hampton• 3,637 .... F6
North Haverhill 400 .... D3
North Stratford 600 .... D2
North Walpole 950 .... C5
North Weare 400 .... D5
North Woodstock 750 .... D3
Northfield-Tilton D5
Northfield• 4,263 .... D5
Northumberland• 2,492 .... D2
Northwood• 3,124 .... E5
Northwood Narrows 325 .... E5
Nottingham• 2,939 .... E5
Orange• 237 .... D4
Orford• 1,008 .... C4
Ossipee 3,309 .... E4
Pelham• 9,408 .... E6
Pembroke• 6,561 .... E5
Peterborough 2,685 .... D6
Peterborough• 5,239 .... D6
Piermont• 624 .... C4
Pike 433 .... C3
Pittsburg• 901 .... E1
Pittsfield 1,717 .... E5
Pittsfield• 3,701 .... E5
Plainfield• 2,056 .... C4
Plaistow• 7,316 .... E6
Plymouth 3,967 .... D4
Plymouth• 5,811 .... D4
Portsmouth 25,925 .... F5
Randolph• 371 .... E3
Raymond 2,516 .... E5
Raymond• 8,713 .... E5
Redstone 300 .... E3
Richmond• 877 .... C6
Rindge• 4,941 .... C6
Rochester 26,630 .... E5
Roxbury• 248 .... C6
Rumney• 1,446 .... D4
Rye• 4,612 .... F5
Rye Beach 600 .... F6
Rye North Beach 700 .... F5
Salem• 25,746 .... E6
Salem Depot 975 .... E6
Salisbury• 1,061 .... D5
Salmon Falls 950 .... F5
Sanbornton• 2,136 .... D5
Sanbornville 750 .... F4
Sandown• 4,060 .... E6
Sandwich• 1,066 .... E4
Seabrook• 6,503 .... F6
Sharon• 299 .... D6
Shelburne 437 .... E3
Shelburne• 318 .... E3
Silver Lake 350 .... E4
Somersworth 11,249 .... F5
South Deerfield 500 .... E5
South Hampton• 740 .... F6
South Lyndeboro 300 .... D6
South Merrimack 650 .... D6
South Seabrook 500 .... F6
South Weare 400 .... D5
Spofford 750 .... C6
Springfield• 788 .... C4
Stark• 518 .... E2
Stewartstown• 1,048 .... E2
Stoddard• 622 .... C5
Strafford• 2,965 .... E5
Stratford• 927 .... D2
Stratham• 4,955 .... F5
Sugar Hill• 464 .... D3
Sullivan• 706 .... C5
Sunapee• 2,559 .... C5
Suncook 5,214 .... C5
Surry• 667 .... C5
Sutton• 1,457 .... D5
Swanzey• 6,236 .... C6
Tamworth• 2,165 .... E4
Temple• 1,194 .... D6
Thornton• 1,505 .... D4
Tilton-Northfield 3,081 .... D5
Tilton• 3,240 .... D5
Troy 2,097 .... C6
Troy• 2,131 .... C6
Tuftonboro• 1,842 .... E4
Twin Mountain 500 .... D3
Unity• 1,341 .... C5
Wakefield• 3,057 .... F4
Walpole• 3,210 .... C5
Warner• 2,250 .... D5
Warren• 820 .... D4
Washington• 628 .... C5
Waterville Valley• 151 .... D4
Weare• 6,193 .... D5
Webster• 1,405 .... D5
Wentworth• 630 .... D4
Wentworths Location 53 .... E2
West Campton 400 .... D4
West Epping 400 .... E5
West Henniker 500 .... D5
West Lebanon C4
West Milan 350 .... E2
West Rye 350 .... F6
West Stewartstown 700 .... E2
West Swanzey 1,055 .... C6
Westmoreland• 1,596 .... C6
Westville 750 .... E6
Whitefield 1,041 .... D3
Whitefield• 1,909 .... D3
Wilmot Flat 450 .... D5
Wilmot• 935 .... D5
Wilton 1,165 .... D6
Wilton• 3,122 .... D6
Winchester• 1,735 .... C6
Windham• 9,000 .... E6
Winnisquam 500 .... E5
Wolfeboro 2,783 .... E4
Wolfeboro• 4,807 .... E4
Wolfeboro Falls 600 .... E4
Woodstock• 1,167 .... D4
Woodsville▲ 1,122 .... C3

OTHER FEATURES

Adams (mt.) E3
Ammonoosuc (riv.) D3
Androscoggin (riv.) E2
Ashuelot (riv.) C6
Back (lake) E1
Baker (riv.) D4
Bearcamp (riv.) E4
Beaver (brook) E6
Belknap (mt.) E5
Blackwater (res.) D5
Blue (mt.) E2
Bond (mt.) E3
Bow (lake) E5
Cabot (mt.) E2
Cannon (mt.) D3
Cardigan (mt.) D4
Carrigain (mt.) E3
Carter Dome (mt.) E3
Chocorua (mt.) E4
Cocheco (riv.) E5
Cold (riv.) C5
Comerford (dam) D3
Connecticut (riv.) B6
Contoocook (riv.) D6
Conway (lake) E4
Crawford Notch (pass) E3
Croydon (peak) C5
Croydon Branch, Sugar (riv.) C5
Crystal (lake) E5
Cube (mt.) D4
Dixville (peak) E2
Dixville Notch (pass) E2
Edward MacDowell (res.) D6
Ellis (riv.) E3
Everett (dam) D5
Exeter (riv.) E6
First Connecticut (lake) E1
Francis (lake) E1
Franconia Notch (pass) D3
Franklin Falls (res.) D4
Gale (riv.) D3
Great (bay) F5
Halls (stream) E1
Hancock (mt.) D3
Highland (lake) C5
Hutchins (mt.) E2
Indian (stream) E1
Jefferson (mt.) E3
Kearsarge (mt.) D5
Kinsman (mt.) D3
Kinsman Notch (pass) D3
Lafayette (mt.) D3
Lamprey (riv.) E5
Liberty (mt.) D3
Lincoln (mt.) D3
Long (mt.) E2
Mad (riv.) D4
Madison (mt.) E3
Mascoma (lake) C4
Massabesic (lake) E6
Merrimack (riv.) D5
Merrymeeting (lake) E5
Mohawk (riv.) E2
Monadnock (mt.) C6
Monroe (mt.) E3
Moore (dam) D3
Moore (res.) D3
Moosilauke (mt.) D3
Nash (stream) E2
Newfound (lake) D4
North Carter (mt.) E3
North Twin (mt.) D3
Nubanusit (lake) C5
Osceola (mt.) E3
Ossipee (lake) E4
Ossipee (mts.) E4
Ossipee (riv.) F4
Passaconaway (mt.) E4
Pawtuckaway (pond) E5
Pease A.F.B. F5
Pemigewasset (riv.) D4
Perry (stream) E1
Pine (riv.) E4
Pinkham Notch (pass) E3
Piscataqua (riv.) F5
Piscataquog (riv.) D5
Presidential (range) E3
Rice (mt.) E2
Saco (riv.) E3

Agriculture, Industry and Resources

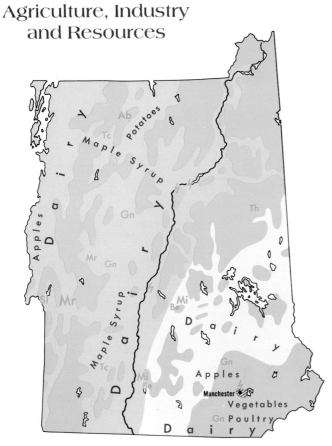

DOMINANT LAND USE

- Specialized Dairy
- Dairy, General Farming
- Dairy, Poultry, Mixed Farming
- Forests

⚡ Water Power

▨ Major Industrial Areas

MAJOR MINERAL OCCURRENCES

Ab	Asbestos	Mr	Marble
Be	Beryl	Sl	Slate
Gn	Granite	Tc	Talc
Mi	Mica	Th	Thorium

AREA 7,787 sq. mi. (20,168 sq. km.)
POPULATION 7,748,634
CAPITAL Trenton
LARGEST CITY Newark
HIGHEST POINT High Point 1,803 ft. (550 m.)
SETTLED IN 1617
ADMITTED TO UNION December 18, 1787
POPULAR NAME Garden State
STATE FLOWER Purple Violet
STATE BIRD Eastern Goldfinch

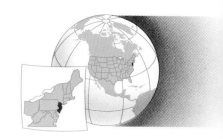

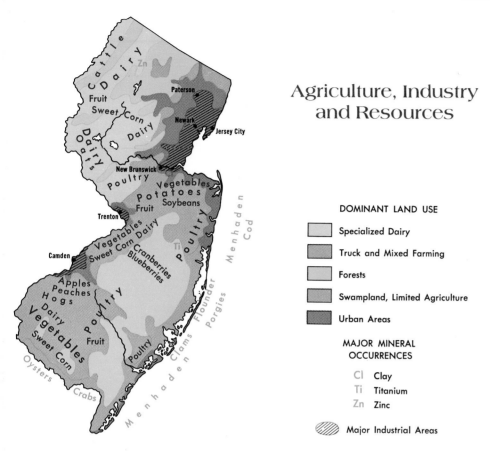

Agriculture, Industry and Resources

DOMINANT LAND USE

- Specialized Dairy
- Truck and Mixed Farming
- Forests
- Swampland, Limited Agriculture
- Urban Areas

MAJOR MINERAL OCCURRENCES

- Cl Clay
- Ti Titanium
- Zn Zinc

- Major Industrial Areas

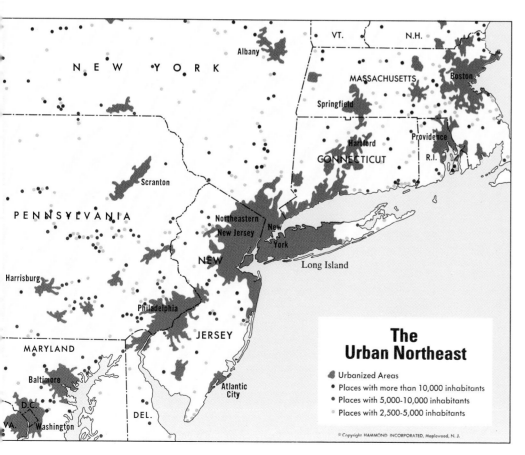

The Urban Northeast

- Urbanized Areas
- Places with more than 10,000 inhabitants
- Places with 5,000-10,000 inhabitants
- Places with 2,500-5,000 inhabitants

© Copyright HAMMOND INCORPORATED, Maplewood, N. J.

COUNTIES

County	Population	Ref
Atlantic	224,327	D5
Bergen	825,380	E2
Burlington	395,066	D4
Camden	502,824	D4
Cape May	95,089	D5
Cumberland	138,053	C5
Essex	778,206	E2
Gloucester	230,082	C4
Hudson	553,099	E2
Hunterdon	107,776	D2
Mercer	325,824	D3
Middlesex	671,780	E3
Monmouth	553,124	E3
Morris	421,353	D2
Ocean	433,203	E4
Passaic	453,060	E1
Salem	65,294	C4
Somerset	240,279	D2
Sussex	130,943	D1
Union	493,819	E2
Warren	91,607	C2

CITIES and TOWNS

Place	Population	Ref
Aberdeen	17,235	E3
Absecon	7,298	D5
Allamuchy	600	D2
Allendale	5,900	B1
Allenhurst	759	F3
Allentown	1,828	D3
Allenwood		E3
Alloway	1,371	C4
Alpha	2,530	C2
Alpine	1,716	C1
Andover	700	D2
Annandale	1,074	D2
Asbury Park	16,799	F3
Ashland		B3
Atlantic City	37,986	E5
Atlantic Highlands	4,629	F3
Audubon	9,205	B3
Audubon Park	1,150	B3
Augusta	500	D1
Aura	500	C4
Avalon	1,809	D5
Avenel	15,504	E2
Avon By The Sea	2,165	E3
Barnegat	1,160	E4
Barnegat Light	675	E4
Barrington	6,774	B3
Basking Ridge		D2
Bay Head	1,226	E3
Bayonne	61,444	B2
Beach Haven	1,475	E4
Beach Haven Crest	500	E4
Beach Haven Terrace	500	E4
Beachwood	9,324	E4
Bedminster •	2,469	D2
Belford		E3
Belle Mead		D3
Belleplain	500	D5
Belleville	34,213	B2
Bellmawr	12,603	B3
Belmar	5,877	E3
Belvidere▲	2,669	C2
Bergenfield	24,458	C1
Berkeley Heights •	11,980	E2
Berlin	5,672	D4
Bernardsville	6,597	D2
Beverly	2,973	D3
Blackwood	5,120	C4
Blackwood Terrace		C4
Blairstown •	4,360	C2
Bloomfield	45,061	B2
Bloomingdale	7,530	E1
Bloomsbury	890	C2
Bogota	7,824	B2
Boonton	8,343	E2
Bordentown	4,341	D3
Bound Brook	9,487	D2
Bradley Beach	4,475	F3
Branchville	851	D1
Brant Beach	500	E4
Breton Woods		E3
Brick •	66,473	E3
Bridgeport	750	C4
Bridgeton▲	18,942	C5
Bridgewater •	29,175	D2
Brielle	4,406	E3
Brigantine	11,354	E5
Brooklawn	1,805	B3
Brookside		D2
Browns Mills	11,429	D4
Budd Lake	7,272	D2
Buena	4,441	D4
Burlington	9,835	D3
Butler	7,392	E2
Caldwell	7,549	B2
Califon	1,073	D2
Camden▲	87,492	B3
Candlewood	6,750	E3
Cape May	4,668	D6
Cape May Court House▲	4,426	D5

Place	Population	Ref
Cape May Point	248	D6
Carlstadt	5,510	B2
Carneys Point	7,686	C4
Carteret	19,025	E2
Cedar Brook	600	D4
Cedar Grove▲	12,053	B2
Cedar Knolls		E2
Cedarville	900	C5
Cedarwood Park		E3
Chatham	8,007	E2
Chatsworth	700	D4
Cheesequake		E3
Cherry Hill •	69,319	B3
Chesilhurst	1,526	D4
Chester	1,214	D2
Chesterfield •	3,867	D3
Cinnaminson •	14,583	B3
Clark •	14,629	A3
Clarksboro		C4
Clarksburg	800	E3
Clayton	6,155	C4
Clementon	5,601	D4
Cliffside Park	20,393	C2
Cliffwood		E3
Clifton	71,742	B2
Clinton	2,054	D2
Closter	8,094	C1
Cold Spring	500	D6
Collingswood	15,289	B3
Cologne	800	D4
Colonia	18,238	E2
Colts Neck	950	E3
Columbia	600	C2
Columbus	800	D3
Convent Station		E2
Corbin City	412	D5
Cranberry Lake	500	D2
Cranbury	1,255	E3
Cranford •	22,624	E2
Cresskill	7,558	C1
Dayton	4,321	D3
Deal	1,179	F3
Deepwater	800	C4
Delanco •	3,316	D3
Delran •	14,811	B3
Demarest	4,800	C1
Dennisville	890	D5
Denville •	14,380	E2
Deptford •	23,473	B4
Dividing Creek	500	C5
Dorchester	500	D5
Dorothy	900	D5
Dover	15,115	D2
Dumont	17,187	C1
Dunellen	6,528	D2
East Brunswick •	43,548	E3
East Hanover •	9,926	E2
East Keansburg		E3
East Millstone	950	D3
East Newark	2,157	B2
East Orange	73,552	B2
East Rutherford	7,902	B2
Eatontown	13,800	E3
Edgewater	5,001	C2
Edgewater Park •	8,388	D3
Edison •	88,680	E2
Egg Harbor City	4,583	D4
Elberon		F3
Elizabeth▲	110,002	B2
Elmer	1,571	C4
Elmwood Park	17,623	B2
Elwood	1,538	D4
Emerson	6,930	B1
Englewood	24,850	C2
Englewood Cliffs	5,634	C2
English Creek	500	D5
Englishtown	1,268	E3
Essex Fells	2,363	B2
Estell Manor	1,404	D5
Ewan	610	C4
Ewing •	34,185	D3
Fair Haven	5,270	E3
Fair Lawn	30,548	B1
Fairfield •	7,615	A2
Fairton	1,359	C5
Fairview	10,733	C2
Fanwood	7,115	E2
Far Hills	657	D2
Farmingdale	1,462	E3
Fieldsboro	579	D3
Flagtown	800	D2
Flanders		D2
Flemington▲	4,047	D2
Florence-Roebling	8,564	D3
Florham Park	8,521	E2
Folsom	2,181	D4
Fords	14,392	E2
Forked River	4,243	E4
Fort Lee	31,997	C2
Franklin	4,977	D1
Franklin Lakes	9,873	B1
Franklin Park •	31,358	D3
Franklinville		C4
Freehold▲ •	10,742	E3
Frenchtown	1,528	C2
Garfield	26,727	B2

(continued on following page)

Topography

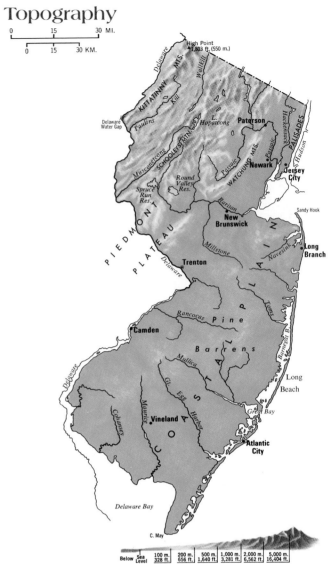

0   15   30 MI.

0   15   30 KM.

High Point
▲1,803 ft.(550 m.)

KITTATINNY MTS.

Delaware Water Gap

Hopatcong

Paterson

PIEDMONT PLATEAU

Newark

Jersey City

Sandy Hook

New Brunswick

Long Branch

Trenton

Camden

Pine Barrens

COASTAL PLAIN

Long Beach

Great Bay

Vineland

Atlantic City

Delaware Bay

C. May

	Below Sea Level	100 m. 328 ft.	200 m. 656 ft.	500 m. 1,640 ft.	1,000 m. 3,281 ft.	2,000 m. 6,562 ft.	5,000 m. 16,404 ft.

New Jersey

SCALE

0   5   10   15   20 MI.

0   5   10   15   20 KM.

State Capitals .... ⊛
County Seats .... ◉
Canals ....
Major Limited Access Hwys. _____
Scale 1:930,000

Copyright HAMMOND INCORPORATED, Maplewood, N.J.

COUNTIES

Bernalillo 480,577....................C4
Catron 2,563.............................A4
Chaves 57,849.........................E5
Cibola 23,794...........................B4
Colfax 12,925...........................E2
Curry 42,207.............................F4
De Baca 2,454.........................E4
Dona Ana 135,510...................C6
Eddy 48,605.............................E6
Grant 27,676.............................A5
Guadalupe 4,156......................E4
Harding 987..............................F3
Hidalgo 5,958...........................A7
Lea 55,765................................F6
Lincoln 12,219..........................D5
Los Alamos 18,115..................C3
Luna 18,110..............................B6
McKinley 60,686.......................A3
Mora 4,264...............................E3
Otero 51,928.............................D6
Quay 10,823.............................F3
Rio Arriba 34,365.....................B2
Roosevelt 16,702......................F4
San Juan 91,605......................A2
San Miguel 25,743...................D3
Sandoval 34,799......................C3
Santa Fe 98,928.......................D3
Sierra 9,912..............................B5
Socorro 14,764.........................C5
Taos 23,118..............................D2
Torrance 10,285.......................D4
Union 4,124...............................F2
Valencia 45,235........................A4

CITIES and TOWNS

Abiquiu 500...............................C2
Acoma 150................................B4
Acomita (Pueblo of
  Acoma) 975.............................B3
Alameda......................................C3
Alamogordo▲ 27,596.............C6
Albuquerque▲ 384,736...........C3
Alcalde 308...............................C2
Algodones 195..........................C3
Allison...A3
Alma 120...................................A5
Alto 285.....................................D5
Amalia 200................................D2
Animas 75.................................A7
Anthony 5,160..........................C6
Anton Chico 400.......................D3
Arrey 367...................................B6
Arroyo Hondo 400....................D2
Arroyo Seco 500......................D2
Artesia 10,610..........................E6
Aztec▲ 5,479.............................B2
Bayard 2,598............................A6
Belen 6,547...............................C4
Bent 294....................................D5
Berino 600.................................C6
Bernalillo▲ 5,960......................C3
Bloomfield 5,214.......................A2
Blanco 200................................B2
Bosque 3,791............................C4
Bosque Farms............................C3
Buckhorn 85..............................A5
Buena Vista 178........................D3
Caballo 225...............................B6
Canjilon 380..............................C2
Canones 300.............................C2
Capitan 842...............................D5
Capulin 100................................F2
Carlsbad▲ 24,952.....................E6
Carrizozo▲ 1,075......................D5
Casa Blanca 560......................B4
Cebolla 100...............................C2
Cedar Crest 600.......................C3
Cedar Hill 145...........................B2
Central 1,835.............................A6
Cerrillos 500..............................D3
Cerro 400...................................D2
Chacon 310...............................D2
Chama 1,048.............................C2
Chamberino 700.......................C6
Chamisal 272............................D2
Chilili 80.....................................C4
Chimayo 2,789..........................D2
Cimarron 774............................E2
Clayton▲ 2,484.........................F2
Cleveland 450...........................D2
Cliff 600.....................................A6
Cloudcroft 636...........................D6
Clovis▲ 30,954..........................F4
Cochiti 434.................................C3
Columbus 641...........................B7
Conchas Dam 240...................E3
Cordova 750..............................D2
Corona 215................................D4
Corrales 5,453...........................C3
Costilla 400................................D2
Coyote 125................................C2
Crownpoint 2,108......................A3
Crystal 200................................A2
Cuba 760...................................B2
Cubero 300................................B3
Cuervo 80..................................E3
Cundiyo 200..............................D3
Datil 150.....................................B4
Deming▲ 10,970........................B6
Derry 175...................................B6
Des Moines 168........................F2
Dexter 898.................................E5
Dilia 100.....................................E3
Dixon 800..................................C2
Dona Ana 1,202........................C6
Dora 167....................................F4
Dulce 2,438...............................B2
Duran 90....................................D4
Eagle Nest 189.........................E2
Edgewood 3,324.......................D3
El Porvenir 150..........................D3
El Prado 200..............................D2
El Rito 475.................................C2
Elephant Butte 500...................B5
Elida 201....................................F5
Embudo 400..............................D2
Encino 131.................................D4

Espanola 8,389 C3
Estancia▲ 792 D4
Eunice 2,676 F6
Fairacres 700 C6
Farmington 33,997 A2
Faywood 100 B6
Fence Lake 150 A4
Fierro 200 A6
Flora Vista 1,021 A2
Floyd 117 F4
Folsom 71 F2
Fort Bayard 400 A6
Fort Stanton 80 D5
Fort Sumner▲ 1,269 E4
Fort Wingate 800 A3
Fruitland 800 A2
Galisteo 125 D3
Gallina 420 C2
Gallup▲ 19,154 A3
Gamerco 800 A3
Garfield 600 B6
Garita 66 E3
Gila 350 A6
Glencoe 125 D5
Glenwood 220 A5
Glorieta 300 D3
Golden 100 C3
Grady 110 F4
Grants▲ 8,626 B3
Guadalupita 300 D2
Hachita 75 A7
Hagerman 961 E5
Hanover 300 A6
Hatch 1,136 B6
Hernandez 500 C2
High Rolls-Mountain Park 555 D5
Hillsboro 175 B6
Hobbs 29,115 F6
Holman 400 D2
Hondo 425 D5
Hope 101 E6
Hot Springs▲ (Truth or Consequences) 6,221 B5
House 85 F4
Humble City 65 F6
Hurley 1,534 A6
Ifeld 68 D3
Isleta 1,703 C4
Jal 2,156 F6
Jarales 700 C4
Jemez Pueblo 1,301 C3
Jemez Springs 413 C3
Kenna 100 F5
Kirtland 3,552 A2
La Cueva 200 D3
La Jara 210 B2
La Luz 1,625 C6
La Madera 200 C2
La Mesa 900 C6
La Plata 150 A2
La Union 200 C7
Laguna 434 B3
Lajoya 97 C4
Lake Arthur 336 E5
Lamy 66 D3
Las Cruces▲ 62,126 C6
Las Vegas▲ 14,753 D3
Ledoux 300 D3
Lemitar 800 B4
Lincoln 100 D5
Lindrith 349 C2
Llano 325 D2
Loco Hills 375 F6
Logan 870 F3
Lordsburg▲ 2,951 A6
Los Alamos▲ 11,455 C3
Los Lunas▲ 6,013 C4
Los Ojos C2
Los Ranchos de Albuquerque 3,955 C3
Loving 1,243 E6
Lovington▲ 9,322 F6
Lumberton 175 C2
Luna 200 A5
Magdalena 861 B4
Malaga 300 E6
Manuelito 200 A3
Manzano 65 C4
Maxwell 247 E2
Mayhill 300 D6
McAlister 320 F4
McDonald 65 F5
McIntosh 325 D4
Meadow Vista 3,377 C7
Melrose 662 F4
Mentmore 315 A3
Mescalero 1,159 D5
Mesilla 1,975 C6
Mesilla Park C6
Mesquite 500 C6
Mexican Springs 242 A3
Miami 112 E2
Milan 1,911 B3
Mimbres 300 B6
Montezuma 250 D3
Monticello 125 B5
Monument 300 F6
Mora▲ D3
Moriarty 1,399 D4
Mosquero▲ 164 F3
Mountainair 926 C4
Mule Creek 62 A5
Nambe 1,246 D3
Nara Visa 250 F3
Navajo 1,985 A3
New Laguna 250 B4
Newcomb 388 A2
Newkirk 54 E3
Nogal 150 D5
Ocate 75 E2
Oil Center 236 F6
Ojo Caliente 600 D2
Ojo Feliz 133 E2
Ojo Sarco 380 D2
Organ 300 C6
Orogrande 80 D6
Otis 200 E6
Paguate 492 B3
Pecos 1,012 D3
Pena Blanca 300 C3
Penasco 648 D2
Peralta 3,182 C4
Petaca 84 C2
Picacho 100 D5
Pie Town 90 A4
Pinos Altos 250 A6
Placitas 1,611 C3
Pleasanton 70 A5
Pojoaque 1,037 C3
Ponderosa 300 C3
Portales▲ 10,690 F4
Prewitt 300 B3
Puerto de Luna 175 E4
Questa 1,707 D2
Radium Springs 150 B6
Rainsville 350 D2
Ramah 574 A3
Ranchos de Taos 1,779 D2
Raton▲ 7,372 E2
Red River 387 D2
Regina 80 B2
Rehoboth 200 A3
Reserve▲ 319 A5
Ribera 84 D3
Rincon 300 C6
Rio Rancho 32,505 C3
Rociada 140 D3
Rodarte 650 D2
Rodeo 200 A7
Roswell▲ 44,654 E5
Rowe 290 D3
Roy 362 E3
Ruidoso 4,600 D5
Ruidoso Downs 920 D5
Rutheron 95 C2
Salem 400 B6
San Acacia 286 B4
San Antonio 359 B5
San Cristobal 350 D2
San Felipe Pueblo 1,557 C3
San Fidel 150 B3
San Ildefonso 447 C3
San Jon 277 F3
San Jose 150 D3
San Juan Pueblo 4,107 C2
San Lorenzo 200 B6
San Mateo 200 B3
San Miguel 400 C6
San Patricio 300 D5
San Rafael 300 A3
San Ysidro 233 C3
Sandia Park 450 C3
Santa Cruz 2,504 D2
Santa Fe (cap.)▲ 55,859 C3
Santa Rita 600 B6
Santa Rosa▲ 2,263 E4
Santo Domingo Pueblo 2,866 C3
Sapello 600 D3
Seboyeta 125 B3
Sedan 60 F2
Sena 150 D3
Serafina 225 D3
Sherman 100 B6
Shiprock 7,687 A2
Silver City▲ 10,683 A6
Socorro▲ 8,159 C4
Soham 104 D3
Solano 114 E3
Springer 1,262 E2
Sunspot 78 D6
Taiban 120 F4
Tajique 145 C4
Taos Pueblo 1,187 D2
Taos▲ 4,065 D2
Tatum 768 F5
Tesuque 1,490 C3
Texico 966 F4
Thoreau 1,099 A3
Tierra Amarilla▲ 850 C2
Tijeras 340 C3
Tinnie 100 D5
Toadlena 200 A2
Tohatchi 661 A3
Tome 500 C4
Torreon 200 C4
Trampas 76 D2
Trementina 80 E3
Tres Piedras 200 D2
Truchas 275 D2
Trujillo 148 E3
Truth or Consequences▲ 6,221 B5
Tucumcari▲ 6,831 F3
Tularosa 2,615 C5
Tyrone 100 A6
University Park 4,520 C6
Ute Park 67 D2
Vadito 283 D2
Vado 325 C6
Valdez 300 D2
Valencia 3,917 C4
Vallecitos 450 C2
Vanadium 150 A6
Vaughn 633 D4
Velarde 950 C2
Vermejo Park 85 D2
Villanueva 500 D3
Virden 108 A6
Wagon Mound 319 E2
Waterflow 475 A2
Watrous 175 D3
White Horse Lake B3
White Rock 6,192 C3
White Sands Missile Range 2,616 C6
Willard 183 D4
Williamsburg 456 B5
Yeso 200 E4
Youngsville 125 C2
Zia Pueblo 637 C3
Zuni 5,551 A3

OTHER FEATURES

Abiquiu (res.) C2
Alamosa (riv.) B5
Animas (riv.) B1
Avalon (res.) E6
Aztec Ruins Nat'l Mon. A2
Baldy (peak) D3
Bandelier Nat'l Mon. C3
Big Burro (mts.) A6
Black (mt.) A6
Black (range) B5
Blanco (creek) F4
Bluewater (creek) B4
Bluewater (creek) D6
Bluewater (lake) A3
Boulder (lake) C2
Brazos (peak) C2
Burford (lake) C2
Caballo (res.) B6
Canadian (riv.) F3
Cannon A.F.B. 3,312 F4
Canyon Blanco (creek) B2
Capitan (mts.) D5
Capitan (peak) D5
Capulin Volcano Nat'l Mon. E2
Carlsbad Caverns Nat'l Park E6
Carrizo (creek) F2
Chaco (mesa) B3
Chaco (riv.) A2
Chaco Culture Nat'l Hist. Park B2
Chico Arroyo (creek) B3
Chivato (mesa) B3
Chupadera (mesa) C5
Chuska (mts.) A2
Cimarron (riv.) E2
Colorado, Arroyo (riv.) B4
Compañero, Arroyo (creek) B2
Conchas (lake) E3
Conchas (riv.) E3
Cookes (range) B6
Corrumpa (creek) F2
Costilla (peak) D2
Cuchillo Negro (creek) B5
Cuervo (creek) E3
Dark Canyon (creek) E6
Datil (mts.) B4
Dry Cimarron (riv.) F2
Eagle Nest (lake) D2
Elephant Butte (res.) B5
El Morro Nat'l Mon. A3
El Rito (riv.) C2
Fifteenmile Arroyo (creek) D4
Florida (mts.) B7
Fort Bliss Mil. Res. C6
Fort Union Nat'l Mon. E3
Gallinas (mts.) B4
Gallinas (riv.) E3
Gila (riv.) A6
Gila Cliff Dwellings Nat'l Mon. A5
Grouse (mt.) A5
Guadalupe (mts.) D6
Hatchet (mts.) A7
Holloman A.F.B. 5,891 C6
Hueco (mts.) D6
Jemez (riv.) C3
Jemez Canyon (res.) C3
Jicarilla Ind. Res. B2
Jornada del Muerto (valley) C5
Kirtland A.F.B. C3
Ladron (mts.) B4
La Plata (riv.) A1
Lake Avalon (res.) E6
Largo, Cañon (creek) B2
Las Animas (creek) B5
Llano Estacado (Staked) (plain) F5
Lucero (lake) C6
Macho, Arroyo del (creek) D5
Magdalena (mts.) B4
Manzano (mts.) C4
Manzano (peak) C4
McMillan (lake) E6
Mescalero (ridge) F6
Mescalero (valley) F5
Mescalero Apache Ind. Res. D5
Mimbres (mts.) B6
Mimbres (riv.) B6
Mogollon (mts.) A5
Mogollon Baldy (peak) A5
Montosa (mesa) E3
Mora (riv.) E3
Nacimiento (mts.) C3
Nacimiento (peak) C2
Navajo (res.) B2
Navajo Ind. Res. A2
North Truchas (peak) D3
Ocate (creek) E2
O'Keeffe Nat'l Hist. Site C2
Oscura (mts.) C5
Osha (peak) C4
Padilla (creek) D5
Pajarito (creek) A2
Pecos (riv.) E5
Pecos Nat'l Mon. D3
Peloncillo (mts.) A6
Perro (lake) D4
Pinos, Rio de los (riv.) B2
Pintada Arroyo (creek) E4
Playas (lake) A7
Potrillo (mts.) B7
Pueblo Ind. Res. B4
Pueblo Ind. Res. C4
Pueblo Ind. Res. D2
Pueblo Ind. Res. D3
Puerco (riv.) A3
Red Bluff (lake) E7
Revuelto (creek) F3
Rio Brazos (riv.) C2
Rio Chama (riv.) C2
Rio Felix (riv.) E5
Rio Grande (riv.) C5
Rio Hondo (riv.) E5
Rio Penasco (riv.) E6
Rio Puerco (riv.) C4
Rio Salado (riv.) B4
Rocky (mts.) C1
Sacramento (mts.) D6
Salinas Pueblo Missions Nat'l Mon. C4
Salt (creek) E5
Salt (lake) F4
San Agustin (plains) B5
San Andres (mts.) C6
San Antonio (peak) C2
Sandia (peak) C3
San Francisco (riv.) A5
Sangre de Cristo (mts.) D3
San Jose (riv.) B3
San Juan (riv.) B2
San Mateo (mts.) B5
Seven Rivers (riv.) E6
Ship Rock (peak) A2
Sierra Blanca (peak) C5
Staked (Llano Estacado) (plain) F5
Sumner (lake) E4
Taylor (mt.) B3
Tecolote (creek) D3
Tequesquite (creek) E2
Thompson (peak) D3
Tierra Blanca (creek) B6
Tramperos (creek) F2
Tularosa (valley) C6
Ute (creek) F3
Ute (peak) D2
Ute (res.) F3
Ute Mountain Ind. Res. A1
Vermejo (riv.) E2
Wheeler (peak) D2
White Sands (des.) C5
White Sands Missile Range C5
White Sands Nat'l Mon. C6
Whitewater Baldy (mt.) A5
Wingate Army Depot A3
Yeso (creek) E4
Zuni (mts.) A3
Zuni (riv.) A3
Zuni-Cibola Nat'l Hist. Park A3
Zuni Ind. Res. A3

▲County seat

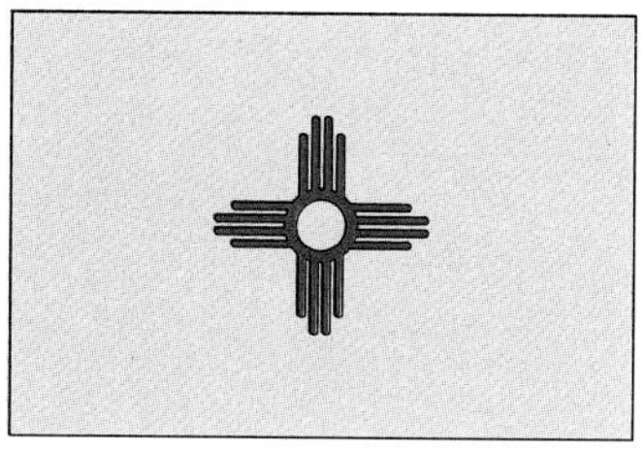

AREA 121,593 sq. mi. (314,926 sq. km.)
POPULATION 1,521,779
CAPITAL Santa Fe
LARGEST CITY Albuquerque
HIGHEST POINT Wheeler Pk. 13,161 ft. (4011 m.)
SETTLED IN 1605
ADMITTED TO UNION January 6, 1912
POPULAR NAME Land of Enchantment
STATE FLOWER Yucca
STATE BIRD Road Runner

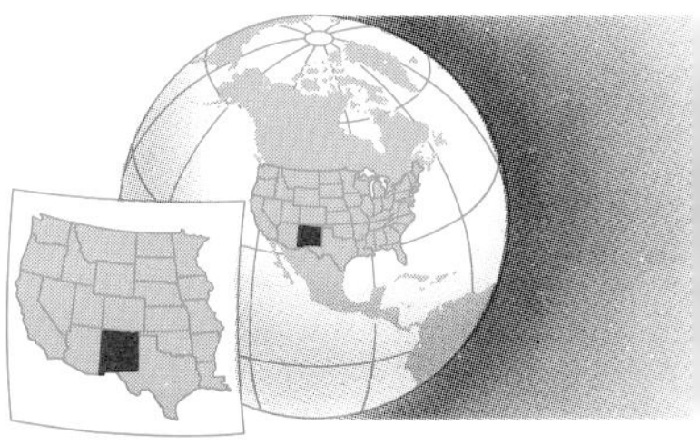

Topography

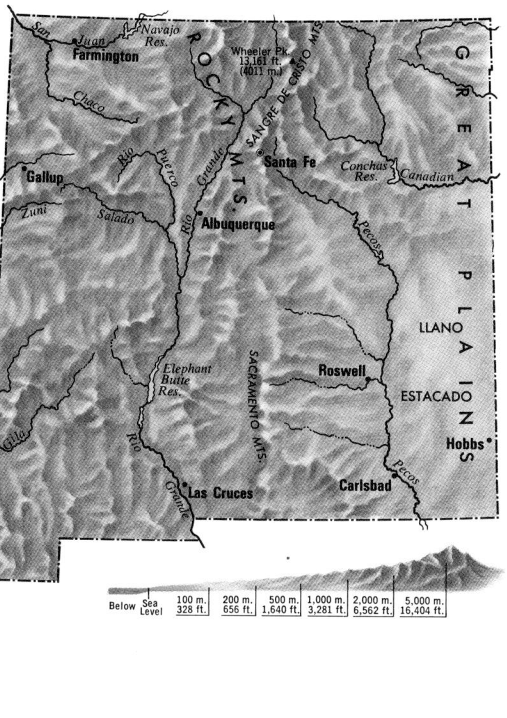

0 50 100 MI.
0 50 100 KM.
San Juan
Navajo Res.
Farmington
Wheeler Pk. 13,161 ft. (4011 m.)
ROCKY MTS.
SANGRE DE CRISTO MTS.
GREAT PLAINS
Chaco
Rio Puerco
Santa Fe
Conchas Res.
Canadian
Gallup
Zuni
Salado
Rio Grande
Albuquerque
Pecos
LLANO
ESTACADO
SACRAMENTO MTS.
Elephant Butte Res.
Roswell
Gila
Hobbs
Las Cruces
Carlsbad
Below Sea Level
100 m. 328 ft.
200 m. 656 ft.
500 m. 1,640 ft.
1,000 m. 3,281 ft.
2,000 m. 6,562 ft.
5,000 m. 16,404 ft.

Agriculture, Industry and Resources

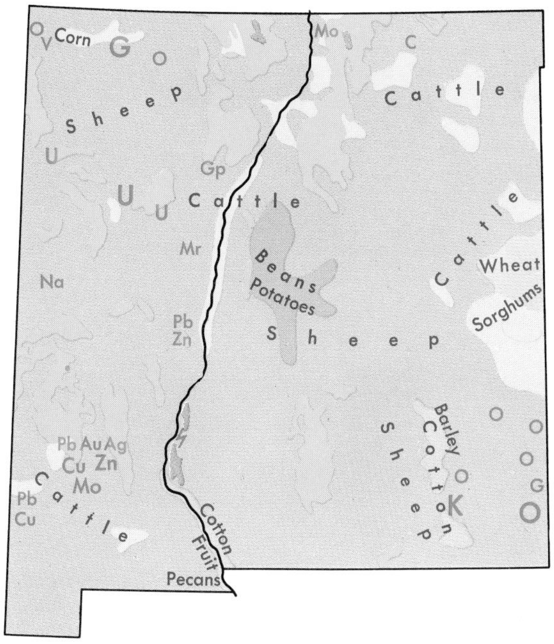

Corn
Sheep
Cattle
Beans
Potatoes
Wheat
Sorghums
Barley
Cotton
Fruit
Pecans

DOMINANT LAND USE

- Wheat, Grain Sorghums, Range Livestock
- General Farming, Livestock, Special Crops
- General Farming, Livestock, Cash Grain
- Dry Beans, General Farming
- Cotton, Forest Products
- Range Livestock
- Forests
- Nonagricultural Land

MAJOR MINERAL OCCURRENCES

Ag	Silver	Gp	Gypsum	O	Petroleum	U	Uranium
Au	Gold	K	Potash	Pb	Lead	V	Vanadium
C	Coal	Mo	Molybdenum			Zn	Zinc
Cu	Copper	Mr	Marble				Water Power
G	Natural Gas	Na	Salt				

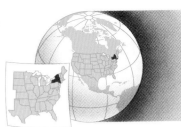

AREA 49,108 sq. mi. (127,190 sq. km.)
POPULATION 18,044,505
CAPITAL Albany
LARGEST CITY New York
HIGHEST POINT Mt. Marcy 5,344 ft.
(1629 m.)
SETTLED IN 1614
ADMITTED TO UNION July 26, 1788
POPULAR NAME Empire State
STATE FLOWER Rose
STATE BIRD Bluebird

Topography

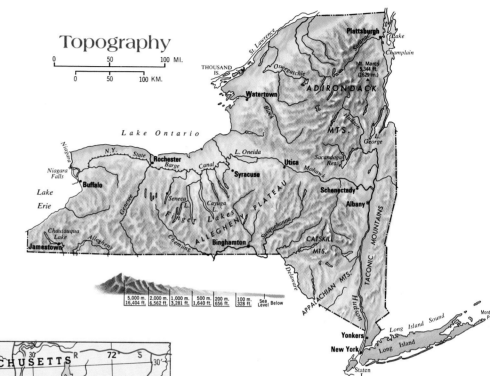

5,000 m.	2,000 m.	1,000 m.	500 m.	200 m.	100 m.	Sea Level
16,404 ft.	6,562 ft.	3,281 ft.	1,640 ft.	656 ft.	328 ft.	Below

© Copyright HAMMOND INCORPORATED, Maplewood, N.J.

Huntington Station 28,247 R6
Hurley 4,644 M7
Hyde Park 2,550 N6
Ilion 8,888 K5
Interlaken 680 G5
Inwood 7,767 P7
Irondequoit 52,322 E4
Irvington 6,348 O6
Island Park 4,860 R7
Islip 18,924 O9
Ithaca▲ 29,541 G6
Jamestown 34,681 B6
Jericho 13,141 R6
Johnson City 16,890 J6
Johnstown▲ 9,058 M4
Jordan 1,325 H4
Keeseville 1,854 O2
Kenmore 17,180 C5
Kerhonkson 1,629 M7
Keuka Park 1,153 F5
Kinderhook 1,293 N6
Kings Park 17,773 O9
Kings Point 4,843 P6
Kingston▲ 23,095 M7
Lackawanna 20,585 B5
Lake Carmel 8,489 N8
Lake Erie Beach 4,509 B5
Lake George▲ 933 N4
Lake Katrine 1,998 M7
Lake Luzerne-Hadley 2,042 N4
Lake Placid 2,485 N2
Lake Pleasant▲ 700 M4
Lake Success 2,484 P7
Lakewood 3,564 B6
Lancaster 11,940 C5
Lansing 3,281 H5
Larchmont 6,181 P7
Latham 10,131 N5
Lattingtown 1,859 R6
Lawrence 6,513 P7
Le Roy 4,974 E5
Levittown 53,286 R7
Lewiston 3,048 B4
Liberty 4,128 L7
Lima 2,165 E5
Lindenhurst 26,879 O9
Little Falls 5,829 L4
Little Valley▲ 1,188 C6
Liverpool 2,624 H4
Livingston Manor 1,482 L7
Livonia 1,434 E5
Lloyd Harbor 3,343 R6
Lockport▲ 24,426 C4
Locust Grove 9,670 R6
Long Beach 33,510 R7
Lowville▲ 3,632 J3
Lynbrook 19,208 P7
Lyndonville 953 D4
Lyons Falls 698 K3
Lyons▲ 4,280 F4
Macedon 1,400 F4
Machias 1,191 D6
Mahopac 7,755 N8
Malone▲ 6,777 M1
Malverne 9,054 R7
Mamaroneck 17,325 P7
Manchester 1,598 F5
Manhasset 7,718 P7
Manhattan (borough) M9
Manlius 4,764 J5
Manorville 6,198 P9
Marathon 1,107 J6
Marcellus 1,840 H5
Margaretville 639 L6
Marion 1,080 F4
Marlboro 2,200 M7
Massapequa 22,018 R7
Massapequa Park 18,044 R7
Massena 11,719 L1
Mastic Beach 10,293 P9
Mattituck 3,902 P9
Maybrook 2,802 M8
Mayfield 817 M4
Mayville▲ 1,636 A6
McGraw 1,074 H5
Mechanicville 5,249 N5
Medina 6,686 D4
Melrose Park 2,091 G5
Melville 12,586 S7
Menands 4,333 N5
Merrick 23,042 R7
Mexico 1,555 H4
Middle Hope 3,229 M7
Middleburgh 1,436 M5
Middleport 1,876 C4
Middletown 24,160 L8
Middleville 624 K4
Mill Neck 977 R6
Millbrook 1,339 N7
Millerton 884 O7
Milton 1,140 M7
Milton 2,063 N4
Mineola▲ 18,994 R7
Minetto 1,252 H4
Mineville-Witherbee 1,740 O2
Minoa 3,745 H4
Mohawk 2,986 L4
Monroe 6,672 M8
Monsey 13,986 J8
Montauk 3,001 S8
Montgomery 2,696 M7
Monticello▲ 6,597 L7
Montour Falls 1,845 G6
Moravia 1,559 H5
Morris 642 K5
Morrisonville 1,742 N1
Morrisville 2,732 J5
Mount Kisco 9,108 N8
Mount Morris 3,102 E5
Mount Vernon 67,153 O7
Nanuet 14,065 K8
Napanoch 1,068 M7
Naples 1,237 F5
Nassau 1,254 N5
New Berlin 1,220 K5
New City▲ 33,673 K8
New Hartford 2,111 K4
New Hyde Park 9,728 P7
New Paltz 5,463 M7
New Rochelle 67,265 P7
New Square 2,605 K8
New Windsor 8,898 N8
New York Mills 3,534 K4
New York▲ 7,322,564 M9
Newark 9,849 G4
Newark Valley 1,082 H6
Newburgh 26,454 M7
Newfane 3,001 C4
Newport 676 K4
Niagara Falls 61,840 C4
Nichols 573 H6
Niskayuna 4,942 N5
Norfolk 1,412 K1
North Boston 2,581 C5
North Collins 1,335 C5
North Hornell 822 E6
North Syracuse 7,363 H4
North Tarrytown 8,152 O6
North Tonawanda 34,989 C4
Northport 7,572 O9
Northville 1,180 M4
Norwich▲ 7,613 J5
Norwood 1,841 L1
Nunda 1,347 E5
Nyack 6,558 K8
Oakfield 1,818 D4
Oceanside 32,423 R7
Odessa 986 G6
Ogdensburg 13,521 K1
Olcott 1,432 C4
Old Forge 1,061 L3
Olean 16,946 D6
Oneida 10,850 J4
Oneonta 13,954 K6
Orangeburg 3,583 K8
Orchard Park 3,280 C5
Oriskany 1,450 K4
Oriskany Falls 795 J5
Ossining 22,582 N8
Oswego▲ 19,195 G4
Otego 1,068 K6
Otisville 1,078 L8
Ovid 660 G5
Owego▲ 4,442 H6
Oxford 1,738 J6
Oyster Bay 6,687 R6
Painted Post 1,950 F6
Palmyra 3,566 F4
Patchogue 11,060 P9
Pawling 1,974 N7
Pearl River 15,314 K8
Peconic 1,100 P8
Peekskill 19,536 N8
Pelham 6,413 O7
Pelham Manor 5,443 O7
Penn Yan▲ 5,248 F5
Perry 4,219 D5
Peru 1,565 N1
Phelps 1,978 F5
Philadelphia 1,478 J2
Philmont 1,623 N6
Phoenix 2,435 H4
Piermont 2,163 K8
Pine Bush 1,445 M7
Pine Plains 1,312 N7
Pine Valley 1,486 G6
Pittsford 1,488 E4
Plainview 26,207 R7
Plattsburgh▲ 21,255 O1
Pleasantville 6,592 N8
Port Byron 1,359 G4
Port Chester 24,728 P7
Port Dickinson 1,785 J6
Port Ewen 3,444 N7
Port Henry 1,263 O2
Port Jefferson 7,455 P9
Port Jervis 9,060 L8
Port Leyden 723 K3
Port Washington 15,387 R6
Portville 1,040 D6
Potsdam 10,251 K1
Poughkeepsie▲ 28,844 N7
Prattsburg• 1,657 F5
Pulaski 2,525 H3
Putnam Valley• 8,994 N8
Queens (borough) N9
Quogue 898 P9
Randolph 1,298 C6
Ransomville 1,542 C4
Ravena 3,547 N6
Red Hook 1,794 N7
Red Oaks Mill 4,906 N7
Rensselaer 8,255 N5
Rhinebeck 2,725 N7
Richfield Springs 1,565 K5
Richmond (borough) (Staten Island) M9
Richmondville 843 M5
Ripley 1,189 A6
Riverhead▲ 8,814 P9
Rochester▲ 231,636 E4
Rockville Centre 24,727 R7
Rome 44,350 J4
Ronkonkoma 20,391 O9
Roosevelt 15,030 R7
Rosendale 1,134 M7
Roslyn 1,965 R6
Rotterdam Junction 1,010 N5
Round Lake 765 N5
Rouses Point 2,377 O1
Rye 14,936 P6
Sackets Harbor 1,313 H3
Sag Harbor 2,134 R8
Saint James 12,703 O9
Saint Johnsville 1,825 L5
Salamanca 6,566 C6
Salem 958 O4
Sand Ridge 1,312 H4
Sands Point 2,477 P6
Sandy Creek 793 H3
Saranac Lake 5,377 M2
Saratoga Springs 25,001 N4
Saugerties 3,915 M6
Savannah• 1,905 G4
Savona 974 F6
Sayville 16,550 O9
Scarsdale 16,987 P6
Schaghticoke 794 N5
Schenectady▲ 65,566 M5
Schoharie▲ 1,045 M5
Schuylerville 1,364 N4
Scotia 7,359 N5
Scottsville 1,912 E4
Sea Cliff 5,054 R6
Seaford 15,597 R7
Seneca Falls 7,370 G5
Sherburne 1,531 K5
Sherman 694 A6
Sherrill 2,864 J4
Shortsville 1,485 F5
Sidney 4,720 K6
Silver Creek 2,927 B5
Silver Springs 852 E5
Sinclairville 708 B6
Skaneateles 2,724 H5
Sloan 3,830 C5
Sloatsburg 3,035 M8
Smithtown 25,638 O9
Sodus 1,904 G4
Sodus Point 1,190 G4
Solvay 6,717 H4
South Corning 1,025 F6
South Fallsburg 2,115 L7
South Glens Falls 3,506 N4
South Nyack 3,352 K8
Southampton 1,302 R9
Southold 5,192 P8
Southport 7,753 G6
Sparrow Bush 1,049 L8
Spencer 815 H6
Spencerport 3,606 E4
Spring Valley 21,802 K8
Springville 4,310 C5
Stamford 1,211 L6
Stannards 1,028 E6
Star Lake 1,092 K2
Staten Island (borough) M9
Stillwater 1,531 N5
Stony Brook 13,726 O9
Stony Point 10,587 M8
Stottville 1,369 N6
Suffern 11,055 J8
Sylvan Beach 1,119 J4
Syosset 18,967 R6
Syracuse▲ 163,860 H4
Tappan 6,867 K8
Tarrytown 10,739 O6
Theresa 889 J2
Thomaston 2,612 P7
Ticonderoga 2,770 N3
Tillson 1,688 M7
Tivoli 1,035 N6
Tonawanda 17,284 B4
Troy▲ 54,269 N5
Trumansburg 1,611 G5
Tuckahoe 6,302 O7
Tully 911 H5
Tupper Lake 4,087 M2
Tuxedo Park 706 M8
Unadilla 1,265 K6
Union Springs 1,142 G5
Uniondale 20,328 R7
Utica▲ 68,637 K4
Valatie 1,487 N6
Valley Cottage 9,007 K8
Valley Stream 33,946 P7
Vestal• 27,238 H6
Victor 2,308 F5
Victory Mills 571 N4
Viola 4,504 J8
Voorheesville 3,225 M5
Waddington 944 K1
Wading River 5,317 P9
Walden 5,836 M7
Wallkill 2,125 M7
Walton 3,326 K6
Wampsville▲ 501 J4
Wantagh 18,567 R7
Wappingers Falls 4,605 N7
Warrensburg 3,204 N3
Warsaw▲ 3,830 D5
Warwick 5,984 M8
Washingtonville 4,906 M8
Waterford 2,370 N5
Waterloo▲ 5,116 G5
Watertown▲ 29,429 J3
Watervliet 11,061 N5
Watkins Glen▲ 2,207 G6
Waverly 4,787 G7
Wayland 1,976 E5
Webster 5,464 F4
Weedsport 1,996 G4
Wellsburg 617 G6
Wellsville 5,241 E6
West Carthage 2,166 J3
West Elmira 5,218 G6
West Glens Falls 5,964 N4
West Hurley 2,252 M6
West Nyack 3,437 K8
West Point 8,024 M8
West Sayville 4,680 O9
West Seneca 47,866 C5
West Winfield 871 K5
Westbury 13,060 R7
Westfield 3,451 A6
Westhampton 2,129 P9
Westhampton Beach 1,571 P9
Westons Mills 1,837 D6
White Plains▲ 48,718 P6
Whitehall 3,071 O3
Whitesboro 4,195 K4
Whitney Point 1,054 J6
Willard 1,339 G5
Williamson 1,768 F4
Williamsville 5,583 C5
Williston Park 7,516 R7
Wilson 1,307 C4
Windsor 1,051 J6
Witherbee-Mineville 1,925 N2
Wolcott 1,544 G4
Woodmere 15,578 P7
Woodridge 783 L7
Woodstock 1,870 M6
Wurtsboro 1,048 L7
Wyandanch 8,950 N9
Yonkers 188,082 O6
Yorkshire 1,340 D5
Yorktown Heights 7,690 N8
Yorkville 2,972 K4
Youngstown 2,075 C4

OTHER FEATURES

Adirondack (mts.) M3
Algonquin (peak) M2
Allegany Ind. Res. C6
Allegheny (res.) C7
Allegheny (riv.) C6
Ashokan (res.) M7
Ausable (riv.) N2
Batten Kill (riv.) O4
Beaver (riv.) K3
Big Moose (lake) L3
Black (lake) J1
Black (riv.) K3
Block Island (sound) S8
Blue Mountain (lake) M3
Bonaparte (lake) K2
Brandreth (lake) L3
Brant (lake) N3
Brookhaven Nat'l Lab. P9
Butterfield (lakes) J2
Canandaigua (lake) F5
Canisteo (riv.) F6
Cannonsville (res.) K6
Catskill (lake) L6
Cattaraugus (creek) C6
Cattaraugus Ind. Res. C5
Cayuga (lake) G5
Champlain (lake) O1
Chateaugay, Upper (lake) M1
Chautauqua (lake) A6
Chazy (lake) N1
Chenango (riv.) J6
Cohocton (riv.) F6
Conesus (lake) E5
Conewango (creek) B6
Cranberry (lake) L2
Deer (riv.) J3
Deer (riv.) L1
Delaware (riv.) K7
East (riv.) N9
Erie (lake) A5
Fire Island Nat'l Seashore P9
Fishers (isl.) S8
Forked (lake) L3
Fort Drum 11,578 J2
Fort Niagara C4
Fort Stanwix Nat'l Mon. J4
Fulton Chain (lakes) K3
Galloo (isl.) H3
Gardiners (bay) R8
Gardiners (isl.) R8
Gateway Nat'l Rec. Area M9
Genesee (riv.) E5
George (lake) N4
Grand (isl.) B5
Grass (riv.) K1
Great Sacandaga (lake) M4
Great South (bay) O9
Great South (beach) O9
Greenwood (lake) M8
Grenadier (isl.) H2
Griffiss A.F.B. K4
Haystack (mt.) N2
Hemlock (lake) E5
Hinckley (res.) K4
Honeoye (lake) F5
Honnedaga (lake) L3
Hudson (riv.) N7
Hunter (mt.) M6
Indian (lake) M3
Jones (beach) R7
Keuka (lake) F5
Lila (lake) L2
Little Tupper (lake) L2
Long (isl.) P9
Long (lake) M2
Long Island (sound) P9
Lower Saranac (lake) M2
Manhattan (isl.) M9
Marcy (mt.) N2
Martin Van Buren Nat'l Hist. Site N6
Meacham (lake) M1
Mohawk (riv.) L5
Montauk (pt.) S8
Moose (riv.) K3
Neversink (res.) L7
New York State Barge (canal) C4
Niagara (riv.) B4
Oil Spring Ind. Res. D6
Oneida (lake) J4
Onondaga Ind. Res. H5
Ontario (lake) F3
Orient (pt.) R8
Oswegatchie (riv.) K2
Oswego (riv.) H4
Otisco (lake) H5
Otsego (lake) L5
Otselic (riv.) J5
Owasco (lake) G
Peconic (bay) R
Peninsula (pt.) H
Pepacton (res.) L
Piseco (lake) M
Placid (lake) N
Plattsburgh A.F.B. 5,483 N
Pleasant (lake) M
Plum (isl.) R
Poosepatuck Ind. Res. P
Raquette (lake) L
Rondout (pt.) M
Round (lake) L
Sacandaga (lake) L
Sackets (harb.) H
Sagamore Hill Nat'l Hist. Site R
Saint Lawrence (lake) K
Saint Lawrence (riv.) J
Saint Regis (riv.) L
Saint Regis Ind. Res. M
Salmon (res.) J
Salmon (riv.) H
Salmon (riv.) M
Saranac (lakes) M
Saranac (riv.) N
Saratoga (lake) N
Saratoga Nat'l Hist. Park N
Schoharie (res.) M
Schroon (lake) N
Seneca (lake) G
Seneca (riv.) G
Shelter (isl.) R
Shinnecock Ind. Res. R
Silver (lake) N
Skaneateles (lake) H
Skylight (mt.) M
Slide (mt.) L
Staten (isl.) M
Statue of Liberty Nat'l Mon. M
Stony (isl.) H
Stony (pt.) H
Susquehanna (riv.) H
Thousand (isls.) H
Tioughnioga (riv.) H
Titus (lake) M
Tomhannock (res.) O
Tonawanda Ind. Res. D
Toronto (res.) L
Tupper (lake) M
Tuscarora Ind. Res. B
Unadilla (riv.) K
Upper Chateaugay (lake) M
Valcour (isl.) N
Wallkill (riv.) L
Whiteface (mt.) N
Whitney Point (lake) J
Woodhull (lake) L

▲County seat
• Population of town or township

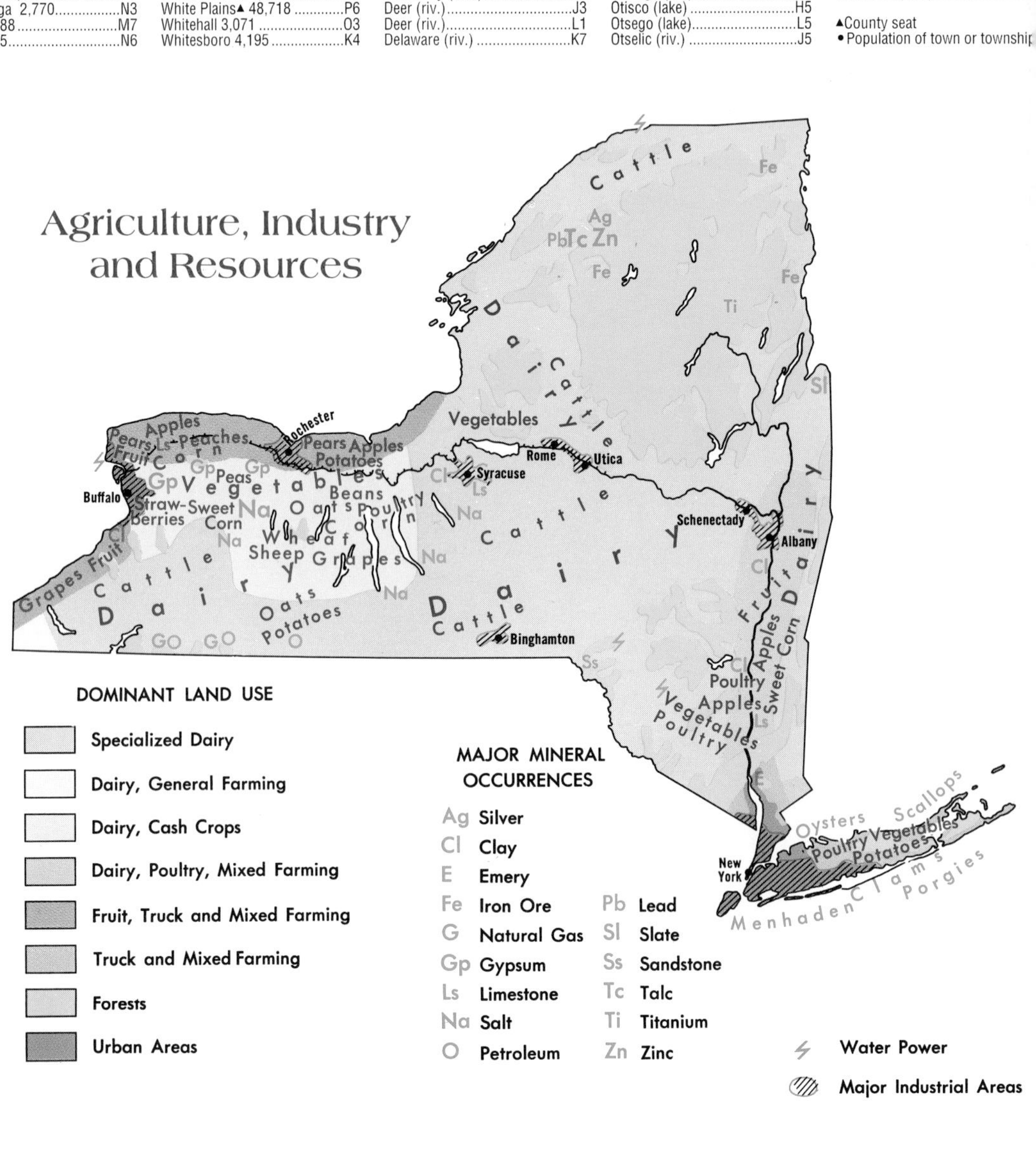

Agriculture, Industry and Resources
Cattle
Dairy
Vegetables
Apples
Pears
Peaches
Fruit
Corn
Rochester
Pears Apples
Potatoes
Peas
Beans
Poultry
Syracuse
Rome
Utica
Buffalo
Straw-berries
Sweet Corn
Wheat
Sheep
Grapes
Oats
Potatoes
Schenectady
Albany
Binghamton
Apples
Sweet Corn
Poultry
Vegetables
New York
Oysters
Scallops
Clams
Porgies
Menhaden
DOMINANT LAND USE
Specialized Dairy
Dairy, General Farming
Dairy, Cash Crops
Dairy, Poultry, Mixed Farming
Fruit, Truck and Mixed Farming
Truck and Mixed Farming
Forests
Urban Areas
MAJOR MINERAL OCCURRENCES
Ag Silver
Cl Clay
E Emery
Fe Iron Ore
G Natural Gas
Gp Gypsum
Ls Limestone
Na Salt
O Petroleum
Pb Lead
Sl Slate
Ss Sandstone
Tc Talc
Ti Titanium
Zn Zinc
Water Power
Major Industrial Areas

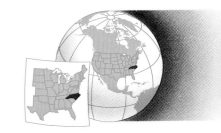

AREA 52,669 sq. mi. (136,413 sq. km.)
POPULATION 6,657,630
CAPITAL Raleigh
LARGEST CITY Charlotte
HIGHEST POINT Mt. Mitchell 6,684 ft. (2037 m.)
SETTLED IN 1650
ADMITTED TO UNION November 21, 1789
POPULAR NAME Tarheel State
STATE FLOWER Flowering Dogwood
STATE BIRD Cardinal

COUNTIES

Alamance 108,213	L3
Alexander 27,544	G3
Alleghany 9,590	G1
Anson 23,474	J4
Ashe 22,209	F2
Avery 14,867	F2
Beaufort 42,283	R4
Bertie 20,388	P2
Bladen 28,663	M5
Brunswick 50,985	N6
Buncombe 174,821	D3
Burke 75,744	F3
Cabarrus 98,935	H4
Caldwell 70,709	F3
Camden 5,904	S2
Carteret 52,556	R5
Caswell 20,693	L2
Catawba 118,412	G3
Chatham 38,759	L3
Cherokee 20,170	A4
Chowan 13,506	R2
Clay 7,155	B4
Cleveland 84,714	F4
Columbus 49,587	M6
Craven 81,613	R4
Cumberland 274,566	M4
Currituck 13,736	S2
Dare 22,746	T3
Davidson 126,677	J3
Davie 27,859	H3
Duplin 39,995	O5
Durham 181,835	M3
Edgecombe 56,558	O3
Forsyth 265,878	J2
Franklin 36,414	N2
Gaston 175,093	G4
Gates 9,305	R2
Graham 7,196	B4
Granville 38,345	M2
Greene 15,384	O4
Guilford 347,420	K3
Halifax 55,516	O2
Harnett 67,822	M4
Haywood 46,942	C3
Henderson 69,285	D4
Hertford 22,523	P2
Hoke 22,856	L4
Hyde 5,411	S3
Iredell 92,931	H3
Jackson 26,846	C4
Johnston 81,306	N4
Jones 9,414	P4

Lee 41,374	L4
Lenoir 57,274	O4
Lincoln 50,319	G3
Macon 23,499	B4
Madison 16,953	D3
Martin 25,078	P3
McDowell 35,681	E3
Mecklenburg 511,433	H4
Mitchell 14,433	E2
Montgomery 23,346	K4
Moore 59,013	L4
Nash 76,677	O2
New Hanover 120,284	O6
Northampton 20,798	P2
Onslow 149,838	P5
Orange 93,851	L2
Pamlico 11,372	R4
Pasquotank 31,298	S2
Pender 28,855	O5
Perquimans 10,447	S2
Person 30,180	M2
Pitt 107,924	P3
Polk 14,416	E4
Randolph 106,546	K3
Richmond 44,518	K4
Robeson 105,179	L5
Rockingham 86,064	K2
Rowan 110,605	H3
Rutherford 56,918	E4
Sampson 47,297	N4
Scotland 33,754	L5
Stanly 51,765	J4
Stokes 37,223	J2
Surry 61,704	H2
Swain 11,268	B3
Transylvania 25,520	D4
Tyrrell 3,856	S3
Union 84,211	H4
Vance 38,892	N2
Wake 423,380	M3
Warren 17,265	N2
Washington 13,997	R3
Watauga 36,952	F2
Wayne 104,666	N4
Wilkes 59,393	G2
Wilson 66,061	O3
Yadkin 30,488	H2
Yancey 15,419	E3

CITIES and TOWNS

Abbottsburg 425	M5
Aberdeen 2,700	L4
Acme	N6
Advance	J3
Ahoskie 4,391	P2
Alamance 258	K2
Alarka 900	C4
Albemarle▲ 14,939	J4
Alexander Mills 662	F4
Alliance 583	R4
Altamahaw 1,076	L2
Andrews 2,551	B4
Angier 2,235	M4
Ansonville 614	J4
Apex 4,968	M3
Arapahoe 430	R4
Archdale 6,913	K3
Arlington 795	H2
Ash 16,362	N6
Asheboro▲ 15,252	K3
Asheville▲ 61,607	D3
Askewville 201	P2
Atkinson 275	N5
Atlantic 1,938	S5
Atlantic Beach 941	R5
Aulander 1,209	P2
Aurora 654	R4
Autryville 166	M4
Avon 500	U4
Avondale	F4
Ayden 4,740	P4
Badin 1,481	J4
Bahama 280	M2
Bailey 553	N3
Bakersville▲ 332	E2
Balfour 1,118	E4
Banner Elk 933	F2
Bannertown 1,028	H1
Barco 325	T2
Barker Heights 1,137	D4
Bat Cave 450	E4
Bath 154	R4
Battleboro 447	O2
Bayboro▲ 733	R4
Bear Creek 500	L3
Beargrass 77	P3
Beaufort▲ 3,808	R5

Belhaven 2,269	R3
Bellarthur 350	O3
Belmont 8,434	H4
Belvidere 275	S2
Belville 66	N6
Belwood 631	F4
Benham 400	G2
Bennett 254	K3
Benson 2,810	N4
Bessemer City 4,698	G4
Beta 500	C4
Bethel 1,842	P3
Beulaville 933	O5
Biltmore Forest 1,327	E3
Biscoe 1,484	K4
Black Creek 615	O3
Black Mountain 5,418	E3
Bladenboro 1,821	M5
Blowing Rock 1,257	F2
Boardman 250	M6
Boger City 1,373	G4
Boiling Spring Lakes 1,650	N7

Boiling Springs 2,445	F4
Bolivia▲ 228	N6
Bolton 531	N6
Bonlee 300	L3
Boomer 250	G2
Boone▲ 12,915	F2
Boonville 1,009	H2
Brevard▲ 5,388	D4
Bridgeton 453	R4
Broadway 973	L4
Brookford 451	G3
Browns Summit 500	K2
Brunswick 302	M6
Bryson City▲ 1,145	C4
Buies 2,085	L5
Buies Creek 1,939	M4
Bullock 525	M2
Bunn 364	N3
Bunnlevel	M4
Burgaw▲ 1,807	N5
Burlington 39,498	K2
Burnsville▲ 1,482	E3
Butner 4,679	M2
Buxton 700	U4
Bynum 312	L3
Calabash 1,210	M7
Calypso 481	N4
Camden▲ 300	S2
Cameron 215	L4
Candler 950	D3
Candor 748	K4
Canton 3,790	D3
Cape Carteret 1,008	P5
Carolina Beach 3,630	O6
Carrboro 11,553	L3
Carthage▲ 976	K4
Cary 43,858	M3
Casar 328	F3
Cashiers 553	C4
Castalia 261	O2
Castle Hayne 1,182	O6
Caswell Beach 175	N7
Catawba 467	G3
Catharine Lake 500	O5
Cedar Falls 400	K3
Cedar Grove 250	L2
Cedar Island 310	S5
Cedar Mountain 250	D4
Centerville 115	N2
Cerro Gordo 227	M6
Chadbourn 2,005	M6
Chadwick Acres 15	P6
Chapel Hill 38,719	L3
Charlotte▲ 395,934	H4
Cherokee 975	C4
Cherry 4,756	R3
Cherryville 4,844	G4
China Grove 2,732	H3
Chinquapin 380	O5
Chocowinity 624	P4
Claremont 980	G3
Clarendon 300	M6
Clark 739	P4
Clarkton 664	M6
Clayton 4,756	N3
Clemmons 6,020	J2
Cleveland 696	H3
Cliffside 950	F4
Climax 475	K3
Clinton▲ 8,204	N5
Clyde 1,041	D3
Coats 1,493	M4
Cofield 407	R2
Coinjock 650	S2

Colerain 139	R2
Collettsville 275	F3
Columbia▲ 836	S3
Columbus▲ 812	E4
Comfort 325	O5
Como 71	P1
Concord▲ 27,347	H4
Conetoe 292	O3
Connellys Springs 500	F3
Conover 5,465	G3
Conway 759	P2
Cooleemee 971	H3
Cornelius 2,581	H4
Council	M6
Cove City 497	P4
Cramerton 2,371	G4
Creedmoor 1,504	M2
Creswell 361	S3
Crisp 435	O3
Crossnore 271	F2
Cruso 800	D4
Culberson	A4
Cullowhee 4,029	C4
Cumberland 400	M5
Currie 294	N6
Currituck▲ 700	T2
Dallas 3,012	G4
Dalton 400	J2
Danbury▲ 119	J2
Davidson 4,046	H4
Davis 612	R5
Delco 450	N6
Denton 1,292	J3
Dillsboro 95	C4
Dobson▲ 1,195	H2
Dortches 840	O2
Dover 451	P4
Drexel 1,746	F3
Dublin 246	M5
Dudley	N4
Dulah 350	M6
Dundarrach	L5
Dunn 8,336	M4
Durham▲ 136,611	M2
Dysartsville 950	F3
Eagle Springs 280	K4
Earl 230	F4
East Arcadia 468	N6
East Bend 619	H2
East Flat Rock 3,218	E4
East Laurinburg 302	L5
East Marion 1,851	F3
East Spencer 2,055	J3
Eden 15,238	K1
Edenton▲ 5,268	R2
Edward	R4
Efland 600	L2
Elizabeth City▲ 14,292	S2
Elizabethtown▲ 3,704	M5
Elk Park 486	E2
Elkin 3,790	H2
Ellenboro 514	F4
Ellerbe 1,132	K4
Elm City 1,624	O3
Elon College 4,394	L2
Emerald Isle 2,434	P5
Enfield 3,082	O2
Engelhard 500	T3
Enka 5,567	D3
Ernul 350	P4
Erwin 4,061	M4
Ether 425	K4
Etowah 1,997	D4
Eure 282	R2

(continued on following page)

Agriculture, Industry and Resources

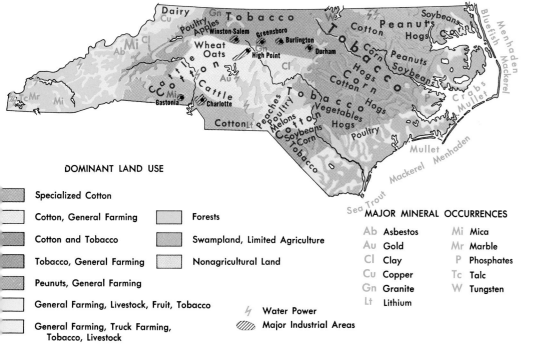

DOMINANT LAND USE

- Specialized Cotton
- Cotton, General Farming
- Cotton and Tobacco
- Tobacco, General Farming
- Peanuts, General Farming
- General Farming, Livestock, Fruit, Tobacco
- General Farming, Truck Farming, Tobacco, Livestock
- Forests
- Swampland, Limited Agriculture
- Nonagricultural Land

⚡ Water Power
▨ Major Industrial Areas

MAJOR MINERAL OCCURRENCES

Ab	Asbestos	Mi	Mica
Au	Gold	Mr	Marble
Cl	Clay	P	Phosphates
Cu	Copper	Tc	Talc
Gn	Granite	W	Tungsten
Lt	Lithium		

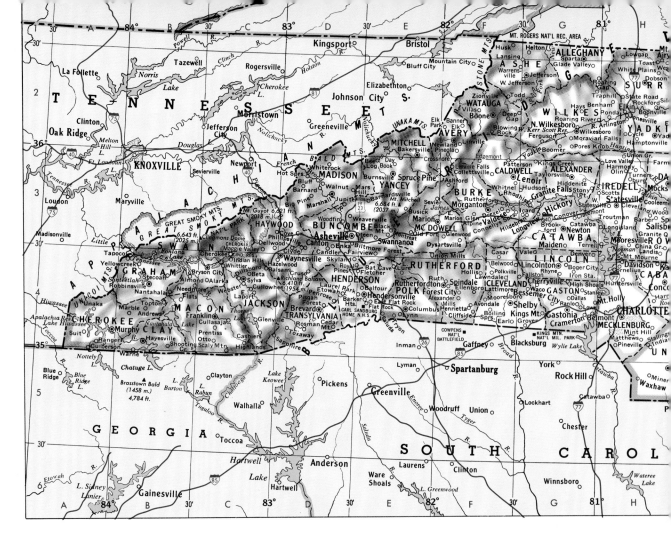

Topography

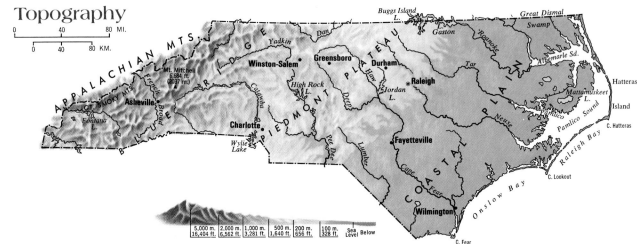

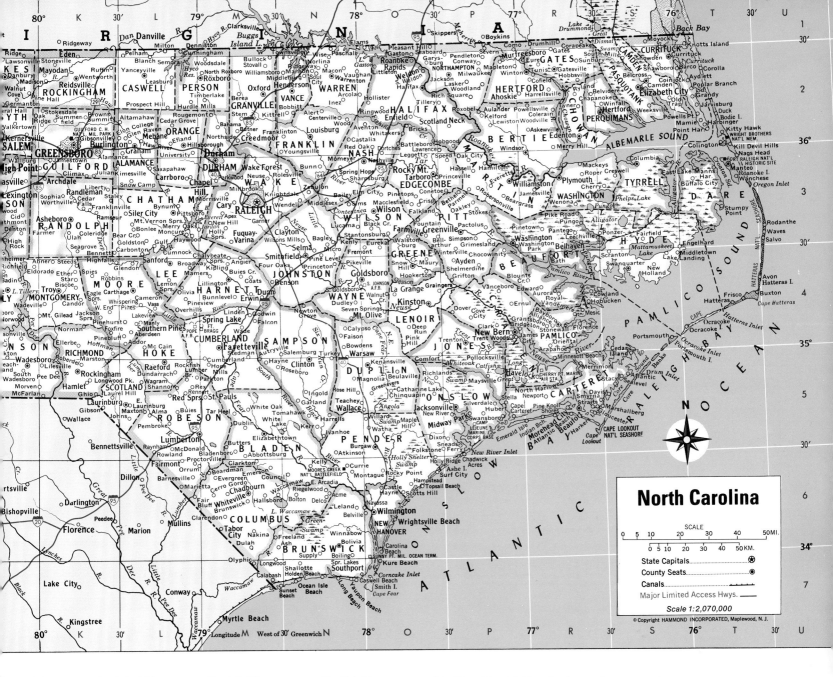

North Carolina

SCALE
0 5 10 20 30 40 50MI.
0 5 10 20 30 40 50KM.

State Capitals .... ⊛
County Seats .... ◉
Canals ....
Major Limited Access Hwys. ———

Scale 1:2,070,000

© Copyright HAMMOND INCORPORATED, Maplewood, N.J.

Rhodhiss 638 ....F3	Sealevel 600 ....S5	Stella 700 ....P5	Wade 238 ....M4	Winston-Salem▲ 143,485 ......J2	Core (sound) S5	New (riv.) O5
Rich Square 1,058 ....P2	Selma 4,600 ....N3	Stem 249 ....M2	Wadesboro▲ 3,645 .....J5	Wintervile 2,816 ....P3	Corncake (inlet) O7	New, South Fork (riv.) G2
Richfield 535 ....J4	Semora 500 ....L2	Stokes 2,134 ....P3	Wagram 480 ....L5	Winton▲ 796 ....P2	Croatan (sound) T3	New River (inlet) P6
Richlands 996 ....O5	Seven Springs 163 ....O4	Stokesdale 1,070 ......K2	Wake Forest 5,769 ....M3	Wise 550 ....N2	Currituck (sound) T2	Nolichucky (riv.) E2
Ridgeway 500 ....N2	Severn 260 ....P2	Stoneville 1,109 ....K2	Walkertown 1,200 .....J2	Wood 2,736 ....N2	Dan (riv.) L1	Norman (lake) H3
Riegelwood 459 ....N6	Sevier 302 ....E3	Stonewall 279 ....R4	Wallace 2,939 ....N5	Woodfin 3,260 ....D3	Deep (riv.) K3	North East Cape Fear (riv.) ...O4
Roanoke Rapids 15,722 ..O2	Shallotte 965 ....N7	Stony Point 1,286 .....G3	Wallburg 300 ....J3	Woodland 760 ....P2	Drum (inlet) S5	Ocracoke (inlet) T5
Roaring Gap 450 ....H2	Sharpsburg 1,536 .....O3	Stovall 409 ....M2	Walnut 1,088 ....D3	Woodleaf 550 ....H3	Fear (cape) O7	Ocracoke (isl.) T4
Roaring River 287 ....G2	Shawboro 300 ....S2	Stumpy Point 250 .....T3	Walnut Cove 1,147 ....J2	Worthville 350 ....K3	Fishing (creek) O2	Onslow (bay) P6
Robbins 970 ....K4	Shelby▲ 14,669 ....G4	Suit 350 ....A4	Walnut Creek 623 .....O4	Wrightsville Beach 2,937 ...O6	Fontana (lake) B2	Oregon (inlet) U3
Robbinsville▲ 709 ....B4	Shoals 350 ....J2	Summerfield 2,051 ....K2	Walstonburg 188 ......O3	Yadkinville▲ 2,525 ....H2	Fort Bragg 34,744 ....M4	Pamlico (riv.) R4
Robersonville 1,940 .....P3	Shooting Creek 250 ...B4	Sunbury 400 ....R2	Wanchese 1,380 ....T3	Yanceyville▲ 1,973 ....L2	Fort Raleigh Nat'l Hist. Site ...T3	Pamlico (sound) S4
Rockingham▲ 9,399 .....K5	Siler City 4,808 ....L3	Supply 300 ....N6	Warrensville F2	Yaupon Beach 734 ....N7	French Broad (riv.) D3	Pee Dee (riv.) J4
Rockwell 1,598 ....J3	Silverdale 250 ....P5	Surf City 970 ....O6	Warrenton▲ 949 ....N2	Youngsville 424 ....N3	Gaston (res.) P2	Phelps (lake) S3
Rocky Mount 48,997 .....O3	Simpson 410 ....P3	Swannanoa 3,538 .....E3	Warsaw 2,859 ....N4	Zebulon 3,173 ....N3	Great (lake) P5	Pigeon (riv.) C3
Rocky Point 975 ....O5	Sims 124 ....N3	Swanquarter▲ 550 ....S4	Washington▲ 9,075 ....R3		Great Dismal (swamp) S1	Pope A.F.B. 2,857 ....L4
Rolesville 572 ....N3	Skyland D4	Swansboro 1,165 ......P5	Washington Park 403 ..R3	OTHER FEATURES	Great Smoky (mts.) B3	Portsmouth T5
Ronda 367 ....H2	Smithfield▲ 7,540 .....N3	Sylva▲ 1,809 ....C4	Watha 99 ....O5		Great Smoky Mts. Nat'l Park..B3	Pungo (lake) S3
Rose Hill 1,287 ....N5	Smyrna 291 ....R5	Tabor City 2,330 ......M6	Waxhaw 1,294 ....H5	Albemarle (sound) S2	Green (swamp) N6	Pungo (riv.) R4
Roseboro 1,441 ....N5	Sneads Ferry 2,031 ...P5	Tar Heel 115 ....M5	Waynesville▲ 6,758 ....D4	Alligator (lake) S3	Guyot (mt.) C3	Raleigh (bay) T4
Rosman 385 ....D4	Snow Hill▲ 1,378 .....O4	Tarboro▲ 11,037 ......O3	Weaverville 2,107 .....D3	Alligator (riv.) S3	Hatteras (cape) U4	Richland Balsam (mt.) D4
Rougemont 400 ....L2	Sophia 350 ....K3	Taylorsville▲ 1,566 ...G3	Webster 410 ....C4	Angola (swamp) O5	Hatteras (inlet) U4	Roanoke (isl.) T3
Rowland 1,139 ....L5	South Goldsboro 2,531 ..N4	Teachey 244 ....N5	Weeksville 500 ....S2	Apalachia (res.) A4	Haw (riv.) K2	Roanoke (riv.) P2
Roxboro▲ 7,332 ....L2	South Mills 950 ....S2	Terrell 319 ....G3	Welcome 3,377 ....J3	Appalachian (mts.) D2	High Rock (lake) J3	Rocky (riv.) H4
Royal 4,418 ....R4	South Wadesboro J5	Thomasville 15,915 ...J3	Weldon 1,392 ....O2	Ashe (isl.) P6	Hiwassee (lake) A4	Santeetlah (lake) A4
Royal Pines D4	South Weldon 1,640 ..O2	Tillery 500 ....O2	Wendell 2,822 ....N3	Bald (mts.) D3	Hiwassee (riv.) A4	Seymour Johnson A.F.B. ...O4
Ruffin 680 ....K2	Southern Pines 9,129 ..L4	Timberlake 500 ....M2	Wentworth▲ 150 ....K2	Blue Ridge (mts.) E3	Holly Shelter (swamp) O6	Six Run (creek) N4
Rural Hall 1,652 ....J2	Southmont 950 ....J3	Toast 2,125 ....H2	West End 950 ....K4	Bodie (isl.) T2	Hunting (riv.) D3	Smith (isl.) O7
Ruth 366 ....E4	Southport 2,369 ....N7	Todd F2	West Jefferson 1,002 ..F2	Broad (riv.) E4	Hyco (lake) L2	South (riv.) M5
Rutherford College 1,126 ..F3	Sparta▲ 1,957 ....G1	Topsail Beach 346 ....O6	West Statesville G3	Buggs Island (lake) M1	James (lake) E4	South Yadkin (riv.) H3
Rutherfordton▲ 3,617 ...E4	Speed 88 ....P3	Traphill 550 ....H2	Westfield 450 ....H2	Camp Lejeune	Jordan, B. Everett (lake)....M3	Stone (mts.) F2
Saint Pauls 1,992 ....M5	Spencer 3,219 ....H3	Trent Woods 2,366 ....P4	Whispering Pines 1,243 ..L4	Marine Corps Base P5	Lanes (creek) J5	Sunny Point
Salemburg 409 ....N4	Spindale 4,040 ....E4	Trenton▲ 248 ....P4	Whitakers 860 ....O2	Cape Fear (riv.) M5	Little (riv.) L4	Mil. Ocean Term. O6
Salisbury▲ 23,087 ......H3	Spring Hope 1,221 ....N3	Troutman 1,493 ....H3	White Lake 390 ....M5	Cape Hatteras Nat'l Seashore..T4	Little (riv.) L4	Tar (riv.) C4
Saluda 488 ....E4	Spring Lake 7,524 .....M4	Troy▲ 3,404 ....K4	White Plains 1,027 .....H2	Carl Sandburg Home	Little Pee Dee (riv.) L6	Tillery (lake) L2
Sandy Ridge 500 ....J1	Spruce Pine 2,010 ....E3	Tryon 1,680 ....E4	Whiteville▲ 5,078 ......M6	Nat'l Hist. Site D4	Little Tennessee (riv.) B4	Trent (riv.) P4
Sanford▲ 14,475 ....L4	Stacy 410 ....S5	Turkey 234 ....N4	Whitnel 975 ....F3	Catawba (lake) G4	Long (lake) S3	Unaka (mts.) E2
Sapphire 350 ....D4	Staley 204 ....K3	Turkey City 34 ....P5	Wilkesboro▲ 2,573 .....G2	Catawba (riv.) G4	Lookout (cape) S5	Unicoi (mts.) A4
Saxapahaw 1,178 ....L3	Stallings 2,132 ....H4	Tyner 264 ....R2	Willard 300 ....O5	Catfish (lake) P5	Lumber (riv.) L6	Waccamaw (lake) N6
Scaly Mountain 250 .....C4	Stanfield 517 ....J4	Ulah 546 ....K3	Williamsboro 59 ....M2	Chatuge (lake) C4	Mackay (riv.) C3	Waccamaw (riv.) M7
Scotland Neck 2,575 ....P2	Stanley 2,823 ....G4	Union Grove 614 ......H2	Williamston▲ 5,503 ....R3	Cherokee Ind. Res. C3	Mattamuskeet (lake) S3	Whiteoak (swamp) P5
Scotts 500 ....H3	Stanleyville 4,779 .....J2	Union Mills 500 ....E4	Wilmington▲ 55,530 ....N6	Cherry Point Marine Air Sta. ..R4	Meherrin (riv.) P1	W. Scott Kerr (lake) G2
Scranton 250 ....S4	Stantonsburg 782 .....O3	Valdese 3,914 ....F3	Wilson▲ 36,930 ....O3	Chowan (riv.) R2	Mitchell (mt.) D3	Wright Brothers Nat'l Mem. ..T2
Seaboard 791 ....O1	Star 775 ....K4	Vanceboro 946 ....R3	Wilsons Mills 300 ......M3	Clingmans Dome (mt.) C3	Moores Creek	Yadkin (riv.) J3
Seagrove 244 ....K3	Stedman 577 ....M4	Vandemere 299 ....R4	Windsor▲ 2,056 ....P2	Nat'l Battlefield N6	Nantahala (lake) B4	
		Vass 670 ....L4	Winfall 501 ....S2	Contentnea (creek) O3	Neuse (riv.) R5	▲County seat.
		Waco 320 ....G4	Wingate 2,821 ....J5	Core (banks) S5		

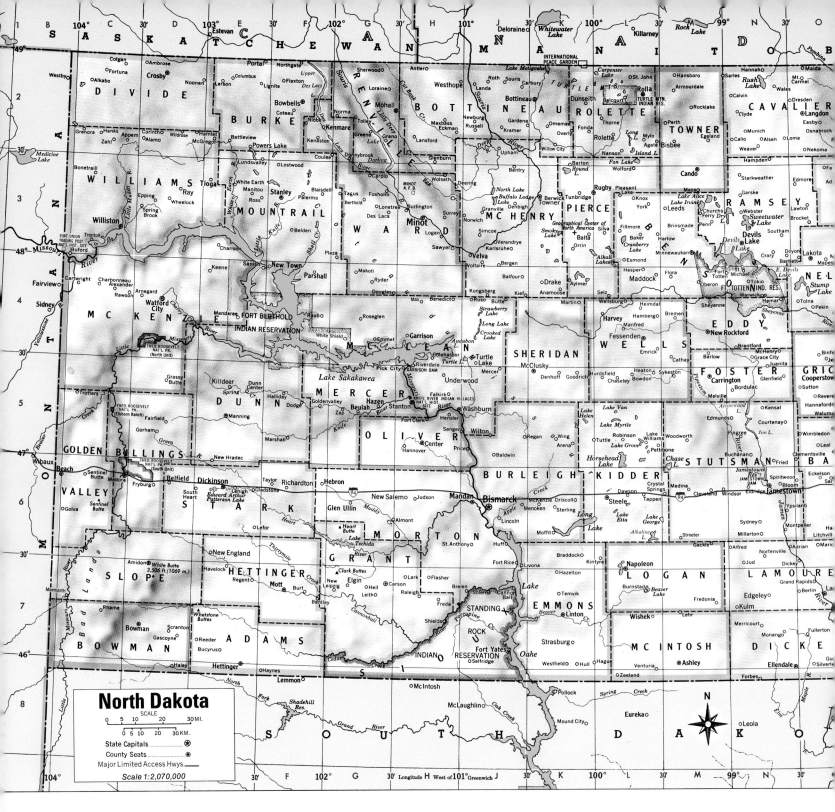

COUNTIES

Adams 3,174 ....F7
Barnes 12,545 ....O5
Benson 7,198 ....M3
Billings 1,108 ....D5
Bottineau 8,011 ....J2
Bowman 3,596 ....C7
Burke 3,002 ....E2
Burleigh 60,131 ....J6
Cass 102,874 ....R5
Cavalier 6,064 ....N2
Dickey 6,107 ....N7
Divide 2,899 ....C2
Dunn 4,005 ....E5
Eddy 2,951 ....N4
Emmons 4,830 ....K7
Foster 3,983 ....N5
Golden Valley 2,108 .....C5
Grand Forks 70,683 ......P3
Grant 3,549 ....G6
Griggs 3,303 ....O5
Hettinger 3,445 ....E7
Kidder 3,332 ....L6
LaMoure 5,383 ....N7
Logan 2,847 ....L7
McHenry 6,528 ....J3
McIntosh 4,021 ....L7
McKenzie 6,383 ....D4
McLean 10,457 ....G4
Mercer 9,808 ....G5
Morton 23,700 ....H6
Mountrail 7,021 ....E3

Nelson 4,410 ....O4
Oliver 2,381 ....H5
Pembina 9,238 ....P2
Pierce 5,052 ....K3
Ramsey 12,681 ....N3
Ransom 5,921 ....P7
Renville 3,160 ....G2
Richland 18,148 ....R7
Rolette 12,772 ....L2
Sargent 4,549 ....P7
Sheridan 2,148 ....K4
Sioux 3,761 ....H7
Slope 907 ....C7
Stark 22,832 ....E6
Steele 2,420 ....P4
Stutsman 22,241 ....M5
Towner 3,627 ....M2
Traill 8,752 ....R5
Walsh 13,840 ....P3
Ward 57,921 ....G3
Wells 5,864 ....L4
Williams 21,129 ....C3

CITIES and TOWNS

Abercrombie 252 ....S7
Adams 248 ....O3
Alexander 216 ....C4
Almont 117 ....H6
Alsen 113 ....N2
Amidon▲ 24 ....D7
Anamoose 277 ....K4
Aneta 314 ....P4

Argusville 161 ....R5
Arnegard 122 ....D4
Arthur 400 ....R5
Ashley▲ 1,052 ....M7
Beach▲ 1,205 ....C6
Belcourt 2,458 ....L2
Belfield 887 ....D6
Berthold 409 ....G3
Binford 233 ....O4
Bisbee 227 ....M2
Bismarck (cap.)▲ 49,256 ..J6
Bottineau▲ 2,598 ....J2
Bowbells▲ 498 ....F2
Bowdon 196 ....L5
Bowman▲ 1,741 ....D7
Buffalo 204 ....R6
Burlington 995 ....G3
Butte 129 ....J4
Buxton 343 ....R4
Cando▲ 1,564 ....M3
Cannon Ball 702 ....J7
Carpio 178 ....G3
Carrington▲ 2,267 ......M5
Carson▲ 383 ....H7
Casselton 1,601 ....R6
Cavalier▲ 1,508 ....P2
Center▲ 826 ....H5
Christine 140 ....R6
Church's Ferry 118 .....M3
Cleveland 121 ....M6
Cogswell 184 ....P7
Coleharbor 88 ....H4

Columbus 223 ....E2
Cooperstown▲ 1,247 .....O5
Crary 145 ....N3
Crosby▲ 1,312 ....D2
Crystal 199 ....P2
Davenport 218 ....R6
Dazey 129 ....O5
Des Lacs 216 ....G3
Devils Lake▲ 7,782 ....N3
Dickinson▲ 16,097 .....E6
Dodge 135 ....F5
Donnybrook 106 ....G2
Drake 361 ....K4
Drayton 961 ....R2
Dunn Center 128 ....E5
Dunseith 723 ....K2
Edgeley 680 ....N7
Edinburg 284 ....P3
Edmore 329 ....O3
Egeland 103 ....M2
Elgin 765 ....G7
Ellendale▲ 1,798 .....N7
Emerado 483 ....R4
Enderlin 883 ....P6
Esmond 196 ....L3
Fairmount 427 ....S7
Fargo▲ 74,111 ....S6
Fessenden▲ 655 ....L4
Fingal 138 ....P6
Finley▲ 548 ....O5
Flasher 317 ....H7
Flaxton 121 ....F2

Fordville 299 ....P3
Forest River 148 .....P3
Forman▲ 586 ....P7
Fort Ransom 111 ......P6
Fort Totten 867 ......M4
Fort Yates▲ 183 .....J7
Frontier 218 ....S6
Fullerton 94 ....O7
Gackle 450 ....M6
Galesburg 161 ....R5
Garrison▲ 1,530 .....H4
Gilby 262 ....R3
Gladstone 224 ....F6
Glen Ullin 927 ....G6
Glenburn 439 ....H2
Glenfield 118 ....N5
Goldenvalley 287 .....F5
Golva 137 ....C6
Goodrich 192 ....K5
Grace City 108 ....N4
Grafton▲ 4,840 .....R3
Grand Forks▲ 49,425 .R4
Grandin 213 ....R5
Granville 236 ....J3
Great Bend 108 ....S7
Grenora 261 ....C2
Gwinner 585 ....P7
Hague 109 ....L7
Halliday 288 ....F5
Hankinson 1,038 ......S7
Hannaford 204 ....O5
Harvey 2,263 ....L4
Harwood 590 ....S6

Hatton 800 ....R4
Havana 124 ....P8
Hazelton 240 ....K7
Hazen 2,818 ....G5
Hebron 888 ....G6
Hettinger▲ 1,574 ....E8
Hillsboro▲ 1,488 ...S5
Hoople 310 ....P3
Hope 281 ....P5
Horace 662 ....S6
Hunter 341 ....R5
Inkster 95 ....P3
Jamestown▲ 15,571 ..N6
Karlsruhe 143 ....J3
Kenmare 1,214 ....G2
Kensal 191 ....N5
Killdeer 722 ....E5
Kindred 569 ....R6
Kulm 514 ....N7
LaMoure▲ 970 ....O7
Lakota▲ 898 ....O3
Langdon▲ 2,241 .....O2
Lankin 152 ....P3
Larimore 1,464 ....Q4
Leeds 542 ....M3
Lehr 191 ....M7
Leonard 310 ....R6
Lidgerwood 799 ....R7
Lignite 242 ....F2
Lincoln 1,132 ....J6
Linton▲ 1,410 ......K7
Lisbon▲ 2,177 ......P7

Litchville 205 ....O6
Maddock 559 ....L4
Makoti 145 ....G4
Mandan▲ 15,177 .....J6
Mandaree 367 ....E4
Manning▲ 75 ....E5
Manvel 333 ....R3
Mapleton 682 ....S6
Marion 169 ....O6
Marmarth 144 ....B7
Martin 117 ....K4
Max 301 ....H4
Maxbass 123 ....H2
Mayville 2,092 ....R4
McClusky▲ 492 ......K4
McVille 559 ....O4
Medina 387 ....M6
Mercer 104 ....J5
Michigan 413 ....O3
Milnor 651 ....P7
Milton 133 ....O2
Minnewaukan▲ 401 ...M3
Minot▲ 34,544 ......H3
Mohall▲ 931 ....G2
Mooreton 193 ....S7
Mott▲ 1,019 ....F7
Mountain 134 ....P2
Munich 310 ....N2
Napoleon▲ 930 ......L6
Neche 434 ....P2
New England 663 ......E6

AREA 70,702 sq. mi. (183,118 sq. km.)
POPULATION 641,364
CAPITAL Bismarck
LARGEST CITY Fargo
HIGHEST POINT White Butte 3,506 ft. (1069 m.)
SETTLED IN 1780
ADMITTED TO UNION November 2, 1889
POPULAR NAME Flickertail State; Sioux State
STATE FLOWER Wild Prairie Rose
STATE BIRD Western Meadowlark

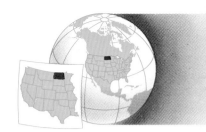

Topography

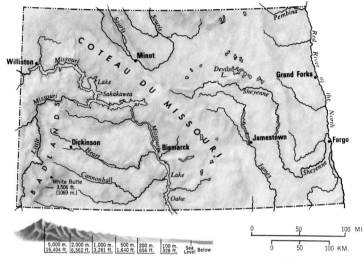

Towner▲ 669	K3
Turtle Lake 681	J4
Tuttle 160	L5
Underwood 976	H5
Upham 205	J2
Valley City▲ 7,163	P6
Velva 968	J3
Verona 103	O7
Wahpeton▲ 8,751	S7
Walcott 178	R6
Walhalla 1,131	P2
Washburn▲ 1,506	J5
Watford City▲ 1,784	D4
West Fargo 12,287	S6
Westhope 578	H2
White Shield 274	G4
Wildrose 193	D2
Williston▲ 13,131	C3
Willow City 281	K2
Wilton 728	J5
Wimbledon 275	O5
Wing 208	K5
Wishek 1,171	L7
Woodworth 102	M5
Wyndmere 501	R7
Zap 287	G5
Zeeland 197	L8

OTHER FEATURES

Alkali (lakes)	L3
Alkaline (lake)	L6
Apple (creek)	J6
Arrowwood (lake)	N5
Ashtabula (Baldhill Res.) (lake)	P5
Audubon (lake)	H4
Bad Lands (reg.)	C7
Baldhill (Ashtabula Lake) (res.)	P5
Bear (creek)	O7
Beaver (creek)	K7
Beaver (creek)	B5
Beaver (lake)	L7
Buffalo Lodge (lake)	J3
Cannonball (riv.)	G7
Carpenter (lake)	L2
Cedar (creek)	G7
Chase (lake)	M5
Cherry (creek)	D4
Clark (buttes)	G7
Coteau du Missouri (plain)	G3
Cranberry (lake)	L3
Crooked (lake)	J4
Cut Bank (creek)	H2
Darling (lake)	G2
Deep (riv.)	J1
Des Lacs (riv.)	G3
Devils (lake)	N3
Dry (lake)	M3
East Devils (lake)	N4
Egg (creek)	H3
Elm (riv.)	N8
Elm (riv.)	R5
Etta (lake)	L6

Fan (lake)	L2
Forest (riv.)	P3
Fort Berthold Ind. Res.	E4
Fort Totten Ind. Res.	N4
Fort Union Trading Post Nat'l Hist. Site	B3
Garrison (dam)	H5
George (lake)	L6
Goose (riv.)	P4
Grand, North Fork (riv.)	E8
Grand Forks A.F.B.9,343	R4
Green (riv.)	D5
Grove (lake)	L5
Heart (butte)	G6
Heart (riv.)	F6
Helen (lake)	K5
Horsehead (lake)	L5
International Peace Garden	K1
Irvine (lake)	M3
Island (lake)	L2
James (riv.)	N6
Jamestown (res.)	N6
Jim (lake)	N5
Knife (riv.)	G5
Knife R. Indian Villages Nat'l Hist. Site	H5
Little Deep (creek)	G2
Little Knife (riv.)	F3

Little Missouri (riv.)	D4
Little Muddy (riv.)	C3
Long (lake)	J4
Long (lake)	K6
Long (lake)	L8
Maple (riv.)	O8
Maple (riv.)	R6
Metigoshe (lake)	K2
Minot A.F.B. 9,095	H3
Missouri (riv.)	H5
Muddy (creek)	G6
Myrtle (lake)	L5
North (lake)	J3
Oahe (lake)	J7
Oak (creek)	J8
Park (riv.)	R3
Patterson, Edward A. (lake)	E6
Pembina (riv.)	O1
Pipestem (riv.)	M5
Porcupine (creek)	J7
Red River of the North (riv.)	S4
Round (lake)	K3
Rush (lake)	N2
Rush (riv.)	R5
Sakakawea (lake)	G5
Sentinel (butte)	C6
Shell (creek)	F3
Sheyenne (riv.)	O6

Smoky (lake)	K3
Souris (riv.)	J2
Spring (creek)	E5
Standing Rock Ind. Res.	J7
Strawberry (lake)	J4
Stump (lake)	O4
Sweetwater (lake)	N3
Theodore Roosevelt Nat'l Park	C5
Theodore Roosevelt Nat'l Park	D4
Theodore Roosevelt Nat'l Park	D6
Thirty Mile (creek)	F6
Tongue (riv.)	P2
Tschida (lake)	G6
Turtle (lake)	H4
Turtle (mts.)	K2
Turtle Mountain Ind. Res.	L2
Upper Des Lacs (lake)	F2
Van (lake)	L5
Whetstone (buttes)	E7
White Butte (buttes)	D7
White Earth (riv.)	E3
Wild Rice (riv.)	R7
Yellowstone (riv.)	B4

▲County seat

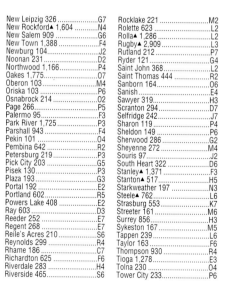

New Leipzig 326	G7
New Rockford▲ 1,604	N4
New Salem 909	G6
New Town 1,388	F4
Newburg 104	J2
Noonan 231	D2
Northwood 1,166	P4
Oakes 1,775	O7
Oberon 103	M4
Oriska 103	P6
Osnabrock 214	O2
Page 266	P5
Palermo 95	F3
Park River 1,725	P3
Parshall 943	F4
Pekin 101	O4
Pembina 642	R2
Petersburg 219	P3
Pick City 203	G5
Pisek 130	P3
Plaza 193	G3
Portal 192	E2
Portland 602	R5
Powers Lake 408	E3
Ray 603	D3
Reeder 252	E7
Regent 268	E7
Reile's Acres 210	S6
Reynolds 299	R4
Rhame 186	C7
Richardton 625	E7
Riverdale 283	H4
Riverside 465	S6

Rocklake 221	M2
Rolette 623	L2
Rolla 1,286	L2
Rugby▲ 2,909	L3
Rutland 212	P7
Ryder 121	G4
Saint John 368	L2
Saint Thomas 444	R2
Sanborn 164	O6
Sanish	E4
Sawyer 319	H3
Scranton 294	D7
Selfridge 242	J7
Sharon 119	P4
Sheldon 149	P6
Sherwood 286	G2
Sheyenne 272	M4
Souris 97	J2
South Heart 322	D6
Stanley▲ 1,371	F3
Stanton▲ 517	H5
Starkweather 197	N3
Steele▲ 762	L6
Strasburg 553	K7
Streeter 161	M6
Surrey 856	H3
Sykeston 167	M5
Tappen 239	L6
Taylor 163	F6
Thompson 930	R4
Tioga 1,278	E3
Tolna 230	O4
Tower City 233	P6

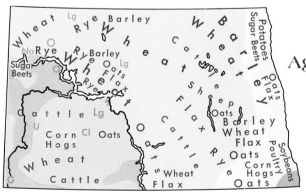

Agriculture, Industry and Resources

DOMINANT LAND USE

- Specialized Wheat
- Wheat, General Farming
- Wheat, Range Livestock
- Livestock, Cash Grain
- Sugar Beets, Dry Beans, Livestock, General Farming
- Range Livestock
- Water Power

MAJOR MINERAL OCCURRENCES

- Cl Clay
- G Natural Gas
- Lg Lignite
- Na Salt
- O Petroleum
- U Uranium

© Copyright HAMMOND INCORPORATED, Maplewood, N. J.

Ohio

SCALE

0 5 10   20   30   40 MI.

0 5 10   20   30   40 KM.

⊛ State Capitals

◉ County Seats

Major Limited Access Hwys. ━━━

Scale 1:1,800,000

© Copyright HAMMOND INCORPORATED, Maplewood, N. J.

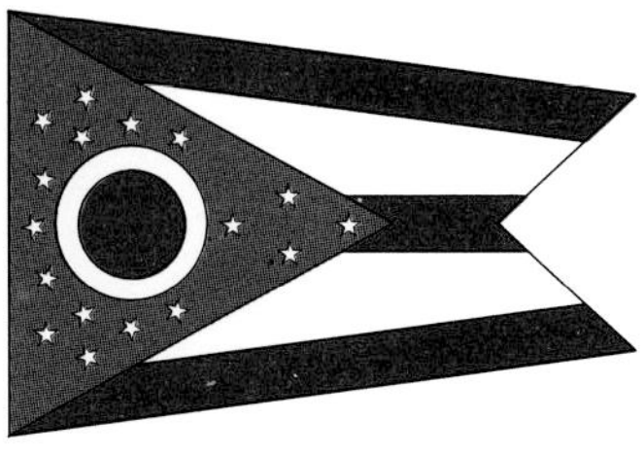

AREA 41,330 sq. mi. (107,045 sq. km.)
POPULATION 10,887,325
CAPITAL Columbus
LARGEST CITY Cleveland
HIGHEST POINT Campbell Hill 1,550 ft. (472 m.)
SETTLED IN 1788
ADMITTED TO UNION March 1, 1803
POPULAR NAME Buckeye State
STATE FLOWER Scarlet Carnation
STATE BIRD Cardinal

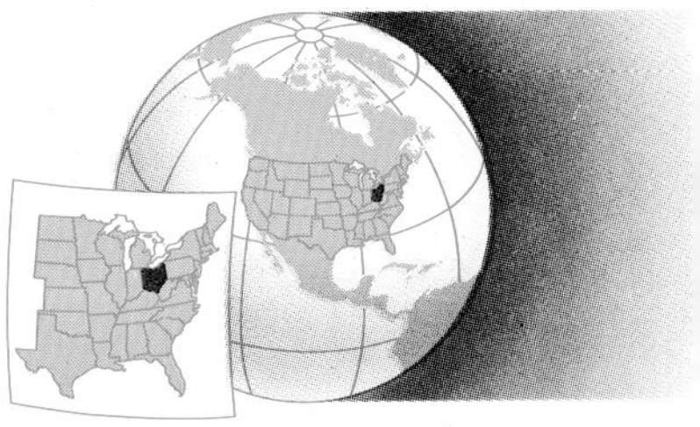

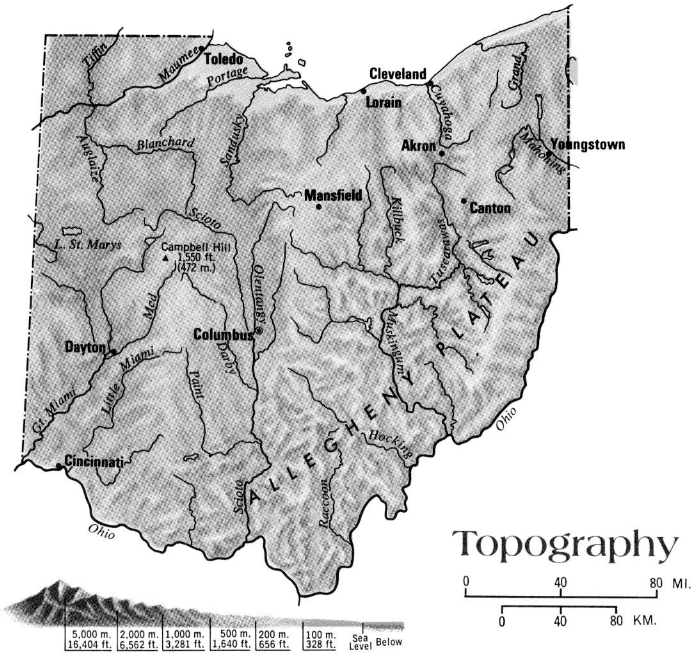

COUNTIES

ams 25,371 D8
en 109,755 B4
hland 47,507 F4
htabula 99,821 J2
hens 59,549 F7
glaize 44,585 B4
lmont 71,074 J5
own 34,966 C8
tler 291,479 A7
rroll 26,521 H4
ampaign 36,019 C5
rk 147,548 C6
ermont 150,187 B7
nton 35,415 C7
lumbiana 108,276 J4
shocton 35,427 G5
awford 47,870 E4
yahoga 1,412,140 G3
rke 53,619 A5
laware 66,929 D5
fiance 39,350 A3
e 76,779 E3
rfield 103,461 E6
yette 27,466 D6
anklin 961,437 E5
ton 38,498 B2
llia 30,954 F8
auga 81,129 H3
eene 136,731 C6
ernsey 39,024 H5
milton 866,228 A7
ncock 65,536 C3
rdin 31,111 C4
rrison 16,085 H5
nry 29,108 B3
ghland 35,728 C7
cking 25,533 F6
lmes 32,849 G4
ron 56,240 E3
ckson 30,230 E7
ferson 80,298 J5
ox 47,473 F5
ke 215,499 H2
wrence 61,834 E8
king 128,300 F5
gan 42,310 C5
rain 271,126 F3
cas 462,361 C2
dison 37,068 D6
honing 264,806 J4
rion 64,274 D4
dina 122,354 G3
igs 22,987 F7
rcer 39,443 A4
ami 93,182 B5
nroe 15,497 H6
ntgomery 573,809 B6
rgan 14,194 G6
rrow 27,749 E4
skingum 82,068 G5
ble 11,336 G6
awa 40,029 D2
ulding 20,488 A3
rry 31,557 F6
Pickaway 48,255 D6
Pike 24,249 D7
Portage 142,585 H3
Preble 40,113 A6
Putnam 33,819 B3
Richland 126,137 E4
Ross 69,330 D7
Sandusky 61,963 D3
Scioto 80,327 D8
Seneca 59,733 D3
Shelby 44,915 B5
Stark 367,585 H4
Summit 514,990 G3
Trumbull 227,813 J3
Tuscarawas 84,090 H5
Union 31,969 D5
Van Wert 30,464 A4
Vinton 11,098 E7
Warren 113,909 B7
Washington 62,254 H7
Wayne 101,461 G4
Williams 36,956 A2
Wood 113,269 C3
Wyandot 22,254 D4

CITIES and TOWNS

Aberdeen 1,329 C8
Ada 5,413 C4
Adamsville 151 G5
Addyston 1,198 B9
Adelphi 398 E7
Adena 842 J5
Akron▲ 223,019 G3
Albany 795 F7
Alexandria 468 E5
Alger 864 C4
Alliance 23,376 H4
Alvordton 298 A2
Amanda 729 E6
Amberley 3,108 C9
Amelia 1,837 D10
Amesville 250 F7
Amherst 10,332 F3
Amsterdam 669 J5
Andover 1,216 J2
Anna 1,164 B5
Ansonia 1,279 A5
Antioch 68 H6
Antwerp 1,677 A3
Apple Creek 860 G4
Aquilla 360 H2
Arcadia 546 D3
Arcanum 1,953 A6
Archbold 3,440 B2
Arlington 1,267 C4
Arlington Heights 1,084 C9
Ashland▲ 20,079 F4
Ashley 1,059 E5
Ashtabula 21,633 J2
Ashville 2,254 E6
Athalia 346 F8
Athens▲ 21,265 F7
Attica 944 E3
Aurora 9,192 H3
Austintown 32,371 J3
Avon 7,337 F3
Avon Lake 15,066 F2
Bailey Lakes 367 F4
Bainbridge 968 D7
Bairdstown 130 C3
Ballville 3,083 D3
Baltic 659 G5
Baltimore 2,971 E6
Barberton 27,623 G4
Barnesville 4,326 H6
Barnhill 313 H5
Barton 1,039 J5
Batavia▲ 1,700 B7
Batesville 95 H6
Bay View 739 E3
Bay Village 17,000 G9
Beach City 1,051 G4
Beachwood 10,677 J9
Beallsville 464 J6
Beaver 336 E7
Beavercreek 33,626 C6
Beaverdam 467 C4
Bedford 14,822 H9
Bedford Heights 12,131 J9
Bellaire 6,028 J5
Bellbrook 6,511 C6
Belle Center 796 C4
Belle Valley 267 G6
Bellefontaine▲ 12,142 C5
Bellevue 8,146 E3
Bellville 1,568 E4
Belmont 471 J5
Belmore 161 B3
Beloit 1,037 J4
Belpre 6,796 G7
Bentleyville 674 J9
Benton 351 G4
Benton Ridge 343 C4
Berea 19,051 G10
Bergholz 713 J4
Berkey 264 C2
Berlin 691 G4
Berlin Heights 756 F3
Bethel 2,407 B8
Bethesda 1,161 H5
Bettsville 752 D3
Beverly 1,444 G6
Bexley 13,088 E6
Blakeslee 128 A2
Blanchester 4,206 B7
Bloomdale 632 D3
Bloomingburg 769 D6
Bloomingdale 227 J5
Bloomville 949 D3
Blue Ash 11,860 C9
Bluffton 3,367 C4
Boardman 38,596 J3
Bolivar 914 G4
Boston Heights 733 J10
Botkins 1,340 B5
Bowerston 343 H5
Bowersville 225 C6
Bowling Green▲ 28,176 C3
Bradford 2,005 B5
Bradner 1,093 C3
Brady Lake 490 H3
Brecksville 11,818 H10
Bremen 1,386 F6
Brewster 2,307 G4
Brice 109 E6
Bridgeport 2,318 J5
Bridgetown 11,748 B9
Brilliant 1,672 J5
Brimfield 3,223 H3
Broadview Heights 12,219 H10
Brook Park 22,865 G9
Brookfield 1,396 J3
Brooklyn 11,706 H9
Brooklyn Heights 1,450 H9
Brookside 703 J5
Brookville 4,621 B6
Broughton 151 B3
Brunswick 28,230 G3
Bryan▲ 8,348 A3
Buchtel 640 F7
Buckeye Lake 2,986 F6
Buckland 239 B4
Bucyrus▲ 13,496 E4
Burbank 289 F4
Burgoon 224 D3
Burkettsville 268 A5
Burlington 3,003 F9
Burton 1,349 H3
Butler 968 F4
Butlerville 188 B7
Byesville 2,435 G6
Cadiz▲ 3,439 J5
Cairo 473 B4
Calcutta 1,212 J4
Caldwell▲ 1,786 G6
Caledonia 644 D4
Cambridge▲ 11,748 G5
Camden 2,210 A6
Campbell 10,038 J3
Canal Fulton 4,157 H4
Canal Winchester 2,617 E6
Canfield 5,409 J3
Canton▲ 84,161 H4
Cardington 1,770 E5
Carey 3,684 D4
Carlisle 4,872 B6
Carroll 558 E6
Carrollton▲ 3,042 J4
Casstown 246 B5
Castalia 915 E3
Castine 163 A6
Catawba 268 C6
Cecil 249 A3
Cedarville 3,210 C6
Celina▲ 9,650 A4
Centerburg 1,323 E5
Centerville 128 B6
Chagrin Falls 4,146 J9
Chardon▲ 4,446 H2
Chatfield 206 E4
Chauncey 980 F7
Cherry Fork 178 C8
Cherry Grove 4,972 C10
Chesapeake 1,073 E9
Cheshire 250 F8
Chester 309 G7
Chesterhill 395 G6
Chesterland 2,078 H2
Chesterville 286 E5
Cheviot 9,616 B9
Chickasaw 378 A5
Chillicothe▲ 21,923 E7
Chilo 130 B8
Christiansburg 599 C5
Cincinnati▲ 364,040 B9
Circleville▲ 11,666 D6
Clarington 406 J6
Clark 523 G5
Clarksburg 483 D7
Clarksville 485 C7
Clay Center 289 D2
Clayton 713 B6
Cleveland Heights 54,052 H9
Cleveland▲ 505,616 H9
Cleves 2,208 B9
Clinton 1,175 G4
Cloverdale 270 B3
Clyde 5,776 E3
Coal Grove 2,251 E9
Coalton 553 E7
Coldwater 4,335 A5
College Corner 379 A6
Columbiana 4,961 J4
Columbus (cap.)▲ 632,910 E6
Columbus Grove 2,231 B4
Commercial Point 405 D6
Conesville 420 G5
Congress 162 F4
Conneaut 13,241 J2
Continental 1,214 B3
Convoy 1,200 A4
Coolville 663 G7
Corning 703 F6
Cortland 5,666 J3
Corwin 225 B6
Coshocton▲ 12,193 G5
Cove 6,669 E8
Covedale 5,830 B10
Covington 2,603 B5
Craig Beach 1,402 H3
Crestline 4,934 E4
Creston 1,848 G3
Cridersville 1,885 B4
Crooksville 2,601 F6
Crown City 445 F8
Cumberland 318 G6
Custar 209 C3
Cuyahoga Falls 48,950 G3
Cuyahoga Heights 682 H9
Cygnet 560 C3
Dalton 1,377 G4
Danville 1,001 F5
Darbydale 825 D6
Darbyville 272 D6
Dayton▲ 182,044 B6
Deer Park 6,181 C9
Deersville 86 H5
Defiance▲ 16,768 B3
Degraff 1,331 C5
Delaware▲ 20,030 E5
Dellroy 314 H4
Delphos 7,093 B4
Delta 2,849 B2
Dennison 3,282 H5
Dent 6,416 B9
Deshler 1,876 C3
Devola 2,736 H7
Dexter City 161 G6
Dillonvale 857 J5
Dover 11,329 G4
Doylestown 2,668 G4
Dresden 1,581 G5
Dublin 16,366 D5
Dunkirk 869 C4
Dupont 279 B3
East Canton 1,742 H4
East Cleveland 33,096 H9
East Liverpool 13,654 J4
East Palestine 5,168 J4
East Sparta 771 H4
Eastlake 21,161 J8
Eaton Estates 1,586 G3
Eaton▲ 7,396 A6
Edgerton 1,896 A3
Edgewood 5,189 J2
Edison 488 E4
Edon 880 A2
Eldorado 549 A6
Elgin 71 B4
Elida 1,486 B4
Elmore 1,334 D3
Elmwood Place 2,937 B9
Elyria▲ 56,746 F3
Empire 364 J5
Englewood 11,432 B6
Euclid 54,875 J9
Evendale 3,175 C9
Fairborn 31,300 B6
Fairfax 2,029 C9
Fairfield 39,729 A7
Fairlawn 5,779 G3
Fairport Harbor 2,978 H2
Fairview Park 18,028 G9
Farmer 932 A3
Farmersville 950 A6
Fayette 1,248 B2
Fayetteville 393 C7
Felicity 856 B8
Findlay▲ 35,703 C3
Fletcher 545 B5
Florida 304 B3
Flushing 1,042 J5
Forest 1,594 C4
Forest Park 18,609 B9
Forestville 9,185 C10
Fort Jennings 436 B4
Fort Loramie 1,042 B5
Fort McKinley 9,740 B6
Fort Recovery 1,313 A5
Fort Shawnee 4,128 B4
Fostoria 14,983 D3
Frankfort 1,065 D7
Franklin 11,026 B6
Franklin Furnace 1,212 E8
Frazeysburg 1,165 F5
Fredericksburg 502 G4
Fredericktown 2,443 F5
Freeport 475 H5
Fremont▲ 17,648 D3
Fulton 325 E5
Fultonham 178 F6
Gahanna 27,791 E5
Galena 361 E5
Galion 11,859 E4
Gallipolis▲ 4,831 F8
Gambier 2,073 F5
Garfield Heights 31,739 J9
Garrettsville 2,014 H3
Gates Mills 2,508 J9
Geneva 6,597 J2
Geneva-on-the-Lake 1,626 H2
Genoa 2,262 D2
Georgetown▲ 3,627 C8
Germantown 4,916 B6
Gettysburg 539 A5
Gibsonburg 2,579 D3
Gilboa 208 C3
Girard 11,304 J3
Glandorf 829 B3
Glendale 2,445 C9
Glenford 208 F6
Glenmont 233 F4
Glenwillow 455 J10
Glouster 2,001 F6
Gnadenhutten 1,226 G5
Golf Manor 4,154 C9
Gordon 206 B6
Grafton 3,344 F3
Grand Rapids 955 C3
Grand River H2
Grandview 1,301 H7
Grandview Heights 7,010 D6
Granville 4,353 E5
Gratiot 195 F6
Gratis 998 A6
Green Camp 393 D4
Green Springs 1,446 E3
Greenfield 5,172 D7
Greenhills 4,393 B9
Greensburg 3,306 G4
Greentown 1,856 H4
Greenville▲ 12,863 A5
Greenwich 1,442 E3
Groesbeck 6,684 B9
Grove City 19,661 D6
Groveport 2,948 E6
Grover Hill 518 B3
Hamden 877 F7
Hamersville 586 C8
Hamilton▲ 61,368 A7
Hamler 623 B3
Hanging Rock 306 E8
Hanover 803 F5
Hanoverton 434 J4
Harbor View 122 C2
Harpster 233 D4
Harrisburg 340 D6
Harrison 7,518 A9
Harrisville 308 J5
Harrod 537 C4
Hartford 418 J3
Hartford 444 E5
Hartville 2,031 H4
Harveysburg 437 C7
Haskins 549 C3
Haviland 210 A3
Hayesville 457 F4
Heath 7,231 F5
Hebron 2,076 E6
Helena 267 D3
Hemlock 203 F6
Hicksville 3,664 A3
Higginsport 298 C8
Highland 275 C7
Highland Heights 6,249 J9
Hilliard 11,796 D5
Hillsboro▲ 6,235 C7
Hiram 1,330 H3
Holgate 1,290 B3
Holland 1,210 C2
Hollansburg 300 A5
Holloway 354 H5
Holmesville 419 G4
Hopedale 685 J5
Hoytville 301 C3
Hubbard 8,248 J3
Huber Heights 38,696 B6
Hudson 5,159 H3
Hunting Valley 799 J9
Huntsville 343 C5
Huron 7,030 F3
Independence 6,500 H9
Indian Hill 5,383 C9
Irondale 382 J4
Ironton▲ 12,751 E8
Ithaca 119 A6
Jackson Center 1,398 B5
Jackson▲ 6,144 E7
Jacksonville 544 F7
Jamestown 1,794 C6
Jefferson (West Jefferson) 3,331 D6
Jefferson▲ 2,952 J2
Jeffersonville 1,281 C6
Jenera 285 C4
Jeromesville 582 F4
Jerry City 517 C3
Jerusalem 144 H6
Jewett 778 H5
Johnstown 3,237 E5
Junction City 770 F6
Kalida 947 B4
Kelleys Island 172 E2
Kent 28,835 H3
Kenton▲ 8,356 C4
Kettering 60,569 B6
Kettlersville 194 B5
Killbuck 809 G5
Kimbolton 134 G5
Kingston 1,153 E7
Kingsville 1,243 J2
Kipton 283 F3
Kirby 155 D4
Kirkersville 563 E6
Kirtland 5,881 H2
Kirtland Hills 628 H2
La Rue 802 D4
Lafayette 449 C4
Lagrange 1,199 F3
Lakeline 210 J8
Lakemore 2,684 H3
Lakeview 1,056 C4
Lakewood 59,718 G9
Lancaster▲ 34,507 E6
Latty 205 A3
Laura 483 B6
Laurelville 605 E7
Lawrenceville 304 C6
Lebanon▲ 10,453 B7
Leesburg 1,063 D7
Leesville 156 H5
Leetonia 2,070 J4
Leipsic 2,203 C3
Lewisburg 1,584 A6
Lewisville 261 H6
Lexington 4,124 E4
Liberty Center 1,084 B3
Lima▲ 45,549 B4
Limaville 152 H4
Lincoln Heights 4,805 C9
Lindsey 529 D3
Linndale 159 G9
Lisbon▲ 3,037 J4
Lithopolis 563 E6
Lockbourne 173 E6
Lockington 214 B5
Lockland 4,357 C9
Lodi 3,042 F3
Logan▲ 6,725 F6
London▲ 7,807 C6
Lorain 71,245 F3
Lordstown 3,404 J3
Lore City 384 H6
Loudonville 2,915 F4
Louisville 8,087 H4
Loveland 9,990 D9
Lowell 617 H6
Lowellville 1,349 J3
Lower Salem 103 H6
Lucas 730 F4
Lucasville 1,575 E8
Luckey 848 D3
Ludlow Falls 300 B6
Lynchburg 1,212 C7
Lyndhurst 15,982 J9
Lyons 579 B2
Macedonia 7,509 J10
Mack 2,816 B9
Macksburg 218 G6
Madeira 9,141 C9
Madison 2,477 H2
Magnetic Springs 373 D5
Magnolia 937 H4
Maineville 359 C9
Malinta 294 B3

(continued on following page)

Agriculture, Industry and Resources

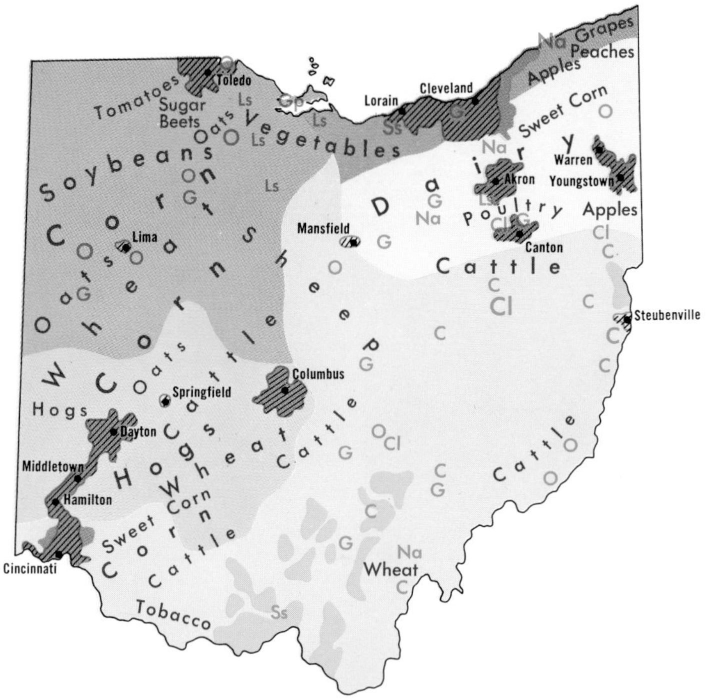

DOMINANT LAND USE

- Hogs, Soft Winter Wheat
- Livestock, Dairy, Soybeans, Cash Grain
- Dairy, General Farming
- General Farming, Livestock, Tobacco
- Fruit, Truck and Mixed Farming
- Forests
- Urban Areas

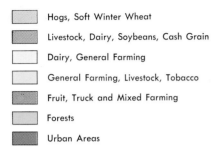

MAJOR MINERAL OCCURRENCES

- C Coal
- Cl Clay
- G Natural Gas
- Gp Gypsum
- Ls Limestone
- Na Salt
- O Petroleum
- Ss Sandstone
- Major Industrial Area

Malta 802 G6
Malvern 1,112 H4
Manchester 2,223 C8
Mansfield▲ 50,627 F4
Mantua 1,178 H3
Maple Heights 27,089 H9
Marblehead 745 E2
Marengo 393 E5
Mariemont 3,118 C9
Marietta▲ 15,026 G7
Marion▲ 34,075 D4
Marseilles 130 D4
Marshall 758 C7
Marshallville 788 G4
Martin 7,990 D2
Martins Ferry 9,331 J5
Martinsburg 213 F5
Martinsville 476 C7
Marysville▲ 9,656 D5
Mason 11,452 B7
Massillon 31,007 H4
Masury 1,836 J3
Maumee 15,561 C2
Mayfield 3,462 J9
Mayfield Heights 19,847 J9
McArthur▲ 1,541 F7
McClure 781 C3
McComb 1,544 C3
McConnelsville▲ 1,804 G6
McDonald 3,526 J3
McGuffey 550 C4
Mechanicsburg 1,803 D5
Medina▲ 19,231 G3
Melrose 307 B3
Mendon 717 A4
Mentor 47,358 H2
Mentor-on-the-Lake 8,271 G2
Metamora 543 C2
Meyers Lake 493 H4
Miamisburg 17,834 B6
Middle Point 639 B4
Middleburg 14,702 C5
Middleburg Heights 16,218 G10
Middlefield 1,898 H3
Middleport 2,725 F7
Middletown 46,022 A6
Midland 319 C7
Midvale 575 H5
Mifflin 162 F4
Milan 1,464 E3
Milford 5,660 D9
Milford Center 651 D5
Millbury 1,081 D2
Milledgeville 120 C6
Miller 173 F8
Miller City 168 B3
Millersburg▲ 3,051 F4
Millersport 1,010 E6
Millville 755 A7
Milton Center 200 C3
Mineral 725 F7
Mineral City 884 H4
Minerva 4,318 H4
Minerva Park 1,463 E5
Mingo 4,297 C5
Mingo Junction 4,834 J5
Minster 2,650 B5
Mogadore 4,008 H3
Monroe 4,490 B7
Monroeville 1,381 E3
Montezuma 199 A4
Montgomery 9,753 C9
Montpelier 4,299 A2
Moraine 5,989 B6
Moreland Hills 3,354 J9
Morral 373 D4
Morristown 296 H5
Morrow 1,206 B7
Moscow 279 B8
Mount Blanchard 491 D4
Mount Carmel 4,462 C10
Mount Cory 245 C4
Mount Eaton 236 G4
Mount Gilead▲ 2,846 E4
Mount Healthy 7,580 B9
Mount Orab 1,929 C7
Mount Pleasant 498 J5
Mount Sterling 1,647 D6
Mount Vernon▲ 14,550 E5
Mount Victory 551 D4
Mowrystown 460 C7
Mulberry 2,856 B7
Munroe Falls 5,359 H3
Murray City 499 F6
Mutual 126 C5
Napoleon▲ 8,884 B3
Nashville 181 F4
Navarre 1,635 H4
Neffs 1,213 J5
Nellie 130 F5
Nelsonville 4,563 F7
Nevada 849 D4
Neville 226 B8
New Albany 1,621 E5
New Alexandria 257 J5
New Athens 370 H5
New Bloomington 282 D4
New Boston 2,717 E8
New Bremen 2,558 B5
New Carlisle 6,049 C6
New Concord 2,086 G6
New Holland 841 D6
New Knoxville 838 B5
New Lebanon 4,323 B6
New Lexington▲ 5,117 F6
New London 2,642 F3
New Madison 928 A6
New Miami 2,555 A7
New Middletown 1,912 J4
New Paris 1,801 A6
New Philadelphia▲ 15,698 G5
New Richmond 2,408 B8
New Riegel 298 D3
New Straitsville 865 F6
New Vienna 932 C7
New Washington 1,057 E4
New Waterford 1,278 J4
New Weston 148 A5
Newark▲ 44,389 F5
Newburgh Heights 2,310 H9
Newcomerstown 4,012 G5
Newton Falls 4,866 J3
Newtonsville 427 B7
Newtown 1,589 C10
Ney 331 B3
Niles 21,128 J3
North Baltimore 3,139 C3
North Bend 541 B9
North Canton 14,748 H4
North College Hill 11,002 B9
North Fairfield 504 E3
North Hampton 417 C5
North Kingsville 2,672 J2
North Lewisburg 1,160 C5
North Madison 8,699 H2
North Olmsted 34,204 G9
North Perry 824 H2
North Randall 977 H9
North Ridgeville 21,564 F3
North Robinson 216 E4
North Royalton 23,197 H10
North Star 246 A5
North Zanesville 2,121 G6
Northfield 3,624 J10
Northridge 5,939 B6
Northwood 5,506 D2
Norton 11,477 G3
Norwalk▲ 14,731 E3
Norwich 133 G6
Norwood 23,674 C9
Oak Harbor 2,637 D2
Oak Hill 1,831 E8
Oakwood 709 H9
Oakwood 886 B3
Oakwood 9,372 B6
Oberlin 8,191 F3
Obetz 3,167 E6
Ohio City 899 A4
Olmsted Falls 6,741 G9
Ontario 4,026 E4
Orange 2,810 J9
Orangeville 253 J3
Oregon 18,334 D2
Orient 273 D6
Orrville 7,712 G4
Orwell 1,258 J2
Osgood 255 A5
Ostrander 431 D5
Ottawa Hills 4,543 C2
Ottawa▲ 3,999 B3
Ottoville 842 B4
Otway 105 D8
Owensville 1,019 B7
Oxford 18,937 A6
Painesville▲ 15,699 H2
Palestine 197 A5
Pandora 1,009 C4
Parma 87,876 H9
Parma Heights 21,448 G9
Parral 255 G4
Pataskala 3,046 E5
Patterson 145 C4
Paulding▲ 2,605 A3
Payne 1,244 A3
Peebles 1,782 D8
Pemberville 1,279 C3
Peninsula 562 G3
Pepper Pike 6,185 J9
Perry 1,012 H2
Perrysburg 12,551 C2
Perrysville 691 F4
Phillipsburg 644 B6
Philo 810 G6
Pickerington 5,668 E6
Piketon 1,717 E7
Pioneer 1,287 A2
Piqua 20,612 B5
Pitsburg 425 A6
Plain City 2,278 D5
Plainfield 178 G5
Pleasant City 419 G6
Pleasant Hill 1,066 B5
Pleasant Plain 138 B7
Pleasantville 926 F6
Plymouth 1,942 E4
Poland 2,992 J3
Polk 355 F4
Pomeroy▲ 2,259 G7
Port Clinton▲ 7,106 E2
Port Jefferson 381 C5
Port Washington 513 G5
Port Wiliam 242 C6
Portage 469 C3
Portsmouth▲ 22,676 D8
Potsdam 250 B6
Powell 2,154 D5
Powhatan Point 1,807 J6
Proctorville 765 F9
Prospect 1,148 D5
Put-in-Bay 141 E2
Quaker City 560 H6
Quincy 697 C5
Racine 729 G8
Rarden 184 D8
Ravenna▲ 12,069 H3
Rawson 482 C4
Ray 490 E7
Rayland 566 J5
Reading 12,038 C9
Reminderville 2,163 J10
Republic 611 D3
Reynoldsburg 25,748 E6
Richfield 3,117 G3
Richmond (Grand River) H2
Richmond 624 J5
Richmond Heights 9,611 H9
Richwood 2,186 D5
Ridgeway 378 C4
Rio Grande 995 F8
Ripley 1,816 C8
Risingsun 659 C3
Rittman 6,147 G4
Riverlea 503 D5
Rochester 206 F3
Rock Creek 553 J2
Rockford 1,119 A4
Rocky Ridge 425 D2
Rocky River 20,410 G9
Rogers 247 J4
Rome 99 J2
Rosemount 1,926 D8
Roseville 1,847 F6
Ross 2,124 B9
Rossburg 250 A5
Rossford 5,861 C2
Roswell 257 H5
Rushsylvania 573 C5
Rushville 229 F6
Russells Point 1,504 C5
Russellville 459 C8
Russia 442 B5
Rutland 469 F7
Sabina 2,662 C7
Saint Bernard 5,344 B9
Saint Clairsville▲ 5,162 J5
Saint Henry 1,907 A5
Saint Louisville 372 F5
Saint Martin 141 C7
Saint Marys 8,441 B4
Saint Paris 1,842 C5
Salem 12,233 J4
Salineville 1,474 J4
Sandusky▲ 29,764 E3
Sarahsville 162 H6
Sardinia 792 C7
Savannah 363 F4
Scio 856 H5
Sciotodale 1,128 E8
Scott 339 A4
Seaman 1,013 C8
Sebring 4,848 H4
Senecaville 434 H6
Seven Hills 12,339 H9
Seven Mile 804 A7
Seville 1,810 G3
Shadyside 3,934 J6
Shaker Heights 30,831 H9
Sharon 13,153 G6
Sharonville 10,108 C9
Shawnee 742 F6
Shawnee Hills 423 D5
Sheffield 1,943 F3
Sheffield Lake 9,825 F3
Shelby 9,564 E4
Sherrodsville 284 H4
Sherwood 828 A3
Shiloh 778 E4
Shreve 1,584 F4
Sidney▲ 18,710 B5
Silver Lake 3,052 G3
Silverton 5,859 C9
Sinking Spring 189 D7
Smithfield 722 J5
Smithville 1,354 G4
Solon 18,548 J9
Somerset 1,390 F6
Somerville 279 A6
South Amherst 1,765 F3
South Bloomfield 900 D6
South Charleston 1,626 C6
South Euclid 23,866 H9
South Lebanon 2,696 B7
South Point 3,823 E9
South Russell 3,402 H3
South Salem 227 D7
South Solon 379 C6
South Vienna 550 C6
South Webster 806 E8
South Zanesville 1,969 F6
Sparta 201 E5
Spencer 726 F3
Spencerville 2,288 B4
Spring Valley 507 C6
Springboro 6,590 B6
Springdale 10,621 B9
Springfield▲ 70,487 C6
Steubenville▲ 22,125 J5
Stockport 462 G6
Stone Creek 181 G5
Stout 518 D8
Stoutsville 537 E6
Stow 27,702 H3
Strasburg 1,995 G4
Stratton 278 J4
Streetsboro 9,932 H3
Strongsville 35,308 G10
Struthers 12,284 J3
Stryker 1,468 B3
Sugar Grove 465 E6
Sugarcreek 2,062 G5
Summerfield 295 H6
Summitville 125 J4
Sunbury 2,046 E5
Swanton 3,557 C2
Sycamore 919 D4
Sylvania 17,301 C2
Syracuse 827 G7
Tallmadge 14,870 H3
Tarlton 315 E6
Taylorsville (Philo) G6
Terrace Park 2,133 D9
The Plains 2,644 F7
Thornville 758 F6
Thurston 539 E6
Tiffin▲ 18,604 D3
Tiltonsville 1,517 J5
Timberlake 833 J8
Tipp City 6,027 B6
Tiro 246 E4
Toledo▲ 332,943 D2
Tontogany 364 C3
Toronto 6,127 J5
Tremont City 493 C5
Trenton 6,189 B7
Trimble 441 F7
Trotwood 8,816 B6
Troy▲ 19,478 B5
Tuscarawas 826 H5
Twinsburg 9,606 J10
Uhrichsville 5,604 H5
Union 5,501 B6
Union City 1,984 A5
Uniontown 3,074 H4
Unionville 238 J2
Unionville Center 272 D5
Uniopolis 261 B4
University Heights 14,790 H9
Upper Arlington 34,128 D6
Upper Sandusky▲ 5,906 D4
Urbana▲ 11,353 C5
Urbancrest 862 D6
Utica 1,997 F5
Valley Hi 217 C5
Valley View 2,137 H9
Valley View 730 D6
Van Buren 337 C3
Van Wert▲ 10,891 A4
Vandalia 13,882 B6
Vanlue 373 C4
Venedocia 158 B4
Vermilion 11,127 F3
Verona 472 A6
Versailles 2,351 A5
Vienna 1,067 J3
Vinton 293 F8
Wadsworth 15,718 G3
Waite Hill 454 H2
Wakeman 948 F3
Walbridge 2,736 C2
Waldo 340 D5
Walton Hills 2,371 J10
Wapakoneta▲ 9,214 B4
Warren▲ 50,793 J3
Warrensville Heights 15,745 H9
Warsaw 699 G5
Washington Court House▲ 12,682 D6
Washingtonville 894 J4
Waterville 4,517 C3
Wauseon▲ 6,322 B2
Waverly▲ 4,477 D7
Wayne 803 C3
Waynesburg 1,068 H4
Waynesfield 831 C4
Waynesville 1,949 B6
Wellington 4,140 F3
Wellston 6,049 F7
Wellsville 4,532 J4
West Alexandria 1,460 A6
West Carrollton 14,403 B6
West Elkton 208 A6
West Farmington 542 J3
West Jefferson D6
West Lafayette 2,129 G5
West Leipsic 244 B3
West Liberty 1,613 C5
West Manchester 464 A6
West Mansfield 830 C5
West Millgrove 171 C3
West Milton 4,348 B6
West Portsmouth 3,551 D8
West Rushville 134 E6
West Salem 1,534 F4
West Union▲ 3,096 C8
West Unity 1,677 B2
Westerville 30,269 D5
Westfield Center 784 G3
Westlake 27,018 G9
Weston 1,716 C3
Wharton 378 D4
Wheelersburg 5,113 E8
Whitehall 20,572 E6
Whitehouse 2,528 C2
Wickliffe 14,558 J9
Wilberforce 2,639 C6
Wilkesville 151 F7
Willard 6,210 E3
Williamsburg 2,322 B7
Williamsport 851 D6
Willoughby 20,510 J8
Willoughby Hills 8,427 J9
Willowick 15,269 J8
Willshire 541 A4
Wilmington▲ 11,199 C7
Wilmot 261 G4
Wilson 136 H6
Winchester 978 C8
Windham 2,943 H3
Wintersville 4,102 J5
Withamsville 2,834 B7
Woodlawn 2,674 C9
Woodmere 834 J9
Woodsfield▲ 2,832 H6
Woodstock 296 C5
Woodville 1,953 D3
Wooster▲ 22,191 G4
Worthington 14,869 E5
Wren 190 A4
Wyoming 8,128 C9
Xenia▲ 24,664 C6
Yankee Lake 88 J3
Yellow Springs 3,973 C6
Yorkshire 126 B5
Yorkville 1,246 J5
Youngstown▲ 95,732 J3
Zaleski 294 F7
Zanesfield 183 C5
Zanesville▲ 26,778 G6
Zoar 177 H4

OTHER FEATURES

Atwood (lake) H4
Auglaize (riv.) B4
Berlin (lake) H4
Big Walnut (creek) E5
Black (riv.) F3
Black Fork, Mohican (riv.) F4
Blanchard (riv.) C4
Blennerhassett (isl.) G7
Buckeye (lake) F6
Campbell (hill) C5
Captina (creek) J6
Cedar (pt.) D2
Chagrin (riv.)
Clear Fork (res.)
Clear Fork, Mohican (riv.)
Clendening (lake)
Cuyahoga (riv.) H
Cuyahoga Valley Nat'l Rec. Area H
Darby (creek)
Deer (creek)
Deer Creek (lake)
Delaware (lake)
Dillon (lake)
Dover (lake)
Duck (creek)
Erie (lake)
Grand (riv.)
Great Miami (riv.) A
Hocking (riv.)
Hoover (res.)
Huron (riv.)
Indian (lake) C
James A. Garfield Nat'l Hist. Site G
Kelleys (isl.)
Killbuck (creek) G
Kokosing (riv.)
Leesville (lake)
Licking (riv.)
Little Beaver (creek)
Little Miami (riv.) E
Little Miami, East Fork (riv.) C
Little Muskingum (riv.)
Loramie (lake)
Mad (riv.) C
Maumee (bay) D
Maumee (riv.) A
Middle Bass (isl.)
Mohican (riv.)
Mosquito Creek (lake)
Mound City Group Nat'l Mon.
Muskingum (riv.) G
North Bass (isl.)
Ohio (riv.) B
Ohio Brush (creek) D
Olentangy (riv.) D
Paint (creek) D
Perry's Victory and Int'l Peace Mem.
Piedmont (lake)
Portage (riv.) D
Pymatuning (res.)
Raccoon (creek)
Rattlesnake (creek) C
Rickenbacker A.F.B.
Rocky (riv.) G
Rocky Fork (lake) D
Saint Joseph (riv.) A
Saint Marys (lake) A
Saint Marys (riv.) A
Salt Fork (creek)
Sandusky (bay)
Sandusky (riv.) D
Scioto (riv.) D
Senecaville (lake)
Sevenmile (creek) A
South Bass (isl.)
Stillwater (riv.) B
Symmes (creek)
Tappan (lake)
Tiffin (riv.) B
Tuscarawas (riv.)
Vermilion (riv.)
Wabash (riv.) A
West Sister (isl.) D
Whiteoak (creek) C
William H. Taft Nat'l Hist. Site C1
Wills (creek) G
Wills Creek (lake) G
Wright-Patterson A.F.B. 8,579 B
Yellow (creek)

▲County seat

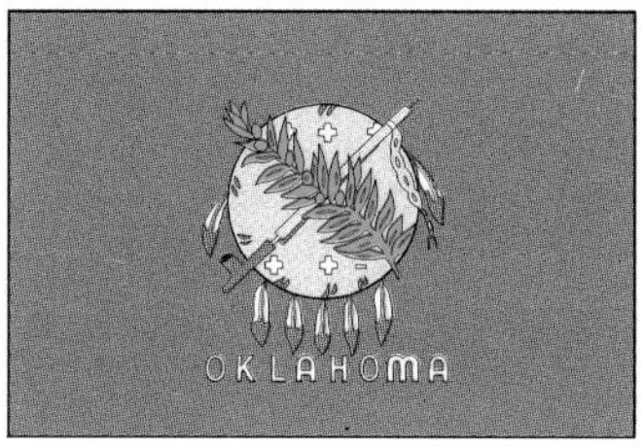

AREA 69,956 sq. mi. (181,186 sq. km.)
POPULATION 3,157,604
CAPITAL Oklahoma City
LARGEST CITY Oklahoma City
HIGHEST POINT Black Mesa 4,973 ft. (1516 m.)
SETTLED IN 1889
ADMITTED TO UNION November 16, 1907
POPULAR NAME Sooner State
STATE FLOWER Mistletoe
STATE BIRD Scissor-tailed Flycatcher

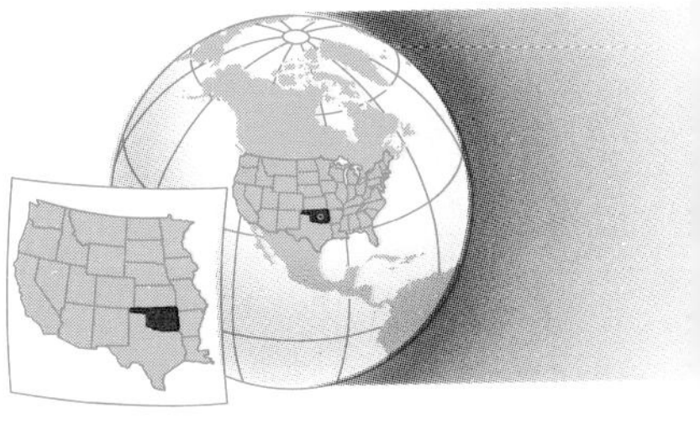

COUNTIES

air 18,421 ... S3
alfa 6,416 ... K1
oka 12,778 ... O6
aver 6,023 ... E1
ckham 18,812 ... G4
aine 11,470 ... K3
yan 32,089 ... O7
ddo 29,550 ... K4
nadian 74,409 ... K3
rter 42,919 ... M6
erokee 34,049 ... R3
octaw 15,302 ... P6
marron 3,301 ... A1
eveland 174,253 ... M4
al 5,780 ... O5
manche 111,486 ... K5
tton 6,651 ... K6
aig 14,104 ... R1
eek 60,915 ... O3
ster 26,897 ... H3
laware 28,070 ... S2
wey 5,551 ... H2
is 4,497 ... G2
rfield 56,735 ... L2
rvin 26,605 ... M5
ady 41,747 ... L5
ant 5,689 ... L1
eer 6,559 ... G5
rmon 3,793 ... G5
rper 4,063 ... G1
skell 10,940 ... R4
ghes 13,023 ... O4
ckson 28,764 ... H5
fferson 7,010 ... L6
hnston 10,032 ... N6
y 48,056 ... M1
ngfisher 13,212 ... L3
owa 11,347 ... J5
timer 10,333 ... R5
Flore 43,270 ... S5
ncoln 29,216 ... N3
gan 29,011 ... M3
ve 8,157 ... M7
ajor 8,055 ... K2
arshall 10,829 ... N6
ayes 33,366 ... R2
cClain 22,795 ... L5
McCurtain 33,433 ... S6
McIntosh 16,779 ... P4
Murray 12,042 ... M6
Muskogee 68,078 ... R3
Noble 11,045 ... M2
Nowata 9,992 ... P1
Okfuskee 11,551 ... O3
Oklahoma 599,611 ... M3
Okmulgee 36,490 ... P3
Osage 41,645 ... O1
Ottawa 30,561 ... S1
Pawnee 15,575 ... N2
Payne 61,507 ... N2
Pittsburg 40,581 ... P5
Pontotoc 34,119 ... N5
Pottawatomie 58,760 ... N4
Pushmataha 10,997 ... R6
Roger Mills 4,147 ... G3
Rogers 55,170 ... P2
Seminole 25,412 ... N4
Sequoyah 33,828 ... S3
Stephens 42,299 ... L6
Texas 16,419 ... C1
Tillman 10,384 ... J6
Tulsa 503,341 ... P2
Wagoner 47,883 ... P3
Washington 48,066 ... P1
Washita 11,441 ... J4
Woods 9,103 ... J1
Woodward 18,976 ... H2

CITIES and TOWNS

Achille 491 ... O7
Ada▲ 15,820 ... N5
Adair 685 ... R2
Adams 150 ... D1
Adamson 150 ... P5
Addington 100 ... L6
Afton 915 ... S1
Agra 334 ... N3
Akins 250 ... S3
Albany 65 ... O7
Albert 100 ... K4
Albion 88 ... R5
Alderson 395 ... P5
Alex 639 ... L5
Alfalfa 70 ... J4
Aline 295 ... K1
Allen 972 ... O5
Altus▲ 21,910 ... H5
Alva▲ 5,495 ... J1
Amber 418 ... L4
Ames 268 ... K2
Amorita 56 ... K1
Anadarko▲ 6,586 ... K4
Antlers▲ 2,524 ... P6
Apache 1,591 ... K5
Apperson 30 ... N1
Aqua Park ... R3
Arapaho▲ 802 ... H3
Arcadia 320 ... M3
Ardmore▲ 23,079 ... M6
Arkoma 2,393 ... T4
Arnett▲ 547 ... G2
Asher 449 ... N5
Ashland 56 ... O5
Atoka▲ 3,298 ... O6
Atwood 225 ... O5
Avant 369 ... O2
Avard 37 ... J1
Avery 35 ... N3
Bache 100 ... P5
Bacone 786 ... R3
Baker 70 ... D1
Balko 100 ... E1
Barnsdall 1,316 ... O1
Baron 300 ... S3
Bartlesville▲ 34,256 ... O1
Battiest 250 ... S6
Bearden 142 ... O4
Beaver▲ 1,584 ... F1
Beggs 1,150 ... P3
Belzoni 50 ... R6
Bengal 300 ... R5
Bennington 251 ... P7
Bentley 75 ... O6
Berlin 50 ... G4
Bernice 330 ... S1
Bessie 248 ... H4
Bethany 20,075 ... L3
Bethel 2,505 ... S6
Bethel Acres 2,314 ... M4
Big Cabin 271 ... R1
Billings 555 ... M1
Binger 724 ... K4
Bison 103 ... L2
Bixby 9,502 ... P3
Blackburn 110 ... N2
Blackgum 150 ... S3
Blackwell 7,538 ... M1
Blair 922 ... H5
Blanchard 1,922 ... L4
Blanco 215 ... P5
Blocker 135 ... P4
Blue 175 ... O7
Bluejacket 247 ... R1
Boggy Depot 100 ... O6
Boise City▲ 1,509 ... B1
Bokchito 576 ... O6
Bokhoma 35 ... S7
Bokoshe 403 ... S4
Boley 908 ... O4
Boswell 643 ... P6
Bowlegs 398 ... N4
Bowring 115 ... O1
Boyd 10 ... E1
Boynton 391 ... P3
Braden 15 ... S4
Bradley 166 ... L5
Braggs 308 ... R3
Braman 251 ... M1
Bray 925 ... L5
Breckinridge 261 ... L2
Briartown 55 ... R4
Bridgeport 137 ... K3
Brinkman ... G4
Bristow 4,062 ... O3
Broken Arrow 58,043 ... P2
Broken Bow 3,961 ... S7
Bromide 162 ... N6
Brooksville 69 ... M4
Bryant 74 ... P4
Buffalo▲ 1,312 ... G1
Bunch 64 ... S3
Burbank 165 ... N1
Burlington 169 ... K1
Burneyville 150 ... M7
Burns Flat 1,027 ... H4
Butler 341 ... H3
Byars 263 ... N5
Byng 755 ... N5
Byron 57 ... K1
Cache 2,251 ... J5
Caddo 918 ... O6
Cairo 50 ... O5
Calera 1,536 ... O7
Calumet 560 ... K3
Calvin 251 ... O5
Camargo 185 ... H2
Cameron 327 ... T4
Canadian 261 ... P4
Canadian City ... L4
Caney 184 ... O6
Canton 632 ... J2
Canute 538 ... H4
Capron 38 ... J1
Cardin 165 ... S1
Carmen 459 ... J1
Carnegie 1,593 ... J4
Carney 558 ... N3
Carrier 171 ... K2
Carter 286 ... H4
Cartersville 79 ... S4
Cashion 430 ... L3
Castle 94 ... O4
Catoosa 2,954 ... P2
Cement 642 ... K5
Center 100 ... N5
Centrahoma 106 ... O5
Centralia ... R1
Chandler▲ 2,596 ... N3
Chattanooga 437 ... J6
Checotah 3,290 ... R4
Chelsea 1,620 ... P1
Cherokee▲ 1,787 ... K1
Chester 104 ... J2
Cheyenne▲ 948 ... G3
Chickasha▲ 14,988 ... L4
Chilocco 400 ... M1
Choctaw 8,545 ... M3
Chouteau 1,771 ... R2
Christie 375 ... S3
Cimarron 71 ... L3
Claremore▲ 13,280 ... R2
Clarita 72 ... O6
Clayton 636 ... R5
Clearview 47 ... O4
Clemscot 52 ... L6
Cleo Springs 359 ... K2
Cleora 45 ... S1
Cleveland 3,156 ... O2
Clinton 9,298 ... H3
Cloud Chief 12 ... J4
Cloudy 175 ... R6
Coalgate▲ 1,895 ... O5
Cogar 40 ... K4
Colbert 1,043 ... O7
Colcord 628 ... S2
Cold Springs 24 ... J5
Cole 355 ... L4
Coleman 200 ... O6
Collinsville 3,612 ... P2
Colony 163 ... J4
Comanche 1,695 ... L6
Commerce 2,426 ... R1
Concho 300 ... L3
Connerville 150 ... N6
Cooperton 15 ... J5
Copan 809 ... P1
Cordell▲ ... H4
Corinne 100 ... R6
Corn 548 ... J4
Cornish 164 ... L6
Council Hill 139 ... P3
Countyline 550 ... L6
Courtney 12 ... L7
Covington 590 ... L2
Coweta 6,159 ... P3
Cowlington 756 ... S4
Cox City 285 ... L5
Coyle 289 ... M3
Crawford 53 ... G3
Crescent 1,236 ... L3
Cromwell 268 ... N4
Crowder 339 ... P4
Cumberland 100 ... N6
Curtis 30 ... H2
Cushing 7,218 ... N3
Custer City 443 ... J3
Cyril 1,072 ... K5
Dacoma 182 ... J1
Daisy 250 ... P5
Dale 160 ... M4
Darwin 50 ... P6
Davenport 979 ... N3
Davidson 473 ... J6
Davis 2,543 ... M5
Deer Creek 124 ... L1
Del City 23,928 ... L4
Dela 434 ... P6
Delaware 544 ... P1
Delhi 41 ... G4
Depew 502 ... O3
Devol 165 ... J6
Dewar 921 ... P4
Dewey 3,326 ... P1
Dibble 181 ... L4
Dickson 942 ... M6
Dill City 622 ... H4
Disney 257 ... S2
Dougherty 138 ... M6
Douglas 55 ... L2
Douthat 30 ... S1
Dover 376 ... L3
Dow 300 ... P5
Driftwood ... K1
Drummond 408 ... L2
Drumright 2,799 ... N3
Duke (E. Duke) 360 ... G5
Duncan▲ 21,732 ... L5
Durant▲ 12,823 ... O6
Durham 30 ... G3
Dustin 429 ... O4
Eagle City 56 ... J3
Eagletown 650 ... S6
Eakly 277 ... K4
Earlsboro 535 ... N4
Edmond 52,315 ... M3
El Reno▲ 15,414 ... K3
Eldorado 573 ... G6
Elgin 975 ... K5
Elk City 10,428 ... G4
Elmer 132 ... H6
Elmore City 493 ... M5
Elmwood 300 ... F1
Empire City 219 ... L6
Enid▲ 45,309 ... L2
Enterprise 130 ... R4
Erick 1,083 ... G4
Eucha 210 ... S2
Eufaula▲ 2,652 ... P4
Fair Oaks 1,133 ... P2
Fairfax 1,749 ... N1
Fairland 916 ... S1
Fairmont 129 ... L2
Fairview▲ 2,936 ... J2
Fallis 49 ... M3
Fanshawe 331 ... S5
Fargo 299 ... G2
Farris 100 ... P6
Faxon 127 ... J6
Fay 140 ... J3
Featherston 75 ... P4
Felt 120 ... A1
Fillmore 60 ... N6
Finley 350 ... R6
Fittstown 500 ... N5
Fitzhugh 196 ... N5
Fleetwood 12 ... L7
Fletcher 1,002 ... K5
Foraker 25 ... O1
Forest Park 1,249 ... M3
Forgan 489 ... E1
Fort Cobb 663 ... K4
Fort Gibson 3,359 ... R3
Fort Supply 369 ... G1
Fort Towson 568 ... R7
Foss 148 ... H4
Foster 100 ... M5
Fox 400 ... M6
Foyil 86 ... R2
Francis 346 ... N5
Frederick▲ 5,221 ... H6
Freedom 264 ... H1
Gage 473 ... G2
Gans 218 ... S4
Garber 959 ... M2
Garvin 128 ... S7
Gate 159 ... F1
Geary 1,347 ... K3
Gene Autry 97 ... N6
Geronimo 990 ... K6
Gerty 95 ... O5
Glencoe 473 ... M2
Glenpool 6,688 ... P3
Glover 244 ... S6
Golden 300 ... S6
Goldsby 816 ... L4
Goltry 297 ... K1
Goodwater 240 ... S7
Goodwell 1,065 ... C1
Gore 690 ... R3
Gotebo 370 ... J4
Gould 237 ... G5
Gowen 75 ... R5
Gracemont 339 ... K4
Grady 85 ... L6
Graham 200 ... M6
Grainola 58 ... N1
Grand Lake Towne 58 ... S1
Grandfield 1,224 ... J6
Granite 1,844 ... H5
Grant ... R7
Gray Horse 60 ... N1
Grayson 66 ... P3
Greenfield 200 ... K3
Griggs 15 ... B1
Grove 4,020 ... S1
Guthrie▲ 10,518 ... M3
Guymon▲ 7,803 ... D1
Haileyville 918 ... P5
Hall Park 1,090 ... M4
Hallett 159 ... N2
Hammon 611 ... H3
Hanna 99 ... P4
Hanson 250 ... S4
Harden City 250 ... N5
Hardesty 228 ... D1
Hardy ... N1
Harjo 35 ... N4
Harmon 27 ... G2
Harrah 4,206 ... M4
Harris 192 ... S7
Hartshorne 2,120 ... R5
Haskell 2,143 ... P3
Hastings 164 ... K6
Haworth 293 ... S7
Haywood 175 ... P5
Headrick 183 ... H5
Healdton 2,872 ... M6
Heavener 2,601 ... S5
Helena 1,043 ... K1
Hendrix 108 ... O7
Hennepin 300 ... M5
Hennessey 1,902 ... L2
Henryetta 5,872 ... O4
Herd 18 ... O1
Hess 29 ... H6
Hester 25 ... H5
Hickory 77 ... N5
Hillsdale 96 ... K1
Hinton 1,233 ... K4
Hitchcock 139 ... K3
Hitchita 118 ... P3
Hobart▲ 4,305 ... J5
Hockerville 125 ... S1
Hodgen 150 ... S5
Hoffman 175 ... P4
Holdenville▲ 4,792 ... O4
Hollis▲ 2,584 ... G5
Hollister 59 ... J6
Homestead 35 ... K2
Hominy 2,342 ... O2
Honobia 80 ... R5
Hooker 1,551 ... D1
Hoot Owl 5 ... R2
Hopeton 42 ... J1
Howe 510 ... S5
Hoyt 160 ... R4
Hugo▲ 5,978 ... P7
Hulah 50 ... O1
Hulbert 499 ... R3
Humphreys 68 ... H5
Hunter 218 ... L1
Hydro 977 ... J3
Idabel▲ 6,957 ... S7
Indiahoma 337 ... J5

(continued on following page)

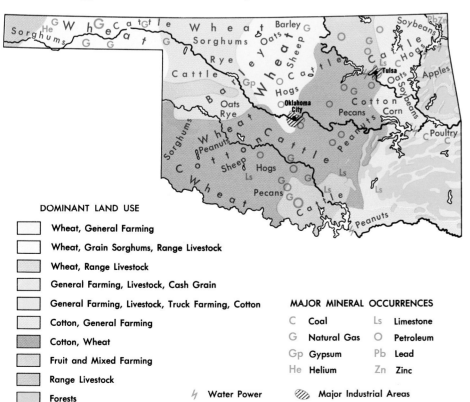

Agriculture, Industry and Resources

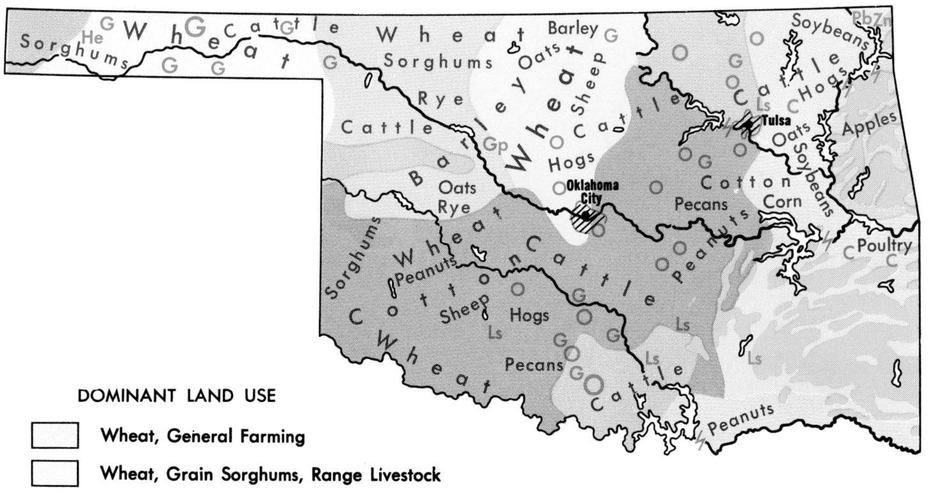

DOMINANT LAND USE

- Wheat, General Farming
- Wheat, Grain Sorghums, Range Livestock
- Wheat, Range Livestock
- General Farming, Livestock, Cash Grain
- General Farming, Livestock, Truck Farming, Cotton
- Cotton, General Farming
- Cotton, Wheat
- Fruit and Mixed Farming
- Range Livestock
- Forests

MAJOR MINERAL OCCURRENCES

C	Coal	Ls	Limestone
G	Natural Gas	O	Petroleum
Gp	Gypsum	Pb	Lead
He	Helium	Zn	Zinc

Water Power

Major Industrial Areas

Oklahoma

SCALE
0 5 10 20 30 40 MI.
0 5 10 20 30 40 KM.

State Capitals..........⊛
County Seats..........◉
Major Limited Access Hwys._____

Scale 1:2,040,000

® Copyright HAMMOND INCORPORATED, Maplewood, N.J.

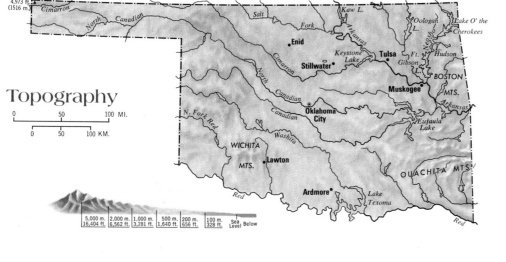

Topography

0 50 100 MI.
0 50 100 KM.

5,000 m. | 2,000 m. | 1,000 m. | 500 m. | 200 m. | 100 m. | Sea
16,404 ft. | 6,562 ft. | 3,281 ft. | 1,640 ft. | 656 ft. | 328 ft. | Level | Below

Slick 124...........O3
Smithville 111........S6
Snow 200...........R6
Snyder 1,619........J5
Soper 305...........P6
South Coffeyville 791...P1
Southard 130........K2
Sparks 202..........N3
Spavinaw 432........R2
Spencer 3,972.......M3
Spencerville 275......R6
Sperry 937..........P2
Spiro 2,146.........S4
Springer 485........M6
Stafford 18.........H3
Stanley 30..........R5
Sterling 684........K5
Stidham 48..........P4
Stigler▲ 2,574......R4
Stillwater▲ 36,676...N2
Stilwell▲ 2,663......S3
Stonebluff 50........P3
Stonewall 519........O5
Strang 141..........O3
Stratford 1,404......M5
Stringtown 366.......P6
Strong City 49.......G3
Stroud 2,666........N3
Stuart 228..........O5
Sugden 65...........L6
Sulphur▲ 4,824......N5
Summerfield 150......S5
Sweetwater 85........G4
Swink...............R6

Tabler 28...........L4
Taft 400............R3
Tahlequah▲ 10,398...R3
Talala 206..........P1
Talihina 1,297.......S5
Taloga▲ 415.........J2
Tamaha 188.........S4
Tatums 176.........M6
Tecumseh 5,750......N4
Temple 1,223........K6
Terlton 121.........O2
Terral 469..........L7
Texhoma 746........C1
Texola 45...........G4
Thackerville 290......M7
Thomas 1,246.......J3
Tiawah 125.........P2
Tipton 1,043.........H6
Tishomingo▲ 3,116...N6
Tom 60.............O3
Tonkawa 3,127......M1
Tribbey 288.........M4
Trousdale 38........M4
Troy 92............N6
Trpin 450...........E1
Tryon 514...........N3
Tullahassee 92.......P3
Tulsa▲ 367,302......O2
Tupelo 323..........O5
Tushka 256..........O6
Tuskahoma 168.......R5
Tussy 150...........L6

Tuttle 2,807.........L4
Tyrone 880..........D1
Union City 1,000.....L4
Utica 38............O7
Valley Brook 744.....M4
Valliant 873.........R6
Vanoss 130.........N5
Velma 661..........M6
Vera 167............P2
Verden 546..........K4
Verdigris 150........P2
Vernon 100..........P4
Vian 1,414..........S4
Vici 751............H2
Vinita▲ 5,804........R1
Vinson 42...........G5
Wade 50............O7
Wagoner▲ 6,894......R3
Wainwright 223.......R3
Wakita 453..........L1
Walters▲ 2,519......K6
Wanette 346.........M5
Wann 126...........P1
Wapanucka 402.......N6
Wardville 52.........P5
Warner 1,479........R4
Warr Acres 9,288.....L3
Warwick 160.........M3
Washington 279......M4
Washita 180.........K4
Watova 35...........P1
Watson 48..........S6
Watts 303...........S2

Waukomis 1,322......K2
Waurika▲ 2,088......L6
Wayne 519..........M5
Waynoka 947........J1
Weatherford 10,124...J4
Weathers 100........P5
Webb City 99........N1
Webbers Falls 722....R3
Welch 499...........R1
Weleetka 1,112.......O4
Welling 115..........S3
Wellston 912.........M3
Welty 80............O3
West Siloam Springs 539..S2
Westport 326........O2
Westville 1,374......S2
Wetumka 1,427......O4
Wewoka▲ 4,050......O4
White Oak 200.......R1
Whitefield 253.......R4
Whitesboro 450......S5
Wilburton▲ 3,092....R5
Williams 110........T4
Willis 250...........N7
Willow 142..........G4
Wilson 1,639........M6
Wirt 350............L6
Wister 956..........R5
Wolco 14...........O1
Wolf 200............N4
Woodford 50........M6
Woodville 31........N7
Woodward▲ 12,340...H2
Wright City 836......R6

Wyandotte 366.......S1
Wynnewood 2,451....M5
Wynona 531.........O1
Yale 1,392..........N2
Yanush 123..........R5
Yeager 40...........O4
Yuba 63............O7
Yukon 20,935.......L3

OTHER FEATURES

Altus (res.)..........H5
Altus A.F.B..........H5
Arbuckles, Lake of the (lake)..M6
Arbuckle Nat'l Rec. Area...N6
Arkansas (riv.).......S4
Atoka (res.).........P5
Beaver (creek).......K6
Beaver (riv.)........F1
Bird (creek).........O1
Black Bear (creek)....M2
Black Mesa (mt.).....A1
Blue (riv.)..........O6
Bluestem (lake)......O1
Boston (mts.)........S3
Broken Bow (lake)....S6
Cache (creek).......K6
Canadian (riv.)......O4
Caney (riv.)........O1
Canton (lake)........J2
Carl Blackwell (lake)..M2
Cherokees, Lake O'The (lake)..S1
Chickasaw Nat'l Rec. Area..N6
Chickasha (lake)......K4

Cimarron (riv.).......N2
Clear Boggy (creek)...O6
Deep Fork, North
 (Canadian) (riv.).....N3
Denison (dam)........M7
Elk (creek)..........H4
Ellsworth (lake)......L4
Eucha (lake).........S2
Eufaula (lake)........P4
Fort Cobb (res.)......J4
Fort Gibson (res.)....R2
Fort Sill 12,107......K5
Fort Supply (lake)....G1
Foss (res.)..........H4
Great Salt Plains (lake)..K1
Heyburn (res.).......O3
Hudson (lake)........R2
Hugo (lake).........R6
Hulah (lake).........O1
Illinois (riv.).......S3
Jackfork (mt.).......P5
Kaw (lake)..........N1
Kerr, Robert S. (res.)..S4
Keystone (lake)......O2
Kiamichi (mts.)......R6
Kiamichi (riv.).......R6
Kiowa (creek)........F1
Lawtonka (lake)......K5
Little (riv.)..........R6
McAlester (lake)......P4
Mountain Fork (riv.)...S6
Mud (creek).........L6
Muddy Boggy (creek)..O5
Murray (lake)........M6

Neosho (riv.).......R1
North Canadian (riv.)..K3
North Carrizo (riv.)...A1
Oologah (lake).......P1
Optima (lake)........D1
Osage Ind. Res.......O1
Ouachita (mts.)......R5
Pine Creek (lake).....R6
Poteau (riv.)........S5
Prairie Dog Town Fork
 Red (riv.)..........F5
Red (riv.)..........R7
Red, North Fork (riv.)..H4
Salt Fork, Arkansas (riv.)..J1
Salt Fork, Red (riv.)..G5
Sans Bois (mts.)......R4
Scott (mt.).........K5
Spavinaw (lake)......S2
Tenkiller Ferry (lake)..S3
Texoma (lake).......M7
Thunderbird (lake)....M4
Tinker A.F.B.........M4
Tom Steed (res.).....J5
Vance A.F.B..........K2
Verdigris (riv.)......P2
Washita (riv.).......M5
Waurika (lake).......K6
Webbers Falls (res.)..R3
Wichita (mts.).......J5
Wildhorse (creek).....L5
Wister (lake)........R5
Wolf (creek).........G2

▲County seat.

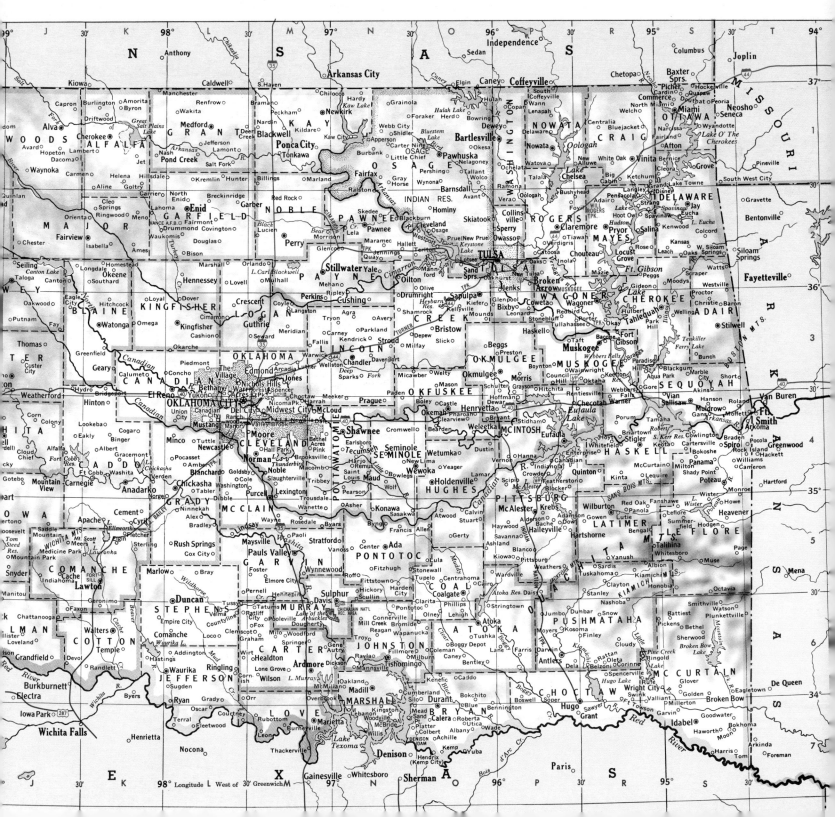

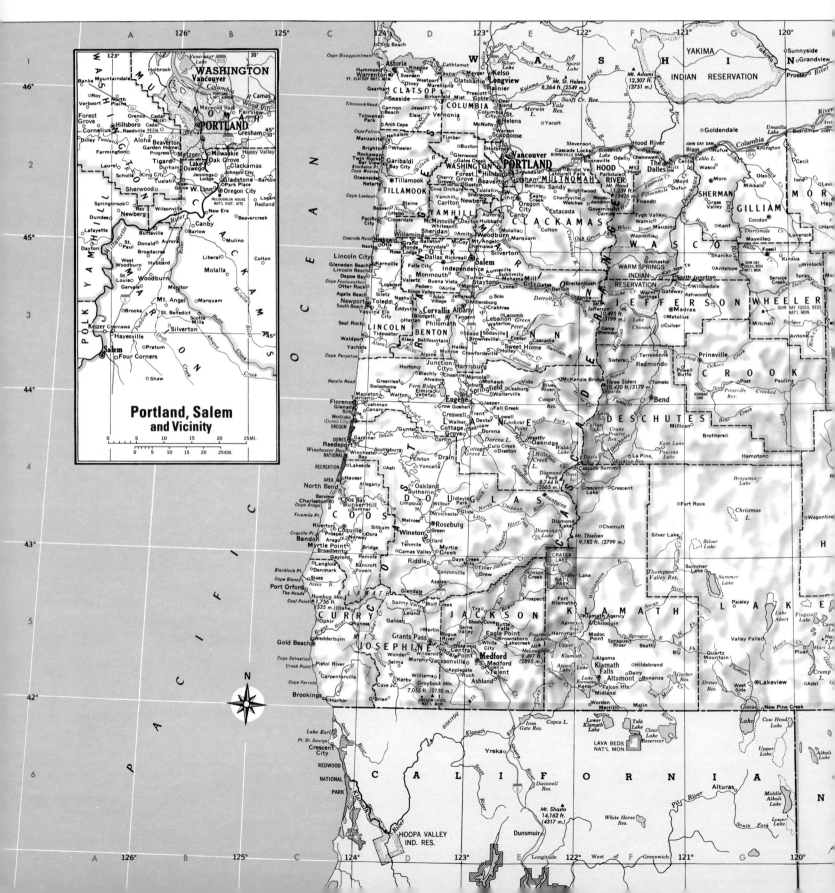

Portland, Salem and Vicinity

STATE OF OREGON
1859

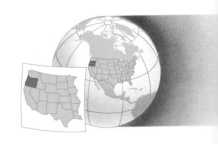

AREA 97,073 sq. mi. (251,419 sq. km.)
POPULATION 2,853,733
CAPITAL Salem
LARGEST CITY Portland
HIGHEST POINT Mt. Hood 11,239 ft.
(3426 m.)
SETTLED IN 1810
ADMITTED TO UNION February 14, 1859
POPULAR NAME Beaver State
STATE FLOWER Oregon Grape
STATE BIRD Western Meadowlark

Crabtree 200		E3
Crane 84		J4
Crater Lake 36		E5
Crawfordsville 350		E3
Crescent 750		F4
Crescent Lake 120		F4
Creswell 2,431		D4
Crow 200		D4
Culp Creek 600		E4
Culver 570		F3
Curtin 350		D4
Cushman 175		D4
Dairy 80		F5
Dale 85		J3
Dallas▲ 9,422		D3
Dalles, The▲ 11,060		F2
Danner 12		K5
Days Creek 550		D5
Dayton 1,526		A3
Dayville 144		H3
Deer Island 225		E2
Denmark 15		C5
Depoe Bay 870		C3
Detroit 331		E3

Dexter 500		E4
Diamond 6		J4
Diamond Lake 56		E4
Dillard 602		D4
Dilley 250		A2
Disston 123		E4
Donald 316		A3
Dora 100		D4
Dorena 200		E4
Drain 1,011		D4
Drew 60		E5
Drewsey		J4
Dufur 527		F2
Dundee 1,663		A2
Dunes City (Westlake)		C4
Durham 748		A2
Durkee 158		K3
Eagle Creek 250		E2
Eagle Point 3,008		E5
Echo 499		H2
Eddyville 564		D3
Elgin 1,586		K2
Elk City 30		D3
Elkton 172		D4

Topography

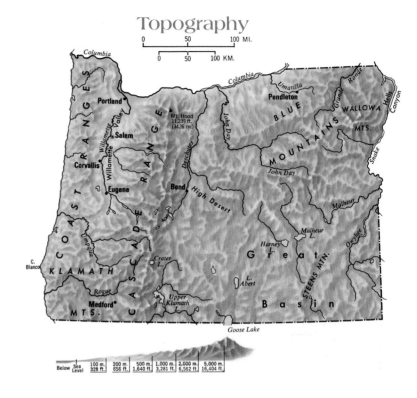

0   50   100 MI.
0   50   100 KM.

Below Sea Level | 100 m. 328 ft. | 200 m. 656 ft. | 500 m. 1,640 ft. | 1,000 m. 3,281 ft. | 2,000 m. 6,562 ft. | 5,000 m. 16,404 ft.

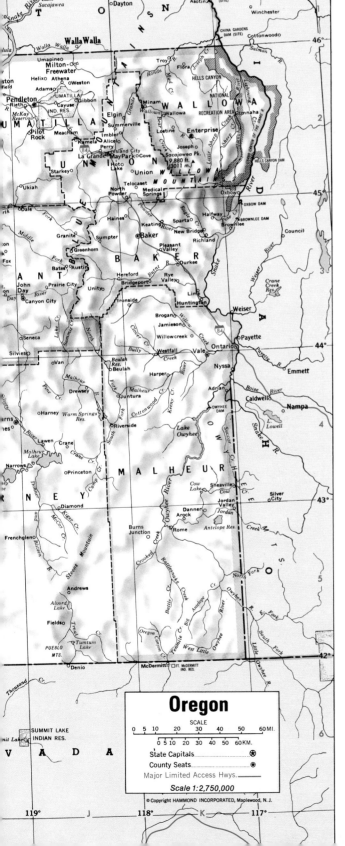

Oregon

SCALE
0 5 10   20   30   40   50   60 MI.
0 5 10   20   30   40   50   60 KM.

⊛ State Capitals
⊚ County Seats
— Major Limited Access Hwys.

Scale 1:2,750,000

© Copyright HAMMOND INCORPORATED, Maplewood, N.J.

Elmira 900		D3
Elsie 30		D2
Enterprise▲ 1,905		K2
Estacada 1,419		E2
Eugene▲ 112,669		D3
Fairview 2,391		B2
Falcon Heights		F5
Fall Creek 58		E4
Falls City 818		D3
Farmington 100		A2
Fields 150		J5
Flora 45		K2
Florence 5,162		C4
Forest Grove 13,559		A2
Fort Klamath 200		E5
Fort Rock 150		G4
Fossil▲ 399		G2
Foster 850		E3
Four Corners 12,156		A3
Fox 30		H3
Frenchglen 45		H5
Fruitdale-Harbeck 4,733		D5
Gales Creek 150		A2
Galice 30		D5
Garden Home-Whitford 6,652		A2
Gardiner 750		C4
Garibaldi 877		D2
Gaston 563		D2
Gates 499		E3
Gateway 108		F3
Gaylord 80		C5
Gearhart 1,027		C1
Gervais 992		A3
Gibbon 100		J2
Gladstone 10,152		B2
Glenada 300		C4
Glendale 707		D5
Gleneden Beach 400		C3
Glenwood 225		D2
Glide 470		D4
Goble 108		E1
Gold Beach▲ 1,546		C5
Gold Hill 964		D5
Goshen 200		D4
Government Camp 230		F2
Grand Ronde 289		D3
Granite 8		J3
Grants Pass▲ 17,488		D5
Grass Valley 160		G2
Green 5,076		D4
Greenhorn 0		J3
Greenleaf 60		D3
Gresham 68,235		B2
Gunter 8		D4
Haines 405		J3
Halfway 311		K3
Halsey 667		D3
Hamilton 12		H3
Hammond 589		C1

Hampton 24		G4
Happy Valley 1,519		B2
Harbor 2,143		C5
Hardman		H2
Harlan 200		D3
Harper 400		K4
Harney 15		J4
Harriman 250		E5
Harrisburg 1,939		D3
Hauser 400		C4
Hayesville 14,318		A3
Heppner▲ 1,412		H2
Hereford 128		K3
Hermiston 10,040		H2
Hildebrand 50		F5
Hillsboro▲ 37,520		A2
Hines 1,452		H4
Holbrook 494		A1
Holley 75		E3
Hood River▲ 4,632		F2
Horton 75		D3
Hubbard 1,881		A3
Huntington 522		K3
Idanha 289		E3
Idleyld Park 300		D4
Illahe 30		C5
Imbler 299		J2
Imnaha 150		L2
Independence 4,425		D3
Ione 255		H2
Ironside 50		K3
Irrigon 737		H2
Island City 696		K2
Jacksonville 1,896		D5
Jamieson 120		K3
Jasper 231		E3
Jefferson 1,805		D3
Jennings Lodge 6,530		B2
Jewell 10		D2
John Day 2,012		J3
Johnson City 586		B2
Jordan Valley 364		K5
Joseph 1,073		K2
Junction City 3,670		D3
Juntura		K4
Kah-Nee-Ta 100		F3
Kamela 11		J2
Keizer 21,884		A3
Keno 500		F5
Kent 200		G2
Kerby 650		D5
Kernville 450		C3
Kimberly 14		H3
King City 2,060		A2
Kings Valley 50		D3
Klamath Agency 10		F5
Klamath Falls▲ 17,737		F5

Knappa 950		D1
La Grande▲ 11,766		J2
La Pine 850		F4
Lacomb 425		E3
Lafayette 1,292		A2
Lake Oswego 30,576		B2
Lakecreek 160		E5
Lakeside 1,437		C4
Lakeview▲ 2,526		G5
Langlois 150		C5
Latourell Falls 40		E2
Lawen 95		J4
Leaburg 150		E3
Lebanon 10,950		E3
Leland 70		D5
Lexington 286		H2
Liberal 300		B3
Lime 25		K3
Lincoln Beach 1,507		C3
Lincoln City 5,892		C3
Logan 80		B2
Logsden 55		D3
Lonerock 11		H2
Long Creek 249		H3
Lostine 231		K2
Lowell 785		E4
Lyons 938		E3
Madras▲ 3,443		F3
Malin 725		F5
Manzanita 513		C2
Mapleton 950		C3
Marcola 900		E3
Marion 300		D3
Marquam 40		B3
Marshland 30		D1
Maupin 456		F2
May Park		J2
Mayger 35		D1
Maywood Park 781		B2
McCoy 40		D2
McKenzie Bridge 500		E3
McMinnville▲ 17,894		D2
McNary 330		H2
McNulty 1,805		B2
Meacham 150		J2
Medford▲ 46,951		E5
Mehama 250		E3
Melrose 30		D4
Merlin 500		D5
Merrill 837		F5
Metolius 450		F3
Metzger 3,149		A2
Midland 520		F5
Mikkalo 40		G2
Mill City 1,555		E3
Millersburg 715		D3
Milo 600		E5
Milton-Freewater 5,533		J2

Milwaukie 18,692		B2
Mist 40		D1
Mitchell 163		G3
Modoc Point 65		F5
Mohawk 50		E3
Molalla 3,651		B3
Monitor 82		B3
Monmouth 6,288		D3
Monroe 448		D3
Monument 162		H3
Moro▲ 292		G2
Mosier 244		F2
Mount Angel 2,778		B3
Mount Hood 2,234		F2
Mount Vernon 538		H3
Mountaindale 25		A1
Mulino 720		B2
Murphy 50		D5
Myrtle Creek 3,063		D4
Myrtle Point 2,712		C4
Nashville 23		D3
Nehalem 232		D2
Neotsu 300		C3
Neskowin 250		D2
Netarts 975		C2
New Bridge 28		K3
New Era 27		B2
New Pine Creek 400		G5
Newberg 13,086		A2
Newport▲ 8,437		C3
North Bend 9,614		C4
North Plains 972		A2
North Powder 448		K2
Norway 50		C4
Nyssa 2,629		K4
O'Brien 850		D5
Oak Grove 12,576		B2
Oakland 844		D4
Oakridge 3,063		E4
Oceanside 300		C2
Odell 450		F2
Olex 40		G2
Olney 75		D1
Ontario 9,392		K4
Ophir 275		C5
Oregon City▲ 14,698		B2
Orenco 220		A2
Otis 200		D2
Otter Rock 450		C3
Oxbow 100		L2
Pacific City 500		C2
Paisley 353		G5
Park Place 500		B2
Parkdale 350		F2
Paulina 80		G3
Pecuee 45		D3
Pendleton▲ 15,126		J2
Perry 50		J2
Perrydale 200		D2

(continued on following page)

Agriculture, Industry and Resources

DOMINANT LAND USE

- Specialized Wheat
- Wheat, Peas
- Specialized Dairy
- Dairy, Poultry, Mixed Farming
- Fruit and Mixed Farming
- Potatoes, General Farming
- General Farming, Dairy, Hay, Sugar Beets
- General Farming, Livestock, Special Crops
- Range Livestock
- Forests
- Nonagricultural Land

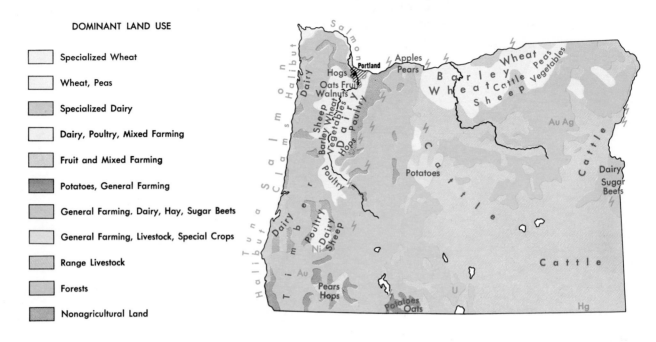

MAJOR MINERAL OCCURRENCES

Ag Silver   Hg Mercury
Au Gold   Ni Nickel
U Uranium

⚡ Water Power
▨ Major Industrial Areas

DOMINANT LAND USE

- Specialized Dairy
- Dairy, General Farming
- Fruit and Mixed Farming
- Fruit, Truck and Mixed Farming
- General Farming, Livestock, Tobacco
- General Farming, Livestock, Fruit, Tobacco
- Forests
- Urban Areas

AREA 45,308 sq. mi. (117,348 sq. km.)
POPULATION 11,924,710
CAPITAL Harrisburg
LARGEST CITY Philadelphia
HIGHEST POINT Mt. Davis 3,213 ft. (979 m.)
SETTLED IN 1682
ADMITTED TO UNION December 12, 1787
POPULAR NAME Keystone State
STATE FLOWER Mountain Laurel
STATE BIRD Ruffed Grouse

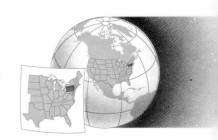

MAJOR MINERAL OCCURRENCES

C	Coal	G	Natural Gas	Sl	Slate
Cl	Clay	Ls	Limestone	Ss	Sandstone
Co	Cobalt	O	Petroleum	Zn	Zinc
Fe	Iron Ore				

⚡ Water Power
▨ Major Industrial Areas

Agriculture, Industry and Resources

(Map of Pennsylvania showing agriculture, industry, and resource symbols, including cities: Erie, Pittsburgh, Johnstown, Scranton, Wilkes-Barre, Hazleton, Easton, Allentown, Bethlehem, Reading, Harrisburg, Lancaster, York, Philadelphia.)

(continued on following page)

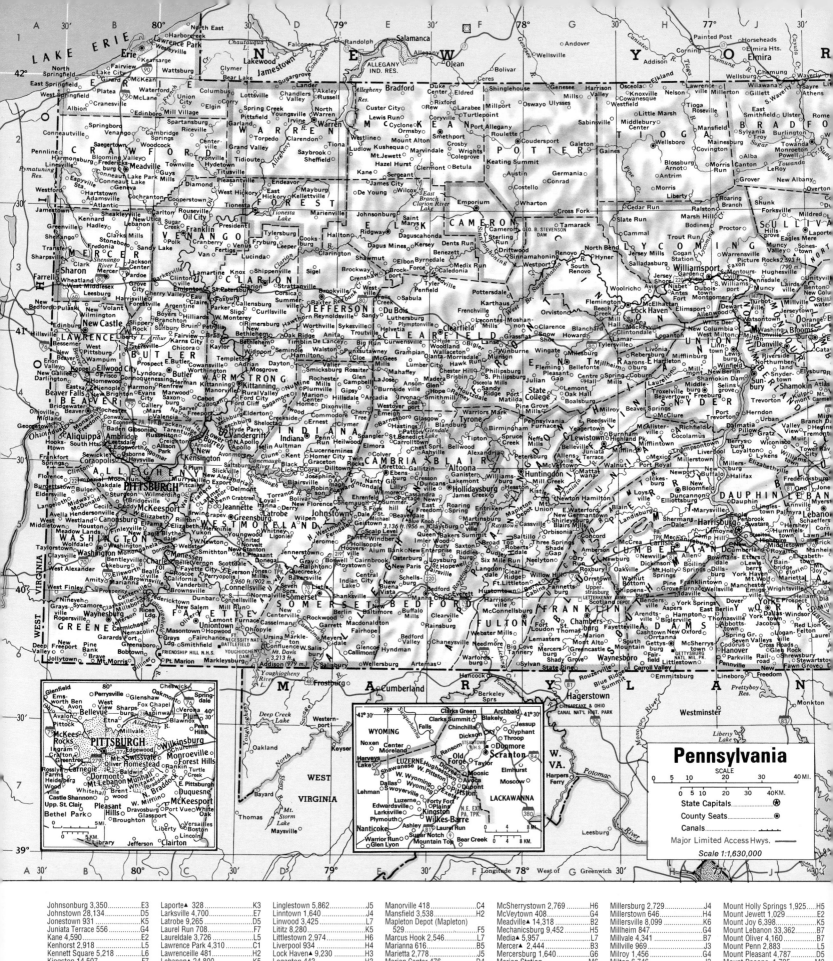

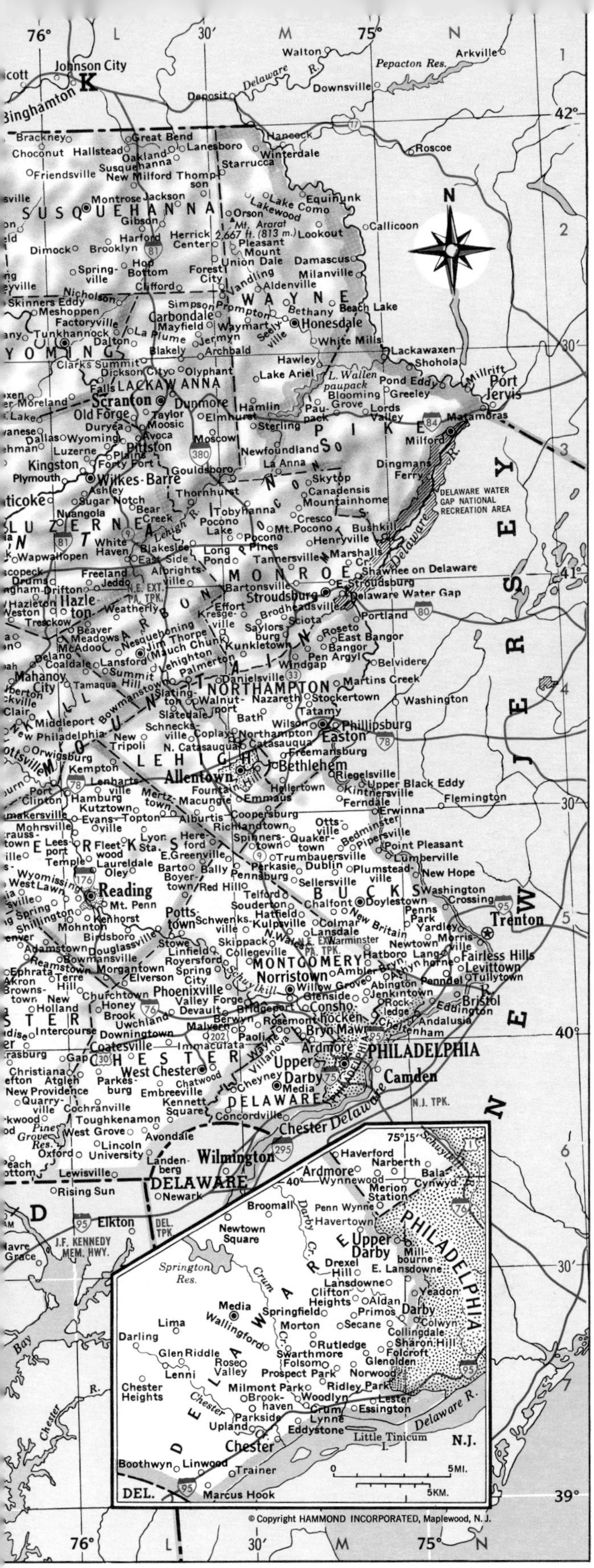

Petersburg 469 G4
Philadelphia▲ 1,585,577 N6
Philipsburg 3,048 F4
Phoenixville 15,066 L5
Picture Rocks 660 J3
Pillow 341 J4
Pine Grove 2,118 K4
Pine Grove Mills 1,129 G4
Pitcairn 4,087 C5
Pittsburgh▲ 369,879 B7
Pittston 9,389 F7
Plains 4,694 F7
Platea 467 B2
Pleasant Gap 1,699 G4
Pleasant Hills 8,884 B7
Plum 25,609 C5
Plumville 390 D4
Plymouth 7,134 E7
Plymptonville 1,074 E3
Pocono Pines 824 M3
Point Marion 1,344 C6
Polk 1,267 C3
Port Allegany 2,391 F2
Port Carbon 2,134 K4
Port Matilda 669 F4
Port Royal 836 H4
Port Vue 4,641 C7
Portage 3,105 E5
Portland 516 M4
Pottstown 21,831 L5
Pottsville▲ 16,603 K4
Prospect 1,122 B4
Prospect Park 6,764 M7
Punxsutawney 6,782 E4
Quakertown 8,982 M5
Quarryville 1,642 K6
Ramey 536 F4
Rankin 2,503 C7
Reading▲ 78,380 L5
Reamstown 2,649 K5
Red Hill 1,794 L5
Red Lion 6,130 J6
Reedsville 1,023 G4
Renovo 1,526 G3
Reynoldsville 2,818 D3
Rices Landing 457 C6
Richland 1,457 K5
Richlandtown 1,195 M5
Ridgway▲ 4,793 E3
Ridley Park 7,592 M7
Riegelsville 912 M4
Rimersburg 1,053 D3
Ringtown 853 K4
Riverside 1,991 J4
Roaring Spring 2,615 F5
Robesonia 1,944 K5
Rochester 4,156 B4
Rockledge 2,679 M5
Rockwood 1,014 D6
Rome 475 K2
Roscoe 872 C5
Rose Valley 982 L7
Roseto 1,555 M4
Rosslyn Farms 483 B7
Rouseville 583 C3
Rouzerville 1,188 G6
Royalton 1,120 J5
Royersford 4,458 L5
Rural Valley 957 D4
Russellton 1,691 C4
Rutledge 843 M7
Saegertown 1,066 B2
Saint Clair 3,524 K4
Saint Marys 5,511 E3
Saint Michael-Sidman 1,189 E5
Saint Petersburg 349 C3
Salisbury 716 D6
Saltillo 347 G5
Saltsburg 990 C4
Sandy 1,795 E3
Sandy Lake 722 B3
Saxonburg 1,345 C4
Saxton 838 F5
Sayre 5,791 K2
Scalp Level 1,158 E5
Schnecksville 1,780 L4
Schuylkill Haven 5,610 K4
Schwenksville 1,326 L5
Scottdale 5,184 C5
Scranton▲ 81,805 F7
Selinsgrove 5,384 J4
Sellersville 4,479 M5
Seven Valleys 483 J6
Seward 522 E5
Sewickley 4,134 B4
Shamokin 9,184 J4
Shamokin Dam 1,690 J4
Sharon 17,493 B3
Sharon Hill 5,771 N7
Sharpsburg 3,781 B6
Sharpsville 4,729 A3
Sheffield 1,294 D2
Shenandoah 6,221 K4
Shickshinny 1,108 K3
Shillington 5,062 K5
Shinglehouse 1,243 F2
Shippensburg 5,331 H5
Shippenville 474 D3
Shoemakersville 1,443 K4
Shrewsbury 2,672 J6
Sinking Spring 2,467 K5
Skippack 2,042 M5
Slatington 4,678 L4
Slickville 1,178 C5
Sligo 706 C3
Slippery Rock 3,008 B3
Smethport▲ 1,734 F2
Smithfield 1,000 C6
Smithton 388 C5
Snow Shoe 800 G3
Snydertown 416 J4
Somerset▲ 6,454 D6
Souderton 5,957 M5
South Bethlehem 479 D4
South Connellsville 2,204 C6
South Fork 1,197 E5
South Heights 647 B4
South Philipsburg 438 F4
South Renovo 579 G3
South Waverly 1,049 J2
South Williamsport 6,496 J3
Spangler 2,068 E4
Spartansburg 403 C2
Spring City 3,433 L5
Spring Grove 1,863 J6
Springboro 557 B2
Springdale 3,992 C6
Springfield 24,160 M7
State College 38,923 G4
State Line 1,253 G6
Steelton 5,152 J5
Stewartstown 1,308 K6
Stockertown 641 M4
Stoneboro 1,091 B3
Stowe 3,598 L5
Stoystown 389 E5
Strasburg 2,568 K6
Strattanville 490 D3
Strausstown 353 K5
Stroudsburg▲ 5,312 M4
Sturgeon 1,312 B5
Sugar Creek 5,532 C3
Sugar Notch 1,044 E7
Sugargrove 630 D1
Summerhill 614 E5
Summerville 675 D3
Summit Hill 3,332 L4
Sunbury▲ 11,591 J4
Susquehanna 1,994 L2
Swarthmore 6,157 M7
Swatara• 18,796 J5
Swissvale 10,637 C7
Swoyerville 5,630 E7
Sykesville 1,387 E3
Tamaqua 7,943 L4
Tarentum 5,674 C4
Tatamy 873 M4
Taylor 6,941 F7
Telford 4,238 M5
Temple 1,491 L5
Terre Hill 1,282 L5
Thompsontown 582 H4
Three Springs 422 G5
Throop 4,070 F7
Tidioute 791 D2
Tioga 638 H2
Tionesta▲ 634 D2
Tipton 1,194 F4
Titusville 6,434 C2
Topton 1,987 L5
Toughkenamon 1,273 L6
Towanda▲ 3,242 J2
Tower City 1,518 J4
Townville 358 C2
Trafford 3,345 C5
Trainer 2,271 L7
Tremont 1,814 K4
Tresckow 1,033 K4
Trevorton 2,058 J4
Troy 1,262 J2
Trumbauersville 894 M5
Tullytown 2,339 N5
Tunkhannock▲ 2,251 L2
Turbotville 675 J3
Turtle Creek 6,556 C7
Tyrone 5,743 F4
Ulysses (Lewisville) 653 G2
Union City 3,537 C2
Uniontown▲ 12,034 C6
Upland 3,334 L7
Upper Darby• 84,054 M6
Upper Saint Claire• 19,023 B7
Valencia 364 C4
Valley Forge 400 L5
Valley View 1,749 J4
Vanderbilt 545 C5
Vandergrift 5,904 D4
Vandling 660 M2
Verona 3,260 C6
Versailles 2,150 C7
Villanova M6
Vintondale 582 E5
Wall 853 C5
Walnutport 2,055 L4
Wampum 666 B4
Warren▲ 11,122 D2
Warrior Run 656 E7
Washington▲ 15,864 B5
Waterford 1,492 B2
Watsontown 2,310 J3
Wattsburg 486 C1
Waymart 1,337 M2
Wayne M6
Waynesboro 9,578 G6
Waynesburg▲ 4,270 B6
Weatherly 2,640 L4
Wellsboro▲ 3,430 H2
Wernersville 1,934 K5
Wesleyville 3,655 C1
West Brownsville 1,170 C5
West Chester▲ 18,041 L6
West Elizabeth 634 C5
West Grove 2,128 L6
West Hazleton 4,136 K4
West Kittanning 1,253 C4
West Lawn 1,606 K5
West Leechburg 1,359 C4
West Middlesex 982 B3
West Mifflin 23,644 C7
West Newton 3,152 C5
West Pittsburg 1,133 B4
West Pittston 5,590 F7
West View 7,734 B6
West Wyoming 3,117 E7
West York 4,283 J6
Westfield 1,119 H2
Westmont 5,789 D5
Westover 446 E4
Wheatland 760 B3
Whitaker 1,416 C7
White Haven 1,132 L3
White Oak 8,761 C7
Whitehall 14,451 B7
Wiconisco 1,321 J4
Wilkes-Barre▲ 47,523 F7
Wilkinsburg 21,080 C7
Williamsburg 1,456 F5
Williamsport▲ 31,933 H3
Williamstown 1,509 J4
Willow Grove 16,325 M5
Wilmerding 2,421 C5
Wilson 7,830 M4
Windber 4,756 E5
Windgap 2,651 M4
Windsor 1,355 J6
Wolfdale 2,906 B5
Womelsdorf 2,270 K5
Woodlyn 10,151 M7
Worthington 713 C4
Wrightsville 2,396 J5
Wyalusing 686 K2
Wyoming 3,255 E7
Wyomissing 7,332 K5
Yardley 2,288 N5
Yeadon 11,980 N7
Yeagertown 1,150 G4
York Haven 758 J5
York Springs 547 H6
York▲ 42,192 J6
Youngsville 1,775 D2
Youngwood 3,372 D5
Zelienople 4,158 B4

OTHER FEATURES

Allegheny (res.) E2
Allegheny (riv.) D2
Allegheny Front (mts.) E5
Appalachian (mts.) H4
Ararat (mt.) M2
Arthur (lake) C4
Beaver (riv.) B4
Blue (mt.) G5
Blue Knob (mt.) E5
Casselman (riv.) D6
Clarion (riv.) D3
Conemaugh (riv.) D5
Conemaugh River (lake) D4
Conewango (creek) D1
Davis (mt.) D6
Delaware (riv.) N3
Delaware Water Gap Nat'l Rec. N3
Erie (lake) B1
Fort Necessity Nat'l Battlefield C6
George B. Stevenson (dam) G3
Gettysburg Nat'l Mil. Park H6
Glendale (lake) F4
Juniata (riv.) G5
Laurel Hill (mt.) D5
Lehigh (riv.) L3
Letterkenny Army Depot G6
Licking (creek) F6
Little Tinicum (isl.) M7
Lycoming (creek) H3
Monongahela (riv.) C6
North (mt.) K3
Ohio (riv.) A4
Oil (creek) C2
Pine (creek) H2
Pine Grove (res.) K6
Pocono (mts.) M3
Pymatuning (res.) A2
Redbank (creek) E3
Schuylkill (riv.) M5
Shenango River (lake) B3
Sinnemahoning (creek) F3
South (mt.) H6
Steamtown Nat'l Hist. Site F7
Susquehanna (riv.) K6
Tioga (riv.) H1
Tionesta Creek (lake) D3
Towanda (creek) J2
Tuscarora (mt.) G5
Wallenpaupack (lake) M3
Youghiogheny River (lake) D6

▲County seat
•Population of town or township

New Beaver 1,736 B4
New Berlin 892 J4
New Bethlehem 1,151 D3
New Bloomfield▲ H5
New Brighton 6,854 B4
New Britain 2,174 M5
New Castle▲ 28,334 B3
New Cumberland 7,665 J5
New Eagle 2,172 B5
New Florence 854 D5
New Freedom 2,920 J6
New Galilee 500 A4
New Holland 4,484 K5
New Hope 1,400 N5
New Kensington 15,894 C4
New Milford 953 L2
New Oxford 1,617 H6
New Philadelphia 1,283 K4
New Salem (Delmont) 669 D5
New Stanton 2,081 C5
New Wilmington 2,706 B3
Newport 1,568 H5
Newtown 2,565 N5
Newtown Square• 11,775 L6
Newville 1,349 H5
Nicholson 857 L2
Norristown▲ 30,749 M5
North Apollo 1,391 D4
North Braddock 7,036 C7
North Catasauqua 2,867 L4
North East 4,617 C1
North Wales 3,802 M5
North Warren 1,232 D2
Northampton 8,717 M4
Northumberland 3,860 J4
Norvelt 2,541 D5
Norwood 6,162 M7
Nuangola 701 L3
Oakdale 1,752 B5
Oakland 641 L2
Oakmont 6,961 C6
Ohioville 3,865 B4
Oil City 11,949 C3
Old Forge 8,834 F7
Oliver 3,271 C6
Olyphant 5,222 F7
Orangeville 504 K3
Orbisonia 447 G5
Orwigsburg 2,780 K4
Osborne 565 B4
Osceola Mills 1,310 F4
Oxford 3,769 K6
Paint 1,091 E5
Palmerton 5,394 L4
Palmyra 6,910 J5
Paoli 5,603 M5
Paradise 1,107 K5
Parker 853 C3
Parkesburg 2,981 L6
Parkside 2,369 M7
Parkville 6,014 J6
Patton 2,206 E4
Pen Argyl 3,492 M4
Penbrook 2,791 J5
Penn 511 C5
Penn Hills 51,430 C7
Penn Wynne 5,807 M6
Penndel 2,703 N5
Pennsburg 2,460 M5
Pennville 1,559 J6
Perkasie 7,878 M5
Perryopolis 1,833 C5

Topography

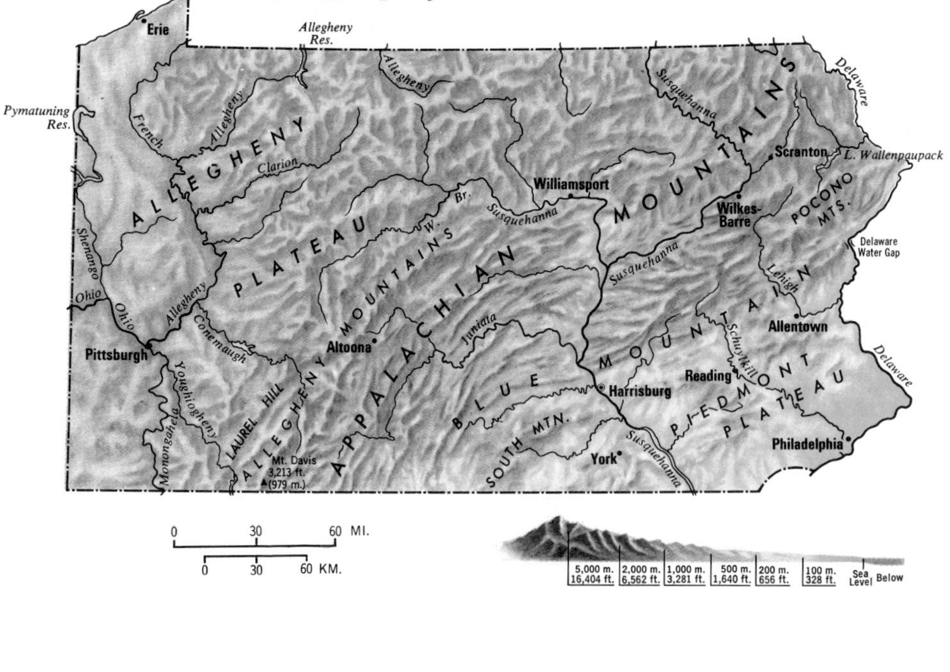

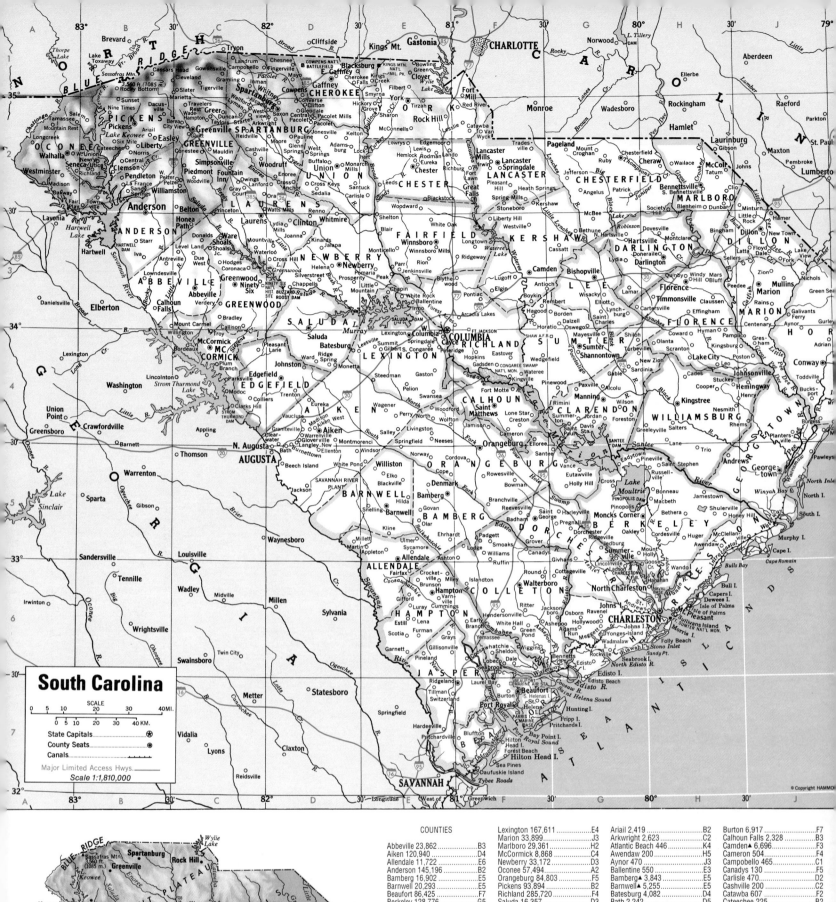

South Carolina

SCALE
0 5 10 20 30 40 MI.
0 5 10 30 40 KM.

State Capitals ⊛
County Seats ⊙
Canals
Major Limited Access Hwys.

Scale 1:1,810,000

© Copyright HAMMOND

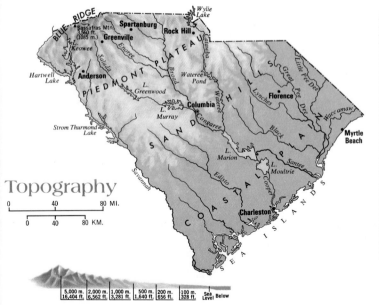

Topography

0 40 80 MI.
0 40 80 KM.

5,000 m. / 16,404 ft. — 2,000 m. / 6,562 ft. — 1,000 m. / 3,281 ft. — 500 m. / 1,640 ft. — 200 m. / 656 ft. — 100 m. / 328 ft. — Sea Level — Below

COUNTIES

Name	Pop.	Grid
Abbeville	23,862	B3
Aiken	120,940	D4
Allendale	11,722	E6
Anderson	145,196	B2
Bamberg	16,902	E5
Barnwell	20,293	E5
Beaufort	86,425	F7
Berkeley	128,776	G5
Calhoun	12,753	F4
Charleston	295,039	H6
Cherokee	44,506	D1
Chester	32,170	E2
Chesterfield	38,577	G2
Clarendon	28,450	G4
Colleton	34,377	F6
Darlington	61,851	H3
Dillon	29,114	J3
Dorchester	83,060	G5
Edgefield	18,375	D4
Fairfield	22,295	E3
Florence	114,344	H3
Georgetown	46,302	J5
Greenville	320,167	C2
Greenwood	59,567	C3
Hampton	18,191	E6
Horry	144,053	J4
Jasper	15,487	E6
Kershaw	43,599	F3
Lancaster	54,516	F2
Laurens	58,092	D2
Lee	18,437	G3
Lexington	167,611	E4
Marion	33,899	J3
Marlboro	29,361	H2
McCormick	8,868	C4
Newberry	33,172	D3
Oconee	57,494	A2
Orangeburg	84,803	F5
Pickens	93,894	B2
Richland	285,720	F4
Saluda	16,357	D3
Spartanburg	226,800	D2
Sumter	102,637	G4
Union	30,337	D2
Williamsburg	36,815	H4
York	131,497	E2

CITIES and TOWNS

Name	Pop.	Grid
Abbeville▲	5,778	C3
Adams Run	500	G6
Adamsburg	300	D2
Aiken▲	19,872	D4
Aiken West	3,083	D4
Alcolu	600	G4
Allendale▲	4,410	E5
Allsbrook	100	K3
Anderson	26,184	B2
Andrews	3,050	H5
Antioch	500	F3
Antreville	500	B3
Appleton	200	E5
Arcadia	899	C2
Arcadia Lakes	611	F3
Ariail	2,419	B2
Arkwright	2,623	C2
Atlantic Beach	446	K4
Awendaw	200	H5
Aynor	470	J4
Ballentine	550	E3
Bamberg▲	3,843	E5
Barnwell▲	5,255	E5
Batesburg	4,082	D4
Bath	2,242	D5
Beaufort▲	9,576	F7
Beech Island	400	D5
Belton	4,646	C2
Bennettsville▲	9,345	H2
Berea	13,535	C2
Bethera	265		H5
Bethune	405	G3
Bingham	200		H2
Bishopville▲	3,560	G3
Blacksburg	1,907	D1
Blackville	2,688	E5
Blenheim	191	H2
Bluffton	738	F7
Blythewood	164	E3
Bonneau	374	H5
Bowman	1,063	F5
Boykin	350	G4
Branchville	1,107	F5
Brunson	587	E6
Bucksport	1,022	J4
Buffalo	1,569	D2
Burgess	250	J4
Burnettown	493	D5
Burton	6,917	F7
Calhoun Falls	2,328	B3
Camden▲	6,696	F3
Cameron	504	F4
Campobello	465	C1
Canadys	130	F6
Carlisle	470	D2
Cashville	200	C2
Catawba	607	E2
Cateechee	225	B2
Central	2,438	B2
Central Pacolet	257	D2
Chapin	282	E3
Chappells	45	D3
Charleston▲	80,414	G6
Cheraw	5,505	H2
Cherokee Falls	250	D1
Chesnee	1,280	D1
Chester▲	7,158	E2
Chesterfield▲	1,373	H2
City View	1,490	C2
Clarks Hill	200	C4
Claussen	500	H3
Clearwater	4,731	D5
Clemson	11,096	B2
Cleveland	800	C1
Clifton	950	D2
Clinton	7,987	D3
Clio	882	H2
Clover	3,422	E1
Columbia (cap.)▲	98,052	F4

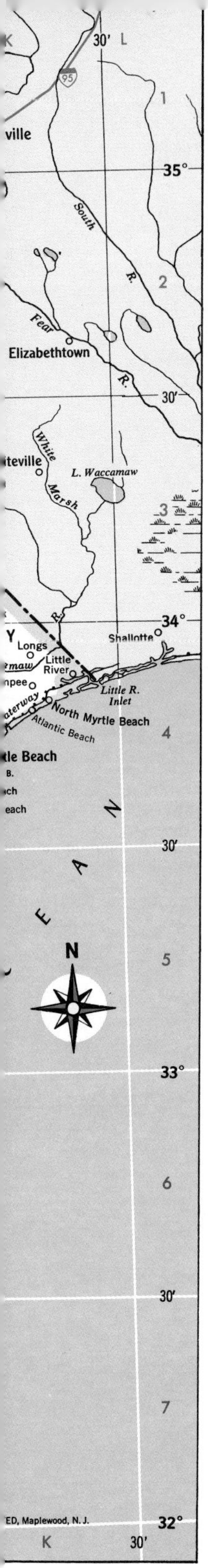

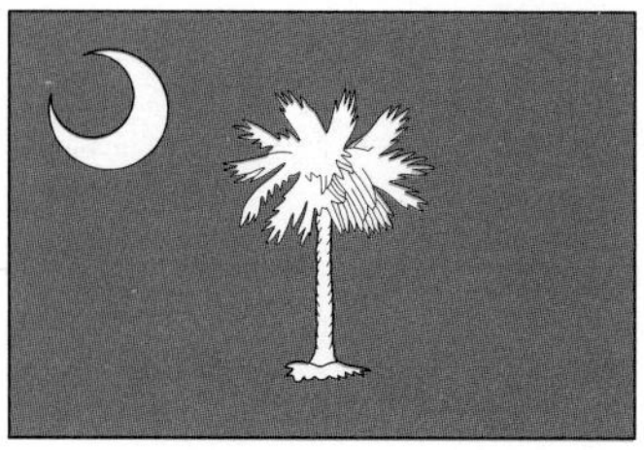

AREA 31,113 sq. mi. (80,583 sq. km.)
POPULATION 3,505,707
CAPITAL Columbia
LARGEST CITY Columbia
HIGHEST POINT Sassafras Mtn. 3,560 ft. (1085 m.)
SETTLED IN 1670
ADMITTED TO UNION May 23, 1788
POPULAR NAME Palmetto State
STATE FLOWER Carolina (Yellow) Jessamine
STATE BIRD Carolina Wren

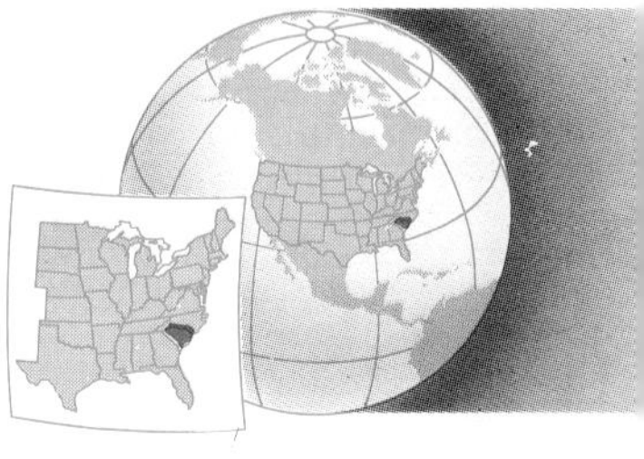

Conestee 500 C2
Converse 1,173 D2
Conway▲ 9,819 J4
Coosawhatchie 250 F6
Cope 124 E5
Cordesville 300 H5
Cordova 135 F5
Coronaca 200 C3
Cottageville 572 G6
Coward 532 H4
Cowpens 2,176 D1
Cross 469 G5
Cross Anchor 350 D2
Cross Hill 604 D3
Cross Keys 250 D2
Cummings 275 E6
Dacusville 350 B2
Dale 500 F6
Dalzell 625 G3
Darlington▲ 7,311 H3
Davis Station 300 G4
Denmark 3,762 E5
Dillon▲ 6,829 J3
Donalds 326 C3
Doneraile 1,276 H3
Dorchester 400 G5
Due West 1,220 C3
Duncan 2,152 C2
Easley 15,195 B2
East Gaffney 3,278 D1
Eastover 1,044 F4
Edgefield 2,563▲ C4
Edgemoor 500 E2
Edisto Beach 340 G7
Edisto Island 900 G6
Effingham 300 H3
Ehrhardt 442 E5
Elgin 622 F3
Elko 214 E5
Elliott 500 G3
Elloree 939 F4
Enoree 1,107 D2
Estill 2,387 E6
Eureka 1,738 E2
Eutawville 350 G5
Fair Play 500 A2
Fairfax 2,317 E6
Filbert 203 E1
Fingerville 320 D1
Florence▲ 29,813 H3
Floyd Dale 450 J3
Folly Beach 1,398 H6
Forest Acres 7,197 E3
Forest Beach 500 F7
Foreston 300 G4
Fort Lawn 718 F2
Fort Mill 4,930 F1
Fort Motte 700 F4
Fountain Inn 4,388 C2
Furman 260 E6
Gable 230 G4
Gadsden 500 F4
Gaffney▲ 13,145 D1
Gantt 13,891 C2
Garden City Beach 300 K4
Garnett 500 E6
Gaston 984 E4
Georgetown▲ 9,517 J5
Gifford 313 E6
Gilbert 324 E4
Gillisonville 350 E6
Givhans 400 G5
Glendale 1,049 D2
Glenn Springs 350 D2
Gloverville 2,753 D4
Goose Creek 24,692 H6
Govan 84 E5
Gowensville 200 C1
Gramling 400 C1
Graniteville 1,158 D4
Gray Court 914 C2
Great Falls 2,307 F2
Greeleyville 464 H4
Greenville▲ 58,282 C2
Greenwood▲ 20,807 C3
Greer 10,322 C2
Gresham 350 J4
Gurley 425 J3
Hamer 588 J3
Hampton 2,997▲ E6
Hanahan 13,176 H6
Hardeeville 1,583 E7
Harleyville 633 G5
Hartsville 8,372 G3
Heath Springs 907 F2
Helena 500 D3
Hemingway 829 J4
Hemlock (Eureka) E2
Hickory Grove 287 E2
Hilda 342 E5
Hilton Head Island 23,694 F7
Hodges 125 C3
Holly Hill 1,478 G5
Hollywood 2,094 G6
Honea Path 3,841 C3
Hopkins 300 F4
Horatio 500 F3
Huger 500 H5
Inman 1,742 C1
Irmo 11,280 D3
Irwin 1,296 F2
Isle of Palms 3,680 H6
Iva 1,174 B3
Jackson 1,681 D5
Jacksonboro 475 G6
Jamestown 84 H5
Jedburg 900 G5
Jefferson 745 G2
Joanna 1,735 D3
Johns Island 200 G6
Johnsonville 1,415 J4
Johnston 2,688 D4
Jonesville 1,205 D2
Kershaw 1,814 G2
Kinards 300 D3
Kingsburg 300 H4
Kingstree▲ 3,858 H4
Kingville 500 F4
Kline 285 E5
La France 875 B2
Ladson 13,540 G6
Lake City 7,153 H4
Lake View 872 J3
Lamar 1,125 G3
Lancaster Mills 2,096 F2
Lancaster▲ 8,914 F2
Lando 250 E2
Landrum 2,347 C1
Lane 523 H5
Langley 1,714 D4
Latta 1,565 J3
Laurel Bay 4,972 F7
Laurens▲ 9,694 C3
Leesville 2,025 E4
Lena 275 E6
Lesslie 1,102 E2
Level Land 100 C3
Lexington▲ 3,289 E4
Liberty 3,228 B2
Lincolnville 716 G6
Little Mountain 235 E3
Little River 3,470 K4
Little Rock 500 J3
Livingston 171 E4
Lobeco 345 F6
Lockhart 58 E2
Lodge 147 F5
Longcreek 200 A2
Longtown 400 F3
Loris 2,067 K3
Lowndesville 162 B3
Lowrys 200 E2
Lugoff 3,211 F3
Luray 102 E6
Lydia 500 G3
Lydia Mills 925 D3
Lyman 2,271 C2
Lynchburg 475 G3
Madison A2
Madison 1,150 D4
Manning▲ 4,428 G4
Marietta-Slater C1
Marion▲ 7,658 J3
Mars Bluff 500 H3
Mauldin 11,587 C2
Mayesville 694 G4
Mayo 1,569 D1
McBee 715 G3
McClellanville 333 H5
McColl 2,685 H2
McConnells 157 E2
McCormick▲ 1,659 C4
Meggett 787 G6
Modoc 300 C4
Monarch Mills 2,353 D2
Moncks Corner▲ 5,607 G5
Monetta 285 D4
Montmorenci 500 D4
Moore 500 D2
Mount Carmel 117 C3
Mount Croghan 131 G2
Mount Holly 200 H5
Mount Pleasant 30,108 H6
Mountain Rest 500 A2
Mullins 5,910 J3
Murrells Inlet 3,334 K4
Myrtle Beach 24,848 K4
Neeses 410 E4
Nesmith 350 H4
New Ellenton 2,515 D5
New Town 950 J3
New Zion 200 H4
Newberry▲ 10,542 D3
Newry 400 B2
Nichols 528 J3
Ninety Six 2,099 C3
Norris 884 B2
North 809 E4
North Augusta 15,351 C5
North Charleston 70,218 G6
North Hartsville 2,906 G3
North Myrtle Beach 8,636 K4
Norway 401 E5
Oakley 250 G5
Olanta 687 H4
Olar 391 E5
Ora 13,739 D2
Orangeburg▲ 14,933 F4
Oswego 500 G3
Pacolet 1,736 D2
Pacolet Mills 696 D2
Pageland 2,666 G2
Pamplico 1,314 H4
Parksville 193 C4
Parr 7,172 E3
Patrick 368 G2
Pauline 750 D2
Pawleys Island 176 J5
Paxville 218 G4
Peak 78 E3
Peedee 350 H3
Pelion 336 E4
Pelzer 81 B2
Pendleton 3,314 B2
Perry 241 E4
Pickens▲ 3,042 B2
Piedmont 4,143 C2
Pineland 800 E6
Pineridge 1,731 E4
Pineville 900 H5
Pinewood 600 G4
Pinopolis 788 G5
Plantersville 231 J4
Plum Branch 101 C4
Pomaria 267 E3
Port Royal 2,985 F7
Poston 250 J4
Princeton 300 C2
Prosperity 1,116 D3
Quinby 865 H3
Rains 450 J3
Ravenel 2,165 G6
Red River F2
Reevesville 244 F5
Reidville C2
Rembert 350 G3
Richburg 405 E2
Ridge Spring 861 D4
Ridgeland▲ 1,071 E7
Ridgeville 1,625 G5
Ridgeway 407 F3
Rimini 525 G4
Rion 300 E3
Ritter 300 F6
Rock Hill 41,643 E2
Rodman 500 E2
Rowesville 316 F5
Ruby 300 G2
Ruffin 400 F6
Saint Andrews 26,692 G6
Saint George▲ 2,077 F5
Saint Matthews▲ 2,345 F4
Saint Paul 725 G4
Saint Stephen 1,697 H5
Salem 192 A2
Salley 451 E4
Salters 300 H4
Saluda▲ 2,798 D4
Santee 638 F5
Sardinia 225 G4
Saxon 4,002 D2
Scotia 182 E6
Scranton 802 H4
Sea Pines 500 F7
Seabrook 948 F6
Sellers 358 H3
Seneca 7,726 A2
Shannontown G4
Sharon 270 E2
Sheldon 225 F6
Shulerville 375 H5
Silverstreet 156 D3
Simpsonville 11,708 C2
Six Mile 562 B2
Slater-Marietta 2,245 C1
Smoaks 142 F5
Smyrna 57 E1
Snelling 125 E5
Society Hill 686 H2
South Bennettsville 1,065 H2
South Congaree 2,406 E4
Spartanburg▲ 43,467 C1
Spring Mills 1,419 F2
Springdale 2,643 F2
Springdale 2,985 E4
Springfield 523 E4
Starr 164 B3
Startex 1,162 C2
Stuckey 311 H4
Sullivans Island 1,623 H6
Summerton 975 G4
Summerville 22,519 G5
Summit 242 E4
Sumter▲ 41,943 G4
Surfside Beach 3,845 K4
Swansea 527 E4
Sycamore 208 E5
Tamassee 320 A2
Tatum 49 H2
Taylors 19,619 C2
Tigerville 975 C1
Tillman 225 E7
Timmonsville 2,182 H3
Toddville 200 J4
Townville 300 B2
Tradesville 500 F2
Travelers Rest 3,069 C2
Trenton 303 D4
Trio 400 H5
Troy 140 C4
Turbeville 698 G4
Ulmer 90 E5
Union▲ 9,836 D2
Utica 1,478 B2
Van Wyck 500 F2
Vance 214 G5
Varnville 1,970 E6
Vaucluse 606 D7
Wade-Hampton 20,014 C2
Wagener 731 E4
Walhalla▲ 3,755 A2
Wallace 500 H2
Walterboro▲ 5,492 F6
Wampee 200 K4
Wando 500 H6
Ward 132 D4
Ware Shoals 2,497 C3
Warrenville 1,029 D4
Waterloo 122 C3
Watts Mill 1,535 D2
Wedgefield 550 F4
Wellford 2,511 C2
West Columbia 10,588 E4
West Pelzer 989 B2
West Springs 500 D2
West Union 260 B2
Westminster 3,120 A2
Westview 1,999 C2
Westville 440 F3
White Pond 200 D5
White Rock 600 E3
Whitmire 1,702 D3
Whitney 4,052 D1
Williams 188 F5
Williamston 3,876 B2
Williston 3,099 E5
Windsor 124 E5
Windy Hill 1,622 H3
Winnsboro Mills 2,275 E3
Winnsboro▲ 3,475 E3
Wisacky 250 G3
Woodford 200 E4
Woodruff 4,365 D2
Woodville C2
Yemassee 728 F6
Yonges Island 500 G6
York▲ 6,709 E1

OTHER FEATURES

Ashepoo (riv.) F6
Ashley (riv.) G6
Bay Point (isl.) F7
Beaufort Marine Air Sta. F7
Big Black (creek) G2
Black (riv.) H4
Blue Ridge (mts.) B1
Broad (riv.) E2
Broad (riv.) F7
Buck (creek) J3
Bull (isl.) H6
Bullock (creek) E2
Bulls (bay) H6
Bush (riv.) D3
Buzzard Roost (dam) D3
Cape (isl.) J5
Capers (isl.) H6
Catawba (riv.) F2
Catfish (creek) J3
Chattooga (riv.) A2
Combahee (riv.) F6
Congaree (riv.) F4
Congaree Nat'l Mon. F4
Cooper (riv.) H6
Coosaw (riv.) G7
Coosawhatchie (riv.) E6
Cowpens Nat'l Battlefield D1
Crooked (creek) H2
Deep (creek) B2
Dewees (isl.) H6
Donaldson A.F.B. C2
Edisto (isl.) G6
Edisto (riv.) G7
Enoree (riv.) C2
Fort Jackson F4
Fort Sumter Nat'l Mon. H6
Four Hole Swamp (creek) F5
Fripp (isl.) G7
Great Pee Dee (riv.) J4
Greenwood (lake) D3
Hartwell (dam) B3
Hartwell (lake) A3
Hilton Head (isl.) F7
Hunting (isl.) G7
Intracoastal Waterway H5
James (isl.) H6
Johns (isl.) G6
Juniper (creek) H2
Keowee (lake) B2
Keowee (riv.) B2
Kiawah (isl.) G6
Kings Mountain Nat'l Mil. Park E1
Little (riv.) C3
Little (riv.) D3
Little Lynches (riv.) G3
Little Pee Dee (riv.) J4
Little River (inlet) L4
Lumber (riv.) J3
Lynches (riv.) H3
Marion (lake) G5
Morris (isl.) H6
Moultrie (lake) G5
Murphy (isl.) J5
Murray (lake) D4
Myrtle Beach A.F.B. K4
Naval Base H6
New (riv.) E6
Ninety Six Nat'l Hist. Site C3
North (inlet) J5
North (isl.) J5
North Edisto (riv.) G6
Pacolet (riv.) D1
Palms, Isle of (isl.) H6
Parris Island Marine Base F7
Pee Dee (riv.) J4
Pocotaligo (riv.) G4
Port Royal (sound) F7
Pritchards (isl.) G7
Reedy (riv.) C2
Robinson (lake) G3
Romain (cape) J6
Saint Helena (isl.) F7
Saint Helena (sound) G7
Salkehatchie (riv.) E5
Saluda (riv.) D3
Sandy (pt.) H6
Sandy (riv.) E2
Santee (dam) G4
Santee (riv.) H5
Sassafras (mt.) B1
Savannah (riv.) E6
Savannah River Plant D5
Sea (isls.) G7
Seabrook (isl.) G6
Seneca (riv.) B2
Shaw A.F.B. F4
South (isl.) J5
Stevens (creek) C4
Stono (inlet) H6
Strom Thurmond (dam) C4
Strom Thurmond (lake) C4
Thompsons (creek) G2
Tugaloo (riv.) A2
Turkey (creek) E2
Tybee Roads (chan.) F7
Tyger (riv.) D2
Waccamaw (riv.) J5
Wadmalaw (isl.) G6
Wando (riv.) H6
Wateree (lake) F3
Winyah (bay) J5
Wylie (lake) E1

▲County seat

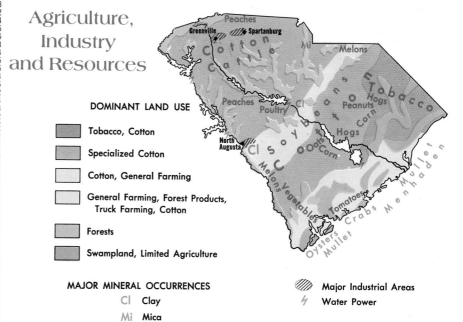

Agriculture, Industry and Resources

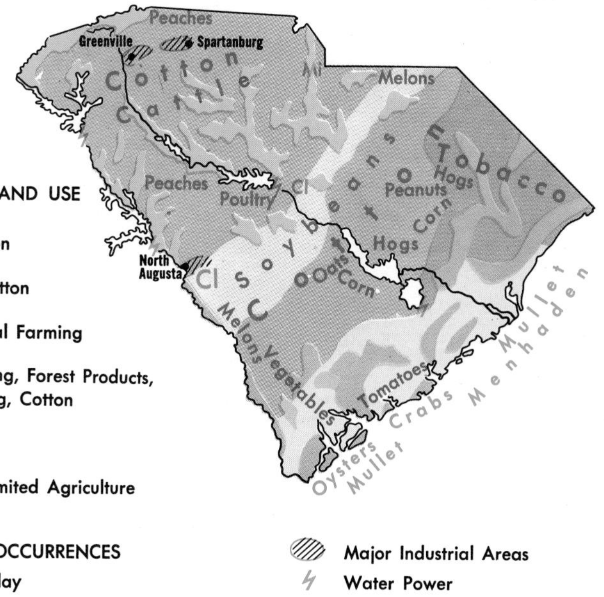

DOMINANT LAND USE

- Tobacco, Cotton
- Specialized Cotton
- Cotton, General Farming
- General Farming, Forest Products, Truck Farming, Cotton
- Forests
- Swampland, Limited Agriculture

MAJOR MINERAL OCCURRENCES

Cl Clay
Mi Mica

Major Industrial Areas
Water Power

298

COUNTIES

Aurora 3,135	M6
Beadle 18,253	N5
Bennett 3,206	F7
Bon Homme 7,089	O7
Brookings 25,207	R5
Brown 35,580	N2
Brule 5,485	L6
Buffalo 1,759	L5
Butte 7,914	B4
Campbell 1,965	J2
Charles Mix 9,131	M7
Clark 4,403	O4
Clay 13,186	P8
Codington 22,698	P4
Corson 4,195	G2
Custer 6,179	B6
Davison 17,503	N6
Day 6,978	O3
Deuel 4,522	R4
Dewey 5,523	G3

Douglas 3,746	N7
Edmunds 4,356	L3
Fall River 7,353	B7
Faulk 2,744	L3
Grant 8,372	R3
Gregory 5,359	L7
Haakon 2,624	F5
Hamlin 4,974	P4
Hand 4,272	L4
Hanson 2,994	O6
Harding 1,669	B2
Hughes 14,817	J5
Hutchinson 8,262	O7
Hyde 1,696	K4
Jackson 2,811	F6
Jerauld 2,425	M5
Jones 1,324	H6
Kingsbury 5,925	O5
Lake 10,550	P5
Lawrence 20,655	B5
Lincoln 15,427	R7
Lyman 3,638	J6

Marshall 4,844	O2
McCook 5,688	P6
McPherson 3,228	L2
Meade 21,878	D5
Mellette 2,137	H6
Miner 3,272	O5
Minnehaha 123,809	R6
Moody 6,507	R5
Pennington 81,343	C6
Perkins 3,932	D3
Potter 3,190	J3
Roberts 9,914	P2
Sanborn 2,833	N5
Shannon 9,902	D7
Spink 7,981	N4
Stanley 2,453	H5
Sully 1,589	J4
Todd 8,352	H7
Tripp 6,924	K7
Turner 8,576	P7
Union 10,189	R8
Walworth 6,087	J3

Yankton 19,252	P7
Ziebach 2,220	F4

CITIES and TOWNS

Aberdeen▲ 24,927	M3
Agar 82	J4
Akaska 52	J3
Albee 15	S3
Alcester 843	R7
Alexandria▲ 518	O6
Allen 300	F7
Alpena 251	N5
Altamont 48	R4
Amherst 75	O2
Andover 106	O3
Ardmore 16	B7
Arlington 908	P5
Armour▲ 854	N7
Artas 28	K2
Artesian 217	O6
Ashton 148	N3

Astoria 155	S4
Aurora 619	R5
Avon 576	N8
Badger 114	P5
Baltic 666	R6
Bancroft 30	O4
Barnard 65	N2
Batesland 124	E7
Bath 175	N3
Belle Fourche▲ 4,335	B4
Belvidere 63	G6
Beresford 1,849	R7
Big Stone City 669	S3
Bison▲ 451	E2
Black Hawk 1,995	C5
Blunt 342	J4
Bonesteel 297	M7
Bowdle 589	K3
Box Elder 2,680	D5
Bradley 117	O3
Brandon 3,543	R6
Brandt 123	R4

Brentford 69	N3
Bridgewater 533	P6
Bristol 419	O3
Britton▲ 1,394	O2
Broadland 40	N4
Brookings▲ 16,270	R5
Bruce 235	R5
Bryant 374	P4
Buffalo▲ 488	B2
Buffalo Gap 173	C6
Bullhead 179	G2
Burbank 90	R8
Burke▲ 756	L7
Bushnell 81	R5
Butler 17	O3
Camp Crook 146	A2
Canistota 608	P6
Canning 40	J5
Canova 172	O6
Canton▲ 2,787	R7
Caputa 50	D5
Carter 7	J7

Carthage 221	O5
Castlewood 549	R4
Cavour 166	N5
Center 887	P6
Centerville 892	R7
Central City 185	B5
Chamberlain▲ 2,347	L6
Chancellor 276	R7
Chelsea 33	M3
Cherry Creek 500	F4
Chester 375	R6
Claire City 85	P2
Clark▲ 1,292	O4
Clear Lake▲ 1,247	R4
Colman 482	R6
Colome 309	K7
Colton 657	R6
Columbia 133	N2
Conde 203	N3
Corona 118	R3
Corsica 619	N7

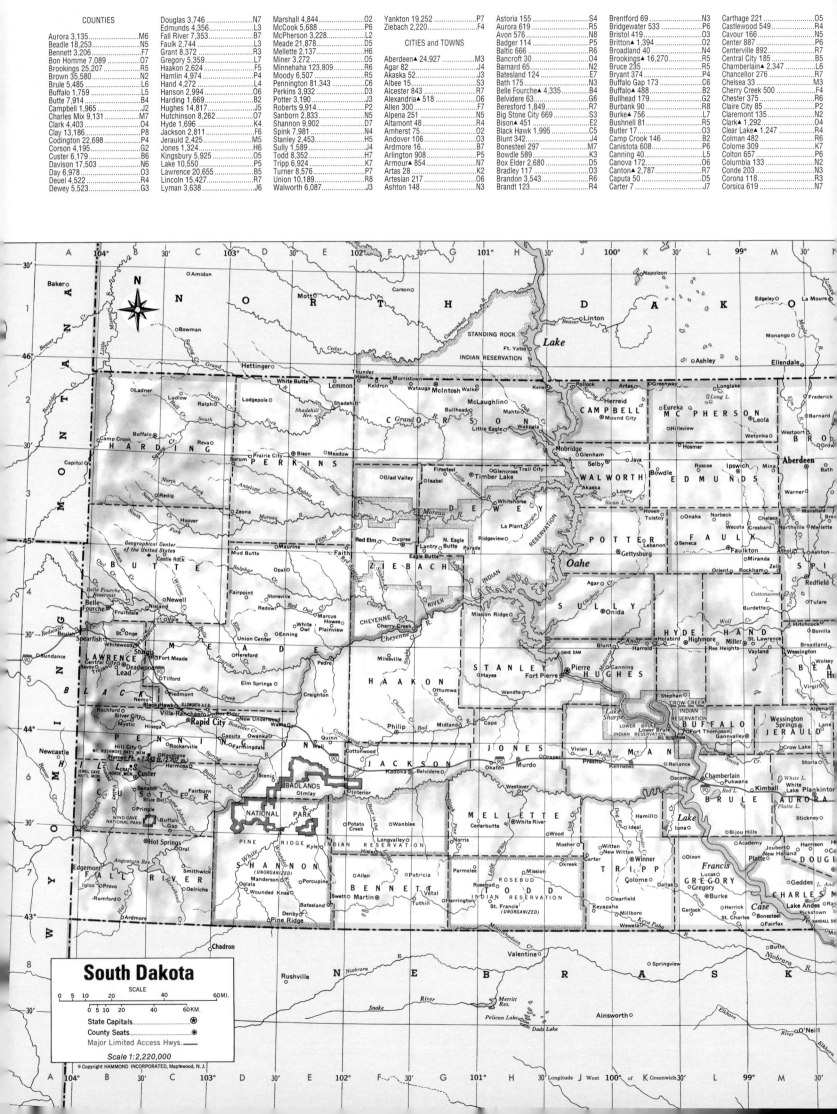

(continued on following page)

AREA 77,116 sq. mi. (199,730 sq. km.)
POPULATION 699,999
CAPITAL Pierre
LARGEST CITY Sioux Falls
HIGHEST POINT Harney Pk. 7,242 ft.
(2207 m.)
SETTLED IN 1856
ADMITTED TO UNION November 2, 1889
POPULAR NAME Coyote State; Sunshine
State
STATE FLOWER Pasqueflower
STATE BIRD Ring-necked Pheasant

Topography

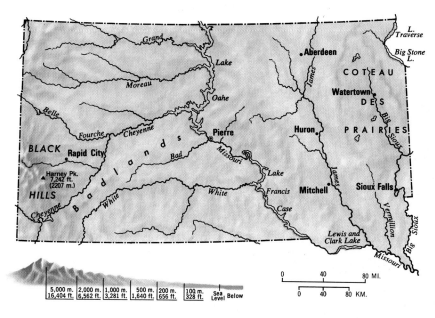

5,000 m.	2,000 m.	1,000 m.	500 m.	200 m.	100 m.	Sea	
16,404 ft.	6,562 ft.	3,281 ft.	1,640 ft.	656 ft.	328 ft.	Level	Below

0   40   80 MI.

0   40   80 KM.

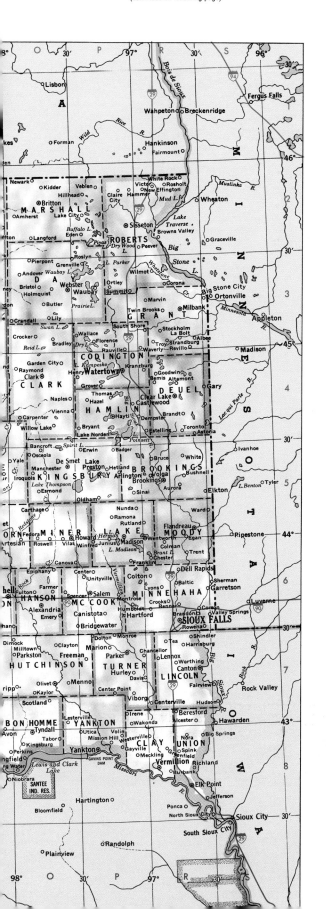

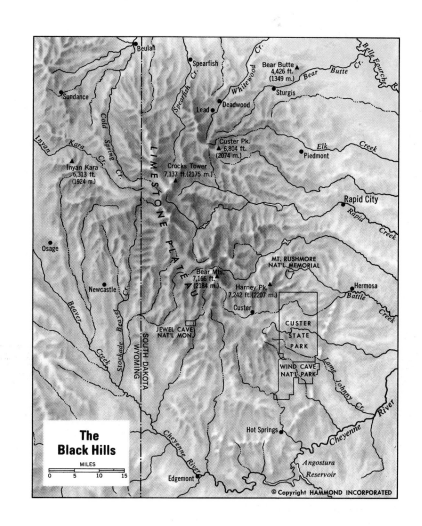

The Black Hills

MILES

0   5   10   15

© Copyright HAMMOND INCORPORATED

Agriculture, Industry and Resources

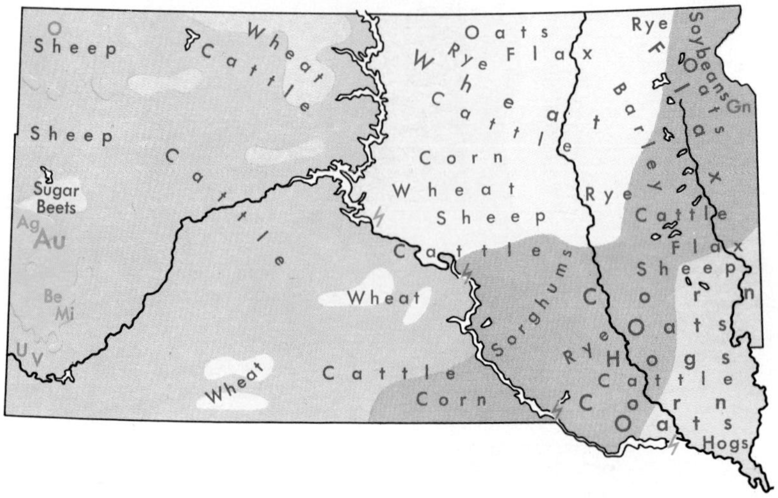

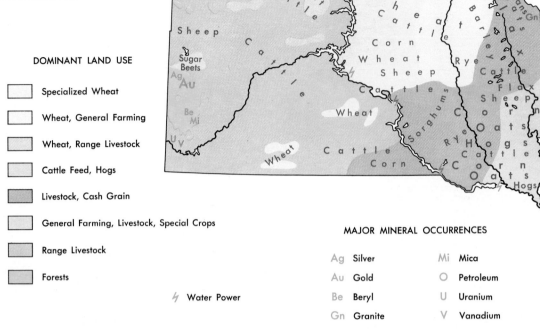

DOMINANT LAND USE

- Specialized Wheat
- Wheat, General Farming
- Wheat, Range Livestock
- Cattle Feed, Hogs
- Livestock, Cash Grain
- General Farming, Livestock, Special Crops
- Range Livestock
- Forests

Water Power

MAJOR MINERAL OCCURRENCES

- Ag Silver
- Au Gold
- Be Beryl
- Gn Granite
- Mi Mica
- O Petroleum
- U Uranium
- V Vanadium

Forestburg 100 ... N5
Fort Meade 900 ... C5
Fort Pierre▲ 1,854 ... H5
Fort Thompson 1,088 ... L5
Frankfort 192 ... N4
Frederick 241 ... N2
Freeman 1,293 ... O7
Fruitdale 43 ... B4
Fulton 70 ... O6
Gannvalley▲ 70 ... L5
Garden City 93 ... O4
Garretson 924 ... S6
Gary 274 ... S4
Gayville 401 ... P8
Geddes 280 ... M7
Gettysburg▲ 1,510 ... K3
Glad Valley 75 ... F3
Glencross 150 ... H3
Glenham 134 ... J2
Goodwin 126 ... R4
Greenway 57 ... K2
Greenwood 90 ... N8
Gregory 1,384 ... L7
Grenville 81 ... O3
Groton 1,196 ... N3
Harrington 54 ... G7
Harrisburg 727 ... R7
Harrison 89 ... M7
Harrold 167 ... K4
Hartford 1,262 ... P6
Hayti▲ 372 ... P4
Hazel 103 ... P4
Hecla 398 ... N2
Henry 215 ... P4
Hereford 50 ... D5
Hermosa 242 ... C6
Herreid 488 ... K2
Herrick 139 ... L7
Hetland 53 ... P5
Highmore▲ 835 ... L4
Hillsview 4 ... L2
Hitchcock 95 ... M4
Hosmer 310 ... L2
Hot Springs▲ 4,325 ... C7
Houghton 80 ... N2
Hoven 522 ... K3
Howard▲ 1,156 ... P5
Hudson 332 ... R7
Humboldt 468 ... P6
Hurley 372 ... P7
Huron▲ 12,448 ... N5
Ideal 250 ... K6
Interior 67 ... F6
Ipswich▲ 965 ... L3
Irene 464 ... P7
Iroquois 328 ... O5
Isabel 319 ... G3
Java 161 ... K3
Jefferson 527 ... S8
Junius 50 ... P6
Kadoka▲ 736 ... F6
Kaylor 120 ... O7
Kenel 245 ... H2
Kennebec▲ 284 ... K6
Keystone 232 ... C6
Kidder 75 ... O2
Kimball 743 ... M6
Kranzburg 132 ... R4
Kyle 914 ... E7
La Bolt 91 ... R3
La Plant 165 ... H3
Lake Andes▲ 846 ... M7
Lake City 43 ... O2
Lake Norden 427 ... P4
Lake Preston 663 ... P5
Lane 71 ... N5
Langford 298 ... O2
Lantry 200 ... G3
Lead 3,632 ... B5
Lebanon 115 ... K3
Lemmon 1,614 ... E2
Lennox 1,767 ... R7
Leola▲ 521 ... M2
Lesterville 168 ... O7
Letcher 164 ... N6
Lily 26 ... O3
Little Eagle 294 ... H2
Longlake 64 ... L2
Loomis 55 ... N6
Lower Brule 655 ... K5
Lowry 15 ... K3
Lyons 100 ... R6
Madison▲ 6,257 ... P6
Manderson 243 ... D7
Mansfield 120 ... N3
Marion 831 ... P7
Martin▲ 1,151 ... F7
Marty 436 ... N8
Marvin 38 ... R3
McIntosh▲ 302 ... G2
McLaughlin 780 ... H2
Meckling 108 ... R8
Mellette 184 ... N3
Menno 768 ... P7
Midland 233 ... G5
Milbank▲ 3,879 ... R3
Miller▲ 1,678 ... L4
Mission 730 ... H7
Mission Hill 180 ... P8
Mission Ridge 46 ... H4
Mitchell▲ 13,798 ... N6
Mobridge 3,768 ... J2
Monroe 151 ... P7
Montrose 420 ... P6
Morristown 64 ... F2
Mound City▲ 89 ... K2
Mount Vernon 368 ... N6
Murdo▲ 679 ... H6
Naples 35 ... O4
Nemo 42 ... B5
New Effington 219 ... R2
New Holland 125 ... M7
New Underwood 553 ... D5
New Witten 87 ... K7
Newell 675 ... C4
Nisland 174 ... C4
North Eagle Butte 1,423 ... G3
North Sioux City 2,019 ... R8
Northville 105 ... M3
Nunda 45 ... P5
Oacoma 367 ... L6
Oelrichs 138 ... C7
Oglala 422 ... D7
Okreek 500 ... J7
Oldham 189 ... P5
Olivet▲ 74 ... O7
Onaka 52 ... L3
Onida▲ 761 ... K4
Oral 60 ... C7
Orient 59 ... L4
Ortley 63 ... P3
Parker▲ 984 ... P7
Parkston 1,572 ... O7
Parmelee 618 ... G7
Peever 195 ... R2
Philip▲ 1,077 ... F5
Pickstown 95 ... M7
Piedmont 500 ... C5
Pierpont 173 ... O3
Pierre (cap.)▲ 12,906 ... J5
Pine Ridge 2,596 ... E7
Plankinton▲ 604 ... N6
Platte 1,311 ... M7
Pollock 379 ... J2
Porcupine 783 ... E7
Potato Creek 40 ... F6
Prairie City 50 ... D2
Presho 654 ... J6
Pringle 96 ... B6
Provo 60 ... B7
Pukwana 263 ... L6
Quinn 72 ... E5
Ramona 194 ... P5
Rapid City▲ 54,523 ... C5
Ravinia 79 ... N7
Raymond 96 ... O4
Redfield▲ 2,770 ... N4
Redig 50 ... C3
Ree Heights 91 ... L4
Reliance 169 ... K6
Renner 320 ... R6
Revillo 152 ... R3
Richland 70 ... R8
Ridgeview 75 ... H3
Rockerville 28 ... C6
Rockham 48 ... M4
Roscoe 362 ... L3
Rosebud 1,538 ... H7
Rosholt 408 ... R2
Roslyn 251 ... P2
Roswell 19 ... O6
Rowena 100 ... R6
Saint Francis 815 ... H7
Saint Lawrence 223 ... M4
Saint Onge 250 ... B4
Salem▲ 1,289 ... P6
Sanator 150 ... B6
Scotland 968 ... O7
Selby▲ 707 ... J3
Seneca 81 ... L3
Shadehill 186 ... E2
Sherman 66 ... S6
Sinai 120 ... P5
Sioux Falls▲ 100,814 ... R6
Sisseton▲ 2,181 ... R2
Smithwick 50 ... C7
South Shore 260 ... P3
Spearfish 6,966 ... B5
Spencer 317 ... O6
Spink 75 ... R8
Springfield 834 ... N8
Stickney 323 ... M6
Stockholm 89 ... R3
Strandburg 74 ... R3
Stratford 85 ... N3
Sturgis▲ 5,330 ... B5
Summit 267 ... P3
Tabor 403 ... O8
Tea 786 ... R7
Tilford 75 ... C5
Timber Lake▲ 517 ... H3
Tolstoy 69 ... K3
Toronto 201 ... R4
Trail City 68 ... H3
Trent 211 ... R6
Tripp 664 ... N7
Trojan 40 ... B5
Tulare 244 ... N4
Turton 76 ... N3
Tuthill 75 ... G7
Twin Brooks 54 ... R3
Tyndall▲ 1,201 ... O8
Union Center 63 ... D4
Utica 115 ... P8
Vale 160 ... C4
Valley Springs 739 ... S6
Veblen 321 ... P2
Verdon 7 ... N3
Vermillion 10,034 ... R8
Viborg 763 ... P7
Vienna 93 ... O4
Vilas 28 ... O6
Villa Ranchaero 1,666 ... C5
Virgil 33 ... N5
Vivian 95 ... J6
Volga 1,263 ... R5
Volin 175 ... P8
Wagner 1,462 ... N7
Wakonda 329 ... P7
Wakpala 500 ... H2
Wall 834 ... E6
Wallace 83 ... P3
Wanblee 654 ... F6
Ward 35 ... R5
Warner 336 ... M3
Wasta 82 ... D5
Watauga 50 ... F2
Watertown▲ 17,592 ... P4
Waubay 647 ... P3
Webster▲ 2,017 ... P3
Wentworth 181 ... R6
Wessington 265 ... M5
Wessington Springs▲ 1,083 ... M5
Westport 112 ... M2
Wetonka 12 ... M2
White 536 ... R5
White Lake 419 ... M6
White River▲ 595 ... H6
White Rock 7 ... R2
Whitehorse 152 ... H3
Whitewood 891 ... B5
Willow Lake 317 ... O4
Wilmot 566 ... R3
Winfred 54 ... P6
Winner▲ 3,354 ... K7
Witten 134 ... J7
Wolsey 442 ... N5
Wood 73 ... J6
Woonsocket▲ 766 ... N5
Worthing 371 ... R7
Wounded Knee 18 ... D7
Yale 128 ... O5
Yankton▲ 12,703 ... P8

OTHER FEATURES

Aeber (creek) ... G4
Andes (lake) ... N7
Angostura (res.) ... B7
Antelope (creek) ... D3
Bad (riv.) ... G5
Badlands Nat'l Park ... E6
Battle (creek) ... C6
Bear in the Lodge (creek) ... F6
Beaver (creek) ... A6
Belle Fourche (res.) ... B4
Belle Fourche (riv.) ... C4
Big Bend (dam) ... K5
Big Sioux (riv.) ... S7
Big Stone (lake) ... R3
Black Hills (mts.) ... B5
Black Pine (creek) ... G6
Bois de Sioux (riv.) ... R1
Boxelder (creek) ... D5
Brant (lake) ... R6
Buffalo (creek) ... F6
Buffalo (lake) ... P2
Bull (creek) ... C2
Bull (creek) ... K6
Byron (lake) ... N4
Cain (creek) ... N5
Cherry (creek) ... F4
Cherry (creek) ... F5
Cheyenne (riv.) ... F4
Cheyenne River Ind. Res. ... F4
Choteau (creek) ... N7
Columbia Road (res.) ... N2
Cottonwood (creek) ... E5
Cottonwood (lake) ... M4
Crazy Horse Mon. ... B6
Crow (creek) ... A4
Crow Creek Ind. Res. ... L5
Dog Ear (creek) ... K6
Dry (creek) ... G4
Dry (lake) ... P3
Dry Wood (lake) ... P2
Elk (creek) ... C5
Ellsworth Air Force Base 7,017 ... C5
Elm (creek) ... D4
Elm (riv.) ... M2
Firesteel (creek) ... N6
Flint Rock (creek) ... E3
Fort Randall (dam) ... N7
Foster (creek) ... N4
Francis Case (lake) ... L7
French (creek) ... C6
Gavins Point (dam) ... P8
Geographical Center of United States ... B4
Grand (riv.) ... F2
Harney (peak) ... B6
Hat (creek) ... B7
Hell Canyon (creek) ... B6
Herman (lake) ... P5
Horsehead (creek) ... C7
Indian (creek) ... B4
James (riv.) ... N5
Jewel Cave Nat'l Mon. ... B6
Kampeska (lake) ... P4
Keya Paha (riv.) ... K7
Lame Johnny (creek) ... C6
Lewis and Clark (lake) ... O8
Little Missouri (riv.) ... B1
Little Moreau (riv.) ... G3
Little White (riv.) ... H7
Long (lake) ... L2
Lower Brule Ind. Res. ... K5
Madison (lake) ... P6
Maple (riv.) ... M1
Medicine (creek) ... J6
Medicine Knoll (creek) ... J5
Minnechaduze (creek) ... H7
Minnesota (riv.) ... S3
Missouri (riv.) ... P8
Mitchell (creek) ... G5
Moreau (riv.) ... G3
Mount Rushmore Nat'l Mon. ... B6
Mud (creek) ... N3
Mud (lake) ... R2
Mud Lake (res.) ... N2
Nasty (creek) ... C2
Oahe (dam) ... J5
Oahe (lake) ... J1
Oak (creek) ... H2
Oak (creek) ... J6
Okobojo (creek) ... J4
Owl (creek) ... B4
Parker (lake) ... P3
Pearl (creek) ... N5
Pine Ridge Ind. Res. ... D7
Piyas (lake) ... P2
Platte (lake) ... M6
Pleasant Valley (creek) ... B6
Poinsett (lake) ... P4
Ponca (creek) ... L7
Prairie (lake) ... P3
Rabbit (creek) ... E3
Red (lake) ... L6
Red Owl (creek) ... E4
Red Scaffold (creek) ... F4
Redstone (creek) ... O5
Redwater (creek) ... A4
Reid (lake) ... O3
Rock (creek) ... O6
Rosebud Ind. Res. ... H7
Sand (creek) ... C3
Sand (creek) ... M5
Shadehill (res.) ... E3
Sharpe (lake) ... J5
Shue (creek) ... N5
Smith (creek) ... L6
Snake (creek) ... F4
Snake (creek) ... F5
Snake (creek) ... M3
Spirit (lake) ... O4
Spring (creek) ... C6
Spring (creek) ... J2
Squaw (creek) ... B3
Sulphur (creek) ... D4
Swan (creek) ... J3
Swan (lake) ... K3
Swan (lake) ... O3
Thompson (lake) ... O5
Thunder (creek) ... N4
Thunder Butte (creek) ... E3
Traverse (lake) ... R2
Turtle (creek) ... M4
Vermillion (riv.) ... P6
Virgin (creek) ... H3
Waubay (lake) ... O3
Whetstone (creek) ... R3
White (lake) ... M6
White (riv.) ... D7
Whitewood (creek) ... B4
Willow (creek) ... C4
Wind Cave Nat'l Park ... B6
Wolf (creek) ... L4
Wounded Knee (creek) ... E7

▲County seat

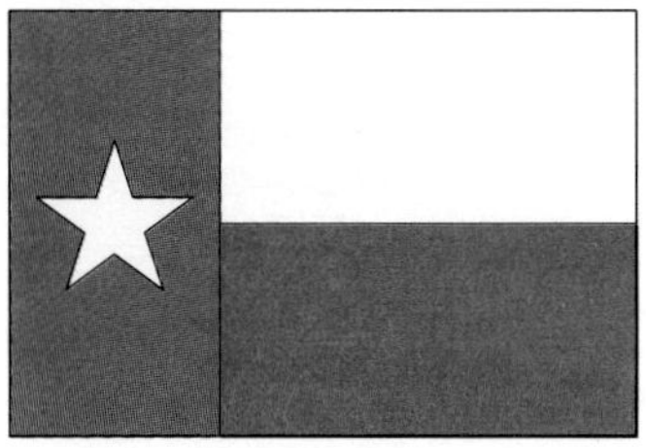

AREA 266,807 sq. mi. (691,030 sq. km.)
POPULATION 17,059,805
CAPITAL Austin
LARGEST CITY Houston
HIGHEST POINT Guadalupe Pk. 8,749 ft. (2667 m.)
SETTLED IN 1686
ADMITTED TO UNION December 29, 1845
POPULAR NAME Lone Star State
STATE FLOWER Bluebonnet
STATE BIRD Mockingbird

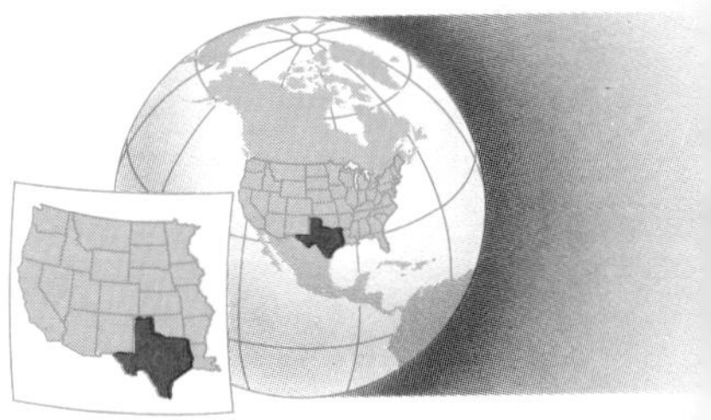

COUNTIES

derson 48,024 .... J6
drews 14,338 .... B5
gelina 69,884 .... K6
ansas 17,892 .... H10
cher 7,973 .... F4
mstrong 2,021 .... C3
ascosa 30,533 .... F9
stin 19,832 .... H8
iley 7,064 .... B3
ndera 10,562 .... E8
strop 38,263 .... G7
ylor 4,385 .... E4
e 25,135 .... G9
ll 191,088 .... G6
xar 1,185,394 .... F8
anco 5,972 .... F8
rden 799 .... C5
sque 15,125 .... G6
wie 81,665 .... K4
azoria 191,707 .... J8
azos 121,862 .... H7
ewster 8,681 .... A8
iscoe 1,971 .... C3
ooks 8,204 .... F11
own 34,371 .... F6
rleson 13,625 .... H7
rnet 22,677 .... F7
aldwell 26,392 .... G8
alhoun 19,053 .... H9
allahan 11,859 .... E5
ameron 260,120 .... G11
amp 9,904 .... K5
arson 6,576 .... C2
ass 29,982 .... K4
astro 9,070 .... B3
hambers 20,088 .... K8
herokee 41,049 .... J6
hildress 5,953 .... D3
lay 10,024 .... F4
ochran 4,377 .... B4
oke 3,424 .... D6
oleman 9,710 .... E6
ollin 264,036 .... H4
ollingsworth 3,573 .... D3
olorado 18,383 .... H8
omal 51,832 .... F8
omanche 13,381 .... F5
oncho 3,044 .... E6
ooke 30,777 .... G4
oryell 64,213 .... G6
ottle 2,247 .... D3
rane 4,652 .... B6
rockett 4,078 .... C7
rosby 7,304 .... C4
ulberson 3,407 .... C11
allam 5,461 .... B1
Dallas 1,852,810 .... H5
Dawson 14,349 .... C5
De Witt 18,903 .... G9
Deaf Smith 19,153 .... B3
Delta 4,857 .... J4
Denton 273,525 .... G4
Dickens 2,571 .... D4
Dimmit 10,433 .... E9
Donley 3,696 .... D2
Duval 12,918 .... F10
Eastland 18,488 .... F5
Ector 118,934 .... B6
Edwards 2,266 .... D7
El Paso 591,610 .... A10
Ellis 85,167 .... H5
Erath 27,991 .... F5
Falls 17,712 .... H6
Fannin 24,804 .... H4
Fayette 20,095 .... H8
Fisher 4,842 .... D5
Floyd 8,497 .... C3
Foard 1,794 .... E3
Fort Bend 225,421 .... J8
Franklin 7,802 .... J4
Freestone 15,818 .... H6
Frio 13,472 .... E9
Gaines 14,123 .... B5
Galveston 217,399 .... K8
Garza 5,143 .... C4
Gillespie 17,204 .... F7
Glasscock 1,447 .... C6
Goliad 5,980 .... G9
Gonzales 17,205 .... G8
Gray 23,967 .... D2
Grayson 95,021 .... H4
Gregg 104,948 .... K5
Grimes 18,828 .... J7
Guadalupe 64,873 .... G8
Hale 34,671 .... C3
Hall 3,905 .... D3
Hamilton 7,733 .... F6
Hansford 5,848 .... C1
Hardeman 5,283 .... E3
Hardin 41,320 .... K7
Harris 2,818,199 .... J8
Harrison 57,483 .... K5
Hartley 3,634 .... B2
Haskell 6,820 .... E4
Hays 65,614 .... F7
Hemphill 3,720 .... D2
Henderson 58,543 .... J5
Hidalgo 383,545 .... F11
Hill 27,146 .... G5
Hockley 24,199 .... B4
Hood 28,981 .... G5
Hopkins 28,833 .... J4
Houston 21,375 .... J6
Howard 32,343 .... C5
Hudspeth 2,915 .... B10
Hunt 64,343 .... H4
Hutchinson 25,689 .... C2
Irion 1,629 .... C6
Jack 6,981 .... F4
Jackson 13,039 .... H9
Jasper 31,102 .... K7
Jeff Davis 1,946 .... C11
Jefferson 239,397 .... K8
Jim Hogg 5,109 .... F11
Jim Wells 37,679 .... F10
Johnson 97,165 .... G5
Jones 16,490 .... E5
Karnes 12,455 .... G9
Kaufman 52,220 .... H5
Kendall 14,589 .... F8
Kenedy 460 .... G11
Kent 1,010 .... D4
Kerr 36,304 .... E7
Kimble 4,122 .... E7
King 354 .... D4
Kinney 3,119 .... D8
Kleberg 30,274 .... G10
Knox 4,837 .... E4
La Salle 5,254 .... E9
Lamar 43,949 .... J4
Lamb 15,072 .... B3
Lampasas 13,521 .... F6
Lavaca 18,690 .... H8
Lee 12,854 .... H7
Leon 12,665 .... J6
Liberty 52,726 .... K7
Limestone 20,946 .... H6
Lipscomb 3,143 .... D1
Live Oak 9,556 .... F9
Llano 11,631 .... F7
Loving 107 .... A6
Lubbock 222,636 .... C4
Lynn 6,758 .... C4
Madison 10,931 .... J6
Marion 9,984 .... K5
Martin 4,956 .... C5
Mason 3,423 .... E7
Matagorda 36,928 .... H9
Maverick 36,378 .... D9
McCulloch 8,778 .... E6
McLennan 189,123 .... G6
McMullen 817 .... F9
Medina 27,312 .... E8
Menard 2,252 .... E7
Midland 106,611 .... B6
Milam 22,946 .... H7
Mills 4,531 .... F6
Mitchell 8,016 .... D5
Montague 17,274 .... G4
Montgomery 182,201 .... J7
Moore 17,865 .... C2
Morris 13,200 .... K4
Motley 1,532 .... D3
Nacogdoches 54,753 .... K6
Navarro 39,926 .... H5
Newton 13,569 .... L7
Nolan 16,594 .... D5
Nueces 291,145 .... G10
Ochiltree 9,128 .... D1
Oldham 2,278 .... B2
Orange 80,509 .... L7
Palo Pinto 25,055 .... F5
Panola 22,035 .... K5
Parker 64,785 .... G5
Parmer 9,863 .... B3
Pecos 14,675 .... B7
Polk 30,687 .... K7
Potter 97,874 .... C2
Presidio 6,637 .... C12
Rains 6,715 .... J5
Randall 89,673 .... C2
Reagan 4,514 .... C6
Real 2,412 .... E8
Red River 14,317 .... J4
Reeves 15,852 .... D11
Refugio 7,976 .... G9
Roberts 1,025 .... D2
Robertson 15,511 .... H6
Rockwall 25,604 .... H5
Runnels 11,294 .... E6
Rusk 43,735 .... K5
Sabine 9,586 .... L6
San Augustine 7,999 .... K6
San Jacinto 16,372 .... J7
San Patricio 58,749 .... G10
San Saba 5,401 .... F6
Schleicher 2,990 .... D7
Scurry 18,634 .... D5
Shackleford 3,915 .... E5
Shelby 22,034 .... K6
Sherman 2,858 .... C1
Smith 151,309 .... J5
Somervell 5,360 .... G5
Starr 40,518 .... F11
Stephens 9,010 .... F5
Sterling 1,438 .... C6
Stonewall 2,013 .... D4
Sutton 4,135 .... D7
Swisher 8,133 .... C3
Tarrant 1,170,103 .... G5
Taylor 119,655 .... E5
Terrell 1,410 .... B7
Terry 13,218 .... B4
Throckmorton 1,880 .... E4
Titus 24,009 .... K4
Tom Green 98,458 .... D6
Travis 576,407 .... G7
Trinity 11,445 .... J6
Tyler 16,646 .... K7
Upshur 31,370 .... K5
Upton 4,447 .... B6
Uvalde 23,340 .... E8
Val Verde 38,721 .... C8
Van Zandt 37,944 .... J5
Victoria 74,361 .... H9
Walker 50,917 .... J7
Waller 23,390 .... J8
Ward 13,115 .... A6
Washington 26,154 .... H7
Webb 133,239 .... E10
Wharton 39,955 .... H8
Wheeler 5,879 .... D2
Wichita 122,378 .... F3
Wilbarger 15,121 .... E3
Willacy 17,705 .... G11
Williamson 139,551 .... G7
Wilson 22,650 .... F8
Winkler 8,626 .... A6
Wise 34,679 .... G4
Wood 29,380 .... J5
Yoakum 8,786 .... B4
Young 18,126 .... F4
Zapata 9,279 .... E11
Zavala 12,162 .... E9

CITIES and TOWNS

Abernathy 2,720 .... B4
Abilene▲ 106,654 .... E5
Addison 8,783 .... G2
Alamo 8,210 .... F11
Alamo Heights 6,502 .... K10
Albany▲ 1,962 .... E5
Alice▲ 19,788 .... F10
Allen 18,309 .... H1
Alpine▲ 5,637 .... D12
Alvarado 2,918 .... G5
Alvin 19,220 .... J3
Amarillo▲ 157,615 .... C2
Anahuac▲ 1,993 .... K8
Anderson▲ 500 .... J7
Andrews▲ 10,678 .... B5
Angleton▲ 17,140 .... J8
Anson▲ 2,644 .... E5
Anthony 3,328 .... A10
Aransas Pass 7,180 .... G10
Archer City▲ 1,748 .... F4
Arlington 261,721 .... F2
Aspermont▲ 1,214 .... D4
Athens▲ 10,967 .... J5
Atlanta 6,118 .... K4
Austin (cap.)▲ 465,622 .... G7
Azle 8,868 .... E2
Bacliff 5,549 .... K2
Baird▲ 1,658 .... E5
Balch Springs 17,406 .... H2
Balcones Heights 3,022 .... J10
Ballinger▲ 3,975 .... E6
Bandera▲ 877 .... F8
Barrett 3,052 .... K1
Bastrop▲ 4,044 .... G7
Bay City▲ 18,170 .... H9
Baytown 63,850 .... L2
Beaumont▲ 114,323 .... K7
Bedford 43,762 .... F2
Beeville▲ 13,547 .... G9
Bellaire 13,842 .... J2
Bellmead 8,336 .... H6
Bellville▲ 3,378 .... H8
Belton▲ 12,476 .... G7
Benavides 1,788 .... F10
Benbrook 19,564 .... E2
Benjamin▲ 225 .... E4
Big Lake▲ 3,672 .... C6
Big Spring▲ 23,093 .... C5
Bishop 3,337 .... G10
Bloomington 1,888 .... H9
Blue Mound 2,133 .... E2
Boerne▲ 4,274 .... J10
Bonham▲ 6,686 .... H4
Borger 15,675 .... C2
Boston▲ 400 .... K4
Bowie 4,990 .... G4
Brackettville▲ 1,740 .... D8
Brady▲ 5,946 .... E6
Brazoria 2,717 .... J9
Breckinridge▲ 5,665 .... F5
Brenham▲ 11,952 .... H7
Briar 3,899 .... E1
Bridge City 8,034 .... L7
Bridgeport 3,581 .... G4
Brookshire 2,922 .... J8
Brownfield▲ 9,560 .... B4
Brownsville▲ 98,962 .... G12
Brownwood▲ 18,387 .... F6
Bryan▲ 55,002 .... H7
Buda 1,795 .... G7
Buna 2,127 .... L7
Bunker Hill Village 3,391 .... J1
Burkburnett 10,145 .... F3
Burleson 16,113 .... F3
Burnet▲ 3,423 .... F7
Caldwell▲ 3,181 .... H7
Cameron▲ 5,580 .... H7
Canadian▲ 2,417 .... D2
Canton▲ 2,949 .... J5
Canutillo 4,442 .... A10
Canyon▲ 11,365 .... C3
Carrizo Springs▲ 5,745 .... E9
Carrollton 82,169 .... G2
Carthage▲ 6,496 .... K5
Castle Hills 4,198 .... J10
Castroville 2,159 .... J11
Cedar Hill 19,976 .... G3
Cedar Park 5,161 .... G7
Center▲ 4,950 .... K6
Centerville▲ 812 .... H6
Channelview 25,564 .... K1
Channing▲ 277 .... B2
Childress▲ 5,055 .... D3
Cisco 3,813 .... E5
Clarendon▲ 2,067 .... C3
Clarksville▲ 4,311 .... K4
Claude▲ 1,199 .... C2
Clear Lake Shores 1,096 .... K2
Cleburne▲ 22,205 .... G5
Cleveland 7,124 .... K7
Clifton 3,195 .... G6
Clute 8,910 .... J9
Clyde 3,002 .... E5
Cockrell Hill 3,746 .... G2
Coldspring▲ 538 .... J7
Coleman▲ 5,410 .... E6
College Station▲ 52,456 .... H7
Colleyville 12,724 .... F2
Colorado City▲ 4,749 .... C5
Columbus▲ 3,367 .... H8
Comanche▲ 4,087 .... F6
Commerce 6,825 .... J4
Conroe▲ 27,610 .... J7
Converse 8,887 .... K11
Cooper▲ 2,153 .... J4
Coppell 16,881 .... G2
Copperas Cove 24,079 .... G6
Corpus Christi▲ 257,453 .... G10
Corsicana▲ 22,911 .... H5
Cotulla▲ 3,694 .... E9
Crane▲ 3,533 .... B6
Crockett▲ 7,024 .... J6
Crosby 1,811 .... J8
Crosbyton▲ 2,026 .... C4
Crowell▲ 1,230 .... E4
Crowley 6,974 .... E3
Crystal City▲ 8,263 .... E9
Cuero▲ 6,700 .... G8
Daingerfield▲ 2,572 .... K4
Dalhart▲ 6,246 .... B1
Dallas▲ 1,006,877 .... G2
Dalworthington Gardens 1,758 .... F2
Dayton 5,151 .... J7
De Kalb 1,976 .... K4
De Leon 2,190 .... F5
De Soto 30,544 .... G3
Decatur▲ 4,252 .... G4
Deer Park 27,652 .... K2
Del Rio▲ 30,705 .... D8
Denison 21,505 .... H4
Denton▲ 66,270 .... G4
Denver City 5,145 .... B4
Devine 3,928 .... E8
Diboll 4,341 .... K6
Dickens▲ 322 .... D4
Dickinson 9,497 .... K3
Dilley 2,632 .... E9
Dimmitt▲ 4,408 .... B3
Donna 12,652 .... F11
Double Oak 1,664 .... F1

(continued on following page)

DOMINANT LAND USE

- Wheat, Grain Sorghums, Range Livestock
- Cotton, Wheat
- Specialized Cotton
- Cotton, General Farming
- Cotton, Forest Products
- Cotton, Range Livestock
- Rice, General Farming
- Peanuts, General Farming
- General Farming, Livestock, Cash Grain
- General Farming, Forest Products, Truck Farming, Cotton
- Fruit, Truck and Mixed Farming
- Range Livestock
- Forests
- Swampland, Limited Agriculture
- Nonagricultural Land
- Urban Areas

MAJOR MINERAL OCCURRENCES

At	Asphalt	He	Helium
Cl	Clay	Ls	Limestone
Fe	Iron Ore	Na	Salt
G	Natural Gas	O	Petroleum
Gn	Granite	S	Sulfur
Gp	Gypsum	Tc	Talc
Gr	Graphite	U	Uranium

Water Power
Major Industrial Areas

Agriculture, Industry and Resources

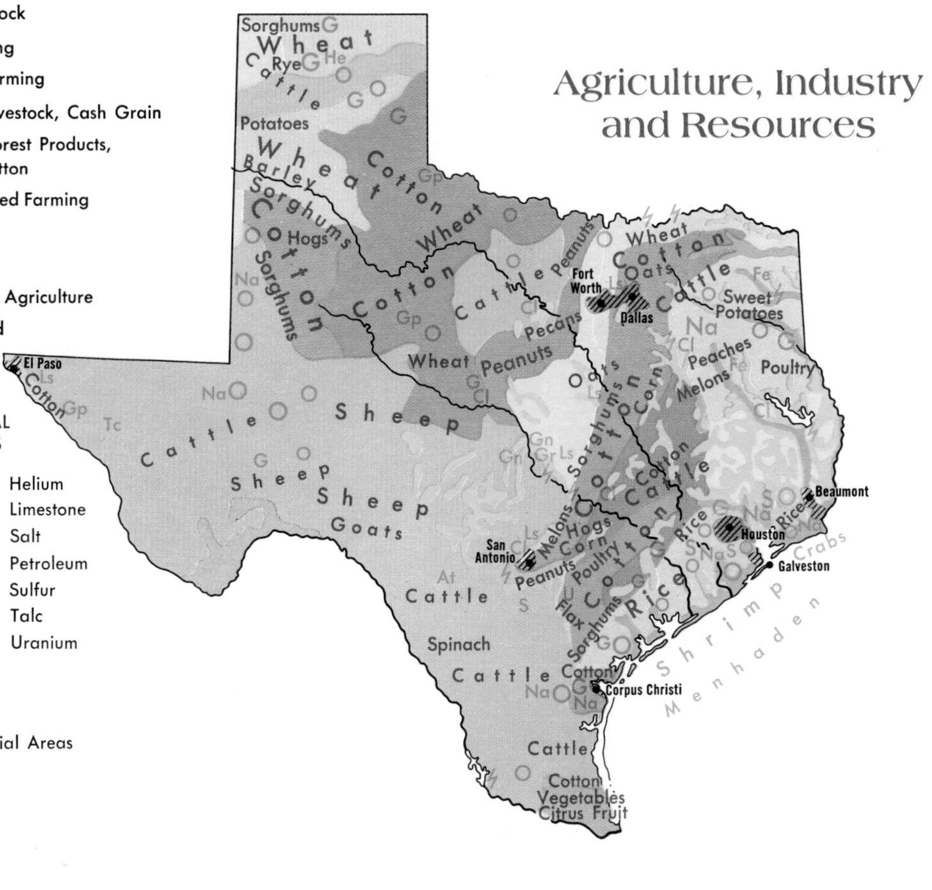

Sorghums
Wheat
Rye
Cattle
Potatoes
Barley
Cotton
Hogs
Fort Worth
Dallas
Oats
Sweet Potatoes
Pecans
Peanuts
Peaches
Poultry
Melons
Corn
El Paso
Sheep
Goats
San Antonio
Houston
Beaumont
Galveston
Rice
Crabs
Shrimp
Menhaden
Flax
Spinach
Corpus Christi
Vegetables
Citrus Fruit

Dublin 3,190.....F5
Dumas▲ 12,871.....C2
Duncanville 35,748.....G3
Eagle Lake 3,551.....H8
Eagle Pass▲ 20,651.....D9
Eastland▲ 3,690.....F5
Edcouch 2,878.....G11
Edgecliff 2,715.....E2
Edinburg▲ 29,885.....F11
Edna▲ 5,343.....H9
El Campo 10,511.....H8
El Lago 3,269.....K2
El Paso▲ 515,342.....A10
Eldorado▲ 2,019.....D7
Electra 3,113.....F4
Elgin 4,846.....G7
Elsa 5,242.....G11
Emory▲ 963.....J5
Ennis 13,883.....H5
Euless 38,149.....F2
Everman 5,672.....F3
Fabens 5,599.....B10
Fairfield▲ 3,234.....H6
Falfurrias▲ 5,788.....F10
Farmers Branch 24,250.....G2
Farmersville 2,640.....H4
Farwell▲ 1,373.....A3
Ferris 2,212.....H3
Floresville▲ 5,247.....K11
Flower Mound 15,527.....F1
Floydada▲ 3,896.....C3
Forest Hill 11,482.....F2
Forney 4,070.....H5
Fort Davis▲ 900.....D11
Fort Stockton▲ 8,524.....A7
Fort Worth▲ 447,619.....F2
Franklin▲ 1,336.....H7
Fredericksburg▲ 6,934.....E7
Fredonia 50.....E7
Freeport 11,389.....J9
Freer 3,271.....F10
Fresno 3,182.....J2
Friendswood 22,814.....J2
Friona 3,688.....B3
Frisco 6,141.....H4
Fritch 2,335.....C2
Gail▲ 171.....C5
Gainesville▲ 14,256.....G4
Galena Park 10,033.....J1
Galveston▲ 59,070.....L3
Ganado 1,701.....H8
Garden City▲ 350.....C6
Garland 180,650.....H2
Gatesville▲ 11,492.....G6
George West▲ 2,586.....F9
Georgetown▲ 14,842.....G7
Giddings▲ 4,093.....H7
Gilmer▲ 4,822.....J5
Gladewater 6,027.....K5
Glen Rose▲ 1,949.....G5
Glenn Heights 4,564.....G2
Goldthwaite▲ 1,658.....F6
Goliad▲ 1,946.....G9
Gonzales▲ 6,527.....G8
Graham▲ 8,986.....F4
Granbury▲ 4,045.....G5
Grand Prairie 99,616.....G2
Grand Saline 2,630.....J5
Grapevine 29,202.....F2
Greenville▲ 23,071.....H4
Groesbeck▲ 3,185.....H6
Groves 16,513.....L8
Groveton▲ 1,071.....J7
Guthrie▲ 170.....D4
Hale Center 2,067.....C3
Hallettsville▲ 2,718.....G8
Hallsville 2,288.....K5
Haltom City 32,856.....F2
Hamilton▲ 2,937.....G6
Hamlin 2,791.....E5
Harlingen 48,735.....G11
Haskell▲ 3,362.....E4
Hearne 5,132.....H7
Hebbronville▲ 4,465.....F10
Hedwig Village 2,616.....H1
Hemphill▲ 1,182.....L6
Hempstead▲ 3,551.....J7
Henderson▲ 11,139.....K5
Henrietta▲ 2,896.....F4
Hereford▲ 14,745.....B3
Hickory Creek 1,893.....F1
Hidalgo 3,292.....F11
Highland Park 8,739.....G2
Highland Village 7,027.....F1
Highlands 6,632.....K1
Hillsboro▲ 7,072.....G5
Hitchcock 5,868.....K3
Hollywood 3,231.....K10
Hondo▲ 6,018.....E8
Honey Grove 1,681.....J4
Hooks 2,684.....K4
Houston▲ 1,630,553.....J2
Howe 2,173.....H4
Hughes Springs 1,938.....K5
Humble 12,060.....J7
Hunters Creek Village 3,954.....J1
Huntington 1,794.....K6
Huntsville▲ 27,925.....J7
Hurst 33,574.....F2
Hutchins 2,719.....G3
Idalou 2,074.....C4
Iowa Park 6,072.....F4
Irving 155,037.....G2
Italy 1,699.....H5
Jacinto City 9,343.....J1
Jacksboro▲ 3,350.....F4
Jacksonville 12,765.....J5
Jasper▲ 6,959.....L7
Jayton▲ 608.....D4
Jefferson▲ 2,199.....K5
Jersey Village 4,826.....J1
Johnson City▲ 932.....F7
Jones Creek 2,160.....J9
Jourdanton▲ 3,220.....F9
Junction▲ 2,654.....E7
Karnes City▲ 2,916.....G9
Katy 8,005.....J8

Kaufman▲ 5,238.....H5
Keene 3,944.....G5
Keller 13,683.....F2
Kenedy 3,763.....G9
Kennedale 4,096.....F3
Kerens 1,702.....H5
Kermit▲ 6,875.....B6
Kerrville▲ 17,384.....E7
Kilgore 11,066.....K5
Killeen 63,535.....G6
Kingsland 2,725.....F7
Kingsville▲ 25,276.....G10
Kirby 8,326.....K11
Kirbyville 1,871.....K7
Kountze▲ 2,056.....K7
Kyle 2,225.....G8
La Feria 3,495.....G11
La Grange▲ 3,951.....G8
La Joya 2,604.....F11
La Marque 14,120.....K3
La Porte 27,910.....K2
Lake Dallas 3,656.....G1
Lake Jackson 22,776.....J8
Lake Worth 4,591.....E2
Lamesa▲ 10,809.....C5
Lampasas▲ 6,382.....F6
Lancaster 22,117.....G3
Laredo▲ 122,899.....E10
League City 30,159.....K2
Leakey▲ 399.....E8
Leon Valley 9,581.....J10
Leonard 1,744.....H4
Levelland▲ 13,986.....B4
Lewisville 46,521.....G1
Liberty▲ 7,733.....K7
Lindale 2,428.....J5
Linden▲ 2,375.....K4
Lipscomb▲ 52.....D1
Littlefield▲ 6,489.....B4
Live Oak 10,023.....K10
Livingston▲ 5,019.....K7
Llano▲ 2,962.....F7
Lockhart▲ 9,205.....G8
Lockney 2,207.....C3
Lomax 2,991.....K2
Longview▲ 70,311.....K5
Los Fresnos 2,473.....G11
Lubbock▲ 186,206.....C4
Lucas 2,205.....H1
Lufkin▲ 30,206.....K6
Luling 4,661.....G8
Lumberton 6,640.....K7
Lyford 1,674.....G11
Lytle 2,255.....J11
Mabank 1,739.....H5
Madisonville▲ 3,569.....J7
Malakoff 2,038.....H5
Mansfield 15,607.....F3
Manvel 3,733.....J3
Marble Falls 4,007.....F7
Marfa▲ 2,424.....C12
Marlin▲ 6,386.....H6
Marshall▲ 23,682.....K5
Mart 2,004.....H6
Mason▲ 2,041.....E7
Matador▲ 790.....D3
Mathis 5,423.....G9
McAllen 84,021.....F11
McCamey 2,493.....B6
McGregor 4,683.....G6
McKinney▲ 21,283.....H4
Memphis▲ 2,465.....D3
Menard▲ 1,606.....E7
Mentone▲ 50.....D10
Mercedes 12,694.....F12
Meridian▲ 1,390.....G6
Merkel 2,469.....E5
Mertzon▲ 778.....C6
Mesquite 101,484.....H2
Mexia 6,933.....H6
Miami▲ 675.....D2
Midland▲ 89,443.....C6
Midlothian 5,141.....G5
Mineola 4,321.....J5
Mineral Wells 14,870.....F5
Mission 28,653.....F11
Missouri City 36,176.....J2
Monahans▲ 8,101.....B6
Montague▲ 1,253.....G4
Morton▲ 2,597.....B4
Mount Pleasant▲ 12,291.....K4
Mount Vernon▲ 2,219.....J4
Muleshoe▲ 4,571.....B3
Nacogdoches▲ 30,872.....J6
Nash 2,162.....K4
Nassau Bay 4,320.....K2
Navasota 6,296.....J7
Nederland 16,192.....K8
Needville 2,199.....J8
New Boston 5,057.....K4
New Braunfels▲ 27,334.....K10
Newton▲ 1,885.....L7
Nixon 1,995.....G8
Nocona 2,870.....G4
North Richland Hills 45,895.....F2
Odessa▲ 89,699.....B6
Olmos Park 2,161.....K11
Olney 3,519.....F4
Olton 2,116.....B3
Orange▲ 19,381.....L7
Overton 2,105.....K5
Ovilla 2,027.....G3
Ozona▲ 3,181.....C7
Paducah▲ 1,788.....D4
Paint Rock▲ 227.....E6
Palacios 4,418.....H9
Palestine▲ 18,042.....J6
Palo Pinto▲ 350.....F5
Pampa▲ 19,959.....D2
Panhandle▲ 2,353.....C2
Pantego 2,371.....F2
Paris▲ 24,699.....J4
Pasadena 119,363.....J2
Pearland 18,697.....J2
Pearsall▲ 6,924.....E9
Pecos▲ 12,069.....D10
Perryton▲ 7,607.....D1

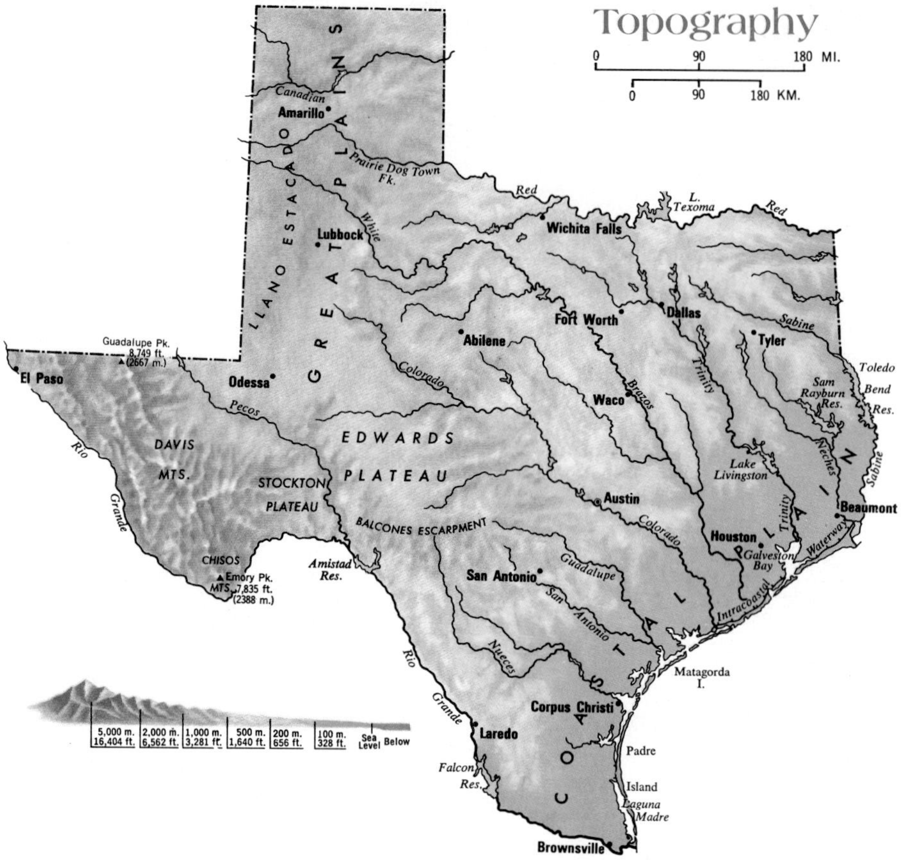

Pflugerville 4,444.....G7
Pharr 32,921.....F11
Pickton 1,729.....C2
Pilot Point 2,538.....H4
Piney Point Village 3,197.....J1
Pittsburg▲ 4,007.....J4
Plains▲ 1,422.....B4
Plainview▲ 21,700.....C3
Plano 128,713.....G1
Pleasanton 7,678.....F9
Port Aransas 2,233.....H10
Port Arthur 58,724.....K8
Port Isabel 4,467.....G11
Port Lavaca▲ 10,886.....H9
Port Neches 12,974.....K7
Portland 12,224.....G10
Post▲ 3,768.....C4
Poteet 3,206.....F8
Prairie View 4,004.....J7
Premont 2,914.....F10
Presidio 3,072.....C12
Quanah▲ 3,413.....E3
Queen City 1,748.....L4
Quitman▲ 1,684.....J5
Ralls 2,172.....C4
Ranger 2,803.....F5
Rankin▲ 1,011.....B6
Raymondville▲ 8,880.....G11
Red Oak 3,124.....H5
Refugio▲ 3,158.....G9
Reno 1,784.....E2
Richardson 74,840.....G2
Richland Hills 7,978.....F2
Richmond▲ 9,801.....J8
Rio Grande City▲ 9,891.....F11
Rio Hondo 1,793.....G11
River Oaks 6,580.....E2
Robert Lee▲ 1,276.....D6
Robstown 12,849.....G10
Roby▲ 616.....D5
Rockdale 5,235.....G7
Rockport▲ 4,753.....H9
Rocksprings▲ 1,339.....D8
Rockwall▲ 10,486.....H5
Roma-Los Saenz 3,384.....E11
Rosenberg 20,183.....J8
Rotan 1,913.....D5
Round Rock 30,923.....G7
Rowlett 23,260.....H2
Royse City 2,206.....H4
Rusk▲ 4,366.....J6
Sachse 5,346.....H2
Saginaw 8,551.....E2
San Antonio▲ 935,933.....J11
San Augustine▲ 2,337.....K6
San Benito 20,125.....G12
San Diego▲ 4,983.....F10
San Elizario 4,385.....A10
San Juan 10,815.....F11
San Leon 3,328.....L2
San Marcos▲ 28,743.....F8
San Saba▲ 2,626.....F6
Sanderson▲ 1,128.....B7
Sanger▲ 3,508.....G4
Sansom Park Village 3,921.....E2
Santa Fe 8,429.....K3
Sarita▲ 200.....G10
Schertz 10,555.....K10
Schulenburg 2,455.....H8
Seabrook 6,685.....K2
Seagoville 8,969.....H3

Seagraves 2,398.....B5
Sealy 4,541.....H8
Seguin▲ 18,853.....G8
Seminole▲ 6,342.....K10
Seymour▲ 3,185.....E4
Shamrock 2,286.....D2
Shepherd 1,812.....K7
Sherman▲ 31,601.....H4
Shiner 2,074.....G8
Sierra Blanca▲ 800.....B11
Silsbee 6,368.....K7
Silverton▲ 779.....C3
Sinton▲ 5,549.....G9
Slaton 6,078.....C4
Smithville 3,196.....G7
Snyder▲ 12,195.....D5
Sonora▲ 2,751.....D7
South Houston 14,207.....J2
South Padre Island 1,677.....F11
Spearman▲ 3,197.....C1
Spring 33,111.....J7
Spring Valley 3,392.....J1
Stafford 8,397.....J2
Stamford 3,817.....E5
Stanton▲ 2,576.....C5
Stephenville▲ 13,502.....F5
Sterling City▲ 1,096.....D6
Stinnett▲ 2,166.....C2
Stratford▲ 1,781.....C1
Sugar Land 24,529.....J8
Sulphur Springs▲ 14,062.....J4
Sundown 1,759.....B4
Sunnyvale 2,228.....H2
Sweeny 3,297.....J8
Sweetwater▲ 11,967.....D5
Taft 3,222.....G9
Tahoka▲ 2,868.....C4
Taylor 11,472.....G7
Taylor Lake Village 3,394.....K2
Teague 3,268.....H6
Temple 46,109.....G6
Terlingua 100.....D12
Terrell 12,490.....H5
Terrell Hills 4,592.....K11
Texarkana 31,656.....L4
Texas City 40,822.....K3
Texhoma 291.....C1
The Colony 22,113.....G1
Three Rivers 1,889.....F9
Throckmorton▲ 1,036.....E4
Tilden▲ 450.....F9
Tomball 6,370.....J7
Trinity 2,648.....J7
Tulia▲ 4,699.....C3
Tyler▲ 75,450.....J5
Universal City 13,057.....K10
University Park 22,259.....F2
Uvalde▲ 14,729.....E8
Van 1,854.....J5
Van Alstyne 2,090.....H4
Van Horn▲ 2,930.....C11
Vega▲ 840.....B2
Vernon▲ 12,001.....E3
Victoria▲ 55,076.....H9
Vidor 10,935.....L7
Waco▲ 103,590.....G6
Wake Village 4,757.....K4
Waskom 1,812.....L5
Watauga 20,009.....F2
Waxahachie▲ 18,168.....H5
Weatherford▲ 14,804.....G5
Webster 4,678.....K2

Weimar 2,052.....H8
Wellington▲ 2,456.....D3
Weslaco 21,877.....F11
West 2,515.....G6
West Columbia 4,372.....J8
West Orange 4,187.....L7
West University Place 12,920...J2
Westworth 2,350.....E2
Wharton▲ 9,011.....J8
Wheeler▲ 1,393.....D2
White Oak 5,136.....K5
White Settlement 15,472.....E2
Whitesboro 3,209.....H4
Whitewright 1,713.....H4
Wichita Falls▲ 96,259.....F4
Willis 2,764.....J7
Wills Point 2,986.....J5
Wilmer 2,479.....H3
Windcrest 5,331.....K11
Winnie 2,238.....K8
Winnsboro 2,904.....J5
Winters 2,905.....E6
Wolfforth 1,941.....C4
Woodsboro▲ 1,731.....G9
Woodville▲ 2,636.....K7
Wylie 8,716.....H1
Yoakum 5,611.....G8
Yorktown 2,207.....G9
Zapata▲ 7,119.....E11

OTHER FEATURES

Alibates Flint Quarries
  Nat'l Mon......C2
Amistad (res.).....C8
Amistad Nat'l Rec. Area.....D8
Angelina (riv.).....K6
Apache (mts.).....C11
Aransas (passage).....H10
Arlington (lake).....F2
Baffin (bay).....G10
Balcones Escarpment (plat.)....E8
Benbrook (lake).....E3
Bergstrom A.F.B......G7
Big Bend Nat'l Park.....A8
Big Thicket Nat'l Preserve...K7
Bolivar (pen.).....K8
Brazos (riv.).....G10
Brooks A.F.B......K11
Brownwood (lake).....E6
Buchanan (lake).....F7
Caddo (lake).....L5
Calaveras (lake).....K11
Canadian (riv.).....D1
Carrizo (creek).....A1
Carswell A.F.B......E2
Cathedral (mt.).....D12
Cavallo (passage).....H9
Cedar (lake).....B5
Cerro Alto (mt.).....B10
Chamizal Nat'l Mon......A10
Chinati (mts.).....C12
Chinati (peak).....C12
Chisos (mts.).....C12
Cibolo (creek).....K11
Clear Fork, Brazos (riv.).....D5
Coldwater (creek).....B1
Colorado (riv.).....D7
Copano (bay).....G9
Corpus Christi (lake).....F9
Corpus Christi N.A.S......G10
Cottonwood Draw (dry riv.)..C10

Davis (mts.).....C11
Deep (creek).....C5
Delaware (creek).....C10
Delaware (mts.).....C10
Denison (dam).....H4
Devils (riv.).....D7
Double Mountain Fork,
  Brazos (riv.).....C4
Dyess A.F.B......D5
Eagle (peak).....C11
Eagle Mountain (lake).....E2
Edwards (plat.).....D7
Elephant (mt.).....D12
Elm Fork, Trinity (riv.).....G2
Emory (peak).....A8
Falcon (res.).....E11
Finlay (mts.).....B10
Fort Bliss 13,915.....A10
Fort Davis Nat'l Hist. Site...D11
Fort Hood 35,580.....G6
Fort Sam Houston.....K11
Frio (riv.).....E8
Galveston (bay).....L2
Galveston (isl.).....K8
Glass (mts.).....A7
Goodfellow A.F.B......D6
Grapevine (lake).....F2
Guadalupe (peak).....B10
Guadalupe (peak).....C10
Guadalupe Mountains
  Nat'l Park.....C10
Houston (lake).....J8
Houston Ship (chan.).....K2
Howard (creek).....C7
Hubbard Creek (lake).....F5
Hueco (mts.).....B10
Intracoastal Waterway.....J9
Johnson Draw (dry riv.).....C7
Kelly A.F.B......J11
Kemp (lake).....E4
Kingsville N.A.S......G10
Kiowa (creek).....D1
Lackland A.F.B. 9,352.....J11
Lake Meredith Nat'l Rec. Area.C2
Lampasas (riv.).....G6
Laughlin A.F.B. 2,556.....D8
Lavon (lake).....H1
Leon (riv.).....F6
Livermore (mt.).....C11
Livingston (lake).....K7
Llano (riv.).....D7
Llano Estacado (plain).....B4
Locke (mt.).....D11
Los Olmos (creek).....F10
Los Olmos (creek).....F11
Lyndon B. Johnson
  Nat'l Hist. Site.....F7
Lyndon B. Johnson Space Ctr. K2
Madre (lag.).....G11
Maravillas (creek).....A7
Matagorda (bay).....H9
Matagorda (isl.).....H9
Matagorda (pen.).....J9
Medina (lake).....E8
Medina (riv.).....J11
Mexico (gulf).....K9
Middle Concho (riv.).....C6
Mountain Creek (lake).....G2
Mustang (creek).....A1
Mustang (isl.).....G10
Mustang Draw (dry riv.).....B5

Navasota (riv.).....
Navidad (riv.).....
Neches (riv.).....
North Concho (riv.).....
North Pease (riv.).....
Nueces (riv.).....
Padre (isl.).....
Padre Island Nat'l Seashore..C...
Palo Duro (creek).....
Palo Duro (creek).....
Pease (riv.).....
Pecos (riv.).....
Pedernales (riv.).....
Possum Kingdom (lake).....
Prairie Dog Town Fork,
  Red (riv.).....
Quitman (mts.).....
Randolph A.F.B......
Ray Hubbard (lake).....
Red (riv.).....
Red Bluff (lake).....
Reese A.F.B......
Rio Grande (riv.).....
Rita Blanca (creek).....
Sabine (riv.).....
Salt Fork, Red (riv.).....
Sam Rayburn (res.).....
San Antonio (bay).....
San Antonio (mt.).....
San Antonio Missions
  Nat'l Hist. Park.....
San Francisco (creek).....
San Luis (passage).....
San Martine Draw (dry riv.).....
San Saba (riv.).....
Santa Isabel (creek).....
Santiago (mts.).....
Santiago (peak).....
Sheppard A.F.B......
Sierra Diablo (mts.).....
Sierra Vieja (mts.).....
Staked (Llano Estacado)
  (plain).....
Stamford (lake).....
Stockton (plat.).....
Sulphur (riv.).....
Sulphur Draw (dry riv.).....
Sulphur Springs (creek).....
Tenmile (creek).....
Terlingua (creek).....
Texoma (lake).....
Thomas (lake).....
Tierra Blanca (creek).....
Toledo Bend (res.).....
Toyah (lake).....
Toyah (lake).....
Travis (lake).....
Trinity (bay).....
Trinity (riv.).....
Trinity, West Fork (riv.).....
Trujillo (creek).....
Washita (riv.).....
West (bay).....
White (riv.).....
White River (lake).....
White Rock (lake).....
Wichita (riv.).....
Wolf (creek).....
Worth (lake).....
Wright Patman (lake).....

▲County seat

Topography

0   90   180 MI.
0   90   180 KM.

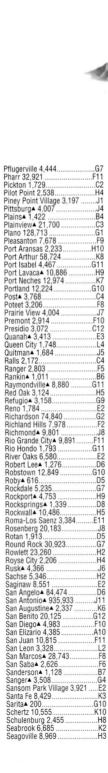

5,000 m. 16,404 ft. | 2,000 m. 6,562 ft. | 1,000 m. 3,281 ft. | 500 m. 1,640 ft. | 200 m. 656 ft. | 100 m. 328 ft. | Sea Level | Below

Texas

State Capitals ⊛
County Seats ◉
Major Limited Access Hwys. ——
Scale 1:4,600,000

Western Part of Texas
Same scale as main map

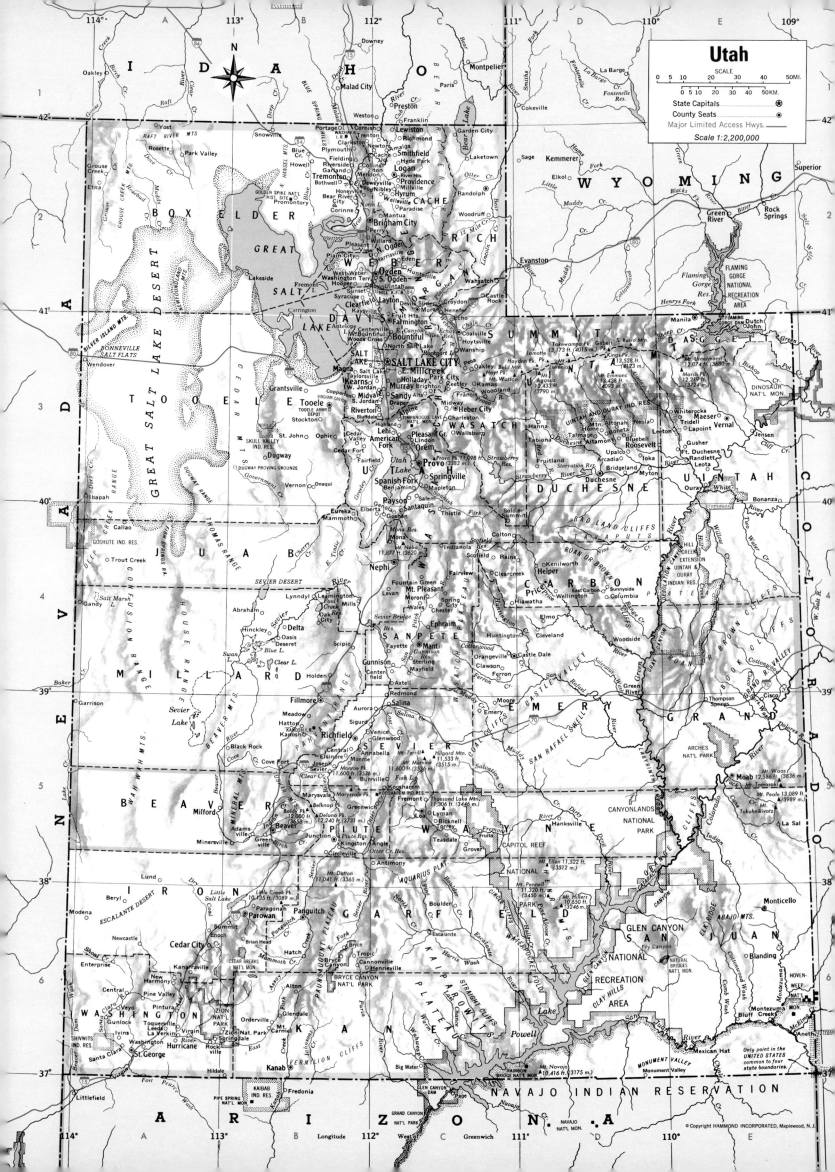

Utah

SCALE

State Capitals ⊛
County Seats ◉
Major Limited Access Hwys. ───

Scale 1:2,200,000

© Copyright HAMMOND INCORPORATED, Maplewood, N.J.

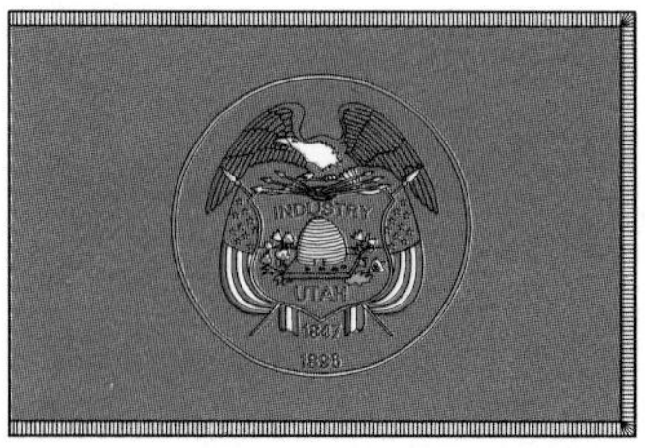

AREA 84.899 sq. mi. (219,888 sq. km.)
POPULATION 1,727,784
CAPITAL Salt Lake City
LARGEST CITY Salt Lake City
HIGHEST POINT Kings Pk. 13,528 ft. (4123 m.)
SETTLED IN 1847
ADMITTED TO UNION January 4, 1896
POPULAR NAME Beehive State
STATE FLOWER Sego Lily
STATE BIRD Sea Gull

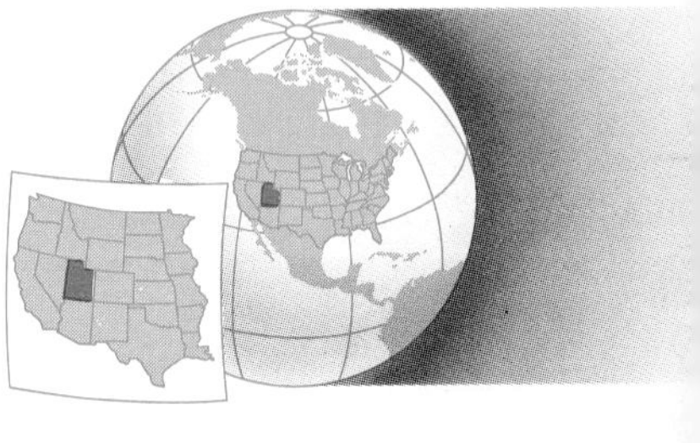

COUNTIES

ıver 4,765 A5
‹ Elder 36,485 A2
che 70,183 C2
·bon 20,228 D4
ggett 690 E3
vis 187,941 B3
chesne 12,645 D3
ery 10,332 D4
·field 3,980 C6
ınd 6,620 E5
ı 20,789 A6
ıb 5,817 A4
ıe 5,169 B6
lard 11,333 A4
ırgan 5,528 C2
te 1,277 B5
h 1,725 C2
t Lake 725,956 B3
ı Juan 12,621 E6
ıpete 16,259 C4
vier 15,431 C5
ımmit 15,518 C3
ɔele 26,601 A3
ıtah 22,211 E3
ıh 263,590 C3
ısatch 10,089 C3
ıshington 48,560 A6
ıyne 2,177 C5
ɔber 158,330 B2

CITIES and TOWNS

ɔine 3,492 C3
a 397 C3
ıalga 366 C2
ıerican Fork 15,696 C3
nabella 487 B5
rora 911 B5
ar River City 700 B2
aver▲ 1,998 B5
ɔknell 327 C5
ı Water 326 C6
ınding 3,162 E6
ıffdale 2,152 B3
ıuntiful 36,659 C3
gham City▲ 15,644 C2
ghton 150 C3
ıstle Dale▲ 1,704 D4
ıstle Rock C2
dar City 13,443 A6
dar Fort 284 B3
ınterfield 766 C4
ınterville 11,500 C3
ıarleston 336 C3
ırcleville 417 B5
ırkston 645 B2
Clearfield 21,435 B2
Cleveland 522 D4
Coalville▲ 1,065 C3
Corinne 639 B2
Delta 2,998 B4
Deweyville 318 B2
Draper 7,257 C3
Duchesne▲ 1,308 D3
Dugway 1,761 B3
East Carbon 1,270 D4
East Millcreek 21,184 C3
Elmo 267 D4
Elsinore 608 B5
Elwood 575 B2
Emery 300 C5
Enoch 1,947 A6
Enterprise 936 A6
Ephraim 3,363 C4
Escalante 818 C6
Eureka 562 B4
Fairview 960 C4
Farmington▲ 9,028 C3
Ferron 1,606 C4
Fielding 422 B2
Fillmore▲ 1,956 B5
Fort Duchesne 655 E3
Fountain Green 578 C4
Francis 381 C3
Fruit Heights 3,900 C2
Garden City 193 C2
Garland 1,637 B2
Genola 803 C4
Glendale 282 B6
Glenwood 437 C5
Goshen 578 C4
Grantsville 4,500 B3
Green River 866 D4
Gunnison 1,298 C4
Harrisville 3,004 C2
Heber City▲ 4,782 C3
Helper 2,148 D4
Henefer 554 C2
Highland 5,002 C3
Hildale 1,325 A6
Hinckley 658 B4
Holden 402 B4
Holladay 22,189 C3
Honeyville 1,112 B2
Hooper 3,468 B2
Howell 237 B2
Huntington 1,875 C4
Huntsville 561 C2
Hurricane 3,915 A6
Hyde Park 2,190 C2
Hyrum 4,829 C2
Ivins 1,630 A6
Joseph 198 B5
Junction▲ 132 B5
Kamas 1,061 C3
Kanab▲ 3,289 B6
Kanarraville 228 A6
Kanosh 386 B5
Kaysville 13,961 B2
Kearns 28,374 B3
Koosharem 266 C5
La Verkin 1,771 A6
Laketown 261 C2
Layton 41,784 C2
Leamington 253 B4
Leeds 254 A6
Lehi 8,475 C3
Levan 416 C4
Lewiston 1,532 C2
Lindon 3,818 C3
Loa▲ 444 C5
Logan▲ 32,762 C2
Lyman 198 C5
Maeser 2,598 E3
Magna 17,829 B3
Manila▲ 207 E3
Manti▲ 2,268 C4
Mantua 665 C2
Mapleton 3,572 C3
Marysvale 364 B5
Mayfield 438 C4
Meadow 250 B5
Mendon 684 B2
Mexican Hat 259 E6
Midvale 11,886 B3
Midway 1,554 C3
Milford 1,107 A5
Millville 1,202 C2
Minersville 608 A5
Moab▲ 3,971 E5
Mona 584 C4
Monroe 1,472 B5
Montezuma Creek 345 E6
Monticello▲ 1,806 E6
Morgan▲ 2,023 C2
Moroni 1,115 C4
Mount Pleasant 2,092 C4
Murray 31,282 C3
Myton 468 D3
Neola 511 D3
Nephi▲ 3,515 C4
Newton 659 C2
Nibley 1,167 C2
North Ogden 11,668 C2
North Salt Lake 6,474 C3
Oak City 587 B4
Oakley 522 C3
Ogden▲ 63,909 C2
Orangeville 1,459 C4
Orderville 422 B6
Orem 67,561 C3
Panguitch▲ 1,444 B6
Paradise 561 C2
Paragonah 307 B6
Park City 4,468 C3
Parowan▲ 1,873 B6
Payson 9,510 C3
Perry 1,211 C2
Plain City 2,722 B2
Pleasant Grove 13,476 C3
Pleasant View 3,603 B2
Plymouth 267 B2
Price▲ 8,712 D4
Providence 3,344 C2
Provo▲ 86,835 C3
Randlett 283 E3
Randolph▲ 488 C2
Redmond 648 C4
Richfield▲ 5,593 B5
Richmond 1,955 C2
River Heights 1,274 C2
Riverton 11,261 B3
Roosevelt 3,915 D3
Roy 24,603 B2
Saint George▲ 28,502 A6
Salem 2,284 C3
Salina 1,943 C5
Salt Lake City (cap.)▲ 159,936 C3
Sandy 75,058 C3
Santa Clara 2,322 A6
Santaquin 2,386 C4
Scipio 291 B4
Sigurd 385 B5
Smithfield 5,566 C2
South Jordan 12,220 B3
South Ogden 12,105 C2
South Salt Lake 10,129 C3
Spanish Fork 11,272 C3
Spring City 715 C4
Springdale 275 B6
Springville 13,950 C3
Stockton 426 B3
Sunnyside 339 D4
Sunset 5,128 B2
Syracuse 4,658 B2
Taylorsville-Bennion 52,351 B3
Tooele▲ 13,887 B3
Toquerville 488 A6
Tremonton 4,264 B2
Trenton 464 B2
Tropic 374 B6
Uintah 760 C2
Vernal▲ 6,644 E3
Wallsburg 252 C3
Washington 4,198 A6
Washington Terrace 8,189 B2
Wellington 1,632 D4
Wellsville 2,206 C2
Wendover 1,127 A3
West Bountiful 4,477 B3
West Jordan 42,892 B3
Whiterocks 312 E3
Willard 1,298 C2
Woods Cross 5,384 B3

OTHER FEATURES

Abajo (mts.) E6
Agassiz (mt.) D3
Antelope (isl.) B3
Aquarius (plat.) C5
Arches Nat'l Park E5
Assay (creek) B6
Bad Land (cliffs) D4
Baldy (peak) B5
Bear (lake) C2
Bear (riv.) B2
Beaver (mts.) A5
Beaver (riv.) A5
Beaver Dam Wash (creek) A6
Birch (creek) B5
Blue (creek) B2
Bonneville (salt flats) A3
Book (cliffs) E4
Bryce Canyon Nat'l Park B6
Canyonlands Nat'l Park D5
Capitol Reef Nat'l Park C5
Castle (valley) D4
Cedar (mts.) B3
Cedar Breaks Nat'l Mon. B6
Chalk (creek) C3
Chinle (creek) E6
Clear (lake) B4
Cliff (creek) E3
Coal (cliffs) C5
Colorado (riv.) E5
Confusion (range) A4
Cottonwood (creek) C4
Cub (creek) C1
Deep (creek) B1
Deep Creek (range) A4
Delano (peak) B5
Desolation (canyon) E4
Dinosaur Nat'l Mon. E3
Dirty Devil (riv.) D5
Dolores (riv.) E5
Dry Coal (creek) A6
Duchesne (riv.) D3
Dugway (range) A3
Dugway Proving Grounds B3
Dutton (mt.) B5
East Canyon (res.) C3
Echo (res.) C3
Elk (ridge) E6
Ellen (mt.) D5
Emmons (mt.) D3
Escalante (des.) A6
Escalante (riv.) C6
Fish (lake) C5
Fish Springs (range) A4
Flaming Gorge (res.) E3
Flaming Gorge Nat'l Rec. Area E2
Fool Creek (res.) B4
Fremont (isl.) B2
Fremont (riv.) C5
Glen Canyon Nat'l Rec. Area D6
Golden Spike Nat'l Hist. Site B2
Goshute Ind. Res. A4
Government (creek) B3
Gray (canyon) D4
Great Salt (lake) B2
Great Salt Lake (des.) A3
Greeley (creek) B3
Green (riv.) D4
Grouse (creek) A2
Grouse Creek (mts.) A2
Gunnison (res.) C4
Henry (mts.) D6
Hilgard (mt.) C5
Hill (creek) E4
Hill A.F.B. C2
Hill Creek Extension, Uintah and Ouray Ind. Res. E4
Hillers (mt.) D6
House (range) A4
Hovenweep Nat'l Mon. E6
Hoyt (peak) C3
Huntington (creek) C4
Indian (creek) B5
Jordan (riv.) C3
Kaiparowits (plat.) C6
Kanab (creek) B7
Kanosh Ind. Res. B5
Kings (peak) D3
Koosharem Ind. Res. C5
Little Creek (peak) B6
Little Salt (lake) A6
Malad (riv.) B1
Marsh (peak) E3
Marvine (mt.) C5
Mineral (mts.) B5
Mona (res.) C4
Monroe (peak) B5
Montezuma (creek) E6
Monument (valley) D6
Muddy (creek) C4
Natural Bridges Nat'l Mon. E6
Navajo (mt.) D6
Navajo Ind. Res. D7
Nebo (mt.) C4
Newfoundland (mts.) A2
Nine Mile (creek) D4
North (lake) B2
Orange (cliffs) D5
Otter (creek) C5
Otter Creek (res.) C5
Paria (riv.) B6
Paunsaugunt (plat.) B6
Pahvant (range) B5
Peale (mt.) E5
Pennell (mt.) D6
Piute (res.) B5
Plumber (creek) C2
Powell (lake) D6
Price (riv.) D4
Provo (peak) C3
Provo (riv.) C3
Raft River (mts.) A2
Rainbow Bridge Nat'l Mon. C6
Roan (cliffs) E4
Rockport (lake) C3
Salvation (creek) C5
San Juan (riv.) D6
San Pitch (riv.) C4
San Rafael (riv.) D4
San Rafael Swell (mts.) D5
Santa Clara (riv.) A6
Sevier (des.) B4
Sevier (lake) A5
Sevier (riv.) B4
Sevier Bridge (res.) C4
Shivwits Ind. Res. A6
Silver Island (mts.) A3
Skull Valley Ind. Res. B3
Spanish Fork (riv.) C3
Strait (cliffs) C6
Strawberry (res.) C3
Strawberry (riv.) D3
Swan (lake) B4
Tavaputs (plat.) D4
Thomas (range) A4
Thousand Lake (mt.) C5
Timpanogos Cave Nat'l Mon. C3
Tokewamna (peak) D3
Tooele Army Depot B3
Two Water (creek) E4
Uinta (mts.) D3
Uinta (riv.) D3
Uintah and Ouray Ind. Res. D3
Utah (lake) C3
Virgin (riv.) A6
Waas (mt.) E5
Wah Wah (mts.) A5
Wasatch (range) C3
Washakie Ind. Res. B2
Waterpocket Fold (cliffs) D6
Weber (riv.) C3
White (riv.) E3
Willow (creek) E4
Zion Nat'l Park A6

▲County seat

Agriculture, Industry and Resources

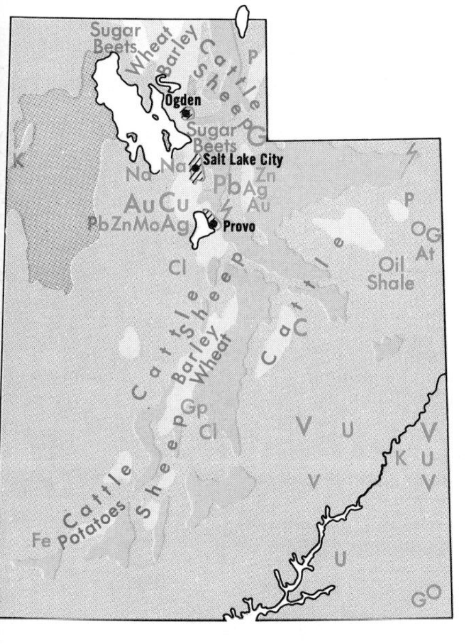

DOMINANT LAND USE

- Wheat, General Farming
- General Farming, Livestock, Special Crops
- Range Livestock
- Forests
- Nonagricultural Land

MAJOR MINERAL OCCURRENCES

Ag	Silver	Fe	Iron Ore	O	Petroleum
At	Asphalt	G	Natural Gas	P	Phosphates
Au	Gold	Gp	Gypsum	Pb	Lead
C	Coal	K	Potash	U	Uranium
Cl	Clay	Mo	Molybdenum	V	Vanadium
Cu	Copper	Na	Salt	Zn	Zinc

Water Power

Major Industrial Areas

Topography

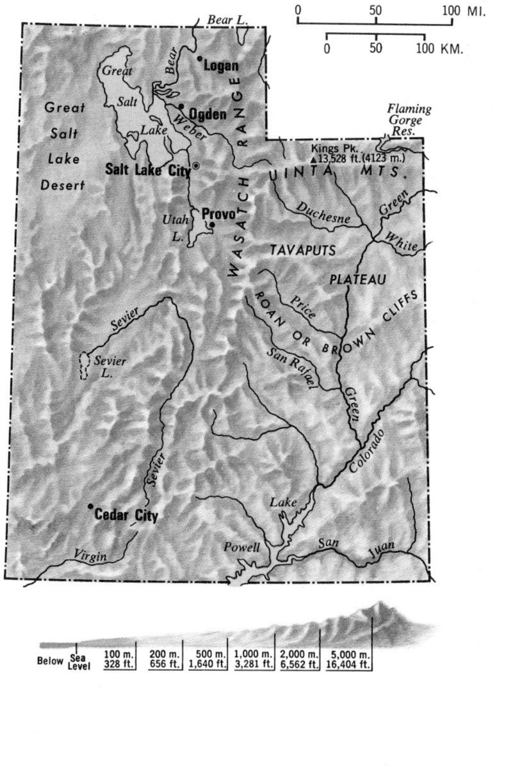

Topography

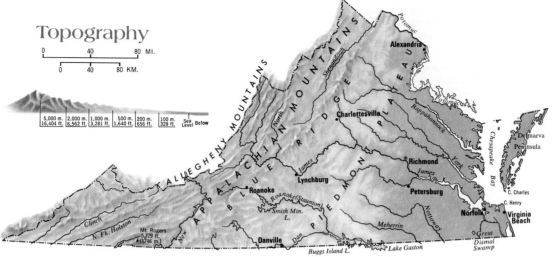

0   40   80 MI.
0   40   80 KM.

| 5,000 m. 16,404 ft. | 2,000 m. 6,562 ft. | 1,000 m. 3,281 ft. | 500 m. 1,640 ft. | 200 m. 656 ft. | 100 m. 328 ft. | Sea Level | Below |

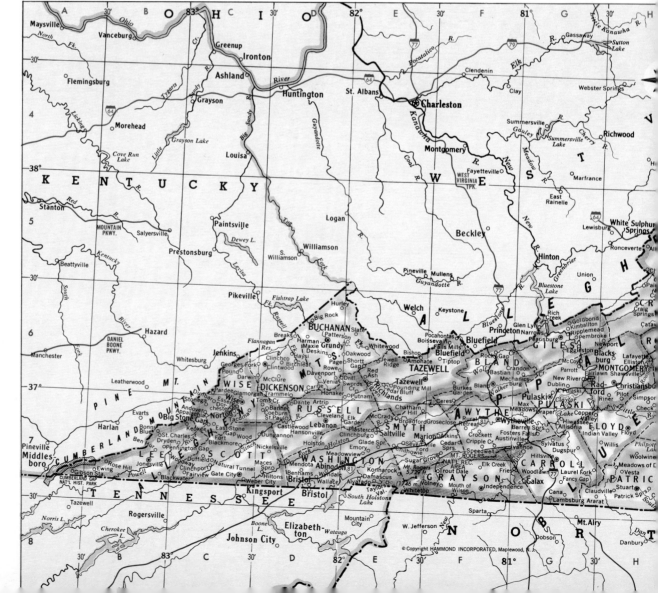

© Copyright HAMMOND INCORPORATED, Maplewood, N.J.

AREA 40,767 sq. mi. (105,587 sq. km.)
POPULATION 6,216,568
CAPITAL Richmond
LARGEST CITY Norfolk
HIGHEST POINT Mt. Rogers 5,729 ft. (1746 m.)
SETTLED IN 1607
ADMITTED TO UNION June 26, 1788
POPULAR NAME Old Dominion
STATE FLOWER Dogwood
STATE BIRD Cardinal

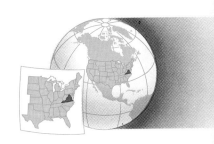

(continued on following page)

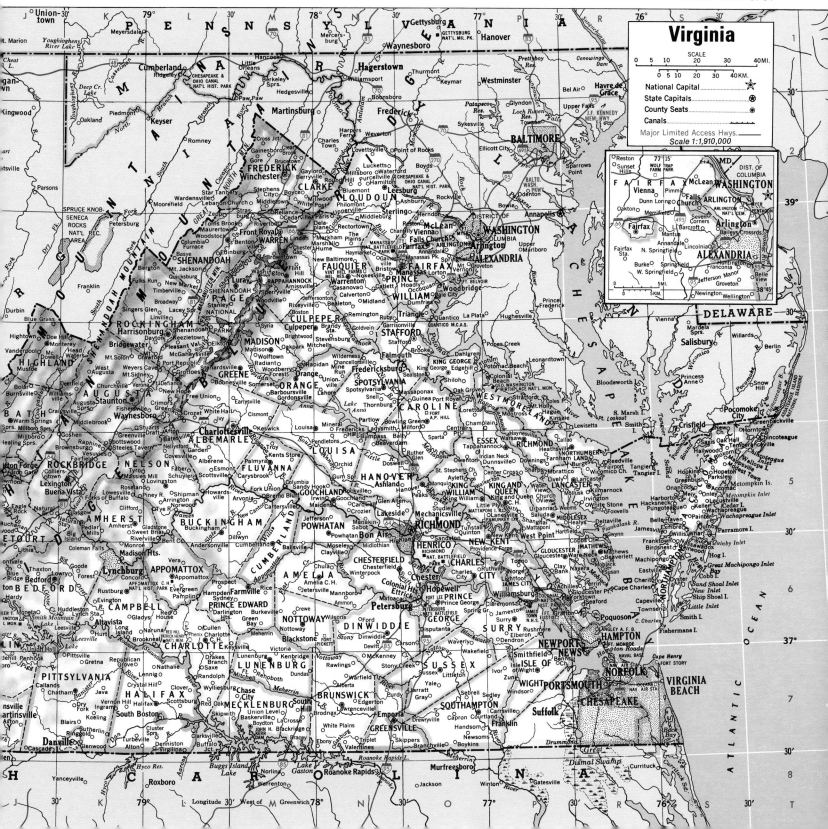

Agriculture, Industry and Resources

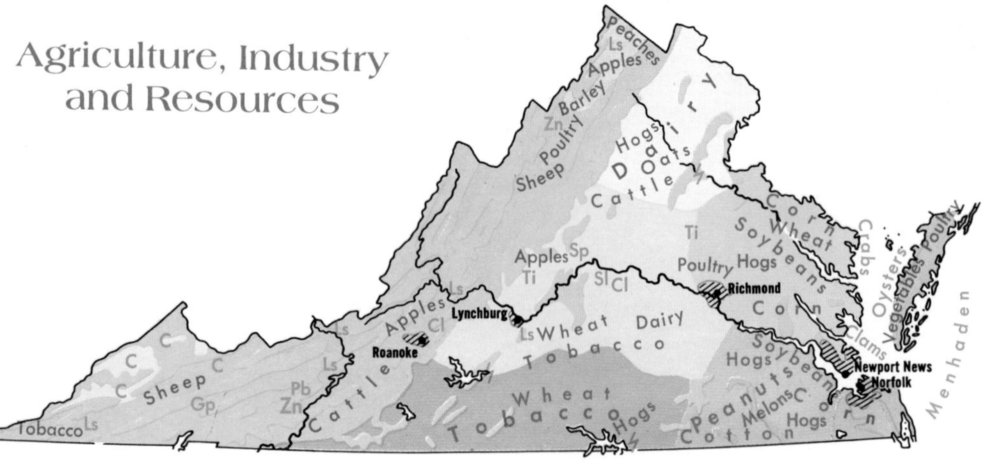

MAJOR MINERAL OCCURRENCES

C Coal
Cl Clay
Gp Gypsum
Ls Limestone
Pb Lead
Sl Slate
Sp Soapstone
Ti Titanium
Zn Zinc

Water Power
Major Industrial Areas

DOMINANT LAND USE

Dairy, General Farming
General Farming, Livestock, Dairy
General Farming, Livestock, Tobacco
General Farming, Livestock, Fruit, Tobacco
General Farming, Truck Farming, Tobacco, Livestock
Tobacco, General Farming
Peanuts, General Farming
Fruit and Mixed Farming
Truck and Mixed Farming
Forests
Swampland, Limited Agriculture

Haysi 222 D6
Healing Springs 175 J5
Heathsville▲ 300 P5
Henry 300 J7
Herndon 16,139 O3
Highland Springs 13,823 O5
Hillsville▲ 2,008 G7
Hiltons 300 D7
Hiwassee 250 G7
Hoadly 400 O3
Hollins College 12,295 H6
Honaker 950 D6
Hopewell (I.C.) 23,101 O6
Horntown 400 T5
Hot Springs 300 J4
Huddleston 200 K6
Hume 350 N3
Huntington 7,489 S3
Hurley 850 D6
Hurt 1,294 K6
Independence▲ 988 F7
Indian Valley 300 G7
Iron Gate 417 J5
Irvington 496 R5
Isle of Wight▲ 185 P7
Ivanhoe 900 G7
Ivor 324 P7
Ivy 900 L4
Jamestown 12 P6
Jamesville 500 S5
Jarratt 556 O7
Jefferson 25,782 N5
Jefferson Manor S3
Jeffersonton 300 N3
Jewell Ridge 600 E6
Jonesville▲ 927 B7
Keeling 680 K7
Keezletown 975 L4
Keller 235 S5
Kenbridge 1,264 M7
Kents Store 130 M5
Keokee 300 C7
Keswick 300 M4
Keysville 606 M6
Kilmarnock 1,109 R5
King George▲ 575 O4
King William▲ 100 O5
King and Queen Court House▲ 500 P5
Kinsale 250 P4
La Crosse 549 M7

Lacey Spring 140 L3
Ladysmith 360 N4
Lafayette-Elliston H6
Lake Barcroft 8,686 S3
Lakeside 12,081 N5
Lambsburg 800 G7
Lancaster▲ 110 R5
Laurel Fork 300 G7
Lawrenceville▲ 1,486 N7
Lebanon Church 300 L2
Lebanon▲ 3,206 D7
Leesburg▲ 16,202 N2
Lewisetta 125 R4
Lexington (I.C.)▲ 6,959 J5
Lincolnia 13,041 S3
Linden 320 M3
Linville 500 L3
Little Plymouth 195 P5
Lively 400 P5
Loretto 150 O4
Lorton 15,385 O3
Louisa▲ 1,088 M4
Lovettsville 749 N2
Lovingston▲ 600 L5
Lowesville 500 K5
Lowmoor 700 J5
Lucketts 500 N2
Lunenburg▲ 13 M7
Luray▲ 4,587 M3
Lynch Station 500 K6
Lynchburg (I.C.) 66,049 K6
Machipongo 400 S6
Madison Heights 11,700 K6
Madison▲ 267 M4
Manakin-Sabot 200 N5
Manassas (I.C.)▲ 27,957 O3
Manassas Park (I.C.) 6,734 O3
Mannboro 175 N6
Manquin 576 O5
Mantua 6,804 S3
Mappsville 700 T5
Marion▲ 6,630 E7
Markham 300 N3
Marshall 800 N3
Martinsville (I.C.)▲ 16,162 J7
Massies Mill 225 K5
Mathews▲ 500 R6
Matoaca 1,967 N6
Mattaponi 300 P5
Maurertown 158 L3
Max Meadows 782 G6

McClure 300 D6
McCoy 600 G6
McGaheysville 600 L4
McKenney 386 N7
McLean 38,168 S2
Meadows of Dan 150 H7
Meadowview-Emory 2,292 D7
Mechanicsburg 350 G6
Mechanicsville 22,027 O5
Meherrin 400 M6
Melfa 428 S5
Mendota 375 D7
Merrifield 8,399 S3
Middlebrook 125 K4
Middleburg 549 B3
Middletown 841 M2
Midland 600 N3
Midlothian 950 N6
Milford 650 O4
Millboro 400 J5
Millboro Springs 200 J4
Millwood 400 N2
Mine Run 450 N4
Mineral 471 N4
Mobjack 210 R6
Modest Town 225 T5
Mollusk 800 P5
Moneta 300 J6
Monroe 500 K6
Monterey▲ 222 K4
Montross▲ 359 P4
Montvale 900 J6
Morattico 225 {5
Moseley 210 N6
Mount Crawford 228 L4
Mount Holly 200 P4
Mount Jackson 1,583 L3
Mount Sidney 500 K4
Mount Solon 124 K4
Mount Vernon 27,485 O3
Mouth of Wilson 400 F7
Mustoe 150 K4
Narrows 2,082 G6
Naruna 175 L6
Nassawadox 564 S6
Nathalie 200 L7
Natural Bridge 200 J5
Natural Bridge Sta. 450 K5
Naxera 300 R6
Nellysford 290 L5
New Baltimore 125 N3

New Castle▲ 152 H5
New Church 427 S5
New Hope 200 L4
New Kent▲ 25 P5
New Market 1,435 L3
New River 500 G6
Newington 17,965 S3
Newport 600 H6
Newport News (I.C.) 170,045 P6
Newsoms 337 O7
Nickelsville 411 D7
Nokesville 520 N3
Nora 550 D6
Norfolk (I.C.) 261,229 R7
Norge 750 P6
North Garden 300 L5
North Pulaski 1,405 G6
North Springfield 8,996 S3
Norton (I.C.) 4,247 C7
Nottoway▲ 170 M6
Oak Hall 221 S5
Oakpark 150 M4
Oakton 24,610 R3
Oakwood 715 E6
Occoquan 361 O3
Onancock 1,434 S5
Onley 532 S5
Orange▲ 2,582 M4
Owenton 400 O5
Oyster 200 S6
Paint Bank 235 H5
Painter 259 S5
Palmyra▲ 250 M5
Pamplin 273 L6
Pardee 190 C6
Parksley 779 S5
Parrott 750 G6
Patrick Springs 800 H7
Peaks 500 D6
Pearisburg▲ 2,064 G6
Pembroke 1,064 G6
Penhook 500 J7
Pennington Gap 1,922 C7
Petersburg (I.C.) 38,386 N6
Phenix 260 L6
Philomont 265 N2
Pilot 360 H6
Pimmit 6,658 S2
Piney River 778 L5
Pittsville 600 K7
Pleasant Valley 150 L4
Pocahontas 513 F6
Poquoson 11,005 R6
Port Royal 204 O4
Portsmouth (I.C.) 103,907 R7
Potomac Beach 200 P4
Pound 995 C6
Pounding Mill 399 E6
Powhatan▲ 600 N5
Prince George▲ 150 O6
Prospect 275 L6
Providence Forge 500 P6
Pulaski▲ 9,985 G6
Pungoteague 500 S5
Purcellville 1,744 N2
Purdy 350 N7
Quantico 670 O3
Quicksburg 160 L3
Quinby 350 S5
Radford (I.C.) 15,940 G6
Radiant 250 M4
Randolph 150 L7
Raphine 500 K5
Rapiden 176 M4

Raven 2,640 E6
Rawlings 200 N7
Rectortown 225 N3
Red Ash 300 E6
Red House 150 L6
Red Oak 250 L7
Reedville 400 R5
Reliance 150 M3
Remington 460 N3
Republican Grove 125 K7
Reston 48,556 R2
Rice 194 M6
Rich Creek 746 G6
Richlands 4,456 E6
Richmond (cap.) (I.C.)▲ 203,056 O5
Ridgeway 752 J7
Riner 360 H6
Ringgold 150 K7
Ripplemead 600 G6
Riverton 500 M3
Rixeyville 150 M3
Roanoke (I.C.) 96,397 H6
Rockville 290 N5
Rocky Gap 200 F6
Rocky Mount▲ 4,098 J7
Rose Hill 12,675 B7
Rosedale 760 E7
Roseland 300 K5
Round Hill 514 N2
Rowe 150 D6
Ruby 188 N3
Rural Retreat 972 F7
Rushmere 1,064 P6
Rustburg▲ 650 K6
Ruther Glen 200 O5
Ruthville 300 P6
Saint Charles 206 B7
Saint Paul 1,007 D7
Saint Stephens Church 500 O5
Salem (I.C.)▲ 23,756 H6
Saltville 2,376 E7
Saluda▲ 150 P5
Sandy Hook 700 M5
Saxis 367 S5
Schuyler 250 L5
Scottsburg 152 L7
Scottsville 239 L5
Sealston 200 O4
Sebrell 160 O7
Sedley 523 P7
Selma 500 J5
Seven Corners 7,280 S3
Seven Mile Ford 425 E7
Shanghai 150 P5
Shawsville 1,260 H6
Shenandoah 2,213 L4
Shiloh 150 O4
Shipman 350 L5
Simpsons 150 H6
Singers Glen 155 K3
Skippers 150 O7
Skipwith 128 L7
Smithfield 4,686 P7
Snell 300 N4
Somerset 200 M4
South Boston (I.C.) 6,997 L7
South Hill 4,217 M7
Sparta 485 o4
Speedwell 650 F8
Spencer 500 J7
Sperryville 500 M3
Spotsylvania▲ 350 N4
Springfield 23,706 S3

Stafford▲ 750 O4
Stanardsville▲ 257 L4
Stanley 1,186 L3
Stanleytown 1,563 H7
Star Tannery 500 L2
Staunton (I.C.)▲ 24,461 K4
Steeles Tavern 200 K5
Stephens City 1,186 M2
Sterling 20,512 O2
Stevensburg 125 N4
Stonega 275 C7
Stony Creek 271 N7
Strasburg 3,762 M3
Stuart▲ 965 H7
Stuarts Draft 5,087 L4
Studley 500 O5
Suffolk (I.C.) 52,141 P7
Sugar Grove 1,027 E7
Surry▲ 192 P6
Susan 500 R6
Sussex▲ 75 O7
Sutherlin 180 K7
Sweet Briar 900 K5
Swords Creek 315 E6
Sylvatus 200 G7
Tacoma 150 C7
Tangier 659 R5
Tappahannock▲ 1,550 O5
Tazewell▲ 4,176 E6
Temperanceville 400 T5
Thaxton 450 J6
The Plains 219 N3
Thornburg 135 N4
Timberville 1,596 L3
Tiptop 175 F6
Toano 950 P6
Toms Brook 227 L3
Townsend 525 R6
Trammel 450 D6
Triangle 4,740 O3
Triplet 300 N7
Trout Dale 248 F7
Troutville 455 J6
Tyro 125 K5
Union Hall 125 J6
Unionville 500 N4
Upperville 250 N2
Urbanna 529 P5
Valentines 400 N7
Vansant 1,187 D6
Vera 150 L6
Vernon Hill 250 K7
Verona 3,479 K4
Vesta 350 H7
Vesuvius 500 K5
Victoria 1,830 M6
Vienna 14,852 R2
Vinton 7,665 J6
Virgilina 161 L7
Virginia Beach (I.C.) 393,069 S7
Wachapreague 291 S5
Wakefield 1,070 O7
Walkerton 985 O5
Warm Springs▲ 325 J4
Warrenton▲ 4,830 N3
Warsaw▲ 961 P5
Washington▲ 198 M3
Water View 265 P5
Waterford 350 N2
Waverly 2,223 O6
Waynesboro (I.C.) 18,549 K4
Weber City 1,377 C7
Weems 500 P5
Weirwood 300 S6
West Augusta 325 K4
West Point 2,938 P5
West Springfield 28,126 S3
Weyers Cave 300 L4
White Hall 250 L4
White Stone 372 R5
Whitetop 860 E7
Whitewood 350 E6
Wicomico Church 500 R5
Wilderness 200 N4
Williamsburg (I.C.)▲ 11,530 P6
Williamsville 145 J4
Willis 170 H7
Willis Wharf 360 S5
Winchester (I.C.)▲ 21,947 M2
Windsor 1,025 P7
Wirtz 500 J6
Wise▲ 3,193 C7
Wolftown 350 M4
Woodberry Forest 450 M4
Woodbridge 26,401 O3
Woodlawn 1,689 G7
Woodstock▲ 3,182 L3
Woodville 200 M3
Woodway 400 C7
Woolwine 150 H7
Wylliesburg 213 L7
Wytheville▲ 8,038 G7
Zuni 300 P7

OTHER FEATURES

Aarons (creek) L7
Allegheny (mts.) H5
Anna (lake) N4
Appalachian (mts.) J5
Appomattox (riv.) M6
Appomattox Court House Nat'l Hist. Park K6
Arlington Nat'l Cemetery T3
Assateague Island Nat'l Seashore T4
Back (bay) S7
Back (creek) J4
Banister (riv.) K7
Big Otter (riv.) K6
Blackwater (riv.) J6
Blackwater (riv.) O6
Blue Ridge (mts.) J6
Bluestone (lake) G5
Booker T. Washington Nat'l Mon. J6
Buggs Island (lake) L8

Bull Run (creek)
Cedar (isl.)
Central Intelligence Agency (C.I.A.)
Charles (cape)
Chesapeake (bay)
Chesapeake and Ohio Canal Nat'l Hist. Park
Chincoteague (bay)
Chincoteague (inlet)
Claytor (lake)
Clinch (riv.)
Cobb (isl.)
Colonial Nat'l Hist. Park
Cowpasture (riv.)
Craig (creek)
Cub (creek)
Cumberland (mt.)
Cumberland Gap Nat'l Hist. Park
Dan (riv.)
Drummond (lake)
Fishermans (isl.)
Flannagan (res.)
Flat (creek)
Fort A.P. Hill
Fort Belvoir 8,590
Fort Eustis
Fort Lee 6,595
Fort Monroe
Fort Myer
Fort Pickett
Fort Story
Gaston (lake)
George Washington Birthplac Nat'l Mon.
Goose (creek)
Goose (creek)
Great Machipongo (inlet)
Great North (mt.)
Hampton Roads (est.)
Henry (cape)
Hog (isl.)
Hog Island (bay)
Holston, North Fork (riv.)
Hyco (riv.)
Jackson (riv.)
James (riv.)
Jamestown Nat'l Hist. Site
John H. Kerr (dam)
Langley A.F.B.
Leesville (lake)
Levisa Fork (riv.)
Little (inlet)
Little (riv.)
Little (riv.)
Manassas Nat'l Battlefield Pk.
Massanutten (mt.)
Mattaponi (riv.)
Mattaponi Ind. Res.
Maury (riv.)
Meherrin (riv.)
Metompkin (inlet)
Metompkin (isl.)
Mobjack (bay)
Mount Rogers Nat'l Rec. Area
New (inlet)
New (riv.)
Ni (riv.)
North Anna (riv.)
Nottoway (riv.)
Oceana N.A.S.
Pamunkey (riv.)
Pamunkey Ind. Res.
Parramore (isl.)
Pentagon
Petersburg Nat'l Battlefield
Philpott (lake)
Piankatank (riv.)
Pigg (riv.)
Po (riv.)
Pocomoke (sound)
Potomac (riv.)
Powell (riv.)
Quantico Marine Corps Air Sta.
Quinby (inlet)
Rapidan (riv.)
Rappahannock (riv.)
Red Hill Patrick Henry Nat'l Mem.
Richmond Nat'l Battlefield Pk.
Rivanna (riv.)
Roanoke (riv.)
Rogers (mt.)
Russell Fork (riv.)
Sand Shoal (inlet)
Shenandoah (mt.)
Shenandoah (riv.)
Shenandoan Nat'l Park
Ship Shoal (isl.)
Slate (riv.)
Smith (isl.)
Smith (riv.)
Smith Mountain (lake)
South Anna (riv.)
South Holston (lake)
South Mayo (riv.)
Stony (creek)
Swift (creek)
Tangier (isl.)
Tangier (sound)
Tug Fork (riv.)
U.S. Naval Base
Vint Hill Farms Mil. Res.
Wachapreague (inlet)
Walker (creek)
Wallops (isl.)
Willis (riv.)
Wolf (creek)
Wolf Trap Farm Park
York (riv.)

I.C. Independent City
▲County seat

AREA 68,139 sq. mi. (176,480 sq. km.)
POPULATION 4,887,941
CAPITAL Olympia
LARGEST CITY Seattle
HIGHEST POINT Mt. Rainier 14,410 ft. (4392 m.)
SETTLED IN 1811
ADMITTED TO UNION November 11, 1889
POPULAR NAME Evergreen State
STATE FLOWER Western Rhododendron
STATE BIRD Willow Goldfinch

COUNTIES

ams 13,603	G3
otin 17,605	H4
nton 112,560	F4
elan 52,250	E3
allam 56,464	B2
ark 238,053	C5
lumbia 4,024	H4
wlitz 82,119	C4
ry 6,295	G2
anklin 37,473	G4
rfield 2,248	H4
ant 54,758	F3
ays Harbor 64,175	B3
and 60,195	C2
fferson 20,146	B3
g 1,507,319	D3
sap 189,731	C3
titas 26,725	E3
ickitat 16,616	E5
wis 59,358	C4
ncoln 8,864	G3
ason 38,341	B3
anogan 33,350	F2
cific 18,882	B4
nd Oreille 8,915	H2
erce 586,203	C3
n Juan 10,035	C2
agit 79,555	D2
amania 8,289	D5

CITIES and TOWNS

Snohomish 465,642	D2
Spokane 361,364	H3
Stevens 30,948	H2
Thurston 161,238	C4
Wahkiakum 3,832	B4
Walla Walla 48,439	G4
Whatcom 127,780	D2
Whitman 38,775	H4
Yakima 188,823	E4

Aberdeen 16,565	B3
Acme 500	C2
Addy 180	H2
Airway Heights 1,971	H3
Albion 632	H4
Alder 300	C4
Algona 1,694	C3
Allyn 850	C3
Almira 310	G3
Aloha 140	A3
Amanda Park 495	A3
Amboy 480	C5
Anacortes 11,451	C2
Appleton 120	D5
Ardenvoir 150	E3
Ariel 386	C5
Arlington 4,037	C2
Ashford 300	C4
Asotin▲ 981	H4
Auburn 33,102	C3

Azwell 152	F3
Bainbridge Island-Winslow (Winslow)	A2
Baring 200	D3
Battle Ground 3,758	C5
Bay Center 187	A4
Bay City 187	B4
Beaux Arts Village 303	B2
Beaver 450	A2
Belfair 500	C3
Bellevue 86,874	B2
Bellingham▲ 52,179	C2
Benton City 1,806	F4
Beverly 200	F4
Biglake 105	C2
Bingen 645	D5
Black Diamond 1,422	D3
Blaine 2,489	C2
Blanchard 125	C2
Bonney Lake 7,494	C3
Bothell 12,345	B1
Bow 200	C2
Boyds 125	G2
Bremerton 38,142	A2
Brewster 1,633	F2
Bridgeport 1,498	F3
Brier 5,633	C3
Brinnon 500	B3
Brownstown 200	E4
Brush Prairie 2,650	C5
Bryn Mawr-Skyway 12,514	B2
Buckley 3,516	C3

Bucoda 536	C4
Buena 590	E4
Burbank 1,745	G4
Burien 25,089	A2
Burley 300	C3
Burlington 4,349	C2
Burton 650	C3
Camas 6,442	C5
Carbonado 495	D3
Carlsborg 500	B2
Carlton 410	F2
Carnation 1,243	D3
Carson 500	D5
Cashmere 2,544	E3
Castle Rock 2,067	B4
Cathlamet▲ 508	B4
Cedar Falls 200	D3
Central Park 2,669	B3
Centralia 12,101	C4
Chattaroy 250	H3
Chehalis▲ 6,527	C4
Chelan 2,969	E3
Chelan Falls 250	E3
Cheney 7,723	H3
Chewelah 1,945	H2
Chimacum 275	C3
Chinook 928	B4
Cinebar 200	C4
Clallam Bay 600	A2
Clarkston 6,753	H4
Clayton 175	H3
Cle Elum 1,778	E3

Clearlake 750	C2
Clearwater 194	A3
Clinton 1,564	C3
Clyde	F4
Clyde Hill 2,972	B2
Coalfield 500	B2
Colbert 225	H3
Colby 150	A2
College Place 6,308	G4
Colton 325	H4
Columbia Heights 2,515	C4
Colville▲ 4,360	H2
Conconully 153	F2
Concrete 735	D2
Connell 2,005	G4
Conway 150	C2
Copalis Beach 600	A3
Copalis Crossing 500	B3
Cosmopolis 1,372	B4
Coulee City 568	F3
Coulee Dam 1,087	G3
Coupeville▲ 1,377	C2
Cowiche 150	E4
Creston 230	G3
Cumberland 250	D3
Curlew 168	G2
Cusick 195	H2
Custer 300	C2
Dallesport 600	D5
Danville 215	G2
Darrington 1,042	H3

Davenport▲ 1,502	G3
Dayton▲ 2,468	H4
Deer Harbor 400	B2
Deer Park 2,278	H3
Deming 200	C2
Des Moines 17,283	B2
Dishman 9,671	H3
Dixie 210	G4
Doe Bay 150	C2
Doty 245	B4
Dryad 125	B4
Dryden 500	E3
Du Pont 592	C3
Dungeness 675	B2
Duvall 2,770	D3
East Olympia 300	B4
East Wenatchee 2,701	E3
Easton 250	D3
Eastsound 800	B2
Eatonville 1,374	C4
Edison 250	C2
Edmonds 30,744	C3
Edwall 150	H3
Electric City 910	F3
Ellensburg▲ 12,361	E3
Elma 3,011	B4
Elmer City 290	G2
Eltopia 200	G4
Endicott 320	H4
Enetai 2,638	A2
Entiat 449	E3
Enumclaw 7,227	D3
Ephrata▲ 5,349	F3
Erlands Point 1,254	A2
Ethel 180	C4
Everett▲ 69,961	C3
Everson 1,490	C2
Fairfield 446	H3
Fairview-Sumach 2,749	E4
Fall City 1,582	D3
Farmington 126	H3
Ferndale 5,398	C2
Fife 3,864	C3
Finley 4,897	F4
Fircrest 5,258	C3
Fords Prairie 2,480	B4
Forks 2,862	A3
Four Lakes 500	H3
Frances 144	B4
Freeland 1,278	C2
Freeman 150	H3
Friday Harbor▲ 1,492	B2
Fruitland 150	G2
Fruitvale 4,125	E4
Galvin 250	B4
Garfield 544	H3
Garrett 1,004	G4
Geiger Heights	H3
George 253	F3
Gig Harbor 3,236	C3
Glacier 150	D2
Glenoma 500	C4
Glenwood 626	D4
Gold Bar 1,078	D3
Goldendale▲ 3,319	E5
Gorst 750	C3
Grand Coulee 984	G3
Grand Mound 1,394	C4
Grandview 7,169	F4
Granger 2,053	E4
Granite Falls 1,060	D2
Grapeview 250	C3
Grayland 750	A4
Grays River 350	B4
Greenacres 4,626	J3
Greenbank 600	C2
Hadlock-Irondale 2,742	C2
Hamilton 228	D2
Hansville 250	C3
Harper 300	A2
Harrah 341	E4
Harrington 449	G3
Hartline 176	F3
Hatton 71	F4
Heisson 200	C5
Hobart 500	D3
Hoodsport 500	B3
Hoquiam 8,972	A3
Humptulips 275	A3
Hunters 200	G2
Hunts Point 513	B2
Husum 200	D5
Ilwaco 815	A4
Inchelium 393	G2
Index 139	D3
Indianola 1,729	A1
Ione 507	H2
Issaquah 7,786	C3
Joyce 375	B2
Juanita 17,232	B1
Kahlotus 167	B4
Kalama 1,210	C4
Kapowsin 500	C4
Keller 195	G2
Kelso▲ 11,820	C4

Kenmore 8,917	B1
Kennewick 42,155	F4
Kent 37,960	C3
Kettle Falls 1,272	H2
Keyport 900	A2
Kingston 1,270	C3
Kiona 230	F4
Kirkland 40,052	B2
Kittitas 843	E4
Klickitat 750	D5
Krupp (Marlin) 53	F3
La Center 451	C5
La Conner 656	C2
La Push 500	A3
Lacey 19,279	C3
Lacrosse 336	H4
Lake Forest Park 4,031	B1
Lake Stevens 3,380	D3
Lakewood 58,412	C2
Lamont 91	H3
Langley 845	C2
Latah 175	H3
Laurel 972	D5
Leavenworth 1,692	E3
Lebam 275	B4
Liberty Lake 2,015	J3
Lind 472	G4
Littlerock 850	B4
Long Beach 1,236	A4
Longbranch 640	C3
Longview 31,499	B4
Loomis 150	F2
Loon Lake 500	H2
Lummi Island 675	C2
Lyle 580	D5
Lyman 275	D2
Lynden 5,709	C2
Lynnwood 28,695	C3
Mabton 1,482	E4
Malaga 125	E3
Malden 189	H3
Malo 240	G2
Malone 175	B4
Malott 350	F2
Manchester 4,031	A2
Mansfield 311	F3
Manson 220	E3
Maple Falls 300	D2
Maple Valley 1,211	C3
Marblemount 300	D2
Marcus 135	H2
Marietta-Alderwood 2,766	C2
Markham 117	B4
Marlin	F3
Marysville 10,328	C2
Matlock 255	B3
Mattawa 941	F4
McCleary 1,235	B3
McKenna 300	C4
Mead	H3
Medical Lake 3,664	H3
Medina 2,981	B2
Menlo 237	B4
Mercer Island (city) 20,816	B2
Mesa 252	G4
Metaline 198	H2
Metaline Falls 210	H2
Mica 105	H3
Milan 150	H3
Millwood 1,559	H3
Milton 4,995	C3
Mineral 550	C4
Moclips 500	A3
Monitor 650	E3
Monroe 4,278	D3
Montesano▲ 3,064	B4
Moses Lake 11,235	F3
Mossyrock 452	C4
Mount Vernon▲ 17,647	C2
Mountlake Terrace 19,320	B1
Moxee City 814	E4
Mukilteo 7,007	C3
Naches 596	E4
Nahcotta 200	A4
Napavine 745	C4
Naselle 500	B4
Navy Yard City 2,905	A2
Neah Bay 916	A2
Neilton 250	B3
Nespelem 291	G2
Newhalem 350	D2
Newman Lake 102	J3
Newport▲ 1,691	H2
Nine Mile Falls 150	H3
Nisqually 558	C3
Nooksack 584	C2
Nordland 706	C2
Normandy Park 6,709	A2
North Bend 2,578	D3
North Bonneville 411	C5
Northport 308	H2
Oak Harbor 17,176	C2
Oakesdale 346	H3
Oakville 493	B4

(continued on following page)

Agriculture, Industry and Resources

DOMINANT LAND USE

- Specialized Wheat
- Wheat, Peas
- Dairy, Poultry, Mixed Farming
- Fruit and Mixed Farming
- General Farming, Dairy, Range Livestock
- General Farming, Livestock, Special Crops
- Range Livestock
- Forests
- Urban Areas
- Nonagricultural Land

MAJOR MINERAL OCCURRENCES

Ag	Silver		Mr	Marble
Au	Gold		Pb	Lead
C	Coal		Tc	Talc
Cl	Clay		U	Uranium
Cu	Copper		W	Tungsten
Gp	Gypsum		Zn	Zinc
Mg	Magnesium			

⚡ Water Power

▨ Major Industrial Areas

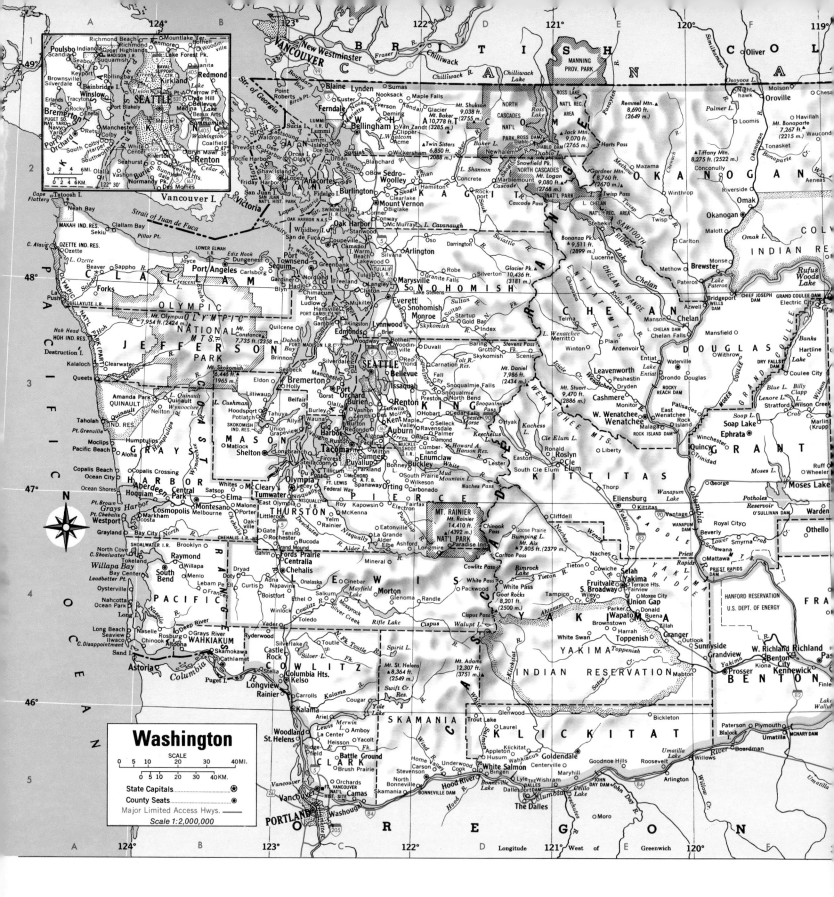

Washington

SCALE

0 5 10 20 30 40MI.

0 5 10 20 30 40KM.

State Capitals .... ⊛

County Seats .... ◉

Major Limited Access Hwys. ——————

Scale 1:2,000,000

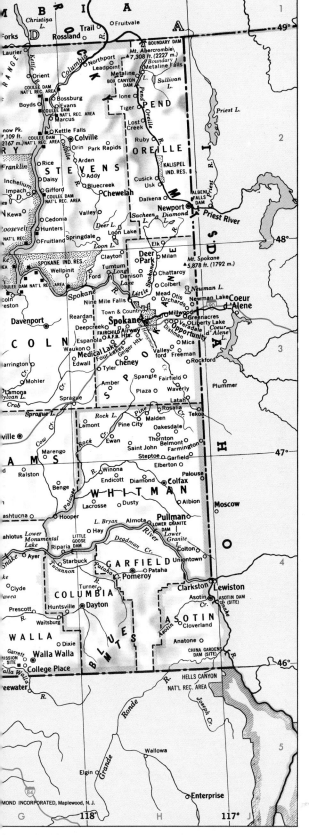

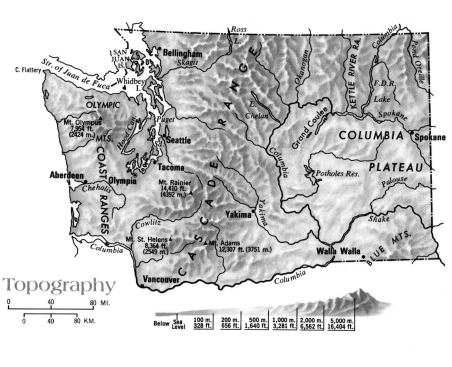

Topography

Below Sea Level — 100 m. 328 ft. — 200 m. 656 ft. — 500 m. 1,640 ft. — 1,000 m. 3,281 ft. — 2,000 m. 6,562 ft. — 5,000 m. 16,404 ft.

RAMMOND INCORPORATED, Maplewood, N.J.

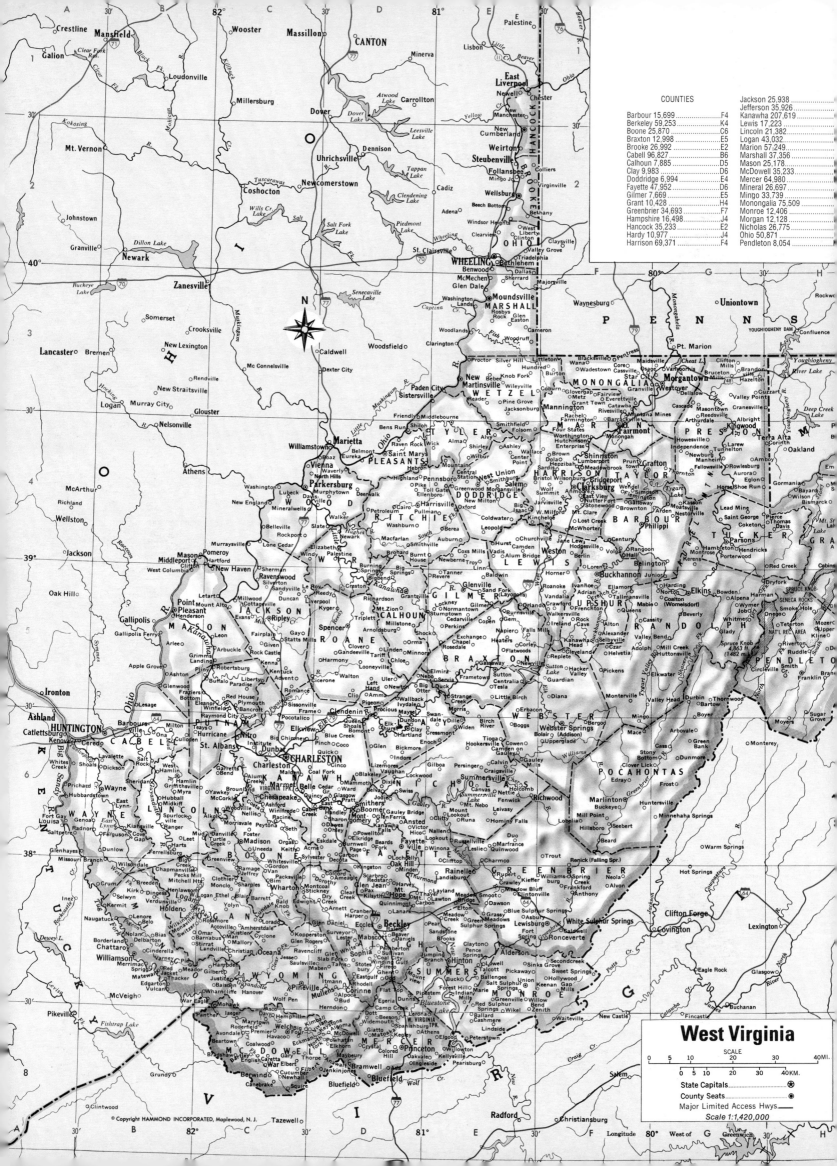

West Virginia

COUNTIES

Barbour 15,699 ....F4	Jackson 25,938
Berkeley 59,253 ....K4	Jefferson 35,926
Boone 25,870 ....C6	Kanawha 207,619
Braxton 12,998 ....E5	Lewis 17,223
Brooke 26,992 ....E2	Lincoln 21,382
Cabell 96,827 ....B6	Logan 43,032
Calhoun 7,885 ....D5	Marion 57,249
Clay 9,983 ....D6	Marshall 37,356
Doddridge 6,994 ....E4	Mason 25,178
Fayette 47,952 ....D6	McDowell 35,233
Gilmer 7,669 ....E5	Mercer 64,980
Grant 10,428 ....H4	Mineral 26,697
Greenbrier 34,693 ....F7	Mingo 33,739
Hampshire 16,498 ....J4	Monongalia 75,509
Hancock 35,233 ....E2	Monroe 12,406
Hardy 10,977 ....J4	Morgan 12,128
Harrison 69,371 ....F4	Nicholas 26,775
	Ohio 50,871
	Pendleton 8,054

SCALE

0 5 10 20 30 40MI.

0 5 10 20 30 40KM.

State Capitals ....✪

County Seats ....◉

Major Limited Access Hwys. ━━━

Scale 1:1,420,000

leasants 7,546	D4
ocahontas 9,008	F6
reston 29,037	G4
utnam 42,835	C6
aleigh 76,819	D7
andolph 27,803	G5
itchie 10,233	D4
oane 15,120	D5
ummers 14,204	E7
aylor 15,144	F4
ucker 7,728	F4
yler 9,796	E4
Jpshur 22,867	F5
Vayne 41,636	B6
Vebster 10,729	F6
Vetzel 19,258	E3
Virt 5,192	D4
Vood 86,915	D4
Vyoming 28,990	C7

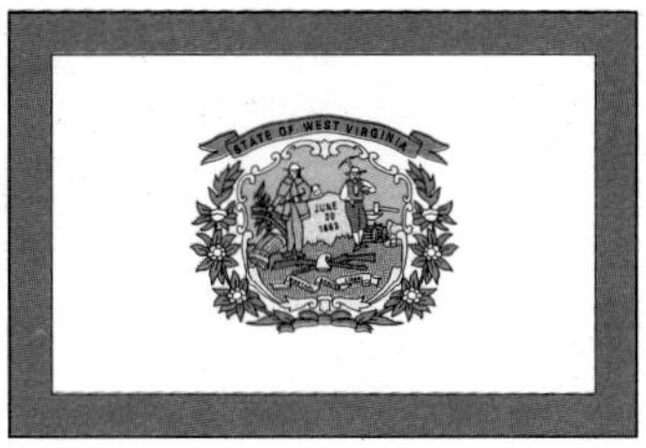

AREA 24,231 sq. mi. (62,758 sq. km.)
POPULATION 1,801,625
CAPITAL Charleston
LARGEST CITY Charleston
HIGHEST POINT Spruce Knob 4,863 ft. (1482 m.)
SETTLED IN 1774
ADMITTED TO UNION June 20, 1863
POPULAR NAME Mountain State
STATE FLOWER Big Rhododendron
STATE BIRD Cardinal

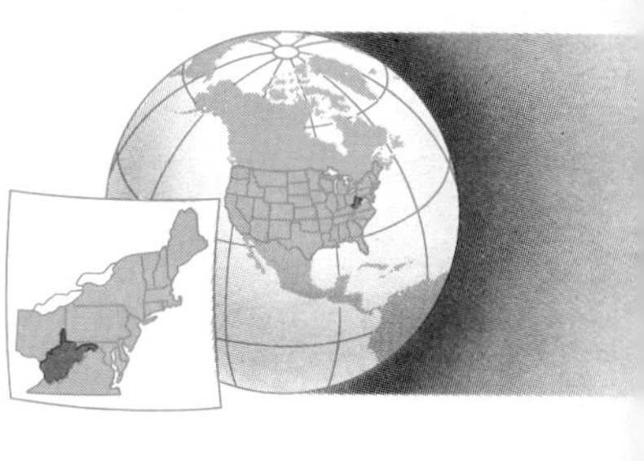

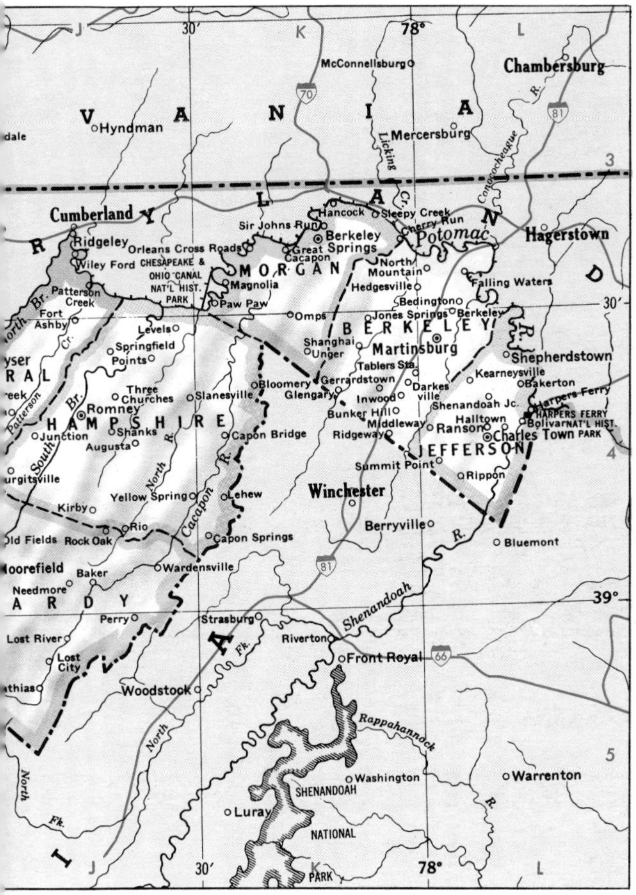

Chambersburg
McConnellsburg
Hyndman
Mercersburg
Cumberland
Hagerstown
Sir Johns Run
Hancock
Sleepy Creek
Berkeley Springs
Great Cacapon
Potomac
Ridgeley
Orleans Cross Roads
Wiley Ford
CHESAPEAKE & OHIO CANAL NAT'L HIST. PARK
MORGAN
North Mountain
Magnolia
Falling Waters
Patterson Creek
Paw Paw
Hedgesville
Bedington
Fort Ashby
Omps
Jones Springs
Berkeley
Levels
Springfield
Points
BERKELEY
Shanghai
Unger
Martinsburg
Shepherdstown
Tablers Sta.
Kearneysville
Bloomery
Gerrardstown
Glengary
Darkesville
Bakerton
Three Churches
Slanesville
Inwood
Romney
Harpers Ferry
HAMPSHIRE
Bunker Hill
Shenandoah Jc.
Halltown
HARPERS FERRY NAT'L HIST. PARK
Bolivar
Middleway
Ransom
Charles Town
Junction
Shanks
Capon Bridge
Ridgeway
Augusta
JEFFERSON
Summit Point
Rippon
Yellow Spring
Lehew
Winchester
Kirby
Rio
Berryville
Bluemont
Rock Oak
Capon Springs
Moorefield
Baker
Wardensville
Needmore
HARDY
Shenandoah
Perry
Strasburg
Lost River
Riverton
Lost City
Front Royal
Woodstock
Rappahannock
Washington
Warrenton
SHENANDOAH
Luray
NATIONAL
PARK

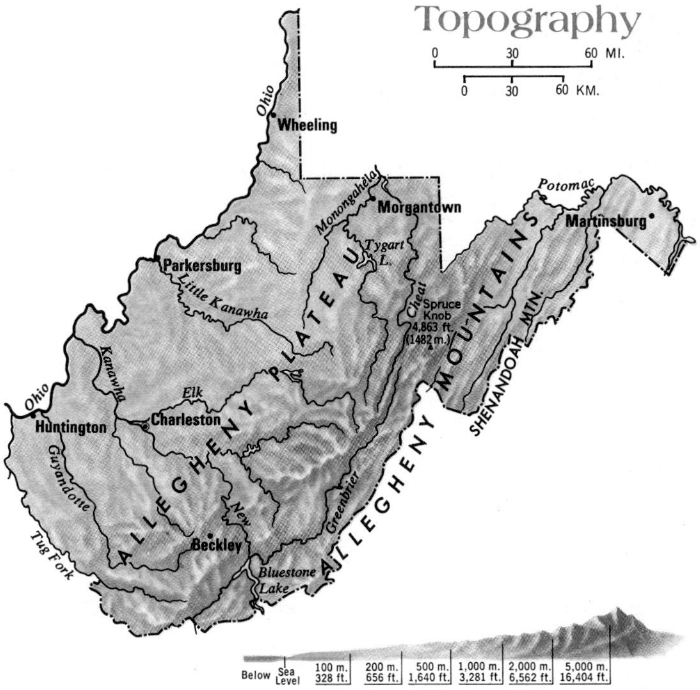

Topography
0 30 60 MI.
0 30 60 KM.
Ohio
Wheeling
Monongahela
Morgantown
Potomac
Martinsburg
Parkersburg
Tygart L.
Little Kanawha
Cheat
Spruce Knob 4,863 ft. (1482 m.)
ALLEGHENY PLATEAU
ALLEGHENY MOUNTAINS
SHENANDOAH MTN.
Kanawha
Elk
Charleston
Huntington
Guyandotte
New
Greenbrier
Beckley
Tug Fork
Bluestone Lake
Below Sea Level
100 m. 328 ft.
200 m. 656 ft.
500 m. 1,640 ft.
1,000 m. 3,281 ft.
2,000 m. 6,562 ft.
5,000 m. 16,404 ft.

CITIES and TOWNS

Accoville 975	C7
Acme 165	D6
Ada 250	D8
Addison▲ (Webster Springs) 674	F6
Adrian 510	F5
Albright 195	G3
Alderson 1,152	E7
Algoma 200	D8
Alkol 500	C6
Alma 197	E4
Alpoca 200	D7
Alum Bridge 150	F5
Alum Creek 1,602	C6
Alvy 150	E4
Ameagle 230	D7
Amherstdale 1,057	C7
Amma 200	D5
Anawalt 329	D8
Anmoore 686	F4
Ansted 1,643	D6
Apple Grove 900	B5
Arbovale 610	G6
Arden 130	G4
Arnett 300	D7
Arnoldsburg 175	D5
Arthur 350	H4
Arthurdale 1,063	G3
Asbury 280	E7
Asco 175	C8
Ashford 400	C6
Ashton 259	B5
Athens 741	E8
Auburn 89	E4
Augusta 750	J4
Aurora 250	G4
Avondale 250	C8
Baisden 500	C7
Baker 200	J4
Bakerton 125	L4
Bald Knob 356	C7
Ballard 220	E8
Ballengee 170	E7
Bancroft 381	C5
Barboursville 2,774	B6
Barnabus 750	C7
Barrackville 1,443	F3
Barrett 950	C7
Baтley 900	C8
Bartow 500	G5
Bayard 414	H4
Beards Fork 400	D6
Beartown 500	C8
Beaver (Glen Hedrick) 1,244	D7
Bebee 125	E3
Beckley▲ 18,296	D7
Bedington 150	L3
Beech Bottom 415	E2
Beeson 300	D8
Belington 1,850	F4
Belle 1,421	C6
Belmont 912	D4
Belva 275	D6
Benwood 1,669	E2
Bergoo 220	F6
Berkeley 600	L4
Berkeley Springs▲ 789	K3
Berwind 615	C8
Bethany 1,139	E2
Bethlehem 2,694	E2
Beverly 696	G5
Bickmore 300	D6
Big Chimney 450	C6
Big Creek 500	B7
Big Four 150	C8
Big Otter 150	D5
Big Springs 485	D5
Bim 500	C7
Birch River 650	E6
Blacksville 168	F3
Blair 800	C7
Bloomery 200	K4
Blue Creek 650	D6
Bluefield 12,756	D8
Boaz 1,137	D4
Boggs 131	E6
Bolair 450	F6
Bolivar 1,013	L4
Bomont 170	D6
Boomer 1,051	D6
Borderland 250	B7
Bowden 135	G5
Bradshaw 394	C8
Bramwell 620	D8
Brandonville 73	G3
Brandywine 300	H5
Breeden 600	B7
Bridgeport 6,739	F4
Brooks 196	E7
Brounland 900	C6
Brownton 400	F4
Bruceton Mills 132	G3
Buck 150	E7
Buckhannon▲ 5,909	F5
Bud 400	D7
Buffalo 969	C5
Bunker Hill 600	K4
Burlington 300	J4
Burning Springs 137	D5
Burnsville 495	E5
Burnt House 175	D4
Burnwell 140	D6
Burton 200	F3
Cabin Creek 900	C6
Cabins 300	H4
Cairo 290	D4
Caldwell 795	F7
Calvin 400	E6
Camden on Gauley 171	E6
Cameron 1,177	E3
Camp Creek 200	D7
Canebrake 300	C8
Canvas 300	E6
Capon Bridge 192	K4
Capon Springs 580	K4
Carbon 300	D6
Caretta 650	C8
Cass 148	G6
Cassity 150	F5
Cassville 1,458	F3
Catawba 186	F3
Cedar Grove 1,213	D6
Center Point 250	E4
Central Station 200	E4
Ceredo 1,916	F4
Chapmanville 1,110	B7
Charles Town▲ 3,122	L4
Charleston (cap.)▲ 57,287	C6
Charmco 800	E6
Chattaroy 1,182	B7
Chesapeake 1,896	C6
Chester 2,905	E1
Christian 200	C7
Cinco 500	D6
Circleville 180	H5
Clarksburg▲ 18,059	F4
Clay▲ 592	D6
Clear Creek 300	D7
Clearview 622	E2
Clendenin 1,203	D5
Clifton 325	B5
Clifton Mills 136	G3
Clifty 250	E6
Clinton 350	E2
Clintonville 250	E7
Clio 300	D5
Clothier 900	C7
Clover 350	D5
Clover Lick 250	F6
Coal City 1,876	D7
Coal Fork 2,100	D6
Coalton 277	G5
Coalwood 650	C8
Coburn 230	F3
Colcord 600	D7
Colliers 864	E2
Colored Hill 900	D8
Core 250	F3
Corinne 900	D7
Corinth 195	H4
Costa 250	C6
Cottageville 300	C5
Cove Gap 650	B6
Cowen 549	E6
Coxs Mills 275	E4
Craigsville 1,955	E6
Cranberry 315	D7
Crawley 395	E7
Crum 500	B7
Crystal 150	D8
Cucumber 274	C8
Culloden 2,907	B6
Cyclone 500	C7
Dallas 450	E2
Daniels 1,714	D7
Danville 595	C6
Darkesville 150	L4
Davis 799	H4
Davisville 200	C4
Davy 403	C8
Dawes 800	D6
Dawson 300	E7
Decota 800	D6
Deerwalk 150	D4
Delbarton 705	B7
Dellslow 300	G3
Diana 300	F5
Dickson 200	B6
Dille 300	E6
Dingess 600	B7
Dixie 985	D6
Dola 200	F4
Dorothy 400	D7
Dry Creek 441	D7
Dryfork 425	H5
Dunbar 8,697	C6
Dunlow 169	B6
Dunmore 280	G6
Durbin 278	G5
East Bank 892	D6
East Lynn 150	B6
East View 1,222	F4
Eastgulf 300	D7
Eccles 1,162	D7
Eckman 750	C8
Edgarton 415	B7
Edray 175	F6
Egeria 150	D7
Elbert 400	C8
Eleanor 1,256	C5
Elizabeth▲ 900	D4
Elk Garden 261	H4
Elkhorn 150	D8
Elkins▲ 7,420	G5
Elkridge 500	D6
Elkview 1,047	C6
Ellenboro 453	F5
Elton 200	E7
English 500	C8
Enterprise 1,058	F4
Erbacon 350	E6
Eskdale 400	D6
Ethel 450	C7
Evans 400	C5
Everettville 175	F3
Fairmont 20,210	F4
Fairplain 200	C5
Fairview 513	F3
Falling Spring (Renick) 191	F6
Falling Waters 130	L3
Farmington 414	F3
Fayetteville▲ 2,182	D6
Fenwick 500	E6
Ferguson 150	B6
Ferrellsburg 300	B6
Filbert 130	D8
Fireco 200	D7
Fisher 500	H4
Flat Top 550	D7
Flatwoods 324	E5
Flemington 352	F4
Follansbee 3,339	E2
Folsom 360	E4
Forest Hill 314	E7
Fort Ashby 1,288	J4
Fort Gay 852	A6
Fort Seybert 200	H5
Fort Spring 250	E7
Foster 500	C6
Four States 500	F4
Frametown 150	E5
Frankford 200	F7
Franklin▲ 914	H5
Fraziers Bottom 250	B5
French Creek 200	F5
Friendly 146	D3
Gallipolis Ferry 325	B5
Galloway 500	F4
Gandeeville 150	D5
Gap Mills 300	F7
Gary 1,355	C8
Gassaway 946	E5
Gauley Bridge 691	D6
Gauley Mills 165	E6
Gay 300	C5
Gerrardstown 240	K4
Ghent 500	D7
Giatto 400	D8
Gilbert 456	C7
Gilboa 500	E6
Glady 175	G5
Glasgow 906	D6
Glen 175	D6
Glen Dale 1,612	E3
Glen Daniel 300	D7
Glen Ferris 200	D6
Glen Hedrick (Beaver)	B7
Glen Jean	D7
Glen Rogers 500	D7
Glen White 300	D7
Glengary 250	K4
Glenhayes 175	A6
Glenville▲ 1,923	E5
Glenwood 400	B5
Gordon 300	C7
Grafton▲ 5,524	G4
Grant Town 694	F3
Grantsville▲ 671	D5
Granville 798	F3
Great Cacapon 750	K3
Green Bank 115	G6
Green Sulphur Springs 225	E7
Greenview 250	C6
Greenwood 750	E4
Griffithsville 300	B6
Grimms Landing 350	B5
Guardian 175	F5
Hacker Valley 440	F5
Halltown 375	L4
Hambleton 265	G4
Hamlin▲ 1,030	B6
Hampden 300	C7
Hancock 175	K3
Handley 334	D6
Hanover 300	C7
Harman 128	G5

(continued on following page)

Agriculture, Industry and Resources

DOMINANT LAND USE

- Dairy, General Farming
- General Farming, Livestock, Dairy
- General Farming, Livestock, Tobacco
- General Farming, Livestock, Fruit, Tobacco
- Fruit and Mixed Farming
- Forests

MAJOR MINERAL OCCURRENCES

- C Coal
- Cl Clay
- G Natural Gas
- Ls Limestone
- Na Salt
- O Petroleum

- ⚡ Water Power
- Major Industrial Areas

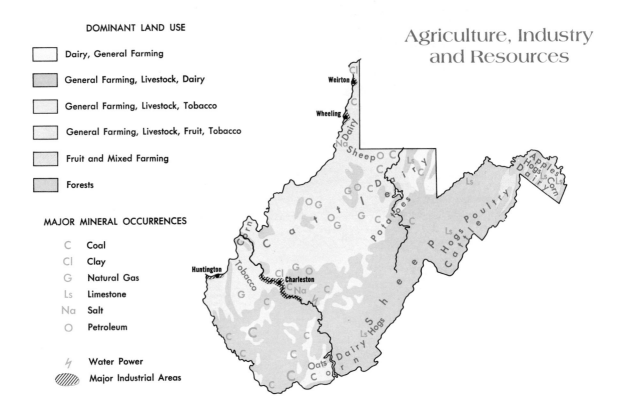

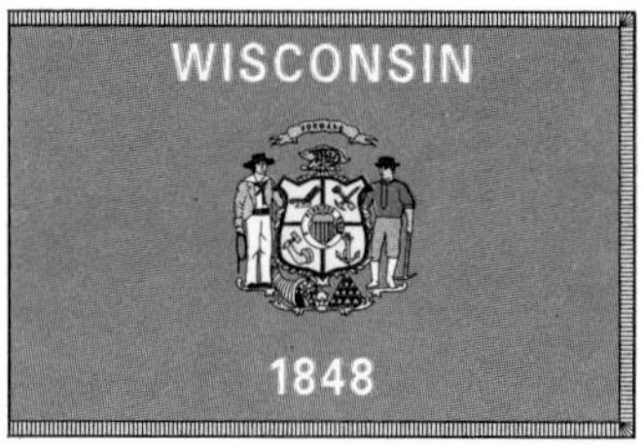

AREA 56,153 sq. mi. (145,436 sq. km.)
POPULATION 4,906,745
CAPITAL Madison
LARGEST CITY Milwaukee
HIGHEST POINT Timms Hill 1,951 ft. (595 m.)
SETTLED IN 1670
ADMITTED TO UNION May 29, 1848
POPULAR NAME Badger State
STATE FLOWER Wood Violet
STATE BIRD Robin

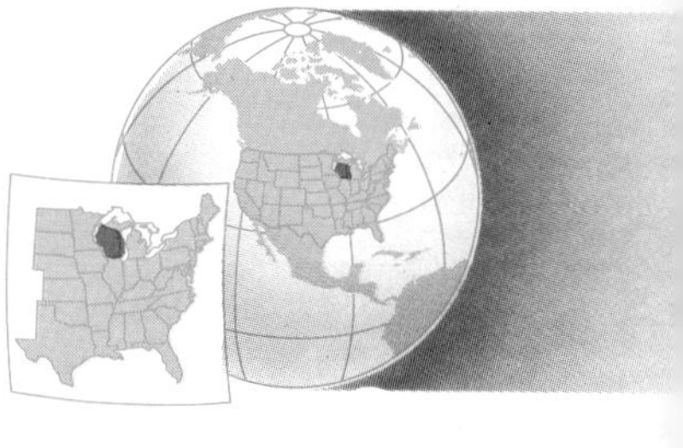

COUNTIES

Adams 15,682 G7
Ashland 16,307 E3
Barron 40,750 C5
Bayfield 14,008 D3
Brown 194,594 L7
Buffalo 13,584 C7
Burnett 13,084 B4
Calumet 34,291 K7
Chippewa 52,360 D5
Clark 31,647 E6
Columbia 45,088 H9
Crawford 15,940 E9
Dane 367,085 H9
Dodge 76,559 J9
Door 25,690 M6
Douglas 41,758 C3
Dunn 35,909 C6
Eau Claire 85,183 D6
Florence 4,590 K4
Fond du Lac 90,083 K8
Forest 8,776 J4
Grant 49,264 E10
Green 30,339 G10
Green Lake 18,651 H8
Iowa 20,150 F9
Iron 6,153 F9
Jackson 16,588 F3
Jefferson 67,783 J9
Juneau 21,650 F8
Kenosha 128,181 K10
Kewaunee 18,878 L6
La Crosse 97,904 D8
Lafayette 16,076 F10
Langlade 19,505 H5
Lincoln 26,993 G5
Manitowoc 80,421 L7
Marathon 115,400 G6
Marinette 40,548 K5
Marquette 12,321 H8
Menominee 3,890 J5
Milwaukee 959,275 L9
Monroe 36,633 E8
Oconto 30,226 K6
Oneida 31,679 G4
Outagamie 140,510 K7
Ozaukee 72,831 L9
Pepin 7,107 C6
Pierce 32,765 B6
Polk 34,773 B5
Portage 61,405 G6
Price 15,600 F4
Racine 175,034 K10
Richland 17,521 F9
Rock 139,510 H10
Rusk 15,079 D5
Saint Croix 43,262 B5
Sauk 46,975 G9
Sawyer 14,181 D4
Shawano 37,157 J6
Sheboygan 103,877 L8
Taylor 18,901 E5
Trempealeau 25,263 D7
Vernon 25,617 E8
Vilas 17,707 G3
Walworth 75,000 J10
Washburn 13,772 C4
Washington 95,328 K9
Waukesha 304,715 K9
Waupaca 46,104 J6
Waushara 19,385 H7
Winnebago 140,320 J8
Wood 73,605 F7

CITIES and TOWNS

Abbotsford 1,916 F6
Abrams 300 L6
Adams 1,715 G8
Adell 510 L8
Afton 225 H10
Albany 1,140 G10
Albion 300 H10
Algoma 3,353 M6
Allenton 915 K9
Allouez 14,431 L7
Alma Center 416 E7
Alma▲ 790 C7
Almena 625 B5
Almond 455 G7
Alto 235 J8
Altoona 5,889 C6
Alvin 160 J4
Amberg 875 K5
Amery 2,657 B5
Amherst 792 H7
Amherst Junction 269 H7
Angelica 200 K6
Angelo 100 E3
Aniwa 249 H6
Antigo▲ 8,276 H5
Appleton▲ 65,695 J7
Arbor Vitae 900 G4
Arcadia 2,166 D7
Arena 525 G9
Argonne 600 G9
Argyle 798 G10
Arkansaw 400 B6
Arlington 440 H9
Armstrong Creek 615 K4
Arpin 312 G6
Ashippun 750 H1
Ashland▲ 8,695 E2
Ashwaubenon 16,376 K7
Athens 951 G5
Auburndale 665 F6
Augusta 1,510 D6
Auroraville 250 H7
Avoca 474 F9
Avon 120 H10
Babcock 250 F7
Bagley 306 D10
Baileys Harbor 250 M5
Baldwin 2,022 B6
Balsam Lake▲ 792 B5
Bancroft 355 G7
Bangor 1,076 E8
Baraboo▲ 9,203 G9
Barnes 225 D3
Barneveld 660 F10
Barron▲ 2,986 C5
Barronett 575 B4
Batavia 125 K8
Bay City 578 B6
Bayfield 686 E2
Bayside 4,789 M1
Bear Creek 418 J6
Beaver 100 K5
Beaver Dam 14,196 J9
Beetown 150 E10
Beldenville 175 A6
Belgium 928 L8
Bell Center 127 E9
Belleville 1,456 G10
Belmont 823 F10
Beloit 35,573 H10
Bennett 350 C3
Benton 898 F10
Berlin 5,371 H8
Bethel 210 F6
Bevent 200 H6
Big Bend 1,299 K2
Birchwood 443 C4
Birnamwood 693 H6
Biron 794 G7
Black Creek 1,152 K7
Black Earth 1,248 G9
Black River Falls▲ 3,490 E7
Blackwell 550 K4
Blair 1,126 D7
Blanchardville 802 G10
Bloom City 167 E8
Bloomer 3,085 D5
Bloomington 776 E10
Blue Mounds 446 G9
Blue River 438 E9
Boardman 100 A5
Boaz 131 E9
Bohners Lake 1,553 K10
Bonduel 1,210 K6
Boscobel 2,706 E9
Boulder Junction 780 G3
Bowler 279 J6
Boyceville 913 C5
Boyd 683 E6
Brackett 150 D6
Bradley 100 G4
Branch 300 L7
Brandon 872 J8
Brantwood 500 F4
Bridgeport 250 D9
Briggsville 250 H8
Brighton 100 K3
Brill 200 C4
Brillion 2,840 L7
Brodhead 3,165 G10
Brokaw 224 G5
Brookfield 35,184 K1
Brooklyn 789 H10
Brooks 103 G8
Brothertown 100 K7
Brown Deer 12,236 L1
Brown's Lake 1,725 K3
Brownsville 415 J8
Browntown 256 G10
Bruce 844 D5
Brule 335 C2
Brussels 500 L6
Buffalo 915 C7
Burlington 8,855 K10
Burnett 260 J9
Butler 2,079 K1
Butte Des Morts J7
Butternut 416 E3
Cable 227 D3
Cadott 1,328 D6
Caldwell 101 J2
Caledonia 100 L2
Cambria 768 H8
Cambridge 963 H9
Cameron 1,273 C5
Camp Douglas 512 F8
Camp Lake 2,291 K10
Campbellsport 1,732 K8
Canton 100 C5
Caroline 450 J6
Carter 100 J5
Cascade 620 K8
Casco 544 L6
Cashton 780 E8
Cassville 1,144 E10
Cataract 200 E7
Catawba 178 E4
Cazenovia 288 F8
Cecil 373 K6
Cedar Grove 1,521 L8
Cedarburg 9,895 L9
Centuria 790 A5
Chaseburg 365 D8
Chelsea 120 F5
Chenequa 601 J1
Chetek 1,953 C5
Chili 185 F6
Chilton▲ 3,240 K7
Chippewa Falls▲ 12,727 D6
City Point 110 F7
Clam Lake 140 E3
Clayton 450 B5
Clear Lake 932 B5
Clearwater Lake 200 H4
Cleveland 1,398 L8
Clinton 1,849 J10
Clintonville 4,351 J6
Clyman 370 J9
Cobb 440 F10
Cochrane 475 C7
Colby 1,532 F6
Coleman 839 L5
Colfax 1,110 C6
Coloma 383 H7
Columbus 4,093 H9
Combined Locks 2,190 K7
Commonwealth 240 K4
Como 1,353 K10
Comstock 160 C5
Concord 200 H1
Conover 480 H3
Conrath 92 E5
Coon Valley 817 E8
Cornell 1,541 D5
Cornucopia 250 D2
Couderay 92 D4
Crandon▲ 1,958 H4
Cream 120 C7
Crivitz 996 L5
Cross Plains 2,098 G9
Cuba City 2,024 F10
Cudahy 18,659 M2
Cumberland 2,163 C4
Curtiss 173 F6
Cushing 150 A4
Cylon 100 B5
Dale 410 J7
Dallas 452 C5
Dalton 300 H8
Danbury 350 B3
Dane 621 G9
Darien 1,158 J10
Darlington▲ 2,235 F10
De Forest 4,882 H9
De Pere 16,569 K7
De Soto 326 D9
Deer Park 237 B5
Deerfield 1,617 H9
Delafield 5,347 J1
Delavan 6,073 J10
Delavan Lake 2,177 J10
Dellwood 120 G7
Denmark 1,612 L7
Dexterville 100 F7
Diamond Bluff 100 A6
Dickeyville 862 E10
Dodge 185 D7
Dodgeville▲ 3,882 F10
Dorchester 697 F5
Dousman 1,277 J1
Downing 250 B5
Downsville 200 C6
Doylestown 316 H9
Draper 125 E4
Dresser 614 A5
Drummond 200 D3
Dunbar 106 K4
Durand▲ 2,003 C6
Dyckesville 300 L6
Eagle 1,182 H2
Eagle River▲ 1,374 H4
East Troy 2,664 J2
Eastman 369 D9
Easton 130 G8
Eau Claire▲ 56,856 D6
Eden 610 K8
Edgar 1,318 G6
Edgerton 4,254 H10
Egg Harbor 183 M5
Eland 247 H6
Elcho 500 H5
Elderon 175 H6
Eldorado 200 J8
Eleva 491 D6
Elk Mound 765 C6
Elkhart Lake 1,019 L8
Elkhorn▲ 5,337 J10
Ellison Bay 112 M5
Ellsworth▲ 2,706 A6
Elm Grove 6,261 K1
Elmwood 775 B6
Elmwood Park 534 M3
Elroy 1,533 F8
Elton 150 J5
Embarrass 461 J6
Emerald 128 B5
Endeavor 316 G8
Ephraim 261 M5
Ettrick 461 D7
Evansville 3,174 H10
Exeland 180 D4
Fair Water 310 J8
Fairchild 504 D6
Fall Creek 1,034 D6
Fall River 842 H9
Fence 200 K4
Fennimore 2,378 E9
Fenwood 214 F6
Ferryville 154 D9
Fifield 310 F4
Fish Creek 119 M5
Florence▲ 780 K4
Fond du Lac▲ 37,757 K8
Fontana 1,635 J10
Footville 764 H10
Forest Junction 140 K7
Forestville 470 L6
Fort Atkinson 10,227 J10
Fountain City 938 C7
Fox Lake 1,269 J8
Fox Point 7,238 M1
Foxboro 360 B2
Francis Creek 562 L7
Franklin 21,855 L2
Franksville 375 M3
Frederic 1,124 B4
Fredonia 1,558 L8
Fremont 632 J7
Friendship▲ 728 G8
Friesland 271 H8
Galesville 1,278 D7
Galloway 200 H6
Gays Mills 578 E9
Genesee 375 J2
Genesee Depot 350 J2
Genoa 266 D8
Genoa City 1,277 K11
Germantown 13,658 K1
Gibbsville 408 L8
Gillett 1,303 K6
Gilman 412 E5
Gilmanton 300 C7
Gleason 200 G5
Glen Flora 108 E4
Glen Haven 160 E10
Glenbeulah 386 L8
Glendale 14,088 M1
Glenwood City 1,026 B5
Glidden 940 E3
Goodman 875 K4
Gordon 600 C3
Gotham 250 F9
Grafton 9,340 L9
Grand Marsh 725 G8
Grand View 447 D3
Granton 379 E6
Grantsburg▲ 1,144 A4
Gratiot 207 F10
Green Bay▲ 96,466 K6
Green Lake▲ 1,064 H8
Green Valley 104 K6
Greendale 15,128 L2
Greenfield 33,403 L2
Greenleaf 300 L7
Greenville 900 J7
Greenwood 969 E6
Gresham 515 J6
Gurney 145 F3
Hager City 110 A6
Hales Corners 7,623 K2
Hallie D6
Hamburg 170 G5
Hammond 1,097 A6
Hancock 382 G7
Hartford 8,188 K9
Hartland 6,906 J1
Hatfield 500 E7

(continued on following page)

Agriculture, Industry and Resources

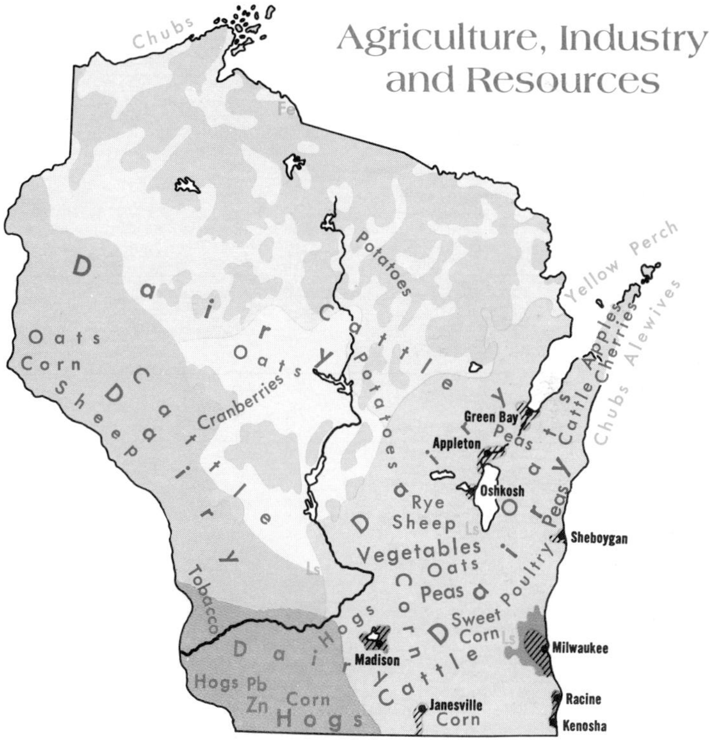

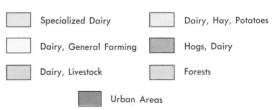

DOMINANT LAND USE

Specialized Dairy
Dairy, Hay, Potatoes
Dairy, General Farming
Hogs, Dairy
Dairy, Livestock
Forests
Urban Areas

MAJOR MINERAL OCCURRENCES

Fe Iron Ore
Pb Lead
Ls Limestone
Zn Zinc

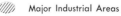

Major Industrial Areas

Topography

0   40   80 MI.
0   40   80 KM.

| Below Sea Level | 100 m. 328 ft. | 200 m. 656 ft. | 500 m. 1,640 ft. | 1,000 m. 3,281 ft. | 2,000 m. 6,562 ft. | 5,000 m. 16,404 ft. |

APOSTLE ISLANDS

Superior

SUPERIOR UPLAND

St. Croix
Namekagon
Chippewa L.
Flambeau Flowage
Menominee
Red Cedar
Chippewa
Flambeau
Rib
Wisconsin
Peshtigo
Washington I.

Timms Hill 1,951 ft. (595 m.)

Eau Claire
Wausau
Black
Yellow
Wolf
Green Bay
Door Pen.
Green Bay
Fox

Chippewa
Petenwell Lake
Castle Rock Lake
L. Poygan
Appleton
Lake Winnebago
Oshkosh

Mississippi

La Crosse
Kickapoo
The Dells
Rock
Fox
Sheboygan

Wisconsin

Madison
Milwaukee

Janesville
Kenosha
Racine

Wisconsin

SCALE
0 5 10   20   30   40 MI.

0 5 10   20   30   40 KM.

State Capitals ....⊛
County Seats ....◉
Canals ....

Major Limited Access Hwys. ————

Scale 1:2,270,000

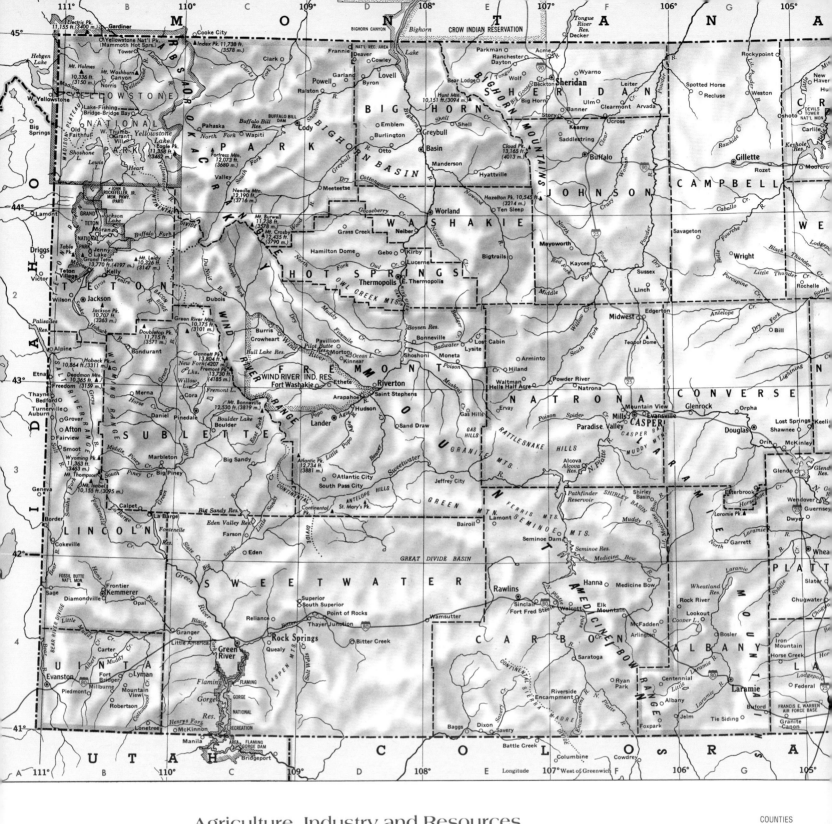

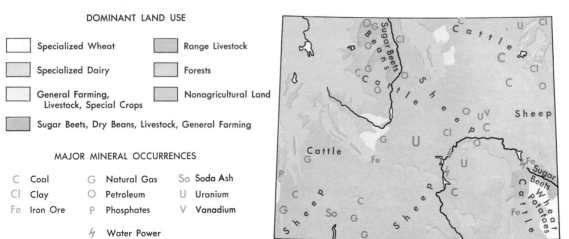

Agriculture, Industry and Resources

DOMINANT LAND USE

- Specialized Wheat
- Specialized Dairy
- General Farming, Livestock, Special Crops
- Sugar Beets, Dry Beans, Livestock, General Farming
- Range Livestock
- Forests
- Nonagricultural Land

MAJOR MINERAL OCCURRENCES

C Coal	G Natural Gas	So Soda Ash
Cl Clay	O Petroleum	U Uranium
Fe Iron Ore	P Phosphates	V Vanadium
	⚡ Water Power	

Wyoming

SCALE
0 5 10   20   30   40 MI.
0 5 10 20 30   40 KM.

State Capitals............................⊛
County Seats.............................◉
Major Limited Access Hwys._____
Scale 1:2,410,000

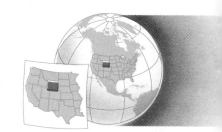

AREA   97,809 sq. mi. (253,325 sq. km.)
POPULATION   455,975
CAPITAL   Cheyenne
LARGEST CITY   Casper
HIGHEST POINT   Gannett Pk. 13,804 ft. (4207 m.)
SETTLED IN   1834
ADMITTED TO UNION   July 10, 1890
POPULAR NAME   Equality State
STATE FLOWER   Indian Paintbrush
STATE BIRD   Meadowlark

Topography

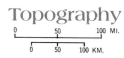

0   50   100 MI.

0   50   100 KM.

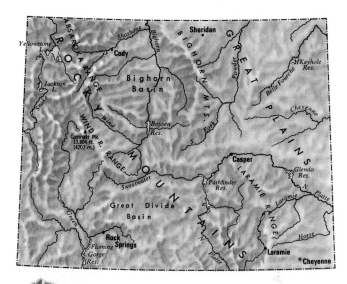

5,000 m.	2,000 m.	1,000 m.	500 m.	200 m.	100 m.	Sea
16,404 ft.	6,562 ft.	3,281 ft.	1,640 ft.	656 ft.	328 ft.	Level	Below

Acquisitions of Territory

WASHINGTON

OREGON COUNTRY 1846
OREGON Treaty with Great Britain

MONTANA

NORTH DAKOTA

RED RIVER
Title Established 1818

MINNESOTA

MICHIGAN

MAINE

VT.
N.H.

NEW YORK

MASS.
CONN.
R.I.

IDAHO

SOUTH DAKOTA

WISCONSIN

WYOMING

L O U I S I A N A 1803
Purchased from France

NEBRASKA

IOWA

PENNSYLVANIA

NEW JERSEY

CALIFORNIA

NEVADA

UTAH

COLORADO

KANSAS

MISSOURI

ILLINOIS

INDIANA

OHIO

WEST VIRGINIA

MD.

DEL.

MEXICAN CESSION 1848

UNITED STATES

KENTUCKY

VIRGINIA

ARIZONA

NEW MEXICO

OKLAHOMA

ARKANSAS

TENNESSEE 1783

NORTH CAROLINA

GADSDEN PURCHASE 1853

T E X A S
Annexed in 1845

TEXAS

LOUISIANA

MISSISSIPPI

ALABAMA

GEORGIA

SOUTH CAROLINA

F L O R I D A 1819
Treaty with Spain

ALASKA
1867
Purchased from Russia

H A W A I I
Annexed in 1898

The United States in 1783 comprised the thirteen original states and included lands acquired by conquest during the Revolution and by the Treaty of 1783.

Rank by Area

20 4 17
10 13 16 12
9 26 43 39
7 11 15 25 23 30 44
3 8 24 38 35 33 45
14 19 37 41 36 46 48 50 49 42
6 5 18 34 28
2 27 32 29 21 40
31 22

1 (Alaska)

47 (Hawaii)

MAP COLORS INDICATE RANKINGS IN GROUPS OF TEN

Rank by Population
1990

18
29 44 47
42 50 20 16 48 38
39 35 36 30 8 2 41 13
1 26 32 15 6 14 7 5 43 9 27
24 37 28 33 23 34 12 46 19
31 22 11 17 25 10
3 21 4
49
40

© Copyright HAMMOND INCORPORATED

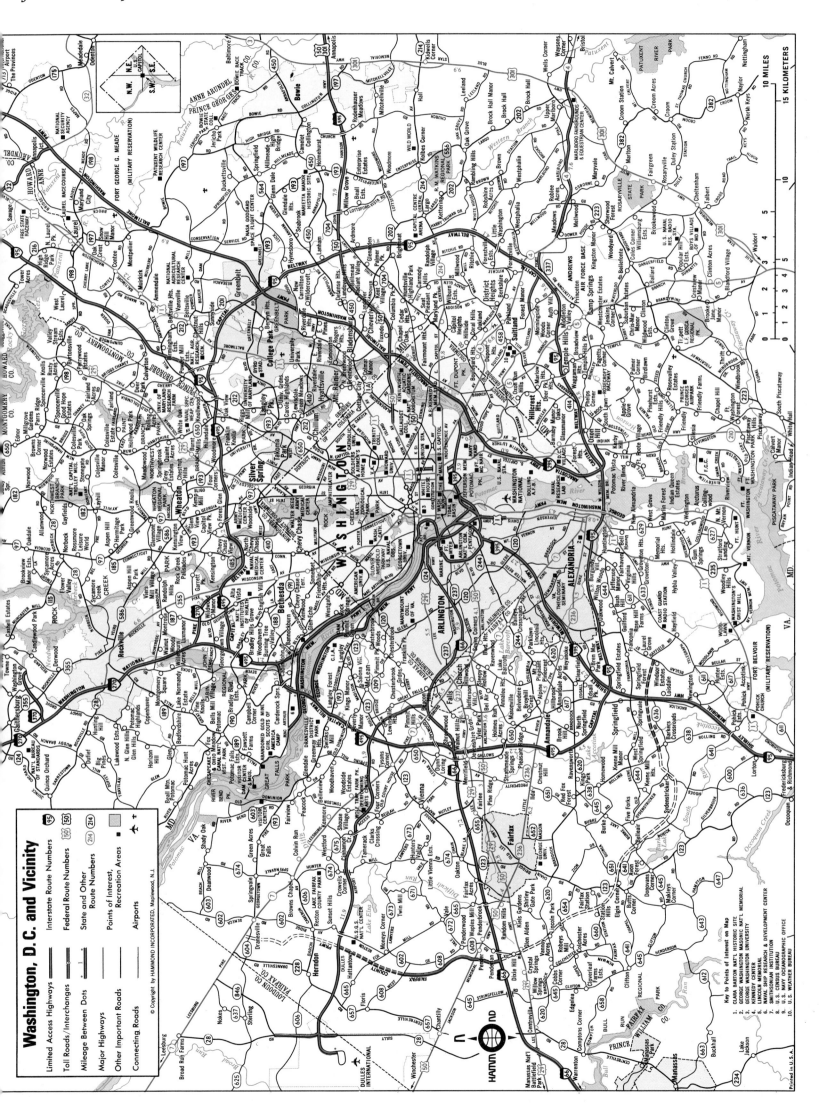

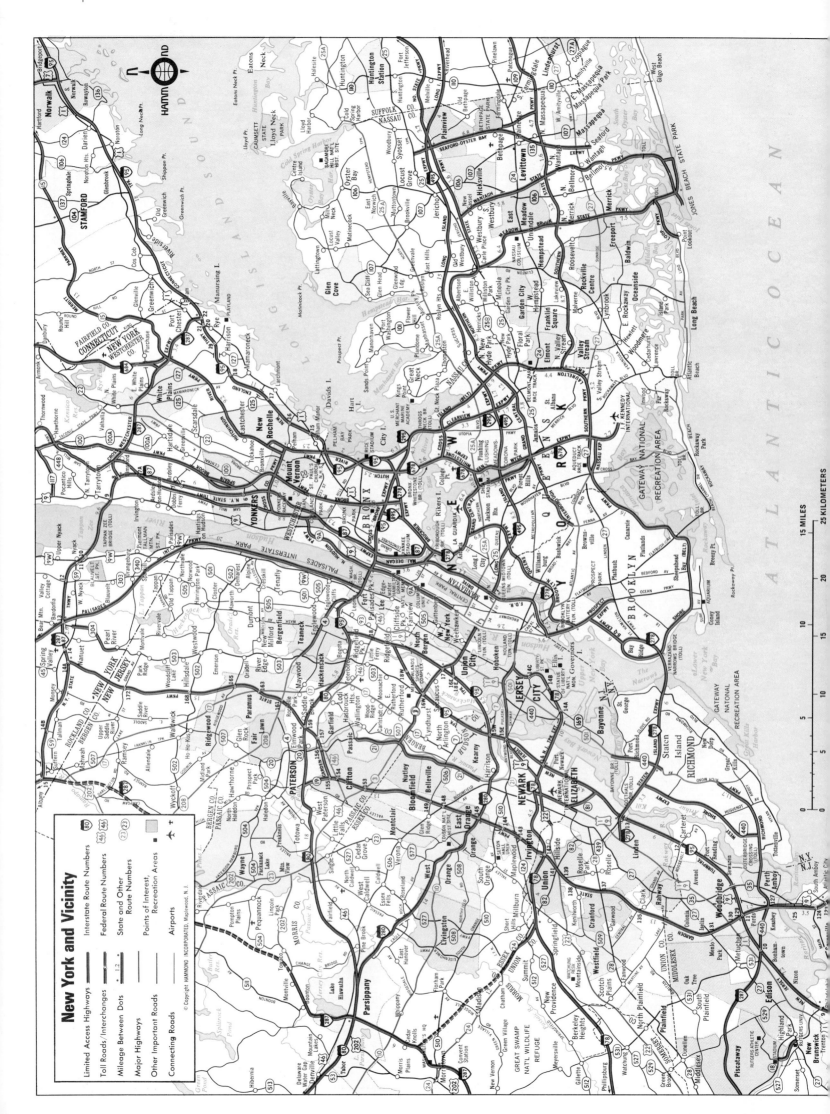

New York and Vicinity

Limited Access Highways
Toll Roads/Interchanges
Mileage Between Dots
Major Highways
Other Important Roads
Connecting Roads

Interstate Route Numbers
Federal Route Numbers
State and Other Route Numbers
Points of Interest, Recreation Areas
Airports

© Copyright HAMMOND INCORPORATED, Maplewood, N.J.

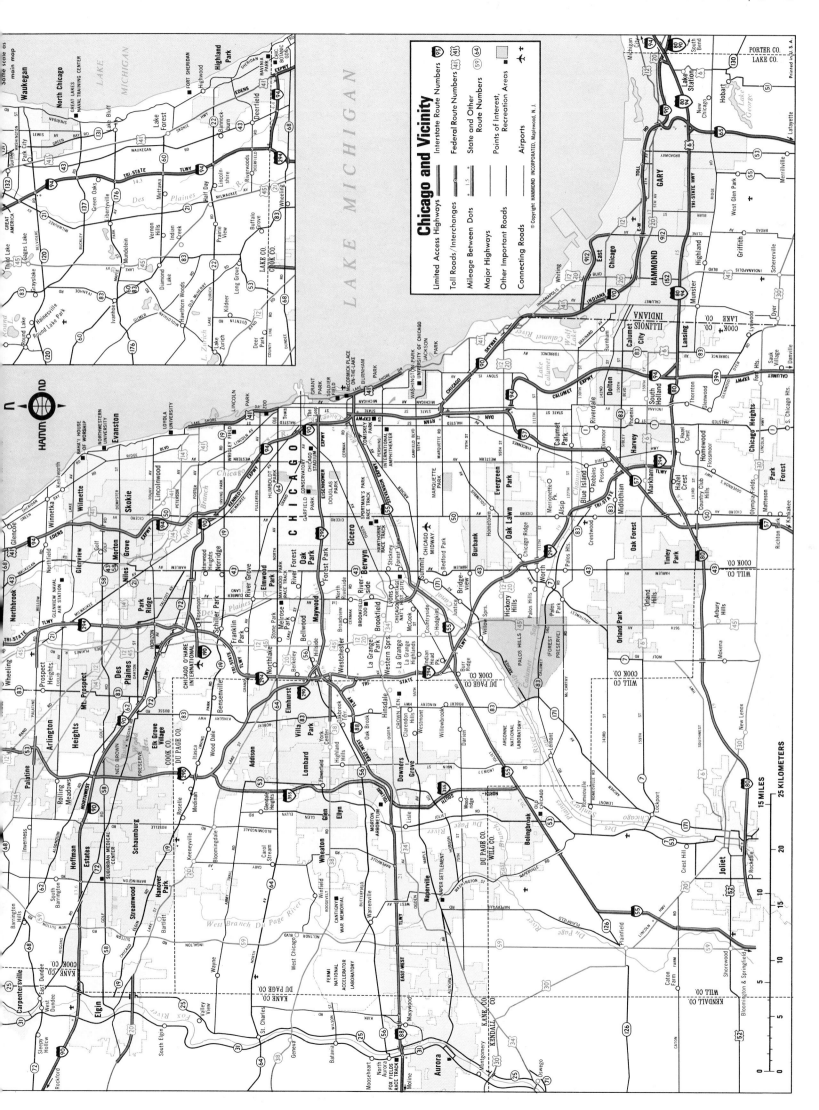

Chicago and Vicinity

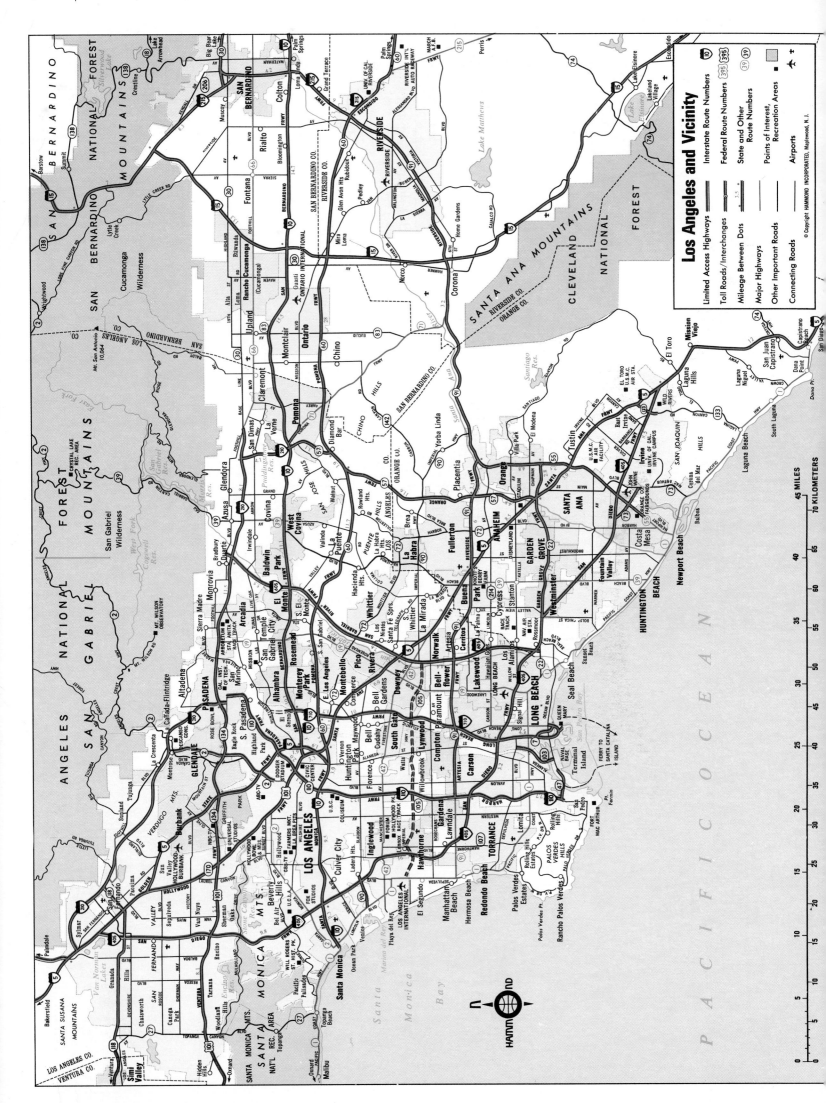

Los Angeles and Vicinity

Limited Access Highways
Toll Roads/Interchanges
Mileage Between Dots
Major Highways
Other Important Roads
Connecting Roads

Interstate Route Numbers
Federal Route Numbers
State and Other Route Numbers
Points of Interest, Recreation Areas
Airports

© Copyright, HAMMOND INCORPORATED, Maplewood, N.J.

UNITED STATES HISTORY ATLAS

SUPPLEMENT

Rank by Area
(Land and water)

Rank by Population

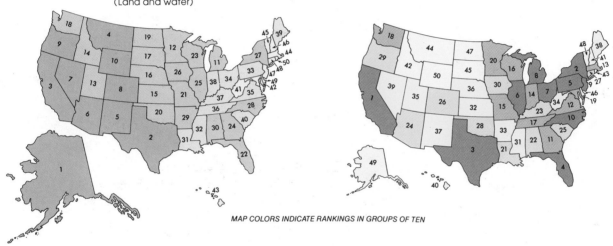

MAP COLORS INDICATE RANKINGS IN GROUPS OF TEN

State or Territory	Area (sq. mi.)	Area (sq. km.)	Population (1990)	State or Territory	Area (sq. mi.)	Area (sq. km.)	Population (1990)
Alabama	52,423	135,775	4,040,587	Montana	147,046	380,850	799,065
Alaska	656,424	1,700,139	550,043	Nebraska	82,282	213,110	1,578,385
American Samoa	77	199	39,000	Nevada	110,567	286,368	1,201,833
Arizona	114,006	295,276	3,665,228	New Hampshire	9,351	24,219	1,109,252
Arkansas	53,182	137,742	2,350,725	New Jersey	8,722	22,590	7,730,188
California	163,707	424,002	29,760,020	New Mexico	121,598	314,939	1,515,069
Colorado	104,100	269,620	3,294,394	New York	54,475	141,089	17,990,456
Connecticut	5,544	14,358	3,287,116	North Carolina	53,821	139,397	6,628,637
Delaware	2,489	6,447	666,168	North Dakota	70,704	183,123	638,800
District of Columbia	68	177	606,900	Ohio	44,828	116,103	10,847,115
Florida	65,758	170,313	12,937,926	Oklahoma	69,903	181,049	3,145,585
Georgia	59,441	153,953	6,478,216	Oregon	98,386	254,819	2,842,321
Guam	209	541	133,152	Pennsylvania	46,058	119,291	11,881,643
Hawaii	10,932	28,313	1,108,229	Puerto Rico	3,515	9,104	3,522,037
Idaho	83,574	216,456	1,006,749	Rhode Island	1,545	4,002	1,003,464
Illinois	57,918	150,007	11,430,602	South Carolina	32,007	82,898	3,486,703
Indiana	36,420	94,328	5,544,159	South Dakota	77,358	200,358	696,004
Iowa	56,276	145,754	2,776,755	Tennessee	42,146	109,158	4,877,185
Kansas	82,282	213,110	2,477,574	Texas	268,601	695,676	16,986,510
Kentucky	40,411	104,665	3,685,296	Utah	84,904	219,902	1,722,850
Louisiana	51,843	134,275	4,219,973	Vermont	9,615	24,903	562,758
Maine	35,387	91,653	1,227,928	Virginia	42,769	110,771	6,187,358
Maryland	12,407	32,135	4,781,468	Virgin Islands	132	342	101,809
Massachusetts	10,555	27,337	6,016,425	Washington	71,303	184,674	4,866,692
Michigan	96,810	250,738	9,295,297	West Virginia	24,231	62,759	1,793,477
Minnesota	86,943	225,182	4,375,099	Wisconsin	65,503	169,653	4,891,769
Mississippi	48,434	125,443	2,573,216	Wyoming	97,818	253,349	453,588
Missouri	69,709	180,546	5,117,073	United States	3,792,575	9,822,769	248,709,873

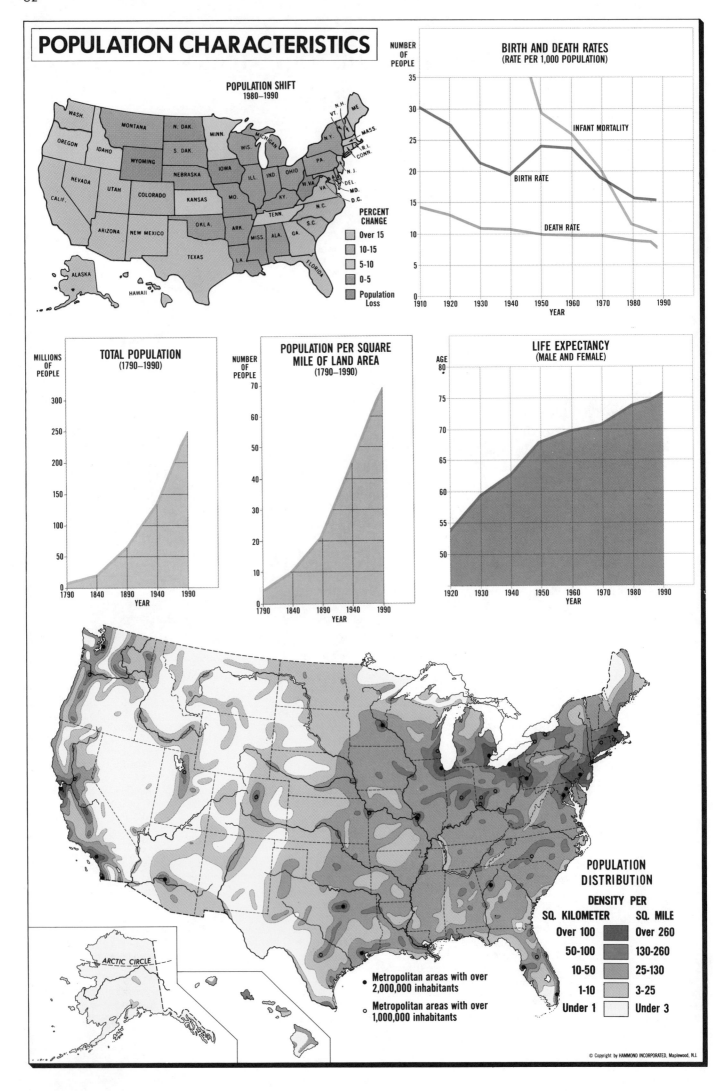

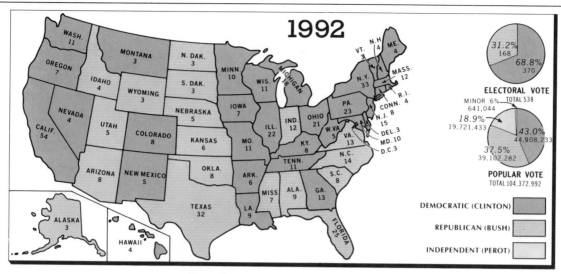

1992

ELECTORAL VOTE TOTAL 538

POPULAR VOTE TOTAL 104,372,992

DEMOCRATIC (CLINTON)
REPUBLICAN (BUSH)
INDEPENDENT (PEROT)

PRESIDENTS OF THE UNITED STATES

No.	Name	Politics	Native State	Age at Inauguration	Age at Death	No.	Name	Politics	Native State	Age at Inauguration	Age at Death
1	George Washington	Federalist	Va.	57	67	22	Grover Cleveland	Democrat	N.J.	47	71
2	John Adams	Federalist	Mass.	61	90	23	Benjamin Harrison	Republican	Ohio	55	67
3	Thomas Jefferson	Rep.-Dem.	Va.	57	83	24	Grover Cleveland	Democrat	N.J.	55	71
4	James Madison	Rep.-Dem.	Va.	57	85	25	William McKinley	Republican	Ohio	54	58
5	James Monroe	Rep.-Dem.	Va.	58	73	26	Theodore Roosevelt	Republican	N.Y.	42	60
6	John Quincy Adams	Rep.-Dem.	Mass.	57	80	27	William Howard Taft	Republican	Ohio	51	72
7	Andrew Jackson	Democrat	S.C.	61	78	28	Woodrow Wilson	Democrat	Va.	56	67
8	Martin Van Buren	Democrat	N.Y.	54	79	29	Warren G. Harding	Republican	Ohio	55	57
9	William Henry Harrison	Whig	Va.	68	68	30	Calvin Coolidge	Republican	Vt.	51	60
10	John Tyler	Whig	Va.	51	71	31	Herbert Clark Hoover	Republican	Iowa	54	90
11	James Knox Polk	Democrat	N.C.	49	53	32	Franklin D. Roosevelt	Democrat	N.Y.	51	63
12	Zachary Taylor	Whig	Va.	64	65	33	Harry S Truman	Democrat	Mo.	60	88
13	Millard Fillmore	Whig	N.Y.	50	74	34	Dwight D. Eisenhower	Republican	Texas	62	78
14	Franklin Pierce	Democrat	N.H.	48	64	35	John F. Kennedy	Democrat	Mass.	43	46
15	James Buchanan	Democrat	Pa.	65	77	36	Lyndon B. Johnson	Democrat	Texas	55	64
16	Abraham Lincoln	Republican	Ky.	52	56	37	Richard M. Nixon	Republican	Calif.	56	—
17	Andrew Johnson	Democrat	N.C.	56	66	38	Gerald R. Ford	Republican	Mich.	61	—
18	Ulysses Simpson Grant	Republican	Ohio	46	63	39	James E. Carter, Jr.	Democrat	Ga.	52	—
19	Rutherford B. Hayes	Republican	Ohio	54	70	40	Ronald W. Reagan	Republican	Ill.	69	—
20	James Abram Garfield	Republican	Ohio	49	49	41	George H. W. Bush	Republican	Mass.	64	—
21	Chester Alan Arthur	Republican	Vt.	50	56	42	William J. Clinton	Democrat	Ark.	46	—

STATISTICAL UPDATES

U-35 GROWTH OF INDUSTRY AND CITIES
Value Added by Manufacture (1990) – $1,326,362 million
Number of Production Workers (1990) – 12,129,000

U-37 EXPORTS, IMPORTS (Value in billions of dollars)
Exports (1989) 363,812 (1990) 393,592 (1991) 421,851
Imports (1989) 473,211 (1990) 495,311 (1991) 488,055

U-54 IMMIGRATION BY COUNTRY OF BIRTH 1981-1990
North America 3,125,000 Asia 2,817,400 Europe 705,600
South America 455,900 Africa 192,300
Australia & Pacific 41,900

U-56,57 GROWTH OF UNITED STATES ECONOMY
POPULATION AND LABOR FORCE
U.S. Percentage of World Population (1990) 4.7%
U.S. Population (1990) 248,709,873
U.S. Labor Force (1990) 122,570,000
Union Membership as Percent of Total Labor Force
(1990) 18.2%
Urban Residency (1990) 75.2%
Rural Residency (1990) 24.8%

AGRICULTURE
Gainful Farm Workers (1990) 2,113,000
Percent of Farm Workers to Total Gainful Labor Force
(1990) 2.1%
Number of Farms (1990) 2,140,000
Value of Farm Machinery and Equipment
(1990) $91.7 billion
TRANSPORTATION
Railroad Mileage (1990) 144,000
Domestic Passenger Miles Flown (1990) 340.2 billion
Miles of Surfaced Roads (1990) 3,524,000
Total Motor Vehicle Registration (1990) 188,655,000
Automobile Registration (1990) 143,026,000
NATIONAL PRODUCT AND INCOME
Gross National Product (1990) $5,524,000 million
Per Capita Disposable Income (current dollars)
(1990) $16,236
Purchasing Power of the Dollar (1982-1984 = $1.00)
(1990) $.734
Consumer Price Index (1982-1984 = 100) (1990) 136.2
One Dollar Purchased in 1990 1 2/5 quarts of milk

UNITED STATES AND WORLD ALLIANCES

Legend:
- North Atlantic Treaty Organization (NATO)
- Organization of American States (OAS)-includes U.S. and Canada
- Countries having defense treaties with the U.S. (excluding NATO and OAS)
- Former Warsaw Pact nations now undergoing democratic reforms
- Former U.S.S.R.
- Communist governments
- League of Arab States
- Association of Southeast Asian Nations (ASEAN)

UNITED STATES AND WORLD ALLIANCES

- ⊡ Organization of Petroleum Exporting Countries (OPEC)
- ● European Community
- ◆ European Free Trade Association
- ▲ Countries with nuclear weaponry
- △ Countries with nuclear weapons potential
- ➤ Strategic waterways

Oceans and Seas: Tasman Sea, Coral Sea, PACIFIC OCEAN, KIRIBATI, INDIAN OCEAN, ATLANTIC OCEAN, ARCTIC OCEAN, Sea of Japan, Sea of Okhotsk, Bering Sea, South China Sea, Bay of Bengal, Arabian Sea, Red Sea, Persian Gulf, Mediterranean Sea, Black Sea, Baltic Sea, North Sea, Gulf of Mexico, Caribbean Sea

Countries/Regions:
NEW ZEALAND, AUSTRALIA, C. Leeuwin, New Caledonia (Fr.), PAPUA NEW GUINEA, VANUATU, SOLOMON ISLANDS, FIJI, NAURU, TONGA, TUVALU, W. SAMOA, AMER. SAMOA, Wake I. (U.S.), Midway Is. (U.S.), U.S. Hawaii, PHILIPPINES, Manila, INDONESIA, Jakarta, MALAYSIA, BRUNEI, SING., LOMBOK STRAIT, SUNDA STRAIT, STRAIT OF MALACCA, MAKASSAR STRAIT, TAIWAN, VIETNAM, CAMBODIA, THAILAND, LAOS, Hong Kong (U.K.), BURMA, JAPAN, Tokyo, S. KOREA, N. KOREA, Beijing, CHINA, KOREA STRAIT, LA PÉROUSE STRAIT, Kuril Is., MONGOLIA, BHUTAN, NEPAL, INDIA, Bombay, C. Comorin, SRI LANKA, MALDIVES, MAURITIUS, Siberia, RUSSIA, KAZAKH., Moscow, AFGHANISTAN, PAKISTAN, KYR., TAJ., UZB., TURKM., IRAN, STRAIT OF HORMUZ, OMAN, U.A.E., QATAR, BAHRAIN, KUWAIT, SAUDI ARABIA, YEMEN, Ras Asér, SOMALIA, MADAGASCAR, COMOROS, AZER., ARM., GEO., IRAQ, SYR., JOR., ISR., TURKEY, EGYPT, SUDAN, ETHIOPIA, DJIB., KENYA, TANZANIA, MOZAMBIQUE, MOZAMBIQUE CHANNEL, BAB EL MANDEB, SUEZ CANAL, DARDANELLES/BOSPORUS, FIN., SWEDEN, NORWAY, UKRAINE, POL., ROM., BUL., MOL., HUN., GR., DEN., GER., CZE., SLV., AUS., SWI., ITALY, FRANCE, SPAIN, PORTUGAL, IRE., UNITED KINGDOM, ICELAND, GREENLAND (Den.), C. Farewell, DANISH STRAITS, NETH., BEL., LUX., CROA., BOS., SER., YUGO., ALB., MAC., ENGLISH CHANNEL, LIBYA, TUN., ALGERIA, MOROCCO, STRAIT OF GIBRALTAR, Azores (Port.), W. SAHARA (Occ. by Morocco), MAURITANIA, MALI, NIGER, CHAD, CENT. AFR. REP., ZAIRE, UGANDA, RWA., BUR., ZAMBIA, ZIMBABWE, SWAZ., LES., BOTSWANA, SOUTH AFRICA, NAMIBIA, ANGOLA, NIGERIA, CAM., CONGO, GABON, E.G., SÃO TOMÉ AND PRÍNCIPE, BURKINA FASO, BENIN, TOGO, GHANA, IVORY COAST, LIBERIA, SIERRA LEONE, GUINEA, G.-B., SEN., CAPE VERDE, Ascension (U.K.), St. Helena (U.K.), Cape Town, Cape of Good Hope

North America / South America:
CANADA, NORTH POLE, U.S. Alaska, Aleutian Is., UNITED STATES, Washington, MEXICO, GUATEMALA, BELIZE, HONDURAS, EL SAL., NIC., COSTA RICA, PANAMA, PANAMA CANAL, CUBA, BAHAMAS, Bermuda (U.K.), JAM., HAITI, DOM. REP., STRAITS OF FLORIDA, WINDWARD PASSAGE, MONA PASSAGE, WEST INDIES, ST. LUCIA CHANNEL, ST. VINCENT & GRENADA-TOBAGO PASSAGES, ECUADOR, COLOMBIA, VENEZUELA, GUYANA, SURINAME, FR. GUIANA, PERU, BOLIVIA, BRAZIL, Rio de Janeiro, C. de São Roque, PARAGUAY, CHILE, ARGENTINA, Buenos Aires, URUGUAY, Cape Horn, Falkland Islands (U.K.-claimed by Arg.)

© Copyright by HAMMOND INCORPORATED, Maplewood, N.J.

UNITED STATES
HISTORY ATLAS

HAMMOND®
INCORPORATED
MAPLEWOOD, NEW JERSEY 07040-1396

Contents

Gazetteer of States, Territories and Possessions

State or Territory	Area (sq. mi.) †	Area (sq. km.) †	Population (1980)	Inhabitants per sq. mi. ‡	Admitted to the Union	Settled at	Date
Alabama	51,705	133 915	3,893,888	76.7	Dec. 14, 1819	Mobile	1702
Alaska	591,004	1 530 700	401,851	0.7	Jan. 3, 1959	Sitka	1801
American Samoa	77	199	32,297	419.4	*Feb. 16, 1900	....	....
Arizona	114,000	295 260	2,718,215	23.9	Feb. 14, 1912	Tucson	1580
Arkansas	53,187	137 754	2,286,435	43.9	June 15, 1836	Arkansas Post	1685
California	158,706	411 049	23,667,902	151.4	Sept. 9, 1850	San Diego	1769
Colorado	104,091	269 595	2,889,964	27.9	Aug. 1, 1876	Near Denver	1858
Connecticut	5,018	12 997	3,107,576	637.8	Jan. 9, 1788	Windsor	1635
Delaware	2,044	5 295	594,338	307.6	Dec. 7, 1787	Cape Henlopen	1627
District of Columbia	69	178	638,333	10,132.3	** 1790-1791	....	1790
Florida	58,664	151 939	9,746,324	180.0	Mar. 3, 1845	St. Augustine	1565
Georgia	58,910	152 576	5,463,105	94.1	Jan. 2, 1788	Savannah	1733
Guam	209	541	105,979	507.1	Dec. 10, 1898	Agana	....
Hawaii	6,471	16 759	964,691	150.1	Aug. 21, 1959	....	....
Idaho	83,564	216 432	943,935	11.5	July 3, 1890	Coeur d'Alene	1842
Illinois	56,345	145 934	11,426,518	205.3	Dec. 3, 1818	Kaskaskia	1720
Indiana	36,185	93 720	5,490,224	152.8	Dec. 11, 1816	Vincennes	1730
Iowa	56,275	145 753	2,913,808	52.1	Dec. 28, 1846	Burlington	1788
Kansas	82,277	213 098	2,363,679	28.9	Jan. 29, 1861	....	1831
Kentucky	40,409	104 660	3,660,777	92.3	June 1, 1792	Harrodsburg	1774
Louisiana	47,752	123 677	4,205,990	94.5	April 30, 1812	Iberville	1699
Maine	33,265	86 156	1,124,660	36.3	Mar. 15, 1820	Bristol	1624
Maryland	10,460	27 092	4,216,975	428.7	April 28, 1788	St. Mary's	1634
Massachusetts	8,284	21 456	5,737,037	733.3	Feb. 6, 1788	Plymouth	1620
Michigan	58,527	151 586	9,262,078	162.6	Jan. 26, 1837	Near Detroit	1650
Minnesota	84,402	218 601	4,075,970	51.2	May 11, 1858	St. Peter's River	1805
Mississippi	47,689	123 515	2,520,638	53.4	Dec. 10, 1817	Natchez	1716
Missouri	69,697	180 516	4,916,686	71.3	Aug. 10, 1821	St. Louis	1764
Montana	147,046	380 848	786,690	5.4	Nov. 8, 1889	....	1809
Nebraska	77,355	200 350	1,569,825	20.5	Mar. 1, 1867	Bellevue	1847
Nevada	110,561	286 352	800,493	7.3	Oct. 31, 1864	Genoa	1850
New Hampshire	9,279	24 032	920,610	102.4	June 21, 1788	Dover and Portsmouth	1623
New Jersey	7,787	20 169	7,364,823	986.2	Dec. 18, 1787	Bergen	1617
New Mexico	121,593	314 925	1,302,894	10.7	Jan. 6, 1912	Santa Fe	1605
New York	49,108	127 189	17,558,072	370.6	July 26, 1788	Manhattan Island	1614
North Carolina	52,669	136 413	5,881,766	120.4	Nov. 21, 1789	Albemarle	1650
North Dakota	70,702	183 119	652,717	9.4	Nov. 2, 1889	Pembina	1780
Ohio	41,330	107 044	10,797,630	263.3	Mar. 1, 1803	Marietta	1788
Oklahoma	69,956	181 186	3,025,290	44.1	Nov. 16, 1907	....	1889
Oregon	97,073	251 419	2,633,105	27.4	Feb. 14, 1859	Astoria	1810
Pennsylvania	45,308	117 348	11,863,895	264.3	Dec. 12, 1787	Delaware River	1682
Puerto Rico	3,515	9 103	3,196,520	924.1	Dec. 10, 1898	Caparra	1510
Rhode Island	1,212	3 140	947,154	897.8	May 29, 1790	Providence	1636
South Carolina	31,113	80 582	3,121,820	103.4	May 23, 1788	Port Royal	1670
South Dakota	77,116	199 730	690,768	9.1	Nov. 2, 1889	Sioux Falls	1856
Tennessee	42,144	109 152	4,591,120	111.6	June 1, 1796	Ft. Loudon	1757
Texas	266,807	691 030	14,229,191	54.3	Dec. 29, 1845	Matagorda Bay	1686
Utah	84,899	219 889	1,461,037	17.8	Jan. 4, 1896	Salt Lake City	1847
Vermont	9,614	24 900	511,456	55.2	Mar. 4, 1791	Ft. Dummer	1764
Virginia	40,767	105 586	5,346,818	134.7	June 26, 1788	Jamestown	1607
Virgin Islands	132	344	96,569	731.6	*Mar. 31, 1917	St. Thomas I.	1657
Washington	68,139	176 479	4,132,156	62.1	Nov. 11, 1889	Astoria	1811
West Virginia	24,231	62 759	1,949,644	80.8	June 20, 1863	Wheeling	1774
Wisconsin	56,153	145 436	4,705,767	86.5	May 29, 1848	Green Bay	1670
Wyoming	97,809	253 326	469,557	4.8	July 10, 1890	Ft. Laramie	1834

*Date of organization as Territory or acquisition by U.S.   **Established under Acts of Congress.   † Land and water.   ‡ Calculation based on land area.

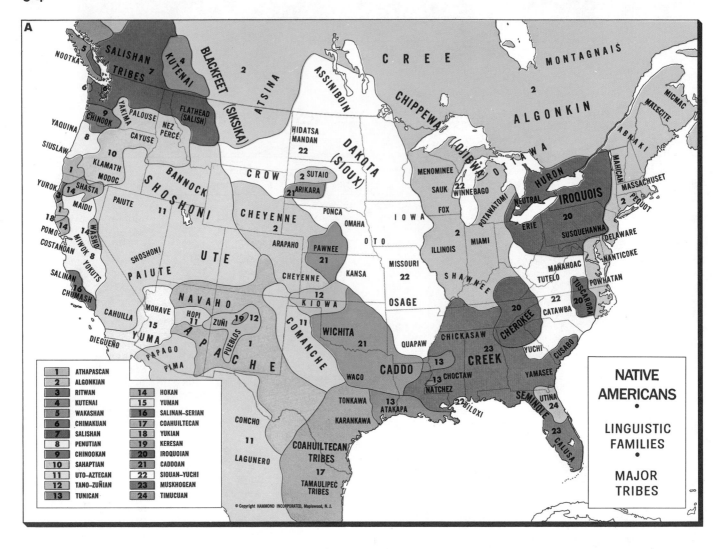

A

NATIVE AMERICANS
·
LINGUISTIC FAMILIES
·
MAJOR TRIBES

1 ATHAPASCAN	
2 ALGONKIAN	
3 RITWAN	14 HOKAN
4 KUTENAI	15 YUMAN
5 WAKASHAN	16 SALINAN–SERIAN
6 CHIMAKUAN	17 COAHUILTECAN
7 SALISHAN	18 YUKIAN
8 PENUTIAN	19 KERESAN
9 CHINOOKAN	20 IROQUOIAN
10 SAHAPTIAN	21 CADDOAN
11 UTO–AZTECAN	22 SIOUAN–YUCHI
12 TANO–ZUÑIAN	23 MUSKHOGEAN
13 TUNICAN	24 TIMUCUAN

© Copyright HAMMOND INCORPORATED, Maplewood, N. J.

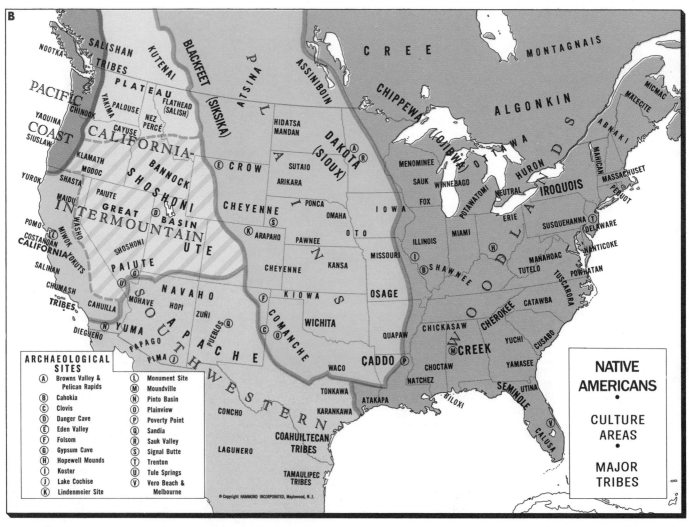

B

NATIVE AMERICANS
·
CULTURE AREAS
·
MAJOR TRIBES

ARCHAEOLOGICAL SITES

Ⓐ Browns Valley & Pelican Rapids	Ⓛ Monument Site
Ⓑ Cahokia	Ⓜ Moundville
Ⓒ Clovis	Ⓝ Pinto Basin
Ⓓ Danger Cave	Ⓞ Plainview
Ⓔ Eden Valley	Ⓟ Poverty Point
Ⓕ Folsom	Ⓠ Sandia
Ⓖ Gypsum Cave	Ⓡ Sauk Valley
Ⓗ Hopewell Mounds	Ⓢ Signal Butte
Ⓘ Koster	Ⓣ Trenton
Ⓙ Lake Cochise	Ⓤ Tule Springs
Ⓚ Lindenmeier Site	Ⓥ Vero Beach & Melbourne

© Copyright HAMMOND INCORPORATED, Maplewood, N. J.

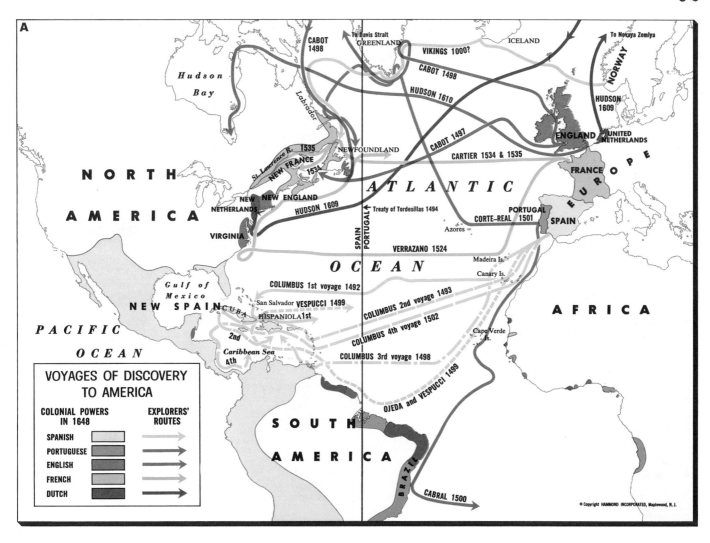

A

To Davis Strait
GREENLAND
CABOT 1498
VIKINGS 1000?
ICELAND
To Novaya Zemlya
NORWAY

Hudson Bay

Labrador

CABOT 1498
HUDSON 1610
HUDSON 1609

CABOT 1497
CARTIER 1534 & 1535

1535
St. Lawrence R.
NEW FRANCE
NEWFOUNDLAND
1534

ATLANTIC

ENGLAND
UNITED NETHERLANDS

NORTH AMERICA

NEW NEW ENGLAND
NETHERLANDS
HUDSON 1609

VIRGINIA

Treaty of Tordesillas 1494
SPAIN
PORTUGAL

FRANCE
EUROPE

OCEAN

PORTUGAL
CORTE-REAL 1501
SPAIN

Azores

VERRAZANO 1524

Madeira Is.

Gulf of Mexico
NEW SPAIN
CUBA

Canary Is.

COLUMBUS 1st voyage 1492

San Salvador VESPUCCI 1499
HISPANIOLA 1st

PACIFIC OCEAN

2nd
Caribbean Sea
4th

COLUMBUS 2nd voyage 1493

COLUMBUS 4th voyage 1502

COLUMBUS 3rd voyage 1498

AFRICA

Cape Verde Is.

OJEDA and VESPUCCI 1499

SOUTH AMERICA

BRAZIL

CABRAL 1500

© Copyright HAMMOND INCORPORATED, Maplewood, N.J.

VOYAGES OF DISCOVERY TO AMERICA

COLONIAL POWERS IN 1648	EXPLORERS' ROUTES
SPANISH	
PORTUGUESE	
ENGLISH	
FRENCH	
DUTCH	

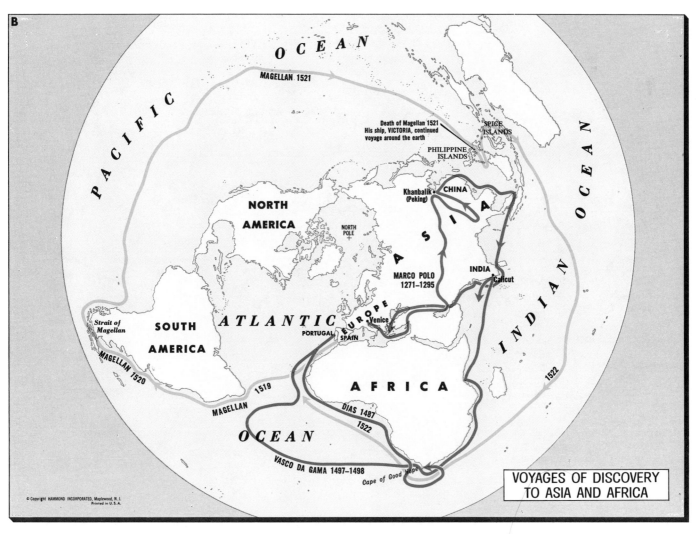

B

OCEAN

MAGELLAN 1521

PACIFIC

Death of Magellan 1521
His ship, VICTORIA, continued voyage around the earth

SPICE ISLANDS

PHILIPPINE ISLANDS

Khanbalik (Peking)
CHINA

ASIA

NORTH AMERICA

NORTH POLE

INDIAN OCEAN

INDIA
Calicut

MARCO POLO 1271–1295

ATLANTIC
EUROPE
Venice

Strait of Magellan

SOUTH AMERICA

PORTUGAL
SPAIN

1519

1522

MAGELLAN 1520

MAGELLAN

AFRICA

DIAS 1487
1522

OCEAN

VASCO DA GAMA 1497–1498

Cape of Good Hope

© Copyright HAMMOND INCORPORATED, Maplewood, N.J.
Printed in U.S.A.

VOYAGES OF DISCOVERY TO ASIA AND AFRICA

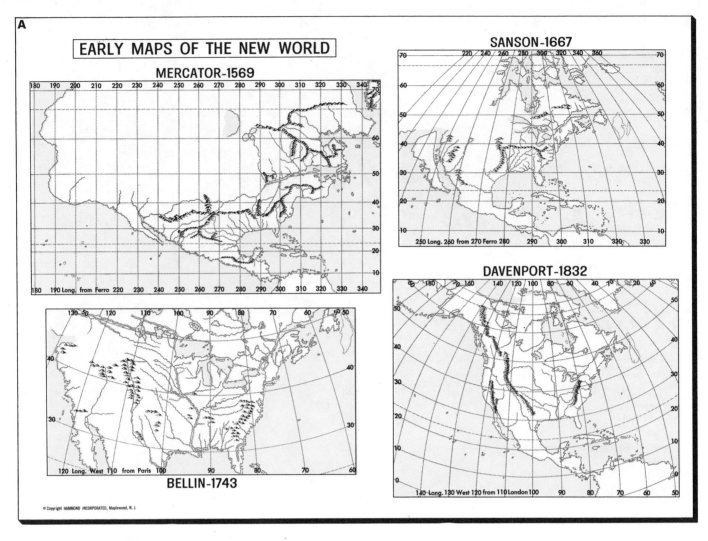

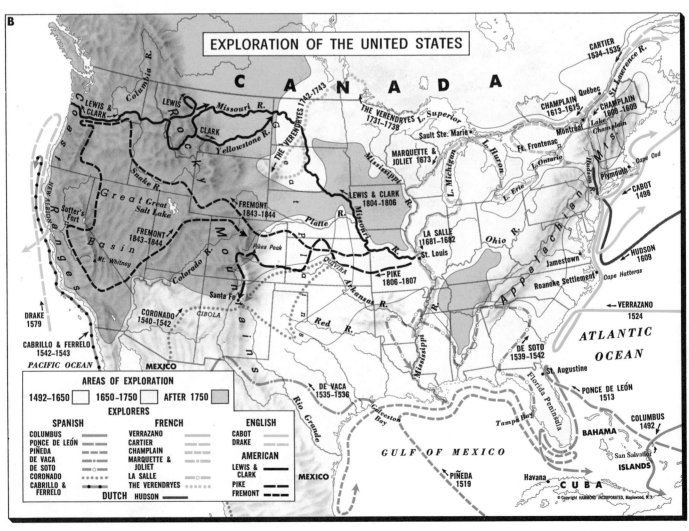

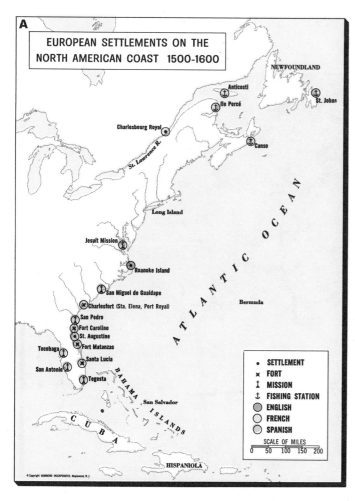

A

EUROPEAN SETTLEMENTS ON THE NORTH AMERICAN COAST 1500-1600

NEWFOUNDLAND

Anticosti

Ile Percé

St. Johns

Charlesbourg Royal

Canso

St. Lawrence R.

Long Island

Jesuit Mission

Roanoke Island

San Miguel de Gualdape

Charlesfort (Sta. Elena, Port Royal)

San Pedro

Fort Caroline

St. Augustine

Fort Matanzas

Tocobaga

Santa Lucia

San Antonio

Tegesta

ATLANTIC OCEAN

Bermuda

BAHAMA ISLANDS

CUBA

San Salvador

HISPANIOLA

- SETTLEMENT
- × FORT
- ⚓ MISSION
- ⚓ FISHING STATION
- ⬤ ENGLISH
- ◯ FRENCH
- ◯ SPANISH

SCALE OF MILES
0 50 100 150 200

© Copyright HAMMOND INCORPORATED, Maplewood, N.J.

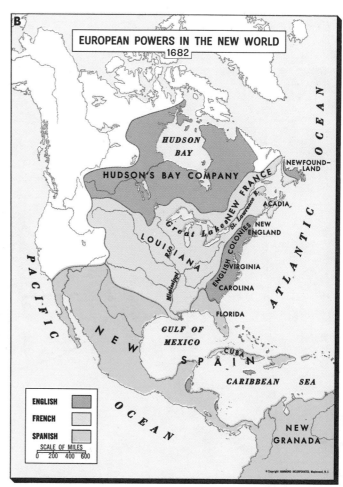

B

EUROPEAN POWERS IN THE NEW WORLD 1682

HUDSON BAY

HUDSON'S BAY COMPANY

NEWFOUND-LAND

ACADIA

NEW FRANCE

Great Lakes

St. Lawrence R.

LOUISIANA

ENGLISH COLONIES

NEW ENGLAND

VIRGINIA

CAROLINA

Mississippi

FLORIDA

PACIFIC

GULF OF MEXICO

NEW SPAIN

CUBA

CARIBBEAN SEA

OCEAN

ATLANTIC OCEAN

NEW GRANADA

- ENGLISH
- FRENCH
- SPANISH

SCALE OF MILES
0 200 400 600

© Copyright HAMMOND INCORPORATED, Maplewood, N.J.

C

EUROPEAN POWERS IN THE NEW WORLD 1713

HUDSON BAY

HUDSON'S BAY COMPANY

NEWFOUND-LAND

ISLE ROYALE

NOVA SCOTIA

NEW FRANCE

Great Lakes

St. Lawrence R.

LOUISIANA

ENGLISH COLONIES

NEW ENGLAND

VIRGINIA

CAROLINA

Mississippi

TEXAS

FLORIDA

PACIFIC

GULF OF MEXICO

NEW SPAIN

CUBA

ST. DOMINGUE (HAITI)

CARIBBEAN SEA

OCEAN

ATLANTIC OCEAN

NEW GRANADA

- ENGLISH
- FRENCH
- SPANISH

SCALE OF MILES
0 200 400 600

© Copyright HAMMOND INCORPORATED, Maplewood, N.J.

D

EUROPEAN POWERS IN THE NEW WORLD 1763

RUSSIANS

HUDSON BAY

HUDSON'S BAY COMPANY

NEWFOUND-LAND

QUEBEC

NOVA SCOTIA

Great Lakes

St. Lawrence R.

NEW ENGLAND

LOUISIANA

ENGLISH COLONIES

VIRGINIA

CAROLINAS

Mississippi

TEXAS

FLORIDA

PACIFIC

GULF OF MEXICO

NEW SPAIN

CUBA

ST. DOMINGUE (HAITI)

CARIBBEAN SEA

OCEAN

ATLANTIC OCEAN

NEW GRANADA

- ENGLISH
- FRENCH
- SPANISH

SCALE OF MILES
0 200 400 600

© Copyright HAMMOND INCORPORATED, Maplewood, N.J.

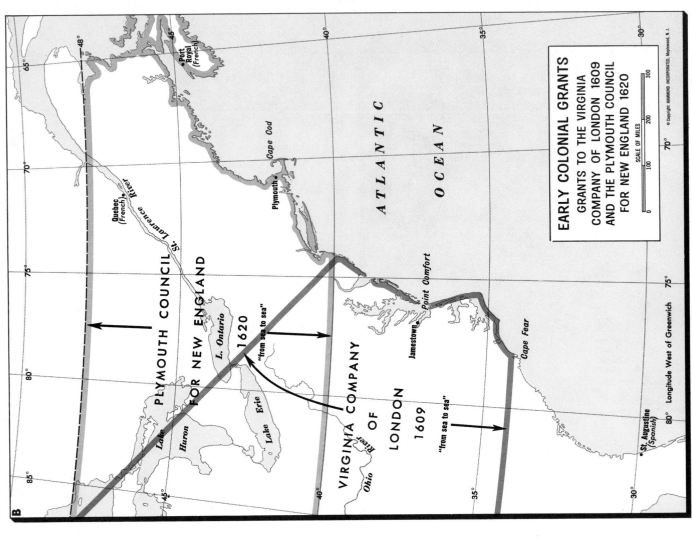

EARLY COLONIAL GRANTS

GRANTS TO THE VIRGINIA
COMPANY OF LONDON 1609
AND THE PLYMOUTH COUNCIL
FOR NEW ENGLAND 1620

SCALE OF MILES

0   100   200   300

© Copyright HAMMOND INCORPORATED, Maplewood, N.J.

PLYMOUTH COUNCIL
FOR NEW ENGLAND
1620

"from sea to sea"

VIRGINIA COMPANY
OF
LONDON
1609

"from sea to sea"

Port
Royal
(French)

Quebec
(French)

St. Lawrence River

L. Ontario

Lake
Huron

Lake
Erie

Ohio River

Cape Cod

Plymouth

ATLANTIC

OCEAN

Jamestown

Point Comfort

Cape Fear

St. Augustine
(Spanish)

Longitude West of Greenwich

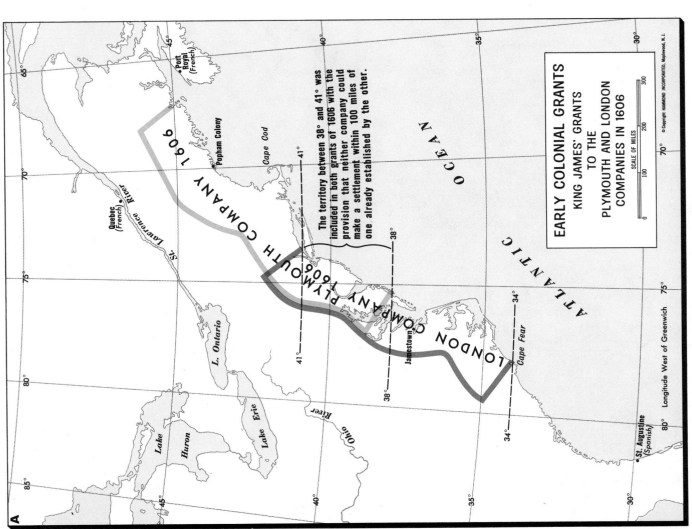

EARLY COLONIAL GRANTS

KING JAMES' GRANTS
TO THE
PLYMOUTH AND LONDON
COMPANIES IN 1606

SCALE OF MILES

0   100   200   300

© Copyright HAMMOND INCORPORATED, Maplewood, N.J.

PLYMOUTH COMPANY 1606

LONDON COMPANY 1606

The territory between 38° and 41° was
included in both grants of 1606 with the
provision that neither company could
make a settlement within 100 miles of
one already established by the other.

Port
Royal
(French)

Quebec
(French)

St. Lawrence River

L. Ontario

Lake
Huron

Lake
Erie

Ohio River

Popham Colony

Cape Cod

Jamestown

ATLANTIC

OCEAN

Cape Fear

St. Augustine
(Spanish)

Longitude West of Greenwich

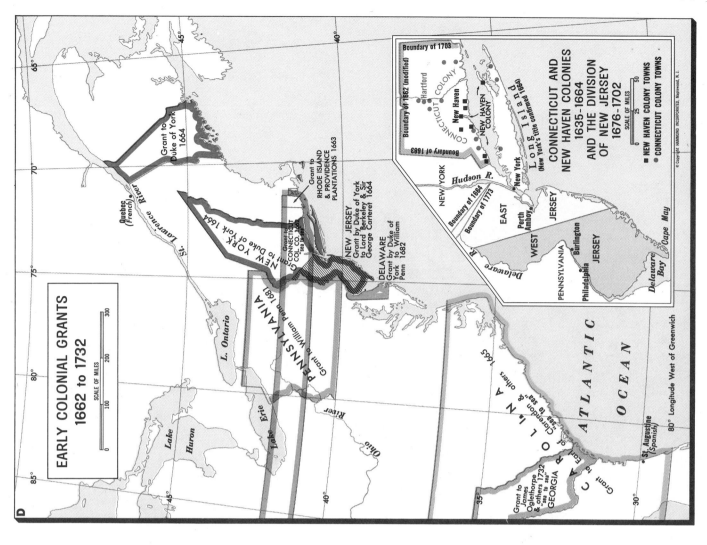

EARLY COLONIAL GRANTS 1662 to 1732

SCALE OF MILES
0   100   200   300

Quebec (French)

St. Lawrence River

L. Ontario

Lake Erie

Lake Huron

Ohio River

Grant to Duke of York 1664

Grant to RHODE ISLAND & PROVIDENCE PLANTATIONS 1663

CONNECTICUT CO. "sea to sea"

NEW YORK Grant to Duke of York 1664

NEW JERSEY Grant by Duke of York to Lord Berkeley & Sir George Carteret 1664

DELAWARE Grant by Duke of York to William Penn 1682

PENNSYLVANIA Grant to William Penn 1681

Grant to Earl of Clarendon & others, "sea to sea" 1665

CAROLINA

Grant to James Oglethorpe & others 1732 "sea to sea" GEORGIA

St. Augustine (Spanish)

ATLANTIC OCEAN

80° Longitude West of Greenwich

CONNECTICUT AND NEW HAVEN COLONIES 1635-1664 AND THE DIVISION OF NEW JERSEY 1676-1702

SCALE OF MILES
0   25   50

Boundary of 1703
Boundary of 1662 (modified)
Hartford
CONNECTICUT COLONY
New Haven
NEW HAVEN COLONY
Boundary of 1662 (New York's title confirmed 1664)
Boundary of 1683
Long Island
New York
NEW YORK
Hudson R.
Boundary of 1773
EAST JERSEY
Perth Amboy
WEST JERSEY
Burlington
Philadelphia
PENNSYLVANIA
Delaware R.
Delaware Bay
Cape May

■ NEW HAVEN COLONY TOWNS
● CONNECTICUT COLONY TOWNS

© Copyright HAMMOND INCORPORATED, Maplewood, N.J.

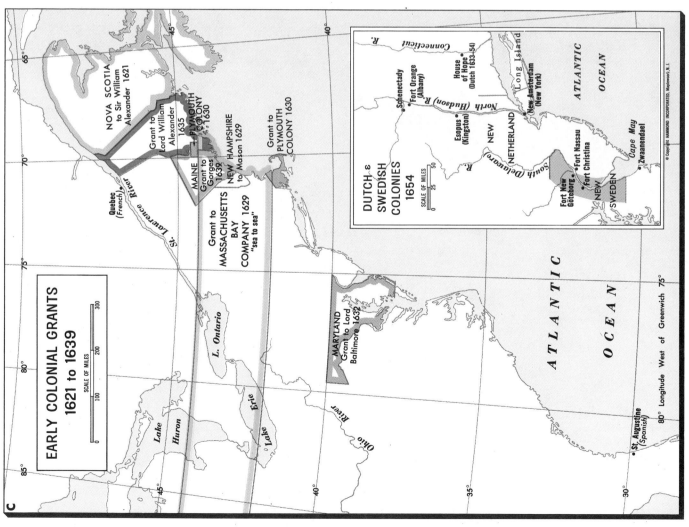

EARLY COLONIAL GRANTS 1621 to 1639

SCALE OF MILES
0   100   200   300

Quebec (French)

St. Lawrence River

L. Ontario

Lake Erie

Lake Huron

Ohio River

NOVA SCOTIA to Sir William Alexander 1621

Grant to Lord William Alexander 1635

MAINE Grant to Gorges 1639

PLYMOUTH COLONY to 1630

NEW HAMPSHIRE to Mason 1629

Grant to MASSACHUSETTS BAY COMPANY 1629 "sea to sea"

Grant to PLYMOUTH COLONY 1630

MARYLAND Grant to Lord Baltimore 1632

St. Augustine (Spanish)

ATLANTIC OCEAN

80° Longitude West of Greenwich

DUTCH & SWEDISH COLONIES 1654

SCALE OF MILES
0   25   50

Connecticut R.
Schenectady
Fort Orange (Albany)
House of Hope (Dutch 1633-54)
Esopus (Kingston)
North (Hudson) R.
NEW (NETHERLAND)
South (Delaware) R.
Long Island
New Amsterdam (New York)
ATLANTIC OCEAN
Fort Nassau
Fort New Göteborg
Fort Christina
NEW SWEDEN
Zwaanendael
Cape May

© Copyright HAMMOND INCORPORATED, Maplewood, N.J.

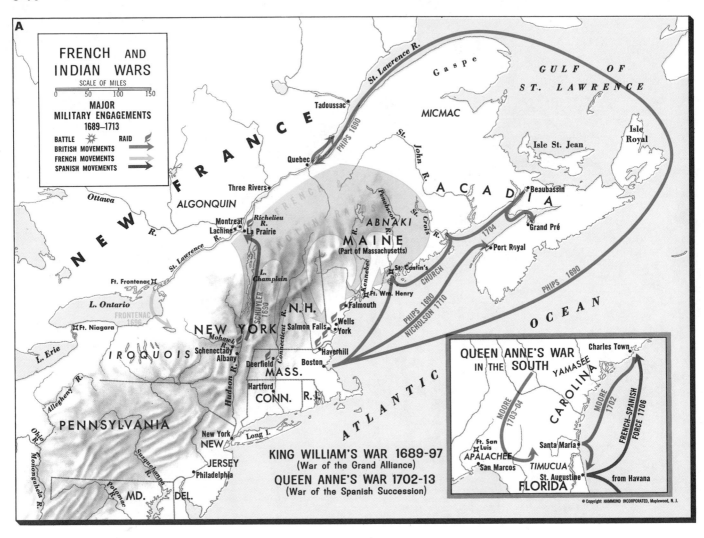

A

FRENCH AND INDIAN WARS

SCALE OF MILES

0 — 50 — 100 — 150

MAJOR MILITARY ENGAGEMENTS 1689–1713

BATTLE · RAID
BRITISH MOVEMENTS →
FRENCH MOVEMENTS →
SPANISH MOVEMENTS →

NEW FRANCE

GULF OF ST. LAWRENCE

St. Lawrence R.

Gaspe

MICMAC

Isle St. Jean

Isle Royal

ACADIA

Tadoussac

PHIPS 1690

Quebec

Three Rivers

ALGONQUIN

Ottawa

Montreal
Lachine · La Prairie
Richelieu R.

ABNAKI

MAINE
(Part of Massachusetts)

Beaubassin

Grand Pré

1704

Port Royal

St. John R.

St. Croix R.

Penobscot R.

Ft. Frontenac

L. Champlain

SCHUYLER 1690

St. Castin's

Ft. Wm. Henry

CHURCH

PHIPS 1690
NICHOLSON 1710

ATLANTIC OCEAN

St. Lawrence

L. Ontario

Ft. Niagara

N.H.

Falmouth

Wells
York

FRONTENAC 1690

L. Erie

NEW YORK

Mohawk R.

Schenectady
Albany

Salmon Falls

Deerfield

Boston

MASS.

Hartford

Haverhill

IROQUOIS

Allegheny R.

Hudson R.

Connecticut R.

CONN.

R.I.

Ohio R.

Monongahela R.

PENNSYLVANIA

Susquehanna R.

New York

NEW

JERSEY

Long I.

Philadelphia

Potomac R.

MD.

DEL.

QUEEN ANNE'S WAR IN THE SOUTH

Charles Town

YAMASEE

CAROLINA

MOORE 1703–04

MOORE 1702

FRENCH-SPANISH FORCE 1706

Ft. San Luis

APALACHEE

San Marcos

Santa Maria

TIMUCUA

St. Augustine

FLORIDA

from Havana

KING WILLIAM'S WAR 1689–97
(War of the Grand Alliance)

QUEEN ANNE'S WAR 1702–13
(War of the Spanish Succession)

© Copyright HAMMOND INCORPORATED, Maplewood, N. J.

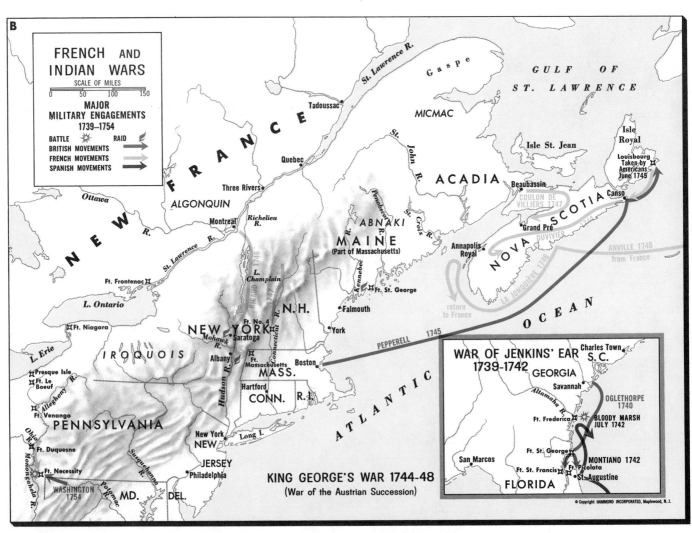

B

FRENCH AND INDIAN WARS

SCALE OF MILES

0 — 50 — 100 — 150

MAJOR MILITARY ENGAGEMENTS 1739–1754

BATTLE · RAID
BRITISH MOVEMENTS →
FRENCH MOVEMENTS →
SPANISH MOVEMENTS →

NEW FRANCE

GULF OF ST. LAWRENCE

St. Lawrence R.

Gaspe

MICMAC

Isle St. Jean

Isle Royal

Louisbourg Taken by Americans June 1745

ACADIA

Tadoussac

Quebec

Three Rivers

ALGONQUIN

Ottawa

Montreal

Richelieu R.

ABNAKI

MAINE
(Part of Massachusetts)

Beaubassin

Canso

COULON DE VILLIERS 1747

Grand Pré

NOVA SCOTIA

DUVIVIER

Annapolis Royal

ANVILLE 1746 from France

St. John R.

St. Croix R.

Penobscot R.

Ft. Frontenac

RICHELIEU 1746

L. Champlain

Ft. St. George

Kennebec R.

LA JONQUIERE 1746

return to France

ATLANTIC OCEAN

St. Lawrence

L. Ontario

Ft. Niagara

N.H.

Ft. No. 4

Falmouth

York

PEPPERELL 1745

L. Erie

NEW YORK

Mohawk R.

Saratoga

Albany

Ft. Massachusetts

Boston

MASS.

Hartford

CONN.

R.I.

IROQUOIS

Presque Isle

Ft. Le Boeuf

Allegheny R.

Ft. Venango

Hudson R.

Connecticut R.

Ohio R.

Ft. Duquesne

Ft. Necessity

Monongahela R.

WASHINGTON 1754

PENNSYLVANIA

Susquehanna R.

New York

NEW

JERSEY

Long I.

Philadelphia

Potomac R.

MD.

DEL.

WAR OF JENKINS' EAR 1739–1742

Charles Town S.C.

GEORGIA

Savannah

Altamaha R.

OGLETHORPE 1740

Ft. Frederica

BLOODY MARSH JULY 1742

Ft. St. George

MONTIANO 1742

San Marcos

Ft. St. Francis

Ft. Picolata

St. Augustine

FLORIDA

KING GEORGE'S WAR 1744–48
(War of the Austrian Succession)

© Copyright HAMMOND INCORPORATED, Maplewood, N. J.

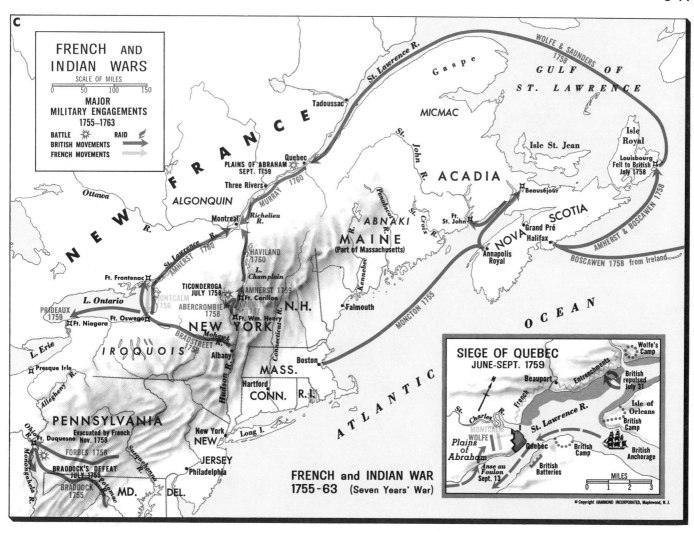

C

FRENCH AND INDIAN WARS

SCALE OF MILES

0   50   100   150

MAJOR MILITARY ENGAGEMENTS 1755–1763

BATTLE ✸ RAID ↯
BRITISH MOVEMENTS →
FRENCH MOVEMENTS →

NEW FRANCE

St. Lawrence R.

Gaspe

GULF OF ST. LAWRENCE

WOLFE & SAUNDERS 1758

Tadoussac

MICMAC

Isle St. Jean

Isle Royal

Louisbourg Fell to British July 1758

St. John R.

ACADIA

AMHERST & BOSCAWEN 1758

BOSCAWEN 1758 from Ireland

PLAINS OF ABRAHAM SEPT. 1759

Quebec

Three Rivers

MURRAY 1760

ALGONQUIN

Ottawa R.

Montreal

Richelieu R.

St. Croix R.

Penobscot R.

ABNAKI

Beauséjour

Ft. St. John

NOVA SCOTIA

Grand Pré
Halifax

Annapolis Royal

St. Lawrence R.

AMHERST 1760

HAVILAND 1760

L. Champlain

MONTCALM 1756

TICONDEROGA JULY 1758

AMHERST 1759
Ft. Carillon

MONTCALM 1757

ABERCROMBIE 1758

Ft. Wm. Henry

MAINE (Part of Massachusetts)

Kennebec R.

Falmouth

MONCTON 1755

Ft. Frontenac

L. Ontario

PRIDEAUX 1759

Ft. Niagara

Ft. Oswego

BRADSTREET 1758

Mohawk R.

N.H.

NEW YORK

Connecticut R.

ATLANTIC OCEAN

L. Erie

Presque Isle

IROQUOIS

Allegheny R.

Albany

Hudson R.

Boston

MASS.

Hartford

CONN.

R.I.

PENNSYLVANIA

Ohio R.

Ft. Duquesne Evacuated by French Nov. 1758

FORBES 1758

Susquehanna R.

New York

NEW JERSEY

Long I.

Monongahela R.

BRADDOCK'S DEFEAT JULY 1755

BRADDOCK 1755

Potomac R.

MD.

DEL.

Philadelphia

SIEGE OF QUEBEC
JUNE–SEPT. 1759

Wolfe's Camp

Beauport

Entrenchments

British repulsed July 31

French R.

St. Lawrence R.

Isle of Orleans

MONTCALM

Charles R.

St. Charles R.

WOLFE

Plains of Abraham

Quebec

Odebec

British Camp

British Camp

British Batteries

Anse au Foulon Sept. 13

British Anchorage

MILES

0   1   2   3

FRENCH and INDIAN WAR 1755-63 (Seven Years' War)

© Copyright HAMMOND INCORPORATED, Maplewood, N.J.

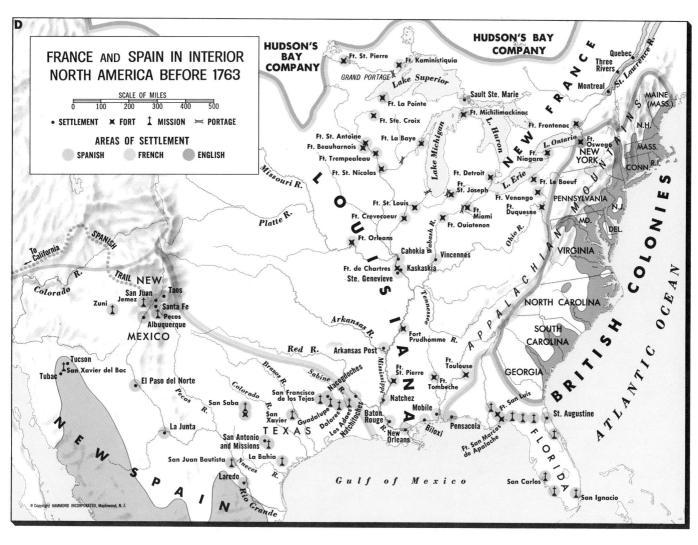

D

FRANCE AND SPAIN IN INTERIOR NORTH AMERICA BEFORE 1763

SCALE OF MILES

0   100   200   300   400   500

• SETTLEMENT ✕ FORT ⚲ MISSION ⋈ PORTAGE

AREAS OF SETTLEMENT
⬤ SPANISH ⬤ FRENCH ⬤ ENGLISH

HUDSON'S BAY COMPANY

HUDSON'S BAY COMPANY

Ft. St. Pierre

Ft. Kaministiquia

GRAND PORTAGE

Lake Superior

Sault Ste. Marie

NEW FRANCE

Quebec

Three Rivers

Montreal

St. Lawrence R.

MAINE (MASS.)

Ft. La Pointe

Ft. Ste. Croix

Ft. Michilimackinac

N.H.

Ft. St. Antoine

Ft. La Baye

L. Huron

Ft. Frontenac

L. Ontario

Ft. Oswego

MASS.

Ft. Beauharnois

Lake Michigan

Ft. Detroit

Ft. Niagara

NEW YORK

CONN. R.I.

Ft. Trempealeau

Ft. St. Nicolas

Ft. St. Joseph

L. Erie

Ft. Le Boeuf

Missouri R.

Ft. St. Louis

Ft. Miami

Ft. Venango

PENNSYLVANIA

N.J.

Ft. Crevecoeur

Wabash R.

Ft. Ouiatenon

Ft. Duquesne

MD.

DEL.

Platte R.

Ft. Orleans

Ohio R.

APPALACHIAN MOUNTAINS

Cahokia

Vincennes

VIRGINIA

L O U I S I A N A

SPANISH

TRAIL

To California

Colorado R.

NEW

Taos

San Juan
Jemez

Santa Fe

Pecos

Albuquerque

MEXICO

Zuni

Ft. de Chartres

Ste. Genevieve

Kaskaskia

Tennessee R.

NORTH CAROLINA

Arkansas R.

Fort Prudhomme

SOUTH CAROLINA

Red R.

Arkansas Post

Ft. Pierre

Ft. Toulouse

GEORGIA

Ft. San Luis

St. Augustine

ATLANTIC OCEAN

BRITISH COLONIES

Tucson

San Xavier del Bac

Tubac

El Paso del Norte

Brazos R.

Naco gdoches

San Francisco de los Tejas

Mississippi R.

Natchez

Ft. Tombeche

Mobile

Pensacola

FLORIDA

Pecos R.

Colorado R.

San Saba

San Xavier

Guadalupe

Dolores

Los Adaes
Natchitoches

Baton Rouge

Biloxi

Ft. San Marcos de Apalache

San Antonio and Missions

La Bahia

TEXAS

New Orleans

N E W   S P A I N

San Juan Bautista

Laredo

Nueces R.

Rio Grande

La Junta

San Carlos

San Ignacio

Gulf of Mexico

Sabine R.

© Copyright HAMMOND INCORPORATED, Maplewood, N.J.

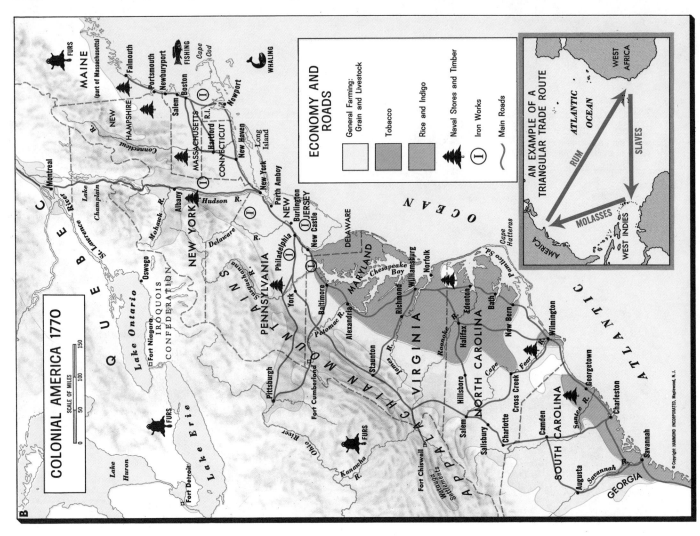

B COLONIAL AMERICA 1770

SCALE OF MILES
0 50 100 150

ECONOMY AND ROADS

General Farming:
Grain and Livestock

Tobacco

Rice and Indigo

Naval Stores and Timber

Ⓘ Iron Works

Main Roads

AN EXAMPLE OF A TRIANGULAR TRADE ROUTE

ATLANTIC OCEAN

WEST AFRICA

RUM

SLAVES

MOLASSES

AMERICA

WEST INDIES

© Copyright HAMMOND INCORPORATED, Maplewood, N.J.

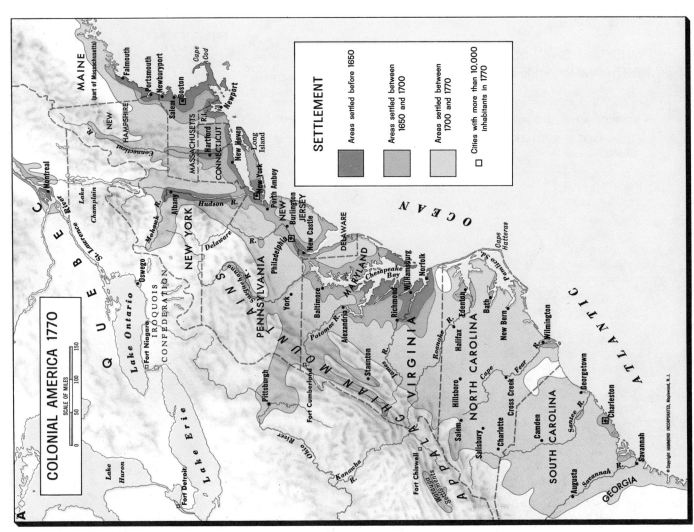

A COLONIAL AMERICA 1770

SCALE OF MILES
0 50 100 150

SETTLEMENT

Areas settled before 1650

Areas settled between 1650 and 1700

Areas settled between 1700 and 1770

▫ Cities with more than 10,000 inhabitants in 1770

© Copyright HAMMOND INCORPORATED, Maplewood, N.J.

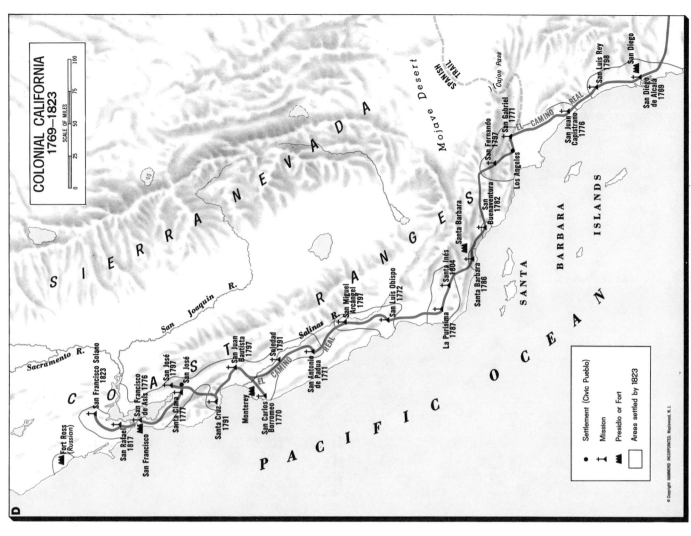

COLONIAL CALIFORNIA 1769–1823

SCALE OF MILES
0   25   50   75   100

Sierra Nevada

San Joaquin R.
San Joaquin R.
Sacramento R.

Fort Ross (Russian)

San Francisco Solano 1823
San Rafael 1817
San Francisco de Asis 1776
San Francisco
San José 1797
San José
Santa Clara 1777
Santa Cruz 1791
Monterey
San Carlos Borromeo 1770
San Juan Bautista 1797
Soledad 1791
San Antonio de Padua 1771
San Miguel Arcángel 1797
San Luis Obispo 1772
La Purísima 1787
Santa Inés 1804
Santa Barbara 1786
San Buenaventura 1782
San Fernando 1797
Los Angeles
San Gabriel 1771
San Juan Capistrano 1776
San Luis Rey 1798
San Diego
San Diego de Alcalá 1769

COAST RANGES

EL CAMINO REAL
Salinas R.
SPANISH TRAIL
Cajon Pass
Mojave Desert

SANTA BARBARA ISLANDS

PACIFIC OCEAN

Legend:
• Settlement (Civic Pueblo)
† Mission
▲ Presidio or Fort
☐ Areas settled by 1823

© Copyright HAMMOND INCORPORATED, Maplewood, N.J.

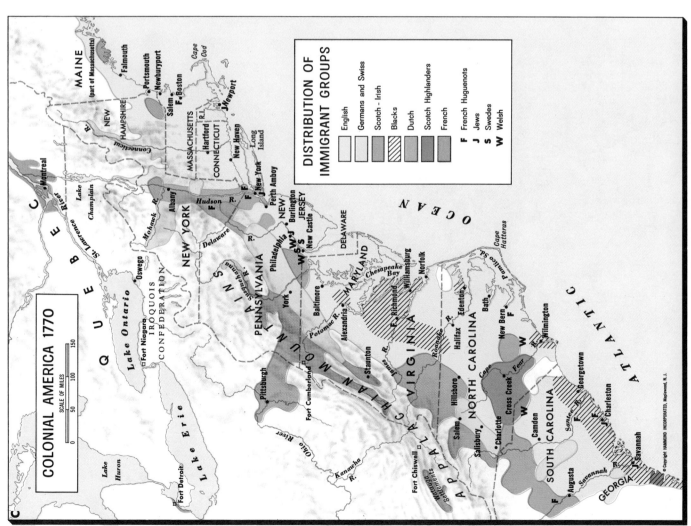

COLONIAL AMERICA 1770

SCALE OF MILES
0   50   100   150

DISTRIBUTION OF IMMIGRANT GROUPS

English
Germans and Swiss
Scotch-Irish
Blacks
Dutch
Scotch Highlanders
French

F French Huguenots
J Jews
S Swedes
W Welsh

QUEBEC
Montreal
St. Lawrence River
Lake Champlain
MAINE (part of Massachusetts)
Falmouth
Portsmouth
NEW HAMPSHIRE
Newburyport
Cape Cod
Salem
Boston
NEW YORK
Oswego
Fort Niagara
IROQUOIS CONFEDERATION
Albany
Mohawk R.
Hartford
R.I.
Newport
New Haven
CONNECTICUT
MASSACHUSETTS
Long Island
New York
Perth Amboy
NEW JERSEY
Burlington
New Castle
PENNSYLVANIA
Philadelphia
Pittsburgh
Fort Cumberland
York
Lancaster
Baltimore
DELAWARE
MARYLAND
Alexandria
Staunton
Fort Chiswell
VIRGINIA
Richmond
Williamsburg
Norfolk
Chesapeake Bay
Cape Hatteras
Edenton
Halifax
Bath
New Bern
NORTH CAROLINA
Hillsboro
Salem
Salisbury
Charlotte
Cross Creek
Wilmington
Camden
SOUTH CAROLINA
Augusta
Georgetown
Charleston
GEORGIA
Savannah
ATLANTIC OCEAN
APPALACHIAN MOUNTAINS
Ohio River
Lake Huron
Lake Erie
Lake Ontario
Fort Detroit

© Copyright HAMMOND INCORPORATED, Maplewood, N.J.

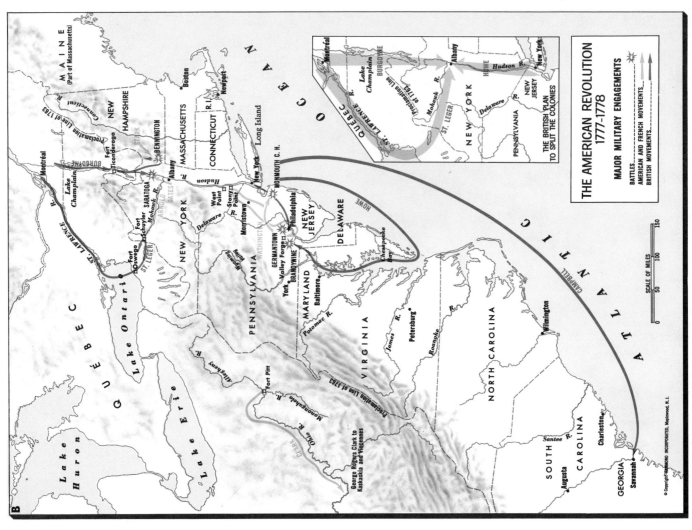

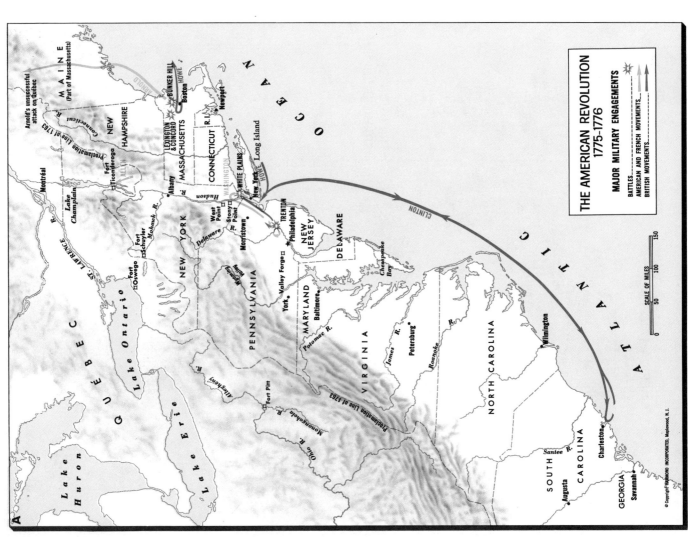

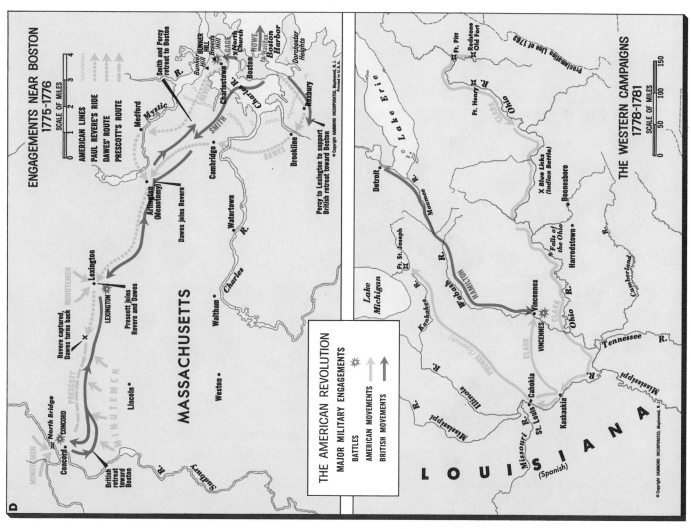

ENGAGEMENTS NEAR BOSTON
1775-1776

SCALE OF MILES
0 1 2 3 4

AMERICAN LINES
PAUL REVERE'S RIDE
DAWES' ROUTE
PRESCOTT'S ROUTE

Smith and Percy retreat to Boston

Bunker BUNKER HILL
Breeds Hill
North Church
GAGE
HOWE
Boston
Boston Harbor
Charlestown
Charles R.
Roxbury
Dorchester Heights
Mystic R.
Medford
Arlington (Menotomy)
Dawes joins Revere
Cambridge
Watertown
Waltham
Charles R.
Brookline
Percy to Lexington to support British retreat toward Boston
Lexington
MINUTEMEN
Prescott joins Revere and Dawes
Revere captured, Dawes turns back
PRESCOTT
North Bridge
Concord
CONCORD
MINUTEMEN
British retreat toward Boston
Lincoln
Weston
Sudbury R.

MASSACHUSETTS

THE AMERICAN REVOLUTION
MAJOR MILITARY ENGAGEMENTS

BATTLES
AMERICAN MOVEMENTS
BRITISH MOVEMENTS

THE WESTERN CAMPAIGNS
1778-1781

SCALE OF MILES
0 50 100 150

Ft. Pitt
Redstone Old Fort
Proclamation Line of 1763
Lake Erie
Detroit
Ft. Henry
Ohio R.
CLARK
Maumee R.
X Blue Licks (Indian Battle)
Boonesboro
Harrodstown
Falls of the Ohio
HAMILTON
Ft. St. Joseph
Wabash R.
Kankakee R.
Lake Michigan
Vincennes
VINCENNES
CLARK
Ohio R.
Cumberland R.
Tennessee R.
Illinois R.
Kaskaskia R.
St. Louis
Cahokia
Kaskaskia
POUCE (Spanish)
CLARK
Missouri R.
Mississippi R.

LOUISIANA
(Spanish)

© Copyright HAMMOND INCORPORATED, Maplewood, N.J.

D

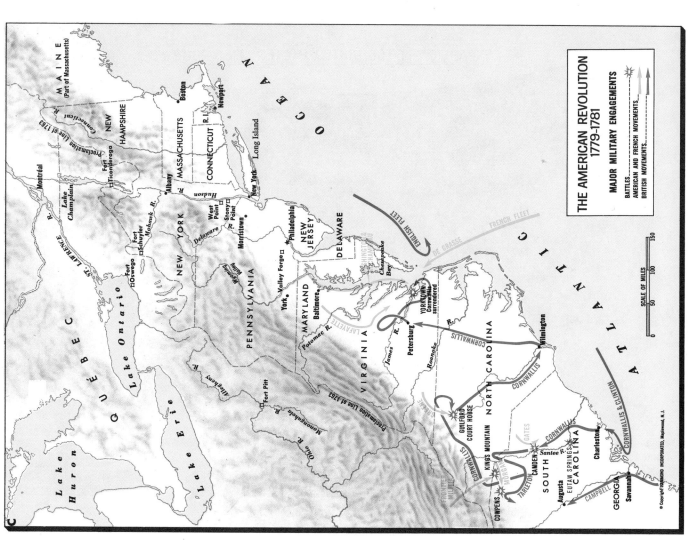

C

THE AMERICAN REVOLUTION
1779-1781

MAJOR MILITARY ENGAGEMENTS

BATTLES
AMERICAN AND FRENCH MOVEMENTS
BRITISH MOVEMENTS

SCALE OF MILES
0 50 100 150

Lake Huron
QUEBEC
Lake Ontario
Lake Erie
St. LAWRENCE R.
Montreal
MAINE (Part of Massachusetts)
NEW HAMPSHIRE
Boston
MASSACHUSETTS
Proclamation Line of 1763
Connecticut R.
Fort Ticonderoga
Lake Champlain
Albany
Hudson R.
NEW YORK
Newport
R.I.
CONNECTICUT
Long Island
New York
West Point
Stony Point
Fort Schuyler
Fort Oswego
Mohawk R.
Morristown
NEW JERSEY
Philadelphia
DELAWARE
PENNSYLVANIA
Valley Forge
York
Allegheny R.
Fort Pitt
Monongahela R.
Ohio R.
Proclamation Line of 1763
MARYLAND
Baltimore
Potomac R.
Delaware R.
ENGLISH FLEET
DE GRASSE
FRENCH FLEET
WASHINGTON
Chesapeake Bay
James R.
VIRGINIA
LAFAYETTE
Petersburg
YORKTOWN
Cornwallis surrendered
Roanoke R.
CORNWALLIS
Wilmington
NORTH CAROLINA
GUILFORD COURT HOUSE
GREENE
GATES
CORNWALLIS
Kings Mountain
MORGAN
Cowpens
TARLETON
Camden
Santee R.
Eutaw Springs
SOUTH CAROLINA
Charleston
Augusta
CORNWALLIS & CLINTON
GEORGIA
Savannah
CAMPBELL

ATLANTIC OCEAN

© Copyright HAMMOND INCORPORATED, Maplewood, N.J.

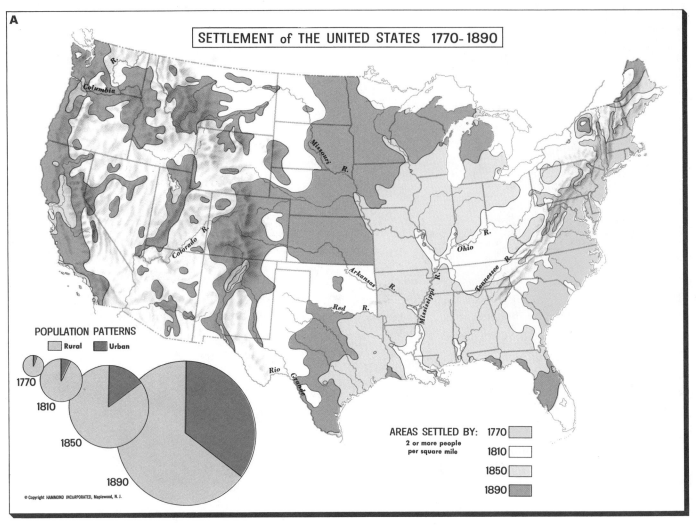

A

SETTLEMENT of THE UNITED STATES 1770-1890

POPULATION PATTERNS

Rural | Urban

1770
1810
1850
1890

© Copyright HAMMOND INCORPORATED, Maplewood, N.J.

AREAS SETTLED BY: | 1770
2 or more people per square mile | 1810
| 1850
| 1890

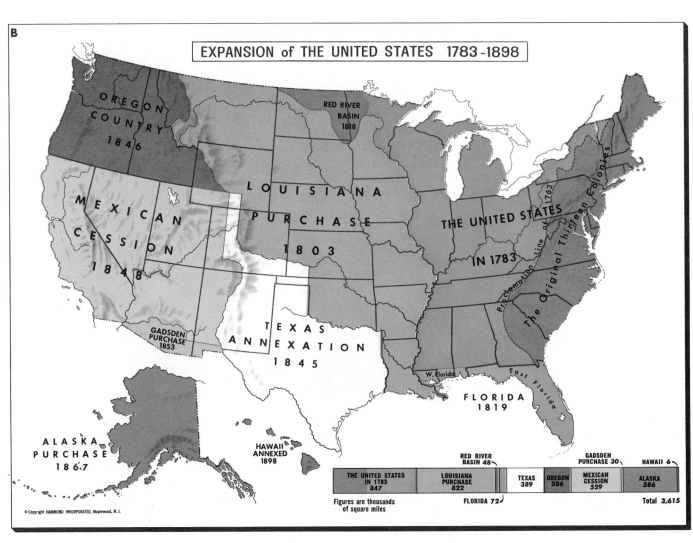

B

EXPANSION of THE UNITED STATES 1783-1898

OREGON COUNTRY 1846

RED RIVER BASIN 1818

LOUISIANA PURCHASE 1803

MEXICAN CESSION 1848

THE UNITED STATES IN 1783

The Original Thirteen Colonies

Proclamation Line of 1763

GADSDEN PURCHASE 1853

TEXAS ANNEXATION 1845

W. Florida

East Florida

FLORIDA 1819

ALASKA PURCHASE 1867

HAWAII ANNEXED 1898

© Copyright HAMMOND INCORPORATED, Maplewood, N.J.

| THE UNITED STATES IN 1783 847 | LOUISIANA PURCHASE 822 | TEXAS 389 | OREGON 286 | MEXICAN CESSION 529 | ALASKA 586 |

RED RIVER BASIN 48

GADSDEN PURCHASE 30

HAWAII 6

Figures are thousands of square miles

FLORIDA 72

Total 3,615

CONFLICTING CLAIMS TO THE WEST
AFTER THE TREATY OF 1783

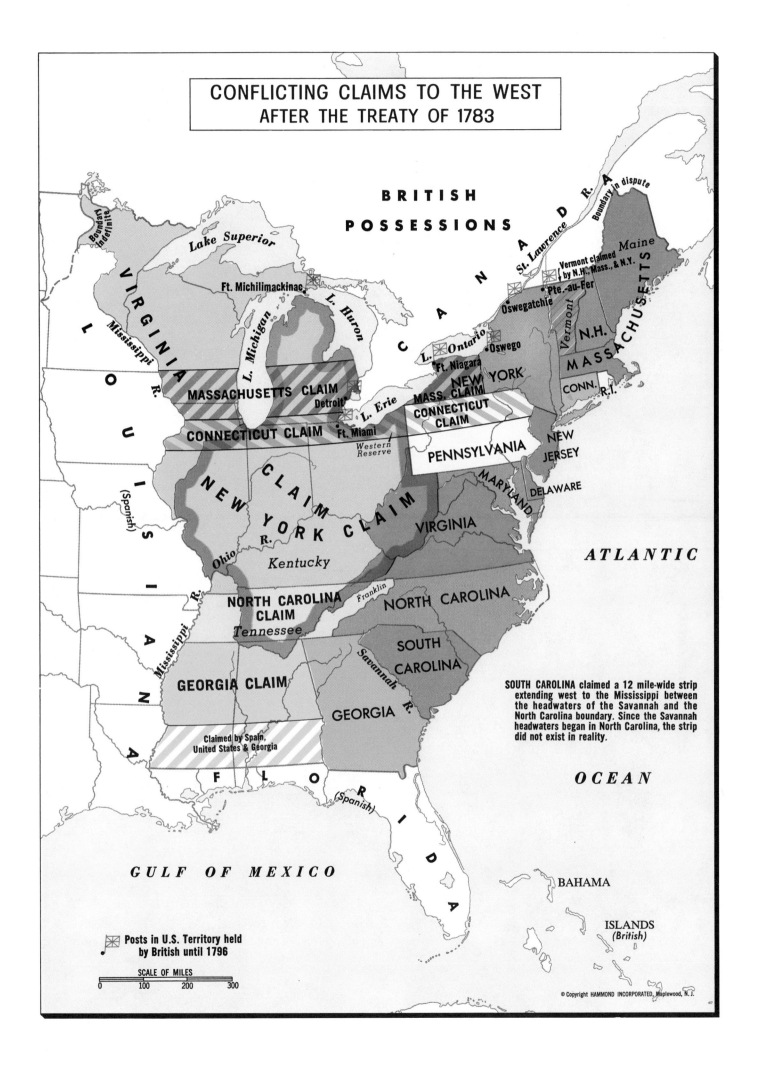

BRITISH

POSVESSIONS

Boundary in dispute

Lake Superior

Maine

Vermont claimed
by N.H., Mass., & N.Y.

Pte.-au-Fer

Ft. Michilimackinac

Oswegatchie

L. Michigan

L. Huron

N.H.

Vermont

MASSACHUSETTS

L. Ontario

Oswego

Ft. Niagara

NEW YORK

Boundary
Indefinite

VIRGINIA

L

O

U

I

S

I

A

N

A

Mississippi R.

MASSACHUSETTS CLAIM

Detroit

L. Erie

MASS. CLAIM

CONN.

R.I.

CONNECTICUT
CLAIM

CONNECTICUT CLAIM

Ft. Miami

Western
Reserve

PENNSYLVANIA

NEW
JERSEY

(Spanish)

NEW

YORK

CLAIM

Ohio R.

Kentucky

VIRGINIA

MARYLAND

DELAWARE

ATLANTIC

NORTH CAROLINA
CLAIM

Franklin

NORTH CAROLINA

Tennessee

Mississippi R.

SOUTH
CAROLINA

Savannah R.

GEORGIA CLAIM

SOUTH CAROLINA claimed a 12 mile-wide strip
extending west to the Mississippi between
the headwaters of the Savannah and the
North Carolina boundary. Since the Savannah
headwaters began in North Carolina, the strip
did not exist in reality.

Claimed by Spain,
United States & Georgia

GEORGIA

OCEAN

F

L

O

R

I

D

A

(Spanish)

GULF OF MEXICO

BAHAMA

ISLANDS
(British)

⊠ Posts in U.S. Territory held
by British until 1796

SCALE OF MILES

0   100   200   300

© Copyright HAMMOND INCORPORATED, Maplewood, N. J.

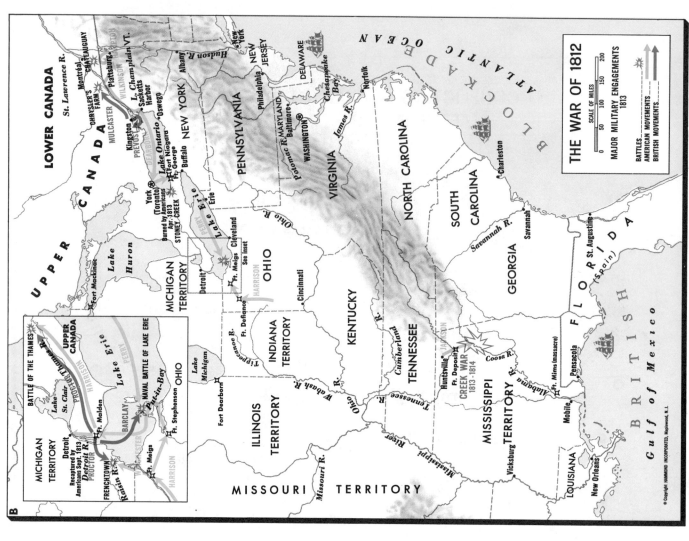

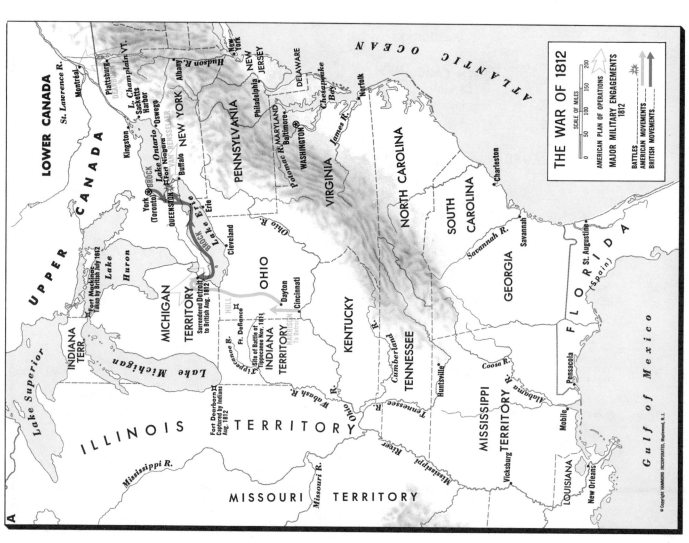

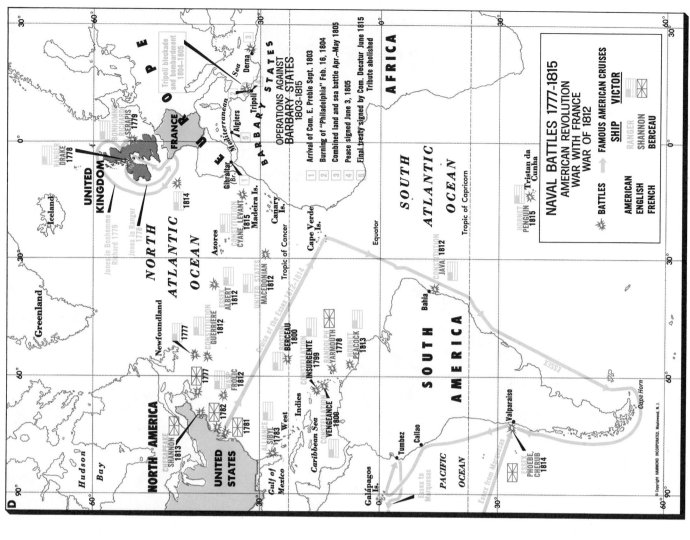

NAVAL BATTLES 1777-1815
AMERICAN REVOLUTION
WAR WITH FRANCE
WAR OF 1812

BATTLES	FAMOUS AMERICAN CRUISES

	SHIP	VICTOR
AMERICAN	RANGER	
ENGLISH	SHANNON	
FRENCH	BERCEAU	

OPERATIONS AGAINST
BARBARY STATES
1803-1815

1 Arrival of Com. E. Preble Sept. 1803
2 Burning of "Philadelphia" Feb. 16, 1804
3 Combined land and sea battle Apr.–May 1805
4 Peace signed June 3, 1805
5 Final treaty signed by Com. Decatur June 1815
   Tribute abolished

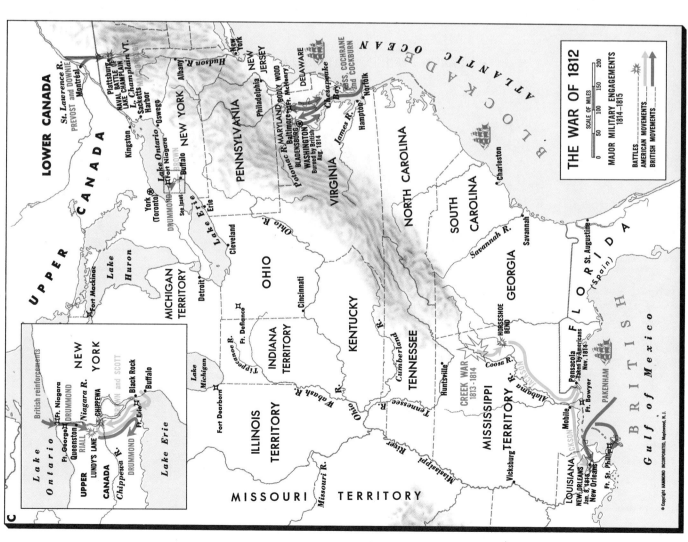

THE WAR OF 1812

SCALE OF MILES
0   50   100   150   200

MAJOR MILITARY ENGAGEMENTS
1814–1815

BATTLES
AMERICAN MOVEMENTS
BRITISH MOVEMENTS

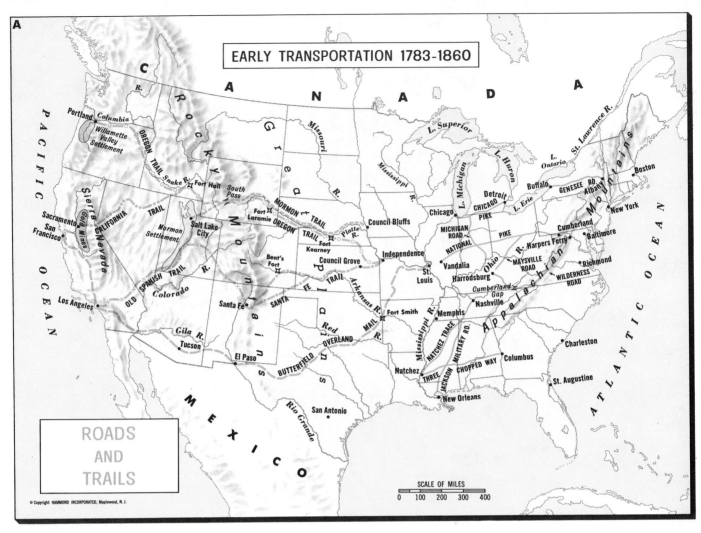

EARLY TRANSPORTATION 1783-1860

ROADS
AND
TRAILS

© Copyright HAMMOND INCORPORATED, Maplewood, N.J.

SCALE OF MILES
0   100   200   300   400

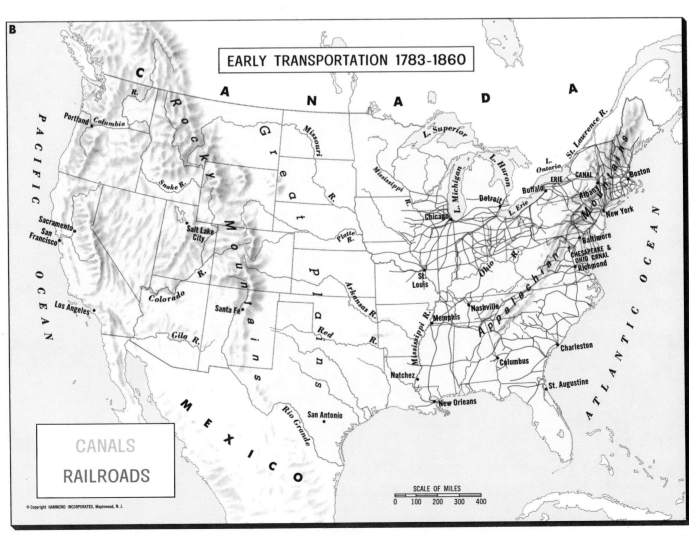

EARLY TRANSPORTATION 1783-1860

CANALS
RAILROADS

© Copyright HAMMOND INCORPORATED, Maplewood, N.J.

SCALE OF MILES
0   100   200   300   400

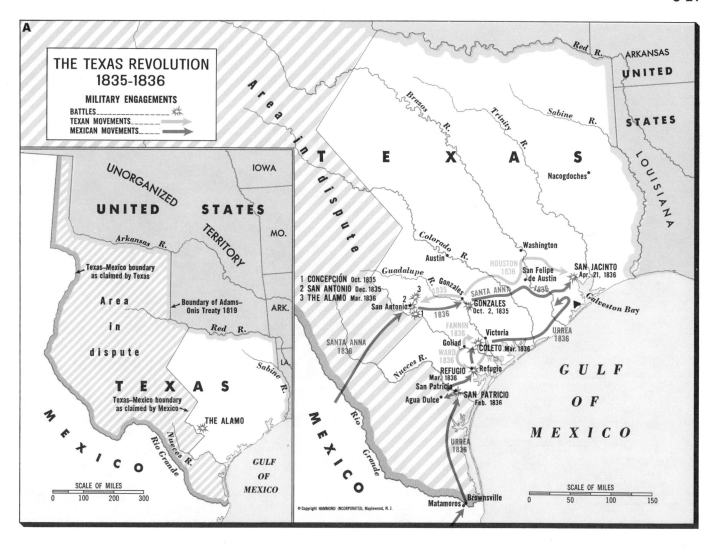

A

THE TEXAS REVOLUTION 1835-1836

MILITARY ENGAGEMENTS

BATTLES _____
TEXAN MOVEMENTS _____
MEXICAN MOVEMENTS _____

UNORGANIZED

UNITED STATES TERRITORY

IOWA

MO.

Arkansas R.

Texas–Mexico boundary as claimed by Texas

ARK.

Boundary of Adams–Onis Treaty 1819

Red R.

Area in dispute

Sabine R.

LA.

TEXAS

Texas–Mexico boundary as claimed by Mexico

THE ALAMO

MEXICO

Rio Grande

Nueces R.

GULF OF MEXICO

SCALE OF MILES
0   100   200   300

T E X A S

Red R.   ARKANSAS

UNITED

STATES

LOUISIANA

Brazos R.   *Trinity R.*   *Sabine R.*

Area in dispute

Nacogdoches

Colorado R.

Washington

Austin

Guadalupe R.   Gonzales

HOUSTON 1836

San Felipe de Austin

SAN JACINTO Apr. 21, 1836

SANTA ANNA 1836

1 CONCEPCIÓN Oct. 1835
2 SAN ANTONIO Dec. 1835
3 THE ALAMO Mar. 1836

San Antonio

GONZALES Oct. 2, 1835

FANNIN 1836

SANTA ANNA 1836

Victoria

Goliad

COLETO Mar. 1836

WARD 1836

Nueces R.

REFUGIO Mar. 1836

San Patricio

Refugio

URREA 1836

Galveston Bay

Agua Dulce

SAN PATRICIO Feb. 1836

URREA 1836

Rio Grande

Matamoros

Brownsville

MEXICO

GULF OF MEXICO

SCALE OF MILES
0   50   100   150

© Copyright HAMMOND INCORPORATED, Maplewood, N.J.

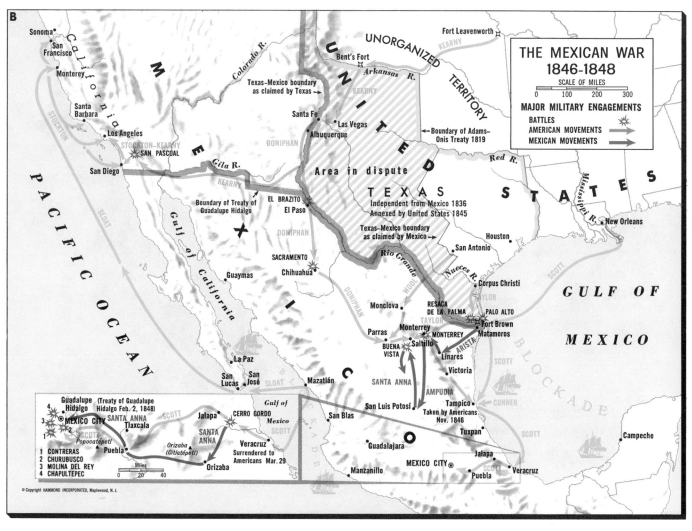

B

THE MEXICAN WAR 1846-1848

SCALE OF MILES
0   100   200   300

MAJOR MILITARY ENGAGEMENTS

BATTLES
AMERICAN MOVEMENTS
MEXICAN MOVEMENTS

Sonoma

San Francisco

California

Monterey

Santa Barbara

Los Angeles

STOCKTON–KEARNY

San Pascual

SAN PASCUAL

San Diego

STOCKTON

KEARNY

Colorado R.

Bent's Fort

Arkansas R.

Fort Leavenworth

KEARNY

UNORGANIZED TERRITORY

UNITED

Texas–Mexico boundary as claimed by Texas

Santa Fe

DONIPHAN

Las Vegas

Albuquerque

Boundary of Adams–Onis Treaty 1819

Red R.

STATES

Area in dispute

Gila R.

KEARNY

Boundary of Treaty of Guadalupe Hidalgo

EL BRAZITO

El Paso

DONIPHAN

SACRAMENTO

Chihuahua

Guaymas

Gulf of California

M E X I C O

TEXAS
Independent from Mexico 1836
Annexed by United States 1845

Texas–Mexico boundary as claimed by Mexico

Houston

San Antonio

Rio Grande

DONIPHAN

Nueces R.

Corpus Christi

WOOL

TAYLOR

Monclova

RESACA DE LA PALMA

PALO ALTO

Fort Brown

Parras

TAYLOR

Monterrey

MONTERREY

Matamoros

BUENA VISTA

Saltillo

ARISTA

Linares

SANTA ANNA

Victoria

Mississippi R.

New Orleans

SCOTT

GULF OF MEXICO

BLOCKADE

CONNER

San Luis Potosí

AMPUDIA

Tampico

Taken by Americans Nov. 1846

SANTA ANNA

San Blas

Mazatlán

Guadalajara

Tuxpan

SCOTT

Jalapa

Campeche

Manzanillo

MEXICO CITY

Puebla

Veracruz

SCOTT

PACIFIC OCEAN

La Paz

San Lucas   San José

SLOAT

SLOAT

BLOCKADE

Guadalupe Hidalgo (Treaty of Guadalupe Hidalgo Feb. 2, 1848)

4
3   MEXICO CITY   SANTA ANNA
2   Tlaxcala
1

Popocatépetl

Puebla

1 CONTRERAS
2 CHURUBUSCO
3 MOLINA DEL REY
4 CHAPULTEPEC

SCOTT

Jalapa

CERRO GORDO

Gulf of Mexico

SANTA ANNA

Orizaba (Citlatépetl)

Veracruz Surrendered to Americans Mar. 29

Orizaba

Miles
0   20   40

© Copyright HAMMOND INCORPORATED, Maplewood, N.J.

A

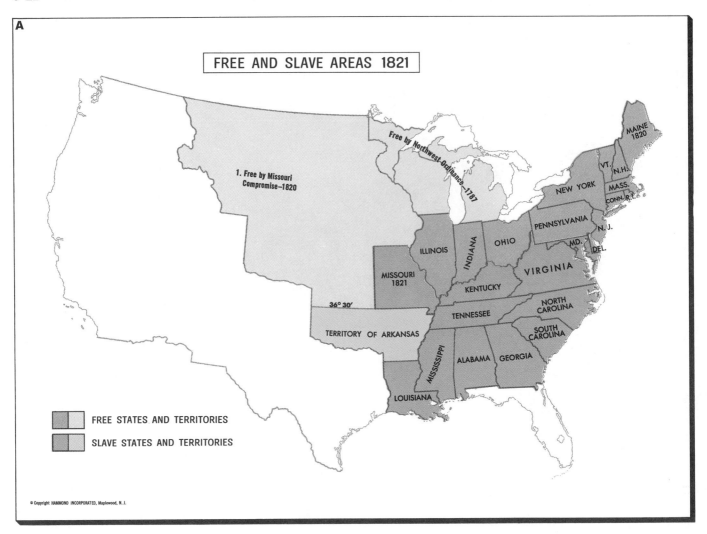

FREE AND SLAVE AREAS 1821

1. Free by Missouri Compromise–1820

Free by Northwest Ordinance–1787

MAINE 1820

VT. N.H.
NEW YORK MASS.
CONN. R.I.
PENNSYLVANIA
N.J.
MD. DEL.

ILLINOIS INDIANA OHIO

VIRGINIA

MISSOURI 1821

KENTUCKY

36° 30'

TENNESSEE

NORTH CAROLINA

TERRITORY OF ARKANSAS

SOUTH CAROLINA

MISSISSIPPI ALABAMA GEORGIA

LOUISIANA

FREE STATES AND TERRITORIES

SLAVE STATES AND TERRITORIES

© Copyright HAMMOND INCORPORATED, Maplewood, N. J.

B

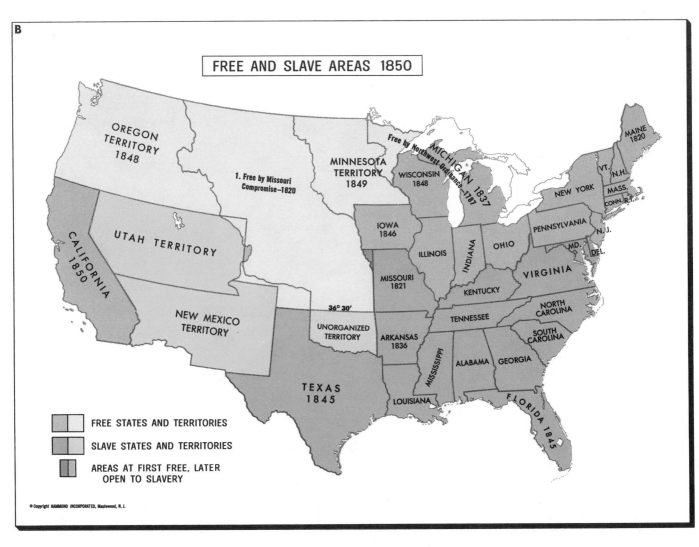

FREE AND SLAVE AREAS 1850

OREGON TERRITORY 1848

1. Free by Missouri Compromise–1820

MINNESOTA TERRITORY 1849

Free by Northwest Ordinance–1787

MICHIGAN 1837

WISCONSIN 1848

MAINE 1820

VT. N.H.
NEW YORK MASS.
CONN. R.I.

CALIFORNIA 1850

UTAH TERRITORY

IOWA 1846

PENNSYLVANIA
N.J.
MD. DEL.

ILLINOIS INDIANA OHIO

MISSOURI 1821

VIRGINIA

KENTUCKY

NEW MEXICO TERRITORY

36° 30'

TENNESSEE

NORTH CAROLINA

UNORGANIZED TERRITORY

ARKANSAS 1836

SOUTH CAROLINA

MISSISSIPPI ALABAMA GEORGIA

TEXAS 1845

LOUISIANA

FLORIDA 1845

FREE STATES AND TERRITORIES

SLAVE STATES AND TERRITORIES

AREAS AT FIRST FREE, LATER OPEN TO SLAVERY

© Copyright HAMMOND INCORPORATED, Maplewood, N. J.

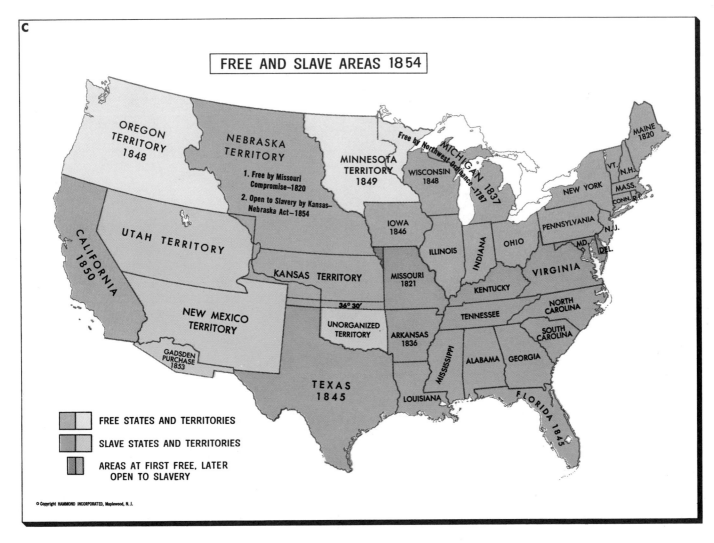

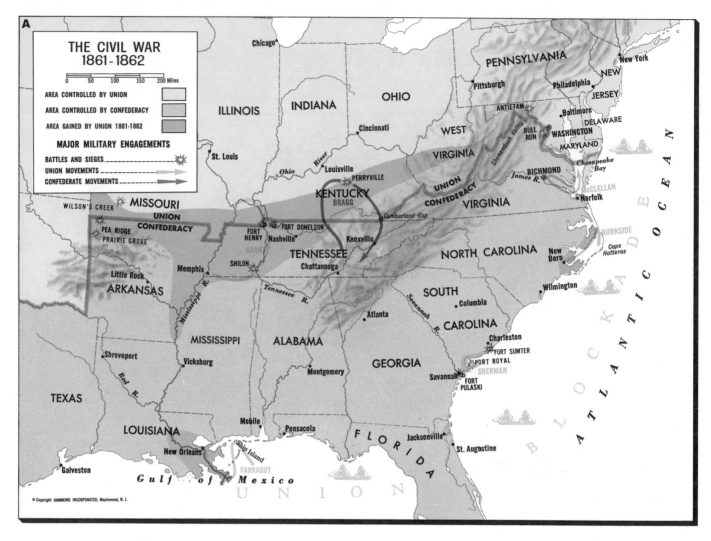

A

THE CIVIL WAR
1861-1862

0   50   100   150   200 Miles

AREA CONTROLLED BY UNION

AREA CONTROLLED BY CONFEDERACY

AREA GAINED BY UNION 1861-1862

MAJOR MILITARY ENGAGEMENTS

BATTLES AND SIEGES _____

UNION MOVEMENTS _____

CONFEDERATE MOVEMENTS _____

© Copyright HAMMOND INCORPORATED, Maplewood, N.J.

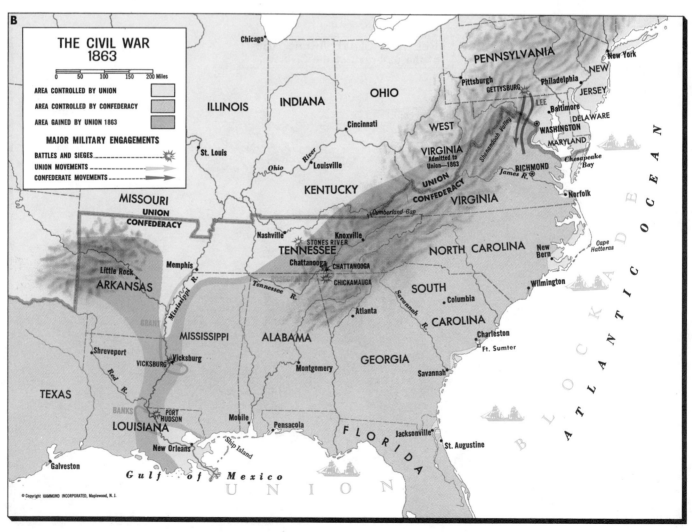

B

THE CIVIL WAR
1863

0   50   100   150   200 Miles

AREA CONTROLLED BY UNION

AREA CONTROLLED BY CONFEDERACY

AREA GAINED BY UNION 1863

MAJOR MILITARY ENGAGEMENTS

BATTLES AND SIEGES _____

UNION MOVEMENTS _____

CONFEDERATE MOVEMENTS _____

© Copyright HAMMOND INCORPORATED, Maplewood, N.J.

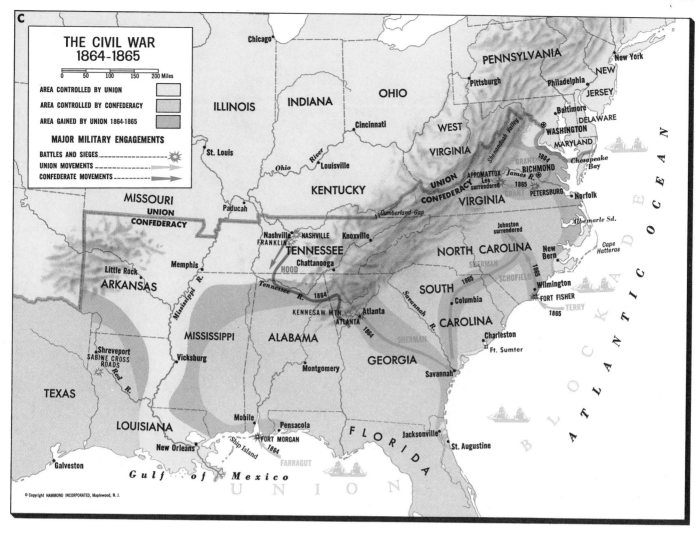

C

THE CIVIL WAR 1864-1865

0 50 100 150 200 Miles

AREA CONTROLLED BY UNION
AREA CONTROLLED BY CONFEDERACY
AREA GAINED BY UNION 1864-1865

MAJOR MILITARY ENGAGEMENTS

BATTLES AND SIEGES
UNION MOVEMENTS
CONFEDERATE MOVEMENTS

© Copyright HAMMOND INCORPORATED, Maplewood, N.J.

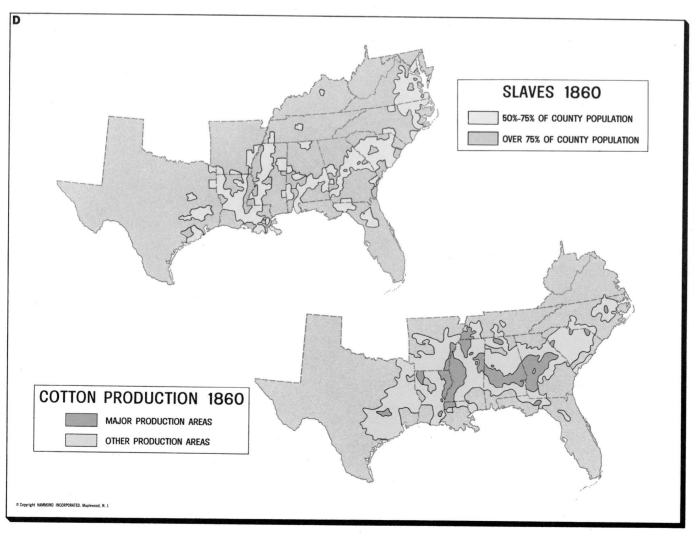

D

SLAVES 1860

50%-75% OF COUNTY POPULATION
OVER 75% OF COUNTY POPULATION

COTTON PRODUCTION 1860

MAJOR PRODUCTION AREAS
OTHER PRODUCTION AREAS

© Copyright HAMMOND INCORPORATED, Maplewood, N.J.

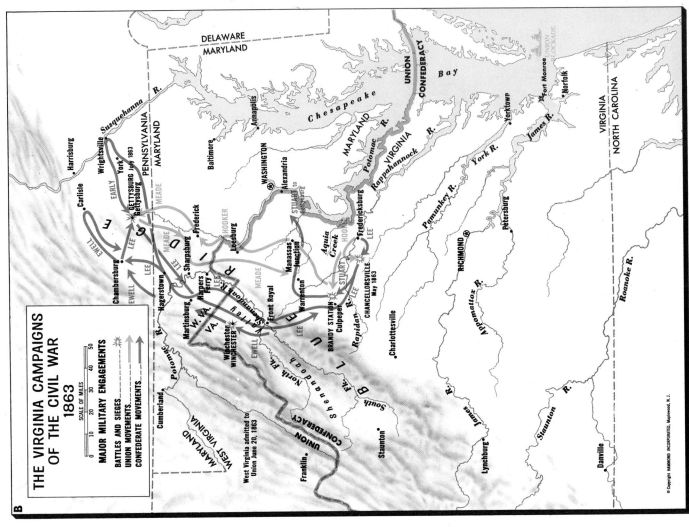

B

THE VIRGINIA CAMPAIGNS OF THE CIVIL WAR 1863

SCALE OF MILES

0   10   20   30   40   50

MAJOR MILITARY ENGAGEMENTS

BATTLES AND SIEGES
UNION MOVEMENTS
CONFEDERATE MOVEMENTS

West Virginia admitted to
Union June 20, 1863

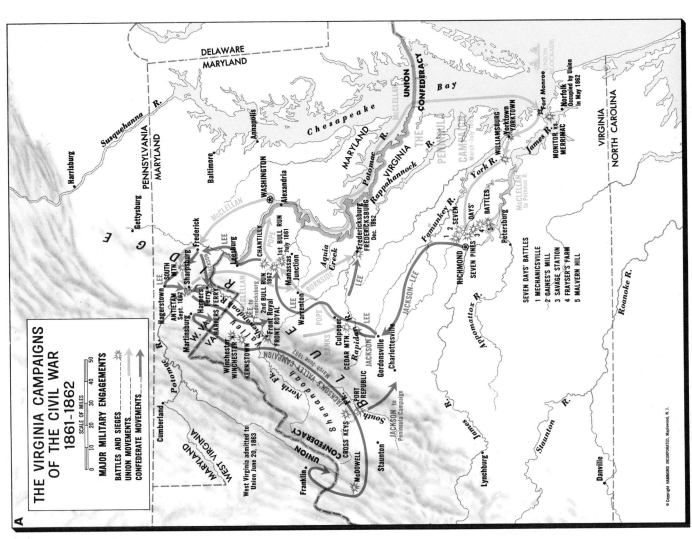

A

THE VIRGINIA CAMPAIGNS OF THE CIVIL WAR 1861-1862

SCALE OF MILES

0   10   20   30   40   50

MAJOR MILITARY ENGAGEMENTS

BATTLES AND SIEGES
UNION MOVEMENTS
CONFEDERATE MOVEMENTS

West Virginia admitted to
Union June 20, 1863

SEVEN DAYS' BATTLES

1 MECHANICSVILLE
2 GAINES'S MILL
3 SAVAGE STATION
4 FRAYSER'S FARM
5 MALVERN HILL

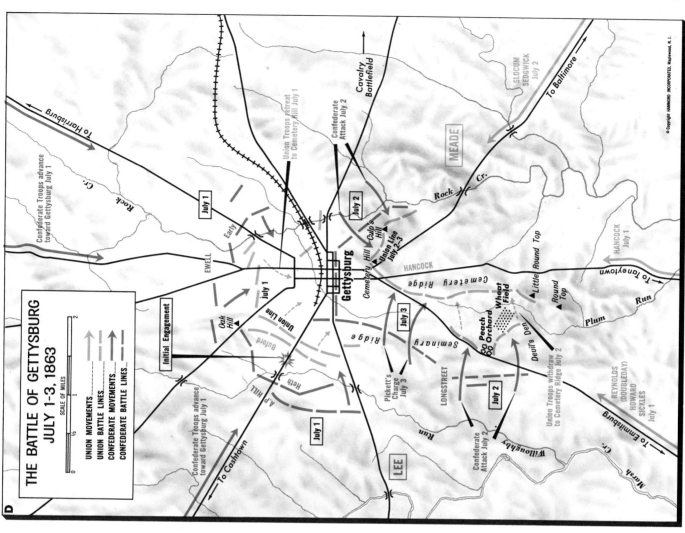

THE BATTLE OF GETTYSBURG
JULY 1-3, 1863

SCALE OF MILES

UNION MOVEMENTS
UNION BATTLE LINES
CONFEDERATE MOVEMENTS
CONFEDERATE BATTLE LINES

D

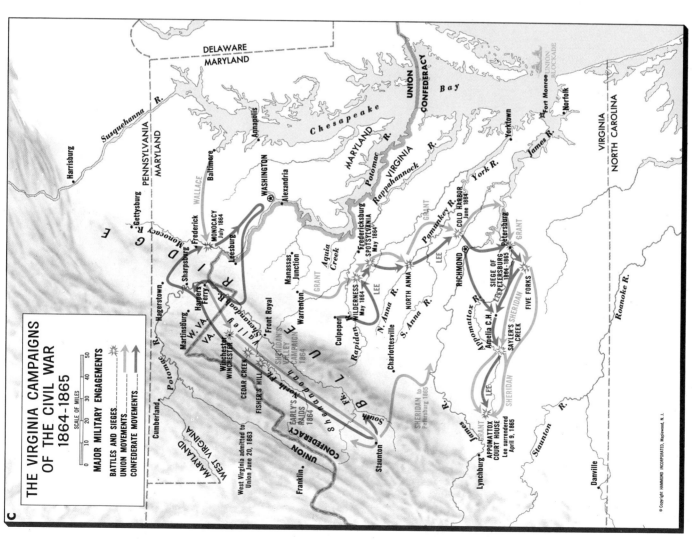

THE VIRGINIA CAMPAIGNS
OF THE CIVIL WAR
1864-1865

SCALE OF MILES

0 10 20 30 40 50

MAJOR MILITARY ENGAGEMENTS

BATTLES AND SIEGES
UNION MOVEMENTS
CONFEDERATE MOVEMENTS

C

© Copyright HAMMOND INCORPORATED, Maplewood, N. J.

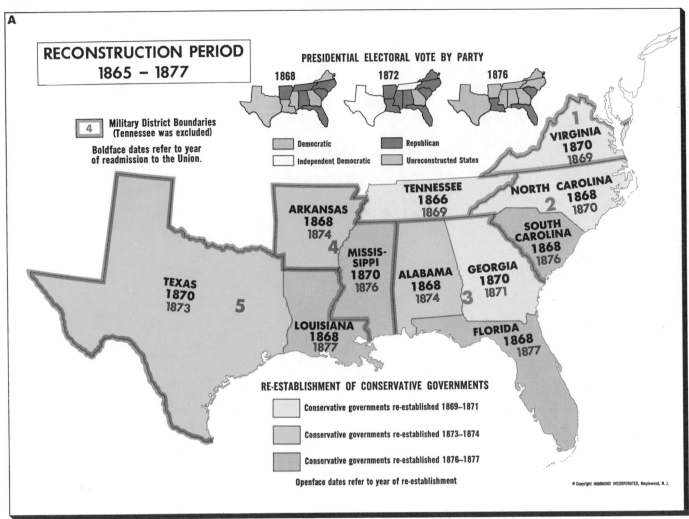

RECONSTRUCTION PERIOD
1865 – 1877

PRESIDENTIAL ELECTORAL VOTE BY PARTY

1868   1872   1876

- Democratic
- Independent Democratic
- Republican
- Unreconstructed States

4 Military District Boundaries (Tennessee was excluded)

Boldface dates refer to year of readmission to the Union.

VIRGINIA 1870 1869

NORTH CAROLINA 1868 1870

SOUTH CAROLINA 1868 1876

TENNESSEE 1866 1869

ARKANSAS 1868 1874

MISSIS-SIPPI 1870 1876

ALABAMA 1868 1874

GEORGIA 1870 1871

TEXAS 1870 1873

LOUISIANA 1868 1877

FLORIDA 1868 1877

RE-ESTABLISHMENT OF CONSERVATIVE GOVERNMENTS

- Conservative governments re-established 1869–1871
- Conservative governments re-established 1873–1874
- Conservative governments re-established 1876–1877

Openface dates refer to year of re-establishment

© Copyright HAMMOND INCORPORATED, Maplewood, N.J.

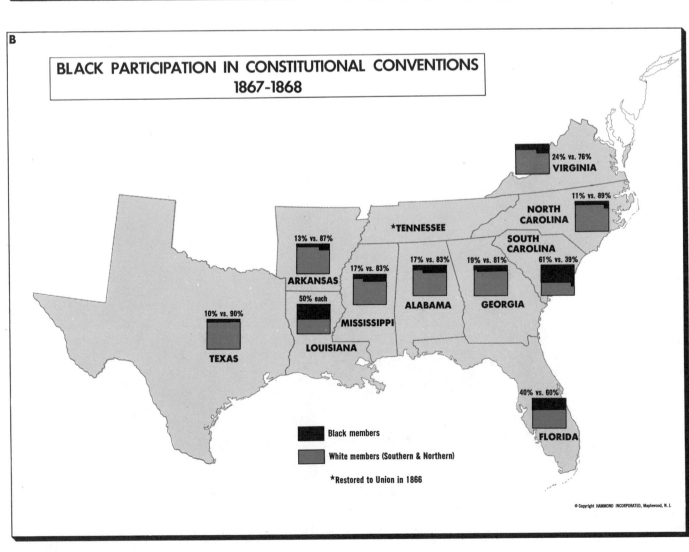

BLACK PARTICIPATION IN CONSTITUTIONAL CONVENTIONS
1867-1868

24% vs. 76% VIRGINIA

11% vs. 89% NORTH CAROLINA

*TENNESSEE

SOUTH CAROLINA 61% vs. 39%

13% vs. 87% ARKANSAS

17% vs. 83% MISSISSIPPI

17% vs. 83% ALABAMA

19% vs. 81% GEORGIA

50% each LOUISIANA

10% vs. 90% TEXAS

40% vs. 60% FLORIDA

- Black members
- White members (Southern & Northern)

*Restored to Union in 1866

© Copyright HAMMOND INCORPORATED, Maplewood, N.J.

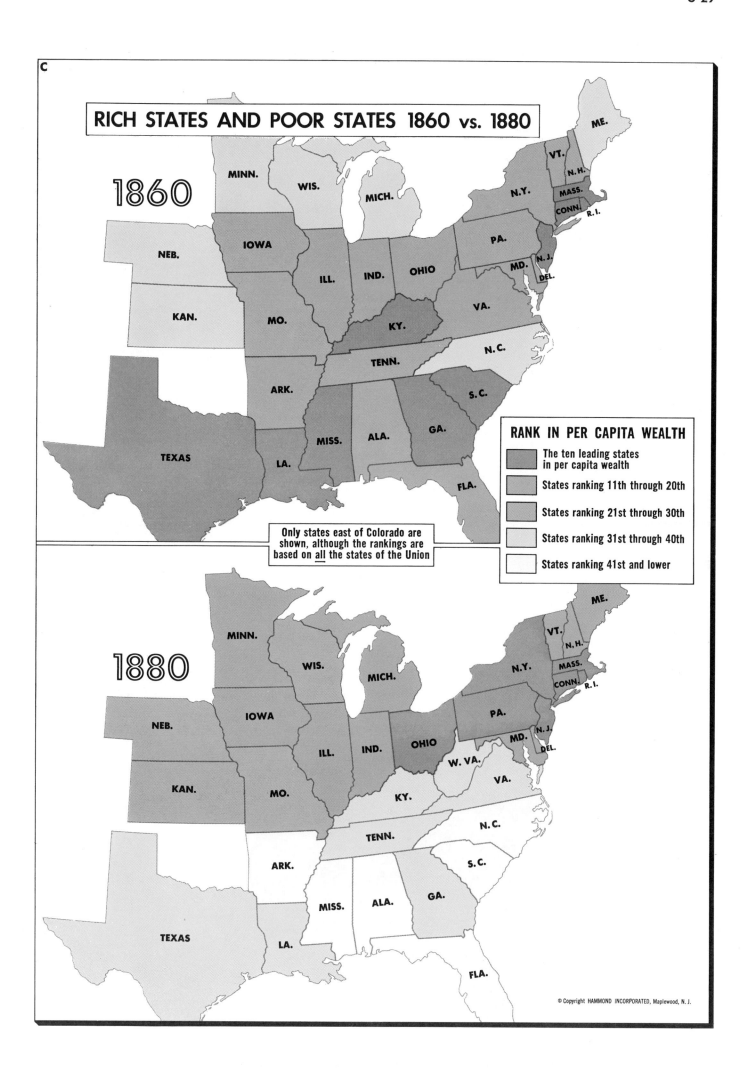

RICH STATES AND POOR STATES 1860 vs. 1880

1860

Only states east of Colorado are shown, although the rankings are based on <u>all</u> the states of the Union

RANK IN PER CAPITA WEALTH

The ten leading states in per capita wealth

States ranking 11th through 20th

States ranking 21st through 30th

States ranking 31st through 40th

States ranking 41st and lower

1880

© Copyright HAMMOND INCORPORATED, Maplewood, N.J.

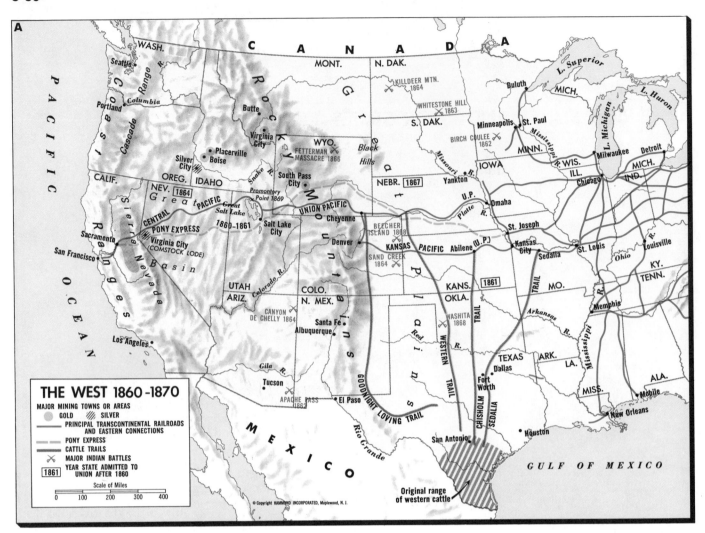

A

THE WEST 1860-1870

MAJOR MINING TOWNS OR AREAS

⬤ GOLD ▨ SILVER

━━━ PRINCIPAL TRANSCONTINENTAL RAILROADS AND EASTERN CONNECTIONS

╌╌ PONY EXPRESS

━━━ CATTLE TRAILS

✕ MAJOR INDIAN BATTLES

[1861] YEAR STATE ADMITTED TO UNION AFTER 1860

Scale of Miles
0   100   200   300   400

© Copyright HAMMOND INCORPORATED, Maplewood, N.J.

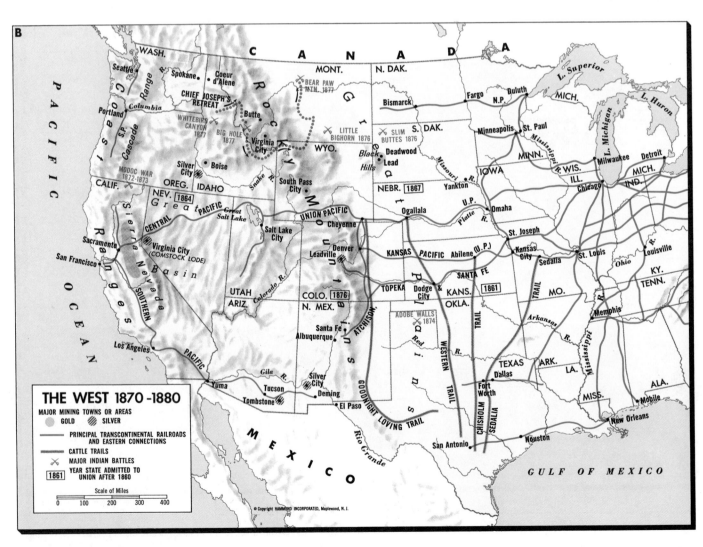

B

THE WEST 1870-1880

MAJOR MINING TOWNS OR AREAS

⬤ GOLD ▨ SILVER

━━━ PRINCIPAL TRANSCONTINENTAL RAILROADS AND EASTERN CONNECTIONS

━━━ CATTLE TRAILS

✕ MAJOR INDIAN BATTLES

[1861] YEAR STATE ADMITTED TO UNION AFTER 1860

Scale of Miles
0   100   200   300   400

© Copyright HAMMOND INCORPORATED, Maplewood, N.J.

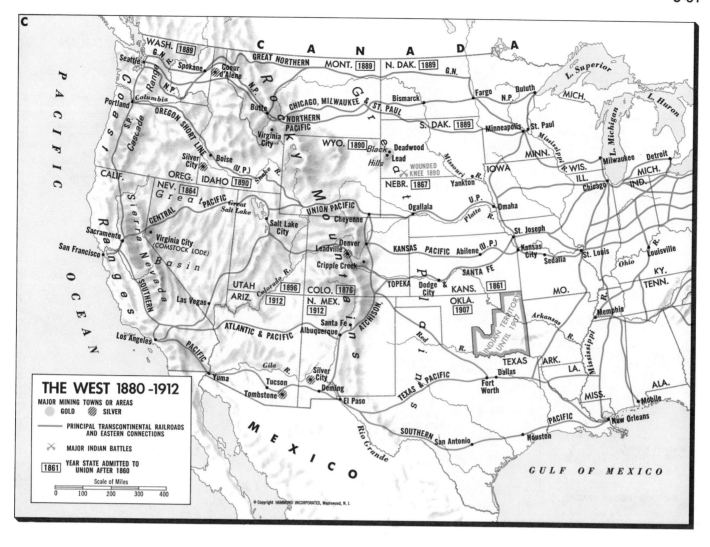

THE WEST 1880-1912

MAJOR MINING TOWNS OR AREAS
GOLD   SILVER

PRINCIPAL TRANSCONTINENTAL RAILROADS
AND EASTERN CONNECTIONS

MAJOR INDIAN BATTLES

1861 YEAR STATE ADMITTED TO
UNION AFTER 1860

Scale of Miles
0   100   200   300   400

© Copyright HAMMOND INCORPORATED, Maplewood, N.J.

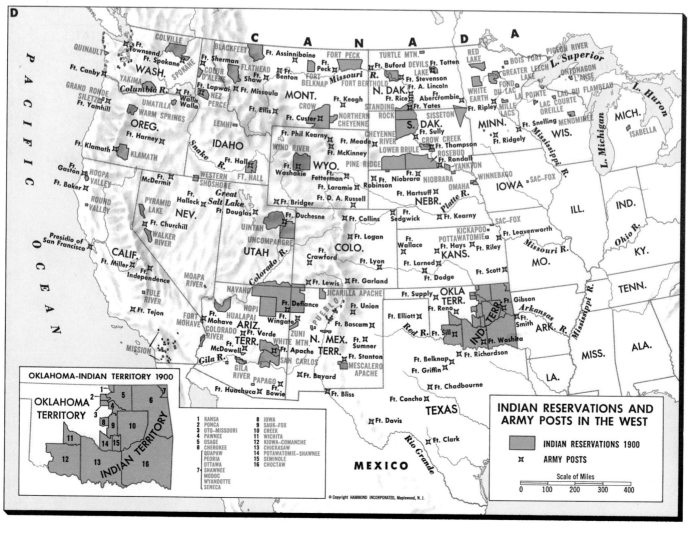

INDIAN RESERVATIONS AND ARMY POSTS IN THE WEST

INDIAN RESERVATIONS 1900

ARMY POSTS

Scale of Miles
0   100   200   300   400

OKLAHOMA-INDIAN TERRITORY 1900

OKLAHOMA TERRITORY

INDIAN TERRITORY

1 KANSA
2 PONCA
3 OTO-MISSOURI
4 PAWNEE
5 OSAGE
6 QUAPAW
   PEORIA
   OTTAWA
7 SHAWNEE
   MODOC
   WYANDOTTE
   SENECA
8 IOWA
9 SAUK-FOX
10 CREEK
11 WICHITA
12 KIOWA-COMANCHE
13 CHICKASAW
14 POTAWATOMIE-SHAWNEE
15 SEMINOLE
16 CHOCTAW

© Copyright HAMMOND INCORPORATED, Maplewood, N.J.

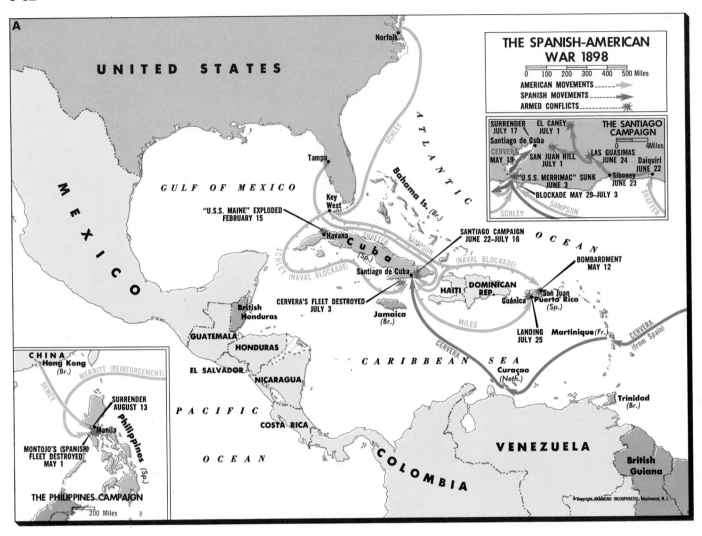

A

UNITED STATES

MEXICO

GULF OF MEXICO

ATLANTIC OCEAN

THE SPANISH-AMERICAN
WAR 1898

0   100   200   300   400   500 Miles

AMERICAN MOVEMENTS
SPANISH MOVEMENTS
ARMED CONFLICTS

THE SANTIAGO
CAMPAIGN

SURRENDER   EL CANEY
JULY 17   JULY 1
Santiago de Cuba
CERVERA   SAN JUAN HILL   LAS GUASIMAS
MAY 19   JULY 1   JUNE 24   Daiquirí
                                                 JUNE 22
"U.S.S. MERRIMAC" SUNK   Siboney
JUNE 3   JUNE 23
BLOCKADE MAY 29–JULY 3

0   4Miles

SCHLEY

SAMPSON

SHAFTER

Norfolk

Tampa

Key West

"U.S.S. MAINE" EXPLODED
FEBRUARY 15

Havana

Cuba (Sp.)

Bahama Is. (Br.)

SHAFTER

SAMPSON

(NAVAL BLOCKADE)

SCHLEY (NAVAL BLOCKADE)

SANTIAGO CAMPAIGN
JUNE 22–JULY 16

Santiago de Cuba

CERVERA'S FLEET DESTROYED
JULY 3

Jamaica (Br.)

HAITI

DOMINICAN REP.

BOMBARDMENT
MAY 12

San Juan
Puerto Rico (Sp.)

Guánica

MILES

LANDING
JULY 25

Martinique (Fr.)

CERVERA (from Spain)

British Honduras

GUATEMALA

HONDURAS

EL SALVADOR

NICARAGUA

COSTA RICA

CARIBBEAN SEA

Curaçao (Neth.)

Trinidad (Br.)

VENEZUELA

COLOMBIA

British Guiana

PACIFIC OCEAN

CHINA
Hong Kong (Br.)

MERRITT (REINFORCEMENT)

DEWEY

SURRENDER
AUGUST 13

Manila

Philippines (Sp.)

MONTOJO'S (SPANISH)
FLEET DESTROYED
MAY 1

THE PHILIPPINES CAMPAIGN

200 Miles

© Copyright, HAMMOND INCORPORATED, Maplewood, N.J.

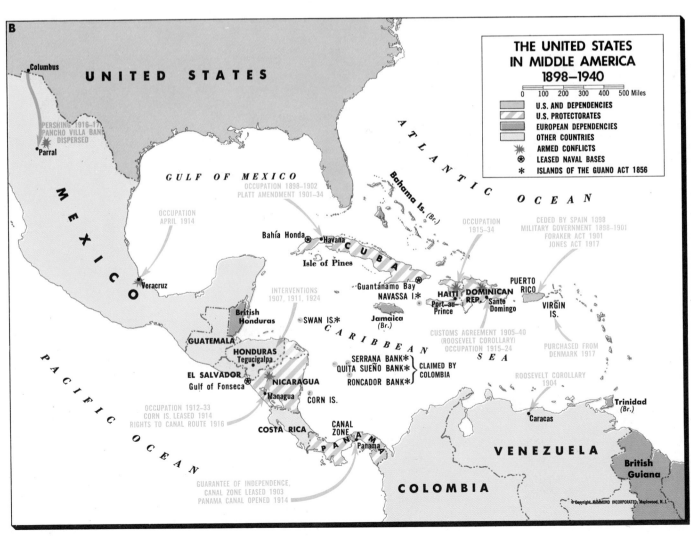

B

Columbus

UNITED STATES

PERSHING 1916–17,
PANCHO VILLA BAND
DISPERSED

Parral

MEXICO

GULF OF MEXICO

THE UNITED STATES
IN MIDDLE AMERICA
1898–1940

0   100   200   300   400   500 Miles

U.S. AND DEPENDENCIES
U.S. PROTECTORATES
EUROPEAN DEPENDENCIES
OTHER COUNTRIES
ARMED CONFLICTS
LEASED NAVAL BASES
ISLANDS OF THE GUANO ACT 1856

ATLANTIC OCEAN

OCCUPATION 1898–1902
PLATT AMENDMENT 1901–34

OCCUPATION
APRIL 1914

Veracruz

Bahía Honda

Havana

CUBA

Isle of Pines

Bahama Is. (Br.)

OCCUPATION
1915–34

CEDED BY SPAIN 1898
MILITARY GOVERNMENT 1898–1901
FORAKER ACT 1901
JONES ACT 1917

INTERVENTIONS
1907, 1911, 1924

Guantánamo Bay
NAVASSA I.*

HAITI
Port-au-Prince

DOMINICAN
REP.
Santo
Domingo

PUERTO
RICO

VIRGIN
IS.

British Honduras

GUATEMALA

HONDURAS
Tegucigalpa

EL SALVADOR
Gulf of Fonseca

NICARAGUA
Managua

SWAN IS.*

Jamaica (Br.)

CARIBBEAN

CUSTOMS AGREEMENT 1905–40
(ROOSEVELT COROLLARY)
OCCUPATION 1915–24

SERRANA BANK*
QUITA SUEÑO BANK* } CLAIMED BY
RONCADOR BANK*   COLOMBIA

SEA

PURCHASED FROM
DENMARK 1917

ROOSEVELT COROLLARY
1904

PURCHASED FROM
DENMARK 1917

CORN IS.

OCCUPATION 1912–33
CORN IS. LEASED 1914
RIGHTS TO CANAL ROUTE 1916

COSTA RICA

CANAL
ZONE

PANAMA
Panama

Trinidad (Br.)

Caracas

VENEZUELA

COLOMBIA

British
Guiana

PACIFIC OCEAN

GUARANTEE OF INDEPENDENCE,
CANAL ZONE LEASED 1903
PANAMA CANAL OPENED 1914

© Copyright, HAMMOND INCORPORATED, Maplewood, N.J.

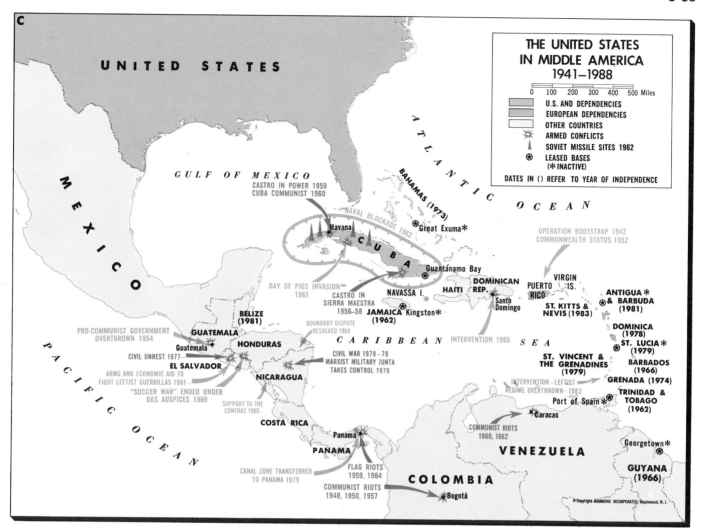

C

UNITED STATES

THE UNITED STATES
IN MIDDLE AMERICA
1941–1988

0 100 200 300 400 500 Miles

U.S. AND DEPENDENCIES
EUROPEAN DEPENDENCIES
OTHER COUNTRIES
✳ ARMED CONFLICTS
▲ SOVIET MISSILE SITES 1962
⊛ LEASED BASES
(✳ INACTIVE)

DATES IN ( ) REFER TO YEAR OF INDEPENDENCE

GULF OF MEXICO

CASTRO IN POWER 1959
CUBA COMMUNIST 1960

ATLANTIC OCEAN

BAHAMAS (1973)

NAVAL BLOCKADE 1962

⊛ Great Exuma ✳

OPERATION BOOTSTRAP 1942
COMMONWEALTH STATUS 1952

M E X I C O

Havana ▲
C U B A

Guantánamo Bay ⊛

BAY OF PIGS INVASION
1961

CASTRO IN
SIERRA MAESTRA
1956–58

NAVASSA I.

JAMAICA Kingston ✳
(1962)

HAITI

DOMINICAN
REP. ✳

Santo
Domingo

PUERTO
RICO

VIRGIN
IS.

ANTIGUA ✳
& BARBUDA
(1981)

P A C I F I C

BELIZE
(1981)

GUATEMALA

PRO-COMMUNIST GOVERNMENT
OVERTHROWN 1954

Guatemala ✳

HONDURAS

BOUNDARY DISPUTE
RESOLVED 1960

CARIBBEAN

INTERVENTION 1965

SEA

ST. KITTS &
NEVIS (1983)

DOMINICA
(1978)

⊛ ST. LUCIA ✳
(1979)

CIVIL UNREST 1977–

EL SALVADOR

ARMS AND ECONOMIC AID TO
FIGHT LEFTIST GUERRILLAS 1981

"SOCCER WAR" ENDED UNDER
OAS AUSPICES 1969

NICARAGUA

CIVIL WAR 1978–79
MARXIST MILITARY JUNTA
TAKES CONTROL 1979

ST. VINCENT &
THE GRENADINES
(1979)

BARBADOS
(1966)

GRENADA (1974)

INTERVENTION—LEFTIST
REGIME OVERTHROWN 1983

TRINIDAD &
TOBAGO
(1962)

O C E A N

SUPPORT TO THE
CONTRAS 1980–

COSTA RICA

Port of Spain ✳⊛

Caracas ✳

COMMUNIST RIOTS
1960, 1962

VENEZUELA

Georgetown ✳

PANAMA
Panama ✳

CANAL ZONE TRANSFERRED
TO PANAMA 1979

FLAG RIOTS
1959, 1964

COLOMBIA

GUYANA
(1966)

COMMUNIST RIOTS
1948, 1950, 1957

✳ Bogotá

© Copyright HAMMOND INCORPORATED, Maplewood, N.J.

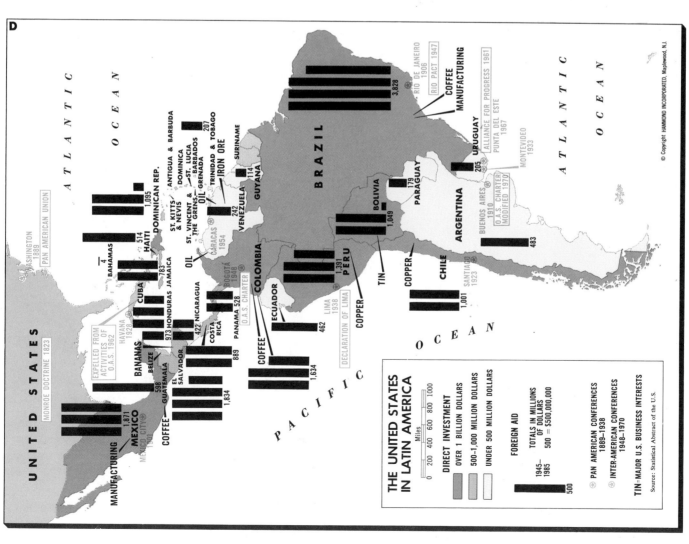

D

© Copyright HAMMOND INCORPORATED, Maplewood, N.J.

ATLANTIC OCEAN

ATLANTIC OCEAN

RIO DE JANEIRO 1906
RIO PACT 1947

COFFEE
MANUFACTURING

3,828

BRAZIL

ALLIANCE FOR PROGRESS 1961
PUNTA DEL ESTE 1967

URUGUAY

MONTEVIDEO
1933

205

WASHINGTON
1889
PAN AMERICAN UNION

ANTIGUA & BARBUDA

207

IRON ORE

ST. LUCIA

DOMINICA

BARBADOS

ST. KITTS
& NEVIS

ST. VINCENT &
THE GRENS.

GRENADA

TRINIDAD & TOBAGO

OIL

DOMINICAN REP.

SURINAME

114

GUYANA

242

VENEZUELA

CARACAS ⊛
1954

O.A.S. CHARTER
MODIFIED 1970

O.A.S. CHARTER

BUENOS AIRES
1910

ARGENTINA

PARAGUAY

179

BOLIVIA

1,049

483

SANTIAGO
1923

CHILE

1,001

COPPER

1,095

514

HAITI

4

BAHAMAS

783

CUBA

HAVANA
1928

EXPELLED FROM
ACTIVITIES OF
O.A.S. 1962

JAMAICA

HONDURAS

973

422 NICARAGUA

528

PANAMA

OIL

BOGOTÁ 1948
O.A.S. CHARTER

COLOMBIA

462

ECUADOR

COFFEE

COFFEE

1,391

PERU

LIMA 1938

DECLARATION OF LIMA

COPPER

TIN

COPPER

UNITED STATES

MONROE DOCTRINE 1823

889

COSTA RICA

598

GUATEMALA

BELIZE

1,834

EL SALVADOR

BANANAS

COFFEE

MEXICO CITY ⊛
1945

1,871

MEXICO

MANUFACTURING

1,634

PACIFIC

OCEAN

THE UNITED STATES
IN LATIN AMERICA

0 200 400 600 800 1000
Miles

DIRECT INVESTMENT

OVER 1 BILLION DOLLARS

500–1,000 MILLION DOLLARS

UNDER 500 MILLION DOLLARS

FOREIGN AID

TOTALS IN MILLIONS
OF DOLLARS
500 = $500,000,000

1945–
1985

500

⊛ PAN AMERICAN CONFERENCES
1889–1938

⊛ INTER-AMERICAN CONFERENCES
1948–1970

TIN=MAJOR U.S. BUSINESS INTERESTS

Source: Statistical Abstract of the U.S.

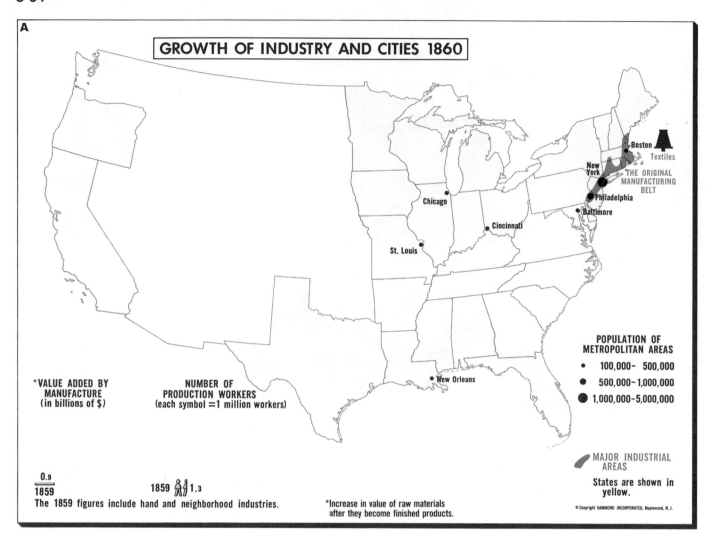

A

GROWTH OF INDUSTRY AND CITIES 1860

Boston
Textiles
New York
THE ORIGINAL MANUFACTURING BELT
Chicago
Philadelphia
Baltimore
Cincinnati
St. Louis
New Orleans

POPULATION OF METROPOLITAN AREAS

· 100,000- 500,000
● 500,000-1,000,000
⬤ 1,000,000-5,000,000

MAJOR INDUSTRIAL AREAS

States are shown in yellow.

© Copyright HAMMOND INCORPORATED, Maplewood, N.J.

*VALUE ADDED BY MANUFACTURE (in billions of $)

NUMBER OF PRODUCTION WORKERS (each symbol =1 million workers)

0.9
‾‾‾
1859

1859 👥 1.3

The 1859 figures include hand and neighborhood industries.

*Increase in value of raw materials after they become finished products.

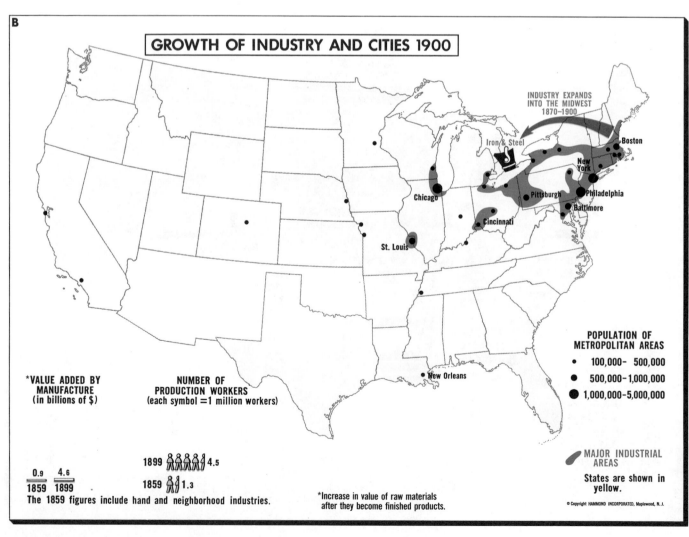

B

GROWTH OF INDUSTRY AND CITIES 1900

INDUSTRY EXPANDS INTO THE MIDWEST 1870-1900
Iron & Steel
Boston
New York
Chicago
Pittsburgh
Philadelphia
Baltimore
Cincinnati
St. Louis
New Orleans

POPULATION OF METROPOLITAN AREAS

· 100,000- 500,000
● 500,000-1,000,000
⬤ 1,000,000-5,000,000

MAJOR INDUSTRIAL AREAS

States are shown in yellow.

© Copyright HAMMOND INCORPORATED, Maplewood, N.J.

*VALUE ADDED BY MANUFACTURE (in billions of $)

NUMBER OF PRODUCTION WORKERS (each symbol =1 million workers)

1899 👥👥👥👥👥 4.5

1859 👥 1.3

0.9   4.6
‾‾‾ ‾‾‾
1859 1899

The 1859 figures include hand and neighborhood industries.

*Increase in value of raw materials after they become finished products.

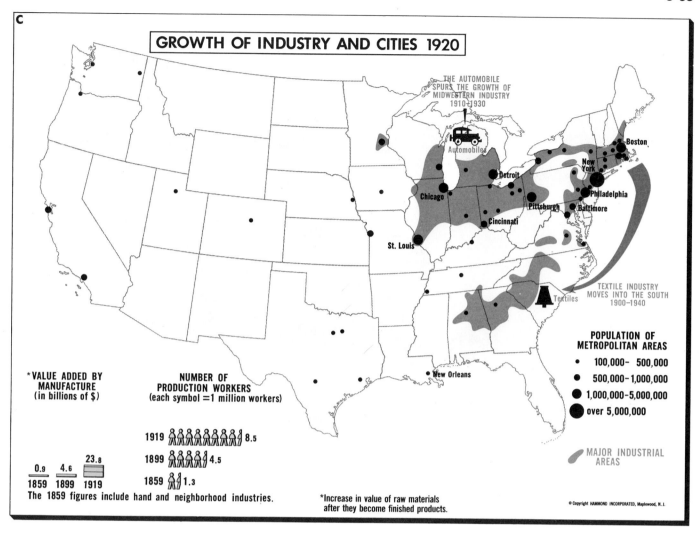

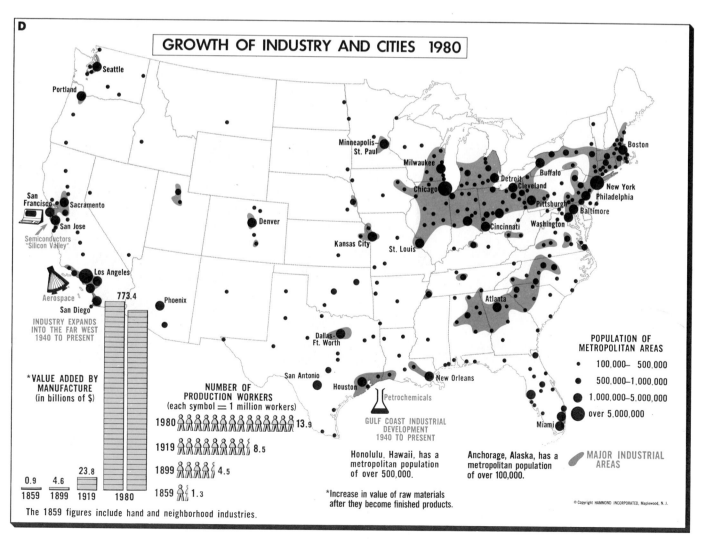

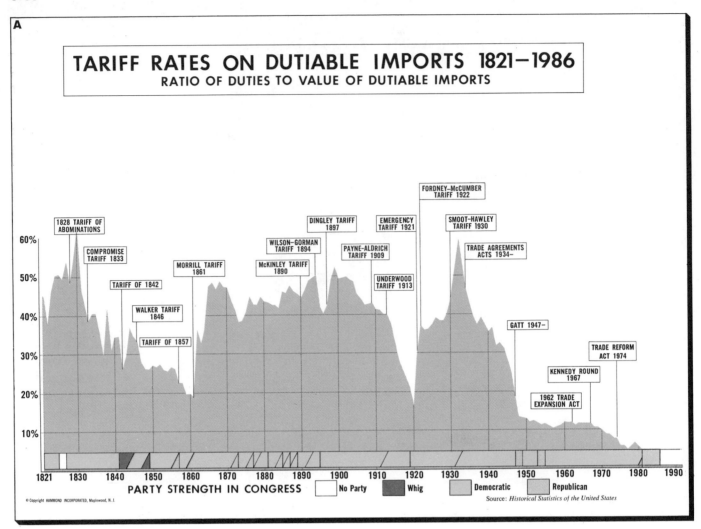

TARIFF RATES ON DUTIABLE IMPORTS 1821–1986
RATIO OF DUTIES TO VALUE OF DUTIABLE IMPORTS

1828 TARIFF OF ABOMINATIONS

COMPROMISE TARIFF 1833

TARIFF OF 1842

WALKER TARIFF 1846

TARIFF OF 1857

MORRILL TARIFF 1861

WILSON–GORMAN TARIFF 1894

McKINLEY TARIFF 1890

DINGLEY TARIFF 1897

PAYNE–ALDRICH TARIFF 1909

EMERGENCY TARIFF 1921

UNDERWOOD TARIFF 1913

FORDNEY–McCUMBER TARIFF 1922

SMOOT–HAWLEY TARIFF 1930

TRADE AGREEMENTS ACTS 1934–

GATT 1947–

TRADE REFORM ACT 1974

KENNEDY ROUND 1967

1962 TRADE EXPANSION ACT

PARTY STRENGTH IN CONGRESS   No Party   Whig   Democratic   Republican

© Copyright HAMMOND INCORPORATED, Maplewood, N.J.

Source: *Historical Statistics of the United States*

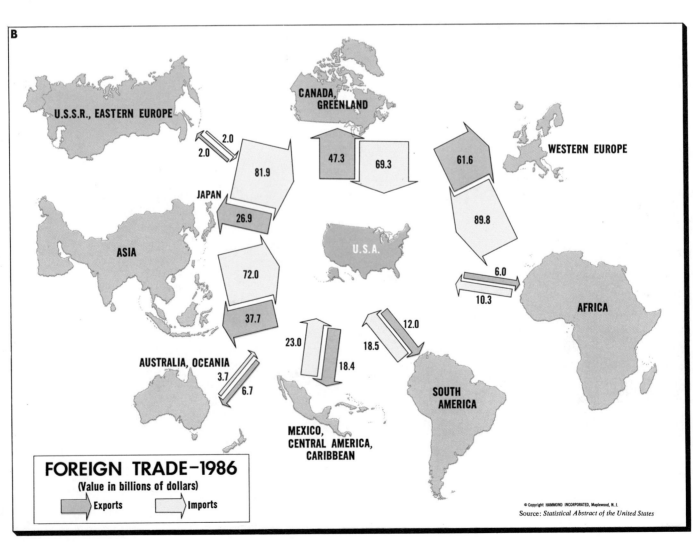

U.S.S.R., EASTERN EUROPE — 2.0 / 2.0

CANADA, GREENLAND — 47.3 / 69.3

WESTERN EUROPE — 61.6 / 89.8

JAPAN — 81.9 / 26.9

ASIA — 72.0 / 37.7

AFRICA — 6.0 / 10.3

AUSTRALIA, OCEANIA — 3.7 / 6.7

MEXICO, CENTRAL AMERICA, CARIBBEAN — 23.0 / 18.4

SOUTH AMERICA — 12.0 / 18.5

U.S.A.

FOREIGN TRADE–1986
(Value in billions of dollars)
Exports   Imports

© Copyright HAMMOND INCORPORATED, Maplewood, N.J.

Source: *Statistical Abstract of the United States*

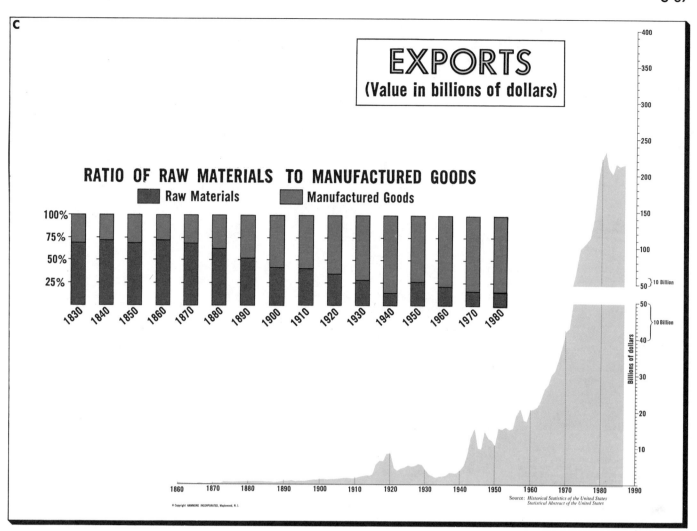

EXPORTS
(Value in billions of dollars)

RATIO OF RAW MATERIALS TO MANUFACTURED GOODS
■ Raw Materials   ■ Manufactured Goods

Source: *Historical Statistics of the United States*
Statistical Abstract of the United States
© Copyright HAMMOND INCORPORATED, Maplewood, N.J.

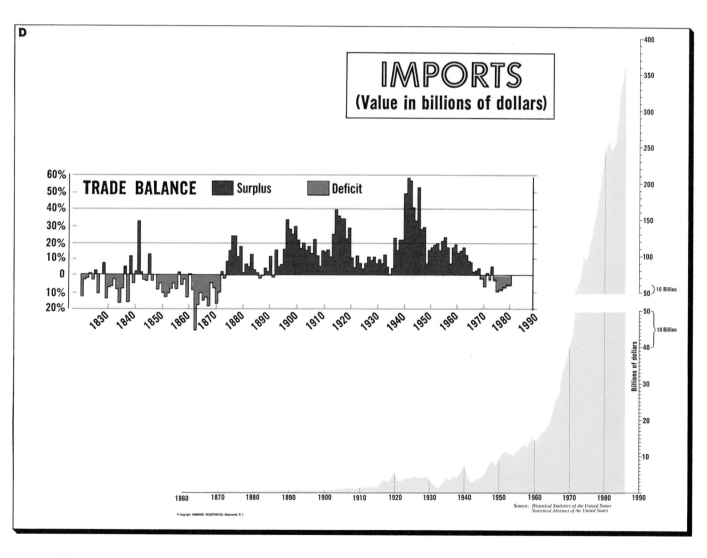

IMPORTS
(Value in billions of dollars)

TRADE BALANCE   ■ Surplus   ■ Deficit

Source: *Historical Statistics of the United States*
Statistical Abstract of the United States
© Copyright HAMMOND INCORPORATED, Maplewood, N.J.

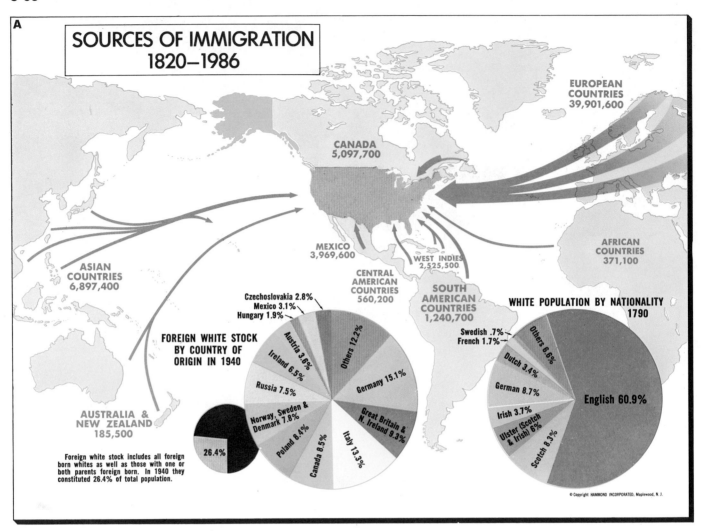

A

SOURCES OF IMMIGRATION 1820–1986

EUROPEAN COUNTRIES
39,901,600

CANADA
5,097,700

ASIAN COUNTRIES
6,897,400

MEXICO
3,969,600

WEST INDIES
2,525,500

CENTRAL AMERICAN COUNTRIES
560,200

SOUTH AMERICAN COUNTRIES
1,240,700

AFRICAN COUNTRIES
371,100

AUSTRALIA & NEW ZEALAND
185,500

FOREIGN WHITE STOCK BY COUNTRY OF ORIGIN IN 1940

- Czechoslovakia 2.8%
- Mexico 3.1%
- Hungary 1.9%
- Austria 3.6%
- Ireland 6.5%
- Russia 7.5%
- Norway, Sweden & Denmark 7.8%
- Poland 8.4%
- Canada 8.5%
- Italy 13.3%
- Great Britain & N. Ireland 9.3%
- Germany 15.1%
- Others 12.2%

26.4%

Foreign white stock includes all foreign born whites as well as those with one or both parents foreign born. In 1940 they constituted 26.4% of total population.

WHITE POPULATION BY NATIONALITY 1790

- Swedish .7%
- French 1.7%
- Others 6.6%
- Dutch 3.4%
- German 8.7%
- Irish 3.7%
- Ulster (Scotch & Irish) 6%
- Scotch 8.3%
- English 60.9%

© Copyright HAMMOND INCORPORATED, Maplewood, N.J.

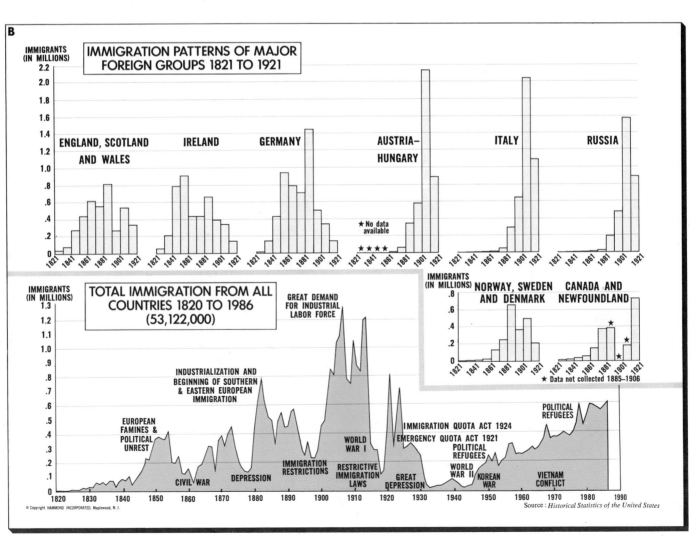

B

IMMIGRATION PATTERNS OF MAJOR FOREIGN GROUPS 1821 TO 1921

IMMIGRANTS (IN MILLIONS)

ENGLAND, SCOTLAND AND WALES

IRELAND

GERMANY

AUSTRIA–HUNGARY

★ No data available

ITALY

RUSSIA

TOTAL IMMIGRATION FROM ALL COUNTRIES 1820 TO 1986 (53,122,000)

IMMIGRANTS (IN MILLIONS)

GREAT DEMAND FOR INDUSTRIAL LABOR FORCE

INDUSTRIALIZATION AND BEGINNING OF SOUTHERN & EASTERN EUROPEAN IMMIGRATION

EUROPEAN FAMINES & POLITICAL UNREST

CIVIL WAR

DEPRESSION

IMMIGRATION RESTRICTIONS

RESTRICTIVE IMMIGRATION LAWS

WORLD WAR I

IMMIGRATION QUOTA ACT 1924

EMERGENCY QUOTA ACT 1921

POLITICAL REFUGEES

GREAT DEPRESSION

WORLD WAR II

KOREAN WAR

VIETNAM CONFLICT

POLITICAL REFUGEES

IMMIGRANTS (IN MILLIONS)

NORWAY, SWEDEN AND DENMARK

CANADA AND NEWFOUNDLAND

★ Data not collected 1885–1906

© Copyright HAMMOND INCORPORATED, Maplewood, N.J.

Source: *Historical Statistics of the United States*

DISTRIBUTION OF FOREIGN BORN IN UNITED STATES
1910

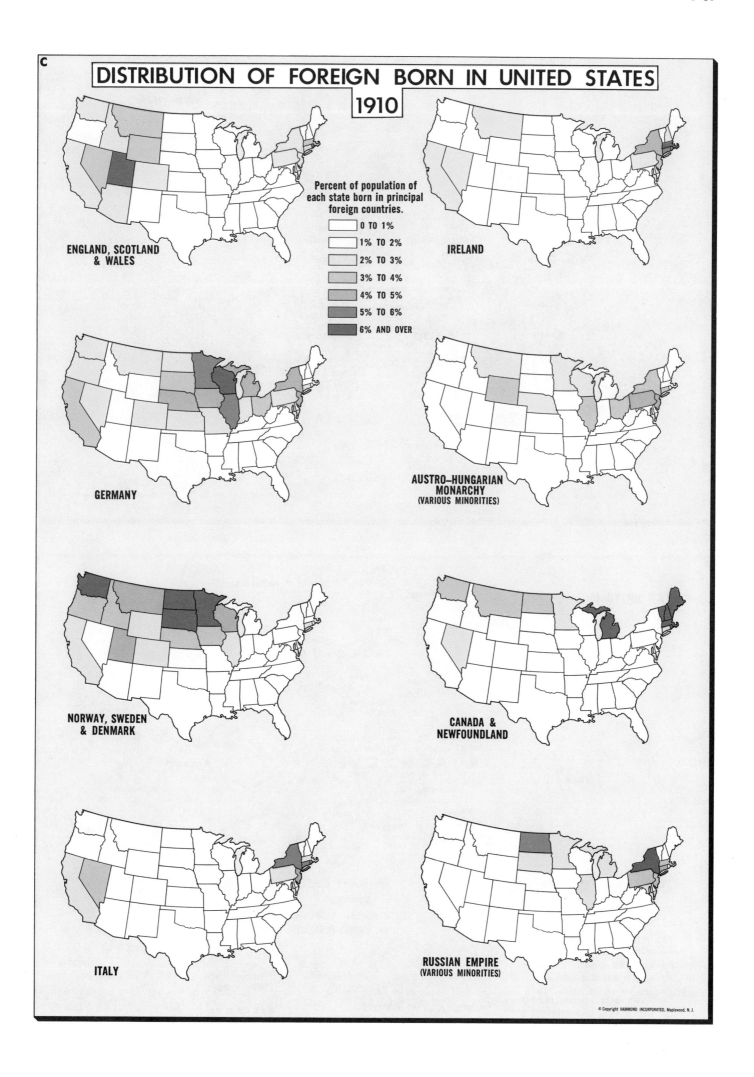

Percent of population of each state born in principal foreign countries.

- 0 TO 1%
- 1% TO 2%
- 2% TO 3%
- 3% TO 4%
- 4% TO 5%
- 5% TO 6%
- 6% AND OVER

ENGLAND, SCOTLAND & WALES

IRELAND

GERMANY

AUSTRO–HUNGARIAN MONARCHY (VARIOUS MINORITIES)

NORWAY, SWEDEN & DENMARK

CANADA & NEWFOUNDLAND

ITALY

RUSSIAN EMPIRE (VARIOUS MINORITIES)

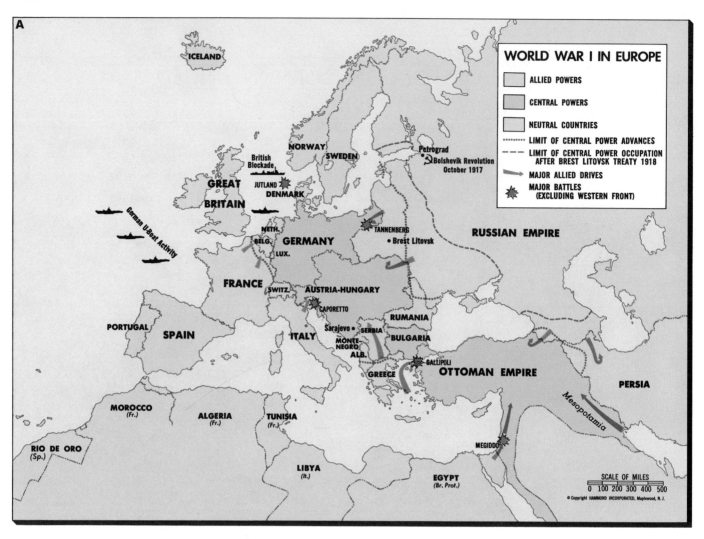

A

WORLD WAR I IN EUROPE

- ALLIED POWERS
- CENTRAL POWERS
- NEUTRAL COUNTRIES
- LIMIT OF CENTRAL POWER ADVANCES
- LIMIT OF CENTRAL POWER OCCUPATION AFTER BREST LITOVSK TREATY 1918
- MAJOR ALLIED DRIVES
- MAJOR BATTLES (EXCLUDING WESTERN FRONT)

ICELAND

NORWAY
SWEDEN

Petrograd
Bolshevik Revolution
October 1917

GREAT
BRITAIN

British
Blockade

JUTLAND
DENMARK

German U-Boat Activity

NETH.
BELG.
LUX.
GERMANY

Tannenberg
Brest Litovsk

RUSSIAN EMPIRE

FRANCE

SWITZ.
AUSTRIA-HUNGARY

CAPORETTO

PORTUGAL

SPAIN

ITALY

Sarajevo
SERBIA
MONTE-
NEGRO
ALB.

RUMANIA

BULGARIA

GREECE

GALLIPOLI

OTTOMAN EMPIRE

PERSIA

MOROCCO
(Fr.)

ALGERIA
(Fr.)

TUNISIA
(Fr.)

Mesopotamia

RIO DE ORO
(Sp.)

LIBYA
(It.)

EGYPT
(Br. Prot.)

MEGIDDO

SCALE OF MILES
0 100 200 300 400 500

© Copyright HAMMOND INCORPORATED, Maplewood, N.J.

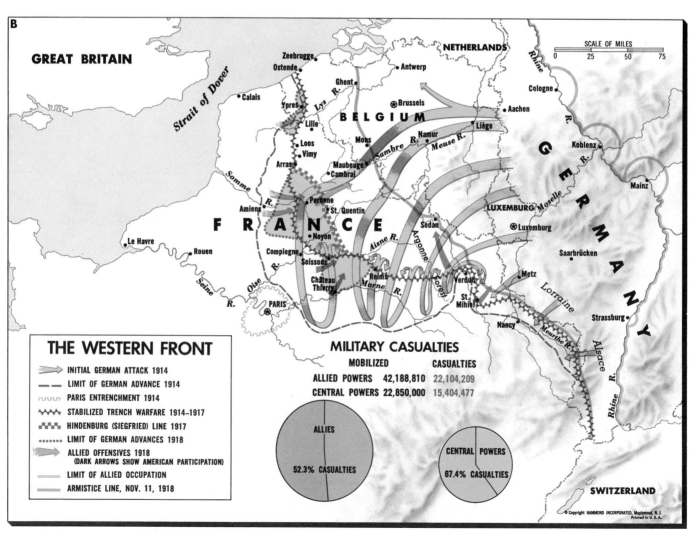

B

GREAT BRITAIN

NETHERLANDS

SCALE OF MILES
0   25   50   75

Strait of Dover

Zeebrugge
Ostende

Antwerp

Rhine R.

Ghent

Cologne

Calais

Ypres

Lys R.

Brussels

Aachen

Liège

GERMANY

Koblenz

R.

Lille

BELGIUM

Loos
Vimy

Mons

Namur

Sambre R.

Meuse R.

Mainz

Arras

Maubeuge
Cambrai

Somme
R.

Péronne
St. Quentin

LUXEMBURG

Moselle R.

Amiens

FRANCE

Noyon

Aisne R.

Sedan

Luxemburg

Saarbrücken

Le Havre

Rouen

Compiègne

Soissons

Oise
R.

Château
Thierry

Reims

Argonne Forest

Verdun

Metz

Lorraine

Strassburg

Seine
R.

PARIS

Marne R.

St.
Mihiel

Meurthe R.

Nancy

Alsace

Rhine R.

SWITZERLAND

THE WESTERN FRONT

- INITIAL GERMAN ATTACK 1914
- LIMIT OF GERMAN ADVANCE 1914
- PARIS ENTRENCHMENT 1914
- STABILIZED TRENCH WARFARE 1914–1917
- HINDENBURG (SIEGFRIED) LINE 1917
- LIMIT OF GERMAN ADVANCES 1918
- ALLIED OFFENSIVES 1918 (DARK ARROWS SHOW AMERICAN PARTICIPATION)
- LIMIT OF ALLIED OCCUPATION
- ARMISTICE LINE, NOV. 11, 1918

MILITARY CASUALTIES

	MOBILIZED	CASUALTIES
ALLIED POWERS	42,188,810	22,104,209
CENTRAL POWERS	22,850,000	15,404,477

ALLIES
52.3% CASUALTIES

CENTRAL POWERS
67.4% CASUALTIES

© Copyright HAMMOND INCORPORATED, Maplewood, N.J.
Printed in U.S.A.

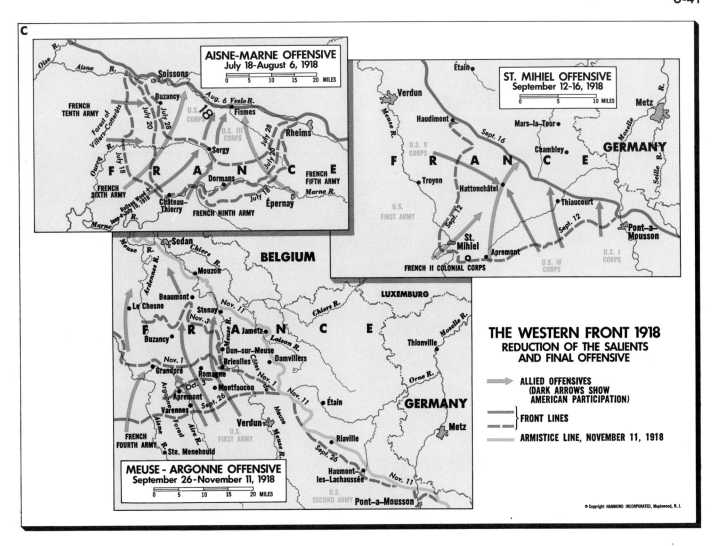

C

AISNE-MARNE OFFENSIVE
July 18-August 6, 1918
0   5   10   15   20 MILES

ST. MIHIEL OFFENSIVE
September 12-16, 1918
0   5   10 MILES

Oise R.
Aisne R.
Soissons
Buzancy
FRENCH TENTH ARMY
Forest of Villers-Cotterêts
July 20
July 28
Aug. 6 Vesle R.
Fismes
U.S. I CORPS
18
U.S. III CORPS
July 28
Rheims
Ourcq R.
July 18
F R A N C E
Sergy
July 20
FRENCH FIFTH ARMY
FRENCH SIXTH ARMY
Dormans
July 18
July 18
Château-Thierry
Belleau West + Imp. Area July 18, 1918
Épernay
Marne R.
FRENCH NINTH ARMY
Marne R.

Verdun
Étain
Haudimont
Mars-la-Tour
Sept. 16
Chambley
GERMANY
Metz
Meuse R.
U.S. V CORPS
F R A N C E
Troyon
Hattonchâtel
Thiaucourt
Moselle R.
Seille R.
U.S. FIRST ARMY
Sept. 12
Sept. 12
Sept. 12
St. Mihiel
Apremont
Pont-a-Mousson
FRENCH II COLONIAL CORPS
U.S. IV CORPS
U.S. I CORPS

Sedan
Chiers R.
Meuse R.
BELGIUM
Mouzon
Beaumont
LUXEMBURG
Le Chesne
Stenay
Nov. 11
Nov. 3
Chiers R.
F R A N C E
Jametz
Buzancy
Meuse R.
Loison R.
Thionville
Moselle R.
Dun-sur-Meuse
Damvillers
Grandpré
Brieulles
Côtes Nov. 1
GERMANY
Romagne
Nov. 1
Orne R.
Oct. 3
Montfaucon
Nov. 11
Apremont
Sept. 26
Étain
Varennes
Argonne Forest
Aire R.
Metz
FRENCH FOURTH ARMY
Verdun
Meuse R.
Aisne R.
U.S. FIRST ARMY
Riaville
Ste. Menehould
Sept. 26
Haumont-les-Lachaussée
Nov. 11
U.S. SECOND ARMY
Pont-a-Mousson

MEUSE - ARGONNE OFFENSIVE
September 26-November 11, 1918
0   5   10   15   20 MILES

THE WESTERN FRONT 1918
REDUCTION OF THE SALIENTS
AND FINAL OFFENSIVE

ALLIED OFFENSIVES
(DARK ARROWS SHOW
AMERICAN PARTICIPATION)

FRONT LINES

ARMISTICE LINE, NOVEMBER 11, 1918

© Copyright HAMMOND INCORPORATED, Maplewood, N.J.

D

EUROPE IN THE 1920'S
PURPLE BANDS INDICATE POST-WAR BOUNDARIES
NEW COUNTRIES ARE UNDERLINED

ICELAND
FINLAND
NORWAY
SWEDEN
ESTONIA
LATVIA
GREAT BRITAIN
EIRE
DENMARK
DANZIG
LITHUANIA
UNION OF SOVIET SOCIALIST REPUBLICS
RUSSIAN EMPIRE
NETH.
GERMANY
BELG.
LUX.
SAAR
POLAND
CZECHOSLOVAKIA
FRANCE
SWITZ.
AUSTRIA-HUNGARY
YUGOSLAVIA
RUMANIA
PORTUGAL
SPAIN
ITALY
SERBIA
MONTE-NEGRO
ALB.
BULGARIA
GREECE
TURKEY
OTTOMAN EMPIRE
PERSIA
SYRIA
(Fr. Mandate)
Mesopotamia
(Italian)
IRAQ
(Br. Mandate)
KUWAIT
(Br. Prot.)
(Neutral Zone)
PALESTINE
(Br. Mandate)
MOROCCO
(Fr.)
ALGERIA
(Fr.)
TUNISIA
(Fr.)
TRANS-JORDAN
(Br. Mandate)
SAUDI ARABIA
RIO DE ORO
(Sp.)
LIBYA
(It.)
EGYPT
(Br. Prot.)

SCALE OF MILES
0 100 200 300 400 500

© Copyright HAMMOND INCORPORATED, Maplewood, N.J.

A

THE GREAT DEPRESSION

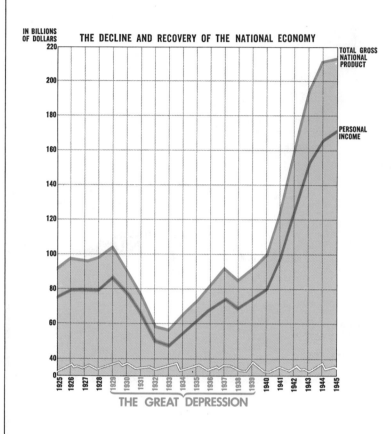

THE DECLINE AND RECOVERY OF THE NATIONAL ECONOMY

IN BILLIONS OF DOLLARS

TOTAL GROSS NATIONAL PRODUCT

PERSONAL INCOME

THE GREAT DEPRESSION

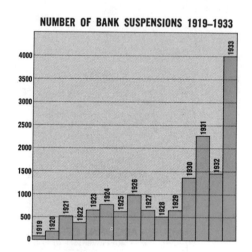

NUMBER OF BANK SUSPENSIONS 1919–1933

UNEMPLOYMENT

THE UNEMPLOYED AS A PERCENT OF THE CIVILIAN LABOR FORCE

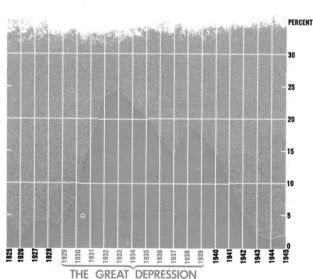

PERCENT

THE GREAT DEPRESSION

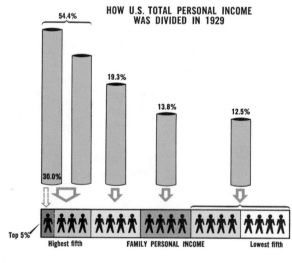

HOW U.S. TOTAL PERSONAL INCOME WAS DIVIDED IN 1929

54.4%

30.0%

19.3%

13.8%

12.5%

Top 5%

Highest fifth

FAMILY PERSONAL INCOME

Lowest fifth

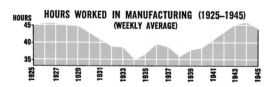

HOURS WORKED IN MANUFACTURING (1925–1945)
(WEEKLY AVERAGE)

HOURS

Source: *Historical Statistics of the United States*

B

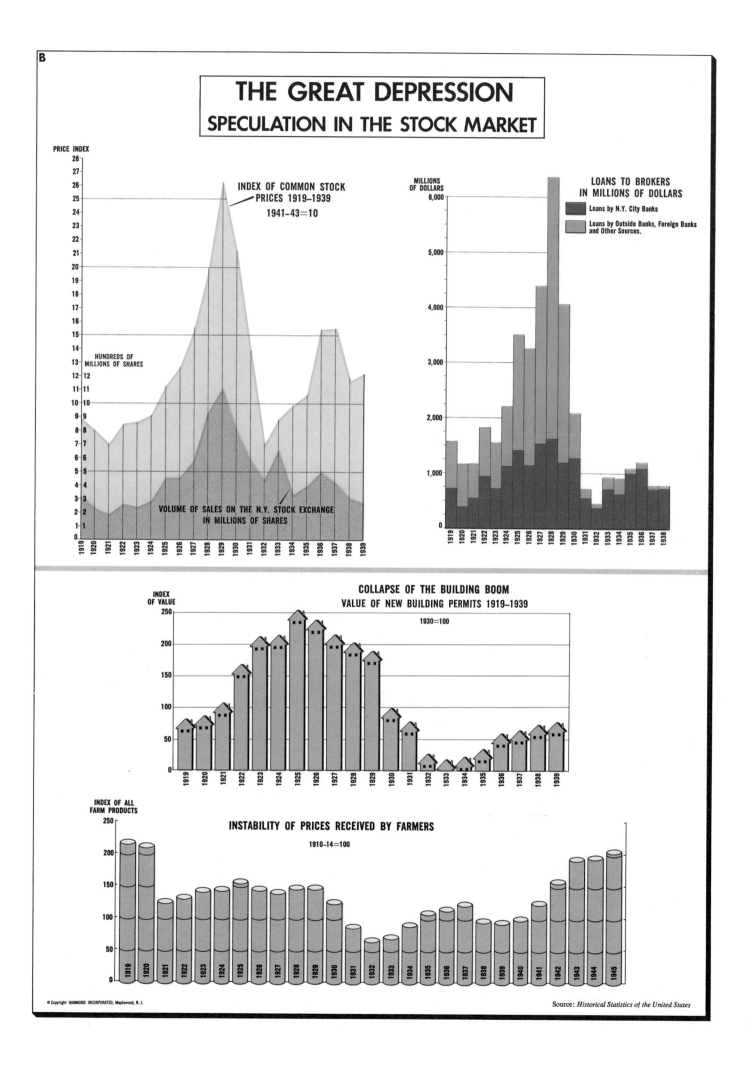

THE GREAT DEPRESSION
SPECULATION IN THE STOCK MARKET

PRICE INDEX

INDEX OF COMMON STOCK
PRICES 1919–1939

1941–43=10

HUNDREDS OF
MILLIONS OF SHARES

VOLUME OF SALES ON THE N.Y. STOCK EXCHANGE
IN MILLIONS OF SHARES

MILLIONS
OF DOLLARS

LOANS TO BROKERS
IN MILLIONS OF DOLLARS

■ Loans by N.Y. City Banks

Loans by Outside Banks, Foreign Banks
and Other Sources.

COLLAPSE OF THE BUILDING BOOM
VALUE OF NEW BUILDING PERMITS 1919–1939

INDEX
OF VALUE

1930=100

INDEX OF ALL
FARM PRODUCTS

INSTABILITY OF PRICES RECEIVED BY FARMERS

1910–14=100

Source: *Historical Statistics of the United States*

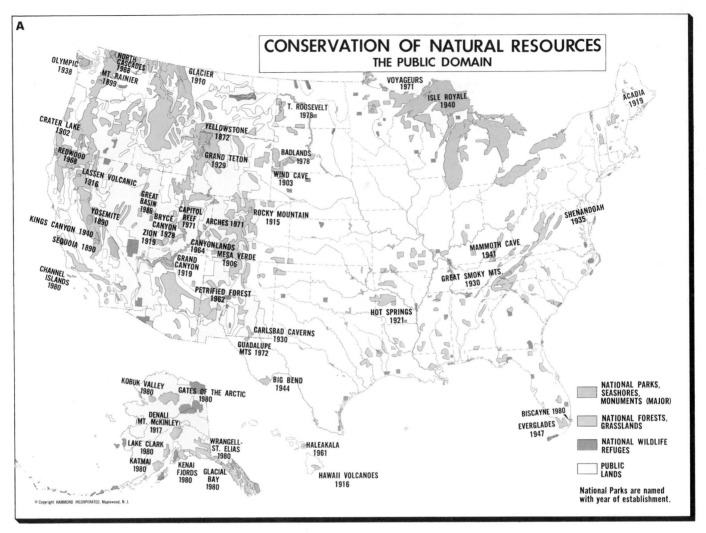

A

CONSERVATION OF NATURAL RESOURCES
THE PUBLIC DOMAIN

OLYMPIC 1938
NORTH CASCADES 1968
MT. RAINIER 1899
GLACIER 1910
VOYAGEURS 1971
ISLE ROYALE 1940
ACADIA 1919
T. ROOSEVELT 1978
CRATER LAKE 1902
YELLOWSTONE 1872
REDWOOD 1968
GRAND TETON 1929
BADLANDS 1978
LASSEN VOLCANIC 1916
WIND CAVE 1903
GREAT BASIN 1986
CAPITOL REEF 1971
BRYCE CANYON 1928
ROCKY MOUNTAIN 1915
SHENANDOAH 1935
YOSEMITE 1890
ZION 1919
ARCHES 1971
KINGS CANYON 1940
CANYONLANDS 1964
MESA VERDE 1906
MAMMOTH CAVE 1941
SEQUOIA 1890
GRAND CANYON 1919
GREAT SMOKY MTS 1930
CHANNEL ISLANDS 1980
PETRIFIED FOREST 1962
HOT SPRINGS 1921
CARLSBAD CAVERNS 1930
GUADALUPE MTS 1972
BIG BEND 1944
BISCAYNE 1980
KOBUK VALLEY 1980
GATES OF THE ARCTIC 1980
EVERGLADES 1947
DENALI (MT. McKINLEY) 1917
LAKE CLARK 1980
WRANGELL-ST. ELIAS 1980
HALEAKALA 1961
KATMAI 1980
KENAI FJORDS 1980
GLACIAL BAY 1980
HAWAII VOLCANOES 1916

NATIONAL PARKS, SEASHORES, MONUMENTS (MAJOR)
NATIONAL FORESTS, GRASSLANDS
NATIONAL WILDLIFE REFUGES
PUBLIC LANDS

National Parks are named with year of establishment.

© Copyright HAMMOND INCORPORATED, Maplewood, N.J.

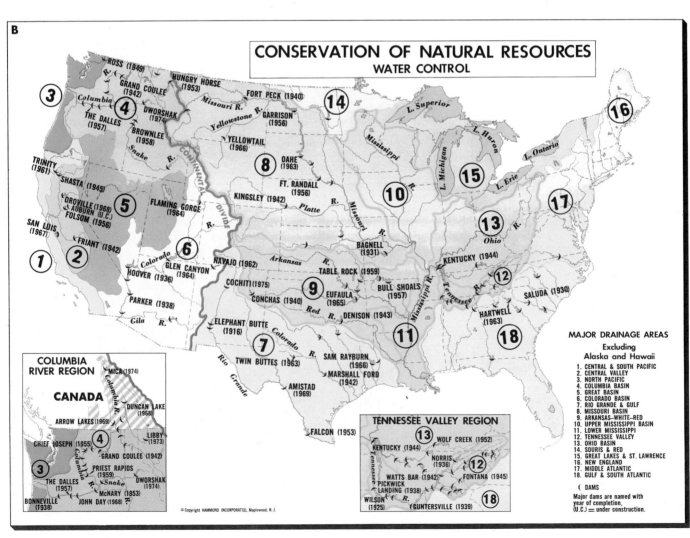

B

CONSERVATION OF NATURAL RESOURCES
WATER CONTROL

ROSS (1849)
HUNGRY HORSE (1953)
GRAND COULEE (1942)
FORT PECK (1940)
③ Columbia
④ DWORSHAK (1974)
THE DALLES (1957)
Missouri R.
GARRISON (1956)
Yellowstone R.
BROWNLEE (1958)
YELLOWTAIL (1966)
⑭
L. Superior
⑯
Snake R.
OAHE (1963)
⑧
Mississippi
L. Huron
TRINITY (1961)
CONTINENTAL DIVIDE
FT. RANDALL (1956)
L. Michigan
L. Ontario
⑮
SHASTA (1945)
KINGSLEY (1942)
Platte R.
Missouri R.
L. Erie
OROVILLE (1968)
⑤
FLAMING GORGE (1964)
⑩
⑰
AUBURN (U.C.)
FOLSOM (1956)
⑬
Ohio R.
SAN LUIS (1967)
R.
BAGNELL (1931)
FRIANT (1942)
⑥
Colorado
NAVAJO (1962)
Arkansas R.
KENTUCKY (1944)
① ②
GLEN CANYON (1964)
TABLE ROCK (1959)
⑫
Tennessee R.
HOOVER (1936)
COCHITI (1975)
BULL SHOALS (1957)
SALUDA (1930)
PARKER (1938)
CONCHAS (1940)
⑨ EUFAULA (1965)
Mississippi R.
HARTWELL (1963)
Gila R.
ELEPHANT BUTTE (1916)
Red R.
DENISON (1943)
⑱
Colorado R.
⑪
⑦
SAM RAYBURN (1966)
TWIN BUTTES (1963)
MARSHALL FORD (1942)
Rio Grande
AMISTAD (1969)
FALCON (1953)

COLUMBIA RIVER REGION
MICA (1974)
CANADA
Columbia R.
DUNCAN LAKE (1968)
ARROW LAKES (1969)
④
LIBBY (1973)
CHIEF JOSEPH (1955)
GRAND COULEE (1942)
PRIEST RAPIDS (1959)
Snake
③
THE DALLES (1957)
DWORSHAK (1974)
McNARY (1953)
BONNEVILLE (1938)
JOHN DAY (1968)

© Copyright HAMMOND INCORPORATED, Maplewood, N.J.

TENNESSEE VALLEY REGION
⑬ WOLF CREEK (1952)
KENTUCKY (1944)
Tennessee
NORRIS (1936)
⑫
WATTS BAR (1942)
FONTANA (1945)
PICKWICK LANDING (1938)
WILSON (1925)
R.
GUNTERSVILLE (1939)
⑱

MAJOR DRAINAGE AREAS
Excluding
Alaska and Hawaii

1. CENTRAL & SOUTH PACIFIC
2. CENTRAL VALLEY
3. NORTH PACIFIC
4. COLUMBIA BASIN
5. GREAT BASIN
6. COLORADO BASIN
7. RIO GRANDE & GULF
8. MISSOURI BASIN
9. ARKANSAS–WHITE–RED
10. UPPER MISSISSIPPI BASIN
11. LOWER MISSISSIPPI
12. TENNESSEE VALLEY
13. OHIO BASIN
14. SOURIS & RED
15. GREAT LAKES & ST. LAWRENCE
16. NEW ENGLAND
17. MIDDLE ATLANTIC
18. GULF & SOUTH ATLANTIC

(DAMS

Major dams are named with year of completion,
(U.C.) = under construction.

C

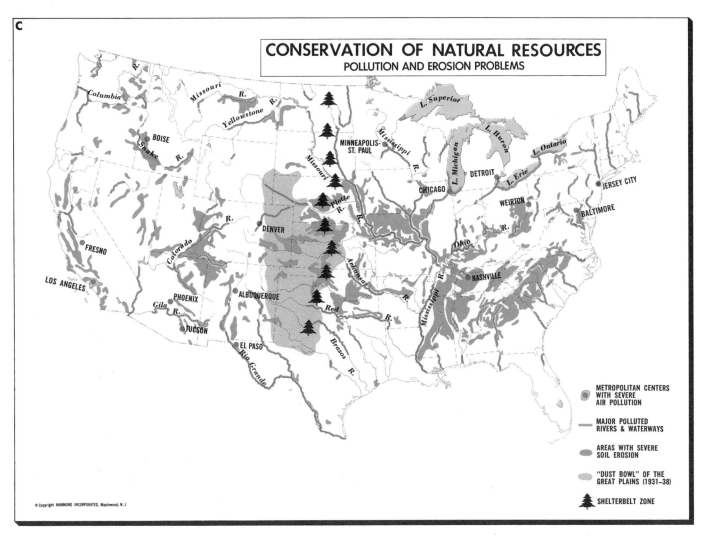

CONSERVATION OF NATURAL RESOURCES
POLLUTION AND EROSION PROBLEMS

METROPOLITAN CENTERS WITH SEVERE AIR POLLUTION

MAJOR POLLUTED RIVERS & WATERWAYS

AREAS WITH SEVERE SOIL EROSION

"DUST BOWL" OF THE GREAT PLAINS (1931–38)

SHELTERBELT ZONE

© Copyright HAMMOND INCORPORATED, Maplewood, N.J.

D

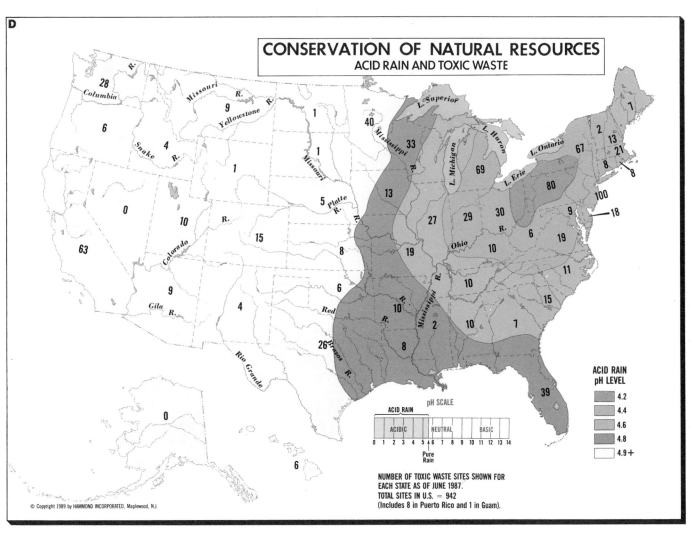

CONSERVATION OF NATURAL RESOURCES
ACID RAIN AND TOXIC WASTE

ACID RAIN pH LEVEL

4.2
4.4
4.6
4.8
4.9+

pH SCALE

ACID RAIN

| ACIDIC | NEUTRAL | BASIC |

0 1 2 3 4 5 6 7 8 9 10 11 12 13 14

Pure Rain

NUMBER OF TOXIC WASTE SITES SHOWN FOR EACH STATE AS OF JUNE 1987.
TOTAL SITES IN U.S. = 942
(Includes 8 in Puerto Rico and 1 in Guam).

© Copyright 1989 by HAMMOND INCORPORATED, Maplewood, N.J.

A

GERMAN EXPANSION 1935-1939*

SCALE OF MILES

0 100 200 300 400

▨ Germany 1933

▦ Area gained by Plebiscite 1935

▥ Areas annexed 1938

▤ Area annexed 1939

☐ German Protectorates

*To Invasion of Poland Sept. 1, 1939

© Copyright HAMMOND INCORPORATED, Maplewood, N. J.

NORWAY

SWEDEN

FINLAND

UNITED KINGDOM

GREAT BRITAIN

NO. IRELAND

IRELAND

NORTH SEA

DENMARK

ESTONIA

LATVIA

LITHUANIA

MEMEL To Germany 1939

DANZIG

BALTIC SEA

East Prussia

UNION OF SOVIET SOCIALIST REPUBLICS

ATLANTIC OCEAN

NETHERLANDS

BELGIUM

LUX.

Rhineland

Saar

Rhineland remilitarized 1936

Berlin ⊛

GERMANY

SAAR To Germany 1935

SUDETENLAND To Germany 1938

Munich ●

Sudeten Area

BOHEMIA & MORAVIA

CZECHOSLOVAKIA

SLOVAKIA

(To Hung. 1939)

BOHEMIA & MORAVIA German Protectorate and occupation 1939

Polish Corridor

POLAND

FRANCE

SWITZ.

AUSTRIA

AUSTRIA To Germany 1938

HUNGARY

SLOVAKIA German Protectorate 1939

RUMANIA

ITALY

ADRIATIC SEA

YUGOSLAVIA

Danube

R.

BLACK SEA

SPAIN

Civil War 1936-1939

PORTUGAL

MEDITERRANEAN SEA

BULGARIA

ALBANIA (To Italy 1939)

GREECE

TURKEY

B

WORLD WAR II 1939-1940*

SCALE OF MILES

0 100 200 300 400

▨ Germany and Slovakia

☐ Allied Nations

☐ Neutral Nations

▥ Areas occupied by Germany

▥ Areas occupied by U.S.S.R.

⇨ German Advances

⇨ British Advances

⇨ Russian Advances

*To July 1, 1940

International Boundaries Sept. 1, 1939

© Copyright HAMMOND INCORPORATED, Maplewood, N. J.

NORWAY

SWEDEN

FINLAND

RUSSO-FINNISH WAR 1939-1940

U.

UNITED KINGDOM

GREAT BRITAIN

NO. IRELAND

IRELAND

NORTH SEA

German invasion of Norway and Denmark April 9, 1940

DENMARK

ESTONIA

Estonia, Latvia and Lithuania annexed by U.S.S.R. 1940

S.

LATVIA

LITHUANIA

BALTIC SEA

DANZIG

East Prussia

S.

London ⊛

German invasion of Low Countries May 10, 1940

NETHERLANDS

BELGIUM

Dunkirk ●

LUX.

Berlin ⊛

GERMANY

Warsaw ⊛

POLAND

U.S.S.R. invasion of Poland September 17, 1939

R.

ATLANTIC OCEAN

Battle of France May-June 1940

● Paris

MAGINOT LINE

German invasion of Poland September 1, 1939 Start of World War II

Bessarabia and northern Bukovina annexed by U.S.S.R. 1940

Vichy Government established July 1940

FRANCE

SWITZ.

Austria

SLOVAKIA

HUNGARY

Partition of Poland September 27, 1939

Bessarabia

● Vichy

ITALY

RUMANIA

Italy declares war on Great Britain and France June 1940

YUGOSLAVIA

Danube

R.

BLACK SEA

SPAIN

PORTUGAL

MEDITERRANEAN SEA

ADRIATIC SEA

BULGARIA

ALBANIA (Italy)

GREECE

TURKEY

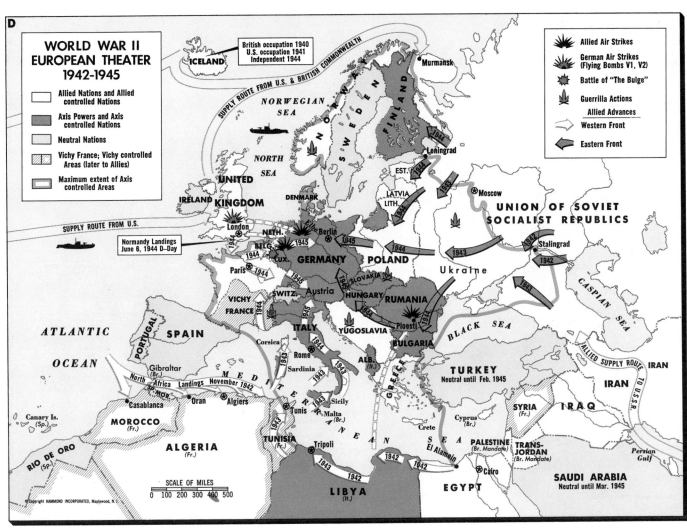

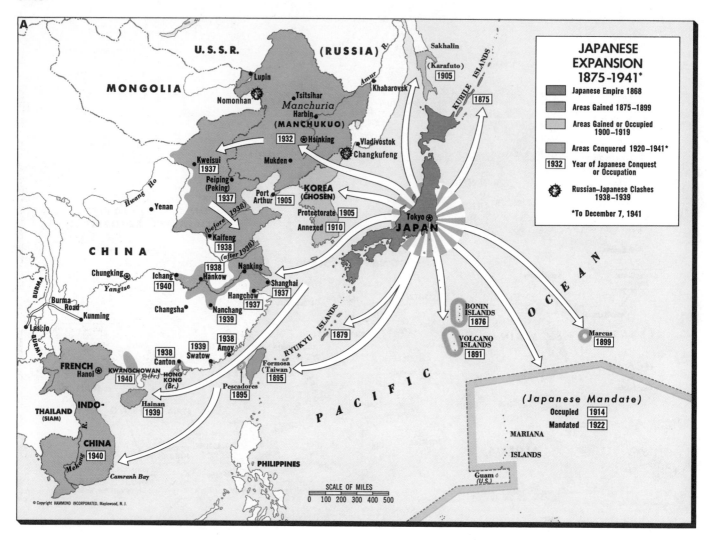

A

JAPANESE
EXPANSION
1875-1941*

Japanese Empire 1868
Areas Gained 1875-1899
Areas Gained or Occupied 1900-1919
Areas Conquered 1920-1941*
1932 Year of Japanese Conquest or Occupation
Russian-Japanese Clashes 1938-1939

*To December 7, 1941

U.S.S.R. (RUSSIA)

MONGOLIA

Sakhalin
(Karafuto) 1905
KURILE ISLANDS
1875

Lupin
Nomonhan
Tsitsihar
Manchuria
Harbin
(MANCHUKUO)
1932 Hsinking
Khabarovsk
Amur R.

Kweisui 1937
Peiping (Peking) 1937
Mukden
Vladivostok
Changkufeng
Port Arthur 1905
KOREA (CHOSEN)
Protectorate 1905
Annexed 1910

Yenan
(before 1938)
Kaifeng 1938
(after 1938)

CHINA

Chungking
Ichang 1940
Hankow 1938
Nanking 1937
Shanghai 1937
Hangchow 1937
Changsha
Nanchang 1939
Amoy 1938
Canton 1938
Swatow 1939

BURMA
Burma Road
Lashio
Kunming

FRENCH
Hanoi
KWANGCHOWAN (Fr.) 1940
HONG KONG (Br.)
Hainan 1939
Pescadores 1895
Formosa (Taiwan) 1895
RYUKYU ISLANDS 1879

THAILAND (SIAM)
INDO-CHINA 1940
Camranh Bay
Mekong R.

Tokyo
JAPAN

BONIN ISLANDS 1876
VOLCANO ISLANDS 1891
Marcus 1899

PACIFIC OCEAN

PHILIPPINES

(Japanese Mandate)
Occupied 1914
Mandated 1922
MARIANA ISLANDS
Guam (U.S.)

SCALE OF MILES
0 100 200 300 400 500

© Copyright HAMMOND INCORPORATED, Maplewood, N.J.

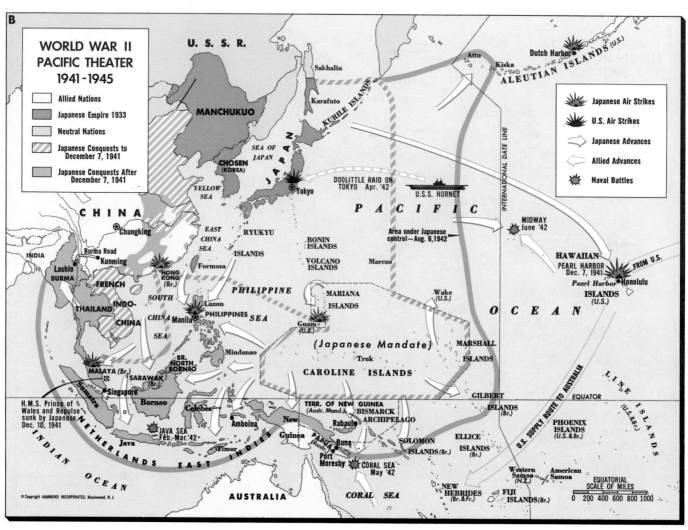

B

WORLD WAR II
PACIFIC THEATER
1941-1945

Allied Nations
Japanese Empire 1933
Neutral Nations
Japanese Conquests to December 7, 1941
Japanese Conquests After December 7, 1941

Japanese Air Strikes
U.S. Air Strikes
Japanese Advances
Allied Advances
Naval Battles

U.S.S.R.

Sakhalin
Karafuto
KURILE ISLANDS

Attu
Kiska
Dutch Harbor (U.S.)
ALEUTIAN ISLANDS (U.S.)

MANCHUKUO

CHOSEN (KOREA)

SEA OF JAPAN

JAPAN

Tokyo

DOOLITTLE RAID ON TOKYO Apr. '42
U.S.S. HORNET

INTERNATIONAL DATE LINE

PACIFIC OCEAN

CHINA

Chungking

INDIA

Burma Road
Kunming
Lashio
BURMA

FRENCH
THAILAND
INDO-CHINA

YELLOW SEA

EAST CHINA SEA

RYUKYU ISLANDS

Formosa

HONG KONG (Br.)
SOUTH CHINA SEA
Luzon
Manila
PHILIPPINES

PHILIPPINE SEA

BONIN ISLANDS
VOLCANO ISLANDS
Marcus

Area under Japanese control—Aug. 6, 1942

MIDWAY June '42

HAWAIIAN
PEARL HARBOR Dec. 7, 1941
Pearl Harbor
Honolulu
ISLANDS (U.S.)
FROM U.S.

MARIANA ISLANDS
Guam (U.S.)
Wake (U.S.)

MARSHALL ISLANDS

Mindanao
BR. NORTH BORNEO
SARAWAK (Br.)
MALAYA (Br.)
Singapore
Borneo

CAROLINE ISLANDS
Truk

H.M.S. Prince of Wales and Repulse sunk by Japanese, Dec. 10, 1941

Sumatra

NETHERLANDS EAST INDIES

Java
JAVA SEA Feb.-Mar. '42
Celebes
Amboina
Timor

TERR. OF NEW GUINEA (Austr. Mand.)
New Guinea
PAPUA (Austr.)
Port Moresby
Buna

BISMARCK ARCHIPELAGO
Rabaul

SOLOMON ISLANDS (Br.)

CORAL SEA May '42

(Japanese Mandate)

GILBERT ISLANDS (Br.)

ELLICE ISLANDS (Br.)

U.S. SUPPLY ROUTE TO AUSTRALIA
EQUATOR

LINE ISLANDS (U.S. & Br.)

PHOENIX ISLANDS (U.S. & Br.)

Western Samoa (N.Z.)
American Samoa

NEW HEBRIDES (Br. & Fr.)
FIJI ISLANDS (Br.)

INDIAN OCEAN

AUSTRALIA

CORAL SEA

EQUATORIAL SCALE OF MILES
0 200 400 600 800 1000

© Copyright HAMMOND INCORPORATED, Maplewood, N.J.

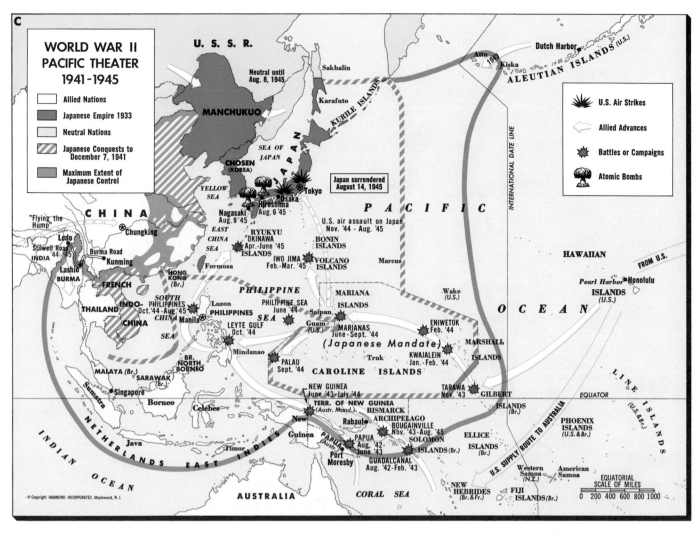

WORLD WAR II PACIFIC THEATER
1941-1945

- Allied Nations
- Japanese Empire 1933
- Neutral Nations
- Japanese Conquests to December 7, 1941
- Maximum Extent of Japanese Control

- U.S. Air Strikes
- Allied Advances
- Battles or Campaigns
- Atomic Bombs

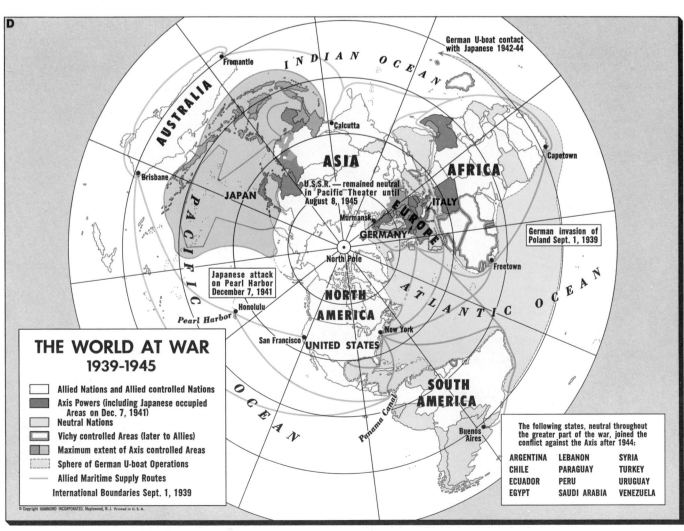

THE WORLD AT WAR
1939-1945

- Allied Nations and Allied controlled Nations
- Axis Powers (including Japanese occupied Areas on Dec. 7, 1941)
- Neutral Nations
- Vichy controlled Areas (later to Allies)
- Maximum extent of Axis controlled Areas
- Sphere of German U-boat Operations
- Allied Maritime Supply Routes
- International Boundaries Sept. 1, 1939

The following states, neutral throughout the greater part of the war, joined the conflict against the Axis after 1944:

ARGENTINA	LEBANON	SYRIA
CHILE	PARAGUAY	TURKEY
ECUADOR	PERU	URUGUAY
EGYPT	SAUDI ARABIA	VENEZUELA

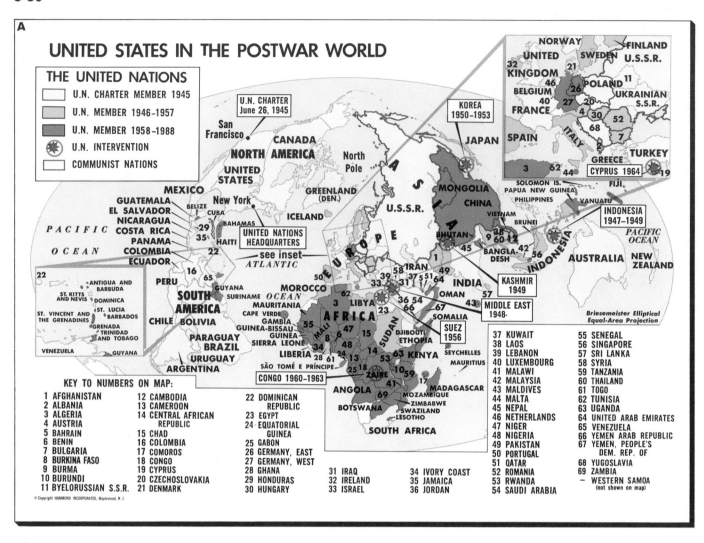

A

UNITED STATES IN THE POSTWAR WORLD

THE UNITED NATIONS

- U.N. CHARTER MEMBER 1945
- U.N. MEMBER 1946–1957
- U.N. MEMBER 1958–1988
- ✳ U.N. INTERVENTION
- COMMUNIST NATIONS

U.N. CHARTER June 26, 1945

San Francisco

NORTH AMERICA

UNITED STATES

MEXICO
GUATEMALA
EL SALVADOR
NICARAGUA
COSTA RICA
PANAMA
COLOMBIA
ECUADOR

BELIZE
CUBA
BAHAMAS
HAITI

New York
GREENLAND (DEN.)
ICELAND

UNITED NATIONS HEADQUARTERS
see inset

North Pole

CANADA

KOREA 1950–1953
JAPAN

NORWAY   SWEDEN   FINLAND
UNITED KINGDOM   U.S.S.R.
32   21
46   POLAND   11
BELGIUM   26   UKRAINIAN S.S.R.
40   27   20
FRANCE   4   30   52
68
7
SPAIN   ITALY
3   62   GREECE   TURKEY
44   CYPRUS 1964   19

MONGOLIA
CHINA

ASIA

U.S.S.R.

EUROPE

ATLANTIC
OCEAN

PACIFIC OCEAN

29
35
22

16   65

PERU

SOUTH AMERICA

GUYANA
SURINAME
CHILE   BOLIVIA

MOROCCO
MAURITANIA
CAPE VERDE
GAMBIA
GUINEA-BISSAU
GUINEA
SIERRA LEONE
LIBERIA

50

62
3   LIBYA
23
MALI
55   6   47   48
8   15   SUDAN
34   24   14
28   61   13   53
25   18   41
CONGO 1960–1963

39
58   IRAN   49
33   31   37   51   64
36   54   66   67   OMAN   57
23   DJIBOUTI
ETHIOPIA   SOMALIA
SUEZ 1956
KENYA   SEYCHELLES
10   59   MAURITIUS
17

INDIA

KASHMIR 1949

MIDDLE EAST 1948-

BHUTAN
38
9   60   12
45   42
BANGLA-DESH   56

BRUNEI
VIETNAM

SOLOMON IS.
PAPUA NEW GUINEA
PHILIPPINES   FIJI
VANUATU
INDONESIA 1947–1949

AUSTRALIA   NEW ZEALAND

PACIFIC OCEAN

Briesemeister Elliptical Equal-Area Projection

22

ST. KITTS AND NEVIS
ST. VINCENT AND THE GRENADINES
VENEZUELA

ANTIGUA AND BARBUDA
DOMINICA
ST. LUCIA
BARBADOS
GRENADA
TRINIDAD AND TOBAGO
GUYANA

PARAGUAY
BRAZIL
URUGUAY
ARGENTINA

SÃO TOMÉ E PRÍNCIPE
ANGOLA
BOTSWANA

ZAIRE
69   ZAMBIA
MOZAMBIQUE
ZIMBABWE
SWAZILAND
LESOTHO

MADAGASCAR

SOUTH AFRICA

KEY TO NUMBERS ON MAP:

1 AFGHANISTAN	12 CAMBODIA	22 DOMINICAN REPUBLIC	
2 ALBANIA	13 CAMEROON	23 EGYPT	
3 ALGERIA	14 CENTRAL AFRICAN REPUBLIC	24 EQUATORIAL GUINEA	
4 AUSTRIA	15 CHAD	25 GABON	
5 BAHRAIN	16 COLOMBIA	26 GERMANY, EAST	
6 BENIN	17 COMOROS	27 GERMANY, WEST	
7 BULGARIA	18 CONGO	28 GHANA	
8 BURKINA FASO	19 CYPRUS	29 HONDURAS	
9 BURMA	20 CZECHOSLOVAKIA	30 HUNGARY	
10 BURUNDI	21 DENMARK		
11 BYELORUSSIAN S.S.R.			

31 IRAQ	34 IVORY COAST
32 IRELAND	35 JAMAICA
33 ISRAEL	36 JORDAN

37 KUWAIT	55 SENEGAL
38 LAOS	56 SINGAPORE
39 LEBANON	57 SRI LANKA
40 LUXEMBOURG	58 SYRIA
41 MALAWI	59 TANZANIA
42 MALAYSIA	60 THAILAND
43 MALDIVES	61 TOGO
44 MALTA	62 TUNISIA
45 NEPAL	63 UGANDA
46 NETHERLANDS	64 UNITED ARAB EMIRATES
47 NIGER	65 VENEZUELA
48 NIGERIA	66 YEMEN ARAB REPUBLIC
49 PAKISTAN	67 YEMEN, PEOPLE'S DEM. REP. OF
50 PORTUGAL	68 YUGOSLAVIA
51 QATAR	69 ZAMBIA
52 ROMANIA	– WESTERN SAMOA (not shown on map)
53 RWANDA	
54 SAUDI ARABIA	

© Copyright HAMMOND INCORPORATED, Maplewood, N.J.

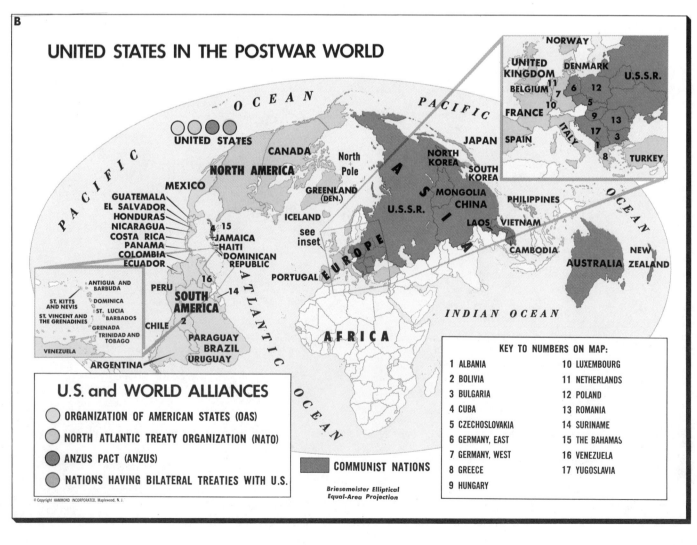

B

UNITED STATES IN THE POSTWAR WORLD

OCEAN

PACIFIC

○ ○ ○ ●
UNITED STATES

CANADA

NORTH AMERICA

North Pole
GREENLAND (DEN.)
ICELAND
see inset

PACIFIC

JAPAN

NORTH KOREA
SOUTH KOREA

ASIA

MONGOLIA
CHINA

U.S.S.R.

LAOS
VIETNAM

PHILIPPINES

MEXICO
GUATEMALA
EL SALVADOR
HONDURAS
NICARAGUA
COSTA RICA
PANAMA
COLOMBIA
ECUADOR

4   15
JAMAICA
HAITI
DOMINICAN REPUBLIC

PORTUGAL

EUROPE

NORWAY
UNITED KINGDOM   DENMARK
11   6   12   U.S.S.R.
BELGIUM   7
10   5
FRANCE   9   13
17   3
SPAIN   ITALY   1   8
TURKEY

CAMBODIA

AUSTRALIA   NEW ZEALAND

16
PERU   14

SOUTH AMERICA

AFRICA

INDIAN OCEAN

ATLANTIC

OCEAN

ANTIGUA AND BARBUDA
ST. KITTS AND NEVIS
DOMINICA
ST. LUCIA
ST. VINCENT AND THE GRENADINES   BARBADOS
GRENADA
TRINIDAD AND TOBAGO
VENEZUELA

CHILE   2

PARAGUAY
BRAZIL
URUGUAY
ARGENTINA

U.S. and WORLD ALLIANCES

- ○ ORGANIZATION OF AMERICAN STATES (OAS)
- ◐ NORTH ATLANTIC TREATY ORGANIZATION (NATO)
- ● ANZUS PACT (ANZUS)
- ◔ NATIONS HAVING BILATERAL TREATIES WITH U.S.

© Copyright HAMMOND INCORPORATED, Maplewood, N.J.

COMMUNIST NATIONS

Briesemeister Elliptical Equal-Area Projection

KEY TO NUMBERS ON MAP:

1 ALBANIA	10 LUXEMBOURG
2 BOLIVIA	11 NETHERLANDS
3 BULGARIA	12 POLAND
4 CUBA	13 ROMANIA
5 CZECHOSLOVAKIA	14 SURINAME
6 GERMANY, EAST	15 THE BAHAMAS
7 GERMANY, WEST	16 VENEZUELA
8 GREECE	17 YUGOSLAVIA
9 HUNGARY	

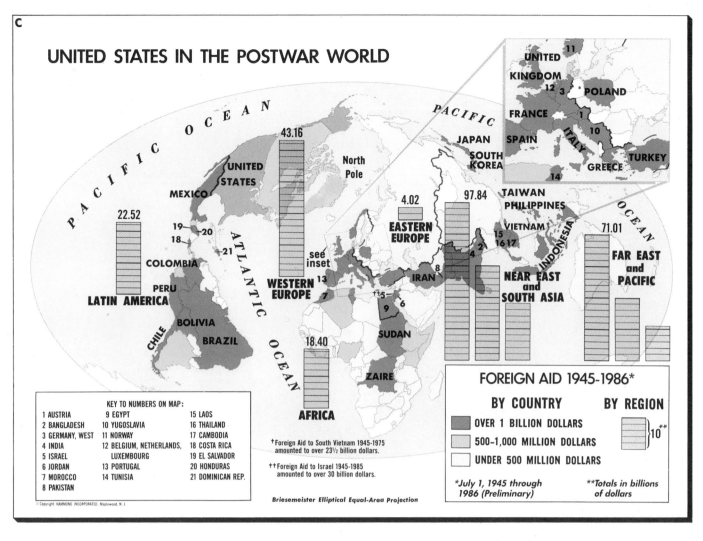

UNITED STATES IN THE POSTWAR WORLD

PACIFIC OCEAN

UNITED KINGDOM 11
12 3 POLAND
FRANCE 1
SPAIN 10 ITALY
14 GREECE TURKEY

North Pole

JAPAN
SOUTH KOREA

43.16

UNITED STATES

MEXICO

22.52

19 20
18
21

COLOMBIA

PERU

LATIN AMERICA

CHILE BOLIVIA BRAZIL

see inset

4.02

EASTERN EUROPE

WESTERN EUROPE

13
7

††5
9 6

IRAN 8

97.84

TAIWAN
PHILIPPINES
VIETNAM
15 1
16 17
4 2

NEAR EAST and SOUTH ASIA

INDONESIA

71.01

FAR EAST and PACIFIC

18.40

SUDAN

ZAIRE

AFRICA

†Foreign Aid to South Vietnam 1945-1975 amounted to over 23½ billion dollars.

††Foreign Aid to Israel 1945-1985 amounted to over 30 billion dollars.

KEY TO NUMBERS ON MAP:

1 AUSTRIA	9 EGYPT	15 LAOS
2 BANGLADESH	10 YUGOSLAVIA	16 THAILAND
3 GERMANY, WEST	11 NORWAY	17 CAMBODIA
4 INDIA	12 BELGIUM, NETHERLANDS,	18 COSTA RICA
5 ISRAEL	LUXEMBOURG	19 EL SALVADOR
6 JORDAN	13 PORTUGAL	20 HONDURAS
7 MOROCCO	14 TUNISIA	21 DOMINICAN REP.
8 PAKISTAN		

© Copyright HAMMOND INCORPORATED, Maplewood, N.J.

Briesemeister Elliptical Equal-Area Projection

FOREIGN AID 1945-1986*

BY COUNTRY   BY REGION

☐ OVER 1 BILLION DOLLARS
☐ 500-1,000 MILLION DOLLARS
☐ UNDER 500 MILLION DOLLARS

}10**

*July 1, 1945 through 1986 (Preliminary)

**Totals in billions of dollars

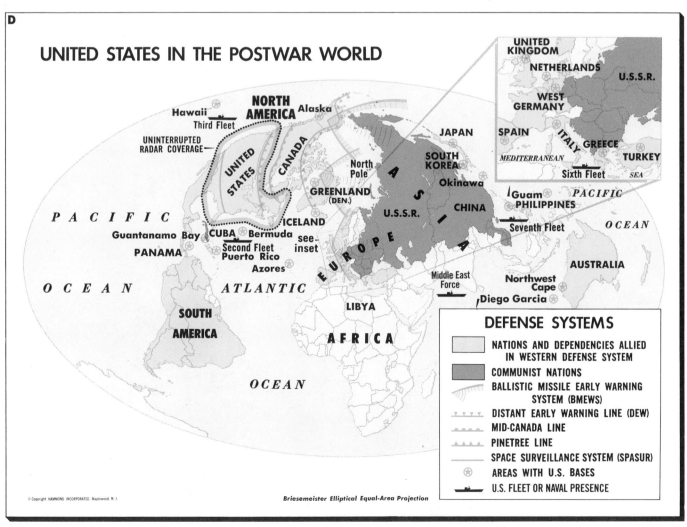

UNITED STATES IN THE POSTWAR WORLD

UNITED KINGDOM
NETHERLANDS
WEST GERMANY
SPAIN ITALY GREECE
MEDITERRANEAN
Sixth Fleet
U.S.S.R.
TURKEY
SEA

Hawaii
NORTH AMERICA Alaska
Third Fleet

UNINTERRUPTED RADAR COVERAGE

UNITED STATES
CANADA

North Pole

GREENLAND (DEN.)

ICELAND

JAPAN

SOUTH KOREA
Okinawa

A S I A

U.S.S.R.
CHINA

Guantanamo Bay
CUBA Bermuda
PANAMA
Second Fleet
Puerto Rico
Azores

see inset

EUROPE

Guam PHILIPPINES
Seventh Fleet

PACIFIC OCEAN

PACIFIC OCEAN

SOUTH AMERICA

ATLANTIC

OCEAN

LIBYA

AFRICA

Middle East Force

Northwest Cape
Diego Garcia

AUSTRALIA

DEFENSE SYSTEMS

☐ NATIONS AND DEPENDENCIES ALLIED IN WESTERN DEFENSE SYSTEM
☐ COMMUNIST NATIONS
〰 BALLISTIC MISSILE EARLY WARNING SYSTEM (BMEWS)
〰 DISTANT EARLY WARNING LINE (DEW)
〰 MID-CANADA LINE
〰 PINETREE LINE
— SPACE SURVEILLANCE SYSTEM (SPASUR)
⊛ AREAS WITH U.S. BASES
▬ U.S. FLEET OR NAVAL PRESENCE

© Copyright HAMMOND INCORPORATED, Maplewood, N.J.

Briesemeister Elliptical Equal-Area Projection

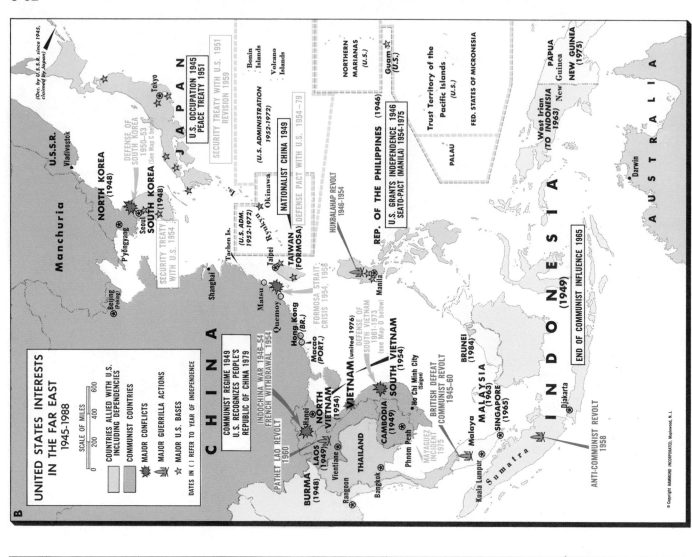

B

UNITED STATES INTERESTS IN THE FAR EAST 1945-1988

SCALE OF MILES
0 200 400 600

COUNTRIES ALLIED WITH U.S. INCLUDING DEPENDENCIES
COMMUNIST COUNTRIES
⊛ MAJOR CONFLICTS
⚔ MAJOR GUERRILLA ACTIONS
☆ MAJOR U.S. BASES

DATES IN ( ) REFER TO YEAR OF INDEPENDENCE

COMMUNIST REGIME 1949
U.S. RECOGNIZES PEOPLE'S REPUBLIC OF CHINA 1979

(Occ. by U.S.S.R. since 1945, claimed by Japan)

JAPAN
Tokyo ☆
U.S. OCCUPATION 1945 PEACE TREATY 1951
SECURITY TREATY WITH U.S. 1951 REVISION 1959

Bonin Islands
Volcano Islands

NORTHERN MARIANAS (U.S.)
Guam ☆ (U.S.)

Trust Territory of the Pacific Islands (U.S.)
FED. STATES OF MICRONESIA
PALAU

U.S.S.R.
Vladivostok •

Manchuria

NORTH KOREA (1948)
P'yŏngyang ⊛
DEFENSE OF SOUTH KOREA 1950-53 (See Map C below)
Seoul ⊛ SOUTH KOREA ☆ (1948)
SECURITY TREATY WITH U.S. 1954

Beijing (Peking) ⊛

Shanghai •

C H I N A

NATIONALIST CHINA 1949
(U.S. ADMINISTRATION 1952-1972)
Okinawa
Ryukyu
(U.S. ADM. 1952-1972)
Tachen Is.
Taipei ☆
TAIWAN (FORMOSA)
DEFENSE PACT WITH U.S. 1954-79
Matsu ○
Quemoy ☆
FORMOSA STRAIT CRISIS 1954, 1958

HUKBALAHAP REVOLT 1946-1954
REP. OF THE PHILIPPINES (1946)
U.S. GRANTS INDEPENDENCE 1946
SEATO-PACT (MANILA) 1954-1975
Manila ⚔ ☆

INDOCHINA WAR 1946-54 FRENCH WITHDRAWAL 1954
Hong Kong ○ (BR.)
Macao ○ (PORT.)

INDONESIA (1949)
Djakarta ⊛

END OF COMMUNIST INFLUENCE 1965

PATHET LAO REVOLT 1960
BURMA (1948)
LAOS (1949) ⊛
Vientiane ⊛
Hanoi ⊛ NORTH VIETNAM (1954)
VIETNAM (united 1976)
DEFENSE OF SOUTH VIETNAM 1961-1973 (See Map D below)
SOUTH VIETNAM (1954)
Ho Chi Minh City (Saigon) •
THAILAND
Bangkok •
Phnom Penh •
CAMBODIA (1949) ⊛
MAYAGUEZ INCIDENT 1975
BRUNEI (1984)
BRITISH DEFEAT COMMUNIST REVOLT 1945-60
Malaya ⊛
MALAYSIA (1963)
Kuala Lumpur ⊛
SINGAPORE (1965)
Sumatra
ANTI-COMMUNIST REVOLT 1958

PAPUA NEW GUINEA (1975)
West Irian (TO INDONESIA 1963) New Guinea

A U S T R A L I A
Darwin •

© Copyright HAMMOND INCORPORATED, Maplewood, N.J.

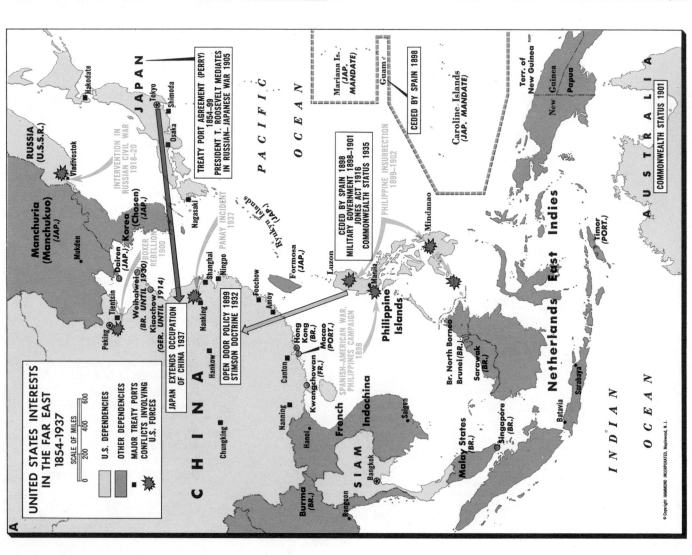

A

UNITED STATES INTERESTS IN THE FAR EAST 1854-1937

SCALE OF MILES
0 200 400 600

U.S. DEPENDENCIES
OTHER DEPENDENCIES
MAJOR TREATY PORTS
⊛ CONFLICTS INVOLVING U.S. FORCES

RUSSIA (U.S.S.R.)
Vladivostok ⊛
Hakodate ■
JAPAN
Tokyo ⊛
Shimoda ■
TREATY PORT AGREEMENT (PERRY) 1854-99
PRESIDENT T. ROOSEVELT MEDIATES IN RUSSIAN–JAPANESE WAR 1905
INTERVENTION IN RUSSIAN CIVIL WAR 1918-20

Manchuria (Manchukuo) (JAP.)
Mukden ■
Korea (Chosen) (JAP.)
Dairen (JAP.)
Weihaiwei (BR. UNTIL 1930)
Kiaochow (GER. UNTIL 1914)
Tientsin ⊛
Peking ⊛
BOXER REBELLION 1900
Osaka •
Nagasaki •
PANAY INCIDENT 1937

(Ryukyu Islands) (JAP.)

C H I N A
Chungking ■
Hankow ■
Nanking ■
Shanghai ⊛
Ningpo ■
Foochow ■
Amoy ■
JAPAN EXTENDS OCCUPATION OF CHINA 1937
OPEN DOOR POLICY 1899 STIMSON DOCTRINE 1932

Formosa (JAP.)

Nanning ■
Canton ■
Kwangchowan (FR.)
Hong Kong (BR.)
Macao (PORT.)

P A C I F I C   O C E A N

Mariana Is. (JAP. MANDATE)
Guam
CEDED BY SPAIN 1898
Caroline Islands (JAP. MANDATE)

CEDED BY SPAIN 1898
MILITARY GOVERNMENT 1898-1901
JONES ACT 1916
COMMONWEALTH STATUS 1935
PHILIPPINE INSURRECTION 1899-1902
Luzon
Manila ⊛
SPANISH-AMERICAN WAR, PHILIPPINES CAMPAIGN 1898
Philippine Islands
Mindanao ⊛

Burma (BR.)
Rangoon •
S I A M
Bangkok ⊛
French Indochina
Hanoi •
Saigon •

Malay States (BR.)
Singapore (BR.)
Br. North Borneo
Brunei (BR.)
Sarawak (BR.)

Netherlands East Indies
Batavia •
Surabaya •
Timor (PORT.)

Terr. of New Guinea
New Guinea
Papua

A U S T R A L I A
COMMONWEALTH STATUS 1901

I N D I A N   O C E A N

© Copyright HAMMOND INCORPORATED, Maplewood, N.J.

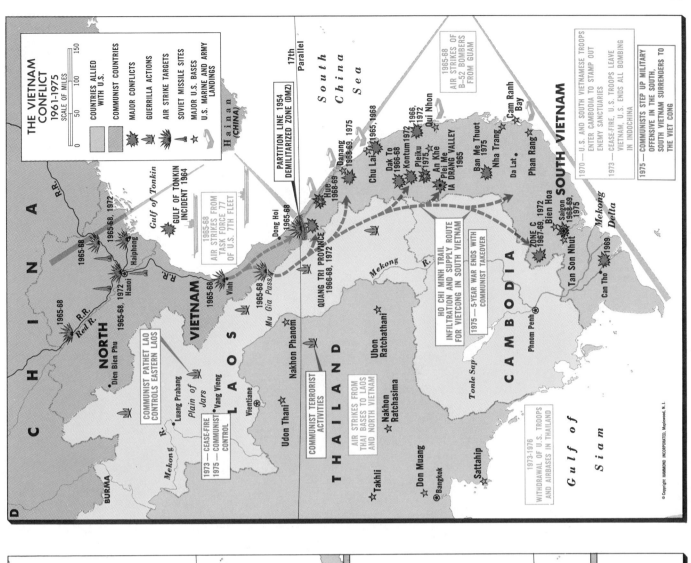

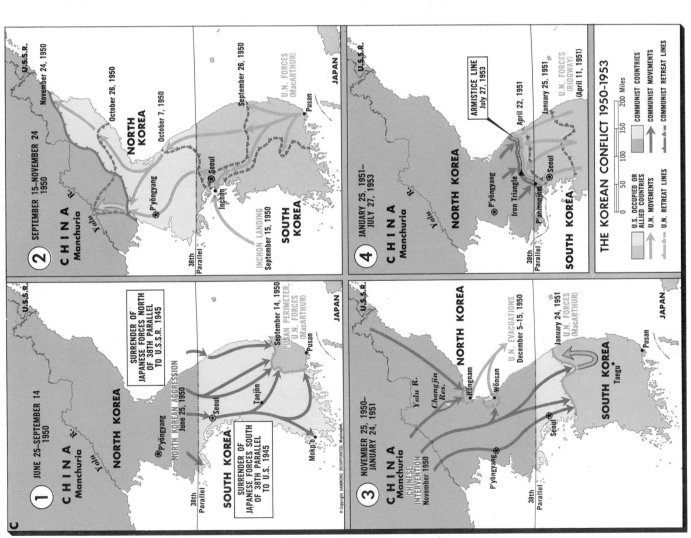

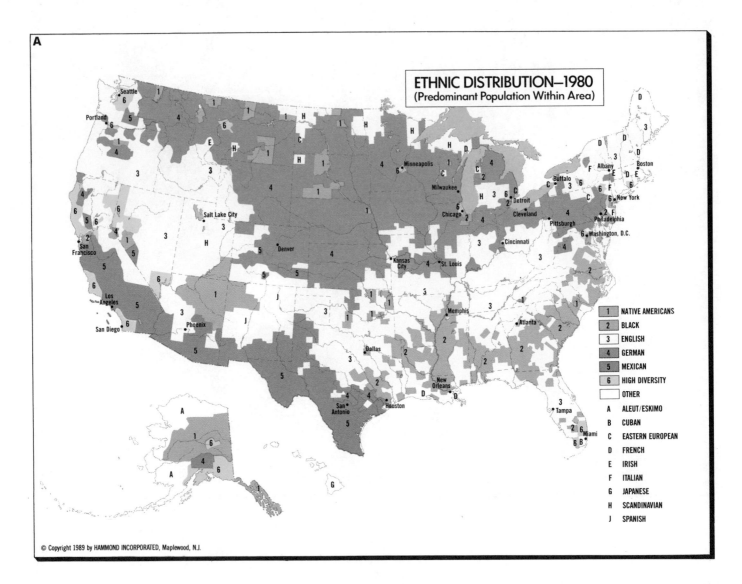

ETHNIC DISTRIBUTION—1980
(Predominant Population Within Area)

1	NATIVE AMERICANS
2	BLACK
3	ENGLISH
4	GERMAN
5	MEXICAN
6	HIGH DIVERSITY
	OTHER
A	ALEUT/ESKIMO
B	CUBAN
C	EASTERN EUROPEAN
D	FRENCH
E	IRISH
F	ITALIAN
G	JAPANESE
H	SCANDINAVIAN
J	SPANISH

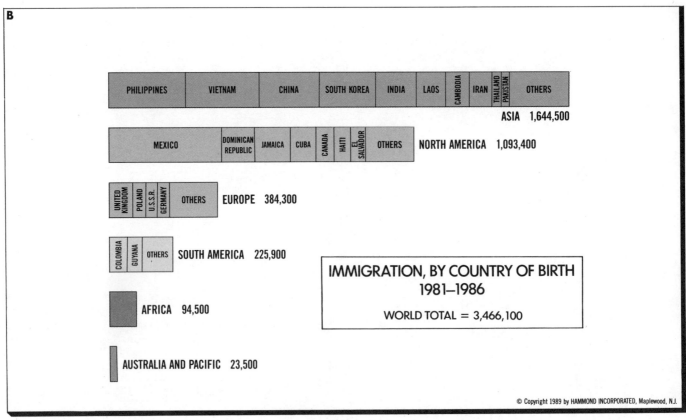

PHILIPPINES | VIETNAM | CHINA | SOUTH KOREA | INDIA | LAOS | CAMBODIA | IRAN | THAILAND | PAKISTAN | OTHERS

ASIA 1,644,500

MEXICO | DOMINICAN REPUBLIC | JAMAICA | CUBA | CANADA | HAITI | EL SALVADOR | OTHERS

NORTH AMERICA 1,093,400

UNITED KINGDOM | POLAND | U.S.S.R. | GERMANY | OTHERS

EUROPE 384,300

COLOMBIA | GUYANA | OTHERS

SOUTH AMERICA 225,900

AFRICA 94,500

AUSTRALIA AND PACIFIC 23,500

**IMMIGRATION, BY COUNTRY OF BIRTH
1981–1986**

WORLD TOTAL = 3,466,100

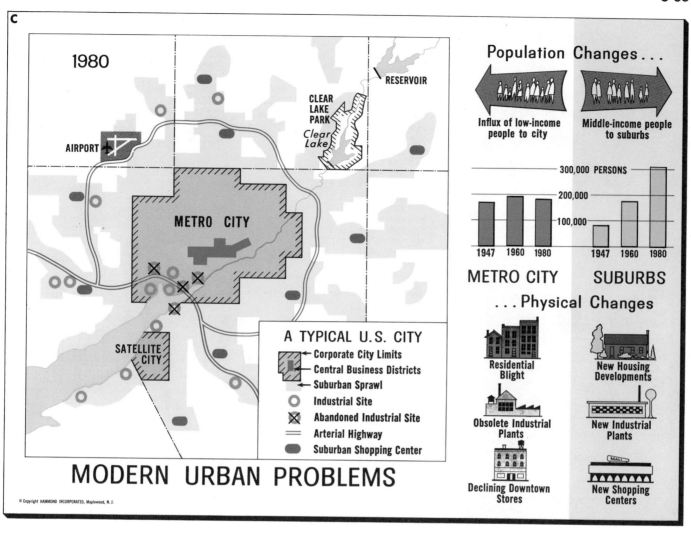

C

1980

RESERVOIR

CLEAR LAKE PARK

Clear Lake

AIRPORT

METRO CITY

SATELLITE CITY

A TYPICAL U.S. CITY

← Corporate City Limits
← Central Business Districts
← Suburban Sprawl
○ Industrial Site
✕ Abandoned Industrial Site
═ Arterial Highway
⬤ Suburban Shopping Center

MODERN URBAN PROBLEMS

© Copyright HAMMOND INCORPORATED, Maplewood, N.J.

Population Changes...

Influx of low-income people to city

Middle-income people to suburbs

300,000 PERSONS
200,000
100,000

1947 1960 1980 — METRO CITY
1947 1960 1980 — SUBURBS

...Physical Changes

Residential Blight

New Housing Developments

Obsolete Industrial Plants

New Industrial Plants

Declining Downtown Stores

New Shopping Centers

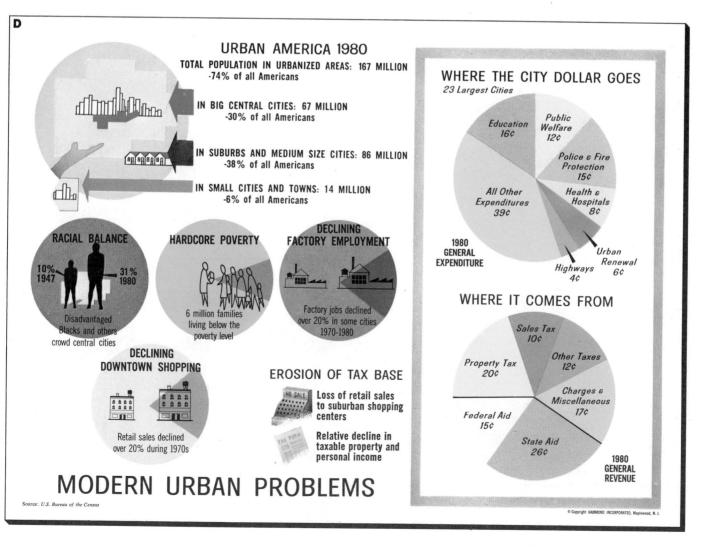

D

URBAN AMERICA 1980

TOTAL POPULATION IN URBANIZED AREAS: 167 MILLION
-74% of all Americans

IN BIG CENTRAL CITIES: 67 MILLION
-30% of all Americans

IN SUBURBS AND MEDIUM SIZE CITIES: 86 MILLION
-38% of all Americans

IN SMALL CITIES AND TOWNS: 14 MILLION
-6% of all Americans

RACIAL BALANCE

10% 1947   31% 1980

Disadvantaged Blacks and others crowd central cities

HARDCORE POVERTY

6 million families living below the poverty level

DECLINING FACTORY EMPLOYMENT

Factory jobs declined over 20% in some cities 1970-1980

DECLINING DOWNTOWN SHOPPING

Retail sales declined over 20% during 1970s

EROSION OF TAX BASE

Loss of retail sales to suburban shopping centers

Relative decline in taxable property and personal income

MODERN URBAN PROBLEMS

Source: *U.S. Bureau of the Census*

WHERE THE CITY DOLLAR GOES
23 Largest Cities

Education 16¢
Public Welfare 12¢
Police & Fire Protection 15¢
Health & Hospitals 8¢
Urban Renewal 6¢
Highways 4¢
All Other Expenditures 39¢

1980 GENERAL EXPENDITURE

WHERE IT COMES FROM

Sales Tax 10¢
Other Taxes 12¢
Charges & Miscellaneous 17¢
State Aid 26¢
Federal Aid 15¢
Property Tax 20¢

1980 GENERAL REVENUE

© Copyright HAMMOND INCORPORATED, Maplewood, N.J.

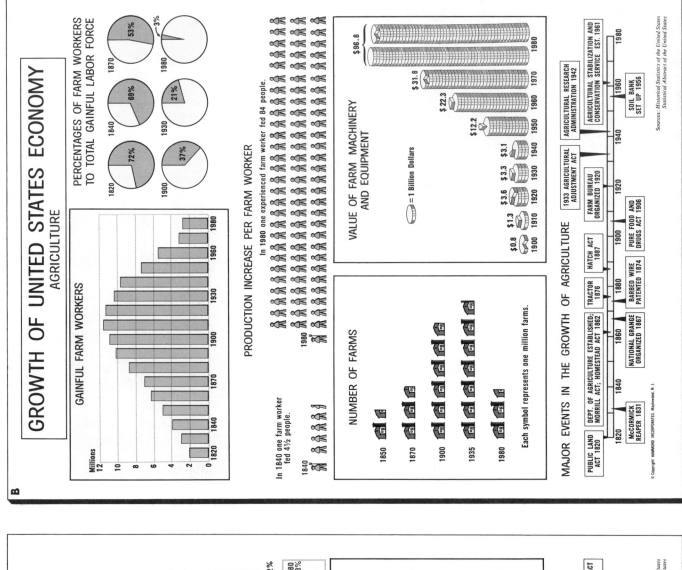

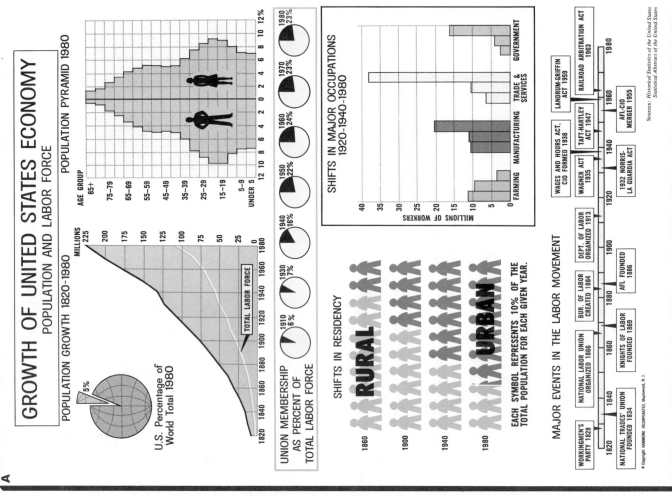

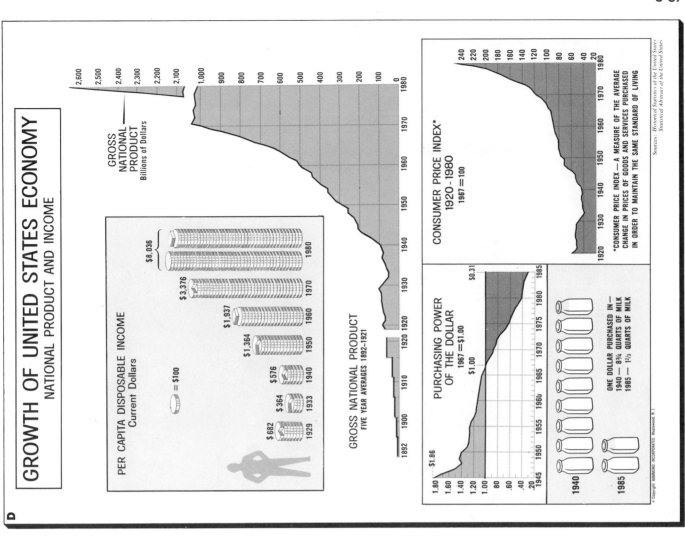

GROWTH OF UNITED STATES ECONOMY
NATIONAL PRODUCT AND INCOME

GROSS NATIONAL PRODUCT
Billions of Dollars

PER CAPITA DISPOSABLE INCOME
Current Dollars

= $100

$682 — 1929
$364 — 1933
$576 — 1940
$1,364 — 1950
$1,937 — 1960
$3,376 — 1970
$8,036 — 1980

GROSS NATIONAL PRODUCT
FIVE YEAR AVERAGES 1892-1921

CONSUMER PRICE INDEX*
1920-1980
1967=100

*CONSUMER PRICE INDEX — A MEASURE OF THE AVERAGE
CHANGE IN PRICES OF GOODS AND SERVICES PURCHASED
IN ORDER TO MAINTAIN THE SAME STANDARD OF LIVING

PURCHASING POWER
OF THE DOLLAR
1967=$1.00

$1.00
$0.31
$1.86

ONE DOLLAR PURCHASED IN —
1940 — 8¾ QUARTS OF MILK
1985 — 1⅓ QUARTS OF MILK

1940
1985

© Copyright HAMMOND INCORPORATED, Maplewood, N.J.

Sources : Historical Statistics of the United States
Statistical Abstract of the United States

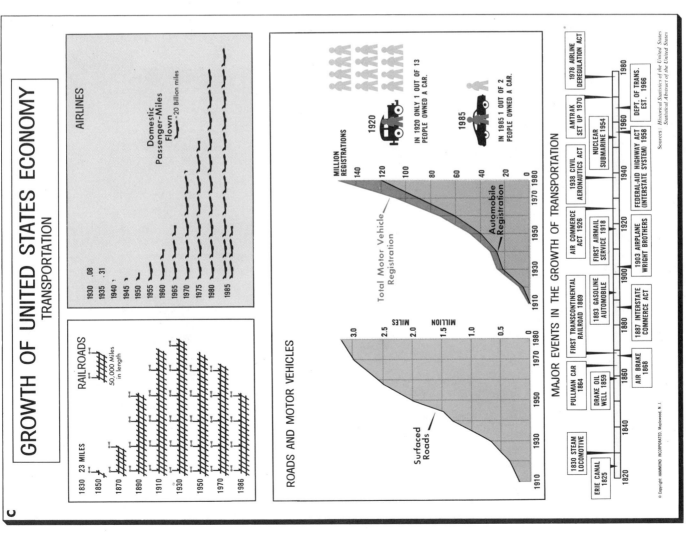

GROWTH OF UNITED STATES ECONOMY
TRANSPORTATION

AIRLINES

Domestic
Passenger-Miles
Flown
= 20 Billion miles

1930 .08
1935 .31
1940
1945
1950
1955
1960
1965
1970
1975
1980
1985

RAILROADS
= 50,000 Miles
in length

1830 23 MILES
1850
1870
1890
1910
1930
1950
1970
1986

ROADS AND MOTOR VEHICLES

MILLION
REGISTRATIONS

1920
IN 1920 ONLY 1 OUT OF 13
PEOPLE OWNED A CAR.

1985
IN 1985 1 OUT OF 2
PEOPLE OWNED A CAR.

Total Motor Vehicle
Registration

Automobile
Registration

Surfaced
Roads

MILLION   MILES

MAJOR EVENTS IN THE GROWTH OF TRANSPORTATION

ERIE CANAL 1825
1830 STEAM LOCOMOTIVE
AIR BRAKE 1868
PULLMAN CAR 1864
DRAKE OIL WELL 1859
FIRST TRANSCONTINENTAL RAILROAD 1869
1887 INTERSTATE COMMERCE ACT
1893 GASOLINE AUTOMOBILE
1903 AIRPLANE WRIGHT BROTHERS
FIRST AIRMAIL SERVICE 1918
AIR COMMERCE ACT 1926
1938 CIVIL AERONAUTICS ACT
NUCLEAR SUBMARINE 1954
FEDERAL-AID HIGHWAY ACT (INTERSTATE SYSTEM) 1958
AMTRAK SET UP 1970
DEPT. OF TRANS. EST. 1966
1978 AIRLINE DEREGULATION ACT

© Copyright HAMMOND INCORPORATED, Maplewood, N.J.

Sources : Historical Statistics of the United States
Statistical Abstract of the United States

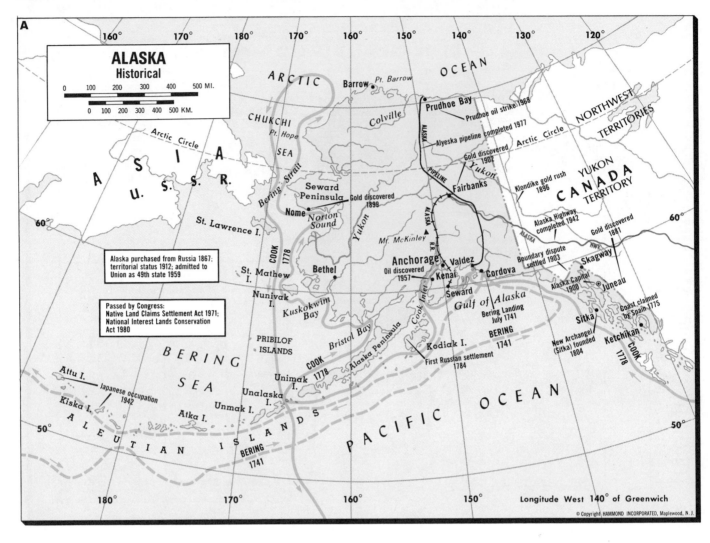

A

ALASKA
Historical

0 100 200 300 400 500 MI.

0 100 200 300 400 500 KM.

ARCTIC OCEAN

Barrow • Pt. Barrow

CHUKCHI SEA

• Prudhoe Bay — Prudhoe oil strike 1968

Colville

Pt. Hope

Arctic Circle

NORTHWEST TERRITORIES

Alyeska pipeline completed 1977

Arctic Circle

Gold discovered 1902

ASIA

U.S.S.R.

Bering Strait

Seward Peninsula

Nome • Gold discovered 1898

Norton Sound

St. Lawrence I.

PIPELINE

Yukon

Fairbanks

YUKON CANADA TERRITORY

Klondike gold rush 1896

60°

60°

Alaska purchased from Russia 1867; territorial status 1912; admitted to Union as 49th state 1959

St. Mathew

COOK 1778

Mt. McKinley ▲

ALASKA R.R.

Anchorage • Oil discovered 1957

Valdez

Alaska Highway completed 1942

Boundary dispute settled 1903

Gold discovered 1881

Passed by Congress: Native Land Claims Settlement Act 1971; National Interest Lands Conservation Act 1980

Nunivak I.

Bethel •

Kuskokwim Bay

Cook Inlet

• Kenai

Seward •

Cordova

Gulf of Alaska

ALASKA HWY.

Alaska Capital 1900

Skagway

• Juneau

Bristol Bay

PRIBILOF ISLANDS

Kodiak I.

Bering Landing July 1741

BERING 1741

Sitka •

New Archangel (Sitka) founded 1804

Coast claimed by Spain 1775

Ketchikan •

BERING SEA

Alaska Peninsula

First Russian settlement 1784

COOK 1778

Attu I. — Japanese occupation 1942

Kiska I.

Atka I.

Unmak I.

Unalaska I.

Unimak I.

COOK 1778

ALEUTIAN ISLANDS

PACIFIC OCEAN

BERING 1741

50°

50°

180°

170°

160°

150°

Longitude West 140° of Greenwich

© Copyright HAMMOND INCORPORATED, Maplewood, N.J.

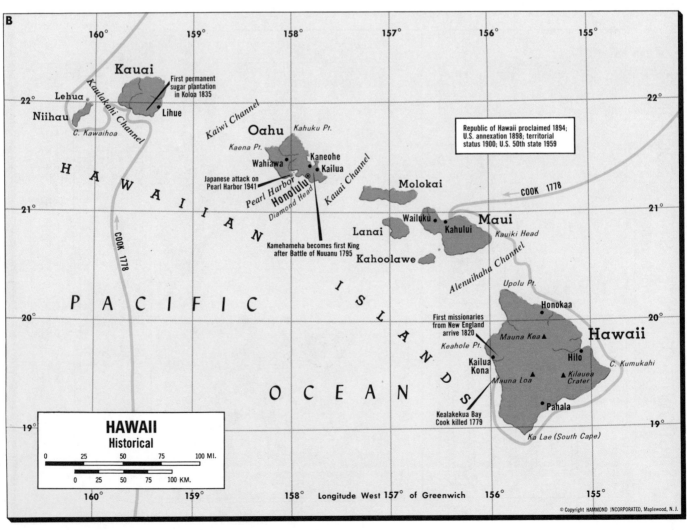

B

Kauai

First permanent sugar plantation in Koloa 1835

Lehua

Niihau

Lihue

C. Kawaihoa

Kaulakahi Channel

22°

22°

Kaiwi Channel

Oahu Kahuku Pt.

Kaena Pt.

Wahiawa

Kaneohe

Kailua

Japanese attack on Pearl Harbor 1941

Pearl Harbor

Honolulu

Diamond Head

Kauai Channel

Republic of Hawaii proclaimed 1894; U.S. annexation 1898; territorial status 1900; U.S. 50th state 1959

Molokai

COOK 1778

HAWAIIAN

Kamehameha becomes first King after Battle of Nuuanu 1795

Lanai

Wailuku

Kahului

Maui

Kauiki Head

21°

21°

Kahoolawe

Alenuihaha Channel

COOK 1778

Upolu Pt.

Honokaa

First missionaries from New England arrive 1820

PACIFIC

ISLANDS

Keahole Pt.

Mauna Kea ▲

Hawaii

20°

20°

Kailua Kona

Mauna Loa ▲

Hilo

Kilauea Crater ▲

C. Kumukahi

COOK 1778

OCEAN

Kealakekua Bay Cook killed 1779

Pahala •

Ka Lae (South Cape)

HAWAII
Historical

0 25 50 75 100 MI.

0 25 50 75 100 KM.

19°

19°

160°

159°

158°

Longitude West 157° of Greenwich

156°

155°

© Copyright HAMMOND INCORPORATED, Maplewood, N.J.

THE FIFTY STATES

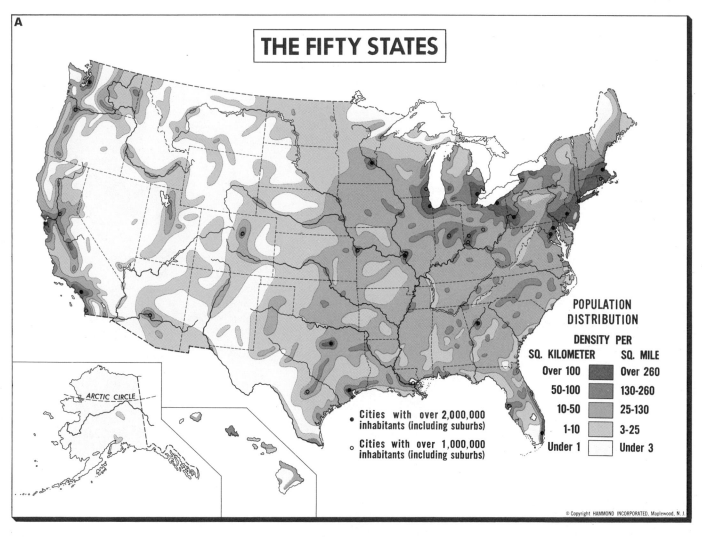

POPULATION
DISTRIBUTION

DENSITY PER

SQ. KILOMETER	SQ. MILE
Over 100	Over 260
50-100	130-260
10-50	25-130
1-10	3-25
Under 1	Under 3

ARCTIC CIRCLE

• Cities with over 2,000,000 inhabitants (including suburbs)
○ Cities with over 1,000,000 inhabitants (including suburbs)

© Copyright HAMMOND INCORPORATED, Maplewood, N. J.

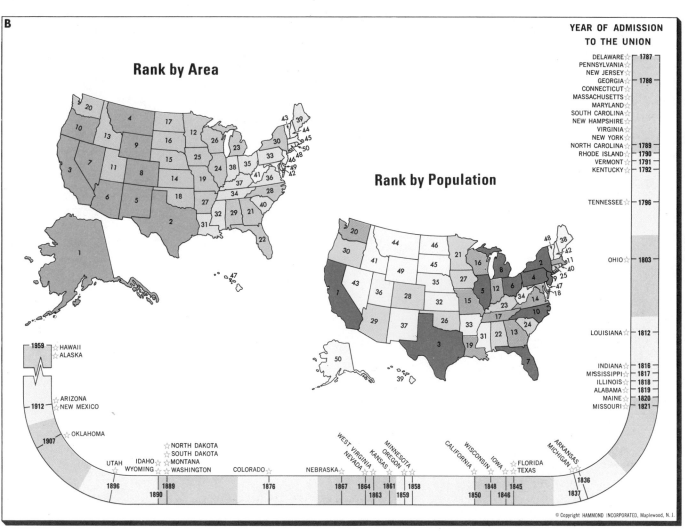

Rank by Area

Rank by Population

YEAR OF ADMISSION
TO THE UNION

© Copyright HAMMOND INCORPORATED, Maplewood, N. J.

POPULATION CHARACTERISTICS

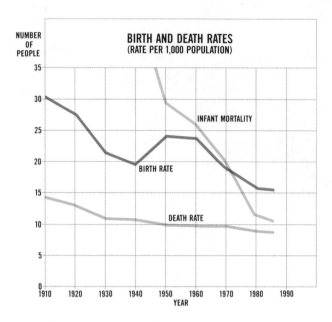

BIRTH AND DEATH RATES
(RATE PER 1,000 POPULATION)

NUMBER OF PEOPLE

INFANT MORTALITY

BIRTH RATE

DEATH RATE

YEAR

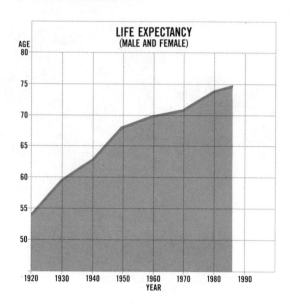

LIFE EXPECTANCY
(MALE AND FEMALE)

AGE

YEAR

POPULATION SHIFT
1970–1980

PERCENT CHANGE
- Over 15
- 10-15
- 5-10
- 0-5
- Population Loss

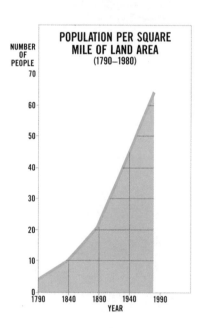

POPULATION PER SQUARE MILE OF LAND AREA
(1790–1980)

NUMBER OF PEOPLE

YEAR

POPULATION SHIFT
1980–1986

PERCENT CHANGE
- Over 15
- 10-15
- 5-10
- 0-5
- Population Loss

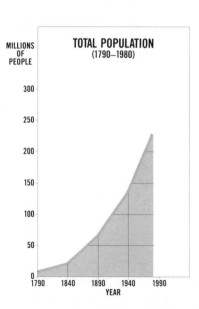

TOTAL POPULATION
(1790–1980)

MILLIONS OF PEOPLE

YEAR

Source: *Statistical Abstract of the United States*

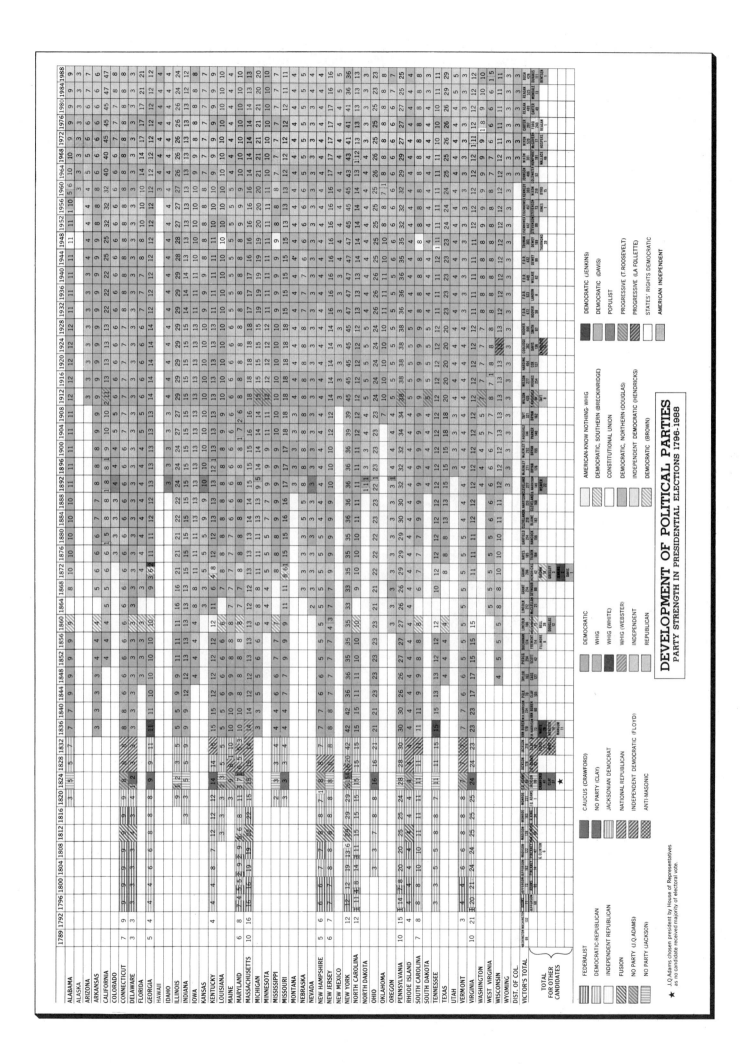

DEVELOPMENT OF POLITICAL PARTIES
PARTY STRENGTH IN PRESIDENTIAL ELECTIONS 1796-1988

POLITICAL SECTIONALISM 1796-1868
PRESIDENTIAL ELECTORAL VOTE BY STATES AND PARTIES

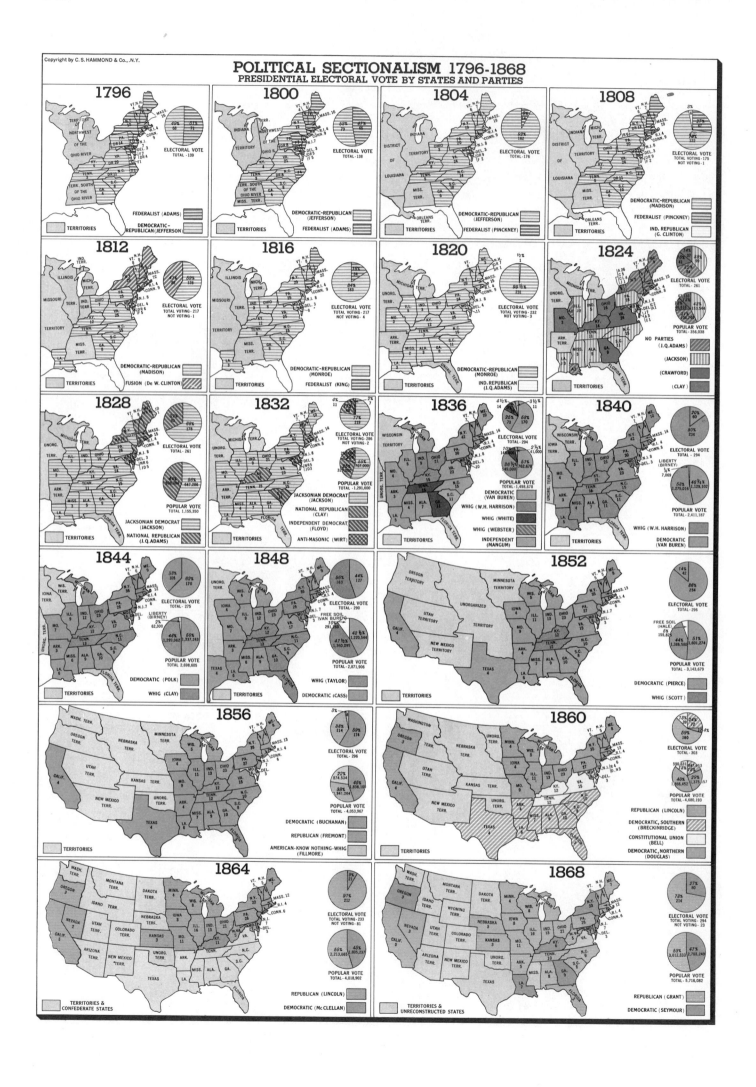

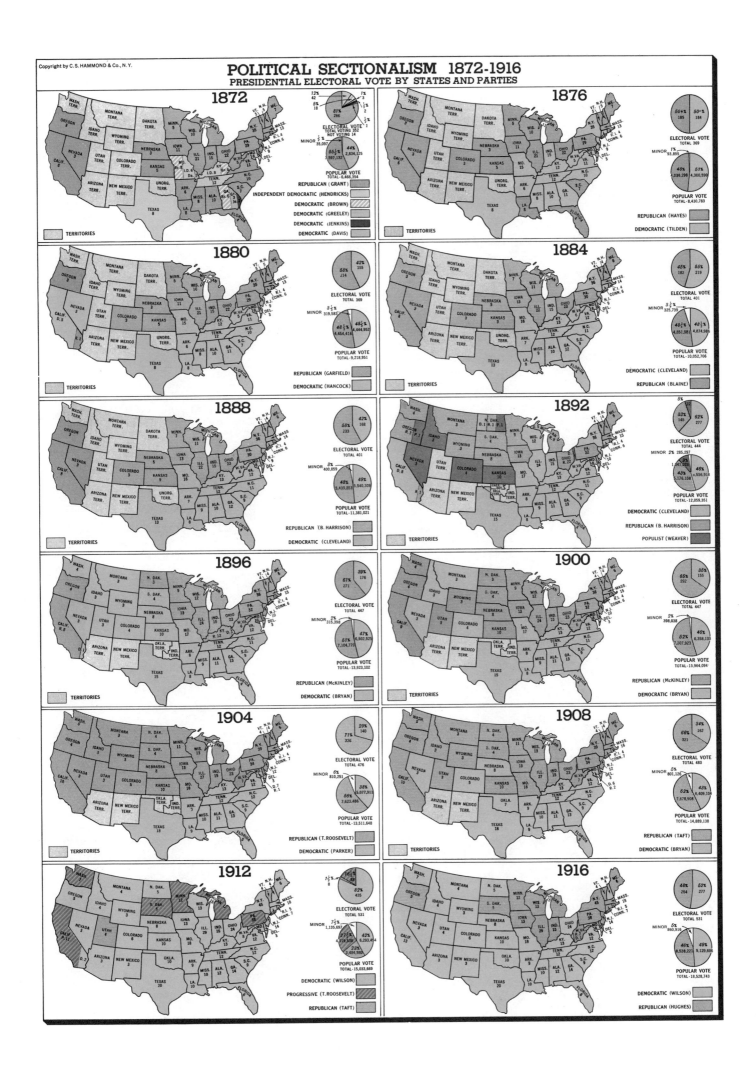

POLITICAL SECTIONALISM 1872-1916
PRESIDENTIAL ELECTORAL VOTE BY STATES AND PARTIES

Copyright by C.S. HAMMOND & CO., N.Y.

POLITICAL SECTIONALISM 1920-1964
PRESIDENTIAL ELECTORAL VOTE BY STATES AND PARTIES

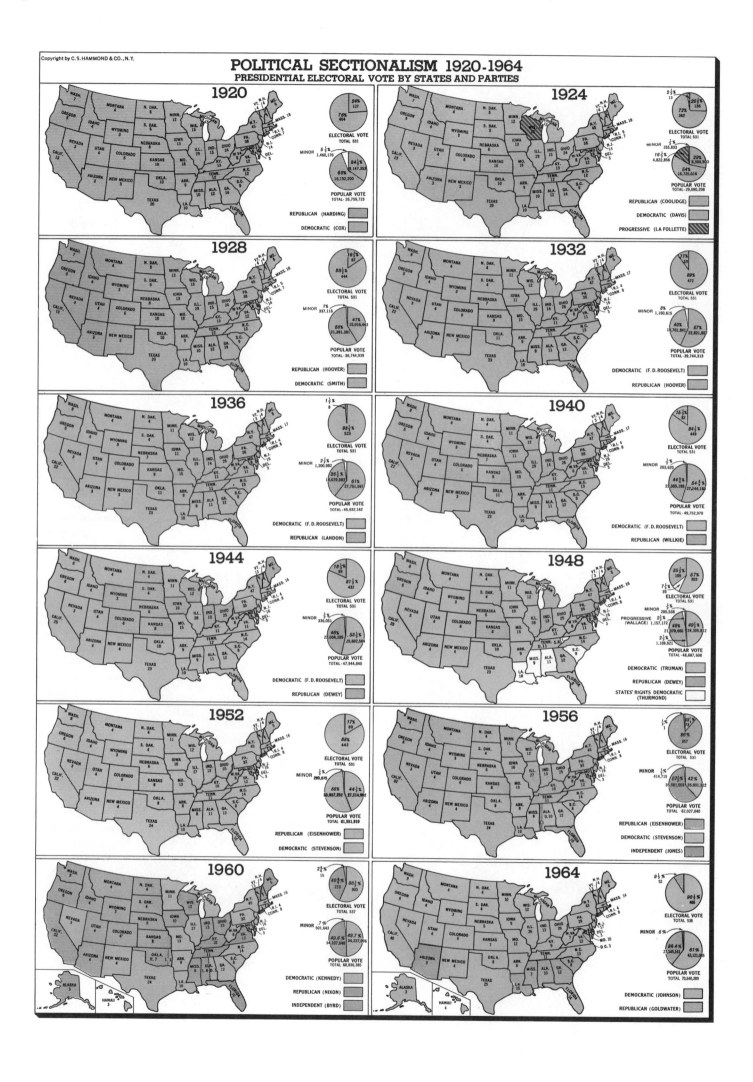

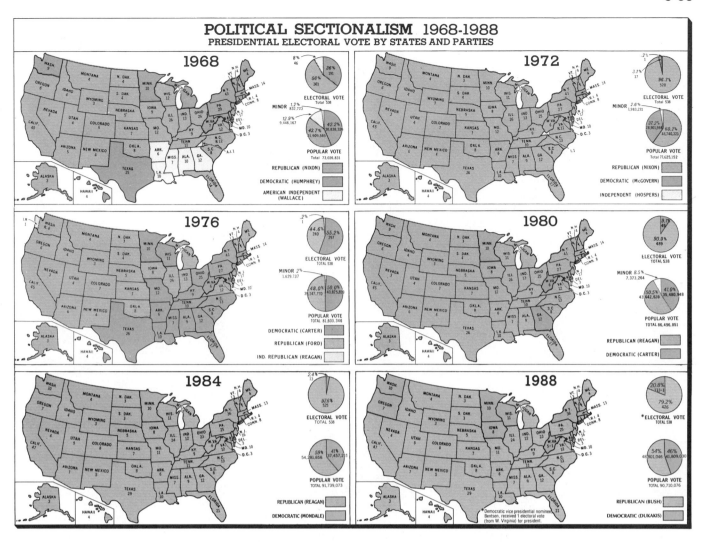

POLITICAL SECTIONALISM 1968-1988
PRESIDENTIAL ELECTORAL VOTE BY STATES AND PARTIES

PRESIDENTS OF THE UNITED STATES

No.	Name	Politics	Native State	Age at Inauguration	Age at Death	No.	Name	Politics	Native State	Age at Inauguration	Age at Death
1	George Washington	Federalist	Va.	57	67	22	Grover Cleveland	Democrat	N.J.	47	71
2	John Adams	Federalist	Mass.	61	90	23	Benjamin Harrison	Republican	Ohio	55	67
3	Thomas Jefferson	Rep.-Dem.	Va.	57	83	24	Grover Cleveland	Democrat	N.J.	55	71
4	James Madison	Rep.-Dem.	Va.	57	85	25	William McKinley	Republican	Ohio	54	58
5	James Monroe	Rep.-Dem.	Va.	58	73	26	Theodore Roosevelt	Republican	N.Y.	42	60
6	John Quincy Adams	Rep.-Dem.	Mass.	57	80	27	William Howard Taft	Republican	Ohio	51	72
7	Andrew Jackson	Democrat	S.C.	61	78	28	Woodrow Wilson	Democrat	Va	56	67
8	Martin Van Buren	Democrat	N.Y.	54	79	29	Warren G. Harding	Republican	Ohio	55	57
9	William Henry Harrison	Whig	Va.	68	68	30	Calvin Coolidge	Republican	Vt.	51	60
10	John Tyler	Whig	Va.	51	71	31	Herbert Clark Hoover	Republican	Iowa	54	90
11	James Knox Polk	Democrat	N.C.	49	53	32	Franklin D. Roosevelt	Democrat	N.Y.	51	63
12	Zachary Taylor	Whig	Va.	64	65	33	Harry S Truman	Democrat	Mo.	60	88
13	Millard Fillmore	Whig	N.Y.	50	74	34	Dwight D. Eisenhower	Republican	Texas	62	78
14	Franklin Pierce	Democrat	N.H.	48	64	35	John F. Kennedy	Democrat	Mass.	43	46
15	James Buchanan	Democrat	Pa.	65	77	36	Lyndon B. Johnson	Democrat	Texas	55	64
16	Abraham Lincoln	Republican	Ky.	52	56	37	Richard M. Nixon	Republican	Calif.	56	....
17	Andrew Johnson	Democrat	N.C.	56	66	38	Gerald R. Ford	Republican	Mich.	61	....
18	Ulysses Simpson Grant	Republican	Ohio	46	63	39	James E. Carter, Jr.	Democrat	Ga.	52	....
19	Rutherford B. Hayes	Republican	Ohio	54	70	40	Ronald W. Reagan	Republican	Ill.	69	....
20	James Abram Garfield	Republican	Ohio	49	49	41	George H. W. Bush	Republican	Mass.	64	....
21	Chester Alan Arthur	Republican	Vt.	50	56						

Flags of American History

FLAGS OF DISCOVERY AND SETTLEMENT

FLAG OF LEIF ERICKSON—1000
RAVEN OF THE VIKINGS, FIRST FLAG CARRIED TO AMERICA'S SHORES.

EXPEDITIONARY FLAG OF COLUMBUS 1492

FLAG OF COLUMBUS 1492—1498
STANDARD OF FERDINAND AND ISABELLA.
RAISED AT SAN SALVADOR 1492, MAINLAND, 1498.

FLAG OF JOHN CABOT—1497
CROSS OF ST. GEORGE, FIRST FLAG RAISED ON MAINLAND. RALEIGH'S FLAG 1585.

FLAG OF CHAMPLAIN—1603
BORNE BY CARTIER, JOLIET, MARQUETTE, LA SALLE AND OTHER INTREPID FRENCH VOYAGEURS.

FLAG OF HUDSON—1607
FIRST FLAG RAISED AT NEW YORK, VERRAZANO DISCOVERED THE RIVER EIGHTY FOUR YEARS EARLIER.

FLAG OF THE MAYFLOWER—1620
FLAG BORNE ON THE MAIN MAST OF THE MAYFLOWER BY THE PILGRIM FATHERS.

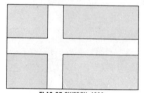

FLAG OF SWEDEN—1638
ENSIGN OF NEW SWEDEN RAISED ON THE DELAWARE RIVER.

FLAGS OF COLONIAL DAYS

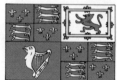

STUART STANDARD 1603—1649, 1660—1689

CROMWELL'S STANDARD 1653—1660

ROYAL STANDARD 1689—1702

ROYAL STANDARD 1707—1714

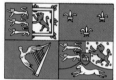

ROYAL STANDARD 1714—1801

ENGLISH RED ENSIGN
THE FAMOUS METEOR FLAG OF OLD ENGLAND AND ENSIGN OF COLONIES 17th CENTURY.

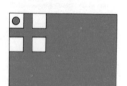

ENDICOTT FLAG—1634
THE SALEM ENSIGN SHOWING RELIGIOUS OPPOSITION TO CROSS IN CANTON.

THREE COUNTY TROUP—1659
FLAG OF THE THREE MASSACHUSETTS COUNTIES AND EMBLEM OF KING PHILIP'S WAR, 1675—1676.

ESCUTCHEONED JACK—1701
FLAG DESIGNED FOR MERCHANT SHIPS OF HIS MAJESTY'S PLANTATIONS.

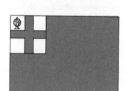

NEW ENGLAND FLAG—1737
THIS ENSIGN SHOWS THE EARLY TENDENCY OF THE COLONIES TO FIND INDIVIDUAL FLAGS.

FLAGS OF THE REVOLUTION

TAUNTON FLAG—1774
ONE OF THE EARLIEST EMBLEMS OF THE REVOLUTION.

BEDFORD FLAG—1775
CARRIED BY REVERE AND DAWES IN AROUSING THE MINUTE MEN.

CULPEPER FLAG—1775
ONE OF THE EARLY RATTLESNAKE FLAGS CARRIED BY THE MINUTE MEN.

PHILADELPHIA LIGHT HORSE
WASHINGTON'S ESCORT TO COMMAND OF THE CONTINENTAL ARMY, 1775.

RHODE ISLAND FLAG—1776
CARRIED AT BRANDYWINE, TRENTON AND YORKTOWN.

FORT MOULTRIE FLAG—1776
NAILED TO STAFF BY SERGEANT JASPER WHEN SHOT AWAY.

LIBERTY TREE FLAG—1776
THE PINE TREE COMES FROM COINS OF THE COLONY OF MASSACHUSETTS, 1652.

BENNINGTON FLAG—1777
FLAG OF VICTORY OF THE GREEN MOUNTAIN BOYS.

BENJAMIN FRANKLIN FLAG
ALSO CALLED "SERAPIS" FLAG. GENERALLY ACCEPTED AS ORIGINATED BY BENJAMIN FRANKLIN AT COURT OF LOUIS XVI.

MERCHANT ENSIGN 1776—1795
AN EMBLEM IN GENERAL USE, ALSO PRIVATEER'S FLAG.

FLAGS OF THE OLD NAVY

GADSDEN FLAG—1775
COMMODORE ESEK HOPKINS' ENSIGN USED IN HIS FIRST FLEET COMMAND.

WASHINGTON'S NAVY ENSIGN—1775
THE FLAG OF THE SIX CRUISERS THAT FORMED THE FIRST AMERICAN NAVAL FLEET.

FIRST NAVY JACK—1775
HOSTED AT THE MAIN MAST BY COMMANDER-IN-CHIEF ESEK HOPKINS, DECEMBER 3, 1775.

FLAGS OF THE YOUNG REPUBLIC

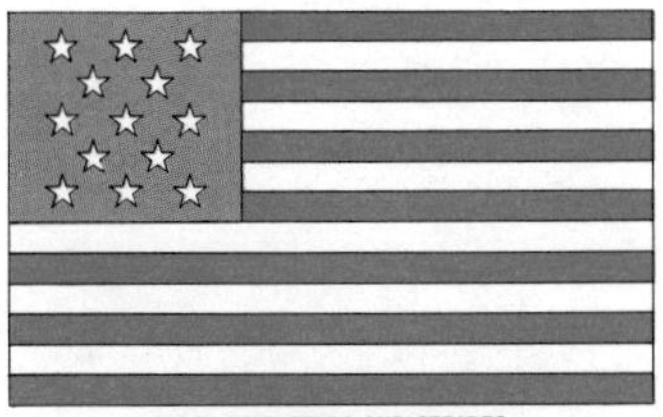

FIRST NAVY STARS AND STRIPES
IN ABSENCE OF SPECIFIC ARRANGEMENT OF STARS BY CONGRESS JUNE 14, 1777 IT WAS CUSTOMARY FOR NAVY TO PLACE THE STARS IN FORM OF CROSSES OF ST. GEORGE AND ST. ANDREW.

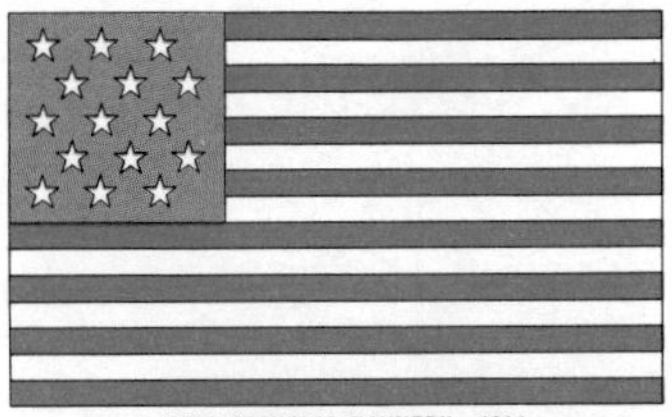

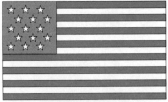

"STAR SPANGLED BANNER" –1814
THE EMBLEM OF INSPIRATION OF OUR NATIONAL ANTHEM, 1814. FLAG OF VICTORY OVER BARBARY PIRATES 1803 TO 1805.

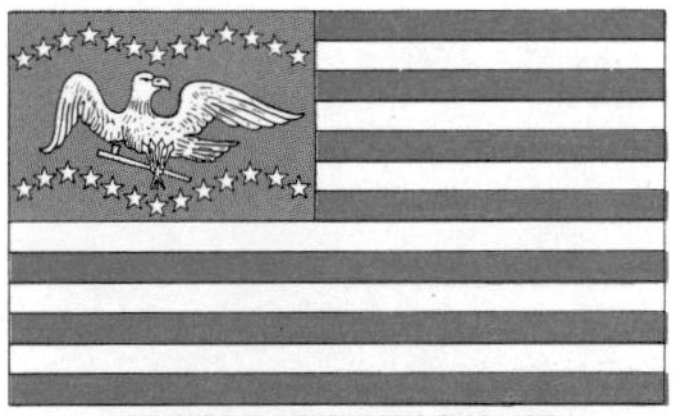

FREMONT THE PATHFINDER'S FLAG–40'S
EMBLEM THAT BLAZED THE TRAIL FOR THE COVERED WAGON IN THE ROARING 40'S. THE EARLY ENSIGN OF THE PLAINS.

FAMOUS BATTLE FLAGS

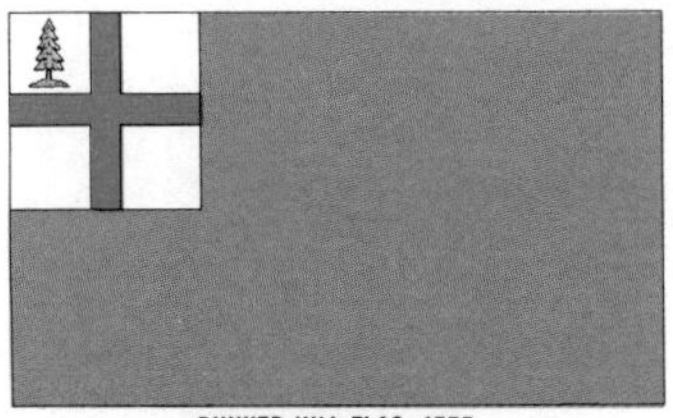

BUNKER HILL FLAG–1775
HISTORIC EMBLEM THAT PROVED THE STRENGTH OF THE SPIRIT OF AMERICAN LIBERTY. CARRIED AT LEXINGTON AND CONCORD.

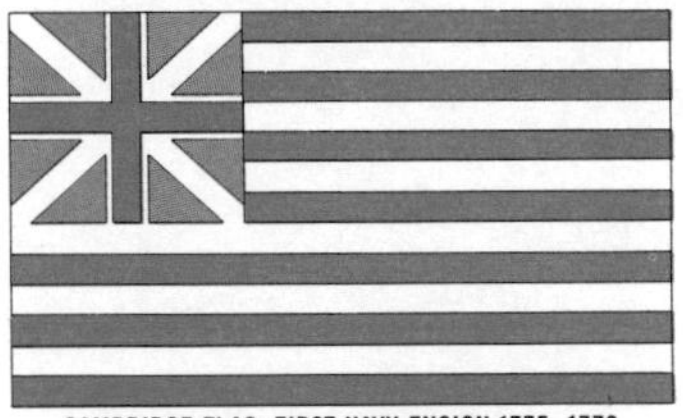

CAMBRIDGE FLAG, FIRST NAVY ENSIGN 1775–1776
HOISTED BY JOHN PAUL JONES, DECEMBER 3, 1775 AND BY GENERAL WASHINGTON, JANUARY 2, 1776.

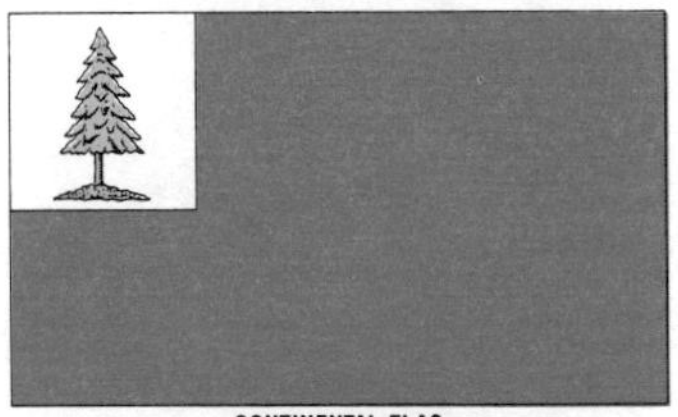

CONTINENTAL FLAG
CARRIED IN 1775–1777, SHOWING PINE TREE, SYMBOL OF MASSACHUSETTS BAY COLONY, IN PLACE OF THE CROSSES OF ST. GEORGE AND ST. ANDREW.

FLAGS OF THE CONFEDERACY

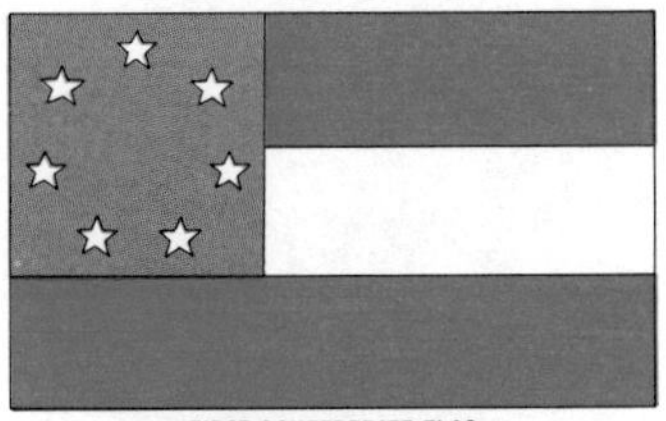

FIRST CONFEDERATE FLAG
FAMOUS "STARS AND BARS" USED FROM MARCH 1861 TO MAY 1863.

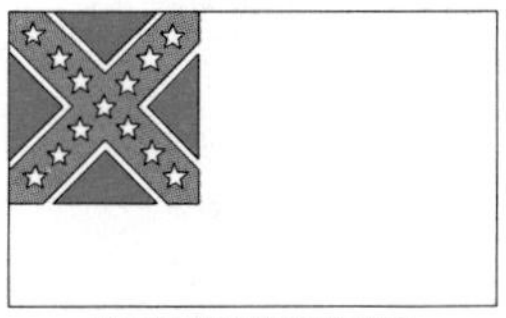

SECOND CONFEDERATE FLAG
NATIONAL EMBLEM FROM MAY 1, 1863 TO MARCH 4, 1865.

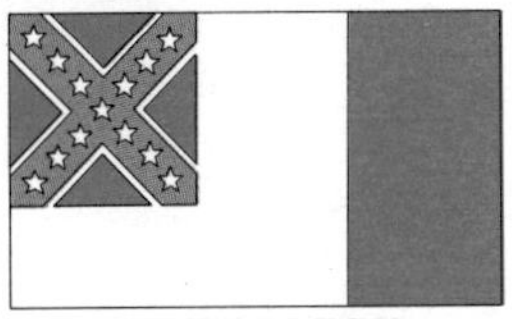

THIRD CONFEDERATE FLAG
NATIONAL EMBLEM ADOPTED MARCH 8, 1865.

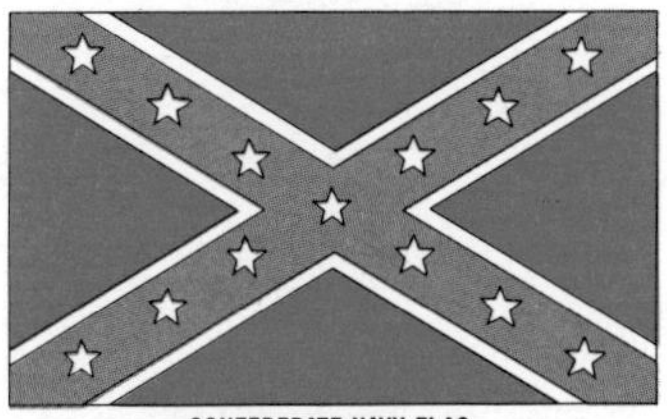

CONFEDERATE NAVY FLAG
USED FROM MAY 1, 1863 TO END OF WAR, 1865. THE BATTLE FLAG WAS SQUARE.

OTHER NOTEWORTHY FLAGS OF AMERICAN HISTORY

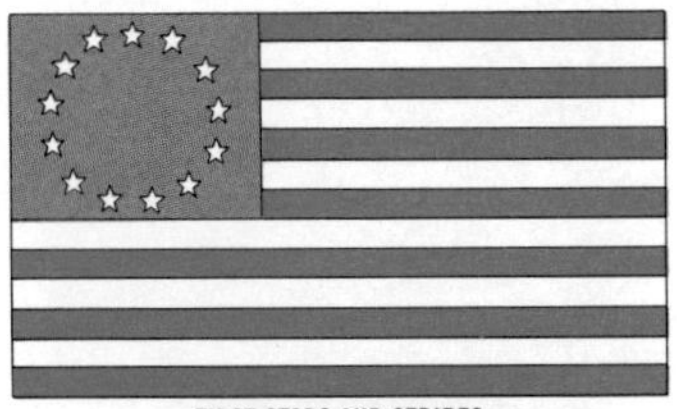

FIRST STARS AND STRIPES
UNITED EMBLEM OF INDEPENDENCE SAID TO HAVE ORIGINATED BY GEORGE WASHINGTON FOLLOWING ACT OF CONGRESS OF JUNE 14, 1777.

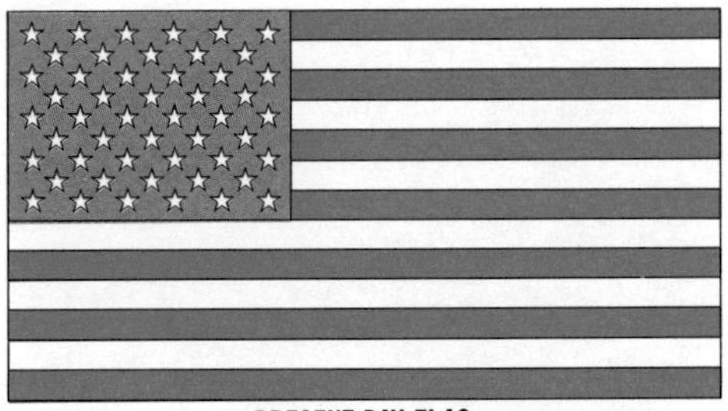

PRESENT DAY FLAG

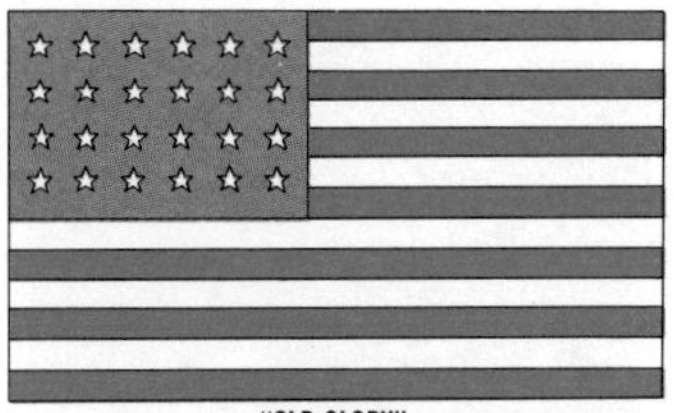

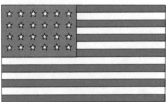

"OLD GLORY"
NAME GIVEN BY CAPTAIN WILLIAM DRIVER, COMMANDING THE BRIG "CHARLES DAGGETT" IN 1831.

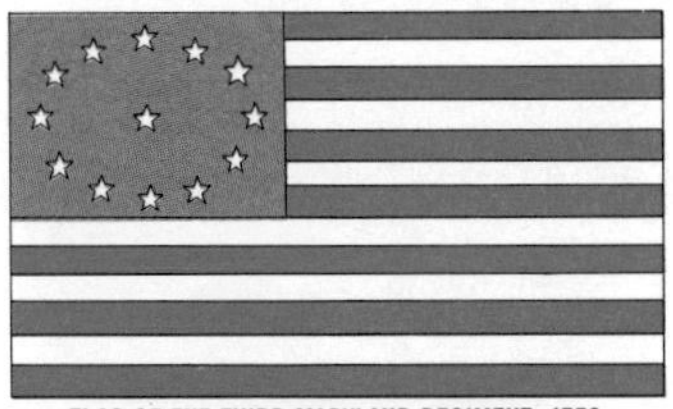

FLAG OF THE THIRD MARYLAND REGIMENT–1778
CARRIED AT THE BATTLE OF COWPENS JANUARY, 1778 AND USED AS COLORS OF AMERICAN LAND FORCES UNTIL MEXICAN WAR.

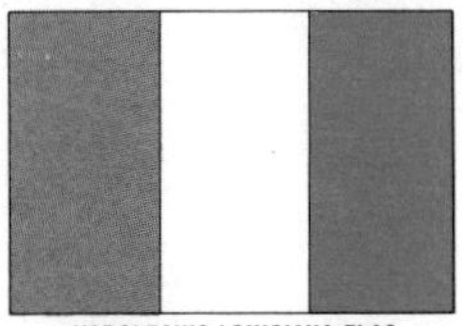

NAPOLEON'S LOUISIANA FLAG
THIS FLAG WAS REPLACED BY "STARS AND STRIPES" FOLLOWING LOUISIANA PURCHASE DECEMBER 24, 1803.

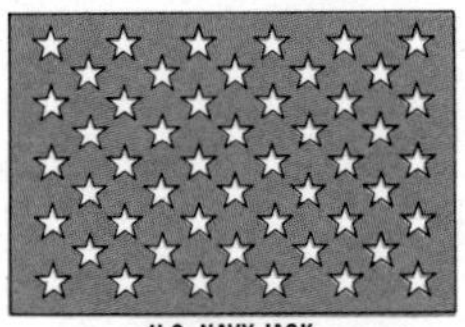

U.S. NAVY JACK
USED BY NAVAL VESSELS AND MARITIME GOVERNORS.

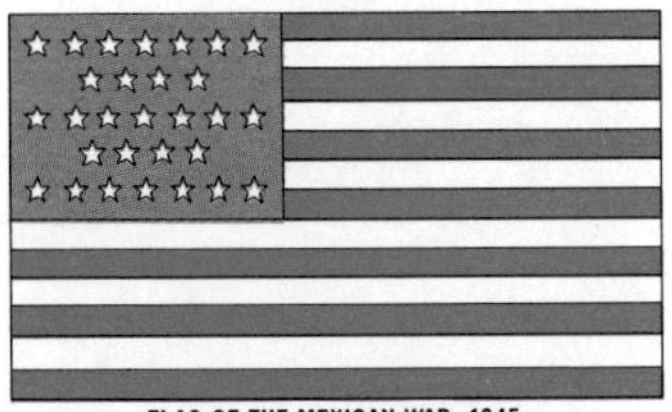

FLAG OF THE MEXICAN WAR–1845
NOT ACTUALLY USED AS REGIMENTAL COLORS BY TROOPS, BUT AS FLAG OF CONQUEST AND OCCUPATION.

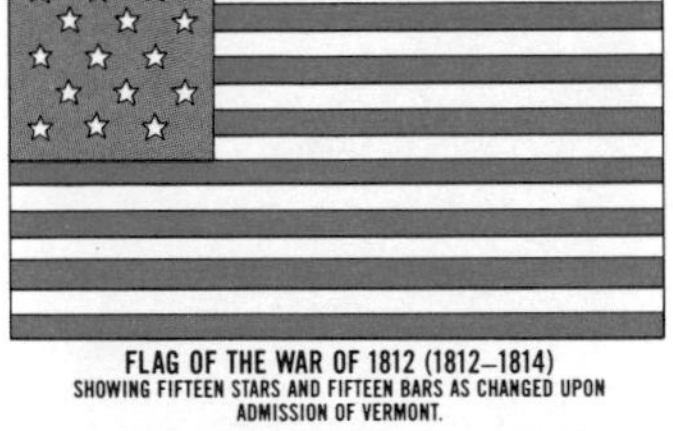

FLAG OF THE WAR OF 1812 (1812–1814)
SHOWING FIFTEEN STARS AND FIFTEEN BARS AS CHANGED UPON ADMISSION OF VERMONT.

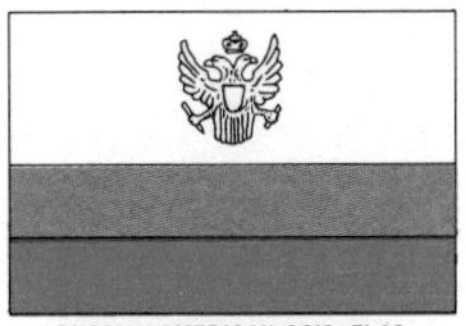

RUSSIAN AMERICAN CO'S. FLAG
EMBLEM RAISED 1799, REPLACED BY "STARS AND STRIPES" 1867.

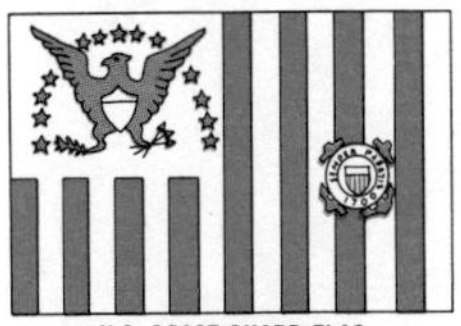

U.S. COAST GUARD FLAG
WITHOUT EMBLEM ON FLY THIS IS U.S. CUSTOMS FLAG.

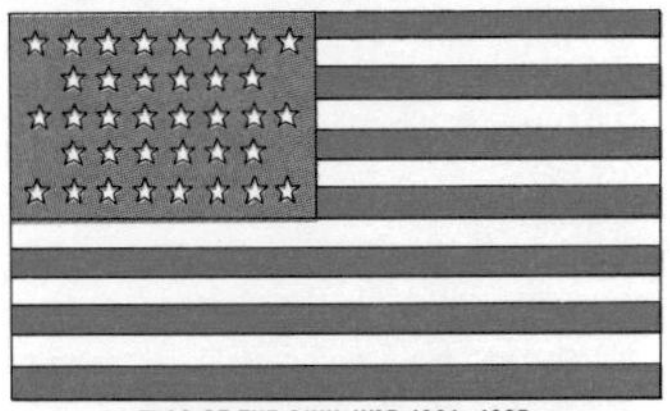

FLAG OF THE CIVIL WAR 1861–1865
THE "STARS AND STRIPES" WITH THIRTY SIX STARS IN THE UNION CARRIED BY THE NORTHERN ARMIES DURING LATER YEARS OF THE CIVIL WAR.

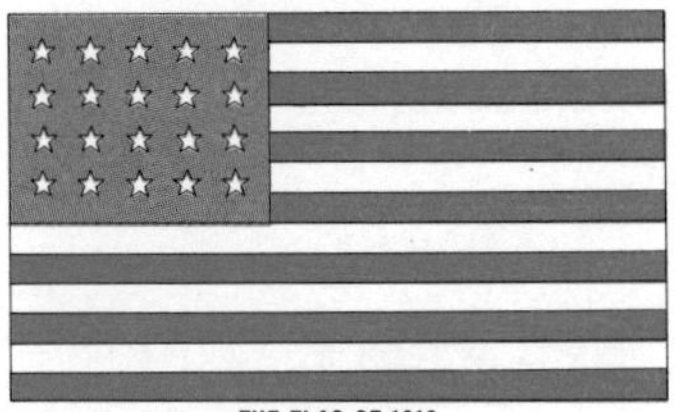

THE FLAG OF 1818
SHOWING RETURN TO THIRTEEN STRIPES AND ADDITIONAL STARS IN CANTON.

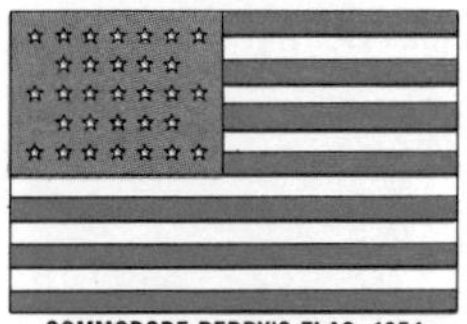

COMMODORE PERRY'S FLAG–1854
THE FLAG THAT OPENED JAPAN TO WESTERN CIVILIZATION.

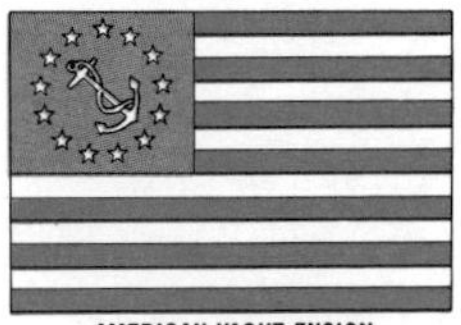

AMERICAN YACHT ENSIGN
AUTHORIZED BY ACT OF CONGRESS AUGUST 7, 1848.

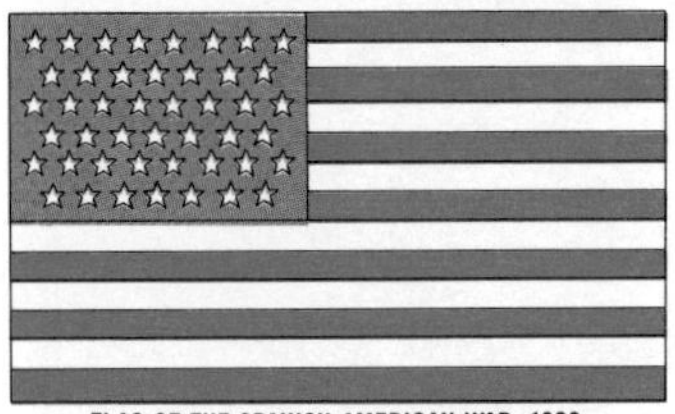

FLAG OF THE SPANISH-AMERICAN WAR–1898
THE EMBLEM OF LIBERTY THAT BROUGHT FREEDOM TO CUBA.

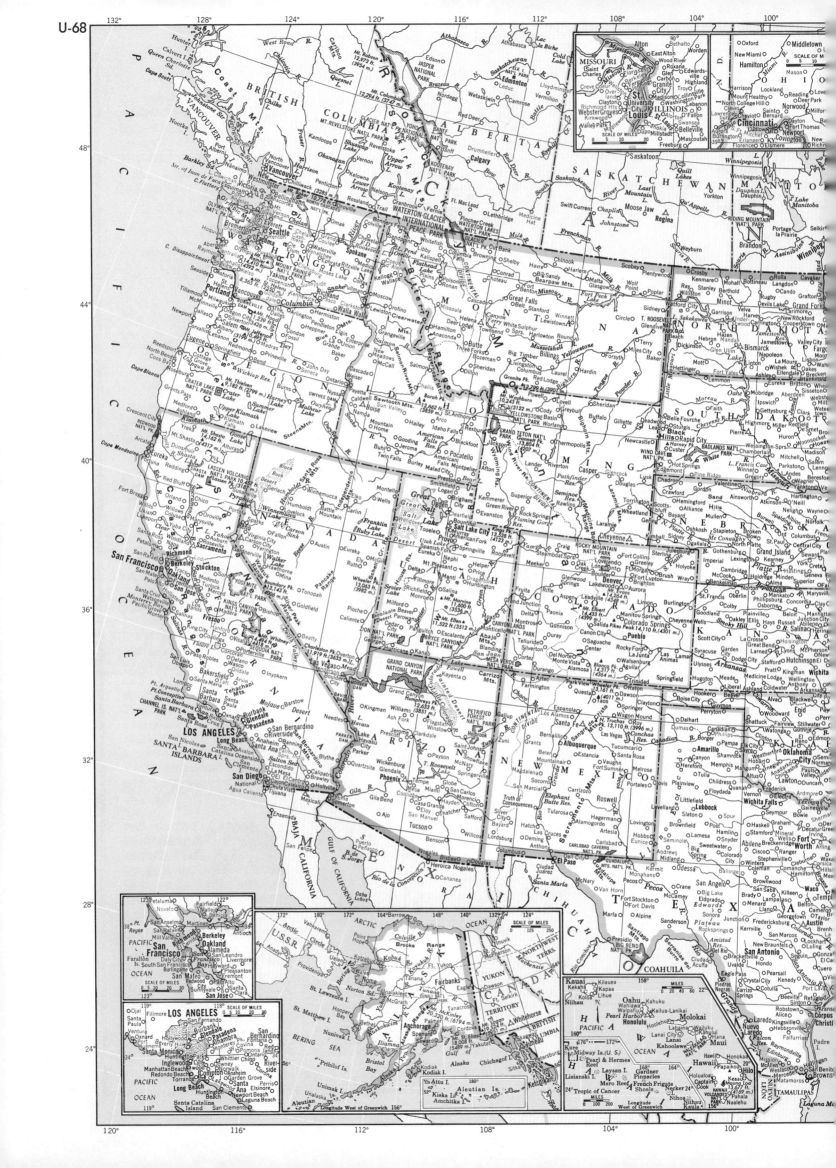

Flags of States, Territories and Possessions

Alabama

Alaska

Arizona

Arkansas

California

Colorado

Connecticut

Delaware

Florida

Georgia

Hawaii

Idaho

Illinois

Indiana

Iowa

Kansas

Kentucky

Louisiana

Maine

Maryland

Massachusetts

Michigan

Minnesota

Mississippi

Missouri

Montana

Nebraska

Nevada

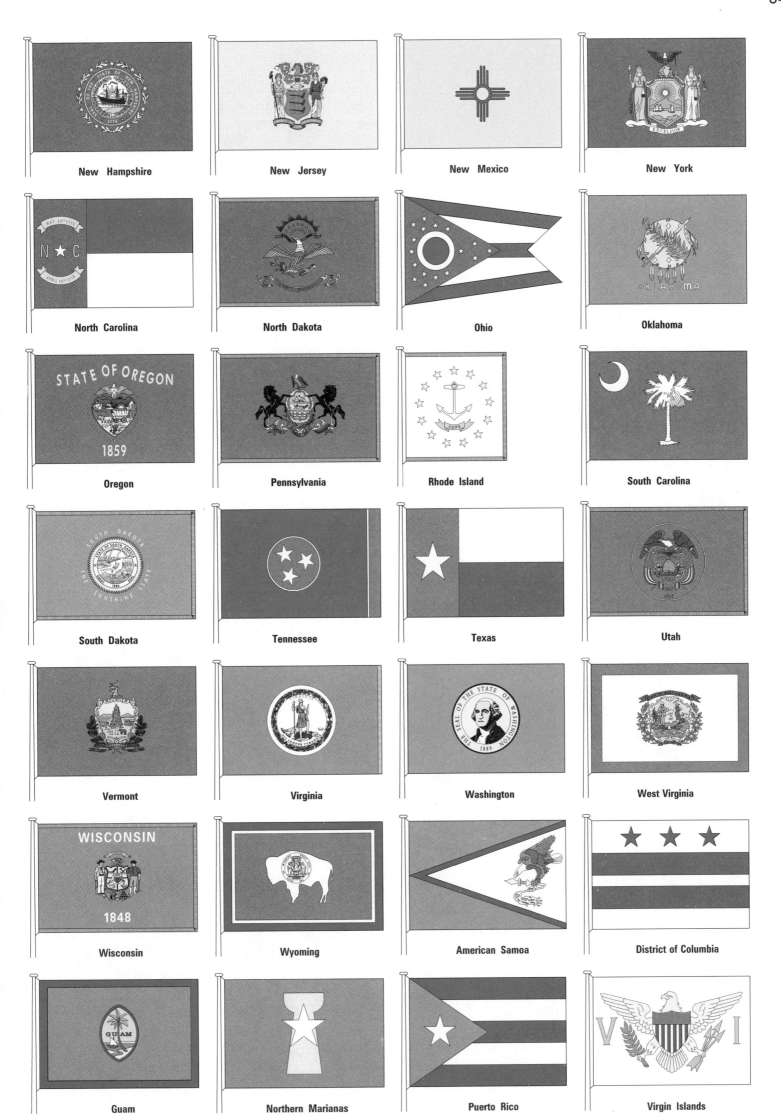

New Hampshire

New Jersey

New Mexico

New York

North Carolina

North Dakota

Ohio

Oklahoma

Oregon

Pennsylvania

Rhode Island

South Carolina

South Dakota

Tennessee

Texas

Utah

Vermont

Virginia

Washington

West Virginia

Wisconsin

Wyoming

American Samoa

District of Columbia

Guam

Northern Marianas

Puerto Rico

Virgin Islands

Index

This index lists historically important places, areas, events and geographical features appearing on the maps of the United States History Atlas. Each entry is followed by the page number on which the name appears. The letters following the page number designate a particular map on pages containing more than one map. Names that appear on more than one map are indexed to the map or maps portraying the place at its most historically significant period.